9
EDITION

BUILDING YOUR DREAM

A CANADIAN GUIDE TO STARTING YOUR OWN BUSINESS

GOOD | MAYHEW

Walter Good

UNIVERSITY OF MANITOBA

Wendy Mayhew

PRESIDENT, BUSINESS LAUNCH SOLUTIONS

McGraw-Hill
Ryerson

McGraw-Hill
Ryerson

BUILDING YOUR DREAM:
A Canadian Guide to Starting Your Own Business
Ninth Edition

Copyright © 2014, 2011; 2008, 2005, 2003, 2000, 1997, 1993, 1989 by McGraw-Hill Ryerson Limited. All rights reserved. No part of this publication may be reproduced or transmitted in any form or by any means, or stored in a data base or retrieval system, without the prior written permission of McGraw-Hill Ryerson Limited, or in the case of photocopying or other reprographic copying, a licence from The Canadian Copyright Licensing Agency (Access Copyright). For an Access Copyright licence, visit www.accesscopyright.ca or call toll free to 1-800-893-5777.

The Internet addresses listed in the text were accurate at the time of publication. The inclusion of a Website does not indicate an endorsement by the authors or McGraw-Hill Ryerson, and McGraw-Hill Ryerson does not guarantee the accuracy of information presented at these sites.

ISBN-13: 978-0-07-133888-2
ISBN-10: 0-07-133888-8

5 6 7 8 9 WEB 1 9 8 7 6 5

Printed and bound in Canada.

Care has been taken to trace ownership of copyright material contained in this text; however, the publisher will welcome any information that enables it to rectify any reference or credit for subsequent editions.

Director of Product Management: Rhondda McNabb
Group Product Manager: Kim Brewster
Marketing Manager: Cathie Lefebvre
Group Product Development Manager: Kelly Dickson
Product Developer: Becky Ranger
Photo/Permissions Research: Lloyd Research and Permissions Editing
Senior Product Team Associate: Christine Lomas
Supervising Editor: Joanne Limebeer
Copy Editor: Erin Moore
Proofreader: Rohini Herbert
Plant Production Coordinator: Michelle Saddler
Manufacturing Production Coordinator: Lena Keating
Cover Design: Greg Devitt
Cover Image: © alphaspirit/Shutterstock
Interior Design: Greg Devitt, Liz Harasymczuk
Composition: Aptara®, Inc.
Printer: Webcom Inc.

Library and Archives Canada Cataloguing in Publication
Good, Walter S., author
      Building your dream : a Canadian guide to starting your own business / Walter S. Good, Wendy Mayhew.—9th edition
Previous editions published under title: Building a dream.

Includes bibliographical references and index.
ISBN 978-0-07-133888-2 (pbk.)

1. New business enterprises—Textbooks.   2. Entrepreneurship—Textbooks.   3. New business enterprises — Canada — Textbooks.
4. Entrepreneurship—Canada—Textbooks.   I. Mayhew Wendy, 1951-, author   II. Title.

HD62.5.G66 2014   C2013-906043-X
658.1'1

ABOUT THE AUTHORS

WALTER GOOD

Walter Good is a Senior Scholar in the Asper School of Business at the University of Manitoba. Dr. Good is the author of the bestselling textbook and self-help guide on entrepreneurship, *Building Your Dream,* now in its ninth edition. He is a past president of the Canadian Council for Small Business and Entrepreneurship, a fellow of the International Council for Small Business and a recent recipient of the Queen Elizabeth II Diamond Jubilee Medal for service in the community. His teaching and research interests include entrepreneurship, business planning, and small business management. Dr. Good's work has appeared in numerous national and international publications. He brings a comprehensive view to the issues facing businesses as they prepare to meet the challenges of an increasingly competitive marketplace.

WENDY MAYHEW

Wendy Mayhew is an accomplished businesswoman with a flair for helping first-time entrepreneurs establish successful businesses. Drawing on early experience in the telecom and satellite technology sectors, Wendy is always on the watch for innovative ways to harness technology in the service of business needs. Among the first to recognize the potential of social media to gather business intelligence, engage clients, and market products and services, Wendy's perspective on web-assisted business development is particularly appealing to today's generation of would-be entrepreneurs.

An example of Wendy's innovative approach is the recent completion of a 13-part reality Web series entitled *Real World Entrepreneur Training.* Incorporated into a digital course on the McGraw-Hill Ryerson *Connect* platform, the behind-the-scenes videos and associated teaching and learning material provide fascinating insights as entrepreneurs and their advisers grapple with the many challenges of establishing a business.

As a professional adviser and as a long-time volunteer contributor to the Canadian Youth Business Foundation and other organizations focused on entrepreneurial development, Wendy continues to share how-to advice and success strategies with business startups across Canada.

BRIEF CONTENTS

CONTENTS

PREFACE

ABOUT THIS BOOK

This self-help guide and workbook is intended to provide a vehicle to lead prospective small-business owners and potential entrepreneurs through the fundamental stages involved in starting a business of their own in a logical and sequential way.

Many people fantasize about being self-employed and having a business of their own at some stage in their lives. For most, this dream never becomes a reality. They do not really know the risks involved and feel very uncomfortable with the uncertainty associated with taking the initial step. There is also a high percentage of businesses that fail. Failure, for the most part, occurs because they do not entirely understand the tasks required to get a new business venture off the ground successfully and that they must continue to work on their business once it is launched.

For the past decade or so, the number of people who have started their own businesses has increased dramatically across North America. People's level of interest in and awareness of the entrepreneurial option has virtually exploded. This has been fostered and reinforced by governments at all levels, which have come to recognize the positive impact small-business startups have on job creation and regional economic development. The Internet, business magazines, the popular press, and the television have fuelled this interest with numerous items on the emotional and financial rewards of having a business of your own. They have glamorized the role of entrepreneurs in our society and established many of them, such as Ryan Holmes of Hootsuite, Tobias Lütke of Shopify, Christine Magee of Sleep Country Canada, Heather Reisman of Indigo Books & Music Inc., and Ron Joyce of Tim Hortons as attractive role models. This has been accentuated over the past few years with the phenomenal success and, in some cases, subsequent failure of many Internet-based companies. However, some businesses, such as Google, Yahoo!, and eBay, have made a number of young entrepreneurs, for example, the owners of BufferBox and DNNresearch, as well as Jeff Skoll and Pierre Omidyar, and many of their employees multi-millionaires or even billionaires within a very short period of time.

STRUCTURE

Building Your Dream has been written for individuals who wish to start a business of their own or want to assess their own potential for such an option. This includes men and women, of all ages, who dream of some type of self-employment, on either a full-time or a part-time basis. This book contains a comprehensive overall framework outlining the entrepreneurial process, descriptive information, practical outlines, checklists, screening questionnaires, and various other tools that will enable you to evaluate your own potential for this type of career and guide you through the early stages of launching a successful business of your own.

This book covers a range of topics that will increase your understanding of what it takes to succeed in an entrepreneurial career. From an overview of entrepreneurship and the entrepreneurial process, the book spreads outward to consider the skills, personality, and character traits possessed by many successful entrepreneurs; how to find and evaluate a possible idea for a business; and how to market and sell your product or service, buy an existing firm, or acquire a franchise. It provides a comprehensive outline for conducting a feasibility study to evaluate the potential of your concept and discusses the ways you can carry on your business, protect your product or service concept or idea, and find the financing necessary to get your new business off the ground. In Stage 5, you will be introduced to Business Plans, where there is a comprehensive framework for preparing a detailed and professional business plan.

PEDAGOGICAL DEVICES TO AID LEARNING

Building Your Dream is divided into "Stages," each of which provides a descriptive overview of a topic, some conceptual material indicating the principal areas to be considered or evaluated, and a series of outlines, worksheets, checklists, and other forms that can be completed in conducting a comprehensive assessment of that stage in the new venture development process.

The **Opening Cases,** new to the ninth edition, highlight entrepreneurs who have come up with brilliant ideas, found a niche that needed to be served, or in some cases, learned the hard way, and yet are all successful entrepreneurs today.

The "**Other Considerations**" boxes highlight some additional material that is directly related to that stage.

STARTUP MYTHS AND REALITIES

Myth 1: I'm smart—I can just wing it.

The "FYI" (For Your Information) boxes refer you to a number of websites that have supplementary material specifically related to the topics discussed in that stage. This enables you to readily obtain further information on subjects that may be of particular interest.

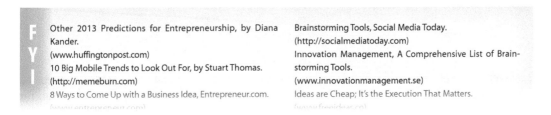

The ninth edition contains an increased number of "**Entrepreneurs in Action**" examples illustrating how people are actually going about building their businesses and are trying to make things work for themselves on a day-to-day basis.

ENTREPRENEURS IN ACTION

TELL US ABOUT US

THE INDUSTRY

Tyler Gompf said there's a growing demand in North America for the kinds of products and services that Tell Us About Us offers.

The firm got its start by developing a software application for the restaurant industry that enabled restaurant customers to an-

Each chapter contains a quote and a photo of a Canadian Entrepreneur answering the question, **What do you like about being an Entrepreneur?,** providing insight into their favourite aspect of their chosen career path.

What do you like about being an Entrepreneur?

Being an entrepreneur is like being a musician, you have to have a natural inclination and the desire, then take lessons and practise, practise, practise.

Marnie Walker, Owner
401 Bay Centre
*Top W100 Canadian
Entrepreneur 2012*
www.401bay.com

Figures and tables are included to illustrate relevant ideas and concepts.

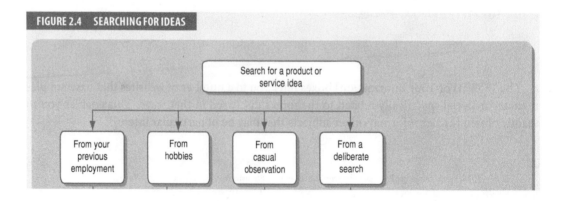

FIGURE 2.4   SEARCHING FOR IDEAS

Search for a product or service idea

- From your previous employment
- From hobbies
- From casual observation
- From a deliberate search

Overall, the book provides a practical opportunity for you to realistically assess the potential opportunity for your concept or idea and enable you to develop a detailed program or plan for your own new venture.

ORGANIZATION

STAGE ONE: ASSESSING YOUR POTENTIAL FOR AN ENTREPRENEURIAL CAREER

This stage provides you with an opportunity to assess your personal attitudes and attributes and to see how they compare with those of "practising" entrepreneurs. It will also enable you to evaluate your managerial and administrative skills and experience and determine your financial capacity for starting a business. The importance of conducting your business affairs in an ethical manner is also emphasized, and an example of a code of ethics developed by a small organization is provided for your information and guidance.

STAGE TWO: EXPLORING BUSINESS IDEAS AND OPPORTUNITIES

This stage describes several sources from which you might obtain ideas for your prospective new venture and identifies a number of areas of opportunity for the future on the basis of dynamic changes now taking place within Canadian society. It also outlines a six-step opportunity selection process, describes the characteristics of an "ideal" or "model" business, and presents a framework for assessing the attributes of your product or service idea in comparison to this ideal. Stage Two also discusses the Venture Opportunity Screening Model (VOSM) for identifying entrepreneurial opportunities on the basis of a series of criteria identified by actual entrepreneurs as being important in their venture selection process. A number of entry strategies that can help you decide on the best way to proceed are outlined as well.

STAGES THREE AND FOUR: MARKET FEASIBILITY STUDY & COST AND PROFITABILITY ASSESSMENT

Stages Three and Four provide a step-by-step process for transforming your chosen new venture concept from the idea stage to the marketplace. This is accomplished by means of a feasibility study. A typical feasibility study considers the following areas:

- The concept of your proposed venture
- The technical feasibility of your idea
- A detailed assessment of your market potential
- Managing the supply situation
- Conducting a cost and profitability assessment
- Your plans for future action

Comprehensive outlines are provided to enable you to assess each of these areas in a preliminary way and to put your thoughts and ideas down on paper as well as online resources to build your feasibility study. Much of this material can be incorporated into your subsequent business plan.

STAGE FIVE: BUSINESS PLANS

This stage, which serves as a capstone for the book, provides a framework for the development of a comprehensive business plan for your proposed new business venture, whether it is a retail or service business, a manufacturing company, a web-based company or a technology company. It lays out the necessary steps in the business planning process such as:

- Developing a vision statement
- Formulating a mission statement
- Defining the fundamental values by which you will run your business
- Setting clear and specific objectives
- Developing a realistic business plan

It also explains what a business plan is, how long it should be, and why it is important that you develop such a plan for your proposed venture and actually write it yourself. It lays out the contents of a typical business plan and provides an outline to follow for developing your plan.

The **Business Plans,** available online with Connect, are "real" business plans that have been prepared by entrepreneurs who have started their own businesses. These plans can easily be used as a guide as you are preparing your business plan following the framework that is outlined in *Building Your Dream*. It is suggested that you work on your Business Plan as you go through the stages of *Building Your Dream*. By the end of the book, you should have a complete, or close to complete plan, and be ready to attract the necessary external resources and support to get your proposed business off the ground.

STAGE SIX: LEGAL CONSIDERATIONS

One of the principal issues to be resolved when starting a new business is the legal form of organization the business should adopt. The most prevalent forms a business might assume include individual or sole proprietorship, general or limited partnership, and incorporation. This stage reviews each of these forms and discusses the advantages and disadvantages of each from the standpoint of the prospective entrepreneur. It discusses how to select and register a name for your business and presents an overview of such issues as the types of licences and permits your business might require, your responsibilities for collecting and remitting a variety of employee contributions and taxes, the impact of provincial employment standards on your business, and protecting your investment.

Many entrepreneurs are also innovators and inventors and are faced with the problem of how to protect the idea, invention, concept, system, name, or design that they feel will be the key to their business success. This stage also discusses the various forms of intellectual property, such as patents, copyrights, trademarks, and industrial design, and what is required to protect your interest in their development.

STAGE SEVEN: FINANCING YOUR BUSINESS AND ACCOUNTING PRACTICES

The principal question relating to any new venture is where the money is going to come from to get the new business off the ground. This stage examines the major sources of funds for new business startups—personal funds, bootstrapping, bank loans, government agencies and programs, angel investors, venture capital, and the latest way to raise funds, web platforms. It also discusses the main issues that need to be addressed when looking to raise capital from private sources. A framework for you to determine just how much money you think you will need to launch your business and where that financing might possibly come from is provided as well. Stage Seven also includes some basic information on Canadian Accounting Practices, including the Canadian Tax Systems and keeping records of your income and expenses.

STAGE EIGHT: MARKETING

New to this edition is Stage Eight, Marketing, a stage completely dedicated to the different aspects of marketing. It is a true statement that if you do not understand the marketing process, you will not be in business for long. In fact, lack of sales, which is related to marketing, is the major cause of business failure. This stage explains the different types of marketing, traditional and nontraditional, including the most up-to-date ways of marketing your business, both online and offline.

The marketing stage explains the different types of online business models for developing an "elevator pitch" and your website; registering a domain name, the importance of content marketing and blogging; ways to build an email list; and how landing pages work and whether your business needs one to drive traffic to your business. The topics in this stage will help build on your marketing strategy. You will be able to choose the information that you think will be most suitable to your business.

STAGE NINE: SALES

Another new addition to this edition is Stage Nine, Sales. As mentioned above, marketing and sales go hand in hand—you cannot have one without the other. By the end of this, you will know the process involved in starting the sales process and how to close the sale.

In this stage, we discuss how to prepare for sales and the different ways of approaching prospective clients through referrals and cold calls, as well as getting an appointment, how to follow-up after the appointment, and how to ask for the sale.

The sales pipeline funnel, how to respond professionally to tough questions asked by a prospective client, the importance of customer service, and when do you give up on the lead before moving on are other topics that are covered. You will also learn the importance of staying in touch with your client once the sale has been solidified.

STAGE TEN: BUYING A BUSINESS

The obvious route to self-employment is to start a business of your own based on a new or distinctive idea. Another route to explore is the possibility of buying an existing firm. This stage deals with such issues as finding a business to buy and the factors to consider in making the acquisition. It also discusses ways to determine an appropriate price to pay for a business and the pros and cons of buying versus starting one. A comprehensive checklist is provided for considering a number of potential business acquisitions.

We also discuss some of the issues involved in working in a family business—a situation that has some unique opportunities and risks and can become very complicated. Planning for succession is typically the most important issue, so it is critical that the business have a viable succession plan in place.

STAGE ELEVEN: BUYING A FRANCHISE

In recent years, franchising has become one of the fastest-growing sectors of North American business. More and more people are considering the franchise alternative as a means of getting into business for themselves. This stage explores the concept of franchising in some detail. It defines franchising so that you know exactly what the concept means. The broad range of types of franchises available is presented, along with an overview of the legal requirements associated with franchising and the terms and conditions contained in a typical franchise agreement. This stage also discusses how to find and apply for a franchise and provides some guidance on franchising your own business. It presents an extensive checklist for evaluating potential franchise opportunities.

This section is followed by a glossary of financial terms as well as a summary listing of all the websites referenced in the book so that you can readily access the source of much of the material referred to in the book without having to flip through all the pages to find it.

Good luck in successfully building your dream.

INSTRUCTOR AND STUDENT RESOURCES

Great care was used in the creation of the supplemental materials to accompany *Building Your Dream,* Ninth Edition. Whether you are a seasoned faculty member or a newly minted instructor, you will find the support materials to be comprehensive and practical.

McGraw-Hill Connect™ is a web-based assignment and assessment platform that gives students the means to better connect with their coursework, with their instructors, and with the important concepts that they will need to know for success now and in the future.

With Connect, instructors can deliver assignments, quizzes, and tests online. Instructors can edit existing questions and author entirely new problems. Track individual student performance—by question, by assignment, or in relation to the class overall—with detailed grade reports. Integrate grade reports easily with Learning Management Systems (LMS).

By choosing Connect, instructors are providing their students with a powerful tool for improving academic performance and truly mastering course material. Connect allows students to practise important skills at their own pace and on their own schedule. Importantly, students' assessment results and instructors' feedback are all saved online—so students can continually review their progress and plot their course to success.

Connect also provides 24/7 online access to an eBook—an online edition of the text—to aid them in successfully completing their work, wherever and whenever they choose.

Key Features
Simple Assignment Management

With Connect, creating assignments is easier than ever, so you can spend more time teaching and less time managing.

- Create and deliver assignments easily with selectable questions and testbank material to assign online.
- Streamline lesson planning, student progress reporting, and assignment grading to make classroom management more efficient than ever.
- Go paperless with the eBook and online submission and grading of student assignments.

Smart Grading

When it comes to studying, time is precious. Connect helps students learn more efficiently by providing feedback and practice material when they need it, where they need it.

- Automatically score assignments, giving students immediate feedback on their work and side-by-side comparisons with correct answers.
- Access and review each response; manually change grades or leave comments for students to review.
- Reinforce classroom concepts with practice tests and instant quizzes.

Instructor Library

The Connect Instructor Library is your course creation hub. It provides all the critical resources you will need to build your course, just how you want to teach it.

- Assign eBook readings and draw from a rich collection of textbook-specific assignments.
- Access instructor resources, including ready-made PowerPoint® presentations and media to use in your lectures.
- View assignments and resources created for past sections.
- Post your own resources for students to use.

eBook

Connect reinvents the textbook learning experience for the modern student. Every Connect subject area is seamlessly integrated with Connect eBooks, which are designed to keep students focused on the concepts key to their success.

- Provide students with a Connect eBook, allowing for anytime, anywhere access to the textbook.
- Merge media, animation, and assessments with the text's narrative to engage students and improve learning and retention.
- Pinpoint and connect key concepts in a snap using the powerful eBook search engine.
- Manage notes, highlights, and bookmarks in one place for simple, comprehensive review.

INSTRUCTOR AND STUDENT SUPPLEMENTS

INSTRUCTOR'S MANUAL The Instructor's Manual, prepared by the author, Wendy Mayhew, includes a wealth of information to assist instructors in presenting this text and their course to its best advantage.

COMPUTERIZED TEST BANK Created by Sandra Wellman, Seneca College, this flexible and easy-to-use electronic testing program allows instructors to create tests from book-specific items. The Test bank contains a broad selection of multiple choice, true/false, and essay questions. Instructors may add their own questions, as well as edit existing questions. Each question identifies the learning objective, page reference, and difficulty level. Multiple versions of the test can be created and printed.

MICROSOFT® POWERPOINT® PRESENTATIONS Prepared by Sandra Wellman, Seneca College, this complete set of PowerPoint® Presentation slides is provided for each chapter. The presentations are based around course learning objectives and include many of the figures and tables from the ninth edition textbook as well as some additional slides that support and expand the text discussions. Slides can be modified by instructors.

INTERACTIVE WORKSHEETS Prepared by Sandra Wellman, Seneca College, these interactive Microsoft® Excel® worksheets and financial templates help students analyze the financial aspects of their new business ideas. These templates also facilitate preparation of financial statements required for their feasibility study and their overall business plan preparation.

ENTREPRENEURSHIP VIDEOS Entrepreneurship videos are available online with Connect and to Instructors on DVD with Closed Captioning. Please contact your Learning Solutions Consultant for more information.

SUPERIOR LEARNING SOLUTIONS AND SUPPORT The McGraw-Hill Ryerson team is ready to help you assess and integrate any of our products, technology, and services into your course for optimal teaching and learning performance. Whether it is helping your students improve their grades, or putting your entire course online, the McGraw-Hill Ryerson team is here to help you do it. Contact your Learning Solutions Consultant today to learn how to maximize all of McGraw-Hill Ryerson's resources!

For more information on the latest technology and Learning Solutions offered by McGraw-Hill Ryerson and its partners, please visit us online: www.mcgrawhill.ca/he/solutions.

ACKNOWLEDGEMENTS

Very comprehensive suggestions for changes and improvements based on the previous edition and drafts of this edition were received from numerous professors across the country, including:

- Cibylla Rakestraw, Grande Prairie College
- Maria Blazkiewicz, Dawson College
- Ron Rubinoff, Seneca College
- Shoja Mazidi, Lethbridge College
- Terry Zinger, Laurentian University
- Ron Pawlowski, Georgian College

Their comments were very helpful in improving and refining the concept of the book to make it even more useful to students and prospective entrepreneurs.

I would like to thank the college and university students and others who have used the earlier editions of this book over the years and have gone on to start new business ventures of their own. Their insatiable desire to explore their personal capacity for an entrepreneurial career and their drive to explore the mysteries of franchising, venture capital, and similar topics associated with the formation of a successful new business have enabled many of them to build their dream. I hope all of us have been able to play a small part in that process.

—WALTER GOOD

There are so many people to thank for their time and assistance in writing the ninth edition of *Building Your Dream*.

The first two that come to mind are Prescott (Scott) Ensign and Walter Good. Without the introduction to McGraw-Hill Ryerson from Scott, *Building Your Dream* would only have been a dream of mine. Thank you, Scott! The second person I need to thank is Walter Good for providing the framework and the help and guidance for me to work from. It made my rewrite much easier than starting the process over again.

To the countless entrepreneurs, Dan Martell, Ron Joyce, Shannon Tessier, Zack Patterson and Casey Grey, Phil Telio, Andy McGuire, and Scott Hallam, who when asked, immediately agreed to share their business experiences through interviews, to form part of this book.

To all the successful business owners who provided me with quotes on why they love being an entrepreneur. To all entrepreneurs who I reached out to for permission to use their articles in the book, and their assistance in clarifying some information to make it easier for students to understand. I could not have done this without you—you are the epitome of true entrepreneurship! I only wish I had room to thank each and every one of you individually.

To my husband, who encouraged me and kept me going, and to my McGraw-Hill Ryerson team, Kim and Becky, for their patience and understanding during the overwhelming times I had as a first-time author.

—WENDY MAYHEW

PROLOGUE

WHAT IS ENTREPRENEURSHIP?

Congratulations on exploring the world of Entrepreneurship! Whether you decide to become an entrepreneur yourself or work for someone else, the skills and information that you will take away from *Building Your Dream* will help guide you in whatever direction you take.

Entrepreneurship has become a worldwide phenomenon. Nations around the world are implementing initiatives to celebrate, inspire, and accelerate entrepreneurship. Startup Canada was started in 2012 with a six-month tour across Canada. The tour provided a platform for the Canadian entrepreneurship community to come together, share ideas, identify gaps and opportunities, and commit to community-level action.

No one has a definitive answer as to why this is happening, but the latest numbers from Industry Canada, Key Small Business Statistics, indicate there are 2.4 million established businesses across Canada. These numbers do not take into account businesses that have not registered with the provincial or federal governments. And a recent report from CIBC[1] indicates that more than half a million Canadians were in the process of starting their own business as of June 2012. The report from CIBC also suggests that this might just be the beginning—the next decade might see the strongest startup activity in the Canadian economy on record!

The gradual shift to a strong culture of individualism and self-betterment, the role of technology in driving the transition from boardrooms to basements, the more global and interconnected markets that require greater specialization, flexibility, and speed, as well as small business–friendly demographic trends are among those forces that are likely to support a net creation of 150,000 new businesses in Canada in the coming years.

New entrepreneurs are choosing self-employment as a career rather than being forced into business by lack of employment opportunities. Being a self-starter increases the probability of the business succeeding. Chances of forced self-employment, as a means of financial survival, will not necessarily succeed. Not all of "forced" businesses will fail, but the likelihood of succeeding are much lower. Being forced to do something does not give you the drive, know-how, and passion that you have when you choose your own destiny.

The overall economic impact of this revolution on Canada is difficult to determine precisely, but it is substantial and suspected to drive longer-term growth. It is being fuelled by such factors as the following:

- It has never been easier to start a business with all the free information and inexpensive tools to help you. The Internet is full of resources for you, as is your local library, where you have access to books and videos on starting your business. Most major cities across Canada have an office of some sort, where you can go to get help by talking to business advisers and entrepreneurs in residence who have been through their own startup.

- Structural changes in the economy, such as organizational downsizing or "rightsizing," with the consequent loss of middle-management positions in many larger companies and government departments—This has led to considerable outsourcing of services previously performed in-house and the growth of self-employment to meet this need.

- Younger Canadians wanting more independence and so becoming more interested in self-employment.

- A growing number of immigrants who have difficulty with conventional employment because of their limited skills and/or language issues or whose academic credentials are not recognized in Canada.

- An aging population and a large number of baby boomers reaching their fifties, an age when people often tend to look toward self-employment. Approximately 30 percent of startups are over 50, the largest segment of startups.[2]

- Increasing consumer demand for more personalized products and services that smaller companies are often better positioned to provide.

The entrepreneurial revolution has been propelled by the explosion of the Internet and technology-based companies. It is difficult to keep up with how fast technology is changing. Smartphones, tablets, apps, cloud computing, crowdfunding, video, and social media are just a few of the current leaders in this revolution and will continue to advance as this relatively new era continues to evolve. However, not all businesses are all about technology. For most businesses, it is imperative that you have a web presence, whether it is for information on your company or selling your product. But many successful companies that have a web presence are not technology companies. One example is Purdy's Chocolatier, located in British Columbia, which has 59 locations across B.C., Alberta, and Ontario. Karen Favelle, CEO & Chocolatier Connoisseur, is a recent recipient of Canada's Most Powerful Women: Top 100 awarded by the Women's Executive Network.

One thing that is clear is that the proportion of total employment in the country accounted for by these smaller firms has increased dramatically. They have created the lion's share of new jobs, while employment levels in large businesses have remained constant or decreased. See Figure 1.

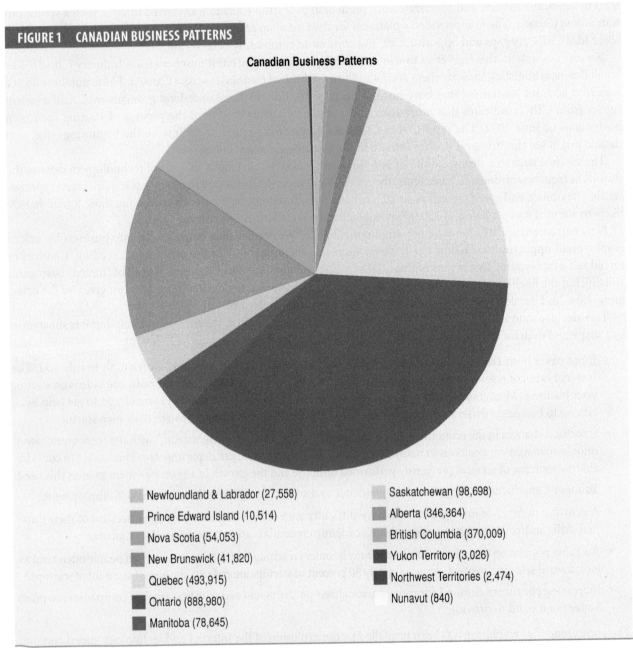

FIGURE 1   CANADIAN BUSINESS PATTERNS

Canadian Business Patterns

Newfoundland & Labrador (27,558)
Prince Edward Island (10,514)
Nova Scotia (54,053)
New Brunswick (41,820)
Quebec (493,915)
Ontario (888,980)
Manitoba (78,645)
Saskatchewan (98,698)
Alberta (346,364)
British Columbia (370,009)
Yukon Territory (3,026)
Northwest Territories (2,474)
Nunavut (840)

Source: Statistics Canada, Table 551-0002, Canadian Business Patterns (www.statcan.gc.ca). Search Table 551-0002.

This book has been developed for people who may be aspiring entrepreneurs and are giving some thought to the possibility of joining the many others who have started some kind of business of their own. Almost everyone has given some thought to owning and managing their own business at some point in their lives. Provided you know what it takes to be successful, it can be a very rewarding way of life. These rewards may be financial, in terms of providing you with a return for the time and money you and others may invest in the business and the risks you take in operating your own firm. Having an independent business also gives you the freedom to act independently, make your own decisions, and be your own boss. This is a very important motivating factor for many people. It can also be a very satisfying way of life, full of the fun and personal satisfaction derived from doing something that you genuinely love to do.

Table 1 shows startups as a share of employed population, by province. British Columbia is the hub for startups, with a nation-leading 3.7 percent of the working population being part of a startup. Alberta is second, largely due to the positive spin-off from the energy sector and the business service sector, followed closely by Saskatchewan. The prosperity to open a business in Ontario is in line with the national average, while Manitoba has the lowest relative level of startup activity.

Starting a new business, however, can be very risky at the best of times. It typically demands long hours, hard work, a high level of emotional involvement and commitment, as well as financial risk and the possibility of failure. Your chances of succeeding will rise if you spend some time carefully evaluating your personal situation and circumstances and trying to anticipate and work out as many potential problems as you can before you invest any money.

This prologue introduces you to the concept of entrepreneurship and gives you some idea of what is required to be successful. It will also discuss some of the folklore and stereotypes that exist around entrepreneurship and dispel a few of the myths that have come to surround entrepreneurs.

Entrepreneurship is difficult to define precisely. Entrepreneurs tend to be identified, not by formal rank or title, but in retrospect—after the implementation of an innovation or idea.

For others, there may be some kind of significant *triggering* event. Perhaps these individuals had no better career prospects than starting businesses of their own. Sometimes the individual has received an inheritance or otherwise come into some money, moved to a new geographic location, been passed over for a promotion, taken an early retirement, been laid off or fired from a regular job, or just does not like the job they are doing. Any of these factors can give birth to a new business.

In *Building Your Dream,* you will read about entrepreneurs from across Canada, some you will know and others you will not, but they are all successful. You do not have to be well known to be a huge success. Take Luc Levesque, for example. Luc started TravelPod, the first web travel blog in 1995. In 2006, Luc TravelPod was acquired by Trip-Advisor, an Expedia company. Luc is now responsible for TripAdvisor's global Search Engine Optimization and is also the general manager for the TravelPod business unit.

Marnie Walker built her first business, Student Express, from a startup in 1990 to a multi-million dollar school business company with a fleet of 250 buses and annual revenues of over $10 million. After selling Student Express, Marnie went on to launch 401 Bay Centre, a shared office centre, located in downtown Toronto. With annual revenue of between $1 million and $2 million, Marnie has turned another business into a successful venture.

TABLE 1 STARTUPS AS A SHARE OF EMPLOYED POPULATION—BY PROVINCE[3]	
Latest information is from 2011.	
British Columbia	3.7
Alberta	3.1
Saskatchewan	2.9
Ontario	2.8
Quebec	2.5
Atlantic provinces	2.4
Manitoba	2.0

And look at the young entrepreneurs that started BufferBox. Do you think they imagined being acquired not only as quickly as they were but by a powerhouse such as Google?

There are unsuccessful entrepreneurs as well. Some, because they did not manage their business properly and others due to circumstances beyond their control. John and Scott Hallam, partners in ParkInMyDriveway, launched a business where owners who had space in their driveway could list their available spaces for rent when these spaces were not being used. John and Scott were passionate and had crunched the numbers and were optimistic that ParkInMyDriveway would succeed. They did everything they were supposed to do. They had talked to city officials to ensure what they were doing fell within the guidelines, and from what they were told, all was good. But, in the end, they found they had not done all the necessary research and closed their business.

This book can only guide you and will not give you the yes or the no about pursuing your dream. After you finish *Building Your Dream*, you will have a better idea about whether you want to take the chance and risk of launching your own business. It is entirely up to you.

The word "entrepreneur" is of French origin, derived from the term "entreprendre," literally translated as "between-taking." This term describes the activities by which an individual takes a position between available resources and perceived opportunities and, because of some unique behaviour, makes something positive happen. One of the first uses of the word was in the late 1700s by economist Jean-Baptiste Say, who is credited with developing the concept of "entrepreneurship."

Over time, many other formal definitions of the term "entrepreneur" have emerged. Many of these modern definitions incorporate the notions of "risk taking" and "innovation," as well as the elements put forward by Say.

For example, Investopedia defines an entrepreneur *as an individual who, rather than working as an employee, runs a small business and assumes all the risk and reward of a given business venture, idea, or good or service offered for sale. The entrepreneur is commonly seen as a business leader and innovator of new ideas and business processes.*[4]

Other definitions are quite simple, such as *an individual who starts his/her own business.*[5]

Perhaps one of the most straightforward definitions is that an entrepreneur is *someone who perceives an opportunity and creates an organization to pursue it.*[6]

And the most thought provoking: *Entrepreneurship is the pursuit of opportunity without regard to resources currently controlled.*[7]

Many people have said that entrepreneurship is really a "state of mind." Though you may be extremely innovative and creative, prepared to work hard, and willing to take risks, both financial and otherwise, these qualities may still be insufficient to guarantee business success. The missing element may be a necessary entrepreneurial mindset: a single-mindedness and dedication to the achievement of a set of personal goals and objectives; confidence in your intuitive and rational capabilities; a capacity to think and plan in both tactical and strategic terms; and an attitude that reflects a penchant for action, frequently in situations in which information is inadequate. One other very important element of being an entrepreneur is to realize that unless you are extremely lucky, you have to understand the marketing and selling process. Many entrepreneurs either do not understand this process or are afraid of it. It does not matter which one it is, it is important to understand you will never be successful if you do not market your product or service. This is the biggest downfall of small business owners.

If you are thinking that freedom is a part of starting your business, then you need to think again. You will have the freedom, for the most part, to act and control your own destiny without any boundaries or limits, unlike working for someone else. However, it is vital to any business to have an advisory board or board of directors. Boards are there to help with the direction and growth of your business. You may not always agree with what they advise, but you need to understand that you brought them into the company to help you with the future growth of your company. If you are going to stay small and do not have any growth plans, then "freedom" may very well work for you.

Entrepreneurship is not the same as management. The principal job of professional managers is to make a business perform well. They take a given set of resources—such as money, employees, machines, and materials—and orchestrate and organize them into an efficient and effective production operation. Managers tend to delegate much of their authority and to rely on the use of formal control systems, and are usually evaluated on the basis of organizationally determined objectives. In contrast, entrepreneurs typically rely more on an informal, hands-on management style and are driven by their personal goals. Their principal job is to bring about purposeful change within an organizational context. They break new ground and, in many cases, each step is guided by some larger plan.

As agents of change, entrepreneurs play, or can play, a number of roles or perform a variety of different functions in the economy. They can, for example:

1. Create new product and/or service businesses

2. Bring creative and innovative methods to developing or producing new products or services

3. Provide employment opportunities and create new jobs as a result of growing their business consistently and rapidly

4. Help contribute to regional and national economic growth

5. Encourage greater industrial efficiency/productivity to enhance our international competitiveness

You should keep in mind, however, that other people also play a significant role in determining who will succeed or fail in our society. For example, entrepreneurs will succeed only when there are customers for the goods and services they provide. But, in most circumstances, it is the entrepreneurs themselves who play the principal role in determining their success or failure. Many still manage to succeed in spite of poor timing, inferior marketing, or low-quality production by combining a variety of talents, skills, and energies with imagination, good planning, and common sense. The entrepreneurial or self-employed option has many attractions, but along with these come risks and challenges and the possibility of failure.

THE COMPONENTS OF SUCCESSFUL ENTREPRENEURIAL VENTURES

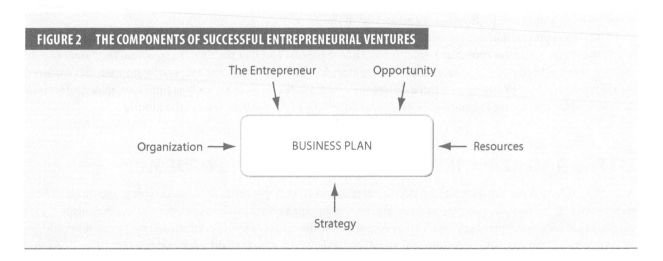

FIGURE 2   THE COMPONENTS OF SUCCESSFUL ENTREPRENEURIAL VENTURES

As illustrated in Figure 2, all of the following elements are outlined and captured in the business plan.

THE ENTREPRENEUR It all begins with the wannabe entrepreneur, the driving force behind the business and the coordinator of all the activities, resources, and people that are needed to get it off the ground. This individual will have conducted some assessment of his or her own resources and capabilities and made a conscious decision to launch the business.

THE OPPORTUNITY The wannabe entrepreneur must have an idea or concept that he or she feels has the potential to develop into a successful enterprise. The concept behind the business must be carefully evaluated to determine whether there is likely to be a market, and if it might represent a viable opportunity. The object is to determine the magnitude of the returns that might be expected with successful implementation.

ORGANIZATION To capitalize on any business opportunity, an organizational structure must be established, with a manager or management team and a form of ownership.

RESOURCES Some essential financial and other resources must be obtained. The key usually is money. Money is the "enabler" that makes everything else happen. Other key resources may include physical plant and equipment, technical capability, and human resources. But for the most part, new business owners work from home or share office space with other like-minded business people. There is a growing trend of incubators/accelerators across Canada, where startups share office space, resources, and advice from the owners of the incubator/accelerator, which, in turn, equates to lower startup costs. Visit the incubator website to find an accelerator/accelerator near you.

STRATEGY Once a startup appears likely, a specific strategy must be developed and a feasibility study conducted. The feasibility study is a way to test your business concept to see whether it actually does have market potential. It is a series of tests you should conduct to discover more and more about the nature and size of your business opportunity. After each test, you should ask yourself whether the opportunity still appears to be attractive and if you still want to proceed. Has anything come up that would make the business unattractive or prevent you from going forward with its implementation? Throughout this process you probably will modify your concept and business strategy several times until you feel that you have it right.

THE BUSINESS PLAN The business plan not only describes your business concept but also outlines the structure that needs to be in place to successfully implement the concept. The plan can be used to assist in obtaining the additional resources that may be needed to actually launch the business and guide the implementation of the strategy. It assumes you have a feasible business concept and have now included the operational components needed to execute the strategy. It describes in some detail the company you are going to create.

Figure 3 illustrates how these components interrelate, the action required at each phase of the implementation of the process, and where these issues are addressed in the book.

This process proceeds in one manner or another to a conclusion, resulting in the implementation of the business. While the model gives the appearance that this is a linear process and that the flow is sequential from one stage to another, this has been done to provide a logical structure for the book and is not necessarily the case. For example, the entrepreneur may pursue two or three different elements at the same time, such as finalizing an organizational structure while also trying to compile the resources necessary to get the business off the ground.

MYTHS AND REALITIES CONCERNING ENTREPRENEURSHIP

According to noted author-lecturer-consultant Peter Drucker, entrepreneurs defy stereotyping. He states, "I have seen people of the most diverse personalities and temperaments perform well in entrepreneurial challenges."[8] This suggests that some entrepreneurs may be true eccentrics, while others are rigid conformists; some are short and fat, while others are tall and thin; some are real worriers, while others are very laid-back and relaxed; some drink and smoke very heavily, while others abstain completely; some are people of great wit and charm, while others have no more personality than a frozen fish.

Despite all that is known about entrepreneurs and entrepreneurship, a good deal of folklore and many stereotypes remain. Part of the problem is that while some generalities may apply to certain types of entrepreneurs and certain situations, most entrepreneurial types tend to defy generalization. The following are examples of long-standing myths about entrepreneurs and entrepreneurship:[9]

- **Myth 1 Entrepreneurs are born, not made.**

  Reality While entrepreneurs may be born with a certain native intelligence, a flair for innovation, a high level of energy, and a core of other inborn attributes that you either have or you do not have, it is apparent that merely possessing these characteristics does not necessarily make you an entrepreneur. The making of an entrepreneur occurs through a combination of work experience, know-how, personal contacts, and the development of business skills acquired over time. In fact, other attributes of equal importance can also be acquired through understanding, hard work, and patience.

FIGURE 3   OUTLINE OF THE ENTREPRENEURIAL PROCESS

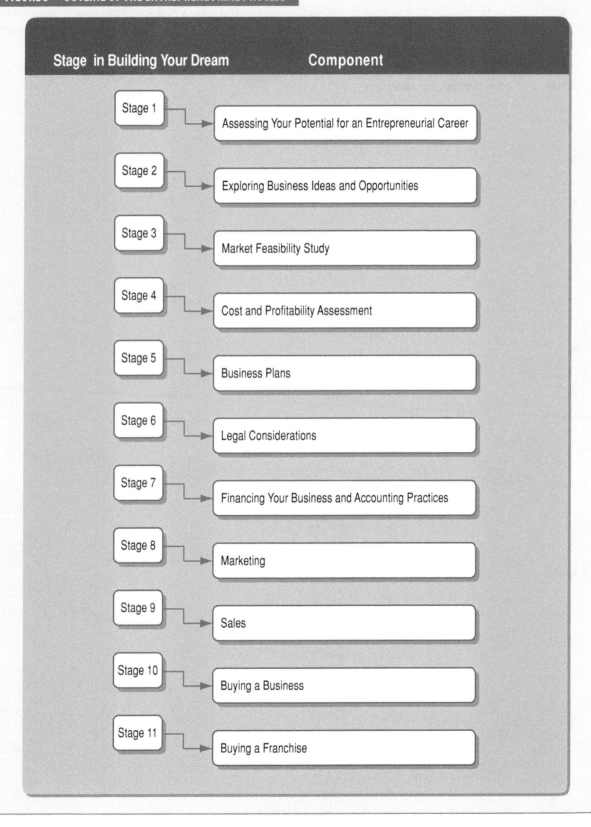

Stage in Building Your Dream   Component

Stage 1 → Assessing Your Potential for an Entrepreneurial Career

Stage 2 → Exploring Business Ideas and Opportunities

Stage 3 → Market Feasibility Study

Stage 4 → Cost and Profitability Assessment

Stage 5 → Business Plans

Stage 6 → Legal Considerations

Stage 7 → Financing Your Business and Accounting Practices

Stage 8 → Marketing

Stage 9 → Sales

Stage 10 → Buying a Business

Stage 11 → Buying a Franchise

- **Myth 2**   **Anyone can start a business. It is just a matter of luck and guts.**

  Reality   Entrepreneurs need to recognize the difference between an idea and a real opportunity to significantly improve their chances of success. If you want to launch and grow a high-potential new venture, you must understand the many things that you have to do to get the odds in your favour. You cannot think and act like a typical bureaucrat or even a manager; you must think and act like an entrepreneur. That often means initiating action, even if conditions are uncertain and existing rules have to be pushed to the limit.

- **Myth 3**   **Entrepreneurs are gamblers.**

  Reality   Successful entrepreneurs only take what they perceive to be very carefully calculated risks. They often try to influence the odds by getting others to share the risk with them or by avoiding or minimizing the risk if they have the choice. They do not deliberately seek to take more risk or to take unnecessary risks, but they will not shy away from taking the risks that may be necessary to succeed.

- **Myth 4**   **Entrepreneurs want to run the whole show themselves.**

  Reality   Owning and running the whole show effectively limits the potential for the business to grow. Single entrepreneurs can make a living, perhaps even a good one, but it is extremely difficult to grow a business by working single-handedly. Most successful ventures typically evolve to require a formal organization, a management team, and a corporate structure.

- **Myth 5**   **Entrepreneurs are their own bosses and completely independent.**

  Reality   Most entrepreneurs are far from independent and have to serve a number of constituencies and a variety of masters, including partners, investors, customers, employees, suppliers, creditors, their families, and pressures from social and community obligations. They do have the choice, however, to decide whether and when to respond to these pressures.

- **Myth 6**   **Entrepreneurs work longer and harder than corporate managers.**

  Reality   There is no evidence at all that entrepreneur's work harder than their corporate counterparts. Some do, and some do not. Both are demanding situations that require long hours and hard work. However, as owners they are tied to the business and responsible in ways that are different from employees' roles.

- **Myth 7**   **Entrepreneurs face greater stress and more pressures and thus pay a higher personal price in their jobs than other managers do.**

  Reality   Being an entrepreneur is undoubtedly stressful and demanding. But there is no evidence it is any more stressful than numerous other highly demanding professional roles, such as being the principal partner in a legal or accounting practice or the head of a division of a major corporation or government agency. Most entrepreneurs enjoy what they do. They have a high sense of accomplishment. For them it is fun rather than drudgery. They thrive on the flexibility and innovative aspects of their job and are much less likely to retire than those who work for someone else.

- **Myth 8**   **Starting a business is risky and often ends in failure.**

  Reality   This statement is undoubtedly true in many instances. Some studies have indicated that upward of 80 percent of new business startups fail within their first five years. However, success tends to be more common than failure for higher-potential ventures because they typically are directed by talented and experienced people able to attract the right personnel and the necessary financial and other resources.

  Vince Lombardi, the well-known former coach of the Green Bay Packers, is famous for the quotation, "Winning isn't everything—it's the *only* thing." But a lesser-known quote of his is closer to the true entrepreneur's personal philosophy. Looking back on a season, Lombardi was once heard to remark, "We didn't lose any games last season, we just ran out of time twice." Entrepreneurs learn from experience and are inclined to believe they have failed if they quit.

  Owning your own business is a competitive game, and entrepreneurs have to be prepared to run out of time occasionally. Businesses fail, but entrepreneurs do not. Many well-known entrepreneurs experience business failure, sometimes several times, before achieving success.

OTHER CONSIDERATIONS

WHY SMALL BUSINESSES FAIL

- Inexperience in running a business
- Not enough financing or too much debt
- Lack of mentors and advisers
- Not understanding you have to know how to market and sell your product/service
- Inability to handle rejection
- Thinking you can do it alone
- Not surpassing your competition in everything you do
- Poor market research
- Poor customer service
- Procrastinating instead of taking action

- **Myth 9   Money is the most important ingredient for success.**

  Reality   If the other important elements and the people are there, the money tends to follow. But it is not true that entrepreneurs are assured of success if they have enough money. Money is one of the least important ingredients of new venture success.

- **Myth 10   New business startups are for the young and energetic.**

  Reality   While youth and energy may help, age is absolutely no barrier to starting a business of your own. However, many people feel there is some threshold for an individual's perceived capacity for starting a new venture. Over time, you gain experience, competence, and self-confidence: These factors increase your capacity and readiness to embark on an entrepreneurial career. At the same time, constraints, such as increases in your financial and other obligations, grow and negatively affect your freedom to choose. The trade-offs between individual readiness and these restraints typically result in most high-potential new businesses being started by entrepreneurs between the ages of 25 and 40.

- **Myth 11   Entrepreneurs are motivated solely by their quest for the almighty dollar.**

  Reality   Growth-minded entrepreneurs are more driven by the challenge of building their enterprise and long-term capital appreciation than by the instant gratification of a high salary and other rewards. Having a sense of personal accomplishment and achievement, feeling in control of their own destiny, and realizing their vision and dreams are also powerful motivators. Money is viewed principally as a tool and a way of "keeping score."

- **Myth 12   Entrepreneurs seek power and control over other people so that they can feel "in charge."**

  Reality   Successful entrepreneurs are driven by the quest for responsibility, achievement, and results rather than for power for its own sake. They thrive on a sense of accomplishment and of outperforming the competition, rather than a personal need for power expressed by dominating and controlling other people. They gain control by the results they achieve.

- **Myth 13   Any entrepreneur with a good idea can raise venture capital.**

  Reality   Very few entrepreneurs get funded by venture capitalists (VCs). To be considered you must have a fantastic idea, know your market and competitors inside and out, and have a great pitch. But, before approaching a VC, build a relationship with them.

ENTREPRENEURS CAN AND DO MAKE GREAT EMPLOYEES

Many people dream of starting their own businesses, but not everyone is willing to take the risks nor the time and energy that is needed to run a business. Being an employee may have several benefits, from health insurance to a regular schedule and paycheque, but just because you do not want to own your own business does not mean you are not entrepreneurial—you are an intrapreneur—someone with the background that can be extremely beneficial to a company. In some cases, intrapreneurs have an edge over other candidates when applying for a position within a company. Why is this the case?

- Intrapreneurs think like their employers and can help ease the day-to-day burdens associated with owning your own business.
- Intrapreneurs are proactive. Intrapreneurs do not need to be told what to do—they see what needs to be done and do it.
- Intrapreneurs take ownership of their jobs. They rarely need supervision.

There is no need to be discouraged if you decide not to become your own boss. The qualities that you have to offer a company may easily help in the growth and success of the business. Being part of a winning team can be just as fulfilling as taking the risk yourself.[10]

Harley Finkelstein, chief platform officer at Shopify, became an entrepreneur while in university, selling T-shirts to help finance his studies. Harley was Shopify's first customer when he moved his company, Smoofer, online. He was so impressed with Shopify that he decided to bring his entrepreneurial experience to the company and closed his business. When asked what entrepreneurial qualities he brings to Shopify, Harley responded by saying he brings the hustle, the autonomy, and the resourcefulness that companies need on a daily basis.

Harley makes an excellent addition to Shopify by bringing his experience and understanding of how a business works.

ARE YOU AN ENTREPRENEUR OR A BUSINESS?

Michael Gerber, author of The *E-Myth*[11] says that a business owner does not really own her business, her business owns her. A business owner works *in* his business, while an entrepreneur works *on* his business.

A business is a business whether you are an entrepreneur or a business owner. The only difference between the two is how you operate the business.

Table 2 shows the differences between being an entrepreneur and a business. Which are you destined to be?

TABLE 2   DIFFERENCES BETWEEN AN ENTREPRENEUR AND A BUSINESS OWNER

Entrepreneur	Business Owner
• Starts a business from a unique idea or concept	• Starts a business from an existing idea or concept
• Innovative and revolutionary	• Traditional
• Customer-oriented	• Profit-oriented
• Excited	• Worried
• Happy	• Distressed
• A market leader	• A market player
• Focuses on cooperation	• Focuses on competition
• Gives life to his or her business	• His business gives him or her a living
• Works for the company	• The company works for him or her
• Thinks about making a sale to get a customer	• Thinks about getting a customer to make a sale
• Works smarter	• Works harder
• Passionate	• Passive
• Delegates	• Micro manages

About: **Small Business: Canada** An extensive source of information and links for Canadians running their own small business or thinking of starting one. This site will give you all the business resources, contacts, financial sources, and tools that you need to be a successful entrepreneur. (www.sbinfocanada.about.com)

Canada Business Service for Entrepreneurs A key network of business information and services and your link to the particular Canada Business Service Centre in your province or territory. (www.canadabusiness.gc.ca)

Industry Canada Canada's principal business and consumer site, containing a wealth of information useful to small business and access to the range of services provided by Industry Canada. (www.ic.gc.ca)

BizPal An online source of information on permits and licences. (www.bizpal.ca)

Canadian Youth Business Foundation CYBF helps young entrepreneurs (18–39 years of age) through the entire business life-cycle from prelaunch planning, to startup, to implementation. (www.cybf.ca)

CanadaOne An online publication for Canadian businesses with articles, resources, promotional tools, a free directory for Canadian companies, and more. (www.canadaone.ca)

PROFIT Magazine Canada's leading media brand dedicated to entrepreneurial business. (www.profitguide.com)

Canadian Business Magazine A business news and information portal for business leaders, entrepreneurs, and investors. (www.canadianbusiness.com)

Entrepreneurship.org Features a vast array of content and resources to assist entrepreneurs, business mentors, policy makers, academics, and investors through each phase of the entrepreneurial process. Entrepreneurship.org is a Kaufman Foundation site. (www.entrepreneurship.org)

The Kauffman Foundation The largest foundation devoted to entrepreneurship. (www.kauffman.org). Search for About the Foundation.

Entrepreneur Magazine The website of *Entrepreneur* magazine with articles about starting a business, money and finance, management and human resources, franchising, and a number of other related topics. (www.entrepreneur.com)

Inc.com The website for *Inc.* magazine that provides advice, tools, and services, to help business owners start, run, and grow their businesses more successfully. Contains information and advice covering virtually every business and management topic, including marketing, sales, finding capital, managing people, and much more. (www.inc.com)

SOHO An online resource that offers articles on small business. (www.soho.ca)

Techvibes A website dedicated to covering social, mobile, and startup news that impacts Canadians. (www.techvibes.com)

Startup North Dedicated to enabling technology entrepreneurs across Canada. (www.startupnorth.ca)

Suggested Reading Material
Redefining Success: Still Making Mistakes by Brett Wilson
The Art of the Start by Guy Kawasaki
The $100 Startup by Chris Guillebeau
Startup Communities by Brad Feld
The E-Myth Revisited by Michael E. Gerber

ASSESSING YOUR POTENTIAL FOR AN ENTREPRENEURIAL CAREER

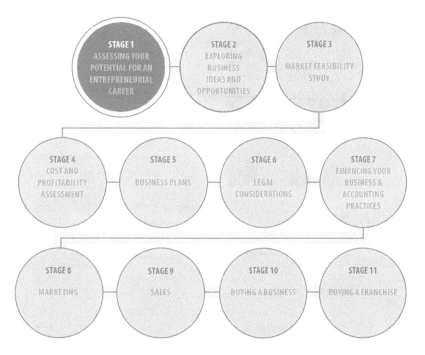

STAGE 1
ASSESSING YOUR POTENTIAL FOR AN ENTREPRENEURIAL CAREER

STAGE 2
EXPLORING BUSINESS IDEAS AND OPPORTUNITIES

STAGE 3
MARKET FEASIBILITY STUDY

STAGE 4
COST AND PROFITABILITY ASSESSMENT

STAGE 5
BUSINESS PLANS

STAGE 6
LEGAL CONSIDERATIONS

STAGE 7
FINANCING YOUR BUSINESS & ACCOUNTING PRACTICES

STAGE 8
MARKETING

STAGE 9
SALES

STAGE 10
BUYING A BUSINESS

STAGE 11
BUYING A FRANCHISE

LEARNING OBJECTIVES

By the end of this stage, you should be able to:

LO1 Evaluate your potential for becoming an entrepreneur through self-assessment quizzes.

LO2 Identify the attitudes and behaviours that will help turn your business dream into a reality.

LO3 Analyze the three different types of entrepreneurs.

LO4 Describe the skills needed by small-business owners.

LO5 Explain the importance of social entrepreneurship, ethics, and being socially responsible in business.

GOOD EARTH

CRAZY CRAFT-BEER CANUCKS ARE GOING WILD WITH FERMENTATION IN AN ONTARIO WINERY

© Elia Najem / Alamy

On a grey October afternoon at the Good Earth vineyard in Beamsville, Ontario, a crowd gathers around a cluster of steaming stainless-steel vats set up a few metres from the rows of swollen grapes. Iain McOustra, a brewer with Toronto's Amsterdam Brewing Co. and one of the architects of this madcap plan, periodically stirs a boiled concoction of grains, hops, and water that has the hue of milky coffee and smells faintly like shredded wheat. If McOustra is giddy, it's because he's exhausted and exhilarated by this, the culmination of three years of research and planning to make a sour beer in the back-breaking style of old-world Belgian breweries.

"This is certainly the craziest brew I've ever done," says the 31-year-old, who's been brewing beer professionally and in backyards for 13 years. "It's the most difficult brew to pull off; so much could go wrong."

Vital to the plan is the winery environment, especially at harvest time, when the air is thick with wild yeast and bacteria that will—it's hoped—float into the open vessels and ferment the grain mixture, or wort. This is a contemporary take on lambic beer, named after the town of Lembeek, Belgium, where the process was refined in the 1300s.

Where modern brewing methods inoculate the wort with lab-cultivated yeast varieties, traditional lambic beers were fermented spontaneously in shallow tubs called "cool ships" in wood structures where the planks were saturated with native micro flora. "This was before there were microscopes, before they even knew what yeast was," says Mike Lackey, a veteran brewer at Toronto's Great Lakes Brewery, who shares McOustra's obsessive devotion to beer making.

For Lackey, McOustra and the three other Ontario brewers involved in this opus (Jason Fisher and Jeff Broeders of Indie Alehouse and Sam Corbeil of Sawdust City Brewery), the old-world brewing process required major new-world expertise. "It takes a whole lot of science to dumb it down to the way it was done back then," McOustra says. "It's like throwing away everything we learned about brewing."

It started at Indie Alehouse with a five-hour boil of Ontario milled wheat, stinky aged hops, and gallons of water. Broeders and Corbeil babysat the boil overnight. In the morning, Lackey and McOustra transferred the hot wort into 20 kegs, loaded everything into a truck, and, in Beamsville, emptied the kegs into the open containers. The next 16 hours, when the wort and yeast were left to mingle in the vineyard, was the fun part. McOustra and Lackey passed around an endless assortment of beers, some from their respective breweries, some wacky creations they cooked up in Lackey's garage. Winemakers from nearby vineyards wandered over to ask technical questions about acidity and fermentation. The rest of the process was all about transport: moving the wort into 20 clean kegs, back to Toronto, and then into four oak wine barrels to ferment for three years. "I'm 100 percent confident this will work," says McOustra. "We've gone overboard on everything. Typically, there would be a five-hour exposure [to the yeast]; we did 16. Typically, the wort would be put into inert barrels; ours went into unwashed barrels. We were within feet of a vineyard; others might have been within three kilometres."

If all goes well, the brewers will end up with 800 litres of wild sour beer, a wholly unique flavour more tart than sour, crisp, and often fruity. They'll name it "Niambic" (McOustra says you can call a beer lambic only if it was brewed in that region of Belgium). Plans are under way for next year's wild brew at the same vineyard. "In a few years we can start blending the different vintages while still maintaining the authentic localness of it."

The craft beer Twittersphere has been abuzz with the news of a lambic-style brew in Canada. "There are no trade secrets in this world between brewers who are interested in pushing the boundaries of beer," says McOustra. "We can't compete with the big guys on pricing, but we can make beers with passion and craft, take chances on stuff, and push the industry forward."

Source: Jasmine Budak, "A Belgian Brew by Way of Beamsville," *MacLean's Magazine,* November 5, 2012, pp. 80–81.

The discussion in the prologue should have served to dispel many of the popular myths concerning entrepreneurship. This section will expand on the theme of entrepreneurial characteristics by proposing and discussing two important questions that are vital to you if you are interested in an entrepreneurial career:

1. Are there certain common attributes, attitudes, and experiences among entrepreneurs that appear to lead to success?
2. If such attributes, attitudes, and experiences exist, can they be learned, or are they inborn and thus available only to those with a "fortunate" heritage?

Research into these questions suggests that the answer to question 1 is yes, while the answer to question 2 is both yes and no. These answers, of course, are of little value to you on their own without some further explanation.

THE ENTREPRENEURIAL PERSONALITY LO1

In 1980, Tom Wolfe wrote a perceptive bestseller that examined the lives of America's leading test pilots and astronauts. According to Wolfe, becoming a member of this select club meant possessing "the right stuff," that is, the proper mix of courage, coolness under stressful conditions, a strong need for achievement, technical expertise, creativity, and so on. While Wolfe was not talking about entrepreneurs, his viewpoint is similar to the basic thesis held by many members of the "people school" of entrepreneurship: A person has to have the "right stuff" to become a successful entrepreneur.

There is considerable evidence, however, that a great deal of the ability and "right stuff" needed to become a successful entrepreneur can be learned (though probably not by everyone).

ENTREPRENEURIAL QUIZ

While most writers in the field of entrepreneurship agree that there is no single profile, no specific set of characteristics, which defines a successful entrepreneur, there do appear to be some common attributes, abilities, and attitudes. Prior to proceeding any further with our discussion of these entrepreneurial characteristics, it is suggested that you take the Entrepreneurial Quiz available online in Connect. The quiz will enable you to compare your personal attitudes and attributes with those of "practising" entrepreneurs.

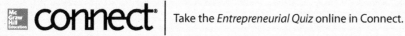 Take the *Entrepreneurial Quiz* online in Connect.

What Does Your Score Mean?

The Entrepreneurial Quiz is *not* intended to predict or determine your likely success or failure. However, if you answer and score the questionnaire honestly, it will provide considerable insight into whether you have the attitudes, lifestyle, and behaviour patterns consistent with successful entrepreneurship.

The higher your number of most desirable responses, the more your responses agree with those of successful entrepreneurs. High levels of agreement indicate that you *may* have the "right stuff" to succeed in an entrepreneurial career. You should make certain, however, that your responses reflect your real opinions and attitudes.

The word *may* is highlighted above because of the overwhelming importance of one particular set of attributes/ characteristics: commitment, determination, and perseverance. Scoring well on the test is not necessarily a guarantee of entrepreneurial success. Anything less than total commitment to your venture, and considerable determination and perseverance, will likely result in failure, regardless of the degree to which you may possess other important attributes. Your total commitment and determination to succeed helps convince others to "come along for the ride." If you are not totally committed, both financially and philosophically, to the venture, it is unlikely that potential partners, your employees, bankers, suppliers, and other creditors will have the confidence in you to provide the level of support your business will require.

What Attributes Are Desirable and Acquirable?

In a study of inductees into the Babson University Academy of Distinguished Entrepreneurs (www.babson.edu), only three attributes and behaviours were mentioned by most as the principal reasons for their success, and they were all learnable:

1. Responding positively to all challenges and learning from mistakes
2. Taking personal initiative
3. Having great perseverance

Other research has uncovered different lists of common learnable attributes. These qualities are also very desirable in the people entrepreneurs want to surround themselves with in building a high-potential business (see Figure 1.1).

ATTITUDES AND BEHAVIOURS   LO2

Following is a summary of the attitudes and behaviours that can be valuable in turning a business dream into reality. The proposed characteristics represent the conclusions of over 50 separate research studies into the essential nature of the entrepreneur.

Commitment, Determination, and Perseverance

More than any other single factor, a combination of perseverance and total dedication is critical. In many cases, these qualities have won out against odds considered impossible to overcome.

Determination and commitment can compensate for other weaknesses you may have. It requires substantial commitment to give up a well-paid job, with its regular paycheques, medical insurance, and pension and profit-sharing plans, and start out on your own.

Success Orientation

Entrepreneurs are driven by an immense desire to achieve the goals they initially set for themselves and then to aim for even more challenging standards. The competitive needs of growth-minded entrepreneurs are to outperform their own previous best results, rather than just to outperform another person. Unlike most people, entrepreneurs do not allow themselves to be concerned with failure. What they think about is not what they are going to do if they do not make it, but what they have to do to succeed.

Opportunity and Goal Orientation

Growth-minded entrepreneurs are more focused on the nature and extent of their opportunity rather than resources, structure, or strategy. They start with the opportunity and let their understanding of it guide these other important issues. Entrepreneurs are able to sense areas of unmet needs and their potential for filling these gaps. Effective entrepreneurs set goals consistent with their interests, values, and talents. These goals are generally challenging but still attainable. Their belief in the "reality" of their goals is a primary factor in their fulfillment of them. Having goals and a clear sense of direction also helps these individuals define priorities and provides them with a measure of how well they are performing.

FIGURE 1.1   WHAT IS YOUR ENTREPRENEURIAL POTENTIAL?

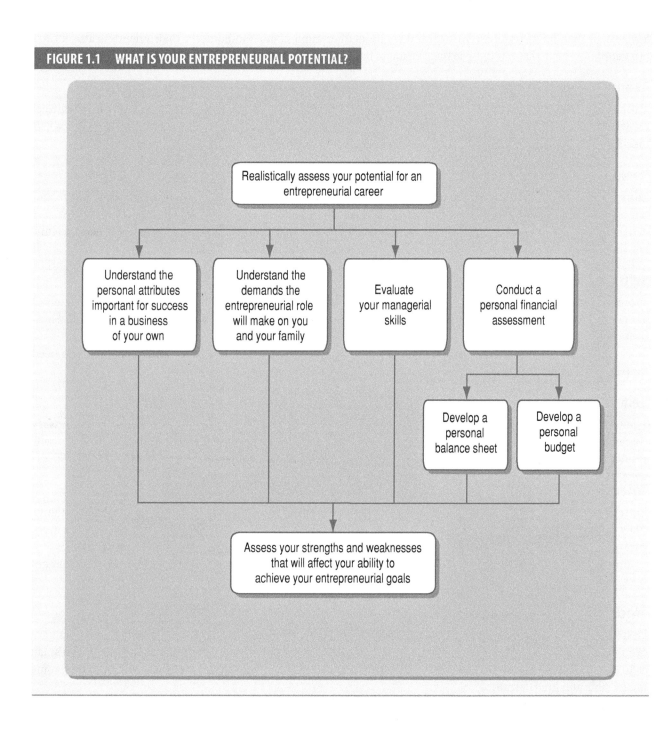

Action Orientation and Personal Responsibility

Successful entrepreneurs are action-oriented people; they want to start producing results immediately. They like to take the initiative and get on with doing it, today. The true entrepreneur is a doer, not a dreamer.

Persistent Problem-Solving, Need to Achieve

Entrepreneurs are not intimidated by the number or severity of the problems they encounter. In fact, their self-confidence and general optimism seems to translate into a view that the impossible just takes a little longer. They will work with a stubborn tenacity to solve a difficult problem. This is based on their desire to achieve the goals they have established for themselves. However, they are neither aimless nor foolhardy in their relentless attack on a problem or obstacle that can impede their business but tend to get right to the heart of the issue.

Reality Orientation

The best entrepreneurs have a keen sense of their own strengths and weaknesses and of the competitive environment in which they operate. In addition, they know when they are in trouble and have the strength to admit when they are wrong. This reality orientation allows them to avoid continuing on an ill-advised course of action.

Seeking and Using Feedback

Entrepreneurs have a burning desire to know how they are performing. They understand that to keep score and improve their performance they must get feedback, digest the results, and use the information they receive to do a better job. In that way, they can learn from their mistakes and setbacks and respond quickly to unexpected events. For the same reason, most entrepreneurs are found to be good listeners and quick learners.

Self-Reliance

Successful entrepreneurs trust the fate of their ventures to their own abilities. They do not believe that external forces or plain luck determine their success or failure. This attribute is consistent with their achievement and motivational drive and desire to achieve established goals.

In a similar vein, entrepreneurs are not joiners. Studies have shown that the need for affiliation, or a high need for friendship, often acts as a deterrent to entrepreneurial behaviour.

Self-Confidence

The self-confidence displayed by entrepreneurs is based on their feeling that they can overcome all the necessary challenges and attain their desired goal. They almost never consider failure a real possibility. While this self-confidence implies a strong ego, it is a different kind of ego—an "I know I'm going to do well" type of attitude.

Tolerance of Ambiguity and Uncertainty

Entrepreneurs tolerate ambiguous situations well and make effective decisions under conditions of uncertainty. They are able to work well despite constant changes in their business that produce considerable ambiguity in every part of their operation.

Entrepreneurs take change and challenge in stride and actually seem to thrive on the fluidity and excitement of such undefined situations. Job security and retirement are generally not of great concern to them.

Moderate Risk-Taking and Risk-Sharing

Despite the myth that suggests entrepreneurs are gamblers, quite the opposite is true. Effective entrepreneurs have been found, in general, to prefer taking moderate, calculated risks, where the chances of losing are neither so small as to be a sure thing nor so large as to be a considerable gamble. Like a parachutist, they are willing to take some measurable and predetermined risk.

The strategy of most entrepreneurs also includes involving other parties in their venture to share the burden of risk: Partners put money and reputations on the line; investors do likewise; and creditors and customers who advance payments, and suppliers who advance credit all share in the financial risk of the business.

Response to Failure

Another important attribute of high-performance entrepreneurs is their ability to treat mistakes and failures as temporary setbacks on the way to accomplishing their goals. Unlike most people, the bruises of their defeats heal quickly. This allows them to return to the business world again soon after their failure.

Rather than hide from or dismiss their mistakes, entrepreneurs concede their errors and analyze the causes. They have the ability to come to terms with their mistakes, learn from them, correct them, and use them to prevent their recurrence. Successful entrepreneurs know that they have to take personal responsibility for either the success or the failure of their venture and not look for scapegoats when things do not work out. They know how to build on their successes and learn from their failures.

Low Need for Status and Power

Entrepreneurs derive great personal satisfaction from the challenge and excitement of creating and building their own business. They are driven by a high need for achievement rather than a desire for status and power. It is important, therefore, to recognize that power and status are a result of their activities and not the need that propels them.

In addition, when a strong need to control, influence, and gain power over other people characterizes the lead entrepreneur, more often than not the venture gets into trouble. A dictatorial and domineering management style makes it very difficult to attract and keep in the business people who are oriented toward achievement, responsibility, and results. Conflicts often erupt over who has the final say and whose prerogatives are being infringed upon. Reserved parking spaces, the big corner office, and fancy automobiles become symbols of power and status that foster a value system and an organizational culture not usually conducive to growth. In such cases, the business's orientation toward its customers, its market, or its competitors is typically lost.

In a recent paper, "Differentiating the Effects of Status and Power: A Justice Perspective," published in the *Journal of Personality and Social Psychology,* Stern School of Business associate professor of management and organizations Steven Blader and co-author Ya-Ru Chen of Cornell University's Johnson School of Management examined the effect of power and status on how fairly individuals act towards others.

Across a series of studies, the authors demonstrated that those who regard themselves as higher in power treat others less fairly, as compared with those who regard themselves as lower in power. In contrast, those who regard themselves as higher in status treat others more fairly, as compared with those who regard themselves as lower in status. In other words, although power and status are often thought of as two sides of the same coin, they, in fact, have opposite effects on the fairness of people's behaviour.

These results have important implications for managers and for organizations more generally, since they inform our understanding of why managers treat those they interact with (including, importantly, their subordinates) fairly or unfairly. The authors suspect that the tendency by organizations to emphasize things that make managers feel more powerful (e.g., headcount, budget control, bonuses) actually leads those managers to treat their subordinates less fairly.[1]

What do you like about being an Entrepreneur?

Being an entrepreneur is like being a musician, you have to have a natural inclination and the desire, then take lessons and practise, practise, practise.

Marnie Walker, Owner
401 Bay Centre
Top W100 Canadian Entrepreneur 2012
www.401bay.com

Photo courtesy of Manie Walker

Successful entrepreneurs appear to have a capacity to exert influence on other people without formal power. They are skilled at "conflict resolution." They know when to use logic and when to persuade, when to make a concession, and when to win one. To run a successful venture, entrepreneurs must learn to get along with many different constituencies, who often have conflicting aims—customers, suppliers, financial backers, and creditors, as well as partners and others inside the company.

Integrity and Reliability

Long-term personal and business relationships are built on honesty and reliability. To survive in the long run, an approach of "Do what you say you are going to do!" is essential. With it the possibilities are unlimited. Investors, partners, customers, suppliers, and creditors all place a high value on these attributes. "Success" resulting from dishonest practices is really long-term failure. After all, anyone can lie, cheat, or steal and perhaps get away with it once, but that is not the way to build a successful entrepreneurial career.

OTHER CONSIDERATIONS

TOP 10 CHARACTERISTICS OF SUCCESSFUL ENTREPRENEURS

1. Independence—a desire to seize control of the future and become one's own boss
2. Persistence and Determination—the doggedness to continue pursuing a goal despite some setbacks and obstacles
3. Self-Confidence—a strong belief in one's own capabilities
4. Creativity—a natural curiosity, inquisitiveness, and the ability to "think outside the box"
5. Being Organized and Goal-Oriented—the ability to consolidate resources
6. Being a Visionary—having a vision for one's own future
7. Risk-Taking and Tolerance for Failure—being ready to take calculated risks and face whatever consequences accompany those risks
8. Perseverance and Hard Work—working at a problem until it is solved or an alternative is found
9. Commitment—remaining focused on an idea or task and not giving up at the first sign of trouble
10. Honesty and Honour—being honest and honourable in all business dealings and interpersonal relationships

Source: Adapted from Hilary Basile, *Entrepreneurs—Top 10 Essential Entrepreneurial Traits* (ezinearticles.com/?Entrepreneurs---Top-10-Essential-Entrepreneurial-Traits&id=531367), accessed January 2, 2013.

Team Builder

Entrepreneurs who create and build successful businesses are not isolated, super-independent types of individuals. They do not feel they have to receive all of the credit for their success, nor do they feel they have to prove they did it all by themselves. Just the opposite situation actually tends to be true. Not only do they recognize that it is virtually impossible to build a substantial business by working alone, but they also actively build a team. They have an ability to inspire the people they attract to their venture by giving them responsibility and by sharing the credit for their accomplishments. This hero-making ability has been identified as a key attribute of many successful corporate managers as well.

In addition to these characteristics, other attributes that have been associated with successful entrepreneurs are the following:

1. They are determined to finish a project once it has been undertaken, even under difficult conditions.
2. They are dynamic individuals who do not accept the status quo and refuse to be restricted by habit and environment.
3. They are able to examine themselves and their ideas impartially.
4. They are not self-satisfied or complacent.
5. They are independent in making decisions while willing to listen to suggestions and advice from others.
6. They do not blame others or make excuses for their own errors or failures.
7. They have a rising level of aspirations and expectations.
8. They have a good grasp of general economic concepts.
9. They are mature, self-assured individuals who are able to interact well with people of varying personalities and values.
10. They are able to exercise control over their impulses and feelings.
11. They have the ability to make the very best of the resources at hand.

AN ENTREPRENEUR'S CREED

1. Do what gives you energy—have fun.

2. Figure out how to make it work.

3. Anything is possible if you believe you can do it.

4. If you do not know it cannot be done, then you will go ahead and do it.

5. Be dissatisfied with the way things are—and look for ways to improve them.

6. Do things differently.

7. Businesses can fail. Successful entrepreneurs learn from failure—but keep the tuition low.

8. It is easier to beg for forgiveness than to ask for permission in the first place.

9. Make opportunity and results your obsession—not money.

10. Making money is even more fun than spending it.

11. Take pride in your accomplishments—it is contagious.

12. Sweat the details that are critical to success.

13. Make the pie bigger—do not waste time trying to cut smaller pieces.

14. Play for the long haul. It is rarely possible to get rich quickly.

15. Remember: Only the lead dog gets a change in scenery.

The consensus among most experts is that all of these personal characteristics can be worked on and improved through concerted practice and refinement. Some require greater effort than others, and much depends on an individual's strength of motivation and commitment to grow. Developing these attributes should not be very different from personal growth and learning in many other areas of your life.

THE NOT-SO-LEARNABLE CHARACTERISTICS

The attributes listed next are those that many experts consider to be innate and, thus, not acquirable to any great degree. Fortunately, the list is quite short. It is from these not-so-learnable characteristics that the conclusion that entrepreneurs are "born, not made" is principally derived. However, while possessing all these attributes would be beneficial, there are many examples of successful business pioneers who lacked some of these characteristics or who possessed them to only a modest degree:

1. High energy, good health, and emotional stability

2. Creativity and an innovative nature

3. High intelligence and conceptual ability

4. The ability to see a better future and a capacity to inspire others to see it

It is apparent from this discussion that entrepreneurs work from a different set of assumptions from those of most "ordinary" people. They also tend to rely more on mental attitudes and philosophies based on these entrepreneurial attributes than on specific skills or organizational concepts.

Many of these points are summed up in "An Entrepreneur's Creed" in the Other Considerations box above, a general philosophy outlining the entrepreneurial approach to doing business.

A DIFFERENT APPROACH

Some people feel this personality approach to identifying entrepreneurial tendencies in individuals is fraught with methodological problems and validity issues. For example, much of the research the Entrepreneurial Quiz (in Connect) is based upon was not specifically intended to be used in measuring entrepreneurship. The results were borrowed from psychology and applied to the area of entrepreneurship. Critics also claim these theories were intended for use across a broad range of situations and to measure general personal tendencies and do not have the level of situational specificity necessary to be any useful predictor of entrepreneurial success. They also feel the traditional assumption in much of this research that personality is formed in an individual's earliest years and essentially remains stable thereafter ignores the fact that entrepreneurship involves an individual operating *in an environment*, so theoretical models to predict entrepreneurial success need to be more interactive. Attributes are susceptible to change over time and circumstances. They are dependent upon the situational context.

To overcome these issues, some authors feel that "attitude" is a better approach to the description of entrepreneurs than personality and personal characteristics. Robinson et al. developed and tested an Entrepreneurial Attitude Orientation (EAO) scale intended to overcome some of the issues related to the personality approach.[2] They defined "attitude" as the predisposition of the individual to respond in a generally favourable or unfavourable manner with respect to the object of the attitude (in this case, organizational creation and innovation). Attitudes, therefore, represent the way we interact with the world around us. Their research also recognized that people relate to the world through three types of reaction:

- Cognition: this includes mental activities such as knowledge, thoughts, beliefs, and opinions.
- Affect: that is, emotions associated with thoughts, actions, or objects in our environment.
- Behaviour: the way we respond to conditions in our environment, including habits and intentions.

"Attitude" is a combination of all three. The EAO focuses specifically on "business" activities and considers what you think or believe about those activities (cognition), how you feel about those activities (affect), and how you might tend to behave regarding business activities (behaviour). Their EAO model is based on this tripartite notion of attitude. It contains four subscales that measure:

1. Achievement in business, referring to the extent of your desire to achieve concrete results in business.
2. Innovation in business, relating to how you perceive you might act upon business activities in new and unique ways.
3. The extent of your desire for personal control over business outcomes.
4. Your sense of self-worth or self-esteem relative to business affairs.

Robinson et al. were able to show that EAO successfully distinguished between existing entrepreneurs and non-entrepreneurs. Other research has further demonstrated that individuals who indicated that they had intentions of starting a business also demonstrated high levels of EAO.[3]

A condensed version of the EAO Business Attitudes Survey is available in Connect. It largely focuses on the four basic subscales. Consistency across these scales is an indicator of your personal, internal focus. You want to determine the extent to which your thoughts, feelings, and behaviour are consistent with each other. When all three are aligned, there is a synergy that enables you to stay on track and continue to perform at a high level. That is very positive from the standpoint of becoming a successful entrepreneur. Try it, and get some idea of the extent to which you have an "entrepreneurial mindset" as well as a comparison with entrepreneurs who have already started and operate their own businesses.

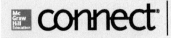 Take the *Entrepreneurial Attitude Orientation (EAO) Survey* online in Connect.

PERSONAL SELF-ASSESSMENT

The purpose of this discussion has been to have you evaluate your personal attitudes, behaviour tendencies, and views to determine the extent to which you seem to fit the typical entrepreneurial profile. Now you should complete the Personal Self-Assessment Questionnaire, which will help you summarize your feelings regarding your potential for self-employment.

Remember, there are no right or wrong answers, and you are not being judged.

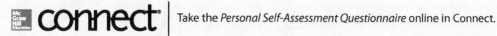 Take the *Personal Self-Assessment Questionnaire* online in Connect.

MANAGERIAL SKILLS INVENTORY

The Managerial Sills Inventory questionnaire can be used to develop an inventory of your skills and capabilities in each of the five areas of management outlined in this stage. For each management area, the questionnaire lists some corresponding skills. Rate your present level of expertise for each skill listed by placing an "X" under the appropriate number in the charts (1 indicates minimal skill, while 5 indicates a great deal of skill). Beneath each section, in the space provided, briefly describe where and when you obtained this experience.

The goal of this inventory is to assess the level of your present skills, with the purpose of identifying areas that may need improvement.

 Complete the *Managerial Skills Inventory* online in Connect.

Many of these attitudes are illustrated by the comments made by Tom Poole in the Entrepreneurs in Action box. Poole, for example, feels the principal character trait common to himself and other entrepreneurs is the "act of faith"—their strong belief that their concept or idea is "fantastic" and their readiness to jump in with both feet. Is this approach always successful? Of course not. But by being flexible and driven by a strong desire to "make it," he feels these individuals succeed more often than they should.

Others may think of business as a "gritty reality" involving constant responsibility and considerable stress rather than the glamourous lifestyle commonly perceived by the general public. Yet they are still prepared to undertake such burdens. Why? Perhaps it is a personal need to challenge themselves, to test their potential, reach goals and fulfill a mission.

WHAT KIND OF ENTREPRENEUR ARE YOU LIKELY TO BE?   LO3

Many references to the term "entrepreneur" seem to presume that there is only one kind of individual who fits the definition. As you can see from the Entrepreneurs in Action examples, however, not all entrepreneurs are the same. John Warrillow, a Toronto-based marketing consultant, spent three years interviewing more than 500 small-business owners. He used that research to develop attitudinal profiles for three entrepreneurial archetypes.

Craftspeople

They comprise less than 70 percent of small business owners and derive their sense of self-worth from their mastery of a craft or trade. While they do not think of themselves as entrepreneurs, they still have the resources and confidence to operate independently. They are more interested in developing their skills than in growing their revenue and generally work alone or employ one other person, often a spouse. They prefer to identify themselves by their

ENTREPRENEURS IN ACTION

THE ENTREPRENEUR EXPOSED

Over the years, people have asked me many questions about my business. But there are two questions I have found myself answering most often: "Why did you give up a promising career to leap into the world of the entrepreneur?" (which my father-in-law continues to ask me weekly) and, "Would you do it again?" For the longest time I was unable to provide good answers, and quite frankly, I never gave them much thought. However, as I grow older and perhaps more philosophical, I have pondered these questions. The answers are slowly beginning to take shape, and I believe my conclusions might shed some light on entrepreneurs in general.

I think the answers lie in a character trait common to most, if not all, entrepreneurs. By "entrepreneur," I do not mean the corporate executive who takes an early retirement package to start a home-based consulting business (not that there's anything wrong with that). I am talking about that crazy s.o.b. who quits his job as a C.A. and sells his mother to secure the capital needed to start a rubbish-collection company. Take a look around you at the entrepreneurs that you know. What do these people have in common? Are they all a little wacky? Eccentric? Unorthodox? Most likely; it goes with the territory.

If the prospective entrepreneur were reasonable and orthodox, he or she would use conventional methods of measuring the risk associated with giving up everything for a leap into the unknown. The consequence of conducting a proper "decision-tree" analysis would be that no one would ever take the step.

So how does an entrepreneur approach the "go/no-go" decision-making process? Well (at the risk of revealing that I never really had a master plan), I think the typical entrepreneur does some initial research, becomes absolutely convinced that his or her idea is fantastic, and jumps. This act of faith is the litmus test for entrepreneurs. Some people may decide that an idea is great but requires more research, and some spend years explaining to their friends how they had developed the concept long before Ms. X (who went on to make a fortune with the idea). But true entrepreneurs leap in with both feet.

I decided to jump in February 1989. I quit my high-paying, secure job with a multinational company, moved my wife and two and one-half children into a camper van, and set out to find a business to run. My gamble paid off—the company I eventually bought has grown from three employees, a 1,800-square-foot "factory," and $350,000 in annual sales to the current 800 employees, five production facilities, and $80 million plus in revenue.

USED WITH PERMISSION OF SEPP'S GOURMET FOODS INC.

Do entrepreneurs always succeed? Of course not. We simply don't hear as much about the failures. But entrepreneurs do succeed more often than circumstances suggest they should. Why? Often for what business schools call the "wrong" reasons: the speed of their decision-making, the dearth of analysis and the fact that they hold nothing back, financially, physically or emotionally. How do these seemingly irrational actions improve the chances of success? By acting quickly, the entrepreneur reduces the likelihood of having the idea "stolen"; the cursory analysis allows the entrepreneur to avoid an analysis-paralysis affliction; and by investing everything, the consequences of failure are so dire that . . . well, they just cannot afford to fail! . . .

Now back to the questions that I have been asked so many times over the years. First, why did I do it? Well, it was a "mix" of about one part crazy and two parts ignorance. And once I had taken the plunge, it was about 100 percent fear. Most entrepreneurs, if pressed for an honest response, would likely acknowledge that their early days were not unlike mine.

Would I do it again? The answer is complicated. In this hypothetical situation, assuming I had the knowledge I have now, the answer is a categorical "No." Of course not. I would know that what I was undertaking was probably close to impossible. Equipped with this information, my analysis would result in a "no-go" decision. I may be crazy, but I'm not stupid!

But if you re-phrase the question and ask whether I would take another entrepreneurial plunge, the answer is "Yes, of course." Why? I think the Steve Martin film *Parenthood* contains the best answer to that question. Toward the end of the movie, a mother explains life to her risk-averse son (Martin). She tells of being young and going to the fair with his father. He always wanted to ride on the merry-go-round, while she preferred the roller coaster. On the merry-go-round, she explained, you saw the same things go by again and again. It became rather boring. The roller coaster, on the other hand, was exhilarating, sometimes even frightening. But once she had ridden the roller coaster, she could never go back to the merry-go-round.

So, having taken the plunge and ridden the roller coaster, I can never return to the merry-go-round. And to those of you who are riding the merry-go-round, mix yourself a cocktail consisting of one part crazy and two parts ignorance. Drink it in one gulp and go for the ride of your life (www.seppsfoods.com).

In June 2010, Ralcorp Holdings, Inc. acquired Sepp's Gourmet Foods Ltd. Terms of the transaction were not disclosed. Sepp's continues to operate in Canada.

Source: Tom Poole, "The Enrepreneur Exposed," PROFIT (PROFITguide.com), July 12, 2001. Updated, January 2, 2013 by Wendy Mayhew. Used with Permission: © 1998–2013 Rogers Publishing Limited. All rights reserved.

craft first and as business owners as an afterthought only. They say "I'm a plumber," for example, or mechanic, film maker, vet, farmer, or grocer, before they say "I'm a business owner."

Freedom Fighters/Lifestyle Business

They seek financial independence above anything else and the freedom to spend their time as they wish. They do not aspire to be the next Terry Matthews, as that would bog them down and distract them from their goal of being free to work hard to control their own destiny. That is because their prime motivator is not growth but simply being in business for themselves. They comprise roughly 28 percent of all small businesses and typically employ three to 50 staff and grow less than 30 percent a year. More than half the freedom fighters are college educated, and 30 percent are women. They are more likely to hire family and tend to treat their staff as family members. Examples of Freedom Fighters/Lifestyle Business are mompreneurs, consultants, and retailers.

Freedom Fighters are generally strong family people and put an emphasis on staff relations and customer care. Freedom Fighters learn to become sophisticated businesspeople because they have to master difficult remote control systems, such as accounting and business-performance analysis, to gain their independence from the day-to-day running of their businesses.

Empire Builders

They are the 10 percent of growth-oriented business owners who are motivated almost solely by achievement, usually measured in terms of company growth. You can usually identify Empire Builders by the fact that their companies grow by more than 30 percent annually. As a result, they are the most high-profile and high-profit group. More than 75 percent have college or university degrees. These go-getters work long hours and expect a lot from themselves and their staff.

The Empire builder is the one most generally associated in popular imagination as the "typical entrepreneur"—always busy with the next project, with an insatiable thirst for growth and wealth, aiming to take over or revolutionize markets and industries. These are people like Terry Matthews (Wesley Clover), Larry Rossy (Dollarama), Guy Laliberté (Cirque du Soleil), and Sandra Wilson (Robeez Footwear). But Warrillow reckons they make up a mere 2 percent of business owners.

Interestingly, he says the Empire Builder is less concerned with money than with power. They tend to see money as simply another tool with which to build their empires.

If you are planning to go into a business of your own, which of these three groups do you think you would fall into? Empire Builders are the people we tend to read about in the newspapers and financial magazines. It is important to recognize, however, that not everyone can be or wants to be an Empire Builder and there are many other opportunities for you to start a business and still be quite happy and do very well.

Similarly, Vesper identified a considerable number of entrepreneurial types.[4] His typology includes:

1. **Solo, self-employed individuals.** These include most independent small business operators, tradespeople, such as agents, technicians, and brokers, and many hourly-rate professionals, such as accountants, dentists, doctors, and lawyers.

2. **Deal-to-dealers.** These small business owners have had more than one venture, often in quite different lines of business.

3. **Team builders.** These entrepreneurs go on to build larger companies through hiring and delegation of authority.

4. **Independent innovators.** These are traditional inventors who hit upon ideas for better products and then create companies to develop, produce, and sell them in the marketplace.

5. **Pattern multipliers.** This group includes entrepreneurs who spot an effective business pattern and multiply it to realize profits on the multiple units. Becoming a franchisor is one effective way of multiplying business patterns for a profit.

6. **Economy-of-scale exploiters.** These entrepreneurs exploit the fact that unit costs tend to shrink as volume expands. This has been practised principally by entrepreneurs in the discount retail merchandising business.

7. **Capital aggregators.** These entrepreneurs are able to pull together a substantial financial stake that enables them to initiate ventures that require large front-end capital, including banks, insurance companies, and mutual funds.

8. **Acquirers.** These entrepreneurs buy a going-concern. They will often take over businesses that are in trouble and try to straighten them out or buy businesses that they can *add value* to in some way, perhaps before selling them off again.

It has been said that entrepreneurship is really a state of mind. An individual may be extremely innovative and creative, be prepared to work long hours, and feel luck is on his/her side, but this is not sufficient to guarantee business success. What is missing is the necessary entrepreneurial mindset: a single-mindedness and dedication to the achievement of a set of personal goals and objectives, a confidence in their intuitive and rational capabilities, a capacity to think and plan in both strategic and tactical terms, and an attitude that reflects a penchant for action. The individuals in the Entrepreneurs in Action boxes definitely seem to possess this mindset.

EVALUATING YOUR BUSINESS SKILLS   LO4

There is a lot more to succeeding as an entrepreneur than just having the proper background, attitudes, and lifestyle. This next section discusses another factor you should consider in assessing your potential for becoming a successful entrepreneur: Do you have the requisite managerial and administrative skills needed to manage and operate a business?

Possessing the necessary managerial skills is an essential ingredient to succeeding in any small venture. It is estimated that the principal reason for the failure of small firms is poor management. Witness the experience of restaurateurs Richard Jaffray and Scott Morison. They thought they had learned a lot in building up their chain of Cactus Club Cafes in the lower mainland of British Columbia. They figured they "could do no wrong," decided to branch out, and opened four additional Clubs, two each in Calgary and Edmonton. Within six months, they knew they had a problem, and six months later it all fell apart.

What could have gone wrong for these relatively seasoned entrepreneurs? "Everything," says Jaffray. Restaurant locations were selected by price rather than by location as they had been in British Columbia. They changed the original concept of the restaurants and abandoned their long-time practice of grooming existing employees to take over the management of new restaurants. They neglected to take local culture into account and charged British Columbia prices, which were 10 percent to 20 percent higher than comparable price levels in Alberta. In the end, three of the four Alberta locations were closed, and the whole experience ended up costing them about $3 million.

Having learned their lesson, the pair has rebuilt the business in British Columbia and Alberta. "Had we not gone right to the very bottom, I don't think we'd be as successful as we are today," says Jaffray. Cactus Club has now grown to over 20 restaurants throughout British Columbia and Alberta.

WHAT SKILLS ARE NEEDED BY SMALL-BUSINESS OWNERS?

Businesses, whether large or small, have to perform in a number of diverse functions to operate successfully. An entrepreneur, because of the limited amount of resources (human and financial) at his or her disposal, faces a particularly difficult time.

The business skills required by an entrepreneur (or some other member of the organization) can be broken down by function, as shown in Table 1.1 above.

INVENTORY OF YOUR MANAGERIAL AND ADMINISTRATIVE SKILLS

Now that you understand the range of skills necessary to enable your new business to succeed, the Managerial Skills Inventory can be used to develop an inventory of your skills and capabilities in several aspects of management. Your present level of expertise may be anything from minimal to having a great deal of skill. The goal of the inventory is to assess your present skills, with the purpose of identifying areas that may need improvement. Since each of these management skills is not required at an equivalent level in all new business situations, completing this inventory might also provide you with some insight into the type of business opportunities for which you are best suited.

WHERE CAN YOU ACQUIRE THE NECESSARY SKILLS?

It should be apparent from the lengthy list in Table 1.1 that few people can expect to have a strong grasp of all of these skills prior to considering an entrepreneurial career. The key question then becomes where and how you can acquire these skills. The available means for developing these business skills are outlined next.

TABLE 1.1 BREAKDOWN OF ENTREPRENEURIAL BUSINESS SKILLS	
1. MANAGING MONEY a. Borrowing money and arranging financing b. Keeping financial records c. Managing cash flow d. Handling credit e. Buying insurance f. Reporting and paying taxes g. Budgeting **2. MANAGING PEOPLE** a. Hiring employees b. Supervising employees c. Training employees d. Evaluating employees e. Motivating people f. Scheduling workers **3. DIRECTING BUSINESS OPERATIONS** a. Purchasing supplies and raw materials b. Purchasing machinery and equipment	c. Managing inventory d. Filling orders e. Managing facilities **4. DIRECTING SALES AND MARKETING OPERATIONS** a. Identifying different customer needs b. Developing new product and service ideas c. Deciding appropriate prices d. Developing promotional strategies e. Contacting customers and making sales f. Developing promotional material and media programs **5. SETTING UP A BUSINESS** a. Choosing a location b. Obtaining licences and permits c. Choosing a form of organization and type of ownership d. Arranging initial financing e. Determining initial inventory requirements

Job Experience

Every job you have had should have contributed to the development of some business skills. For example, working as an accountant might teach you:

1. How to prepare financial statements
2. How to make financial projections and manage money
3. How to determine the business's cash requirements, among other things

Working as a sales clerk might teach you:

1. How to sell
2. How to deal with the public
3. How to operate a cash register

In fact, many aspiring entrepreneurs consciously follow a pattern of "apprenticeship," during which they prepare themselves for becoming entrepreneurs by working in a family business or obtaining job experience directly related to their particular interests.

Perhaps the best experience, however, is working for another entrepreneur. In that case, you will learn to understand the overall process and skills required to operate your own business.

Club Activities

Many of the functions that service clubs and similar organizations perform in planning and developing programs are similar to those performed by small businesses. Some examples of what can be learned from volunteer activities are:

1. How to organize and conduct fundraising activities
2. How to promote the organization through public service announcements and free advertising
3. How to manage and coordinate the activities of other members of the organization

Education

Universities, community colleges, high schools, and government agencies, such as local business development organizations, provide many programs and individual courses in which essential business-related skills can be acquired. Some examples of applicable skills that can be learned from these programs include:

1. Business skills (from particular business classes)
2. Socialization and communication skills (from all school activities)
3. Bookkeeping and record-keeping skills (from accounting classes)

Your Friends

Most of us have friends who through their job experience and education can teach us valuable business skills. Some examples of useful information we may acquire from this source are:

1. Possible sources of financing
2. Assistance in selecting an appropriate distribution channel for your products
3. Information on the availability of appropriate sites or locations for your business
4. Sources for finding suitable employees

Your Family

Growing up with an entrepreneur in the family is perhaps the best learning experience of all, even though you may not be aware of the value of this experience at the time. Some examples of what you might learn from other members of your family are:

1. How to deal with challenges and problems
2. How to make personal sacrifices and why
3. How to keep your personal life and business life separate
4. How to be responsible with money

Home Experiences

Our everyday home experiences help us develop many business skills. Some examples of such skills are:

1. Budgeting income
2. Planning finances
3. Organizing activities and events
4. Buying wisely
5. Managing and dealing with people
6. Selling an idea

It can be hard for a single individual to wear all these "hats" at once. Partnerships or the use of outside technical or general business assistance can be an excellent supplement for any deficiencies in characteristics and skills a small business owner may have. Thus, it often becomes essential to identify an individual, or individuals, who can help you when needed. This outside assistance might come from one of the following sources:

1. A spouse or family member
2. A formal partnership arrangement
3. Hired staff and employees
4. External professional consultants
5. A formal course or training program
6. Regular idea exchange meetings or networking with other entrepreneurs

ASSESSING YOUR PERSONAL FINANCIAL SITUATION

In addition to your managerial capabilities, your financial capacity will be a very important consideration in your decision as to whether an entrepreneurial career is right for you. It will certainly be a critical factor to those you may approach for a loan to provide investment capital for your venture.

YOUR PERSONAL BALANCE SHEET

Your personal balance sheet provides potential lenders with a view of your overall financial situation so that they can assess the risk they will be assuming. Generally, if you are in a strong financial position, as indicated by a considerable net worth, you will be considered a desirable prospect. On the other hand, an entrepreneur with a weak financial position and a large number of outstanding debts may not meet the standards of most lenders.

From a personal standpoint, you might also want to reconsider becoming a small business owner if you cannot afford a temporary or perhaps even a prolonged reduction in your personal income.

Your personal balance sheet includes a summary of all your assets—what you own that has some cash value—and your liabilities or debts. Preparing a personal balance sheet is a relatively simple process:

- **Step 1** Estimate the current market value of all your "assets"—the items you own that have cash value—and list them.
- **Step 2** Add up the value of these assets.

- **Step 3**   List all your debts, also known as "liabilities."
- **Step 4**   Add up your liabilities.
- **Step 5**   Deduct your total liabilities from your total assets to find your "net worth."

You can use the Sample Balance Sheet Form, available in Connect, to help organize your assets and liabilities. The items listed are not exhaustive; the form is provided only as a guide for thinking about your present position. Since every business opportunity has its own unique capital (money) requirements, there is no specific dollar value for the personal net worth necessary to start a business. However, you should keep in mind that most private lenders or lending institutions typically expect a new small business owner to provide at least 40 to 50 percent of the capital required for startup. In addition, lenders consider the net worth position of prospective borrowers to determine their ability to repay the loan should the new business fail.

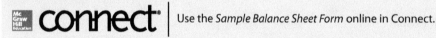 Use the *Sample Balance Sheet Form* online in Connect.

DEVELOPING A PERSONAL BUDGET

As well as determining your present net worth, you must also consider your personal living expenses when assessing your ability to provide the total financing needed to start a new business. In fact, you should evaluate your personal financial needs while in the process of determining whether an entrepreneurial career is right for you.

In some situations, you will need to take money from the business each month to pay part or all of your personal living expenses. If such is the case, it is crucial that this amount be known and that at least that much be set aside to be paid out to you each month as a salary.

If your new business is starting off on a limited scale, you might wish to continue holding a regular job to cover your basic living expenses and provide some additional capital to your fledgling operation. In some cases, your spouse's income may be sufficient to cover the family's basic living expenses, and it may not be necessary to consider your personal financial needs in making a go/no-go decision.

The Personal Living Expenses Worksheet is an effective means of estimating your present cost of living. From the totals on the worksheet, you can calculate the minimum amount of money you and your family will require on a regular monthly basis and determine from what sources this regular income will be obtained.

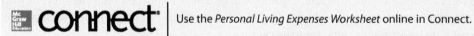 Use the *Personal Living Expenses Worksheet* online in Connect.

CHECK YOUR CREDIT RATING

One thing that may significantly impact your ability to obtain a loan or other financing for your venture is your *credit rating*. Your rating is based on your prior history in borrowing and repaying money. By regularly paying your bills, including credit cards, telephone bills, mortgages, lines of credit, and similar debts, on time you are building your credit rating. Without a good credit rating, few institutions will lend you money.

Your credit rating is maintained by two consumer reporting agencies in Canada, including Equifax Canada Inc. (www.Equifax.ca) and TransUnion Canada (www.transunion.ca). Lenders, such as retailers and financial institutions, provide these agencies with information about how you pay your bills. The agencies then assemble this information into your credit file indicating whether your bills are being paid on time (R1) or late (R4) or have not been paid and been placed with an agency for collection (R9). This information can dramatically affect your ability to obtain a personal loan or any other credit for personal or business purposes.

The information in the files of these reporting agencies is not always entirely accurate. You have a right to know what is in your file, so you should check the file periodically. Contact either of the above agencies, and they will tell you how you can obtain a copy of your personal report. If you notice any errors, report them back to the agency right away, and they will investigate the situation with the lender who reported the item. If the file is inaccurate, it will be changed right away.

ARE YOU READY FOR AN ENTREPRENEURIAL CAREER?
EXTERNAL ROLE DEMANDS

It is not enough simply to possess a large number and high level of the characteristics previously discussed as prerequisites for a successful entrepreneurial career. There are also certain external conditions, pressures, and demands inherent in the small business ownership role itself.

While successful entrepreneurs may share several characteristics with successful people in other careers, entrepreneurs' preference for and tolerance of the combination of requirements unique to their role is a major distinguishing feature.

Many of these requirements were mentioned earlier. What follows is a discussion of a few of the most relevant issues you should consider concerning your degree of readiness and preparedness for such a career.

Need for Total Commitment

As an entrepreneur, you must live with the challenge of trying first to survive in the business world, then to stay alive, and always to grow and withstand the competitive pressures of the marketplace. Almost any venture worth considering requires top priority on your time, emotions, and loyalty. As an entrepreneur you must be prepared to give "all you've got" to the building of your business, particularly during the initial stages of its development. Anything less than total commitment will likely result in failure.

Management of Stress

Stress, the emotional and physiological reaction to external events or circumstances, is an inevitable result of pursuing an entrepreneurial career option. Depending on how it is handled, stress can be either good or bad for an entrepreneur. The better you understand how you react to stressful situations, the better you will be able to maximize the positive aspects of these situations and minimize the negative aspects, such as exhaustion and frustration, before they lead to a serious problem.

Stress, in the short term, can produce excellent results because of its relationship to the type of behaviour associated with entrepreneurial activities, especially during the startup stage of a new business. There is some evidence that once individuals become accustomed to producing under stressful conditions, they seem to continue to respond in a positive manner; entrepreneurs tend to create new challenges to replace the ones they have already met, and to continue to respond to those challenges with a high level of effectiveness.

Economic and Personal Values

Entrepreneurs engaged in "for-profit" organizations, as opposed to social or "not-for-profit" organizations, must share the basic values of the free enterprise system: private ownership, profits, capital gains, and growth. These dominant economic values need not exclude social or other values. However, the nature of the competitive market economy requires belief in, or at least respect for, these values.

THE CONCEPT OF SOCIAL ENTREPRENEURSHIP   LO5

Up to now, our focus has been on "economic" entrepreneurship: the discovery, evaluation, and exploitation of opportunities for financial profit. However, we are hearing more and more about the concept of "social" entrepreneurship. This can be thought of as the discovery, evaluation, and pursuit of opportunities for social change. While both types of entrepreneurs are visionaries, tend to be opportunistic, and pay a lot of attention to building networks of contacts, social entrepreneurs tend to communicate their visions in moral terms, driven by a desire to achieve some form of social justice rather than make a dollar.[5]

Jeff Skoll, eBay's first president, has established a foundation specifically to support the efforts of social entrepreneurs. Since its founding in 2002, his foundation has given away millions of dollars to support the efforts of social entrepreneurs, including Craig and Mark Kielburger of Toronto and their Free the Children organization. As a 12-year-old, Craig was inspired by an article in the newspaper about a South Asian boy who was sold into slavery at the age of four and chained to a carpet-weaving loom but still had the courage to speak out for children's rights. Craig gathered together a group of his classmates in Grade 7, and Save the Children was born with a mission to free children of the world from poverty and exploitation. To date, Free the Children has worked with almost two million youth involved in 45 countries to educate and empower young people to act locally and globally as agents of change for their peers around the world. It is the world's largest network of children helping children through education.[6]

The benefit of incorporating Corporate Social Responsibility (CSR) into a small business versus a large corporation is the same: It is the right thing to do, and customers flock to the businesses that are giving back. For lack of a better phrase, it is a win–win situation—you are helping the community by making it a better place, and you are building your business at the same time. However, you need to understand that CSR is a long-term commitment and needs to be brought into your business strategy at the early stages of your business.

More and more of today's youth are becoming very socially responsible, even before they start their own business and can easily incorporate their charity into their business when it is up and running.

Excellent examples of successful student social entrepreneurs are Shannon Tessier and Zack Patterson. While on a school trip to Vietnam, Shannon saw poverty like she had never seen before—children without shirts and shoes and living in caves. Before leaving the country, Shannon emptied her suitcase and left everything but a pair of sandals behind for the children.

To add to these emotions, shortly after returning home from Vietnam, the father of a friend died. Shannon attended the funeral and kept hearing stories about the father from his friends—all about the acts of kindness he did and how much giving he had done. Shannon knew she had to do something herself to give back and called on a few friends to help lay the groundwork for a foundation called CHANCE (Charity of Hope to Assist Needy Children Everywhere).

Today Shannon and co-founder Zack Patterson (see the Entrepreneurs in Action box), along with family and volunteers, are working on their fourth project—building an orphanage and school in Haiti. Shannon and Zack started CHANCE when they were undergrads at Carleton University and are both currently working on their theses but have indicated, it does not matter what the future brings, that they are both dedicated to continuing with CHANCE.

Social entrepreneurs are not necessarily just involved with not-for-profit ventures. They can also work on behalf of for-profit community development banks and similar initiatives, and hybrid organizations mixing not-for-profit elements, such as homeless shelters that start small businesses of various kinds to train and employ their clients or sheltered workshops working with the disabled. These individuals also have to have a vision and be ambitious, mission-driven, resourceful, and results-oriented, just like conventional entrepreneurs.

DEALING WITH THE ETHICAL CHALLENGE

With the collapse of Enron and WorldCom, the coming to light of Ponzi schemes by Bernie Madoff and others, and exposure of similar incidents in the world of big business in recent years, there has been a dramatic increase in the ethical expectations from all businesses and professionals. Increasingly, consumers, clients, employees, and others are seeking out those who define the basic ground rules of their businesses on a day-to-day basis.

Entrepreneurs are typically faced with many ethical decisions. These may relate to such issues as potential conflicts of interest between your personal situations and the interests of your business; temptations to provide gifts, expensive entertainment, or even bribes or kickbacks to certain people or organizations to attract or influence their business activity; or the use of proprietary or confidential information to influence the outcome of a deal or a sale. To be successful as an entrepreneur, it is important that you act and conduct your business in an ethical manner, and the significance of ethics when initiating a new venture must be emphasized.

ENTREPRENEURS IN ACTION

SHANNON TESSIER AND ZACK PATTERSON: CHANCE FOUNDATION

"As Canadians we have so much to be thankful for, and it is important that we help others who are not as fortunate."—Shannon Tessier

This is what Shannon Tessier, founder of CHANCE, thought after becoming a volunteer with the Volunteer Abroad program and studying in Ecuador, South America. Soon after becoming a volunteer, Shannon's attention focused in on San Cristobal, the second largest human settlement of Ecuador's volcanic island chain, which is in the Galapagos Islands. After learning that 50 percent of San Cristobal's population falls below the poverty line and that infant mortality is roughly five times higher than in Canada, Shannon's sights were set on helping improve the lives of the children living in this community.

In May 2007, Shannon's vision developed into something much bigger when she founded CHANCE, which at the time stood for the Charity of Hope to Assist the Needy Children of Ecuador. For CHANCE's first project, Shannon chose to bring help to the Oscar Jandl hospital. This hospital, which serves 90 percent of the community in San Cristobal, was in desperate need of medical equipment and supplies. Shannon recruited like-minded individuals for CHANCE, and these volunteers immediately began turning this goal into a reality.

Shannon and Zack, her friend and co-founder of CHANCE, organized a couple of events to raise money. In talking to the Ecuador embassy staff, they were advised not to give any money to the hospital, as more than likely the funds would not be used for supplies but would more than likely benefit the owners of the hospital. Instead of giving money, Shannon and Zack focused on finding used hospital equipment and used the money to pay the shipping costs of the crate of equipment. The arrival of the crate in Ecuador was not without problems, but Zack and Shannon persevered and got $250,000 worth of medical equipment and supplies to the hospital.

Since then, CHANCE evolved and became the Charity of Hope to Assist Needy Children Everywhere, and in 2009 began its second project. CHANCE formed a partnership with School-Box Inc., a Canadian charity that empowers impoverished

COURTESY OF SHARON TESSIER

children through education. Since 2007, SchoolBox had been supporting the children of the Jezreel School in Managua, Nicaragua, and needed CHANCE's support to build a new permanent school for the community.

The third CHANCE project was one closer to home—Ottawa—where they focused on recreation to support families in need so that their children can undertake extra curricular recreational activities, such as hockey, soccer, gymnastics, and so on. In addition, CHANCE partnered with the City of Ottawa to refurbish a park in the Ottawa area.

Their fourth project, building an orphanage and school in Haiti, is well underway.

Both Shannon and Zack are honours students, and while writing their theses, they still find the time to balance everything. Time management works for them both. When the alarm goes off in the morning they do not turn it off—they get up and start their day. As CFO of CHANCE, Zack has periods where he is not as busy with his duties, and thus he can be a bit flexible with this time; but Shannon spends at least an hour a day on CHANCE so as to not get behind.

According to Shannon, although there are lots of youth doing lots, there still is not enough being done to help the less fortunate.

Shannon and Zack's goal is to help children on every continent. They are well on their way of making this a reality.

Source: Interview with Wendy Mayhew. Used with permission, courtesy of Shannon Tessier.

What specifically do we mean by "ethics"? One dictionary defines it as *the moral quality of a course of action; fitness; propriety.*[7] One could think of ethics as a set of principles outlining a behavioural code that lays out what is good and right or bad and wrong. Ethics may also outline obligations and appropriate moral actions for both the individual and the organization.[8] The problem with these kinds of definitions, however, is that they describe ethics as a static factor, implying that society universally agrees on certain fundamental principles that everyone

THE ACSESS CODE OF ETHICS AND STANDARDS

As members of the Association of Canadian Search, Employment & Staffing Services we commit to uphold this Code of Ethics & Standards and to display it prominently in our place of business. We support the principles set forth below and acknowledge that compliance with these principles is in the best interests of ACSESS member companies, their candidates, employees, client organizations, and the reputation of the search, employment and staffing services profession in Canada.

- We will observe the highest principles of integrity, professionalism and fair practice in dealing with clients, candidates, employees and all regulatory authorities; and will respect the confidentiality of records in accordance with law and good business practices.

- We will provide leadership in the adherence to both the spirit and letter of all applicable human rights, employment laws and regulations. We will treat all candidates and employees without prejudice and will not accept an order from any client that is discriminatory in any way.

- We will take all reasonable steps to provide clients with accurate information on each candidate's employment qualifications and experience; and will only present those candidates who have given us authorization to represent their application for employment.

- We will supply candidates and employees with complete and accurate information as provided by the client, regarding terms of employment, job descriptions and workplace conditions.

- We will not recruit, encourage or entice a candidate whom we have previously placed to leave the employ of our client, nor will we encourage or coerce an individual to leave any temporary assignment before the stated completion date.

- We will not restrict the right of a candidate or employee to accept employment of their choice.

- We will not misuse membership privileges for the purpose of recruiting a member's staff, or in any way that may otherwise injure our candidates, employees or competitors.

- We will derive income only from clients and make no direct or indirect charges to candidates or employees unless specified by a license.

- We will maintain the highest standards of integrity in all forms of advertising, communications and solicitations; and will conduct our business in a manner designed to enhance the operation, image and reputation of the employment, recruitment and staffing services industry.

- We will recognize and respect the rights and privileges of competitors in the true fashion of individual initiative and free enterprise, and will refrain from engaging in acts of unfair competition.

- We will ensure that our clients, candidates and employees are aware of our duty to abide by this Code of Ethics & Standards and such supporting policies and guidelines as may from time to time be adopted by the Association; and will undertake to bring any potential infringements before the appropriate Association body.

Source: Used with the permission of Acsess.com. Acsess Code of Ethics found at: http://www.acsess.org/about/ethics.asp

regards as being "ethical." With society being a dynamic and rapidly changing environment, however, such a consensus clearly does not exist. In fact, considerable conflict and general disagreement over what would be considered "ethical" in most decision situations is probably more typical.

Another dilemma for the entrepreneur is the issue of legal versus ethical considerations. Survival of their business is a strong motivating factor for most entrepreneurs and the question arises as to how far they can go to help their business become established and successful. The law provides the boundaries defining just what activities are illegal (although they are often subject to some interpretation), but it does not provide any specific guidance for ethical considerations. So what is legal and illegal is usually very clear, but what is ethical and unethical is frequently not obvious. Rather, situations involving ethical issues are often very ambiguous.

OTHER CONSIDERATIONS

OUTLINE FOR A CODE OF ETHICS

Over all, a code of ethics should be a formal statement of a business's values concerning ethics and social issues. It commonly speaks to acceptable norms of behaviour, guided by six areas of concern:

1. Honesty: to be truthful in all your endeavours; to be honest and forthright with one another and with customers, communities, suppliers, and other stakeholders.

2. Integrity: to say what you mean, to deliver what you promise, and to stand up for what is right.

3. Respect: to treat others with dignity and fairness, appreciating the diversity of the people you deal with and their uniqueness.

4. Trust: to build confidence through teamwork and open, candid communication.

5. Responsibility: to speak up—without fear of retribution—and report concerns in the workplace and elsewhere, including violations of laws, regulations, and company policies.

6. Citizenship: to obey all laws of the countries where you do business and to improve the communities where you live and work.[9]

Because the system is so unclear and filled with situations involving potential conflicts, entrepreneurs need to commit to a general strategy for ethical responsibility. Most professional organizations and business associations have a code of ethics that members are expected to follow. Failure to do so can result in expulsion from the organizations. AIM Personnel Services Inc. (www.aimpersonnel.ca), a full-service employee recruiting and staffing organization in Ottawa, for example, is a member of the Association of Canadian Search, Employment & Staffing Services and prominently displays the association's code of ethics on its website. This code is reproduced in the Other Considerations box.

Many organizations, on the other hand, prefer to develop their own codes of ethics or conduct. These documents often lay out in considerable detail just how the company's management and employees are expected to behave in particular situations and what the company feels is the right thing to do in such circumstances.

Having a code of ethics can be a great start, but it may not be sufficient to take the greyness out of an ethical situation and help you to determine a solution. It is easy to charge ahead without thinking and then rationalize your decision after the fact. Kenneth Blanchard and Norman Vincent Peale suggest using an *Ethics Check* that helps you to sort out dilemmas by examining the situation at several different levels. Their Ethics Check is intended to help you clarify issues by addressing three questions when confronted by an ethical problem:

1. *Is it legal?*

    Will you be violating either civil law or your organization's code of ethics?

2. *Is it balanced?*

    Is it fair to all concerned in the short term as well as the long term? Does it promote win–win relationships?

3. *How will it make you feel about yourself?*

    Will it make you proud?

    Would you feel good if your decision was published in the newspaper?

    Would you feel good if your family knew about it?[10]

Regardless of the approach, having a code of ethics can be the foundation for the success of your business. By being honest and truthful and adhering to a clearly defined set of principles, not only will you feel good about yourself, but you will also gain the respect of your customers, suppliers, bankers, and other business associates.

BEING SOCIALLY RESPONSIBLE

Companies today are expected to go beyond just being "ethical" in their dealings with customers, employees, and other stakeholders. They are expected to generally act in a *socially responsible* manner. That means their behaviour should reflect not only their efforts to make money and achieve a high level of financial performance but that they need to be good citizens as well and give something back to the societies in which they exist.

What is the basis for this argument that companies should "give back"? First, all firms make use of society's basic infrastructure—land, plants, animals, and so on—to earn a profit. Second, companies should reimburse society for the negative consequences their activities might create—noise, smell, traffic congestion, and toxic emissions. Just as individuals have a "moral duty" to contribute to the community they live in, companies are also obliged to contribute to their community through corporate volunteering, charitable donations, sponsoring community and cultural events, providing school equipment, funding university buildings and libraries, and so forth.[11] This is based on the belief there is an integral link between the strength of the community and the strength of the company.

Why should businesses be concerned about being more socially responsible? The argument is that activities in this area can have positive financial benefits to the organization as well, resulting in better long-term, more stable profits, and a higher level of employee, stakeholder, and company well-being. This can result from:

- Cost savings due to more efficient operations
- Development of a more positive organizational image and reputation
- Creation of a clearly identifiable market niche with consumers who are interested in health and the environment, social justice, and sustainable living
- Being forced to become more innovative to accommodate these values within the company's organizational strategy.

Rather than just focusing on the company's financial performance as reflected in its income statement, the success of organizations in being socially responsible is commonly measured against a *triple bottom line* assessment of financial performance, environmental impact, and social well-being. The idea is to make a positive contribution to the environment and society in a financially responsible manner. Even though the assessment of social and environmental performance is largely subjective, many large companies are reporting their performance in this area in a CSR report, or a non financial report, although smaller firms are jumping on this bandwagon as well and this number is likely to increase substantially over time. Bridgehead, an Ottawa coffee company with over a dozen coffeehouses in the Ottawa area, has been socially responsible since the business started. Their business is a complex web of relationships, which begins with the grower and the land, extends to the shippers and suppliers, and, in the end, connects their premium fairly traded products through their employees to their customers. Their vision and values guide their day-to-day decision making.

Their vision is quite simple: linking their customers with small-scale farmers in the developing world through sustainable fair trade and demonstrating that business can be socially responsible and profitable. They strive to provide the highest quality products and service for their customers, while honouring their core values.

Bridgehead's Vision and Values Statements:

- We maintain fair trade as the founding principle of our business.
- We encourage community building locally and globally.
- We create premium products for our customers.
- We use organic and locally produced products, wherever possible.
- We consciously reduce our environmental impact.
- We encourage a healthy, open, and inclusive work environment.
- We provide ongoing education and growth for employees and customers.

BRIDGEHEAD COFFEE'S SOCIAL RESPONSIBILITY SCORECARD

Vision and Values Statements	How Do We Measure This?	How Are We Doing?	What Have We Committed to Do to Improve?
• We maintain fair trade (FT) as the founding principle of our business.	• % FT purchases for coffee, tea, sugar, cocoa • Maintaining certification with Fair Trade Canada (FLO)	• 100% FT purchases of coffee, tea, retail chocolate, cane sugar • Kitchen utilizes a mix of fair trade and conventional products re: quality, availability, and price • Successful microlot purchases from Guatemala and Mexico in 2012 and 2013	• Work with co-ops of small-scale farmers to disaggregate their coffee and develop an incentive system for quality premiums in addition to fair trade or organic premiums
• We encourage community building locally and globally.	• Local donations and partnerships • Assistance to farmer organizations • Participation of employees in community events	• Value of donations in 2013 exceeded $70,000 • Fundraising blend for Codech in Guatemala for cupping lab in Winter 2012/13, $8,000 target achieved • Bridgehead employees helped found Fair Trade Ottawa group in 2011, and its reach has grown to nearly 50 people in 2013 • Over one-third of employees participated in community events over the past year as volunteers, including Earth Hour, Sole Responsibility shoe collection, River cleanup	
• We create premium products for our customers.	• % of coffees and teas purchased over 84 points	• 100% of coffees and teas purchased were rated 84 points or higher • Moved to seasonal coffee program • Increased freshness to within seven days off roast at all shops	• Additional microlots • Seasonal tea program
• We use organic and locally produced products, wherever possible.	• % of coffee and tea purchases which are organic • Local farmer program at bakery and kitchen • Organic cream, milk, and sugar at shops	• 100% of coffee and tea purchases are certified organic (OCIA) • 14 local farmers supply kitchen, all year round or seasonally • Organic cream, milk, soy, and sugar available in shops	• Increase number of local farmers, and engage them to develop a product pipeline to stimulate recipe development

continued

Vision and Values Statements	How Do We Measure This?	How Are We Doing?	What Have We Committed to Do to Improve?
• We consciously reduce our environmental impact.	• Waste audits every two years • Recycling, composting programs • Discount for own mug • Commitment to 100% compostable packaging • Promoting coffee origins closer to home • Energy saving lighting and HVAC protocols • Shop locations restricted to urban core on walking routes • Use of china and cutlery at condiment stands	• Last waste audit: 94% streaming efficiency Increasing "own mug" participation by customers (est. 12,000) • All but coffee and tea retail packaging is bio degradable • Over 60% of coffees are from Meso or Central America • LED bulb exchange program in place • New shops meet criteria for LEED commercial interiors (but designation not sought) • Protocols for HVAC and dim or off lights in place and effective	• Biodegradable retail coffee and tea packaging (in testing phase) • Migrate paper-based loyalty to technological solution of card, fob, and mobile wallet (expected Summer 2013) • Sandwich-making will be centralized to commissary and will reduce use of transport containers and warewashing substantially
• We encourage a healthy, open, and inclusive work environment.	• Employee satisfaction survey administered once each year • Manager effectiveness survey administered once each year • Promote-from-within policy • Diversity policy • Commitment to training and development • Open-door policy • Managers practise "servant leadership" • Lower-than-average turnover • Match or lead compensation	• Completed review of vision and values with managers in early 2013 • High levels of employee satisfaction in 2013 survey • Hire Immigrants Ottawa award for mid-size employer in 2013 • One grievance in all of past year • 55% turnover, significantly less than industry average (100%) • Salary review/benchmarking conducted, and corrective action taken on selected position wage scales for 2014 • Quarterly staff meetings foster team development and understanding	• Vision and values "review" to be completed by front line by end of September 2013

Source: Tracey Clark, Bridgehead Coffee. Used with permission.

A FINAL ANALYSIS

The Personal Self-Assessment Questionnaire is designed to help you summarize your thinking concerning what you need to do to become a successful entrepreneur. The questions get you to focus on areas of strength and weakness you have identified from the previous questionnaires and to think about how compatible you seem to be with the typical requirements of an entrepreneurial lifestyle. If you have answered all the questions carefully, you have done some hard work and careful thinking. Try to do as much of this as you can for yourself, but do not hesitate to also ask for help from family and friends who may know you very well to get their perspective, too.

Several other instruments are available that will also enable you to assess your potential for an entrepreneurial career. You might check out:

Business Startup Quiz An interactive entrepreneurship quiz hosted by Youth Employment Services (YES) Montreal to help determine if you are ready for self-employment. (www.yesmontreal.ca/yes.php?section=entrepreneurship/tools/quiz)

Entrepreneurial Self-Assessment A questionnaire from the Business Development Bank of Canada on attitude and lifestyle that will enable you to assess how consistent your character is with that of proven successful entrepreneurs. (www.bdc.ca/EN/advice_centre/benchmarking_tools/Pages/entrepreneurial_self_assessment.aspx)

The Entrepreneur Test Do you have what it takes to succeed as an entrepreneur? This interactive quiz will help you assess your entrepreneurial skills and indicate to what extent you have the personal traits important to a business owner. (www.bizmove.com/other/quiz.htm)

Are You Tough Enough? This quiz from *The Small Business Bible* helps determine if you have the chops to be a successful entrepreneur. (www.success.com/articles/581-entrepreneurship-quiz)

This assessment of your entrepreneurial potential is based on a series of self-evaluations, and for it to reveal anything meaningful, an absolute requirement is for you to be completely honest with yourself. This, however, is only the first step. The road to entrepreneurship is strewn with hazards and pitfalls, and many who start on it fall by the wayside for one reason or another. However, those who persevere and reach the end by building a successful venture may realize considerable financial and psychological rewards, as well as a lot of personal satisfaction.

The remainder of this book can help you evaluate other important parts of this process and improve your chances for success. It will help you decide what else you need to consider and enable you to go after it. Good luck!

LO1 **The various quizzes, surveys, and forms that you completed in Stage 1 will have given you a good idea of your potential for becoming an entrepreneur:**

- the Entrepreneurial Quiz did a comparison of your personal attitudes and attributes with those of practising entrepreneurs
- the Entrepreneurial Attitude Orientation Survey focused on attitude that was broken down into achievement in business, innovation in business, personal control over business outcomes, and your sense of self-worth or self-esteem relative to business affairs
- the Personal Self-Assessment Questionnaire summarized your feelings about your potential for self-employment
- the Managerial Skills Inventory assessed the level of your present skills and identified areas that may need improvement
- the Sample Balance Sheet Form provided your overall financial situation that you can take to a financial institution
- the Personal Living Expenses Worksheet will help you calculate the amount of money you will need on a regular monthly basis and determine where the monthly source of income will come from

LO2 **You learned the attitudes and behaviours that will help turn your business dream into a reality. With a critical combination of perseverance and total dedication, entrepreneurs:**

- are driven by the desire to achieve the goals they set
- are focused on the nature and extent of the opportunity rather than the resources, structure, or strategy, of the business
- are action-oriented
- are not easily intimidated
- understand their own strengths and weaknesses
- seek feedback to know they are performing well
- are self-reliant and self-confident

- tolerate ambiguity and uncertainly and make effective decisions
- are risk-takers
- have the ability to accept mistakes and failures as temporary set-backs
- do not strive for status and power; they are excited about the challenge and creating and building their own business

LO3 **You will have decided the type of entrepreneur that you will be:**

- a Craftsperson who is skilled in a particular craft or trade and is more concerned about the business than making large amounts of money
- a Freedom Fighter/Lifestyle Business that seeks financial independence and the freedom to spend your time when and how you want
- an Empire Builder who wants to make it bigger and better

LO4 **There are many facets involved in starting a business:**

- are you willing to put in the amount of time needed to run a business?
- are you a risk taker?
- do you have the support of your family and friends?

LO5 **Social entrepreneurship, ethics, and social responsibility:**

- the social entrepreneur business model is about social change not making a profit
- prevent possible situations by incorporating a code of ethics into your business and follow them
- it is routinely expected that all corporations are socially responsible in some way—many large corporations have initiatives that serve to help the less fortunate; the initiative normally brings attention to the company which, in turn, increases profits for their main products and or services

For more information on the resources available from McGraw-Hill Ryerson, go to www.mcgrawhill.ca/he/solutions.

STAGE 2

EXPLORING BUSINESS IDEAS AND OPPORTUNITIES

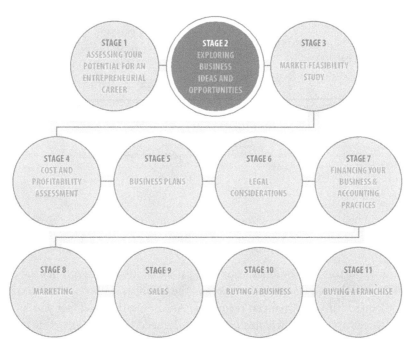

STAGE 1
ASSESSING YOUR POTENTIAL FOR AN ENTREPRENEURIAL CAREER

STAGE 2
EXPLORING BUSINESS IDEAS AND OPPORTUNITIES

STAGE 3
MARKET FEASIBILITY STUDY

STAGE 4
COST AND PROFITABILITY ASSESSMENT

STAGE 5
BUSINESS PLANS

STAGE 6
LEGAL CONSIDERATIONS

STAGE 7
FINANCING YOUR BUSINESS & ACCOUNTING PRACTICES

STAGE 8
MARKETING

STAGE 9
SALES

STAGE 10
BUYING A BUSINESS

STAGE 11
BUYING A FRANCHISE

LEARNING OBJECTIVES

By the end of this stage, you should be able to:

LO1 Explain the process of an entrepreneurial opportunity.

LO2 Identify where to look for business ideas.

LO3 Evaluate your business idea.

LO4 Choose what business model suits your idea.

DATAWIND LTD.

SELLING TO THE WORLD'S POOR OFFERS HUGE POTENTIAL

THE CANADIAN PRESS/Ryan Remiorz

It might seem counterintuitive, but setting your sights on the world's four billion poorest people can be remarkably lucrative. Just ask Suneet Singh Tuli. The CEO of wireless-device manufacturer DataWind Ltd. says his Montreal-based company's revenue could soar from less than $10 million last year to more than $300 million next year, thanks to the stripped-down tablet computer it developed to sell in India: "It's an astonishing rate of growth."

His management team figured that if they could offer tablets for a price similar to the $30 to $60 that most cellphones cost in India, they could sell enormous numbers of tablets there. (Indians buy 15 million cellphones *per month*.) DataWind has pulled off this feat, selling bare-bones tablets for $60 a pop at Indian retailers. The company already has sold 100,000 units at $47 each to India's government, which, in turn, sells them to students for $35—and ultimately plans to sell tens of millions more. Tuli says DataWind already has more than 1.5 million pre-orders from individual Indians and could move five million units this year.

By whittling down the price as low as possible, DataWind has put its tablets within reach not only for affluent Indians but also the endless ranks of the poor. Many poverty-stricken Indians are willing to part with a large chunk of one month's income for a tool they can use to help educate themselves and their families. DataWind is now discussing deals similar to the one in India with governments in Thailand, Sri Lanka, Turkey, and Brazil.

In an increasingly global economy, companies that figure out how to serve the poor can develop immense client bases serving a market that most firms overlook. DataWind certainly has proven that being first has its rewards. After all, a little foresight enabled the small Canadian firm to blaze a trail in a potentially mammoth new tablet market.

Source: Adapted from profitguide.ca (www.profitguide.com/opportunity/selling-to-the-worlds-poor-offers-huge-potential-30348).

In Stage One, you had an opportunity to evaluate your own potential for an entrepreneurial career from the standpoint of your personal fit with the requirements for success, the business skills required to start and run a business of your own, and the adequacy of your financial resources. Assuming that you feel you have the "right stuff" to continue to explore this career option, you will need an idea—the seed that will germinate and, hopefully, grow and develop into a profitable enterprise. This is the topic of Stage Two.

RECOGNIZING THE OPPORTUNITY   LO1

Before getting into that, however, it is important that you have some understanding of the relationship between the entrepreneur and the actual startup of a business. One of the major steps in this process is the recognition of an appropriate opportunity by the entrepreneur. This "opportunity recognition" has been described as perceiving a possibility for new profit potential through (a) the founding of a new business, or (b) the significant improvement of an existing business.[1]

Figure 2.1 illustrates a conceptual model of the relationship between an entrepreneur, his or her environment, and an opportunity to potentially start a new business.

An entrepreneur's personal characteristics and environment influence the process of proceeding from a new venture idea to an entrepreneurial opportunity. An important issue that relates to this process is timing; specifically, when does an idea become an opportunity, and how long after the opportunity is recognized are the necessary resources acquired and a business actually founded?[2]

As you can see from Figure 2.1, an idea is the first thing you will require to start a business. Ideas that succeed are difficult to find and evaluate, but they are critical to the entire process. So, while an idea is at the centre of every opportunity, not every idea represents an opportunity to start a viable business.

How entrepreneurs recognize opportunities has been a matter of considerable academic debate. Perhaps this can best be summarized by thinking in terms of two basic approaches: economic events and process models. The economic approach assumes that events occur in the economy that give rise to new opportunities. These may be conditions such as demographic changes, for example, aging baby boomers; sociopolitical trends, such as the increasing recognition and acceptance of gay consumers or the explosive growth currently taking place in certain market areas; or changes in government regulations. Changes of this nature create situations of disequilibrium in the economy that may be first recognized by certain people who have unique knowledge of marketplace conditions. This knowledge enables them to find and exploit opportunities to capitalize on these changing circumstances.

The second major approach to opportunity recognition views it as a multi stage and often very complex process. There have been any number of models proposed to explain this process, but one of the more comprehensive was developed by Lumpkin, Hills, and Shrader.[3] They viewed the opportunity recognition process as a type of creativity consisting of five basic elements—preparation, incubation, insight, evaluation, and elaboration. This framework is illustrated in Figure 2.2.

Preparation refers to the background, experience, and prior knowledge the entrepreneur brings to the opportunity recognition process. Such preparation is typically an effort by the individual to develop expertise in some particular area. This may include such things as previous work experience, technical or market knowledge, social contacts and networks, and conscious research or general information scanning for prospective ideas. It may also include knowledge and experience that has been gathered unintentionally without any particular aim to discover some business opportunity.

Incubation refers to that part of the process where the individual contemplates an idea or a specific problem. This is typically the time when the individual is mulling over the general concept or idea unconsciously in his or her mind.

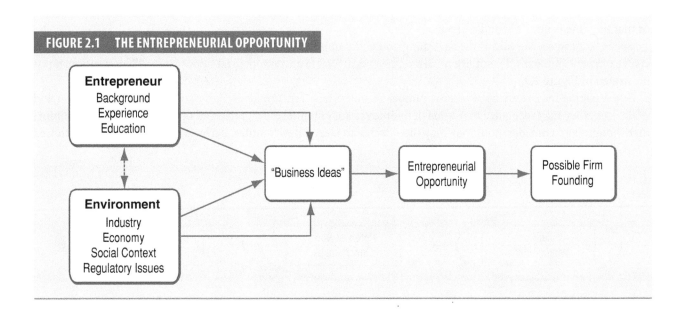

FIGURE 2.1   THE ENTREPRENEURIAL OPPORTUNITY

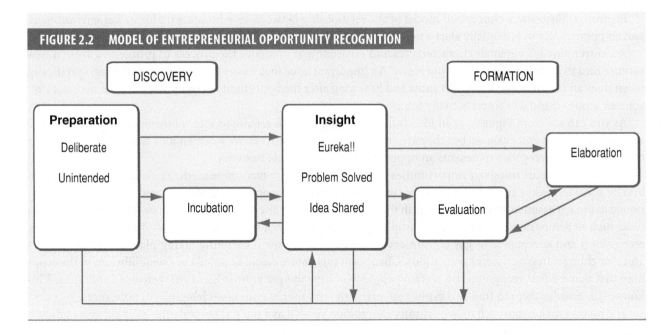

FIGURE 2.2   MODEL OF ENTREPRENEURIAL OPPORTUNITY RECOGNITION

DISCOVERY

FORMATION

Preparation

Deliberate

Unintended

Incubation

Insight

Eureka!!

Problem Solved

Idea Shared

Evaluation

Elaboration

Insight may refer to what is commonly called the "eureka" or the "aha" moment. This is the moment of insight or conscious awareness that the idea may, in fact, represent an entrepreneurial opportunity. This may be reflected in a sudden confidence that an idea will actually work or will actually solve a problem the individual has been contemplating.

Evaluation is when these insights are analyzed for their viability. This is when the entrepreneur investigates whether a concept is actually workable, whether he or she has the skills and capabilities to implement it, and whether it is really worthwhile for him or her to pursue. This evaluation often involves a feasibility study where the ideas are "put to the test" by means of concept testing, a preliminary market analysis, an initial financial assessment, and preliminary discussion of the merits of the idea with professionals and other people.

Elaboration involves moving the concept forward if it survives the evaluation stage. This means continuing the process of business planning, finalizing choices regarding business strategy and structure, organizing resources, and all other activity that may be required to actually start up the venture.

The process in this model appears linear; it is not. There is constant iteration and feedback during the process. At any time the entrepreneur may decide that the opportunity is not a good one, that the resources are not available, or that the time is not right and bail out.

So, as you can see, an idea is the first thing you will require to start a business. However, while an idea is at the centre of every opportunity, not every idea represents a "viable entrepreneurial opportunity." This relationship is illustrated in Figure 2.3.

Some people may come up with any number of initial new venture ideas. After some additional thought and evaluation, they may recognize that some of their ideas are potential entrepreneurial opportunities. With even further thought and consideration, they may then decide to start a new venture. Perhaps only one idea in a hundred

FIGURE 2.3

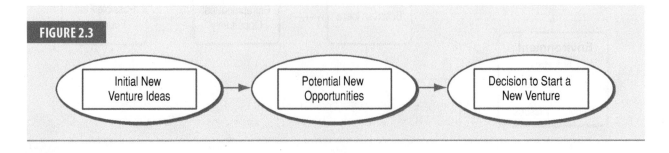

Initial New Venture Ideas → Potential New Opportunities → Decision to Start a New Venture

will possess the elements required to make it a success. But how do you tell an idea from an entrepreneurial opportunity? Harvard professor J.A. Timmons says *an opportunity has the qualities of being attractive, durable, and timely and is anchored in a product or service that creates or adds value for its buyer or end user.*[4] Many ideas for a prospective new business do not add much value for customers or users. To help you distinguish between a list of ideas and real opportunities, you might start by asking yourself the following questions:

- Does the idea solve some fundamental consumer or business want or need?
- Is there a demand? Are there enough people who will buy the product to support a business, and how much competition exists for that demand?
- Can the idea be turned into a business that will be *profitable*?
- Do you have the skills needed to take advantage of the opportunity? Why hasn't anyone else tried this concept? If anyone has, what happened to them?

In some instances, what was felt to be a good idea was the key element stimulating an individual to think of going into business. In others, it was the lack of an acceptable concept that was the principal factor holding back an aspiring entrepreneur. Perhaps you fall into this category. If so, it is important not to be impatient. It may take several years to fully develop and evaluate an idea that is suited to your particular circumstances and that you feel represents a real opportunity. Do not try to force the issue. Actively pursue a range of possible options, but wait until the right situation presents itself before investing your time and money.

There is no shortage of real opportunities. For example, the recipients of the 2012 Canadian Youth Business Foundation Best Business Awards were involved in a wide range of different businesses, including a retail store selling footwear manufactured in Africa, a job site for students, affordable orthopedic solutions and a surgical tool for surgeons, a composting and recycling company, and a lifestyle store for kids. To illustrate:

- **Tal Hehtiar,** owner of retail footwear Oliberté Limited (www.oliberte.com), partners with factories, suppliers, farmers, and workers to produce premium footwear in Africa.
- **Lauren Friese** is the founder of TalentEgg (www.talentegg.ca), Canada's leading job site and career resource for students and new graduates.
- **Armen Bakirtzian, Richard Fanson, and Andre Hladio** are the co-founders of Avenir Medical Inc. (www.avenirmedical.com) Avenir's main product is PelvAssist™, a surgical tool that measures the precise position and orientation of hip replacements.
- **Lisa von Sturmer** is the founder and CEO of Growing City (www.GrowingCity.ca), North America's first and only premium office composting service. Her company makes it easy for any business to reduce their waste by up to 50 percent, overnight.
- **Lisa Donaldson** is a co-founder of Fiddleheads (www.gofiddleheads.com), a new kind of lifestyle store for children ages 0 to 4 that brings together excellent gifts, gear, and accessories to help make the job a little easier.[5]

In this stage, we will describe a number of sources from which you might obtain ideas for a prospective new venture and present a variety of techniques you can use to evaluate the conceptual, technical, and financial aspects of your idea to determine whether it might represent a real opportunity.

These ideas will not all be equal and will originate from a number of different sources. There are three basic categories into which most of these concepts fall. They:

1. Cater to consumers in new markets (Type A);
2. Introduce new technologies to the marketplace (Type B); or
3. Provide consumers with new or more benefits than competitive offerings currently available in the marketplace (Type C).

Type A ideas typically provide customers with a product or service that does not exist in their market but already exists somewhere else. This could be something as simple as a bar or restaurant concept that you observed while on a trip and thought would be well received in your home market area.

OTHER CONSIDERATIONS

STARTUP MYTHS AND REALITIES

Myth 1: I'm smart—I can just wing it.

Reality: Face it—you need a plan. One of the few things that small-business lenders, advisers, and consultants agree on is the need for a business plan.

Myth 2: I can do it on a shoestring.

Reality: While no one ever has enough money, having too little can spell doom. You have to have enough money for you and the company to survive until it can support itself.

Myth 3: No sweat. I have a great idea.

Reality: Great ideas are an important start for businesses, but ideas alone will not get you far. You also need the resources, skills, and products to make a business grow. About 5 percent of the success equation is having a good idea.

Myth 4: I've got nothing better to do.

Reality: You cannot start a successful small business half-heartedly. The level of commitment associated with "making a quick buck" is a long way from the reality needed for success in starting a new business.

Myth 5: Maybe starting a business will help our marriage.

Reality: A risky bet. The stress involved in starting a business can amplify marital weaknesses.

Myth 6: A bad economy will mean fewer competitors.

Reality: Maybe. But it can also make the survivors more fierce competitors.

Myth 7: I'm mad as hell, and I'm not going to take it anymore.

Reality: The frustration that you may feel with your current job can be a good rationale for starting your own business, but only if your anger is focused on finding a positive outcome.

Myth 8: If I can't think of anything else, I'll open a bar.

Reality: Despite common opinion, restaurants and bars are not easy businesses to start or run.

Source: Dave Kansas, "Don't Believe It," The Wall Street Journal—Small Business, October 15, 1993, p. R8. "Reprinted by permission of The Wall Street Journal, Copyright © 1993. Dow Jones & Company, Inc. All Rights Reserved Worldwide.

Type B ideas involve a technically new product or process. Software you have developed to solve some business problem or a new invention or innovation that provides a better way of performing certain functions.

Type C ideas are concepts for performing old functions in new and/or better ways. They probably account for the largest number of new startups. These are often "me too" kind of ideas that try to differentiate themselves from other businesses by offering better service, higher quality, better performance, or lower cost.[6]

LONG-TERM EXPECTATIONS FOR YOUR BUSINESS

Whether your plans are to own and operate a business for a number of years or sell it shortly after it becomes operational, you will want to consider the long-term prospects of your venture. If you plan to keep the business, you are bound to have an interest in how it is expected to prosper; if you plan to sell the business, the prospective buyer will consider the long-term viability of the business in his or her purchase offer. So, either way, the long-term performance—the kind of firm your business may become—is important in evaluating alternatives. Opportunities with higher growth potential generally offer greater economic payoffs. However, those are not the only kind of payoffs that are important. Some small but stable ventures provide very enjoyable situations and lucrative benefits to their owners.

For purposes of assessing the expected long-term prospects of your venture, three types of possibilities should be considered:

1. Lifestyle ventures
2. Small, profitable ventures
3. High-growth ventures

LIFESTYLE VENTURES

These include most "one-man shows," mom-and-pop stores, and other lifestyle businesses, such as gas stations, restaurants, dry cleaning shops, and small independent retail stores. Typically, their owners make modest investments in fixed assets and inventory, put in long hours, and earn considerably less income than the average unskilled auto worker or union craftsperson. The profit in reselling these businesses tends to be quite low.

The operator of a lifestyle business often risks his or her savings to capitalize the enterprise and works longer hours with less job security than the average employee. Most lifestyle businesses have a high risk of failure. Unless you are willing to put up with these inherent conditions, such types of businesses should probably be avoided in favour of staying with your job until a more attractive opportunity can be identified.

SMALL, PROFITABLE VENTURES

Small manufacturing firms, larger restaurants and retail firms, small chains of gas stations, and other multi-establishment enterprises commonly fall into this category. Usually they involve a substantial capital investment—$500,000 or more. Some owners put in long hours, while others do not. Once established, many owners enjoy a comfortable life. The profit in reselling the business can be high to a buyer who sees both an attractive job and a profitable investment.

You might be surprised at how many small, virtually unnoticed businesses around your city or town have managed to provide a very comfortable life for their founders. Almost always there is a very particular reason that they are able to do so: a contract the entrepreneur was able to land at favourable terms; or a market that was unknown to others or too small to attract competitors, which therefore permitted a high profit margin; or special skills or knowledge on the part of the proprietor that enabled him or her to charge high rates for his or her time. The business's advantage may be its location, perhaps purchased for a low price many years earlier, or a patented process others are not able to copy. It may even be simply a brand that is protected by trademark and has become well known over time or through successful advertising.

HIGH-GROWTH VENTURES

Much rarer than lifestyle ventures or small, profitable ventures, but typically more highly publicized, are small firms that have the capability of becoming large ones. They include many high-technology companies formed around new products with large potential markets and also some of the small, profitable firms that, due to such factors as having amassed substantial capital or having hit on a successful formula for operating, can be expanded many times. Ventures of this type are often bought and absorbed by larger companies. The potential for significant capital gain on resale of such a business can be substantial.

A key factor in starting a high-growth venture is choosing the right industry to enter. The rate of growth of the industry as a whole often plays a large role in determining the growth patterns of startups within it. In addition, however, there has to be some property of the business that can readily be multiplied by that company but cannot easily be duplicated by others for there to be significant growth potential. In franchising, for example, it can be a format for doing business that has proven exceptionally effective and can be taught. In high-technology firms, it is specialized know-how in creating something at a hard-to-reach frontier of engineering for which there is a demand. If a technology is common knowledge and not too capital-intensive, then companies providing it generally do not grow very rapidly.

In Stage One, it was suggested that your previous jobs, hobbies, personal experiences, and the like could provide you with some of the requisite business and technical skills needed to operate your own business. Similarly, your past work experience, hobbies, and acquaintances can provide a starting point for developing a list of business ventures you might wish to consider for further investigation. The following is a brief description of some of the sources most often used by entrepreneurs in search of new business opportunities. Also see Figure 2.4.

Photo courtesy of
Terry Matthews

What do you like about being an Entrepreneur?

Terry Matthews
Chairman, Wesley Clover
www.wesleyclover.com

I am passionate about creating technology companies from scratch and building them into global businesses. It is a pleasure for me to work with young well-educated engineers, scientists, and business graduates and form a committed team that builds on new market opportunities. This provides great enjoyment for me and the people I work with at Wesley Clover. I create structures where the team members share the risks, rewards, and ownership. I work with customers and channel partners around the world helping to drive the new teams, turning them into rocket ships, growing rapidly and learning to become big business. I am persistent in my drive to create value for customers, success for the teams, and their companies. The other thing—I have a lot of fun doing it.

PREVIOUS EMPLOYMENT

Prior work experience is the most common source of new business ideas. It has been estimated that as many as 85 percent of new businesses started are based on product ideas similar to those of prior employers of the founders. When you think about it, the attractions of starting a business in a field in which you have experience and expertise are obvious. You are already familiar with the products and services you will provide, you understand the competitive environment, you have some knowledge and understanding of customer requirements, you may already know several prospective clients, and so on.

Ideas from your previous employment can take several forms. For example, you might set yourself up as a consultant in some technical area using the background and experience you acquired in a previous job. You might develop a product or service for which your prior employer might be a prospective customer. You might even be interested in providing a product or service similar or related to that provided by your previous employer. In this last case, you should check with a lawyer to ensure your plans do not violate the legal rights of that employer. You must be certain your actions do not infringe on any patent, trademark, or other proprietary rights, break any non-competition clause or other agreements you may have signed, involve the direct solicitation of your former employer's customers, or raise similar legal or ethical problems.

FIGURE 2.4   SEARCHING FOR IDEAS

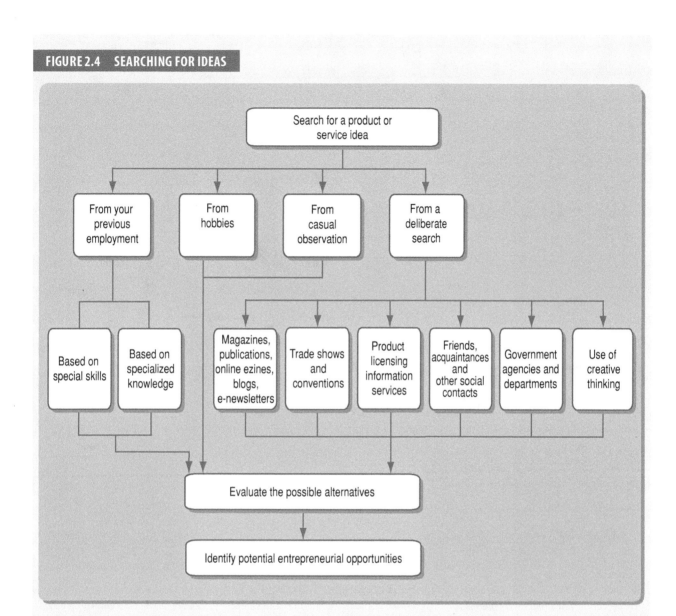

Mandy Kan (see the Entrepreneurs in Action box) had always wanted to start her own business involving something to do with food. After graduating with a Commerce degree, she worked in a number of professional kitchens to gain some experience and attended the French Culinary Institute of New York to become a pastry chef. With more experience under her belt, gained at a number of Toronto restaurants and a stint at the Ritz Carlton hotel in Florida, she returned to Toronto to take a job as a pastry chef at an upscale grocer and put together her business plan to open her own shop. Her plan was to sell high-quality ice cream, truffles, homemade cookies, and similar items. A year later, she finally found a location in Toronto's trendy Yorkville area that fit her concept of her business, quit her job, and started to implement her dream. Dessert Lady was an instant hit, and sales took off, even though the only marketing she did was distributing invitations in the local neighbourhood for the grand opening to generate some word-of-mouth and offering samples to passersby on the street. Undoubtedly her prior experience in the food service field stood her in good stead in coping with the challenges of getting Dessert Lady successfully off the ground.

DESSERT LADY

Choosing a name for her new Toronto bakery was a no-brainer for Mandy Kan. The 28-year-old had spent two years working as the pastry chef at the Ritz Carlton in Florida, where her loyal customers nicknamed her " Dessert Lady."

When Ms. Kan graduated from university, she knew she wanted to open her own business—and she knew that business would involve food. She'd already worked in a couple of professional kitchens, but to give herself a real edge, she decided to attend the French Culinary Institute of New York. Six months and $26,000 later, Ms. Kan was a professional pastry chef.

She returned to Toronto, her hometown, in 2002, and while working as a pastry chef at a high-end grocer, she began to put together a business plan for her own shop. In February 2004, she started shopping for a location.

Her plan was to sell high-quality products at her bakery, so she had to find a space in a neighbourhood that could support her business. It took an entire year to find the right spot. "I got 22 rejections before I found my location," says Mandy, who says her lack of experience as a retailer put landlords off. "I kept getting no, no, no."

One year later, Ms. Kan saw a space in Toronto's trendy Yorkville neighbourhood. She instantly knew it was right for her. "It was love at first sight," she says. And the landlord liked her idea of selling homemade cookies, cakes, truffles, and ice cream.

She quit her job at the grocer. Then she researched and ordered her equipment—an oven, mixers, a fridge and freezer, and an Italian ice cream machine—all of which took nearly two months to arrive. While she waited, she began designing and renovating the 800-square-foot space, which was a blank canvas. Luckily, she had lots of friends (among them an interior designer) willing to lend a hand. They did everything themselves, except the electrical work. A graphic designer pal helped her design a logo. Doing the work herself not only saved lots of cash, but it gave her a sense of ownership as well. "It made me love my shop even more," she says.

With construction underway, Ms. Kan took care of the details: She bought a used cash register and ordered her sign and packaging. She also tracked down suppliers and hired two employees.

Two months after taking over the space, Mandy was ready to open her doors. There was just one problem: She hadn't done any marketing, and money was tight. "When you open a small business, it's all about money," she says. Instead of buying ads, she launched her own word-of-mouth campaign by hosting a grand-opening party. "I printed 500 invitation cards. I

COURTESY OF DESSERT LADY CAFÉ.

went door-to-door in the neighbourhood, and passed them out to anyone who walked by," she says. Hundreds of guests showed up.

Two days before opening day, Ms. Kan and three friends began preparing inventory. In just 48 hours, they whipped up 14 flavours of ice cream, 15 kinds of truffles, and 20 varieties of cookies and biscotti, plus half a dozen cakes.

Dessert Lady was a hit. Ms. Kan still hasn't spent a cent on marketing—instead, she relies on her repeat customers to spread the word. To lure passersby into the shop, a staff member often stands outside handing out samples.

Now the reality of running a business has finally sunk in. "I go for a month without a single day off sometimes," says Ms. Kan. And meeting sales targets can be tricky. She quickly realized that the bakery business is seasonal—holidays like Christmas and Valentine's Day are crucial. "So when you have a chance to make money, you have to work hard and plan for those times."

Her favourite part of owning a pastry shop is coming up with original creations. It makes good business sense, too. "You can't offer the same things everyone else has," she says. "I come up with a new product at least once a month."

Ms. Kan wasn't sure how customers would take to her smoked chili chocolate cookies or her cappuccino cinnamon biscotti, but those are the products that keep regulars coming back again and again.

What really takes the cake for Ms. Kan is the pleasure she brings to her customers. "I'm a real people person," she says. "I love making each customer's day, and seeing them smile after they've tried my products."
(www.dessertlady.ca)

YOUR HOBBIES

Some people are deeply involved with their hobbies, often devoting more time to them than to their regular job. There are many instances of such secondary interests leading to new business ventures. For example, serious athletes may open sporting goods stores, amateur photographers open portrait studios, hunters offer guiding services and run hunting lodges and game farms, pilots start fly-in fishing camps, bakers open bakeries, philatelists open coin and stamp stores, and so forth.

Witness the case of Sue Harmer. Sue is the "Suzy" of SuzyQ Doughnuts (www.suzyq.ca). Sue has been making doughnuts since she started having children. She would take them to school craft shows where they were an instant hit. She then started taking them to work for her colleagues to sample. Within three months, she was overwhelmed with the orders from workers at Canada Post. Then she moved on to the selling her doughnuts at local farmers' markets. She kept being asked the same thing over and over: When are you opening a store? Her first retail location was opened in 2012, and Sue has plans to open more locations. As well as making doughnuts, Sue continues to work full time as a postal carrier.

Many such ventures do very well, but there can be considerable conflict. Hobbies are typically activities that you and others are prepared to do at your own expense. This can exert downward pressure on the likely profitability of your business. As a result, margins are quite low in such areas as the production of arts and crafts; small-scale farming; trading in stamps, coins, and other collectibles; antique automobile restorations; and similar hobby-based operations.

PERSONAL OBSERVATION

For many people personal observation is the most practical way of identifying a business idea. Personal observations may arise from either casual observation or deliberate search.

Casual Observation

Often, ideas for a new product or service result from chance observation of daily living situations. This commonly occurs when people travel and observe product or service concepts being provided that are not yet available in the United States, Canada, or, perhaps, the person's local market area.

Restaurant themes and concepts, such as Thai, Mexican, health food, and salads, typically are established in most cities only after they have proven successful somewhere else. Sporting trends, such as wakeboarding and rollerblading, and fashion colours and styles are also usually imported from outside the country.

For this type of observation to yield results, you have to recognize the need for a new type of product or service offering and then work out some kind of solution.

Tyler Gompf had a bad customer service experience while purchasing a home-electronics product, which gave him and his brother the idea to start a business when they graduated from university, one that could provide companies with a better way of communicating with their customers and collecting customer feedback data. Tell Us About Us (TUAU) started by developing a software application for the restaurant industry that enabled customers to answer a short questionnaire about the business using their telephone rather than by filling out the traditional comment card found on the table. The company expanded its service to include customer surveys, employee surveys, dial-in-and-win promotional campaigns, and mystery-shopper services for clients, such as Dunkin Donuts, Dairy Queen, Arby's, and Baskin-Robbins. (See the Entrepreneurs in Action box.)

The observation may emerge from your own experience in the marketplace, be expressed by someone else who has recognized some opportunity or problem, or be the result of observing the behaviour of other people. Regardless of its source, this type of simple observation can be the source of numerous excellent new business ideas.

Deliberate Search

While deliberate search may seem to be the most rational way of finding viable business ideas, in fact, most new ventures do not start in this manner. The majority of business startups arise almost incidentally from events relating to work or everyday life. However, this approach should not be completely ignored, as it can be fruitful if you

TELL US ABOUT US

THE INDUSTRY

Tyler Gompf said there's a growing demand in North America for the kinds of products and services that Tell Us About Us offers.

The firm got its start by developing a software application for the restaurant industry that enabled restaurant customers to answer a short questionnaire about the establishment using their telephones, rather than by filling out a traditional comment card.

Since then, TUAU has expanded its product offering to include customer surveys, employee surveys, 1-800 customer-support services, dial-in-and-win promotional campaigns, and mystery-shopper services.

"We're now a multi-tiered resource company," Gompf said.

While restaurant chains like Dunkin Donuts, Dairy Queen, Arby's and Baskin-Robbins have been a big part of TUAU's business, its customer base has since expanded to include large corporations in the telecommunications, entertainment, retailing, and financial-services sectors.

And while Tell Us About Us got its start in Canada, that market now accounts for only about 10 percent of its yearly revenues. The rest comes from the United States, which Tell Us entered into within its first year in business after a Montana casino operator stumbled upon its website, liked what it saw, and hired the firm to do market research.

"Up until then, we had no thought of working in the States," Gompf said. "But after that, we just never looked back." He said the company's main focus now is south of the border.

THE ENTREPRENEURS

Tyler and Kirby Gompf were fresh out of university—Tyler was 23 years old and had a sociology degree and Kirby was 22 and had a degree in information systems management—when they launched Tell Us About Us.

Tyler sounded like he wasn't quite sure how to answer when asked recently why they opted to become entrepreneurs, rather than go to work for someone else.

"It's just the way it was," he said after a brief hesitation. "Right out of school, I just knew it was something I wanted to do."

PHOTO: MIKE DEAL, WINNIPEG FREE PRESS.

He admitted that because of their young age, they sometimes had trouble persuading prospective clients that they knew what they were doing.

"But being a technology-driven business helped," he said, because those kinds of businesses tend to be dominated by younger people who have grown up using technology and are comfortable with it.

Gompf said a bad experience while purchasing a home-electronics product gave him the idea to start a business that could provide companies with a better way of communicating with their customers and collecting customer feedback data.

He said there seemed to be a need for such a service, and not a whole lot of firms providing it. Gompf said the company has managed to double its revenues every year since it was launched, and he and Kirby expect that to continue.

He added that when people ask him if he's surprised at how successful TUAU has become, "I tell them we're not there yet. There is still lots of room for growth."

Tell Us About Us was acquired by Market Force in 2011 for an undisclosed amount. Read the article (www.winnipegfreepress.com/business/customer-feedback-firm-sold-118826334.html).

Source: Murray McNeill, "A Plan for Making a Happy Workplace," *Winnipeg Free Press*, February 6, 2007, p. B3. Reprinted with permission. Updated January 2013.

are committed to investigating the possibilities of starting a new business but lack the seed of any real, likely idea. For example, while studying commerce in university, Chad Fischl and Dan Robinson decided to research a natural and safe product that could kill bacteria and bad odours arising from intensive sports-related activities. They found a Korean manufacturer with a patent for nano silver technology. Nano silver is an antibacterial technology that uses silver nanoparticles in water as a sterilizing agent. After visiting the facility and further investigation, the pair commissioned a nano silver body wash, a deodorant, a sports equipment spray, and a detergent to be marketed under the brand name of Shutout Solutions (www.shutoutsolutions.com). Shutout Solutions has worked hard since the business started in 2007—on their website, they have a list of testimonials from athletes who use their product, which has no doubt helped in the development of them reaching the retail market across Canada.

A deliberate search process can be initiated by consulting the following sources.

MAGAZINES AND OTHER PUBLICATIONS

Reading business publications and other printed and online sources, such as newspapers, specialty magazines, newsletters, and trade publications, can provide ideas that might stimulate your entrepreneurial thinking. Some of the more important of these sources are listed below.

Newspapers and Magazines

The Globe and Mail (www.theglobeandmail.com), the *National Post* (www.nationalpost.com), and *The Wall Street Journal* (www.wsj.com) offer business and classified sections that provide a listing or make other reference to available small business opportunities. A number of Canadian magazines, such as *Canadian Business* (www.canadianbusiness.com), *PROFIT* (www.profitguide.com), *The Globe and Mail Report on Business Magazine* (www.theglobeandmail.com/report-on-business), and the *Financial Post Magazine* (www.financialpost.com), and U.S. publications, such as *Inc.* (www.inc.com), *Entrepreneur* (www.entrepreneur.com), and *Fortune* (www.money.cnn.com), provide further descriptions of a range of business possibilities. All of the above resources have digital versions available, and in most cases, you can subscribe to receive daily updates.

Newsletters

Thousands of newsletters are available, covering almost every conceivable subject. The information they contain is current and specialized and can provide valuable access to opportunities in any field. For further information, contact the reference librarian at your public library, and ask for *Newsletters in Print*. You can also find many resources online that you can subscribe to. The FYI box at the end of this stage lists some of the most popular sites for online news, information, and resources for the business owner.

Trade Publications

A list of available trade publications can be obtained from WebWire (www.webwire.com), or similar publications are available in most libraries. You can also do an online search for publications that are specific to what you are interested in. Trade magazines are usually the first to publicize a new product. In many cases, the manufacturer is looking for help in distributing a new line. The ads will also provide information about potential competitors and their products. These trade publications are some of the best sources of data about a specific industry and frequently print market surveys, forecasts, and articles on needs the industry may have. All this information can serve as a stimulating source of ideas.

TRADE SHOWS AND CONVENTIONS

Inventors' Shows

These shows provide inventors and manufacturers with a place to meet to discuss potential products for the marketplace. Major inventors' shows are held annually in the larger cities throughout Canada and the United States. Information on upcoming shows may be available from online sources, such as InventNET (www.inventnet.com), the Inventor's Network, which provides a list of the major shows held throughout the United States. The Inventors College (www.inventorscollege.org) holds an annual Great Canadian Inventions Show. Information on the show is available on their website. Recently the W network started airing the Back Yard Inventor—a reality show where inventors from across Canada are in competition to impress innovation expert Doug Hall. Whoever impresses him the most is invited to Eureka! Ranch, where their invention is reworked, re tooled, and turned into a marketable product and then pitched to a big business. Check your local W station for airing times.

Trade Shows

Shows covering the industry you want to enter can also be an excellent way to examine the products and services of many of your potential competitors. It can also be a way for you to meet distributors and sales representatives, learn of product and market trends, and identify potential products or services for your venture. Trade shows usually take place several times a year, in various locations. You will find trade show information in the trade magazines servicing your particular field or industry, or you could refer to the following sources:

- Biz Trade Shows (biztradeshows.com) provides a comprehensive list of trade shows around the world by industry.
- Global Sources Trade Show Centre (tradeshowcalendar.globalsources.com) also provides a detailed listing of trade shows all over the world by industry.
- EventsEye (www.eventseye.com) provides a friendly, searchable database of almost 7,000 trade shows, exhibitions, and conferences scheduled to be held all over the planet.

Conventions

Fairs or conventions are also an excellent place to stimulate your creative thinking. At a convention, you are exposed to panels, speakers, films, and exhibitions. You also have an opportunity to exchange ideas with other people attending. Information on conventions and meetings scheduled to take place around the world can be obtained from:

- All Conferences.com (www.allconferences.com) is a directory focusing on conferences, conventions, trade shows, and workshops. The information ranges from specialized scientific, medical, and academic conferences to all kinds of general events.
- Biz Trade Shows (www.biztradeshows.com) provides a comprehensive list of conferences around the world by industry.

PRODUCT LICENSING INFORMATION SERVICES

An excellent way to obtain information about the vast number of new product ideas available from inventors, corporations, or universities is to subscribe to a service that periodically publishes data on products offered for licensing. Licensing means renting the right to manufacture or distribute a product within agreed rules or guidelines. For example, you might purchase the right to manufacture T-shirts and sweaters with the logo of Batman, Dilbert, or other popular fictional characters or use the trademark of a popular product, such as Labatt's or Coca-Cola or sports teams from the NFL, NHL, MLB, or other organizations on similar apparel. The owner of the licence retains ownership and receives a royalty or fixed fee from you as the licensee. Here are some of the information services you can contact to locate product or service licensing opportunities:

- Flintbox (www.flintbox.com) an intellectual property matchmaking system started by UBC Research Enterprises and now managed by Wellspring Worldwide LLC linking industry, researchers, and others from over 100 countries around the world.
- Canadian Patents Database (patents1.ic.gc.ca) administered by the Canadian Intellectual Property Office as a vehicle for inventors and entrepreneurs to get together. This database includes the full content of all patent files, including an indication of which patent-holders wish to make patents available for sale or licensing. The site includes access to similar databases for trademarks, copyrights, and industrial designs as well.

FRIENDS, ACQUAINTANCES, AND OTHER SOCIAL NETWORKS

Discussions with those you know should not be overlooked as a source of insight into needs that might be fulfilled by a new venture. Comments, such as "Wouldn't it be nice if someone came up with something to do away with . . . " or "what this place needs is . . . , " and other complaints and observations can provide a number of potential ideas.

Social networks are recognized as one of the key factors in assisting many entrepreneurs in determining whether their idea may represent a real opportunity for them.

Julian Brass developed his concept for Notable TV (notable.ca) after returning to Toronto from San Francisco where he had worked at Engage.com, a social networking site for singles. He was impressed with the number of activities and events that targeted young professionals like him and the ease with which information about those events was disseminated through his peer group. On his return to Toronto, he wanted to develop some means of promoting similar events there. Initially, that involved setting up a Facebook page to publish a calendar of events for his friends and colleagues and anyone else who wanted to join. When that proved successful, he launched Notable.ca, financing it with savings and a loan from the Canadian Youth Business Foundation. After only five months, Notable.ca was revenue positive, with a growing number of businesses coming on board as content partners.

GOVERNMENT AGENCIES AND DEPARTMENTS

Industry Canada (www.ic.gc.ca), the provincial departments of economic development, the Business Development Bank of Canada (BDC), university entrepreneurship centres, small business development centres, community colleges, and various other federal and provincial government agencies are all in the business of helping entrepreneurs by means of business management seminars and courses, advice, information, and other assistance. You can also get feedback on the viability of your business idea, or even suggestions. The Canadian Innovation Centre (www.innovationcentre.ca), for example, has a program to help inventors and entrepreneurs crystallize their ideas and commercialize and market the resulting products. The cost, in most cases, is nominal.

Numerous other government agencies, such as the Canada Business Services Centres of Industry Canada (www.canadabusiness.ca), also have publications and resources available to stimulate ideas for new business opportunities. Your public library can provide you with further information on all the government departments relevant to your area of interest. It is possible to get your name on mailing lists for free material or even a government source list so that others can find out about goods or services that you may want to provide.

USE OF CREATIVE THINKING

Tremendous opportunities can materialize from the simple exchange of ideas among a number of people. A variety of analytical techniques and creative thinking concepts can be used to facilitate this exchange. They help to generate and subjectively evaluate a number of prospective new business opportunities. These include such approaches as the use of decision trees, force field analysis, Plus/Minus/Interesting (PMI) assessment, the Simplex Problem Solving Process, and similar concepts. Perhaps the most popular approach used for this purpose is "brainstorming."

Brainstorming is a method for developing creative solutions to problems. It works by having a group of people focus on a single problem and come up with as many deliberately unusual solutions as possible. The idea is to push the ideas as far as possible to come up with distinctly creative solutions. During a brainstorming session, there is no criticism of the ideas that are being put forward—the concept is to open up as many ideas as possible and to break down any previously held preconceptions about the limits of the problem. Once this has been done, the results of the brainstorming session can be explored and evaluated using further brainstorming or other analytical techniques.

Group brainstorming requires a leader to take control of the session, encourage participation by all members, and keep the dialogue focused on the problem to be resolved. It is helpful if participants come from diverse backgrounds and experiences, as this tends to stimulate many more creative ideas. A brainstorming session should be fun as the group comes up with as many ideas as possible from the very practical to the wildly impossible, without criticism or evaluation during the actual session.

Ross McGowan and his friends used a brainstorming session to generate ideas for a prospective golf-related business they might start. Eventually, someone hit on the idea of establishing a golf-training centre devoted entirely to the short game. From there, they were able to go out and do a market analysis to see if the concept had any potential and the nature and extent of the competition. That analysis revealed that outside of one school in Florida, no one had thought to open a short game facility anywhere in North America, and there seemed to be a tremendous need for such a centre. That was the motivation McGowan and his group needed to move forward with the implementation of their plan and the opening of their first centre.

However, not all ideas, even good ones, necessarily succeed. The Short Game facility in Winnipeg closed for good early in the summer of 2002. The concept definitely seemed to work, but the owners miscalculated the length of the season. Rather than an April-to-October season, as they expected, they discovered their season was really from May to the end of July. Manitoba golfers were just not interested in practising in August and September. They were principally interested in getting their real games in. All was not lost, however. The U.S. Short Game rights were sold to a group looking to open a facility in Las Vegas, which has a much longer season.

The following is an example of a modified brainstorming exercise that you could use to help identify opportunities you might choose to develop for a new business.

A Four-Step Process

1. Meet with someone you trust (a close friend, relative, or other person) for one hour. With this individual, discuss your strengths, weaknesses, personal beliefs, values, and similar topics. In other words, focus on what you enjoy doing because you do it well (jobs, hobbies, sports, pastimes, etc.) and where your limits are in terms of interests, ethics, capabilities.

2. After considering your strengths and weaknesses, pick the activity (job, hobby, etc.) that you enjoy the most. Think of a number of problem areas that affect you when you engage in that activity. Then meet with a group of personal acquaintances (three to five) and actively brainstorm a number of potential products or services that could solve those problems (no criticism or negative comments). In an hour, you should be able to come up with 80 to 100 potential product/service ideas.

3. Take this list of potential ideas back to the same person you met with in (1). Reflect back on what you previously identified as your strengths and weaknesses and use that information to develop a framework to narrow the 80 to 100 ideas down to what you think are the five best new business ideas for you.

4. By yourself, take the five ideas, and refine them down to the *one* that you feel relates most closely to your individual interests. Answer the following questions about that top idea:
   - Why did you select it?
   - Where did the idea come from?
   - What are the principal characteristics or attributes of the idea?
   - In what context did it come up during the brainstorming session?
   - What is your ability to carry out the idea?
   - What resources would you need to capitalize on the idea?
   - How profitable is a business venture based on the idea likely to be?
   - Who else might you need to involve?
   - What do you feel is the success potential of the idea you have proposed on a scale of 1 to 5 (with 5 being a very profitable venture)?[7]

The range of sources discussed here is certainly not exhaustive. Through careful observation, enthusiastic inquiry, and systematic searching, it is possible to uncover a number of areas of opportunity.

As you go about this kind of search, it is important to write down your ideas as they come to mind. If not, a thought that might have changed your life may be lost forever.

You should understand that although you are the one that came up with the idea you may not have the desire or the skills that are required to start and run the business. There is absolutely nothing wrong with this. In fact, it is to your advantage to understand this from the onset and realize that you need help. Perhaps at this point, you need to partner with someone or apply to an incubator/accelerator program that will offer the support and guidance you need. You will meet others in the same situation as well as mentors who will help you through the startup process. Remember, you do not have to do this alone. And you should only do what you are real good at! If you do not have the social skills that are needed for marketing and selling your product, then you need to find someone who can. There is no use having a great idea if you do not know how to get it out to the market.

TABLE 2.1	WHERE ENTREPRENEURS FIND THE IDEAS FOR THEIR NEW VENTURES

SOURCE OF IDEA

- Prior business experience
- Business associates
- Seeing a similar business somewhere else
- Suggestion by friends or relatives
- Hobby/personal interest
- Personal research
- An idea just coming to mind
- Seeing something in a magazine/newspaper
- Seeing or hearing something on radio/television

WHERE DO NEW VENTURE IDEAS COME FROM?

Although there is no one answer to where new ideas come from, Table 2.1 does show areas where the many ideas do come from.

Phil Telio came up with the idea for The International Startup Festival while walking alone on a frozen lake. Shannon Tessier came up with her idea while on a school trip, and Sue Harmer got the idea from the demand for the doughnuts she loved to make. Most will agree that ideas come to you when you stop thinking about them—they come to you.

Entrepreneurs need to keep up with market demands by making changes and adjustments to their products. Canada's fastest-growing companies depend on new ideas for their continued growth.

AREAS OF FUTURE OPPORTUNITY

In searching for a unique business idea, the best thing to keep in mind is the dynamic changes taking place within our society, our economy, and our everyday way of doing things. These changes are usually difficult to get a handle on, and it is hard to understand their implications for new business possibilities, but they represent the principal areas of opportunity available today. If you think about it for a minute, most of the major growth areas in business—such as computers and information technology; satellite television systems; fast food; a wide range of personal services; smartphones; and the Internet—did not even exist just a few years ago. But now they are so commonplace we take them for granted. Getting information on emerging trends and assessing their implications for various business situations can be a major road to significant business success.

What can we expect in the future? No one has a crystal ball that can predict these changes with 100 percent accuracy, but many books and business publications provide projections of future trends and changes that could be useful to the insightful observer. For example, over 10 years ago Faith Popcorn, the consumer trend diva, first prophetically envisioned a number of evolving social trends she felt would have a major impact in North American society. These included:

- **99 Lives** Too fast a pace and too little time causes societal schizophrenia and forces us to assume multiple roles. Popcorn says that time is the new money—people would rather spend money than time—and predicted that 90 percent of all consumer goods will soon be home delivered.

- **Anchoring** A reaching back to our spiritual roots, taking what was secure from the past to be ready for the future. Popcorn noted that more and more people are returning to traditional Western religions, feeling that religion is an important part of their lives, or are exploring non-Western alternatives in their search for spirituality and healing.

OTHER CONSIDERATIONS

STAYING INNOVATED

1. Raise your Periscope. Keep up-to-date on what your competitors are doing in the marketplace.

2. Partner with an Innovator. Research-driven institutions, such as colleges and universities, and innovation-minded companies can help you open your eyes to new ideas that can be adapted for your business.

3. Form Innovation Teams. Form groups within your business that will brainstorm ideas and bring them forward for consideration.

4. Borrow Great Ideas. Form a group with businesses in the same industry and share ideas —something that may have worked for one and not another.

5. Leverage an Advisory Board. Ask for their advice and feedback on innovation that will make you stand out from the rest.

6. Don't Let it Bring You Down. Spend time with your employees as a group on a regular basis asking for their ideas and feedback on new innovative ideas.

Source: Adapted from *Profit Magazine* (www.profitguide.com/manage-grow/innovation/growing-great-ideas-36633).

- **AtmosFEAR** Polluted air, contaminated water, and tainted food stir up a storm of consumer doubt and uncertainty. Headlines scream about E. coli, "mad cow" disease, anthrax threats, and other environmental problems. Bottled water has become a billion-dollar business in North America alone.

- **Being Alive** Awareness that good health extends longevity and leads to a new way of life. Look at the tremendous surge in the sales of organic products and herbal additives and remedies, and the popularity of fitness clubs and gyms, acupuncture, magnets, meditation, and other forms of alternative medicine.

- **Cashing Out** Working women and men, questioning personal/career satisfaction and goals, opt for simpler living. Stressed consumers, she says, are searching for fulfillment and simplicity by going back to basics in their lifestyles, consciously opting for more leisure time, or getting out of the rat race by starting a home-based or other small business.

- **Clanning** Belonging to a group that represents common feelings, causes, or ideals; validating one's own belief system. People are banding together to form common-interest clubs, groups, and other organizations, where they can share opinions, beliefs, complaints, or whatever else they are feeling with other like-minded individuals.

- **Down-Aging** Nostalgic for their carefree childhood, baby boomers find comfort in familiar pursuits and products from their youth. Music, automobile brands, movies, and a variety of other names and products from the 1960s and 1970s are all being resurrected in response to this demand.

- **Egonomics** To offset a depersonalized society, consumers crave recognition of their individuality. This has created opportunities for improved customer service by increasingly recognizing the specific needs of individuals or for the "ultracustomization" of products and services to the specific requirements of particular customers.

- **EVEolution** The way women think and behave is impacting business, causing a marketing shift away from a traditional, hierarchical model to a relationship model. As Popcorn notes, women have far more financial influence than has traditionally been recognized. They own one-third of all North American businesses and control 80 percent of all household spending in the country. As a consequence, marketing to them in an appropriate manner can mean a significant business opportunity.

1. **Organic food:** Increasing numbers of people care about the quality of the food they eat, wanting it to be both healthy and safe.

2. **Bike store:** Bicycling is the second most popular outdoor activity in America by frequency of participation. Many North American cities are trying hard to increase the number of people using bikes, rather than cars, to commute to work.

3. **Senior transportation services:** Many seniors are being forced to give up their driving privileges and rely on being transported by others. Many of them are not able to just hop on a bus or take other public transit because of physical limitations; transporting seniors is a huge business opportunity that is only going to get bigger over the next few years.

4. **Hot lunch delivery:** If you have been to India, you are probably familiar with the custom of hot lunches delivered to working people in "tiffins" (metal food containers). Now take that idea, and apply it to the office buildings full of working people in your city. Think how much people working in offices would appreciate the convenience of having a hot meal delivered.

5. **General contracting services for home renovations:** It takes a small army of tradespeople just to renovate one room. A person with superior organizational skills and contacts with tradespeople could make a fortune overseeing the renovations of other people's bathrooms, kitchens, house extensions, and so on.

6. **Patient advocacy:** The growing demands on our increasingly fragmented, dysfunctional healthcare system create an urgent need for people who can help individual patients and their families navigate our medical system.

7. **Irrigation systems:** Selling and installing irrigation systems is a good business opportunity because of the large group of potential clients. Residential homeowners with their green lawns, businesses, golf courses, greenhouse growers, and farmers—they all want or need irrigation. But the truly great thing about this business is the potential to make money from the maintenance of the irrigation systems you sell, such as shutting down systems in the winter.

8. **Mobile apps development:** Increasing numbers of businesses will want branded apps, and there is still the chance of making the big score by developing an app for consumers that becomes wildly popular.

9. **Pet farewell products and services:** To many North Americans, pets are not animals; they are family members. Therefore, when a beloved pet dies, they will want to express their grief in a similar way as for the death of a loved person.

10. **Scooter sales and repair:** In Canada, in 2009 to 2011, 67 percent of Canadian men and 54 percent of Canadian women aged 18 to 79 were overweight or obese. It is not just older people who are using scooters to get around anymore.[8]

- **Fantasy Adventure** The modern age whets our desire for roads untravelled. Exotic theme hotels (such as those in Las Vegas), theme parks, cruise lines, and adventure and eco tourism are all growing tremendously, and theme rooms and suites in hotels are becoming increasingly popular as people strive to satisfy their exotic fantasies.

- **Icon Toppling** A new socioquake transforms mainstream North America and the world as the pillars of society are questioned and rejected. Increasingly skeptical consumers are ready to bring down the long-accepted monuments of business, government, and society. Large companies no longer hold our trust. Loyalty to a single employer has gone the way of the dinosaur. Governments are now a source of cynicism and distrust. And the views of doctors, lawyers, and other professionals are no longer accepted without question.

- **Pleasure Revenge** Consumers are having a secret bacchanal. They are mad as hell and want to cut loose again. They are tired of being told what is good for them and so are indifferent to rules and regulations and want to enjoy some of the more "forbidden" aspects of life. Steakhouses, martini bars, and similar diversions are all popular reflections of this trend.

- **Small Indulgences** Stressed-out consumers want to indulge in affordable luxuries and seek ways to reward themselves. Premium-priced products, such as ice cream, sunglasses, chocolate, liqueur, and similar items, have become one way for consumers to reward themselves at moderate expense at the end of a hard day or week.

- **SOS (Save Our Society)** The country has rediscovered a social conscience of ethics, passion, and compassion. We are seeing more corporations make a commitment to return some proportion of their profits to the community; consumers are becoming more responsive to companies that exhibit a social conscience attuned to ethical concerns, education, or the environment; and there has been a increase in the popularity of "ethical" and "socially responsible" mutual funds.

- **Vigilante Consumer** Frustrated, often-angry consumers are manipulating the marketplace through pressure, protest, and politics. Consumers seek real products, benefits, and value. When they are disappointed, they can be formidable enemies. At any one time, there are typically a number of boycotts in progress against some company. This has really been facilitated by the growth of the Internet, where consumers can set up chat rooms, news groups, and websites to carry on their complaint against some particular company or brand.[9]

The kind of social changes mentioned by Popcorn have largely materialized and evolved over the past few years and will help define the future orientation of our society. And while being aware of such changes is interesting, how does it translate into an entrepreneurial opportunity? Keeping on top of such trends can provide the inspiration for many significant new businesses for an observant entrepreneur. As the futurist John Naisbitt said, "Trends, like horses, are easier to ride in the direction they are going."

SOME SPECIFIC IDEAS AND CONCEPTS FOR THE FUTURE

In view of all these evident trends, a number of specific business ideas might be expected to do well in the marketplace of the future.

The list that follows will expand on some of the possible implications of these trends and give you some idea of specific businesses they indicate should be potential opportunities. The list is by no means complete, but it will give you a few things to think about.

E-Business

The Internet has changed the way business is done across the globe. With a potential customer base of 875 million active Internet shoppers, small businesses cannot afford to ignore e-business.

The Internet continues to change the way we communicate and conduct business. Regardless of whether your venture is web based or not, you will still likely have a web page for customer support and communication, to complement your advertising and marketing program, to offer product information, to conduct research and obtain competitive intelligence, or to network with other business owners. New venture opportunities using the Internet could include:

- Designing, hosting, and maintaining websites
- Internet marketing consulting services
- Social networking sites
- Social media consulting services
- Social media analytics
- Software development for very specific applications
- E-commerce—selling products to both the consumer and business, such as small-business equipment, health-related equipment and supplements, cosmetics and anti-aging products, home-delivered meals and specialty foods, gaming services and related products, travel and leisure products and services, educational products, e-books, videos, mobile applications, multimedia packages and programs, and almost anything you can think of that serves narrow markets around the globe, 24/7.

Many forecasters predict that business-to-business (B2B) e-commerce will grow more than 10 times faster than business-to-consumer (B2C) commerce, with most of the attractive opportunities likely to be found in this arena.

Maintaining "Wellness"

This is an emerging theme that will create a growing demand for a variety of fitness and health-related products. People are focusing on experiencing a better quality of life by shaping up and healing their minds and bodies. New venture opportunities exist in the following areas:

- Healthier and organically grown food products
- Alternative medicine and homeopathic remedies
- Spas and cosmetic surgery centres
- Holistic health clubs and fitness centres
- Holistic healing and the use of ancient remedies
- Restaurants emphasizing low-fat and other types of "healthy" foods

Personal Indulgence

Personal Indulgence is almost the opposite of the "wellness" trend, with people wanting to reward themselves periodically with small, affordable luxuries. New venture opportunities here could include:

- Individual portions of gourmet foods
- Specialty ice cream and other exotic desserts
- Specialty coffee, tea, and wine shops
- Exotic meats, such as elk, wild boar, bison, ostrich, and venison
- Bed-and-breakfast places or small hotels with specialty services
- Aromatherapy

Home Health Service and Eldercare

These services will continue to be a rapidly growing market with the aging of the baby boomers and the ever-increasing costs and declining quality of healthcare. Opportunities for businesses in this area include:

- Home healthcare providers, such as physiotherapists, occupational therapists, and nursing assistants
- Door-to-door transportation services for the elderly
- Homemaking services
- Daycare centres for the elderly
- Seniors' travel clubs
- Independent, residential, and assisted-living centres
- Products and services for the physically challenged

Pet Care and Pampering

Pet services represent a significant market opportunity as well for specialized care products and services. Some opportunities for businesses here include:

- Pet daycare centres and hotels
- Pet snacks and treats
- Home grooming services for pets
- 24/7 veterinary care
- Baked products for dogs
- Pet furniture and clothing stores

OTHER CONSIDERATIONS

Retail Boutiques

Boutiques with narrow sales niches will increase in number as the category-killer box stores and discount department stores expand across the country and come to dominate most conventional retail markets, such as building materials, lawn and garden supplies, books, computers and office supplies, consumer electronics, food products, and other categories. Opportunities for one-of-a-kind stores include:

- Second-hand goods
- Bakery cafés
- Specialty shoe stores
- Home decorating
- Birding
- Gardening centres
- Stress relief
- Craft stores
- Travel-related products and services
- Homeopathic remedies
- Microbreweries

Personal Services of All Types

Personal services will grow in popularity as people spend more time at work and have fewer leisure hours. As a result, they will be willing to pay others to run their errands and handle many time-consuming home and family-related matters. Providers of these personal errand services could perform a variety of tasks, such as grocery shopping, picking up laundry, buying theatre tickets, having shoes repaired, and other jobs. They could also arrange for the repair and servicing of cars, take care of pets, choose gifts, consult on the selection of clothes, and handle similar personal matters. Other opportunities in this area include:

- Personal concierge service
- Gift services
- Pick-up and delivery service for guests and clients
- Rent-a-driver
- Rent-à-chef
- Personal escort service

F
Y
I

SECTOR BY SECTOR
What Canada's leading growth stars do

SECTOR	NO. OF COMPANIES
Business services	79
Information technology	22
Marketing	22
Human resources	9
Communications	6
Other	20
Software development	30
Business management	8
Marketing	5
Other	17
Manufacturing	23
Wholesale or distribution	15
Financial services	14
Construction	12
Consumer services	12
Natural resources services	6
Retail	5
Food production or distribution	3
Media	1

A PROVINCIAL BREAKDOWN OF PROFIT 200 FIRMS

BRITISH COLUMBIA
Companies on the list: 37

SASKATCHEWAN
Companies on the list: 2

ALBERTA
Companies on the list: 23

MANITOBA
Companies on the list: 2

QUEBEC
Companies on the list: 33

ONTARIO
Companies on the list: 101

ATLANTIC CANADA
Companies on the list: 2

Source: Profitguide.com, Canada's Fastest-Growing Companies (www.profitguide.com/news/canada%E2%80%99s-fastest-growing-companies-35015). Used with permission.

EVALUATING YOUR IDEAS LO3

As you have seen, generating ideas for a prospective new business is a relatively simple procedure—the end result of which is a number of potential business opportunities that may, or may not, have a chance of becoming successful ventures.

Discovering ideas is only part of the process involved in starting a business. The ideas must be screened and evaluated and a selection made of those that warrant further investigation. It is essential that you subject your ideas to this analysis to find the "fatal flaws" if any exist (and they often do). Otherwise, the marketplace will find them when it is too late, and you have spent a great deal of time and money.

But how can you determine which ideas you should evaluate? Of the multitude of possible alternatives, which are likely to be best for you? Knowles and Bilyea suggest that you think of the process of selecting the right opportunity for yourself a huge funnel equipped with a series of filters. You pour everything into this funnel—your vision, values, long-term goals, short-term objectives, personality, problems, and so on—and a valuable business idea drains out the bottom.[10]

This opportunity selection process contains six steps:

1. Identify your business and personal objectives.
2. Learn more about your favourite industries.
3. Identify promising industry segments.
4. Identify problem areas, and brainstorm solutions.
5. Compare possible solutions with your objectives and opportunities in the marketplace.
6. Focus on the most promising opportunities.

STEP 1: IDENTIFY YOUR BUSINESS AND PERSONAL GOALS

List your personal and business goals. What do you want from your business? Money? Personal fulfillment? Independence? Being your own boss? Freedom? Control over your own destiny? Think back to what stimulated your interest in thinking about going into a business of your own in the first place. List everything you would like to accomplish and what you expect your business to be able to provide.

At this stage, it might help to meet with someone whom you trust—a close friend, relative, or other person—for an hour or so. With this individual, you can discuss your strengths and weaknesses, goals, values, ethical standards, and similar personal issues. He or she can help you focus your goals and refine your thinking in relation to what you enjoy doing, what you are good at, and where your limits are in terms of interests and capabilities.

STEP 2: RESEARCH YOUR FAVOURITE INDUSTRIES

As you considered the variety of trends we discussed earlier in this stage, there were undoubtedly a number of possibilities that captured your interest. Now you should explore a couple of these situations in more detail. These industries should be ones that interest you and about which you have some first-hand knowledge. They could be food service, travel, manufacturing, retailing, construction, or whatever.

After you have picked your industries, investigate all the information you can find about them from business publications, government agencies and departments, trade magazines, the Internet, and similar sources. The Industry Canada website and online databases, such as ABI/Inform and Canadian Business and Current Affairs (CBCA), available at your local university library can point you to hundreds of articles related to almost any field. Focus on such areas as the history of the business, the nature and degree of competition, recent industry trends and breakthroughs, number and distribution of customers, and similar topics. It will help to write a brief industry overview of each situation after you have completed your investigation.

STEP 3: IDENTIFY PROMISING INDUSTRY SEGMENTS

With a thorough understanding of one or more industry situations you are now in a position to identify possible market segments where you think you could survive and prosper. Profile your typical target customer—a person or business who needs a particular product or service you could provide.

If you are looking at the consumer market, identify what this prospect will look like in terms of demographic factors, such as age, gender, location, income, family size, education, and so on, and in terms of psychographic and other factors, such as interests, values, lifestyle, leisure activities, and buying patterns. If you are looking at a commercial/industrial market, use company size, industry, geographic location, number of employees, and so on.

STEP 4: IDENTIFY PROBLEM AREAS, AND BRAINSTORM SOLUTIONS

Identify the problem areas for some of these groups of customers that you feel are currently being met ineffectively. What "gaps" are there in terms of the needs of these customers that you feel you can address? Get together with a group of people who know something about business and the industry. Try to actively brainstorm a list of products and services that could represent potential ways to solve these problems. Keep your discussion positive. Let your imagination roam. Do not be concerned about the merits or demerits of an idea at this stage. Just try to make note of as many potential ideas as you can. You should be able to come up with 80 to 100 or more prospective ideas in an hour.

Refine your list. Try to narrow it down to the five or ten best ideas for you based on your interests, goals and objectives, strengths and weaknesses, and available resources.

STEP 5: COMPARE POSSIBLE SOLUTIONS WITH YOUR OBJECTIVES AND OPPORTUNITIES IN THE MARKETPLACE

The "Ideal" or "Model" Business Model

Richard Buskirk of the University of Southern California designed a framework you can use to evaluate the pros and cons of your potential business ideas.[11] It is built around what he calls the "Ideal" or "Model" business. The framework contains 19 distinct factors that affect the chances of success for any new business. Very few ideas will conform precisely to the specifications of the model, but the more a business idea deviates from the "ideal," the more difficulties and greater risks you will encounter with that venture. Testing your concepts against the model will also help identify the areas in which you might expect to have difficulties with your business.

The model is presented in Table 2.2. Let us briefly discuss each of the factors listed.

Requires No Investment

If you do not have to put any money into your business, then you cannot lose any if it fails. You lose only the time you have invested. The more money that must be committed to the venture, the larger is the risk and the less attractive the business becomes. Some new businesses, such as fancy theme restaurants, may require so much initial capital; there is really no way they can be financially profitable. Smart businesspeople tend to avoid businesses that require a large investment of their own money.

Has a Recognized, Measurable Market

The ideal situation is to sell a product or service to a clearly recognized market that can be relied on to buy it. This may require doing a preliminary investigation of the market acceptance of your idea or concept. Look for some market confirmation of what you propose to offer before proceeding any further.

A Perceived Need for the Product or Service

Ideally, your intended customers should already perceive a need for what you intend to sell them. They should know they need your product or service now, thus simplifying your marketing efforts. If they do not recognize their need, you have to first persuade them they need the product and then convince them to buy it from you. Try to avoid products or services that require you to educate the market before you can make a sale.

A Dependable Source of Supply for Required Inputs

Make certain you can make or provide what it is you plan to sell. Many businesses have failed because they were unable to obtain essential raw materials or components under the terms they had originally planned. Sudden changes in price or availability of these key inputs can threaten the viability of your entire venture. Large corporations commonly try to directly control or negotiate long-term contracts to ensure reliable and consistent supplies. You have to be just as concerned if there are only one or two sources for the materials you require.

No Government Regulation

The ideal business would not be impacted at all by government regulation. This is impossible in today's world, but some industries are more subject to government involvement than others. Food, drugs, financial services, transportation, communications, and so on, are all examples of businesses that require extensive government approval. If your business falls into this category, make sure you understand how government regulations will affect you in terms of time and money.

Requires No Labour Force

The ideal business would require no labour force. This is possible in one-person operations—the "one-man show." Once you hire an employee, you have a lot of government paperwork to deal with relating to Employment Insurance, Canada Pension Plan contributions, and other legal requirements. You are also subject to a broad range of regulations concerning such things as occupational health and safety, human rights, and pay equity. Few small business operators enjoy dealing with these requirements, as these can be quite time consuming. If your business demands the hiring of additional employees, you must be prepared to take on the responsibility for managing these people effectively.

Provides 100 Percent Gross Margin

While virtually no businesses provide a 100 percent gross margin, the idea is that the larger the gross margin, the better is the business. Gross margin is what you have left after paying the *direct* material and labour costs for whatever it is you are selling. For example, say, you are running an appliance repair business. A typical service call takes one hour, for which you charge the customer $50. However, this call costs you $15 in direct labour and $5 in parts and materials; therefore, your gross margin is $30, or 60 percent. Service industries like this generally have larger gross margins than manufacturing businesses.

In businesses with low gross margins, small errors in estimating costs or sales can quickly lead to losses. These businesses also tend to have a high break-even point, making it very difficult to make a lot of money. High-margin businesses, on the other hand, can break even with very small sales volumes and generate profits very quickly once this volume of business is exceeded.

Buyers Purchase Frequently

The ideal business would provide a product or service that customers purchase very frequently. This gives you more opportunities to sell to them. Frequent purchasing also reduces their risk in case your offering does not live up to their expectations. You are much more likely to try a new fast-food restaurant that has opened in town than you are to purchase a new brand or type of washing machine, printer, home theatre system, or other such item.

Receives Favourable Tax Treatment

Firms in certain industries may receive tax incentives, such as accelerated depreciation on capital assets, differential capital cost allowances, investment tax credits, or various other tax breaks. The ideal business will receive some sort of favourable or differential tax treatment. This sort of advantage can make your business more profitable and attractive to other investors should you require outside capital.

Has a Receptive, Established Distribution System

Ideally, your business would sell to established intermediaries and distributors who are eager to handle your product. If you have to develop a new method of distribution or are unable to obtain access to an existing one, getting your product to market can be a long and costly process. If traditional wholesalers and retailers are not prepared to carry your line, achieving any reasonable level of market coverage can be extremely difficult.

Has Great Publicity Value

Publicity in magazines, in newspapers (print and online), and on television has great promotional value, and it is free! If your offering is sufficiently exciting and newsworthy, the resulting publicity may be sufficient to ensure a successful launch for your business. The publicity given to concepts, such as Sue Harmer's SuzyQ Doughnuts, the International Startup Festival, and favourable reviews of local restaurants by newspaper food critics are all examples of tremendously helpful public notice of new products.

Customers Pay in Advance

A major problem facing most new businesses is that of maintaining an adequate cash flow. Typically, small firms are chronically short of cash, the lifeblood they require to pay their employees, their suppliers, and the government on an ongoing basis. The ideal business would have customers who pay in advance. This is, in fact, the case for many small retail service firms, the direct-mail industry, and manufacturers of some custom-made products. Businesses where customers pay in advance are usually easier to start, have smaller startup capital requirements, and do not suffer losses from bad debts incurred on credit sales.

No Risk of Product Liability

Some products and services are automatically subject to high risk from product liability. Anything ingested by the customer; amusement facilities, such as go-cart tracks and water slides; and many manufactured products that possibly could cause injury to the user are all loaded with potential liability. Liability can occur in unexpected situations, such as the serious injury sustained by a golfer whose golf club shattered and impaled him in the chest.

Try to avoid such high-risk businesses, or take every precaution to reduce risk, and carry lots of insurance.

No Technical Obsolescence

The ideal product or service would not suffer from technical obsolescence. The shorter the product's expected technical life expectancy, the less desirable it is as an investment. Such products as popcorn, shampoo, garden tools, and electric drills seem to have been with us for as long as most of us can remember. On the other hand, the Blue-ray player, MP3 player, and smartphone are of recent origin and are undergoing rapid technological transformation. Businesses built around these products are extremely risky for smaller firms and have a very high probability of failure.

No Competition

Too much competition can be a problem, since aggressive price competitors can make it very difficult for you to turn a profit. Not having any competition can certainly make life much easier for a new small business. But if you ever find yourself in this happy situation, you should ask yourself why. True, your offering may be so new to the marketplace that no other firms have had a chance to get established. But maybe it is just that other firms have already determined there really is no market for what you are planning to provide.

No Fashion Obsolescence

Fashion products usually have extremely short life cycles. You must be sure you can make your money before the cycle ends, or be prepared to offer an ongoing series of acceptable products season after season, if you hope to build your business into a sizeable enterprise. Fashion cycles exist not only for clothing and similar products but also for such items as toys—consider what happened with the hula hoop, Wacky Wall Walker, Rubik's Cube, and Cabbage Patch dolls.

No Physical Perishability

Products with a short physical life have only a limited window available for their disposition. This applies not only to most food items but also to a wide variety of other such goods as printer ink. If your product is perishable, your business concept must include some method of selling your inventory quickly or a contingency plan to dispose of aged merchandise before it spoils.

Impervious to Weather Conditions

Some businesses are, by their very nature, at the mercy of the weather. If the weather is right for them, they prosper; if not, they may go broke. Pity the ski resort owner without any snow, the waterslide operator with a year of unseasonably cold weather, the beach concession during a summer of constant rain, the market gardener in the midst of an unexpected drought. The ideal business would not be impacted by these unpredictable changes in the weather.

Possesses Some Proprietary Rights

The ideal business would possess significant proprietary rights that give it some unique characteristic and protection against competition. These rights can be in the form of registered patents, trademarks, copyrighted material, protected trade secrets, licensing agreements that provide some sort of exclusive manufacturing arrangements, or perhaps rights for exclusive distribution of certain products in particular markets. Gendis Corporation, for example, was largely built on the rights to distribute first Papermate pens and then Sony products in Canada on an exclusive basis.

TABLE 2.2   CHARACTERISTICS OF THE "IDEAL" BUSINESS

- Requires no investment
- Has a recognized, measurable market
- A perceived need for the product or service
- A dependable source of supply for required inputs
- No government regulation
- Requires no labour force
- Provides 100 percent gross margin
- Buyers purchase frequently
- Receives favourable tax treatment
- Has a receptive, established distribution system
- Has great publicity value
- Customers pay in advance
- No risk of product liability
- No technical obsolescence
- No competition
- No fashion obsolescence
- No physical perishability
- Impervious to weather conditions
- Possesses some proprietary rights

Of the ideas that you have generated, you might want to pick three and evaluate each of them against the factors described in the Buskirk model "Compare your Ideas to the 'Ideal' Business" available online in Connect. This evaluation will illustrate how well these ideas fit with all the characteristics of the "ideal" business. How would you rate each idea on each of Buskirk's 19 factors? On the basis of this evaluation, which of these ideas do you feel represents the most significant new venture opportunity for you? Can you justify your response? Did the idea you picked score less than five on any of Buskirk's factors? If so, can you think of any way to overcome the situation or find other solutions to the problem?

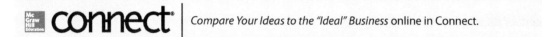

For a more formal evaluation of an invention, software concept, or other innovative idea, the Canadian Innovation Centre will conduct a comprehensive assessment to assist you in the decisions you must make regarding your idea. For more information, contact Canadian Innovation Centre at www.innovationcentre.ca.

STEP 6: FOCUS ON THE MOST PROMISING OPPORTUNITIES

Which of the ideas you have evaluated seems to be the best fit with the "ideal" business and is most consistent with your goals and values? This is probably the one you should be looking to pursue. However, no matter how exhaustive your evaluation, there is no guarantee of success. The challenge is to do the best you can in conducting an assessment of each of your principal ideas, knowing that at some point you will have to make a decision with incomplete information and less than scientific accuracy. As a good friend of mine commented during a dinner speech not long ago, "Entrepreneurship is like bungee jumping. Both require an act of faith."

THE VENTURE OPPORTUNITY SCREENING MODEL

While the Buskirk model can be very useful for doing a "quick and dirty" evaluation of any prospective business idea and understanding how it might deviate from your notion of the "Ideal" or "Model" business, it is a simplification of the process. It gives you some insight into the issues you may have to wrestle with or overcome in implementing a particular business idea but does not tell you how it stacks up to such strategic issues as:

- Market size and growth potential
- Current relationship with any customer base
- The degree of innovation and how related the concept is to customer needs
- The expected speed to market and difficulty with actual implementation
- The overall business strategy and strength of the business model
- The capabilities of the CEO and strength of the management team
- Anticipated risks and expected return on the investment as well as a number of other important factors.

To overcome these issues and provide a more comprehensive process for identifying entrepreneurial opportunities, you might also consider using the Venture Opportunity Screening Model (VOSM). It is based on Rae's work in the realm of opportunity recognition and his proposed Opportunity Recognition Model.[12] The VOSM is intended to give you a clearer idea of the relative attractiveness of a number of new venture opportunities you may be considering. This is not a cut-and-dried process. Most of the time, there will be considerable uncertainty and numerous unknowns and risks. Going through this exercise, however, will help you understand some of the uncertainties and risks as you make a decision about an idea. It may even help you devise ways to overcome some of these uncertainties and risks and make them more acceptable to you. Every potential venture is unique. As a result, you may find that certain issues are more pertinent in some situations than in others. Or you may need to tailor some questions and issues to your particular circumstances. Do not be afraid to do so. The idea is to determine if your opportunity is attractive enough, according to the various criteria in the model, to go ahead and conduct a comprehensive feasibility study or develop a business plan.

The model is based on a series of constructs identified by entrepreneurs as being important in their venture selection process. It aims to distinguish between high value opportunities that are worthy of exploration and low value opportunities less likely to be worth pursuing. These constructs have been clustered into a number of categories to facilitate their assessment. These include:

- The assessment of the market opportunity
- The role of innovation
- Strategic potential
- The investment, risk, and return situation
- The effectiveness of the people involved in the venture

An outline for the VOSM is available online in Connect. You can make as many copies as you need to assess the variety of potential opportunities you have in mind. Indicate for each of the criteria just where you feel the venture is located on the Value scale from low (1) to high (10). Once you have evaluated the idea according to each of the criteria, you can determine its total raw score for each of the five major constructs. Since some of these constructs may be more relevant to your idea than others or may be more important to you from a personal standpoint, you can weight each of them to reflect your preferences. You can then determine the weighted score and the Total Aggregate Score for that concept. This will be helpful in forming your overall assessment of the venture idea and determining whether you believe it may or may not hold attractive possibilities as a real entrepreneurial opportunity for you.

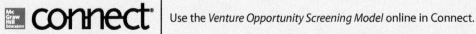

Use the *Venture Opportunity Screening Model* online in Connect.

Once you have finished the VOSM, return to this page, and answer the questions under Conclusions below:

Conclusions

- What is your overall assessment of this opportunity? Articulate your reasons for believing it may have some attractive possibilities.
- If positive, why does this opportunity exist now?
- What major problems or difficulties are you likely to encounter in moving the venture forward?
- What market entry strategy appears to best suit the opportunity? Why?
- What indications do you have that there is a fit between the current external environment and the factors assessed above that seem to create your opportunity?

DECIDING HOW TO PROCEED   LO4

Once satisfied you have identified an idea that represents a significant business opportunity, you must determine the best way to proceed. There are all sorts of *entry strategies*—ways people start new enterprises.

Reflecting on these alternatives and judging how they fit with your specific idea and your particular abilities and circumstances will enable you to turn them into real opportunities. No general rules have been developed to guarantee success or even to indicate which concepts and strategies will work best in different situations, but being aware of the possibilities will give you a clearer picture of the job you need to do to succeed.

BUY A BUSINESS

One possibility is to find a business presently operating in your area of interest, buy it, and take over its operations. You may want to buy the business either because it is already quite successful but the current owners want to get out for some reason or because the business is not doing very well under the current owners and you feel you can turn it around.

This can be a good entry strategy. A good deal of time and effort is involved in the startup phase of any business. This stage can be bypassed when you buy a going-concern. You also acquire a location, customers, established trade relationships, and a number of other positive elements.

These advantages do not come for free, however. Buying an existing business may cost you more than getting into a similar business on your own. The current owner may expect to receive "goodwill" for certain assets already acquired or the effort devoted to the business so far. You may also inherit some problem, such as obsolete equipment, the bad image and reputation of the previous owners, or labour difficulties.

For a more complete discussion of this entry strategy, refer to Stage Ten of this book.

ACQUIRE A FRANCHISE

Another alternative is to buy the rights to operate a business that has been designed and developed by someone else, that is, to acquire a *franchise*. Under a franchise agreement, an established company, the *franchisor*, with one or more successful businesses operating in other locations, provides assistance to a new firm in breaking into the marketplace. In return, the new owner, or *franchisee*, pays a fee for the assistance, invests money to set up and operate the business, pays a percentage of sales as a royalty to the franchisor, and agrees to operate the business within the terms and conditions laid out in the franchise agreement.

The assistance provided by the franchisor can take many forms, such as:

- The right to use the franchisor's brand names and registered trademarks
- The right to sell products and services developed by the franchisor
- The right to use operating systems and procedures developed by the franchisor
- Training in how to run the business
- Plans for the layout of the business facilities and the provision of specialized equipment
- A regional or national advertising program
- Centralized purchasing and volume discounts
- Research and development support

While the failure rate of franchised businesses is reported to be lower than that for independently established firms, there are a number of disadvantages associated with the concept.

For more detailed information, refer to Stage Eleven of this book.

START A BUSINESS OF YOUR OWN

The third and probably most common means of getting into business for yourself is to start a business of your own from scratch. This is the route most frequently travelled by the true entrepreneur who wants a business that is really his or her own creation. Starting your own business can take many forms and involve a variety of entry strategies. While we are unable to discuss all the possibilities here in any detail, a few alternatives will be mentioned to get you thinking about their fit with your particular situation. Some of the possibilities available to you are:

1. Develop an entirely new product or service unlike anything else available in the market.
2. Acquire the rights to manufacture or sell someone else's product or use someone else's name or logo under licence. These rights could be exclusive to a product category, a geographic area, or a specific market.

3. Find a customer who wants to buy something. Then create a business to make that sale or serve that need.

4. Take a hobby, and develop it into a business.

5. Develop a product or service similar to those currently on the market but that is more convenient, less expensive, safer, cleaner, faster, easier to use, lighter, stronger, more compact, or has some other important distinguishing attribute.

6. Add incremental value to a product or service already available by putting it through another production process, combining it with other products and services, or providing it as one element in a larger package.

7. Become an agent or distributor for products or services produced by someone else. These may be domestically produced or imported from other countries.

8. Open a trading house or become a selling agent for Canadian firms who may be interested in selling their products or services abroad.

9. Develop a consulting service or provide information to other people in a subject area you know very well.

10. Become a supplier to another producer or large institutional customer. Large organizations require an extensive range of raw materials, supplies, and components to run their business. A small portion of their requirements could represent a significant volume of sales for you. This type of "outsourcing" is an excellent opportunity to pursue either through a contract or a strategic alliance with a larger organization.

11. Identify a situation where another firm has dropped what may be profitable products or product lines. They may have abandoned customer groups or market segments that are uneconomic for them to serve effectively but that may still be quite lucrative for a smaller company.

12. Borrow an idea from one industry or market and transfer it to another. A product or service that has been well accepted in one situation may well represent a substantial opportunity in other circumstances as well.

13. Look for opportunities to capitalize on special events and situations or unusual occurrences. You may be able to "piggyback" your business onto these situations.

F
Y
I

Other 2013 Predictions for Entrepreneurship, by Diana Kander. (www.huffingtonpost.com)

10 Big Mobile Trends to Look Out For, by Stuart Thomas. (http://memeburn.com)

8 Ways to Come Up with a Business Idea, Entrepreneur.com. (www.entrepreneur.com)

How to Find New Business Ideas in Everyday Life, Entrepreneur.com. (www.entrepreneur.com)

Is It Time to Let Go of Your Business Idea, Entreprepreneur.com. (www.entrepreneur.com)

Key Characteristics of Innovative Startup Teams, Startup Professional Musings. (http://blog.startupprofessionals.com)

Brainstorming Tools, Social Media Today. (http://socialmediatoday.com)

Innovation Management, A Comprehensive List of Brainstorming Tools. (www.innovationmanagement.se)

Ideas are Cheap; It's the Execution That Matters. (www.freeideas.co)

Make Money Online, Donna Fontenot. (www.donnafontenot.com)

Reading Material

The Big Idea by Donny Deutsch

The Idea Hunter by Andrew Boynton

One Simple Idea for Startups and Entrepreneurs by Stephen Key

LO1 The Entrepreneurial Opportunity is a process of proceeding from a new idea to an opportunity. The process consists of five steps:

- preparation—the background, experience, and prior knowledge the entrepreneur brings to the opportunity
- incubation—contemplation of the idea or problem unconsciously done in your mind
- insight—the idea potentially becomes an opportunity
- evaluation—the idea is analyzed for viability
- elaboration—if viable, the product moves to business planning

LO2 Business ideas come from many places:

- previous employment, hobbies, personal observations, a deliberate search
- when you are alone or with a group of friends and start throwing around ideas that will somehow make a difference in some way, shape, or form

LO3 Evaluate your idea. The six steps in evaluating your prospective new business are:

- identify your business and personal goals
- research your favourite industries
- identify promising industry segments
- identify problem areas, and brainstorm solutions
- compare possible solutions in the marketplace
- focus on the most promising opportunities

LO4 Choose a business model:

- buy a business
- acquire a franchise
- start a business of your own

For more information on the resources available from McGraw-Hill Ryerson, go to www.mcgrawhill.ca/he/solutions.

MARKET FEASIBILITY STUDY

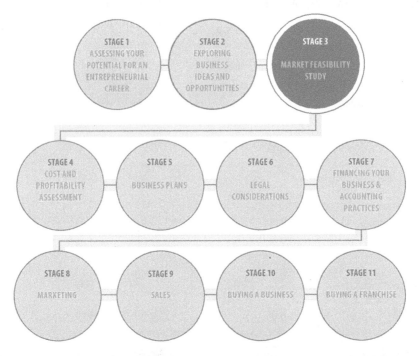

PYTHIAN
GOING AROUND THE WORLD TO GET AROUND THE CLOCK

Joël Côté-Cright / Ottawa Business Journal.

Pythian first headed to India because its employees needed sleep.

The Ottawa remote database administration services company was working around the clock to fix and maintain its customers' data. Its engineers not only needed to collaborate with clients during business hours but also service databases during the night.

So co-founder and *Ottawa Business Journal* Forty Under 40 recipient Paul Vallée travelled to Hyderabad, India, in 2002 to set up an office where infrastructure management was booming and the difference in time zones beneficial. Pythian had no more than 20 employees at the time.

"The whole idea of setting up a subsidiary in India for a 20-person company was ridiculous," Mr. Vallée says. "I didn't know that I couldn't do it because nobody told me that I couldn't do it." He did it anyway, and it was not long before a contact in Sydney, Australia, passed along a resumé after noticing a gap in the (North American) evening shift where more employees for database administration were needed.

That was when Pythian decided to become a global company using global resources. This year, as the company celebrates its 15th anniversary, its 215 employees are spread across 21 countries and speak as many languages.

But it is not about having boots on the ground—Pythian does not serve customers in as many countries as it has employees. It is more about allowing the company to access the best and brightest in the field internationally.

"We can hire out of a candidate pool that is global instead of limiting ourselves to a pool that happens to be living where we have offices," Mr. Vallée says.

Managing a Global Team

Working as a remote company, Pythian had to develop software that would make its services visible to customers, showing what it did and why.

Serendipitously, that same software (which Mr. Vallée developed himself) can be used to manage remote employees.

Inspired by charting and continuous documentation in healthcare, Pythian's work management software prompts its engineers to document observations, actions, and results. Even email correspondences can be included. A clock measures exactly how much time is spent on each task performed.

The software can also be filtered by employee, to see what each engineer has accomplished in a day.

"All the things that are difficult about managing home workers was relatively easy for us," he says.

Clockwork

One challenge that cannot be fixed by technology is dealing with time zones. "We've come a long way in telepresence technology to create collaboration," Mr. Vallée says. "But if they're asleep or would rather be having dinner with their families, this is a very tough challenge."

Staff meetings are often held outside of Ottawa office hours, and there is a nap room that can be booked by employees. It is named Hyderabad after the Indian city into which the company first expanded. Mr. Vallée says he has booked that room plenty of times.

The Future of Remote I.T.

Even with Pythian's advanced work documentation software, concerns remain about employees having access to private information. There is no way of knowing if an engineer administering an email system takes a peek at others' private correspondence.

And as systems become more valuable, pressure is mounting to create additional accountability. Mr. Vallée draws similarities to the surge in banks installing cameras as soon as the technology became available in the 1940s, with most implementing the technology within a decade.

"We think something similar will happen in our space, and we'd rather be leaders and trendsetters," he says, without elaborating on what software Pythian has in the works. For now, its 100 Ottawa-based employees will continue to work around the clock, ring a cowbell hanging in the office to celebrate every new contract, and sign up for the occasional nap.

Source: Courtney Symons, *Ottawa Business Journal*, October 24, 2012 (www.obj.ca).

So far, we have considered and evaluated your new venture primarily from a conceptual point of view. That is, we have concentrated on the following questions:

1. What product/service businesses would you be interested in pursuing?
2. How attractive are these venture ideas?
3. What options should you consider in getting into a business of your own?

Now, in Stage Three, a step-by-step process will be presented to help you transform your *chosen* venture concept from the idea stage to the marketplace. This is accomplished by means of a *feasibility study* to determine the probability of your product or service idea successfully getting off the ground by subjecting it to solid analysis and evaluation. You must put your ideas through this type of evaluation to discover whether they contain any fatal flaws that are likely to impact their viability. Sometimes people get all excited about the prospects of a new business without thoroughly researching and evaluating its potential. Sometime later, they may discover that while the idea was good, the market was too small, the profit margins too narrow, the competition too tough, and the financing insufficient or that there are other reasons that cause the business to fail. If the individuals involved had thoroughly researched their idea and conducted a feasibility study before starting, many of these failed businesses would never have been started in the first place.

A feasibility study is the first comprehensive plan you need in contemplating any new venture (Figure 3.1). It proves both to you and others that your new venture concept can become a profitable reality. If the feasibility study indicates that the business idea has potential, then you can proceed to write a business plan. A typical feasibility study considers the following areas:

1. The concept for your venture
2. An assessment of your market
3. The technical feasibility of your idea
4. The supply situation
5. Cost–profit analysis
6. Your plans for future action

Much of the same information can be incorporated into your subsequent business plan (see Stage Five) if it appears that your venture warrants commercial development.

The contents of a typical feasibility study are outlined in A Typical Feasibility Study in Figure 3.2. You can use this guide to assist you in evaluating the feasibility of your new venture idea.

Doing a feasibility study takes time and patience and can be very frustrating; however, a feasibility study is a must for anyone starting a business. When frustration kicks in, take a deep breath, and excuse yourself from it for a while. You will come back with a clear mind and be ready to go again. When you hit a roadblock, reach out to someone you know who is in business. Most cities across Canada have some type of business centre that has an entrepreneur in residence or someone from whom you can seek assistance. The FYI box presents a list of Incubators and Seed Accelerators across Canada, including their contact information. Contact them directly to introduce yourself, and arrange a face-to-face meeting.

YOUR VENTURE CONCEPT

It is critical that you be able to clearly and concisely explain, verbally, the principal concept underlying your venture—what sets it apart from other businesses of similar character. This is what is sometimes called your "elevator pitch"—a conversation that begins when the elevator door closes and ends when the door opens at your floor. That means you have only a few seconds to capture your listener's interest, so you had better be able to explain your

FIGURE 3.1   FEASIBILITY STUDY

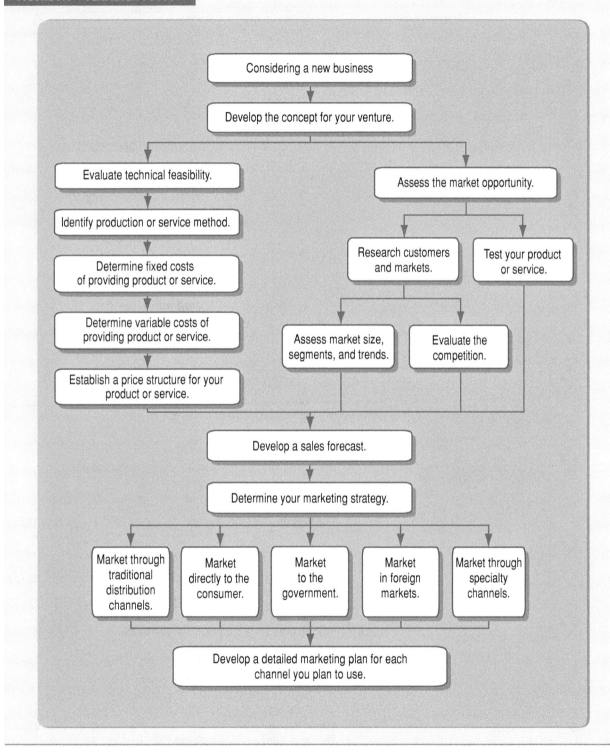

FIGURE 3.2   A TYPICAL FEASIBILITY STUDY

Feasibility Study Contents

Concept for your venture

- Explain clearly and concisely the principal concept underlying your venture and what sets it apart from other businesses.

Market assessment

- Describe the profile of your principal target customers.
- Indicate current market size, trends, and seasonal patterns.
- How do you plan to test your idea?
- Describe any market research or customer surveys you plan to conduct.
- Assess the nature of your competition.
- Estimate your expected sales and market share.

Technical feasibility of your Idea

- Indicate the degree of innovativeness of your venture idea and the risks associated with it.
- Does it need to be subjected to some form of technical evaluation or assessment?

Your marketing plan

- Detail the marketing strategy you plan to use.
- Describe your marketing plan, including your sales strategy, advertising and promotion plans, pricing policy, and channels of distribution.

Managing the supply situation

- How do you plan to assure continuing access to critical supplies of raw materials and component parts at reasonable prices?
- Will you produce or subcontract your production?

Cost and profitability assessment

- Determine the funds required to set up your business.
- Develop short-term financial projections, including:
  - Cash flow forecasts
  - Pro forma profit and loss statements
  - Pro forma balance sheet
  - Break-even analysis

Plan for future action

- What were the strong and weak points of your venture idea?
- Did your assessment indicate the business was likely to be profitable?
- Is it sufficiently attractive to proceed with the development of a complete business plan?

A Partial Listing of Business Incubators and Seed Accelerators in Canada		Updated March 2013		
You may contact CABI to add the name of a business incubation or seed acceleration program that follows industry best practices. The organizations and programs below are listed for informational purposes only.				
Name	**Website Address**	**City**	**Prov**	**Tel #**
Banff Accelerator	www.banffcentre.ca	Banff	AB	403-762-6475
Alastair Ross Technology Centre, Innovate Calgary	www.innovatecalgary.com	Calgary	AB	403 284-6422
Advanced Technology Centre	www.edmonton.com	Edmonton	AB	780-462-2121
Duncan McNeill Centre for Innovation	www.nait.ca/dmci/dmci.htm	Edmonton	AB	780 378-6168
NRC National Institute for Nanotechnology	www.nint.ca	Edmonton	AB	780-641-1600
TEC Centre	www.tecedmonton.com	Edmonton	AB	780-492-2494
TRLabs	www.trlabs.ca/trlabs	Edmonton	AB	780-441-3800
Fort McKay Business Incubator	http://fmbi.ca	Fort McKay	AB	780-828-2494
881 Business Incubation Centre	http://www.881bic.com	Lac La Biche	AB	780-520-1426
Ag Food Processing Development Centre	www1.agric.gov.ab.ca	Leduc	AB	780-980-4860
Agrivalue Processing Business Incubator	www1.agric.gov.ab.ca	Leduc	AB	780-980-4244
Foothills Business Incubator	http://www.okotoks.ca	Okotoks	AB	403-995-4151
Northern Alberta Business Incubator	www.nabi.ca	St Albert	AB	780-460-1000
Accelerate Okanagan	www.accelerateokanagan.com	Kelowna	BC	250-870-9028
SFU Venture Labs Student Business Incubator	www.ventureconnection.sfu.ca	Surrey	BC	778-782-8101
Centre4Growth	www.bctia.org	Vancouver	BC	604-683-6159
Entrepreneurship@ubc	www.entrepreneurship.ubc.ca	Vancouver	BC	205-807-9853
GrowLab	www.growlab.ca	Vancouver	BC	604-652-3230
Institute B	www.instituteb.com	Vancouver	BC	604-689-9659
NRC Institute for Fuel Cell Innovation -IPF	www.ifci.nrc-cnrc.gc.ca	Vancouver	BC	604 221-3013
TIME Ventures Innovation Incubator	www.sfu.ca	Vancouver	BC	604-268-7970
Wavefront	www.wavefrontac.com	Vancouver	BC	778-331-7500
Engineering Entrepreneurship@UVIC	www.ece.uvic.ca	Victoria	BC	n/a
Biomedical Commercialization Canada Inc. (BCC)	www.biomedcanada.com	Winnipeg	MB	204-272-2403
CDEM	www.cdem.com	Winnipeg	MB	204-235-3414
Eureka Project	www.eurekaproject.ca	Winnipeg	MB	204-474-8758
Genesys Venture Inc.	www.genesysventure.com	Winnipeg	MB	204-487-7412

continued on next page ...

A Partial Listing of Business Incubators and Seed Accelerators in Canada		Updated March 2013		
You may contact CABI to add the name of a business incubation or seed acceleration program which follows industry best practices. The organizations and programs below are listed for informational purposes only.				
Name	Website Address	City	Prov	Tel #
NRC Institute for Information Technology	http://iit-iti.nrc-cnrc.gc.ca	Fredericton	NB	506 444-0394
Genesis Centre	www.genesis.mun.ca	St Johns	NF	709 737-2365
NRC Institute for Ocean Technology -IPF	http://iot-ito.nrc-cnrc.gc.ca	St Johns	NF	709 772-4939
Innovacorp Technology Innovation Centre	http://innovacorp.ca	Dartmouth	NS	902-424-6670
Innovacorp Enterprise Centre	http://innovacorp.ca	Halifax	NS	902-424-6670
NRC Insititute for Marine Biology -IPF	www.imb.nrc-cnrc.gc.ca	Halifax	NS	902-426-1040
Perennia Innovation Centre	http://perennia.ca	Truro	NS	902-896-7275
Springboard Innovation Centre	www.springboardinnovation.com	Barrie	ON	707-719-7564
Innovation Guelph	www.innovationguelph.ca	Guelph	ON	519-265-4495
Haliburton Creative Business Incubator	www.haliburtoncdc.ca	Haliburton	ON	705-754-9996
Hamilton Technology Centre	www.hitcentre.ca	Hamilton	ON	905-689-2400
Innovation Factory	www.innovationfactory.ca	Hamilton	ON	905-667-2611
The McMaster Biosciences Incubation Centre	www.mcmaster.ca	Hamilton	ON	905-525-9140
Lawson Health Research Institute	www.lhrionhealth.ca	London	ON	519-646-6005
London Biotechnology Commercialization Centre	www.stillercentre.com	London	ON	519-858-5050
VentureLAB	http://venturelab.ca	Markham	ON	905-248-2727
Research Innovation Commercialization Centre (RICC)	http://riccentre.ca	Mississauga	ON	289-373-3050
Communications Research Innocation Centre	www.crc.ca	Ottawa	ON	613-991-1635
Invest Ottawa	http://investottawa.ca	Ottawa	ON	613-828-6274
NRC Institute for Microstructural Sciences - IPF	http://ipf-ipi.nrc-cnrc.gc.ca	Ottawa	ON	613-998-6755
NRC Steacie Institute for Molecular Sciences - IPF	http://steacie.nrc-cnrc.gc.ca	Ottawa	ON	613 990-0970
NRCan Innovation Acceleration Centre	http://ess.nrcan.gc.ca	Ottawa	ON	613-996-9398
The Code Factory	http://thecodefactory.ca	Ottawa	ON	613-321-3831
IDEAHUB	www.myideahub.ca	Port Hope	ON	905-885-0303
Sault Ste Marie Innovation Centre	www.ssmic.com	Sault Ste Marie	ON	705-942-7927
nGEN	http://ngen-niagara.com	St Catherines	ON	905-685-3460
Innovation Centre for Entrepreneurs	www.iceinnovation.ca	St Thomas	ON	519-633-7597

continued on next page ...

A Partial Listing of Business Incubators and Seed Accelerators in Canada		Updated March 2013		
You may contact CABI to add the name of a business incubation or seed acceleration program which follows industry best practices. The organizations and programs below are listed for informational purposes only.				
Name	Website Address	City	Prov	Tel #
Northwestern Ontario Innovation Centre	www.nwoinnovation.ca	Thunder Bay	ON	807-768-6682
Centre for Social Innovation	http://socialinnovation.ca	Toronto	ON	416-979-3939
Digital Media Zone	http://digitalmediazone.ryerson.ca	Toronto	ON	416-979-5000
Extreme Startups	http://www.extremestartups.com	Toronto	ON	Not listed
George Brown Digital Media and Gaming Incubator	http://www.gaminginc.ca	Toronto	ON	416-415-5000
Incubes	http://incubes.ca	Toronto	ON	416-521-5318
Jolt Accelerator	http://jolt.marsdd.com	Toronto	ON	not listed
MaRS Centre	http://www.marsdd.com	Toronto	ON	416-673-8112
Microskills Business Incubator	http://www.microskills.ca	Toronto	ON	416-247-7181
Mobile Experience Innovation Centre	http://meic.ca/home	Toronto	ON	416-977-6000
Multiplicity Accelerator	http://multiplicityaccelerator.com	Toronto	ON	Not listed
The Entrepreneurship Hatchery	www.engineering.utoronto.ca	Toronto	ON	not listed
Toronto Business Development Centre	www.tbdc.com	Toronto	ON	416-345-9437
Toronto Fashion Incubator	www.fashionincubator.com	Toronto	ON	416-971-7117
Toronto Food Business Incubator	www.tfbi.ca	Toronto	ON	416-401-8888
Accelerator Centre	www.acceleratorcentre.com	Waterloo	ON	519-513-2400
Communitech	www.communitech.ca	Waterloo	ON	519-888-9944
Velocity	http://velocity.uwaterloo.ca	Waterloo	ON	226-338-4046
Spark Centre	http://www.sparkcentre.org	Whitby	ON	905-432-3399
We-Tech Alliance	www.wetech-alliance.com	Windsor	ON	519-997-2865
LaunchPad Incubator - Atlantic Technology Centre	www.peibusinessdevelopment.com	Charlottetown	PEI	902-894-0381
NRC Institute for Nurtisciences and Health - IPF	http://inh-isns.nrc-cnrc.gc.ca	Charlottetown	PEI	902-566-7444
NRC Industrial Materials Institute - IPF	http://imi.cnrc-nrc.gc.ca	Boucherville	QC	450-641-5490
Technoparc Bromont	www.technoparcBromont.com	Bromont	QC	450-534-2020
Drummondville Economic Development Authority	www.sded-drummond.qc.ca	Drummond-ville	QC	819-477-5511
Centre de développement d'entreprises technologiques	www.cdet.ca	Gatineau	QC	819-595-0338
Centre Quebecois d'Innovation en Biotechnologie	www.cqib.org	Laval	QC	450-688-8377
Ag-Bio Centre	www.agbiocentre.com	Lévis	QC	418-835-2110

continued on next page ...

A Partial Listing of Business Incubators and Seed Accelerators in Canada			Updated March 2013	
You may contact CABI to add the name of a business incubation or seed acceleration program which follows industry best practices. The organizations and programs below are listed for informational purposes only.				
Name	Website Address	City	Prov	Tel #
Incubateur industriel de la MRC de Maskinongé	www.choosemaskinonge.com	Louisville	QC	819-228-2744
Centech	http://centech.etsmtl.ca	Montréal	QC	514-396-8827
Centre d'entreprises et d'innovation de Montreal	www.ceim.org	Montréal	QC	514-866-0575
Flow Ventures	http://flowventures.com	Montréal	QC	514-933-7356
Founder Fuel	http://founderfuel.com	Montréal	QC	n/a
Incubateur J.-Armand-Bombardier	www.polymtl.ca	Montréal	QC	514 340-4711
Inno-Centre	www.inno-centre.com	Montréal	QC	514-987-9550
TandemLaunch Technologies Inc.	www.TandemLaunchTech.com	Montréal	QC	438-380-5435
TechBA - Montreal	www.techba.org	Montréal	QC	514-987-9550
Year One Labs	www.yearonelabs.com	Montréal	QC	n/a
L'incubateur bioalimentaire de La Pocatière	www.ita.qc.ca	Pocatière	QC	416-856-1110
Entrepreneuriat Laval Inc	www.el.ulaval.ca	Québec	QC	418-656-5883
National Optics Institute	www.ino.ca/en-ca	Québec	QC	418-657-7006
Agribionet	www.bioalimentaire.ca	Saint-Hyacinthe	QC	450-773-4232
BioTechnopole	www.st-hyacinthetechnopole.qc.ca	Saint-Hyacinthe	QC	450-773-4232
Centre de productique intégrée du Québec	www.productique.qc.ca	Sherbrooke	QC	819-822-8998
Springboard West Innovations	www.springboardwest.ca	Regina	SK	306-789-0535
NRC Plant Biology Institute -IPF	www.pbi.nrc-cnrc.gc.ca	Saskatoon	SK	306-975-5568
Saskatchewan Ideas Inc.	http://saskideas.com	Saskatoon	SK	306-653-2007

The list is updated regularly by CABI. Check their website (www.cabi.ca) for updates for a location close to you.

Source: Canadian Association of business Incubators (www.cabi.ca).

concept quickly, completely, and confidently. If you have difficulty explaining to other people precisely what your business proposes to do, it is a clear sign that your concept still needs development and refinement.

An idea is not yet a concept but only the beginning of one. A fully developed concept includes not only some notion as to the product or service the business plans to provide but also a description of the proposed pricing strategy, promotional program, and distribution plans. It will also consider such aspects of the business as what is unique or proprietary about your product or service idea, any innovative technology involved in its production or sale, and the principal benefits it is expected to deliver to customers.

Developing a good description of your concept can be difficult. Many concepts are too broad and general, not clearly communicating the really distinctive elements of the venture—for example, "a retail sporting goods outlet" or "a tool and equipment rental store." Other concepts may use such words as "better service," "higher quality," "new," "improved," or "precision machined," which are either ambiguous or likely to have different meanings for different people. It is much better to have a detailed, clear, definitive statement—for example, "a retail outlet providing top-of-the-line hunting and fishing equipment and supplies for the serious outdoors person" or "a tool and equipment rental business for the professional, commercial, and residential building contractor." Such descriptions are easier to visualize and allow the uninformed to really understand what it is you propose to do.

Your business concept is not necessarily etched in stone. It may need to change and evolve over time as you come to better understand the needs of the marketplace and the economics of the business. Sharpening and refining of your concept is normal and to be expected.

TECHNICAL FEASIBILITY

You should keep in mind that not all businesses are started on the basis of new or original ideas. Many, in fact, merely attempt to copy successful ventures. To simplify matters, all product and service ideas can be placed along a continuum according to their degree of innovativeness or may be placed into one of the following categories:

1. **New invention** This is something created for the first time through a high degree of innovation, creativity, and experimentation. Examples include fibre optics, electric cars, bionic prostheses for replacement arms and legs, diagnostic and research tools, and wireless technologies.

2. **Highly innovative** This term means that the product is somewhat new and as yet not widely known or used. Examples are mobile apps, near field communication, cloud computing, wide-ranging consumer products incorporating global positioning system (GPS) technology, and non invasive testing techniques for various kinds of cancer.

3. **Moderately innovative** This refers to a product that is a significant modification of an existing product or service or combines different areas of technology, methods, or processes. Examples include microprocessors used to control various automobile systems or single-person cars. The term could also refer to such ideas as the redesign of bicycles to make them easier to ride for people with physical disabilities, thus developing a new market.

4. **Slightly innovative** This term means that a small, yet significant, modification is made to an established product or service, as in larger-scale or more exotic recreational water slides or amusement parks.

5. **"Copycatting"** This is simply imitating someone else's business idea.

The degree of innovation inherent in a business idea has strong implications for the risk, difficulty in evaluation, and profit potential of the venture. *Risk* refers to the probability of the product or service's failing in the marketplace. *Evaluation* is the ability to determine its worth or significance. *Profit potential* is the level of return or compensation that you might expect for assuming the risks associated with investing in this business.

In general, the following relationships hold:

1. New inventions are extremely risky and difficult to evaluate, but if they are accepted in the marketplace they can provide enormous profits.

2. For moderately innovative and slightly innovative ideas, the risks are lower and evaluation is less difficult, but profit potential tends to be more limited.

3. In the "copycat" category, risks are often very high and profit potential tends to be quite low. Such businesses usually show no growth, or very slow growth, and there is little opportunity for profit beyond basic wages.

Every new product must also be subject to some form of evaluation to ensure that the benefits intended for prospective customers can, indeed, be delivered. In developing a working prototype or an operating model of a product with this criterion in mind, some of the most important technical requirements to consider include the following:

- Functional design of the product and the attractiveness of its appearance
- Flexibility of the product in permitting ready modification of its external features to meet customer requirements or competitive pressures
- Durability of the materials from which the product is made
- Expected product reliability under normal operating circumstances
- Safety of the product under normal operating conditions
- Expected rate of obsolescence
- Ease and cost of maintenance
- Ease and cost of processing or manufacture
- Ease of handling and use by the customer

If a product does not fare well on some of these requirements, it should be reworked until it does.

One key approach for testing a new product is to subject it to the toughest conditions that might be experienced during actual use. In addition to this kind of test, there may be standard engineering tests to which the product will have to be subjected to receive Canadian Standards Association (CSA) (www.csa.ca) or Underwriters Laboratory (UL) (www.ul.com) certification. You might also undertake an evaluation of alternative materials from which the product could be made. Further assistance in conducting a technical evaluation may be available from various agencies of your provincial government as well as some colleges and universities and the Canadian Innovation Centre (www.innovationcentre.ca).

MARKET ASSESSMENT

Assessing the potential market for your concept is a critical part of any feasibility study. At the very least, you need to demonstrate that a market does, in fact, exist, or there is not much point in developing a full-scale business plan. In some cases, the potential market may be large and obvious; in others, considerable research and investigation may be required to demonstrate if there is likely to be any significant level of demand. It is essential to determine that a sufficiently large market exists to make the concept financially viable.

WHO IS YOUR CUSTOMER?

To tailor your marketing program to the needs of your market, you must have a very clear idea of who your customers are likely to be. To do this, you will need to gather some information in the marketplace. The more information you have about your target market, the better you will be able to develop a successful marketing plan.

Types of Markets

The first thing to recognize is that the term "market" does not refer to only a single type of possible customer. The two types of markets are Business to Consumer (B2C) and Business to Business (B2B). You will see from the information below that B2C is one area, while B2B consists of different markets:

1. **(B2C) The consumer market** Individual users of products and services, such as you and me
2. **(B2B) The institutional market** Organizations, such as hospitals, personal care homes, schools, universities, and similar types of institutions

3. **(B2B) The industrial market** Other firms and businesses in your community and across the country

4. **(B2B) The government market** Various agencies and departments of the municipal, provincial, and federal governments

5. **(B2B) The international market** Markets similar to the above examples outside the national boundaries of the country

What Is Your Market?

Very few businesses initially operate in all of these markets. Most analyze the possibilities available to them in each situation to determine which offers the best potential. This involves asking broad questions, such as:

1. Who is your customer?
2. How big is the market?
3. Where is it located geographically?
4. How fast is it growing?
5. What organizations and/or individuals are most likely to buy this kind of product or service?
6. Why do they buy it?
7. Where and how do they buy it?
8. How often do they buy it?
9. What are their principal requirements in selecting a product or service of this type?

To determine which of these markets is likely to represent the best opportunity for you, you need to understand just what your product or service has to offer to a group of people or businesses. To do this, you need to understand the primary features of your product or service offering and the benefits it can provide. A *feature*, for example, is some characteristic of a product or service that is part of its basic makeup, while a *benefit* is what motivates people to actually buy it. If an automobile has air bags or anti lock brakes, they are features of the car, but the benefit they provide to the consumer is increased safety. By knowing what your product or service has to offer in terms of features and what will make customers buy it, you can begin to determine characteristics that may be common across the members of your potential market. This kind of assessment will serve to identify some broad areas of opportunity for you.

Failure to understand your customer, however, can be terminal. Ralph Giancola thought he had a surefire winner (see the Entrepreneurs in Action box). No one else in Quebec was offering a service to hockey players that would clean their smelly gear. The market was untapped. He installed his industrial-strength cleaning equipment at a high-traffic rink in Montreal and offered his service to local players at $40 a wash. He figured he would be making money in no time. However, the business did not materialize as he expected. It was never able to generate sufficient revenue to cover the monthly expenses, and things did not improve even when he dropped his price to $20.

So what went wrong? Ralph gradually came to realize that some players did not want to leave their expensive hockey equipment with the business; others did not want to have to come back after four hours to pick it up. Many parents thought it was too expensive just to clean equipment their kids were going to outgrow in any case, and some players just did not think cleaning their equipment was all that important. As Giancola says, "You just can't change the way people think. If someone hasn't washed their equipment in 20 years, why would they wash it now?" In March 2006, the company closed its doors. Some basic research and talking to a few prospective customers to determine whether there was a need for his service before jumping in might have helped Ralph avoid this financial disaster.

Segment Your Market

It is natural to want to target as many people and groups as possible with your business offering. However, in most circumstances, it is not very practical to do so. For example, you are not likely to have the promotional budget to be able to communicate effectively with many different groups at once. Even if you had a large enough

ENTREPRENEURS IN ACTION

HE SHOOTS, HE MISSES

After watching a Discovery Channel program about Esporta Wash Systems, Ralph Giancola came up with a business plan that he was sure would be a winner. Esporta, based in Kelowna, B.C., sold an industrial-strength cleaning system that worked on firefighter equipment, football pads, and hockey gear. It was once the official cleaner for Hockey Canada and was even endorsed by the Great One's dad, Walter Gretzky.

Giancola was already running a commercial cleaning business (with seven employees) in hockey-obsessed Montreal, and he'd been inside enough rank dressing rooms to know that most recreational players aren't all that diligent when it comes to cleaning their equipment. "It seemed to us that nobody was washing hockey gear in Quebec," says 36-year-old Giancola. "The market was untapped."

He and a partner drafted a plan to install an Esporta machine at a high-traffic rink and offer the equipment cleaning services to players. They took their idea to TD Bank, which gave them a $100,000 small business loan; $75,000 of that went to buying the system, plus supplies like mesh bags, cage inserts, stain removers, and a special hockey-glove dryer. In November, 2004, NETS Inc. (Nettoyeur Equipment Travail Sport) rented a storefront at a rink in the Montreal borough of Pierrefond that draws about 5,000 players and fans a week during peak season. At $40 a wash, Giancola figured NETS would be making money in no time. With Giancola and his partner splitting shifts, their monthly costs—including rent, loan payments, and a phone line—ran to about $3,000. To supplement their clientele, NETS would also cut deals with two other rinks and a local sports store that would act as drop-off points for dirty gear.

It took just a few months for Giancola to see where they'd gone wrong. Some players didn't want to leave expensive equipment with NETS; others didn't want to come back after four hours to pick it up. Hockey parents thought it was too expensive—why spend 40 bucks cleaning gear that wouldn't even fit the kid next season? Then there were the guys who simply spritzed their gear with Febreze after each game—if that.

DREAMSTIME/ ROYALTY FREE

"You can't change the way people think," says Giancola. "If someone hasn't washed their equipment in 20 years, why would they wash it now?"

"There was no way this business could make money," he says, "unless we had another three or four years, plus tens of thousands of dollars we could throw into marketing to change the way people think about cleaning their gear." He admits he didn't do enough interviews with hockey parents and players to gauge interest before starting up.

By March, 2006, the company was out of commission. Giancola sold the Esporta system back to the company for $17,000. Because the $100,000 bank loan had been guaranteed through a provincial small-business program, Giancola only had to repay 25 percent. But he and his partner had racked up $55,000 on a line of credit, which they're still trying to pay back.

promotional budget, your promotional message would not likely talk directly to any one group, thus having much less impact. So in addition to doing the broad analysis described above, you also need to question whether within these major market types there are groups of potential customers with different preferences, requirements, and purchasing practices or that are concerned about different benefits. For example, toddlers, teenagers, businesspeople, and older adults all have quite different clothing needs, although all are members of the consumer market. Retailers, designers, and manufacturers must take these different needs into account when developing and marketing their product lines. Each of these groups should be considered a separate *target market*. This process of breaking down large, heterogeneous consumer or industrial markets into more homogeneous groups is known as *market segmentation*. Most markets can be segmented on the basis of a number of variables:

1. **Geographic location,** such as part of a city or town, county, province, region, or country. If you are selling farm equipment, geographic location is obviously a major factor in segmenting your target markets, since your customers will be located in particular rural areas. Climate is a commonly used geographic segmentation variable that affects such industries as sporting equipment, lawn and garden equipment, snowblowers and snowmobiles, and heating and air-conditioning equipment. If this is a factor in your business, you need to identify the geographic area where your market is located and identify the specific boundaries within which you will do business.

2. **Demographic description,** such as age, gender, marital status, family size, race, religion, education level, income, and occupation. Non consumer markets might be classified on the basis of their total purchases or sales, number of employees, or type of organizational activity. Choose those demographic characteristics of your target market that relate to their interest, need, and ability to purchase your product or service. For example, a market for luxury condominiums would include professional married couples approximately 35 to 55 years old with incomes of more than $100,000 and either no children or grown children.

3. **Psychographic or sociological factors,** such as lifestyle, status, timing and means of purchasing, and reasons for buying products or services similar to yours. The desire for status or enhanced appearance, the pursuit of fun and excitement, and the desire to be socially responsible and environmentally conscious are all examples of these kinds of variables. Many products—for example, a variety of extreme sports, such as skydiving and bungee jumping; organically grown foods; and environmentally friendly insect-control methods—would appeal or not appeal to different people largely on the basis of these types of factors.

RESEARCH YOUR MARKET

LO2

WHAT IS MARKET RESEARCH?

Market research can be defined as the gathering, processing, reporting, and interpretation of market information. It is essential that all businesses engage in this process to some degree to prepare a realistic marketing plan. The market research process involves four basic steps:

1. Define the need for information.
2. Search for secondary data.
3. Gather primary data.
4. Interpret the information.

We will discuss each of these steps as they relate to obtaining the information you will require to put together your market assessment.

Define the Need for Information

Before you take the time to gather any data, you need to first decide how you are going to use the information and what you need to demonstrate or show with the information. For example, do you need to:

- Estimate the total expected size of the market for your product or service and the nature and extent of any trends in expected demand?

- Determine the expected level of demand for your product or service?
- Provide a description of who you feel will be your primary customer?
- Outline how your customers are expected to buy your product or service, and with what frequency?
- Understand the nature and extent of the competition you may face in the marketplace?

Search for Secondary Data

The easiest place to start to try to answer these questions is by searching through available sources of secondary data. Secondary data comprise information that others have put together relating to your industry and/or your customers. Using secondary data is usually considerably less expensive than gathering new information, so you should exhaust all readily available sources of secondary information before moving on to gather new data of your own.

Secondary data can come from a tremendous variety of sources. Often they may not exist in the exact form you require, but by combining data from a number of secondary sources, you may be able to compile the information you require, at much lower cost than going out and gathering your own information.

Sources of Secondary Market Information

There are a number of sources you might consult to get a handle on the approximate size of the market you are considering entering. Some of these sources are Statistics Canada publications; various industry reports, trade journals, and investment journals; and financial statements of your leading competitors. You must be careful to make some provision for error in your estimate of market size. Most of the information sources you will consult will not be able to provide complete up-to-date figures, and forecasts of future sales are always subject to error. One key source of demographic data on the Canadian market can be found on Statistics Canada website (www5.statcan.gc.ca) through CANSIM. CANSIM is Statistics Canada's key socioeconomic database. Updated daily, CANSIM provides fast and easy access to a large range of the latest statistics available in Canada. Of particular interest is Table 551-0002, Canadian business patterns. Table 551-0002 provides information on several statistics, such as number of businesses in each province, employment size, and types of businesses. You are able to manipulate the table to include only areas that are of interest to you. A wealth of other information is available from Statistics Canada as well. For example, it breaks the country up into 36 Census Metropolitan Areas (CMAs). For each CMA, there is a series of referenced maps providing an index from which it is possible to get a tract number for almost any neighbourhood in the country. From this tract number, you can get a detailed breakdown of the number of people and their characteristics within a single local neighbourhood or for a combination of tracts comprising a region of a city or for the entire metropolitan area. These data can be a valuable resource, providing a wide variety of information on a large number of geographic markets. The major drawback, however, is that it is largely derived from census data and may be a little stale. This should not be surprising, given the constantly changing tastes of consumers and ongoing technological advancement.

Following are listings of some of the more popular sources of market information. Much of this material is available at your local public, college, or university library.

Industry and Trade Associations

In most situations the best place to start is with the industry or trade associations for the industry in which your business will compete. For example, if you were thinking of starting a retail sporting goods store, you could find a lot of data on the industry and other useful information available from a number of industry associations, depending on your particular emphasis.

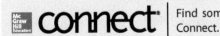 Find some examples of industry and trade associations and organizations online in Connect.

Virtually all organizations have websites where you may be able to access market studies, cost-of-doing business reports, industry fact sheets, and other statistical data that can help you research the potential market for your business.

Trade Publications

Just to give you an idea of the number and diversity of the trade publication, blogs, forums and e-newsletters, take a minute to review the list available online in Connect. It is by no means a listing of all trade-oriented publications but is merely a sampling of the range of material available to you. Depending on the nature of your new venture, any one or more of innumerable publications could represent a source of market-related information or a means for you to communicate with potential customers. Included in the list are digital versions, blogs, forums, and e-newsletters.

 A partial listing of publications, blogs, forums, and e-newsletters that currently are available are posted online in Connect.

General Publications

In addition to trade publications, there are numerous general publications that can be extremely useful in compiling relevant market data. Some of the more important of these are available online in Connect.

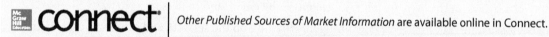 *Other Published Sources of Market Information* are available online in Connect.

In addition to all these publications, other sources that you should look to for information include:

1. Your local Chamber of Commerce
2. Your city or municipal government
3. Local or regional development corporations
4. District school board offices
5. Provincial government offices
6. Business associations
7. Shopping centre developers
8. Advertising agencies
9. Newspapers, and radio and television stations
10. Competitors
11. Sales representatives and trade suppliers
12. Similar businesses in another location
13. Other business associates

Canada Business Services for Entrepreneurs

One prospective source of market information that should not be overlooked is Canada Business Services for Entrepreneurs. In addition to accessing a wealth of information on their main site, you can also link directly to the Canada Business Service Centre (CBSC) (www.CanadaBusiness.ca) in your own province or territory. CBSCs are a collaborative effort of the federal, provincial, and territorial governments, designed to provide businesses and entrepreneurs with a single point of access to a wide range of useful information relating to government services, programs, and regulations that might impact their businesses. Each CBSC offers a broad range of products and services, as well as access to general information tailored to meet the needs of its specific clients. These include:

- Availability of services on the Web, by toll-free telephone, by email, and in person
- Access to databases and other material containing information on the services and programs of the participating departments and various community organizations
- Info-Guides and Fact Sheets that provide descriptions of services and programs that relate to a particular topic (e.g., exporting, e-business, franchising, business startup, financing)
- Other business services, which could include interactive software for business planning, videos, business directories, how-to manuals, DVD/CD-ROM library search capability, and access to external databases

CBSCs are located in one major urban centre in each province and territory and have partnership arrangements with local groups in most other communities as a way to provide regional access to their services.

The Internet

Another place where you will find a great deal of information about any idea you plan to pursue is the Internet. Just about everything is available on the Internet, and you should easily be able to search the Net's millions of web pages and thousands of newsgroups for topics of general interest or to help find precise pieces of specific data.

Almost every industry has a website where you will be able to find the information that you are looking for. In the past, most industries regularly published trade magazines; however, this is no longer the case. Search the industry online, and you will more than likely find either a blog or a subscription to their e-publication that can be downloaded. The most known and used search engines are Google (www.google.ca), Bing (www.bing.com), and Yahoo (ca.yahoo.com). Remember to search for words or phrases that relate to the information you are looking for. Google provides a wealth of information on how to search the Internet. Type "Google Inside Search" in your browser, which will take you to the site where you can explore what is available to help you with your search for information.

In addition to the basic search engines, there are other search tools you should consider as well. These include:

- **Subject guides** can be an excellent source of information about a particular topic, since someone who has a lot of knowledge about a subject has usually prepared the index. There are literally thousands of subject guides that contain links to a number of other websites. Many of them can be found by searching in directories like Yahoo! or Google. Some of the best ones for information relevant to small business include the websites of the Canadian Youth Business Foundation (CYBF) (www.cybf.ca), Canadian Business Online (www.canadianbusiness.com), and the Kauffman Foundation Entrepreneurship website (www.entrepreneurship.org). These guides can be excellent starting points to begin your search for more specific information.

- **Commercial research databases,** such as ProQuest (www.proquest.com) and Northern Light (www.northernlight.com). These databases contain information from newspapers, magazines, journals, and other hard-to-find information sources and make it available for a fee. This can be a flat fee per month, a per document charge, or a combination of a monthly or annual fee and a per-document charge.

There are many fundamental problems you need to be aware of in gathering research information off the Internet. First, the quality of some of the information may be of questionable value or use. There is a lot of useless information posted online, since literally anyone can create a website. Second, the information you come across may be misleading. Since anyone can set up a website and publish information, fraud and misrepresentation have become real problems. Third, the information may be out of date. There is no assurance that information on the Web is the most recent or reflects current research or theory.

GATHER PRIMARY DATA

Doing your own research—called *primary research*—may be the best way to get the most current and useful information regarding your potential market. A number of techniques can be used to obtain primary data. These can be classified into two basic research approaches: observational methods and questioning methods.

Observational Methods

This is the gathering of primary data by observing people and their actions in particular situations. It may entail such approaches as observing the behaviour of shoppers in a store as they go about purchasing a range of different products, counting traffic flows through a mall or past a particular location, or observing patterns in traffic flows around a store or other facility.

Questioning Methods

These include both the use of surveys and experimentation that involves contact with respondents. Survey research involves the systematic collection of data from a sample of respondents to better understand or explain some aspect of their behaviour. This data collection can occur by personal contact, through the mail, by telephone, or on the Internet. In addition, the information may be gathered from people individually as in an individual interview or in a group, such as a focus group.

Survey research is the most widely used method of primary data collection. Its principal advantages are its relatively low cost and flexibility. It can be used to obtain many different kinds of information in a wide variety of situations.

However, there are also some problems associated with survey research. Constructing a good survey is not necessarily an easy thing to do. Sometimes people are unable or unwilling to answer survey questions, so the response rate is not always as high as you might like to see. In addition, a number of technical issues relating to survey research, such as appropriate sample size, reliability, validity, and statistical significance, need to be considered as well. These issues go beyond the scope of this book but definitely need to be considered when gathering any primary data. Before rushing out to conduct a survey, however, it is a good idea to formulate a systematic research design that addresses the following issues:

Problem statement	1. What is the decision you have to make?
	2. What information will assist you in making that decision?
Questionnaire design	1. Precisely what information do you want to collect in the interviews?
	2. What interview questions will get you that response from respondents?
	3. How should those questions be phrased?
	4. How are you going to contact prospective respondents?

TIPS FOR WRITING EFFECTIVE QUESTIONS[1]

Perhaps the most important factor in carrying out a successful survey is the quality and structure of the questions you ask. At the end of the day, it is what will determine whether you get back useful feedback or not. Poorly structured questions can result in incomplete, biased, and/or unfocused responses, and ultimately lead your research to be ineffective. We will now take a look at some of the "Do's" and "Do Not's" of question creation to assure that you get the most out of your survey.

THE "DO'S"

Each question should be focused on a single topic or issue: *Questions need to be concise and specific while only asking respondents about one issue at a time. This will reduce uncertainty on the respondent's part and assure that you receive the information you are looking for.*

BAD QUESTION: How do you feel about Walmart?

GOOD QUESTION: Please rank each aspect of Walmart on a scale of 1–5.

Questions should be brief: *Long drawn out questions can increase confusion and the risk that a question is misinterpreted by the respondent. To guard against this, keep questions short and sweet.*

BAD QUESTION: When some appliance in your home breaks, do you call Sears repair service to come and fix it?

GOOD QUESTION: When you need it, do you call Sears repair service?

Questions should be as simple as possible: *Make questions easy to understand by keeping them simple in their wording and syntax.*

BAD QUESTION: If the Sears repair service schedule was not convenient for you, would you consider or not consider calling a competing repair organization to fix the problem you have?

GOOD QUESTION: If you did not use Sears repair service, would you use another repair service?

Questions should be crystal clear: *What the question is asking should be obvious. Questions should be presented in their rawest form possible, without any unnecessary words and phrases.*

BAD QUESTION: How much do you think you would have to pay to have Sears fix something that needs to be repaired?

GOOD QUESTION: How much do you think Sears charges for a repair service call?

THE "DO NOT'S" OF QUESTION WRITING

Questions should not "lead" respondents to a particular answer: *A leading question is one that suggests an answer. These should be avoided to prevent biased responses.*

BAD QUESTION: Shouldn't concerned parents use car seats?

GOOD QUESTION: Do you think infant car seats are useful?

Questions should not have "loaded" wording or phrasing: *Avoid using "loaded" language in questions, or words that might have an emotive implication. Questions should be neutral in language.*

BAD QUESTION: Should car seats be used for our loved ones?

GOOD QUESTION: Do you think car seats are useful for family members?

Questions should not be "double barrelled": *Questions that could have two possible responses should not be asked. They should be split up into two parts and asked separately.*

BAD QUESTION: Do good parents and responsible citizens use car seats?

GOOD QUESTION: Do you think parents who use car seats are responsible?

Questions should not use "dramatics" or words that overstate the condition: *Questions should be worded as neutrally as possible. Descriptive words that could exaggerate the scenario should be avoided, as these could coax the respondent towards a particular answer.*

BAD QUESTION: Do you believe infant car seats can protect riders from being maimed?

GOOD QUESTION: Do you think child car seats are useful?

Avoid extreme absolutes: *It is best to avoid words that suggest extreme absolutes. These place respondents in a situation where they must fully agree or disagree with the position in the question. Some of these words are:* ***all, any, anybody, best, ever, every, never,*** *etc.*

BAD QUESTION: Do you always observe traffic rules?

GOOD QUESTION: Do you observe traffic rules?

The questions in a survey are like the meat in a hamburger. They really are the most important part. Take your time crafting each one to make sure you are asking exactly what you want to ask while following the rules above, and you will be sure to get some great feedback!

Sampling procedure	1. Who should your respondents be?
	2. How many respondents should you use?
Data analysis	1. How will you tabulate, summarize, and analyze your data?

An example of a relatively simple survey developed by a woman who wanted to open a fitness centre and offer one-on-one training is illustrated in the Other Considerations box, Fitness Centre Questionnaire.

Market-Testing Your Idea

In addition to obtaining information from prospective customers, there are also some primary research methods you can use to gauge market reaction to your particular concept or idea. These techniques are more subjective

OTHER CONSIDERATIONS

DEVELOPING A CUSTOMER SURVEY

GO IN WITH A PLAN

Carrying out a customer survey isn't something that should be done on a limb—you need to establish well defined goals. What is it that you're trying to learn? Do you want to know what they think of your product or service? Will they use it? It is important to know what you're trying to find out before writing the survey, otherwise you risk being unfocused and finding out nothing at all. What will you do with the results? Are you going to like what you hear? Before putting pen to paper on a feedback survey, you have to determine your feedback goals.

GROW THICK SKIN

It's always great to receive positive feedback. It reaffirms that what you are doing is right and you'll receive some well appreciated responses. However, you're also bound to get some more negative views, ones that may completely surprise and upset you. These are just as valuable as other responses. You have to place as much importance on the negative as the positive. You can't hide, you have to be prepared to deal with any amount of criticism. The end goal is to transform these negatives into positives.

BE PREPARED TO ACT

Once you have received the feedback, it's important to act on what you've learned. Gathering feedback only to ignore the results not only wastes time and money, but also alienates and discourages potential customers.

STAY IN TOUCH

Maintain a constant conversation with respondents. If they see you are implementing their suggested changes they may very well become your customers. The human connection between you and your potential clients cannot be replaced or forgotten. Be prepared to accept feedback in any situation. You can never stop listening.

Source: FluidSurveys, adapted from Developing a Customer Survey (www.fluidsurveys.com) Used with permission.

OTHER CONSIDERATIONS

FITNESS CENTRE QUESTIONNAIRE

1. Do you exercise regularly? YES ___ NO ___

   If NO, please go to Part A.

   If YES, please go to Part B.

PART A. PLEASE CHECK YOUR REASONS FOR NOT EXERCISING:

___ Lack of time ___ Lack of motivation ___ Cost

___ No convenient fitness centres ___ Medical reasons

___ Other. Please specify _____

PART B. CHECK THE TYPE OF EXERCISE YOU DO:

___ Aerobic ___ Nautilus ___ Free weights ___ Yoga

___ Pilates ___ Tai Chi ___ Running ___ Swimming

___ Other. Please specify _____

2. Are you: ___ Male ___ Female

3. What is your age group?

   ___ Under 25 ___ 26–35 ___ 36–50 ___ Over 50

4. Where do you normally exercise?

   ___ At home ___ Fitness centre

   ___ Other. Please specify _____

5. How far do you live from (location of proposed centre)?

   ___ Nearby ___ 5–10 km ___ over 10 km

6. Do you think your community needs a new fitness centre? YES ___ NO ___

7. Would you be interested in one-on-one training? YES ___ NO ___

8. Do you have any comments or suggestions about the need for a fitness centre in your community?

Source: Adapted from "How to Prepare a Market Analysis," Edward Lowe Foundation, *Entrepreneurial Edge* (edge.lowe.org).

and cannot be analyzed statistically. However, most of them provide instant feedback. Usually one opinion leads to another so that overall you will receive some interesting and useful information. These techniques include prototype development, obtaining opinions from prospective distributors, comparing your idea directly with competitors' offerings, conducting in-store tests, and demonstrating at trade shows.

Developing a Prototype

A *prototype* is a working model of your product. If you are considering selling a product that, when mass-produced, could cost you $5 per unit to manufacture, prototypes may cost you hundreds of dollars each. However, this could be an inexpensive investment because with just one prototype, you can get photographs, make up a brochure or flyer, show the idea to prospective buyers, and put out publicity releases. You do not need 1,000 or 10,000 units at this stage.

Even though you are interested in producing only a few units at this point, it is still important to get manufacturing prices from a number of (approximately five) different suppliers. You should find out how much it will cost to produce various quantities of the product (1,000 units, 5,000 units, 10,000 units) and what the terms, conditions, and costs of the production process would be. Once you have this information, you will be able to approach buyers and intelligently and confidently discuss all aspects of the product.

Obtaining Opinions from Prospective Distributors

A second way to test your product idea is to ask a professional buyer's personal opinion. For example, most major chain stores are organized into departments, each department having its own buyer. After arranging to see the buyer representing the product area in which you are interested, arm yourself with the cost information you received from potential suppliers. Remember, a buyer is a very astute person. He or she has seen thousands of items before yours and, in most cases, will be able to tell you if products resembling yours have ever been on the market, how well they sold, what their flaws were, and so on. You can get a tremendous amount of free information from a buyer, so it is advisable to solicit his or her independent opinion before you become too involved with your product.

Comparing with Competitors' Products

Most of us have only limited exposure to the vast array of products available in the marketplace and so could end up spending a lot of money producing a "new" product that is already being marketed by someone else. Test your product idea by comparing it with other products already on the market, before you invest your money.

One-Store Test

Another way to test your product is to run a one-store test. This can be done by arranging with a store owner or manager to put a dozen units of your product on display. The purpose of this test is to learn what the public thinks about your product. You can often get the store owner's cooperation because the store does not have to put any money up front to purchase your product. However, problems can be associated with such tests. If you are very friendly with the owner, he or she may affect the results of the test in your product's favour by putting it in a preferred location or by personally promoting it to store customers. You should request that your product be treated like any other because you are looking for unbiased information.

Also, you should keep in mind that one store does not constitute a market; the one store in which you test may not be representative of the marketplace in general. Nevertheless, the one-store test is a good way to gather information on your product.

Trade Shows

Another way to test your product idea is at a trade show. It makes no difference what your field is—there is a trade show involving it. At a trade show, you will have your product on display, and you can get immediate feedback from sophisticated and knowledgeable buyers—people who know what will sell and what will not. There are approximately 15,000 trade shows in Canada and the United States every year, covering every imaginable product area, so there is bound to be one that could serve as a reasonable test site for you. Exhibiting at trade shows can be expensive. Check with your local entrepreneurship centre, Chamber of Commerce, and other organizations that you know about to see if they are attending. In some cases, these organizations offer sharing of exhibit space, which will reduce your costs. If they are a recognized organization, it will draw more traffic to your exhibit as well.

Conducting a Customer Survey

A critical factor in successfully launching a new venture is understanding who your customers are and what needs your product or service might satisfy. It is important to consider that not all potential customers are alike or have similar needs for a given product. For example, some people buy toothpaste primarily to prevent cavities, while others want a toothpaste that promotes whiter teeth, fresher breath, or "sex appeal" or has been designed specifically for smokers or denture wearers. You have to determine which of these segments (i.e., cavity prevention, whiter teeth, etc.) your product or service can best satisfy.

As previously mentioned, most major markets can be broken down into more homogeneous groups or *segments* on the basis of a number of different types of variables. In developing a plan for your proposed business venture, you must consider who your potential customers are and how they might be classified, as in the toothpaste example, into somewhat more homogeneous market segments. You should be clear in your own mind just which of these segments your venture is attempting to serve. A product or service that is sharply focused to satisfy the needs and wants of a specifically defined customer group is typically far more successful than one that tries to compromise and cut across the widely divergent requirements of many customer types. Small businesses are often in a position to search for "holes" in the market representing the requirements of particular customer types that larger companies are unwilling or unable to satisfy. Developing a Market or Customer Profile provides a framework you can complete to develop a market profile of your prospective customer.

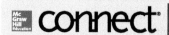 | A *Developing a Market or Customer Profile* template is available online in Connect.

To be successful, you should seek a *competitive advantage* over other firms—look for something especially desirable from the customer's perspective, something that sets you apart and gives you an edge. This may be the quality of your product, the speed of your service, the diversity of your product line, the effectiveness of your promotion, your personality, your location, the distinctiveness of your offering, or perhaps even your price.

Accomplishing all this may require some basic market research. This might be thought of as one of the first steps in testing your product or service idea with potential customers.

Since you will want to provide as good a description of your offering as possible (preferably via a prototype), personal, face-to-face interviews are the best method for gathering the information. Developing an outline for a customer survey you might conduct will help when conducting your survey. An Outline for a Customer Survey is available online in Connect. It would be wise to interview at least 30 to 40 potential customers to ensure that the responses you receive are probably representative of the marketplace in general. This approach can be used effectively for either consumer or industrial products/services.

This customer survey will provide you with important information that will allow you to further develop and fine-tune your marketing strategy. For example, if you discover that the most customers will pay for your product is $10 and you had planned on charging $12, you will have to reconsider your pricing strategy. Similarly, if customers prefer to purchase products like yours by mail, you will have to keep that in mind as you set up a distribution system. The responses to each of the questions posed in the survey should be analyzed and their impact on areas of marketing strategy noted. These will be brought together later in your preliminary marketing plan.

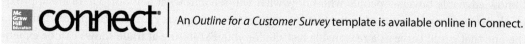 | An *Outline for a Customer Survey* template is available online in Connect.

INTERPRET THE INFORMATION

Once this secondary and primary data have been gathered, they must be analyzed and translated into usable information. The research needs to help you in making, management decisions related to such issues as:

- Who should be your target customer?
- What product or service should you be selling?
- What is the total size of your potential market, and how can it be broken down?
- Who are your competitors, and what are their strengths and weaknesses?
- What is your estimated sales forecast?
- Where should you locate your business?
- How should you promote, price, and distribute your product?

Fluidware, an Ottawa-based survey company has developed templates that make it easy for you to develop your own survey.

Creating an Online Survey The following are screen shots from the 'Product Feasibility' FluidSurveys template and a few tips on making a professional online survey. This specific template was developed to provide a survey structure designed for businesses wanting to predict the value of their product before it is introduced to the market.

Introduction The introduction is one of the most important parts of the survey. The majority of potential respondents will decide whether or not to spend the time filling out the questionnaire based solely on the first page. To create an excellent first page a researcher should ensure that the introduction contains four key parts: (1) A thank-you statement: This should reflect the surveyor's gratitude as well as highlight the importance of the respondent's input. (2) The topic of the study: Respondents are more likely to participate if they know the reason for the study. (3) The expected time to complete the survey: Respondents will be more likely to take part in a study if they have an idea of how much time they can expect to spend on the questionnaire. (4) A confidentiality statement: This allows respondents to answer more honestly, knowing that their answers will not be traced back to them.

Survey Questions It used to be that online surveys had many questions per page to limit the chances of computer crashes and avoid slow loading times, both of which dramatically increase respondent dropout rates. With the rapid advances of computer speed, switching from page to page has become almost instantaneous and has made one question per page the most effective survey technique. This limits scrolling, allows the progress bar to be more accurate, and provides the respondent with a feeling of progress. However, with multiple paged surveys, it is essential to include a progress bar. Without it, respondents can feel discouraged, since they have no way to gauge their progression to the end of the questionnaire.

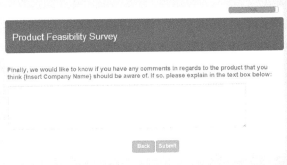

Feedback Page Before the obligatory "Thank You and Exit" last page that is automatically included in most online survey tools, it is a great idea to include a final comments textbox. This is a catch all section that allows respondents to speak their mind on the issue you spent the last 15 minutes questioning them about. Many times, the respondent will have something unique to say that does not fit in any of the questions the surveyor designed, but this does not make the information any less useful! In fact, this exploratory research can reveal new problems or opportunities that were overlooked in the past.

Find and Use Any FluidSurveys Templates If you would like to see the full template or other entrepreneur survey templates, such as 'Service Feasibility,' 'Business to Business Product Feasibility,' or 'Business to Business Service Feasibility' templates, follow the link to FluidSurveys' website or use the QR-code below. http://fluidsurveys.com/templates/market-research-surveys/

Getstock

FluidSurveys also provides an easy to use, low-cost solution for conducting surveys. Often you do not have the database that is needed to get the response you are looking for. Fluidware surveys makes it easy to reach your target market through an integration tool called *Cint,* and once you have received your responses, you only need to click on a tab, and your data appears. (www.fluidsurveys.com)

OTHER CONSIDERATIONS

DO-IT-YOURSELF MARKET RESEARCH

Here are some things you should keep in mind when doing your own market research.

1. In conducting a survey, your information will be only as good as your sample. To be useful, your sample group needs to be relevant to and representative of your target population.

2. Design your survey or questionnaire carefully. Make sure it's focused specifically on the information you need to know.

3. Keep your survey or questionnaire as short as possible, preferably a single page.

4. Always provide some opportunity for the respondent to provide detailed answers.

5. Work out how you intend to record the information and analyze the data as you are developing the questionnaire.

6. Before you administer the survey, establish the criteria that you will use to make decisions based on the information obtained from the survey.

7. Remember, market research is needed at all stages of a business's life to keep you in touch with your customers and their needs and desires.

Some conclusions based on the analysis of this data may be obvious. Others may be more difficult to decipher, or you may feel the data you need to answer the question are just not available. Nonetheless market research can provide you with some of the information you need to be more proactive and help you decide what you should be doing in the future rather than just relying on what has happened in the past.

Failure to employ some of these basic techniques to try to assess consumer response and the expected level of market demand for your business concept can be an expensive lesson.

ESTIMATING TOTAL MARKET SIZE AND TRENDS

A large part of market assessment is determining the volume of *unit sales* or *dollar revenue* that might flow from a market and what proportion of this you might expect to capture. At first glance "unit sales" seems to mean simply how many potential customers there are in the market for your product/service. However, this would overlook the possibility that some customers may buy more than one unit of the product/service. Estimates of total market size must take these *repeat purchases* into account. Total demand is determined by multiplying the number of customers who will buy by the average number of units each might be expected to purchase. To determine the total market size in dollars, simply multiply this total number of units by the average selling price.

A form for estimating market size is available online in Connect. This form helps you estimate the approximate total market size (past, present, and future) and the expected trends for your product/service type.

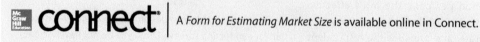

A *Form for Estimating Market Size* is available online in Connect.

THE NATURE OF YOUR COMPETITION

Unless your product or service is a "new to the world" innovation, which is unlikely, it will have to compete with other products or services that perform a similar function.

Who Are Your Competitors?

In the customer survey, your respondents probably identified the names of a number of firms that offer products or services designed to serve the same function or meet the same customer need as yours. Some will be considered *direct competitors* because they offer products or services that are very similar to yours. Others could be thought of as *indirect competitors* because they offer a substitute for your product or service or combine your product with something else they provide. In addition to those mentioned by your respondents, you should seek out other potential competition by watching newspapers and magazines for ads, talking to people who live or work in the area of your business, and searching on the Internet. Identifying the competition in this way will give you some idea of just how crowded your market is and who appear to be the principal players in customers' minds at the present time.

How Do They Compete?

Once you have identified who you feel are your principal direct and indirect competitors, you need to ask specific and detailed questions regarding this competition. The answers will help you gain a better understanding of the level of sales and market share you could achieve, the kind of strategy you might pursue, and the type of marketing program (person, place, pricing, product, and promotion) you might employ. The kind of information you need to gather for the top three or four competitors in your business will relate to such issues as:

- Their estimated sales and market positions
- How they are viewed by consumers and what consumers think of their products or services
- How their products/services compare with what you are planning
- Their apparent strengths and weaknesses
- The key elements of their marketing strategy in terms of:
  - Pricing
  - Promotion
  - Place (Distribution/location)

The Form for Analyzing Your Competition, available online in Connect, will help you organize your assessment of each of these competitors. Fill out a copy of this form for each major competitor you have identified. You should be on the lookout for areas where you can gain a sustainable competitive advantage and carve out a market for yourself. For example, can you provide the best quality, the lowest cost, and a higher level of service or be the most innovative?

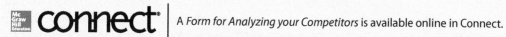

A *Form for Analyzing your Competitors* is available online in Connect.

Where Will You Get The Information?

Naturally, your competitors will probably not cooperate by providing you with this information directly. Sources that can be useful in obtaining this information include:

- Secondary sources, such as patent and trademark filings, general business and trade publications, trade associations, annual reports for public companies, and websites, chat rooms, and blogs on the Internet.
- Primary sources, such as talking to prospective customers and suppliers, attending trade shows, and buying or trying competitors' products to assess their quality and features in order to benchmark them against what you have planned, and touring the facilities of their businesss, if possible.

Using the information you have gathered, you can summarize the results in a Competitive Profile Matrix available online in Connect, to see how your plans compare with the competition on each of the dimensions listed in the matrix. This will enable you to compare your firm's strengths with those of the competition and start thinking of ways to utilize those strengths and exploit your competitors' weak areas.

One approach that might be helpful in enabling you to get a better understanding of your relative competitive situation is to perform a formal SWOT (Strengths, Weaknesses, Opportunities, and Threats) analysis, which is available in Connect. This analysis helps you to see how your strengths stack up against your competitors' weaknesses and suggests ways to take advantage of opportunities out in the marketplace.

In carrying out a SWOT analysis to determine how you rate against a competitor, consider the following points:

Strengths

What are your business's strong points? They should be considered both from your own and your customers' points of view. Be realistic in your assessment, and consider the following questions:

- What distinct advantages does your company offer?
- What do they like about your product or service?
- Why do your customers say they enjoy doing business with you?
- Is there anything you currently offer that can not be copied by a competitor, now or in the future?

Weaknesses

Evaluate your company's weaknesses not only from your perspective, but also from the perspective of your customers and competitors. It is sometimes difficult to think about and discuss your weaknesses, but it is best to be realistic now and face any unpleasant truths as soon as possible. For example:

- What does your company do now that has room for improvement?
- What do your customers dislike about your product or service relative to the competition?
- What does your company do poorly?
- What do your competitors do better than you?
- Do competitors have a particular market or segment locked up?

Opportunities

Next, consider the areas in your market that offer room to grow. Opportunities can come from changes in technology and markets on both broad and narrow scales; changes in government policy related to your industry; changes in social patterns, demographics or consumer lifestyle. Are any special events scheduled to take place, such as the Olympics, or local events, such as the closing of a competitor's store near you that may create a unique opportunity at the moment? Think about the following questions:

- What and where are the interesting opportunities in your marketplace?
- What are the important trends occurring in your local area as well as across the country which could positively impact your business?
- What do you anticipate happening in the future that may represent an opportunity?

Threats

Although we do not like to think about them, we all face threats in our businesses. Many times they are out of our control, such as the recent downturn in the economy, a shift in market demographics, or perhaps a new Target or other major competitor opening in your local area. It is critical to think about and be prepared for such events.

- What are the current obstacles that your business faces?
- What is your competition doing that could negatively impact your business's growth?

- Are the required specifications or government regulations relating to your products or services changing?
- Is changing technology threatening your position in the market?
- Do you have financial problems that could keep you from being able to effectively compete?

The primary purpose of a SWOT analysis is to give you a vehicle to compare your internal factors in terms of strengths and weaknesses with specific external factors to help identify areas of potential opportunity for you. The matching process can be facilitated by the construction of a SWOT matrix, constructed by creating a table showing the strengths, weaknesses, opportunities and threats that you have just identified and evaluating the interrelationships among them. An example of a SWOT matrix is available online in Connect.

You can use the matrix to methodically compare each relevant pair of factors to generate logical matches. The four SWOT cells enable you to make comparisons of opportunities with your strengths (O/S), threats with your strengths (T/S), opportunities with your weaknesses (O/W) and threats with your weaknesses (T/W). Analyzing each of the four SWOT cells of the matrix should yield a variety of matches that will help you generate some possible strategic alternatives. For example, if an opportunity exists in the marketplace for a firm that can provide faster and more reliable service but your business is only comparable with the competition on this dimension (i.e., customer service is not one of your strengths), then you will quickly see when you do the O/S match that you must focus on improving this aspect of your business if you hope to capitalize on this market opportunity.

There are four basic categories of matches for which strategic alternatives can be considered:

- S/O matches show the company's strengths and opportunities. Essentially, the company should attempt to use its strengths to exploit these opportunities.

- S/T matches show the company's strengths in light of major threats from competitors. The company should use its strengths to avoid or defuse such threats.

- W/O matches illustrate the company's weaknesses coupled with major opportunities. The company might try to overcome its weaknesses to take advantage of such opportunities.

- W/T matches show the company's weaknesses against existing market threats. Essentially, the company must attempt to minimize its weaknesses and avoid threats. These strategy options are generally defensive.[2]

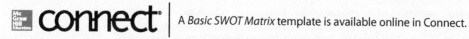

A *Basic SWOT Matrix* template is available online in Connect.

What do you like about being an Entrepreneur?

The uniqueness of being an entrepreneur is that you create something that was not there before—a company. There is no greater sense of accomplishment than being able to create at that level. You create wealth and employment and break new ground.

Adam Chowaniec,
Chair
Solantro Semiconductor
www.solantro.com

YOUR COMPETITIVE STRATEGY

Once you have completed your SWOT analysis, you can then think about developing a strategic plan for dealing with your competitors and other market forces. Although there are many areas where you might obtain an edge over the competition, the primary means are through:

1. **Cost advantage** Having a significantly lower cost so that you can charge lower prices while still achieving reasonable profit margins. These lower costs may arise from maintaining a lower variable cost per unit

sold, having a lower level of marketing expenses, or having a lower level of overhead or operating expenses. Businesses focused on a niche market often have lower overhead and lower marketing costs.

2. **Differentiation advantage** Having a meaningful difference between your products and those of the competition, which creates a higher level of perceived customer benefits. This could be in terms of the physical characteristics of the product itself, the range or level of services provided, or the image and reputation of your business. A business with a meaningful differential advantage can often charge higher prices and generate higher unit profits.

3. **Marketing advantage** Undertaking a marketing effort that dominates the competition in terms of distribution, sales coverage, or weight and type of promotion. You might choose to focus on a specific region, or a particular channel of distribution that you can dominate. Such businesses can often attract new customers more easily and maintain their presence with existing ones.

4. **Focus on a market niche** By identifying a position in the market that has been overlooked, neglected, or abandoned by one or more of your competitors. This can be particularly effective for smaller firms trying to escape direct competition with larger companies with more resources while trying to build their own competitive advantage. This niche could be a particular customer segment with very particular needs or requirements, limiting sales to a single geographic location or concentrating your efforts on a single, specialized product or service offering.

Considering these issues and your position relative to other firms can enable you to begin to envision an ideal strategy for building a competitive edge for your business.

DEVELOPING A SALES FORECAST

Sales forecasting is the process of organizing and analyzing all the information you have gathered in a way that makes it possible to estimate what your expected sales are likely to be. Your sales forecast will probably be one of the most difficult and yet the single most important business prediction you ever make. If you get it wrong, the error can lead to plenty of unsold inventory and problems generating sufficient cash to keep the business going or to a number of disappointed customers.

But how do you get it right? One way is to consider the following formula:

$$\text{Sales Forecast} = \text{Total Estimated Market Size} \times \text{Estimated Growth Rate} \times \text{Market Share Target}$$

ESTIMATING MARKET SIZE

Fairly accurate market data are available from trade associations and other secondary sources for certain industries. However, companies in many other industries have to operate without any concrete information concerning the total size of the market for their products or services. Nonetheless, information on market size is vital to develop a meaningful marketing plan.

It is especially important when introducing new products that you have a good estimate of the size of the total market, but this is exactly the situation for which obtaining an accurate forecast is most difficult. For example, suppose that you were considering setting up a distribution business to sell garbage bags and shopping bags made from recycled plastic (polyethylene) in Halifax. To estimate the total potential market that might be available, you would need to know the total demand for such products in the four Atlantic Provinces, if that was how you had geographically defined you market. In addition, you would also be interested in determining the size of the various segments of the market. Three obvious segments that should be considered might be: (1) garbage bags for household use sold by retail stores; (2) heavy-duty garbage bags sold in bulk for commercial and industrial use; and (3) printed plastic shopping bags for independent retail stores and chains. You may not wish to compete in the entire market but decide to focus on the needs of one particular segment, such as printed shopping bags for chain stores.

It is usually much easier to determine market data for established products. Data on total market sales may already exist, or they can be developed using either a *top-down* or a *bottom-up* approach.

Top-Down Approach

The top-down approach utilizes published data on such statistics as total market size and weights them by an index that may be some such factor as the percentage of the population within your designated geographic area. For example, our distributor of plastic bags needs an estimate of the total size of the potential market for these bags in Atlantic Canada. Since the four Atlantic Provinces account for approximately 10 percent of the total Canadian population, a rough estimate of the size of the plastic bag market in that region would be 10 percent of the total Canadian market. Data concerning the entire Canadian market may be available from such sources as Statistics Canada or from trade associations or other industry sources. One word of caution, however, in using this approach: This estimate of the total market for plastic bags in the Atlantic provinces is accurate only if usage patterns of plastic bags are the same in that region of Canada as they are in the country as a whole.

Bottom-Up Approach

The bottom-up approach involves aggregating information from the customer level to the total market level. Information on past or current purchase or usage of a product or service may be collected from a sample of customers by a mail or telephone survey or through personal interviews. For frequently purchased consumer products, such as plastic garbage bags, the survey may simply ask how much of the product is used either by individuals or the entire household during an average week or month. These individual or household statistics are then aggregated based on population or household statistics that are available from Statistics Canada and other sources to develop an estimate of the total size of the potential market. An overview of both these approaches is illustrated in the following Other Considerations box.[3]

For your business plan, these sales estimates for your first year of operation should be monthly, while the estimates for subsequent years can be quarterly. A serious miscalculation many aspiring entrepreneurs make is to assume that because their new product or service appeals to them, other consumers will buy it as well. It is important to be aware of this tendency. This type of thinking is often reflected in what is known as the "2 percent syndrome." This syndrome follows a certain line of reasoning, such as, "The total market for a product is $100 million. If my firm can pick up just 2 percent of this market, it will have sales of $2 million per year."

There are, however, two things wrong with this line of reasoning. The first is that it may be extremely difficult for you to capture 2 percent of this market unless your business has a unique competitive advantage. The second is that a 2 percent market share may still be unprofitable, since competing firms with greater market share may benefit from *economies of scale*—lower unit cost due to mass production—and other cost advantages unavailable to your firm.

A number of external factors can affect your sales, including:

- Seasonal changes
- Holidays
- Special events
- Political activities and events
- General economic conditions
- Weather
- Fashion trends and cycles
- Population shifts
- Changes in the retail mix

In addition, a number of internal factors must be considered, such as:

- Level of your promotional effort
- Your ability to manage inventory levels effectively
- The distribution channels you decide to use
- Your price level relative to the competition
- Any labour and personnel problems you might encounter

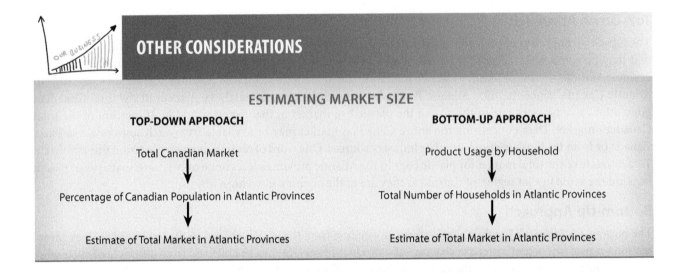

OTHER CONSIDERATIONS

ESTIMATING MARKET SIZE

TOP-DOWN APPROACH

Total Canadian Market

↓

Percentage of Canadian Population in Atlantic Provinces

↓

Estimate of Total Market in Atlantic Provinces

BOTTOM-UP APPROACH

Product Usage by Household

↓

Total Number of Households in Atlantic Provinces

↓

Estimate of Total Market in Atlantic Provinces

It is impossible to predict all these situations, but you should try to take them into account in developing your sales forecast.

One approach to gaining some insight into your business's potential market is to develop a sales forecast (available online in Connect). Refer to the *market profile* you developed earlier. How do you feel your prospective customers would decide whether or not to buy your offering? This estimate should also consider the likely frequency and volume of a typical customer's purchases over a certain period of time.

In implementing this process, you should think about how prospective customers will likely hear about the opportunity to buy your product/service, whether from a salesperson, from an advertisement, Internet searches, or through a chain of intermediaries. Estimates can then be made of how many of the people you have described are good prospects and, consequently, what your total sales volume might be. This can be an "armchair" procedure involving the use of some library references or personal knowledge of similar businesses. The estimate of market potential developed using this method can be quite crude; however, it is important that you think your way through such a process and not sidestep it in favour of simply hoping a market exists for you.

A *Developing a Sales Forecast* template is available online in Connect.

Selecting a Location

It is often said that the three most important factors in the success of any retail business are "location, location, and location." Every new business faces the problem of where to locate its facilities. This problem is much more critical to retailers than to other types of businesses. Much of their business typically comes from people who are walking or driving by. As a consequence, a customer's decision to shop or not shop at a particular store may depend on such factors as what side of the street you are on, ease of access and egress, availability of parking, or similar concerns. This means that in determining the best location for your business, you will have to concern yourself with a variety of issues.

1. **Zoning regulations** Zoning bylaws govern the kind of activities that can be carried on in any given area. Classifications vary from locality to locality, but many municipalities categorize activities as residential, commercial office, commercial retail, institutional, and industrial. When considering a location, make certain the business activities you plan to pursue are permitted under the zoning restrictions for that area.

2. **Municipal licences and taxes** Businesses must typically buy a municipal business licence. In the city of Winnipeg, for example, more than 115 types of businesses require a licence, which costs from $15 to over $2,000. In general, businesses in some amusement fields or that affect public health and safety require a licence.

   Businesses, such as homeowners, must usually pay a business tax—a tax assessed as a percentage of the rental value of the premises or on the basis of a standard assessment per square foot of space utilized. These requirements vary from municipality to municipality.

3. **Municipal services** You should make sure that municipal services, such as police and fire protection, adequate sewer and water supplies, public transit facilities, and an adequate road network, are available to meet your business's requirements.

4. **Other considerations** Other things to consider are such site-specific issues as:

   - Cost
   - The volume and timing of traffic past the location
   - The nature of the location, whether on a downtown street, in a strip mall, or in an enclosed mall
   - The nature of the area surrounding your location and its compatibility with your business
   - The kind and relative location of surrounding businesses
   - The volume of customer traffic generated by these other firms and the proportion that might "spin off" to your store
   - The growth potential of the area or community
   - The number and location of curb cuts and turnoffs

You can use the rating form for selecting a retail location, available online in Connect, to help choose the most favourable location for a retail business.

Most of these same location factors also apply to service businesses, although perhaps not to the same degree. If your service business requires you to visit prospective customers at home or place of business, a central location providing easy access to all parts of your market area may be preferred.

Location has a quite different meaning for manufacturing firms. Manufacturers are principally concerned about locating their plant where their operations will be most efficient. This means considering such issues as:

- General proximity to primary market areas
- Access to required raw materials and supplies
- Availability of a suitable labour force
- Accessibility and relative cost of transportation and storage facilities
- Availability and relative cost of power, water, and fuel supplies
- Financial incentives and other inducements available from municipal, provincial, or federal government agencies

The importance of each of these factors in the location decision will depend on the nature of your manufacturing business and your own preferences and requirements.

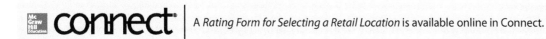 A *Rating Form for Selecting a Retail Location* is available online in Connect.

Buying or Leasing Facilities

Many new businesses already own or decide to purchase the land and building in which their ventures or the machinery and equipment they will require to operate are located. With today's extremely high costs, however, this may not be a wise decision. The majority of new firms are not principally in the business of speculating in real estate and should not acquire their own property. During their early stages, most businesses tend to be short of cash, and many have failed because they had their capital tied up in land and buildings when it could have been more effectively used to provide needed working capital for the business itself. In addition, a business that owns its own building may be more difficult to sell at a later date, since a smaller number of potential buyers will have enough capital to buy both the business and the property. While building your own facility enables you to more carefully tailor the property to the specific requirements of your business, it tends to be a much more costly alternative.

If you are planning to rent or lease your facilities, it is a good idea to have your lawyer review the terms and conditions of the agreement. You will want to ensure satisfactory arrangements in such matters as:

1. **The duration of the agreement** A business lease can last a year, three years, five years, or any other mutually agreed-on term. A short-term lease may be preferable if your situation is likely to change soon. However, the lease conditions can be a valuable asset of your business, and a short-term lease may reduce the sale value of your business (if you ever sell it) because of loss of the goodwill associated with maintaining your present location. The ideal lease arrangement should enable you to stay in the location for some time, in case your venture is successful, but give you the flexibility to move after a reasonable period of time if it does not work out.

   You also need to consider the terms and conditions for renewing the lease. Are there provisions for automatic renewal? Is there a maximum to any rent increase applied on renewal of your lease?

2. **The rent** Rental costs for commercial property are commonly stated in terms of the annual cost per square foot of floor space. For example, a 1,500-square-foot location rented for $8 per square foot will cost $12,000 per year, or $1,000 per month. This may be a *net lease*, in which you pay a single monthly fee that is all-inclusive (rent, utilities, maintenance costs, property taxes, etc.), or a "net-net-net," or *triple net lease*, in which you pay a base rent plus a share of all the other expenses incurred by the landlord in operating the building. In the latter situation, your operating costs may fluctuate each year because of changing tax, maintenance, insurance, and other costs.

   In retail shopping malls, *participating* (or *percentage*) *leases* are common. Instead of a fixed monthly rent, the landlord receives some percentage of your sales or net profit. There are several types of participating leases. You may pay either a percentage of the total monthly sales of your business, a base rent plus some percentage of your gross sales, or a percentage of your net profit before interest and taxes. Shopping centre leases can be quite complex documents, so be certain to check with your accountant and lawyer before committing yourself.

3. **The ownership of any additions or improvements you might make to the facilities** Under the terms of most leases, all improvements and fixtures that you add to the premises are considered as belonging to the landlord. They immediately become part of the building and cannot be removed without his or her consent. If you need to install expensive fixtures to launch your business, you should try right up front to negotiate permission to remove specific items.

4. **Any restrictions on the use of the property** Most leases specify the kind of business activity you can carry on in the location. Before signing, you should think not only about the activities you now plan to engage in but also about those you might wish to engage in the future. Many leases also contain a non-competition clause to protect you from competitive firms coming into the premises and taking away your business.

5. **Whether you are permitted to sublet some or all of the property to a third party** This is commonly permitted, but only with the prior written consent of the landlord, and it is subject to any use restrictions and non competition clauses in your agreement.

   A closely related issue is your ability to assign any remaining time left on your lease to another party. If you decide to sell your business, this can be an attractive part of the package. In some cases, assignment of the lease is not permitted; in others, an assignment may be acceptable with the prior written consent of the landlord, which may then not be unreasonably withheld.

6. **The nature of any default and penalty clauses** The lease will spell out the situations that constitute a breach of its conditions and the recourse available to the landlord. Obvious grounds for default include failure on your part to pay the rent, the bankruptcy of your business, violation of the use conditions or non competition clauses, and so on. Should you default on the lease, the landlord may be able to claim accelerated rent for the time remaining on the lease. For example, if you were to move out two years before your lease expires, the landlord may claim the full two years' rent. In this situation, however, the landlord legally must try to limit his or her damages by renting out your space to another party as soon as possible.

Your lease may or may not contain a *penalty clause* limiting your exposure should you breach the lease. A penalty of three months' rent is common in many situations, although the landlord will want you or the directors of an incorporated business to sign personal guarantees for the amount of the penalty.

Home-Based Businesses

For many kinds of businesses, working out of the home has become a very popular and attractive option. There are a number of advantages to running your business out of your home, the most obvious of which is the cost.

Not only can you save on the rent for your business premises by operating in this manner, but the Canada Revenue Agency will also let you write off part of your home expenses for income tax purposes. Possible write-offs are utility costs, mortgage interest, municipal taxes, and other expenses related to maintaining that part of your premises used for your business. You can also save on the cost and time of travelling to and from work every day, and you have greater flexibility in planning and organizing your work and personal life. In addition, a home-based business may have a number of other benefits, such as being able to work in more comfortable clothes and having more time to look after and be with your family. There are, however, a number of disadvantages.

1. It takes a lot of self-discipline to sustain a regular work schedule and resist distractions from family, friends, television, and other sources. You may find that there are too many interruptions to work effectively, that you tend to mix work with family life too much, or that you become distracted by household chores. Conversely, you may find it very difficult to get away from your work when you would like to, since it is so close at hand, and you may have trouble stopping after a full day.

2. Suppliers and prospective customers may not take you as seriously. You may have to rent a post office box or make other arrangements to give the appearance of operating from a more conventional commercial location.

3. The space available in your home may not be appropriate for your business, and you may not have access to facilities and equipment, such as boardrooms and copy machines, that you need to conduct your business effectively.

4. If your house is in a typical residential area, operating a business from your home will probably contravene local zoning bylaws.

5. You can feel lonely and very alone without anyone to talk to or exchange ideas with.

It is true that most municipal governments have become reasonably flexible in this regard and do not go looking for violations; they will, however, respond to complaints from immediate neighbours and others in the vicinity. It is a good idea to check with these people before starting any kind of visible business activity from your home. Activities that may lead to complaints are posting a large sign on the front lawn; constant noise; a steady stream of customers, suppliers, or others going in and out of your home; or the clutter of parked vehicles in your driveway or on the street.

FLESHING OUT YOUR MARKETING PROGRAM   LO3

The purpose of this section is to bring together what you have learned about the total market potential for your product or service, customer attitudes toward your particular offering, and the nature of the competitive environment you will be facing. The goal is to put down on paper a preliminary marketing strategy or plan for your new venture concept. This involves making some decisions regarding what you feel is an appropriate *marketing mix* for your business. Put simply, the principal ingredients of your marketing program that must be blended together to form your overall strategy can be grouped under the following headings:

1. Person
2. Place
3. Product
4. Pricing
5. Promotion

Person (Target Market)

The person is your target market. You need to know your customer profile, the characteristics of your customer, and how big your target market is.

Place (Method of Distribution)

Your channel of distribution is the path your product or service takes to market. Physical products typically follow one or more complex paths in getting from the point at which they are produced to the hands of their final consumer. These paths involve the use of several different kinds of wholesalers and retailers who perform a variety of functions that are essential to making this flow of products reasonably efficient. These functions include buying, selling, transporting, storing, financing, and risk taking.

Distribution channels consist of channel members that are independent firms that facilitate this flow of merchandise. There are many different kinds, and they have quite different names, but the functions they perform may not be that dramatically different. For example, wholesalers are generally classified according to whether they actually take title or ownership of the products they handle (*merchant wholesalers*) or not (*agents*). Merchant wholesalers are further classified as *full-service, limited-function, drop shippers, truck wholesalers,* and *rack jobbers.* Agents are commonly referred to as *brokers, manufacturer's agents, selling agents, food* or *drug brokers*, and so on. For small manufacturers, all of these types of wholesalers, alone or in combination, represent possible paths for getting their product to market.

Retailers, too, cover a very broad spectrum, starting with the large department stores that carry a broad product selection and provide an extensive range of customer services; through specialty stores, such as electronics, men's clothing, and furniture stores; to discount department stores, grocery stores, drug stores, catalogue retailers, and convenience stores. All represent possible members that could be included in your channel of distribution.

In addition to opportunities for marketing your products or services in conjunction with these traditional and conventional distribution channel members, you should not overlook more unconventional possibilities for reaching your potential customers. For example, over the past few years, we have seen a tremendous growth of various forms of non store retailing, including:

1. Mail-order catalogues
2. Direct-response advertising on television and in newspapers and magazines
3. Direct-selling door to door
4. Party plan or home demonstration party selling
5. Direct-mail solicitations
6. Vending machines
7. Trade shows
8. Fairs and exhibitions
9. The Internet
10. Face-to-face meetings with prospective clients

Product or Service Offering

The product area involves the planning and development of the product or service you are planning to offer in the marketplace. This involves defining the breadth and depth of your offering, the length of your line, how it will be packaged and branded, the variety of colours and other product features, and the range of complementary services (delivery, repair, warranties, etc.) that will be made available to the customer.

Pricing Program

Your pricing strategy involves establishing the right base price for your offering so that it is appealing to customers and profitable to you. This base price may be adjusted to meet the needs of particular situations, such as to encourage early acceptance of your offering during its introductory stages; to meet aggressive or—exceptional competition; to provide for trade, functional, seasonal, and other discounts; or to introduce your product/service into new market situations.

A number of approaches can be used to determine a base price for your planned market offering. These include *cost-based pricing, value-based pricing*, and *competition-based pricing*.

Cost-Based Pricing

One of the most commonly used strategies by retailers and small manufacturers is *cost-based pricing* or *markup pricing*. The cost of your product or service is determined and used as the base, and then a markup is added to determine what your selling price should be. *Markups* are generally expressed as a percentage of the selling price—for example, a product costing $2.50 and selling for $5 has a 50 percent markup.

To illustrate, let us assume that you have come up with a new formula for an automobile engine treatment that will be sold through auto parts jobbers to service stations for use in consumers' cars. Table 3.1 illustrates what the price markup chain for this product might look like.

As you can see, in this illustration a product with a factory cost of $1.50 has a retail selling price of $5 to the final consumer. The markup percentages shown here are merely examples of a typical situation, but in most wholesale and retail businesses, standard markups tend to prevail in different industry sectors. Food products and other staple items usually have a low unit cost and high inventory turnover, so the markups tend to be fairly low, 15 to 25 percent;

TABLE 3.1　PRICE MARKUP CHAIN

	Per Bottle	Markup
Direct factory costs	$1.00	
Indirect factory costs	0.50	
Total factory cost	$1.50	
Manufacturer's markup	0.50	25%
Manufacturer's selling price	$2.00	
Jobber's markup	0.50	20%
Jobber's selling price	$2.50	
Service station markup	2.50	50%
Service station selling price	$5.00	

such products as jewellery and highly advertised specialty products typically have higher markups, perhaps as much as 50 or 60 percent or even more.

This type of markup pricing is simple and easy to apply and can be very successful if all competitors have similar costs of doing business and use similar percentages. On the other hand, this approach does not take into account variations in the demand for the product that may occur with a different final price. For example, how much more or less of the engine treatment would be sold at a price of $4 or $6 rather than the $5 price determined by the standard markup chain?

Most manufacturers do not employ markup pricing in the same way that many wholesalers and retailers do. However, if you plan to manufacture a product that will be sold through wholesalers and various types of retail outlets, it is important for you to know the markups these distributors will likely apply to your product. For instance, in the above example, if the manufacturer of the engine treatment thinks $5 is the right retail price, he or she can work backward and determine that it must be able to sell profitably to the jobbers for $2 to succeed. If that is not possible, perhaps the overall marketing strategy for the product should be reconsidered.

Value-Based Pricing

Instead of using costs, more and more companies are basing their prices on their estimate of the market's perceived value of their market offering. This is particularly true in determining the most appropriate price to charge in a service business. This perceived value is the overall value the customer places on a product or service. The process begins by analyzing customer needs and value perceptions. This may involve much more than just the basic product or service itself and include other features, such as availability, image, delivery, after-sales service, warranty considerations, and other issues. With this approach, the price is set by determining the price that people are willing to pay, while making sure that you can still cover all your costs.

The way businesses are able to price more effectively on "value" is by differentiating themselves in some way from the competition. This differentiation can be based on any number of factors, such as promotion and advertising, availability, or the addition of value-added services. People are prepared to pay more for products produced by brand-name designers, such as Bill Blass, Calvin Klein, or Tommy Hilfiger, for example, than they are for similar items produced by others. Similarly, a computer store that provides emergency service to customers on a 24/7 basis might be able to charge more for its computers or extended warranty package than an outlet that is open only from 9:00 a.m. to 6:00 p.m. five days a week.

Competition-Based pricing

In some situations, consumers base their judgments of a product's or service's value on the prices that competitors charge for similar offerings. You might decide to base your price largely on competitors' prices with less attention to your own costs or expected demand. For example, you might decide to charge the same as, more than, or less than your principal competitors. Some of this may depend on the image you are trying to achieve in the marketplace. If you want to create an image of a bargain or discount operation, such as Dollar Store Plus or Ultracuts, then your prices should be consistent with that image. Similarly, if you are trying to establish an image of a luxury operation, such as Holt Renfrew or an exclusive hair salon, people may be prepared to pay more, and your prices should be consistent with that position. Your target market might not be attracted to a cheaper product or service.

In addition to establishing a base price for your product or service line, you may permit some customers to pay less than this amount in certain circumstances or provide them with a discount. The principal types of discounts are quantity discounts, cash discounts, and seasonal discounts. *Quantity discounts* are commonly provided to customers who buy more than some minimum quantity or dollar value of products or services from you. This discount may be based either on the quantity or value of each individual order (noncumulative) or on the total value of their purchases over a certain period of time, such as a month (cumulative).

Cash discounts are based on the typical terms of trade within an industry and permit customers to deduct a certain percentage amount from the net cost of their purchases if payment is made in cash at the time of purchase or full payment is made within a specified number of days. Different types of businesses have their own customary cash discounts. For example, a typical discount is expressed as "2/10 net 30." In this situation, a customer who is invoiced on October 1 for an outstanding bill of $2,000 need pay only $1,960 if payment is made before October 10. This is a 2 percent cash discount for making payment within the 10 days. Otherwise the full face value of the invoice ($2,000) is due by October 31, or 30 days after the invoice date.

Seasonal discounts of 10 percent, 15 percent, 20 percent, or more on your normal base price may be offered to your customers if their purchases are made during your slow or off-season. This gives you a method of moving inventories that you may otherwise have to carry over to the following year or of providing your dealers, agents, and other distributors with some incentive to stock up on your products well in advance of the prime selling season.

Promotion

The budget that you allocate for the promotion of your new venture must be distributed across the following activities:

1. Advertising
2. Personal selling
3. Sales promotion
4. Public relations

Each of these activities differs along a number of important dimensions, such as their cost to reach a member of the target audience and the degree of interaction that can take place with that audience. Table 3.2 summarizes how these activities compare on a number of different criteria.

TABLE 3.2 A COMPARISON OF VARIOUS PROMOTIONAL ACTIVITIES				
	Advertising	**Sales Promotion**	**Public Relations**	**Personal Selling**
Cost per Audience Member	Low	Low	Very Low	Very High
Focus on Target Markets	Poor to Good	Good	Moderate	Very Good
Ability to Deliver a Complicated Message	Poor to Good	Poor	Poor to Good	Very Good
Interchange with Audience	None	None	Low to Moderate	Very Good
Credibility	Low	Low	High	Moderate to High

Source: Adapted from Gerald E. Hills, "Market Opportunities and Marketing," in William D. Bygrave, *The Portable MBA in Entrepreneurship*, 2nd ed. (Hoboken, NJ: John Wiley & Sons, Inc., 1999). This material is used by permission of John Wiley & Sons Inc.

The distribution of your expenditures should be made to obtain the maximum results for your particular circumstances. It is impossible to generalize about the optimum distribution of your dollars to each of these activities. Different businesses use quite different combinations. Some companies put most of their money into hiring a salesforce and their sales promotion program; others put most of their budget into a media advertising campaign. The proper combination for you will depend on a careful study of the relative costs and effectiveness of each of these types of promotion and the unique requirements of your business.

We often think of promotion as being directed strictly toward our final prospective customer, and, in fact, the largest share of most promotional activity is channelled in that direction. However, promotion can also be used to influence your dealers, your distributors, and other members of your distribution channel. This may persuade them to adopt your offering more rapidly and broaden the breadth of your distribution coverage.

Advertising

Advertising is one of the principal means you have of informing potential customers about the availability and special features of your product or service. Properly conceived messages presented in the appropriate media can greatly stimulate demand for your business and its offerings. A wide range of advertising media is available to carry your messages, of which the most important are those listed in Table 3.3. The choice of media for your advertising program will depend on the consumers you are trying to reach, the size of the budget you have available, the nature of your product or service, and the particular message you hope to communicate.

Advertising on the Internet is gaining in popularity. The World Wide Web is open for business, and small firms, particularly retail businesses, have jumped on board in ever-increasing numbers. Before joining this throng, however,

---

TABLE 3.3   THE MOST COMMON ADVERTISING MEDIA

1. **MAGAZINES**
   a. Consumer magazines
   b. Trade or business publications
   c. Professional magazines
   d. E-zines

2. **NEWSPAPERS**
   a. Daily newspapers
   b. Weekly newspapers
   c. Digital newspapers
   d. Shopping guides
   e. Special-interest newspapers

3. **TELEVISION**
   a. Local TV
   b. Network TV
   c. Special-interest cable TV

4. **RADIO**
   a. Local stations
   b. Network radio

5. **DIRECTORY**
   a. Community
   b. Special-interest
   c. Professional organizations

6. **DIRECT-MAIL ADVERTISING**
   a. Letters
   b. Catalogues

7. **OUTDOOR ADVERTISING**
   a. Billboards
   b. Posters
   c. Bench

8. **TRANSPORTATION ADVERTISING**
   a. Interior car cards
   b. Station posters
   c. Exterior cards on vehicles

9. **POINT-OF-PURCHASE DISPLAYS**

10. **ADVERTISING NOVELTIES AND SPECIALTIES**

11. **THE INTERNET**
    a. Google Adwords
    b. LinkedIn
    c. Social Media Sites—Facebook and Twitter
    d. e-Bay
    e. Blogs
    f. YouTube
    g. e-newsletters

you should consider whether a Web presence will really serve your business interests. If so, you need to formulate a clear strategy or plan, rather than just developing another web page to join the millions that already exist on the Net.

If you decide to proceed with implementing a website, remember that the Web is not a passive delivery system like most other media but is an active system where the user expects to participate in the experience. Your virtual storefront must be genuinely interesting, and the interactivity of the Web should be used to your advantage to attract and hold the interest of your target consumers.

Personal Selling

Personal selling involves direct, face-to-face contact with your prospective customer. A personal salesperson's primary function is usually more concerned with obtaining orders than informing your customers about the nature of your offering, as in the case of advertising. Other types of salespeople are principally involved in providing support to different components of your business or filling routine orders rather than more persuasive kinds of selling.

Sales Promotion

Sales promotion includes a broad range of promotional activities other than advertising and personal selling that stimulate consumer or dealer interest in your offering. While advertising and personal selling tend to be ongoing activities, most sales promotion is sporadic or irregular in nature. Sales promotion includes activities related to:

1. Free product samples
2. Discount coupons
3. Contests
4. Special deals and premiums
5. Gifts
6. Special exhibits and displays
7. Participation in trade shows
8. Off-price specials
9. Floats in parades and similar events

Sales promotion consists of typically nonrecurring activities. They are intended to make your advertising and personal selling effort more effective and may be very intimately involved with them. For example, your advertising may be used to promote a consumer contest or certain special deals and incentives may be offered to your salespeople to encourage them to increase their sales to your dealers or final consumers. These activities can be an effective way for businesses with a small budget and some imagination to reach potential sales prospects and develop a considerable volume of business.

Public Relations

Public relations relates to your business's general communications and relationships with its various interest groups, such as your employees, stockholders, the government, and society at large, as well as your customers. It is concerned primarily with such issues as the image of you and your business within the community rather than trying to sell any particular product or service. Publicity releases, product introduction notices, news items, appearances on radio and television, and similar activities are all part of your public relations program.

DEVELOPING A PRELIMINARY MARKETING PLAN

A Framework for Developing a Preliminary Marketing Plan, available online in Connect, presents a template to help you prepare a preliminary marketing plan for the product or service idea behind your prospective venture. It will guide you through the process and indicate the kind of information you will need to do a thorough job. It will get you thinking about the size and nature of the market opportunity that may exist for your concept or idea. It will also focus your thoughts on the marketing program you will require to take advantage of the opportunity and achieve your personal goals. The marketing plan is a key part of your feasibility study and your subsequent business plan. Much of the work you do here can be incorporated into your business plan.

Keep in mind, however, that marketing plans are not static documents. Businesses normally have to reformulate their marketing strategy several times over their active life. Economic conditions change, additional competitors come onto the scene, and customer's interests and requirements change. Consequently, the business must plan marketing programs appropriate to each stage in its development. For example, Scott and Bruce identified five stages in the growth of a typical small business: inception, survival, growth, expansion, and maturity.[4] The basic features of each stage are different and the objectives of the business's marketing plan will vary as well. Table 3.4 provides an overview of some of the basic features of each stage and how the firm's marketing efforts may need to be modified to address the principal issues typical of each stage.

Take the case of Bobby Pasternak and Geoff Tait, for example (see the Entrepreneurs in Action box). They established Quagmire Golf to market their line of bold-patterned, hip, and youthful golf fashions to appeal to a younger market than the traditional clothing lines favoured by older golfers. By hitting the road and personally calling on individual golf shops, they were able to place their clothing in a number of shops across the country. At the beginning of 2008, they had the good fortune of signing little-known PGA tour rookie Chez Reavie to a sponsorship deal to wear their clothes. Later that season, Chez won Canada's biggest golf tournament, the RBC Canadian Open, and things changed overnight for Quagmire. All of a sudden, they were in the news and had to come up with a new marketing plan to take advantage of the situation. Instead of calling on golf pro shops themselves, they hired a number of regional sales reps to do the job. They also contacted a professional public relations firm to spread the word about their new line of clothes and were able to sign promotional deals with national firms, such as Golf Town and Molson Canada, to broaden their distribution and create more market awareness. These moves seen to be paying off as sales now approach seven figures, and the game has changed for these young men as the company becomes more mature.

TABLE 3.4 A MODEL FOR SMALL BUSINESS GROWTH

	Stage 1 Inception	Stage 2 Survival	Stage 3 Growth	Stage 4 Expansion	Stage 5 Maturity
Key Issue	Obtaining customers	Increasing competition	Expansion into new products or markets	Greater external emphasis	Finding growth opportunities
Product and Market Research	None	Little	Some new product development	New product development, market research	Production innovation
Product Market	Single basic product Line	Single product line and market, but greater scale	Broader but limited product line, single market	Extended Range of products, broader markets	Contained product lines, multiple markets
Emphasis of Marketing Plan	Limited channels of distribution, cost-plus pricing, heavy sales promotion	Reach expanding markets, broader channels of distribution	Emphasis on cost-efficiency, penetration pricing, build market awareness and distribution	Greater focus on customer Needs and adapting the marketing plan (including promotion) to meet those needs	Major investment in the marketing effort, phase out weak products, cut prices, focus on profitable niches

Source: M. Scott and R. Bruce, "Five Stage of Growth in Small Business," *Long-Range Planning*, June 1987, pp. 45–52.

ENTREPRENEURS IN ACTION

IT'S IN THE FOLLOW-THROUGH

It wasn't exactly a five-star steak house, but for Bobby Pasternak and Geoff Tait, dinner with a new friend at a Keg in downtown Toronto at the end of July was proof that any business, even their upstart golf clothing company, has to be prepared for the unexpected.

In this case, Tait and Pasternak, founders of Toronto-based Quagmire Golf, were toasting their sudden good fortune with RBC Canadian Open champion Chez Reavie. In a stroke of luck, Quagmire had inked a sponsorship deal with the PGA Tour rookie at the start of this year. The little-known Reavie made few headlines leading into the Open. But then, wearing Quagmire's hip and youthful golf fashions, he surprised everyone, holding off conservatively attired fairway stars like Mike Weir to win Canada's biggest golf tournament. In an afternoon, Quagmire shed its startup status and was being heralded as a Next Big Thing. Just as fast, Tait and Pasternak were dealing with a new business problem—how to build on their opportunity so that their fame wouldn't be fleeting.

The first step? Tait and Pasternak hired a U.S. public-relations firm that specializes in golf-related business to spread their story as widely as possible. Next, they went on a hiring spree, expanding their sales staff to 12 reps from one, including six in the U.S. They also leveraged their new-found celebrity to ink important deals, including a test-market program with Golf Town, Canada's largest golf retailer, that's put Quagmire products in 15 of the chain's 39 stores, and a marketing deal with Molson Canada Inc. attached to its Coors Light brand. Finally, they've been hiring staff to handle the routine duties—bookkeeping and answering the phones—that they had previously done themselves.

Tait and Pasternak came up with the idea for Quagmire back in 2004 while working at a youth golf camp in Florida. They noticed that the kids at the camp eschewed traditional clothing lines favoured by older golfers, preferring instead clothes more typically associated with surfer dudes and skater boys. They launched Quagmire the following year, putting together $6,000 they had in savings to hire a designer and register a company

COMSTOCK IMAGES/JUPITERIMAGES

name. Then they hit the road to hustle their bold-patterned fashions. "Everyone said 'no' to us at the start. The banks said 'no.' The golf shops said 'no.'" Pasternak recalls. But the duo nevertheless managed to place their clothing in 12 shops, generating $72,000 in revenue in that first year of business.

Sales have been doubling annually since then. Now, with Reavie as celebrity endorser, they are heading towards the seven figures. "We have credibility and people know us. It is a question of what we can do," Tait says.

These days, that involves acting like the heads of a rapidly maturing company. Tait and Pasternak, for instance, no longer travel from golf club to golf club to pitch their clothing to pro shops. Regional sales reps are doing that job so that Quagmire's founders—who continue to present themselves as the face of the company—can focus on national retail, attend major trade shows, and develop the strategic aspects of the business. "We need to take off 20 hats and only wear two. We need to oversee the company, and not run its operations," Tait says. "We can't be plugging in orders at 2 o'clock in the morning. It is about taking Quagmire to where we know it can go."

(www.quagmiregolf.com)

MANAGING THE SUPPLY SITUATION

A key factor in the success of any new venture is some assurance of continuing access to critical supplies of raw material and component parts at reasonable prices. Many new businesses have floundered due to changing supply situations that impacted their ability to provide products of acceptable quality or that drastically increased their costs of production. These conditions are seldom correctable and tend to be terminal for the smaller firm. It is critical that you investigate the range of possible sources for these key elements well in advance of starting your venture.

Assessing your supply situation requires an understanding of the manufacturing cycle for your product or service and an in-depth appreciation of the market for equipment, materials, and parts. One strategy being followed by more and more smaller firms is to subcontract their production requirements instead of making their own products. This strategy has a number of significant advantages:

- Your business can use the subcontractor's money instead of having to raise the funds to build your own production facilities.
- You can take advantage of the expertise and technical knowledge possessed by the subcontractor without having to develop it yourself.
- Using a subcontractor may enable you to bring your business on stream more rapidly. There is no need to delay while your production facilities are being built and broken in.
- You can concentrate your time on developing a market for your products and running your business rather than on trying to produce a satisfactory product.
- You may be able to benefit from the reputation and credibility of the subcontractor; having your products produced by a firm with an established reputation will rub off on your business.
- A reliable subcontractor can also keep you up to date with technical advances in that field so that your products do not become obsolete.
- Perhaps the most important advantage of using a subcontractor is that it establishes your costs of production in advance, reducing the uncertainty and unpredictability of setting up your own facilities. A firm, fixed-price contract from a reliable subcontractor nails down one of your most important costs of doing business and facilitates your entire planning process.

As you can see, there are a number of strong advantages to subcontracting certain aspects of your operations, but that does not necessarily mean this strategy should be employed in all situations. There are a number of disadvantages that should be considered as well:

- The cost of having a job done by a subcontractor may not be as low as if you did the work yourself. Subcontractors may have antiquated equipment; high-cost, unionized labour; or other problems to deal with that make their operations very expensive. Subcontractors also factor in some margin of profit for themselves into a job. The end result may be a total production cost that would make it very difficult for you to successfully compete.
- Your business may be jeopardized if the subcontractor fails to meet commitments to you or divulges critical trade secrets about your product or process.

In any case, sometimes a suitable subcontractor is just not available. If you want your product produced, you may have no alternative but to do it yourself.

Regardless of the approach you decide to take, to cover your supply situation there are a number of key factors that have to be considered. These include:

- Delivered cost (total cost, including transportation etc.)
- Quality
- Delivery schedules
- Service level

All have to be at an acceptable level for you to have confidence that your supply situation is under reasonable control.

Once you have completed this series of worksheets, you will have a better understanding of the likely market opportunity for your concept or idea, and you will have thought through the process of determining how you feel it can be most effectively marketed. This is an essential step in deciding whether the concept really does represent a worthwhile opportunity that ought to be aggressively pursued or whether it should be abandoned. This is also a key part of your business plan. Most of this information represents the foundation on which the business plan is built and can be directly transferred to that document.

F Y I

The following are some helpful websites for developing your marketing plan:

Guidelines for Taking Your Idea to Market A case study of the approach used by chip maker Nazomi Communications to bring their new Java accelerator chip successfully from conception to launch. (www.design-reuse.com)

About: Small Business: Canada A series of articles dealing with marketing strategies relating to a number of aspects of your marketing program, such as advertising, networking, business promotion, Internet marketing, market research, trade shows, personal selling, and marketing plans. (sbinfocanada.about.com)

Canada Business Network A guide to help you learn the basics of market research for your business. (www.canadabusiness.ca) Enter "market research" in the search box.

The Business Link—Where to Find the Market Information You Need A listing of some of the key market research resources you need to help identify your target market, assess your competition, and develop your marketing plan. (www.canadabusiness.ab.ca)

Advertising A series of guides to help you plan your advertising budget, select media, prepare ads, and determine the results of your advertising expenditures. (www.canadabusiness.ca) Enter "advertising" in the search box.

Marketing Basic A web-based program sponsored by Canada Business that discusses such issues as identifying your customer, finding the right product, determining your price, forecasting your sales, and advertising and promotion. (www.canadabusiness.ca) Enter "marketing basic" in the search box.

e-Business Marketing A series of guides for conducting e-business dealing with such topics as marketing your website, marketing on the Internet, marketing with newsgroups, and viral and email marketing. (www.ic.gc.ca) Enter "e-business" in the search box.

Business Information by Industrial Sector A comprehensive overview of Canadian business information by industry sector. (www.ic.gc.ca) Enter "industry sectors" in the search box.

Canadian Statistics A business resource of online statistics for, and publications about, various business sectors, plus other information. (www.statcan.gc.ca) Use the search box to locate the specific area of interest.

Canadian Economic and Market Research/Statistics A statistical overview of current Canadian economic conditions and a number of industry and trade-related statistics. (www.ic.gc.ca) Enter "Canadian Economic and Market Research/Statistics" in the search box.

Corporations Canada A division of Industry Canada, where you can search for companies in your industry (www.ic.gc.ca) Enter "corporations branch" in the search box—once there, you will be able to enter keywords of the industry for which you are looking for information.

Corporate Information Information on world securities markets, including company profiles from 55 countries worldwide. (corporateinformation.com)

Home-Based Business Home-based business ideas, home business opportunities, home business resources, advice for starting a home business or to help you work at home—everything you need to run a successful home-based business. (sbinfocanada.about.com) Enter home-based business in the search box.

Start and Run Your Own Business The inspiration and information you can use to start and run a profitable small and home-based business. (www.lifemedia.ca)

Exporting Everything you need to know to take advantage of international trade and compete in a global marketplace with your goods and services. (www.canadabusiness.ca) Enter "exporting" in the search box.

The Step-By-Step Guide to Exporting The *Step-by-Step Guide to Exporting* is intended to help you learn about the world marketplace and how your company can do business there. (www.tradecommissioner.gc.ca)

Customized Market Research Reports for International Trade Over 600 detailed industry sector analysis reports for countries all over the world. (www.tradecommissioner.gc.ca)

Export Development Canada A series of guides on exporting, market, and industry. (www.edc.ca)

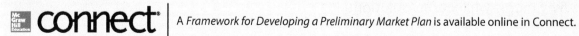

A *Framework for Developing a Preliminary Market Plan* is available online in Connect.

LO1 A feasibility study is a comprehensive plan that proves whether your new venture concept can be profitable. A feasibility study includes:

- the concept idea
- an assessment of your target market and your competition
- the technical feasibility of your idea
- the supply situation
- cost-profit analysis
- future plans

LO2 Market research tells you:

- whether there is a need for your concept
- who your competitors are
- what potential you have for entering the market

LO3 A marketing plan outlines your marketing strategy:

- product—what your product or service is
- person—your target market
- place—where is your market located
- pricing—the price you put on your product/service
- promotion—what avenues you going to use to tell the world about your business

For more information on the resources available from McGraw-Hill Ryerson, go to www.mcgrawhill.ca/he/solutions.

COST AND PROFITABILITY ASSESSMENT

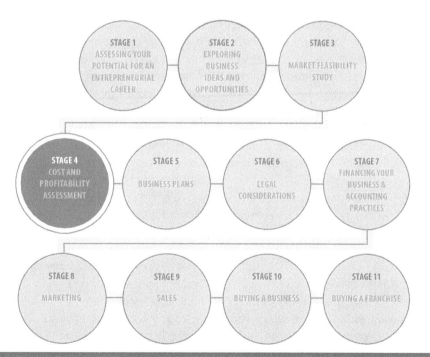

STAGE 1
ASSESSING YOUR POTENTIAL FOR AN ENTREPRENEURIAL CAREER

STAGE 2
EXPLORING BUSINESS IDEAS AND OPPORTUNITIES

STAGE 3
MARKET FEASIBILITY STUDY

STAGE 4
COST AND PROFITABILITY ASSESSMENT

STAGE 5
BUSINESS PLANS

STAGE 6
LEGAL CONSIDERATIONS

STAGE 7
FINANCING YOUR BUSINESS & ACCOUNTING PRACTICES

STAGE 8
MARKETING

STAGE 9
SALES

STAGE 10
BUYING A BUSINESS

STAGE 11
BUYING A FRANCHISE

LEARNING OBJECTIVES

By the end of this stage, you should be able to:

LO1   Explain what is involved in a cost and profitability assessment.

LO2   Complete a feasibility study for your business.

PHOTO COURTESY OF
PHIL TELIO

Phil Telio has been an entrepreneur since 2004 but never considered himself one until he started the Montreal International Startup Festival in 2011.

Phil fell into being an entrepreneur when the company that he worked for started closing its offices around the world—with Montreal being one of them. Shortly after, Phil was approached by a friend who asked if he would help him with his business. Selling his services to a friend gave him the confidence to launch his own consulting business—Embrace. Phil says, "I fell into entrepreneurship with circumstances that I didn't control." Even though he had the burning desire to be an entrepreneur, he considered himself a late starter in the startup universe—he was in his mid-thirties. When Phil started Embrace, he considered himself a business owner, not an entrepreneur. He said, "Entrepreneurs take risks, and there is very little risk in being a consultant."

This changed when Phil founded the International Startup Festival—a festival that takes place each year in Montreal and is all about the business of startups. Every year, the Festival brings together aspiring founders, ground-breaking innovators, and veteran entrepreneurs from around the world to meet, talk, and listen to others who are passionate about entrepreneurship.

The Festival was Phil's first entrepreneurial challenge—taking an idea and making it happen. "That's when entrepreneurship kicks in," he says. "You need to have a whack of investment—there is a certain amount of risk involved to make this happen."

Phil was quite involved in the Montreal startup community—arranging free events where startups could network with other like-minded people. The Startup Festival was an evolution from these events. Entrepreneurs are always looking or striving for more and better—local events were successful—but he needed to reach further. The idea for the Festival came to him when he was alone on a lake, and reflecting. He says, "That's when a lot of ideas come to you. When you stop thinking about it—it just comes."

He had always liked startups and had the startup mentality, so now all he had to do was build the minimum viable product. He had the idea—now what? He needed to convince the people who currently attended the events and the international startup community to come to Montreal. To make this happen, he needed partners that would add value and at the very least advise on the idea. He put together a presentation that consisted of six PowerPoint® slides and presented the idea to three people, who all came on board.

The next step was to find funding—Phil did not have any idea how much it would take to fund the Festival and did not have any budget to do it. He had to somehow convince sponsors to come on board with only his dream. Phil was successful in his endeavours to find the capital to make his dream a reality.

It is truly amazing how social media can make things happen. Without a marketing budget for the first two years of the Festival, Phil turned to social media to spread the word. Eleven hundred people attended the first year and 1,200 the second year, but Phil is not worried about the numbers—it is all about getting the right people to attend. Now with three full-time employees and a marketing budget, the team is building on increasing the Festival's profile that will, in turn, attract more startups from cities and countries around the world.

Within seven months of standing on a lake with an idea to launch, Phil has proven that if you want to do something badly enough you can make it happen. As with any business, there were many ups and downs, with funding being the biggest hurdle. After proving that the Festival was viable, it has been easier to find support—both financial and otherwise.

Phil asks himself everyday what his long-term vision is for the Festival. His ultimate goal is to have a large-scale event in Montreal for thousands of entrepreneurs, which will be run by others as a business like other events in Montreal.

When asked if Phil loves being an entrepreneur, he responded by saying, "I don't know if I love being an entrepreneur—it's something that torments me to a certain extent—always on guard—having to take the risk, but, I love what I am doing."

At this point, the Festival takes a large chunk of time away from Embrace, but Phil is happy for the time being, spending his time working on it.

To find out more or register to attend the International Startup Festival, visit www.start-upfestival.com.

Source: International Startup Festival. Interview by Wendy Mayhew. Used with permission.

COST AND PROFITABILITY ASSESSMENT LO1

In addition to determining the size and nature of the market for your new venture idea, it is also important to consider the financial components of your business. The costs associated with operating your business may include labour, materials, rent, machinery, and so on. Collecting potential sales and cost information should put you in a better position to make reasonably accurate financial forecasts that can be used not only as a check on the advisability of proceeding with the venture but also for raising capital, if required. As an example, Bill Buckwold wants to evaluate the financial feasibility of opening a Tough Guys Sporting Goods store and sets out to do a comprehensive analysis of its expected viability.

DETERMINE YOUR STARTUP FINANCIAL REQUIREMENTS

The process of financial analysis begins with an estimate of the funds required to set up the business. The startup financial requirements can be broken down into two components:

1. **One-time expenditures** that must be made before the business can open its doors. These include both *capital expenditures* for the purchase or lease of furniture, fixtures, equipment, and the purchase of beginning inventory or supplies and *soft costs* relating to such items as utility deposits and fees, pre-opening advertising and promotion expenses, and other prepaid expenses. In the case of a retail or manufacturing business, these requirements can be considerable, while a service business may not require a very large initial expenditure to get started. Remember, what we are trying to determine here is the amount of *cash* that will be needed to get the business launched. For example, a piece of required equipment may cost $20,000, but if the seller is prepared to take a deposit of $5,000 and finance the rest or if the business will be leasing the equipment for $500 per month rather than buying it outright, only the out-of-pocket cash cost needs to be factored in and not the total cost of the item. The estimated one-time financial requirements for the startup of Tough Guys Sporting Goods is illustrated in Figure 4.1.

2. **Operating expenses,** such as payments for Bill's and his employees' wages, rent, operating supplies, telephone, and postage, promotion, and other ongoing expenses, that must be incurred until the business begins to show a profit. Many new businesses take several months or even years before they operate "in the black." Sufficient funds must be available to cover a minimum of two to three months' operations and provide a cash reserve for emergency situations. One way to determine just how much cash might be required is to review the cash flow statement to see how long it takes before the business reaches a positive cash flow situation. If, for example, it is not until the sixth month after opening the doors, Bill will need enough cash to cover the expected losses up to that time plus some additional cash as a safety factor. The estimated funds required to cover these initial operating expenses for Tough Guys is also illustrated in Figure 4.1.

Note that a sporting goods store, like many retail businesses, is a relatively capital-intensive business to start. The bulk of the money is required to finance the initial inventory Bill will need to stock the store, while most of the remaining one-time funds go to decorating and providing the necessary fixtures for the store. In addition, he should have approximately $52,000 available to cover his estimated monthly expenses until the business starts generating a positive cash flow. He does not necessarily have to have the entire cash requirements available strictly from his own resources; $100,000 to $150,000 may be sufficient. Suppliers may be prepared to grant him credit terms so that he does not necessarily have to pay for some of the stock for 30 or 60 days. Or the bank may be prepared to extend him a term loan or line of credit that he can draw on to meet some of his working capital requirements as they arise.

Insufficient financing is a major cause of new business failure, so Bill should be certain he has sufficient financing to cover both his estimated one-time and initial operating expenses.

FIGURE 4.1   ESTIMATED STARTUP COSTS FOR TOUGH GUYS SPORTING GOODS STORE

ESTIMATED MONTHLY EXPENSES

Item	Column 1 Bill's Estimate of Monthly Expenses Based on Sales of $800,000 per Year	Column 2 Number of Months of Cash Required to Cover Expenses*	Column 3 Estimated Cash Required to Start Business (Column 1 × Column 2)*
Salary of Owner-Manager	$3,400	2	$6,800
All Other Salaries and Wages	$6,000	3	$18,000
Rent	$3,200	3	$9,600
Advertising	$1,000	3	$3,000
Delivery Expense/Transportation	$100	3	$300
Supplies	$0	3	$0
Telephone, Fax, Internet Service	$100	3	$300
Other Utilities	$580	3	$1,740
Insurance	$500	3	$1,500
Taxes, Including Employment Insurance	$0	4	$0
Interest	$250	3	$750
Maintenance	$750	3	$2,250
Legal and Other Professional Fees	$700	3	$2,100
Miscellaneous	$1,800	3	$5,400
Total Cash Requirements for Monthly Recurring Expenses: (A)			**$51,740**

STARTUP COSTS YOU ONLY HAVE TO PAY ONCE	Cash Required to Start Business
Capital Costs	
Fixtures and Equipment	$40,000
Decorating and Remodelling	$10,000
Installation of Fixtures and Equipment	$5,600
Starting Inventory	$220,000
Soft Costs	
Deposits with Public Utility	$2,000
Legal and Other Professional Fees	$1,500
Licences and Permits	$1,000
Advertising and Promotion for Opening	$1,000
Accounts Receivable	$8,000
Cash	$5,000
Miscellaneous	$5,000
Total One-time Cash Requirements: (B)	**$299,100**
Total Estimated Cash Required to Start Business: (A) + (B)	**$350,850**

*These figures may be typical for one kind of business. You will have to decide how many months to allow for your business to offset expected shortages of cash flow.

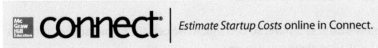

Estimate *Startup Costs* online in Connect.

DEVELOP SHORT-TERM FINANCIAL PROJECTIONS
PRO FORMA INCOME STATEMENT

Bill's next step is to develop a projected operating statement, or *pro forma income statement*. This involves estimating the initial profit or loss expected by the business. Simply put, the basic formula to calculate profit and loss is:

Revenue − Expenses = Net Profit before Taxes

This means he will have to estimate the total expected revenue and expenses for at least the first year of operation of his business.

An income statement then measures the company's sales and expenses during a specified period of time—usually a month or a year. Its function is to total all sources of revenue for the business and subtract all expenses related to generating that revenue. It shows a company's financial performance over a period of time, and the heading of the income statement should always indicate the time period that is being examined (i.e., for the month ending, for the year ending, etc.).

The information Bill must be able to provide to construct a pro forma income statement includes:

1. The predicted sales volume for the period for which he is making the forecast or his projected *Net Sales*
2. How much it is expected to cost to produce or purchase the products he will sell or his projected *Cost of Goods Sold*
3. His *Fixed Operating Expenses,* such as rent, utilities, insurance premiums, and interest costs
4. His controllable or *Variable Operating Expenses,* such as advertising and promotion expenses, wages and salaries, and delivery expenses
5. His expected *Net Operating Profit or Loss*

Net Sales is the total sales plus any transportation costs he expects to make during the month or year being examined *minus* any cash discounts, trade discounts, or expected returns.

Cost of Goods Sold is often called *Cost of Sales*. For retail and wholesale businesses, it is the total price paid for the products Bill expects to sell during the period for which he is developing the forecast. It is just the price of the goods. It does not include selling and other expenses. These are shown elsewhere on the income statement.

For most service and professional businesses, there will be no cost of goods sold. These businesses receive their income from fees, commissions, and royalties, so they do not typically have inventories of physical products. Their costs to provide these services are included in the fixed and variable operating expense sections of the statement.

Most small retail and wholesale businesses determine their cost of goods sold by:

- Determining the value of their inventory at the beginning of the period being projected
- Adding the value of any products purchased during the period
- Subtracting the value of any inventory left at the end of the period

This calculation will provide a value for the amount of inventory actually sold during the period for which the projection is being developed. Net sales minus cost of goods sold yields Bill's expected *Gross Margin* or *Gross Profit Margin*.

Fixed Expenses are operating expenses or overhead that he must pay regardless of his expected level of sales. These include expenses, such as rent, telephone, insurance premiums, business taxes and licences, and interest, as well as some provision for depreciation on any capital assets used in the business.

Variable Expenses are those that are expected to rise and fall in proportion to Bill's sales. These include most of his selling expenses, such as sales salaries and commissions, travel costs, advertising and promotion, delivery and vehicle expenses, and similar costs.

Net Operating Profit or Loss is the difference between his gross margin and his fixed and variable operating expenses. This is his expected net profit or loss before any consideration of federal or provincial income taxes.

The creation of a pro forma income statement is an important event for a small business. It provides a summary of many of the important activities of the company and provides valuable information to both the prospective owner and to others who may be looking to lend money or potentially invest in a business.

One means Bill might use to develop a pro forma income statement for his business is to follow the *desired income approach* suggested by Szonyi and Steinhoff.[1] This approach enables him to develop financial projections on the basis of the actual operating performance of firms similar to the business he is contemplating. It also suggests that his business should provide him with not only a return for the time he will spend running the business but also a return on the personal funds he has to invest to launch the business. For example, instead of starting a business, he could keep his present job or obtain another one and earn a salary working for someone else. He could also invest his money in common stocks, bonds, guaranteed income certificates, or other investments, where it would yield some kind of return. Both possibilities should be kept in mind for comparison purposes when determining the expected minimum level of acceptable profit performance of your new venture.

To illustrate this approach, assume Bill has determined that he would like to have a salary of $40,000 per year from the business, plus $15,000 as a reasonable return on the investment he will have to make in the business. These represent his desired income and return levels. By referring to the Industry Canada SME Benchmarking Tool profiles, he can obtain comprehensive financial data on sporting goods stores as well as dozens of other different lines of business.

Combining the information about his desired income and return goals with some of this published data will enable him to develop a pro forma income statement highlighting the level of operations he will have to reach to achieve his goals. The additional information he requires is as follows:

- **The average inventory turnover for this type of business** is the number of times a typical firm's inventory is sold each year. If the business carries an inventory of $25,000 and its overall net revenue is $150,000, inventory turnover is six times per year.

- **The average gross margin** is the difference between the firm's net sales and cost of goods sold, expressed as a percentage. For example, if the business's net sales are $200,000, while cost of goods sold totals $140,000, its gross margin is $60,000, or 30 percent of sales.

- **Net profit** as a percentage of sales is relatively self-explanatory. It can be determined either before or after the application of any federal or provincial taxes. In the case of Industry Canada's SME Benchmarking Tool profiles, it is shown before the application of any taxes.

Developing the Statement

With these data and an estimate of his desired salary and return levels, Bill can construct a pro forma income statement for a sporting goods store. For example, checking the 2006 Industry Canada SME Benchmarking Tool profile for a typical performing store in NAISC Classification code 45111—Sporting Goods Stores[2] could provide us with the following information:

Inventory turnover	3.6 times per year
Gross margin	34.7% of sales
Net profit as a percentage of sales	1.8%

Figure 4.2 illustrates how these data, along with the information about Bill's desired salary and return, can be used to develop a pro forma income statement. This statement indicates the minimum level of sales his business will have to generate to provide him with his desired salary and level of profitability. Sales above this level will probably provide a higher level of profits, while lower sales will likely mean he will not make as much money as he had hoped. It is assumed in this evaluation that his business will be operated as efficiently as, and in a similar manner to, other sporting goods stores across the country.

All the figures in this statement have been computed from our ratio data and our stated desired salary and return on investment. For example:

1. Our $15,000 desired profit is inserted in line (E).

2. Profits for a typical retail sporting goods store are very slim, at only 1.8 percent of sales. To determine the sales level required to provide our desired level of profitability, we divide $15,000 by 0.018 to obtain our estimate of the required level of $833,333 for net sales in line (A).

FIGURE 4.2 SAMPLE PRO FORMA INCOME STATEMENT

TOUGH GUYS SPORTING GOODS PRO FORMA INCOME STATEMENT
For the Year Ending (date)

Net Sales		$833,333 **(A)**
Less: Cost of goods sold		
Beginning Inventory	$220,000	
Plus: Net purchases	555,647	
Goods available for sale	$775,647	
Less: Ending Inventory	231,481	
Cost of goods sold		544,166 **(B)**
Gross margin		$289,167 **(C)**
Operating Expenses		274,167 **(D)**
Net Profit (Loss) before Income Tax		**$15,000 (E)**

3. Our statistics indicate that sporting goods stores typically have an average gross margin of 34.7 percent of net sales. In our situation, this would provide a gross margin estimate of $289,167 in line (C).

4. The difference between our estimated net sales and gross margin has to provide for our cost of goods sold. In this example, our cost of goods sold will be $833,333 − $289,167 = $544,166 in line (B).

5. Sporting goods stores have a relatively low level of inventory turnover in comparison with other types of retail business. A typical retail firm will turn over its inventory from six to seven times per year, while our statistics indicate a turnover ratio of only 3.6 times for a sporting goods store. This means we need to have more money tied up in inventory to support our estimated level of net sales than most other retailers. Our projected average inventory level can be determined by dividing our net sales revenue by the inventory turnover rate, or $833,333/3.6 = $231,481.

6. The difference between our expected gross margin and the net operating profit (before taxes) necessary to provide our desired income level represents our total operating expenses in line (D). In this case, $289,167 − $15,000 = $274,167 should be available to cover such expenses as Bill's salary and those of his employees, rent, insurance, promotion, interest, and similar expenses. Note that his expected salary of $40,000 has to be included in this amount.

This pro forma statement shows Bill the level of sales, investment in inventory, and similar information he needs to know to generate the level of income he feels he needs to obtain from the business.

Photo courtesy of
Nancy Knowlton

What do you like about being an Entrepreneur?

There are several reasons why I love being an entrepreneur. Creating something from nothing is the biggest kick for me. Having an idea and then bringing that idea to life against the odds is exhilarating. Doing something that transforms the way that something is done gives me a sense of satisfaction. Creating value in a company, jobs for people, and exports for Alberta and Canada are good measures as the game progresses.

Nancy Knowlton
Co-founder and Vice Chair,
SMART Technologies Inc.
President and CEO, Byye Group
www.smarttech.com

The statement constructed in Figure 4.2 is based on the distinct financial characteristics of a small retail sporting goods business and relates only to that situation. A pro forma income statement for a store in another line of business could look very different due to variations in inventory turnover, gross margin percentage, and other factors reflecting the different character of that business.

This is even truer if we are considering the startup of a service business or a manufacturing company. Service firms, such as drycleaners and management consultants, typically do not carry an inventory of goods for resale and so do not have a "cost of goods sold" section on their income statements. Manufacturing companies, on the other hand, may have several types of inventory—raw materials, work in process, and finished goods. Appropriate levels for all three types of inventories should be determined and reflected in the projected income statement. The statement also tries to determine the value of raw materials and components, direct labour, factory overhead, and other inputs required to manufacture a product suitable for sale. This "cost of goods manufactured" replaces the cost of goods sold component on the pro forma statement.

Determining Reasonable Operating Expenses

So far, our pro forma income statement has lumped all of Bill's business's projected operating expenses together under a single heading. For example, Figure 4.2 shows the overall, estimated operating expenses to be $274,167. This means that all operating expenses must be covered by this amount if he is to achieve his desired level of profitability.

The same statistical sources used to obtain the data for the overall pro forma statement can be used to obtain a breakdown of the typical operating expenses for his type of business. For example, the SME Benchmarking Tool provides data on the operating results of sporting goods stores. It indicates the following breakdown of operating expenses as a percentage of sales for the average incorporated firm:

Labour and commissions	15.1%
Amortization and depreciation	1.2%
Repairs and maintenance	0.6%
Utilities and telephone	1.1%
Rent	4.6%
Interest and bank charges	0.8%
Professional fees	1.3%
Advertising and promotion	2.2%
Delivery, shipping, and warehouse expenses	0.2%
Insurance	0.6%
Other expenses	5.5%

These expenses total approximately 33.2 percent of sales. If we translate these percentages to our pro forma income statement, Bill can obtain an approximation of the detailed breakdown of his operating expenses in dollar terms. His finalized pro forma income statement would look like Figure 4.3.

This complete pro forma statement can now serve as part of your plan for outlining the requirements of your proposed new business venture or as a guide or schedule to monitor the ongoing performance of your new business during its early stages.

The need for a cash flow analysis originates from the reality that in most businesses there is a time discrepancy between when your expenditures are incurred and when the cash is actually realized from the sale of the products or services you provide. This analysis is particularly important at the startup stage, when businesses typically have lower revenues and higher expenditures. In fact, it is not uncommon for a new startup to incur expenses requiring the outlay of cash several months prior to actually opening its doors. This outflow of cash should be taken into account in preparing the initial pro forma cash flow forecast.

A typical pro forma income statement that you can use for projecting the first-year operating performance of your new business is available online in Connect.

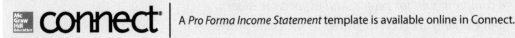

A *Pro Forma Income Statement* template is available online in Connect.

TOUGH GUYS SPORTING GOODS PRO FORMA INCOME STATEMENT
For the Year (date)

1.	Gross Sales	$833,333
2.	*Less:* Cash Discounts	0
A.	**NET SALES**	**833,333**
	Cost of Goods Sold:	
3.	Beginning Inventory	$220,000
4.	*Plus:* Net Purchases	555,647
5.	Total Available for Sale	$775,647
6.	*Less:* Ending Inventory	231,481
B.	**COST OF GOODS SOLD**	**$544,166**
C.	**GROSS MARGIN**	**$289,167**
	Less: Variable Expenses	
7.	Owner's Salary	40,000
8.	Employees' Wages and Salaries	85,133
9.	Supplies and Postage	0
10.	Advertising and Promotion	18,330
11.	Delivery Expense	1,670
12.	Bad Debt Expense	0
13.	Travel	0
14.	Legal and Accounting Fees	10,830
15.	Vehicle Expense	0
16.	Miscellaneous Expenses	45,833
D.	**TOTAL VARIABLE EXPENSES**	**$201,796**
	Less: Fixed Expenses	
17.	Rent	38,333
18.	Repairs and Maintenance	5,000
19.	Utilities (Heat, Light, Power)	8,170
20.	Telephone	1,000
21.	Taxes and Licences	0
22.	Depreciation	10,000
23.	Interest	6,667
24.	Insurance	5,000
25.	Other Fixed Expenses	0
E.	**TOTAL FIXED EXPENSES**	**$ 74,170**
F.	**TOTAL OPERATING EXPENSES**	**$274,167***
G.	**NET OPERATING PROFIT (LOSS)**	**$ 15,000**

*Numbers may not exactly match operating expense percentages due to rounding.

FORECAST YOUR CASH FLOW

Your next step is to bring closer to reality the operating profit or loss Bill has projected by developing a cash flow forecast. It traces the expected flow of funds into and out of his business over some period of time. Cash flow is the lifeblood of any business. Therefore, this cash flow analysis is the most important document you will compile in assessing the financial feasibility of your business idea, and it enables you to control the financial affairs of your business. It is quite a complex financial statement, so you will need to have some basic understanding of general accounting concepts to prepare it properly. As illustrated in the Entrepreneurs in Action box, Hit the Green, failure to plan adequately for future cash requirements is one of the principal reasons small businesses fail. Although Robert Bobbett and his two brothers-in-law had developed what seemed to be an excellent idea from a technological perspective, they grossly overestimated the ongoing revenue their business model for the TeePod scoring system could generate for their company. Over five years, the company burned through over $3 million of their and other investors' money and eventually ended up in bankruptcy.

Even the best of plans can go awry. Nico and Karri Schuermans thought they had everything under control for the opening of their Chambar restaurant in Vancouver (see the Entrepreneurs in Action box). They estimated they needed $400,000 to open the doors. They had developed a detailed business plan, laying out how much money they needed to get started, how much to subsequently run the place, and even how much cash they needed to keep in reserve. Unfortunately, things did not work out quite as they had planned. A couple of investors they were counting on backed out, costs were higher than expected, and a change to the original concept meant higher expenses. But by counting on friends and doing a lot of the work themselves, they were able to pull it off. Upon reflection, Karri suggests that unlike them, anyone looking to open a restaurant business have at least six months' worth of expected cash requirements available before they start. An accurate cash flow forecast can be your best means of ensuring continued financial solvency and the survival of your business.

Cash flow statements are similar to but differ from income statements, in a number of ways. Cash flow is exactly as the name implies. The statement measures only the flow of cash into and out of the business. Non-cash accounting entries that may show up on an income statement, such as depreciation, amortization, and asset transfers, are ignored in forecasting the cash flow statement. Similarly, expenses that have been incurred but not yet paid and income that has been earned but not yet received are not included in the cash flow statement either.

In a typical small business, sales revenue and expenses vary throughout the year. Your cash flow forecast tries to predict all the funds that you will receive and disburse within a certain period of time—for example, a month, quarter, or year—and the resulting surplus or deficit. It allows you to estimate the total amount of cash you actually expect to receive each period and the actual bills that have to be paid. At times, your cash inflows will exceed your outflows; at other times, your cash outflows will exceed your inflows. Knowing your expected position and cash balance will enable you to plan your cash requirements and negotiate a line of credit with your bank or arrange other external financing.

Your completed cash flow forecast will clearly show to the bank loans officer what additional working capital, if any, your business may need and demonstrate that there will be sufficient cash on hand to make the interest payments on a line of credit or a term loan for purchasing additional machinery or equipment or expanding the business.

There are three sections in a typical cash flow statement:

1. Operating activities
2. Investment activities
3. Financing activities

These three sections work together to show the expected net change in cash that will occur in the business over a particular period of time. Cash inflows into the business are *added* on the statement, while outflows are *subtracted* to determine total net cash flow.

Cash Flow from Operating Activities

Cash flow from operating activities is probably the most complicated section to develop. It is important to distinguish between sales revenue and cash receipts in most businesses. They are typically not the same unless all the

ENTREPRENEURS IN ACTION

HIT THE GREEN

Golf is known as a game uniquely suited to people in business. Perhaps that's because the two disciplines share similar requirements for success: a solid strategy, calculated risk, and precise execution.

Robert Bobbett has learned this lesson the hard way—in both pursuits. Although he describes himself as a "duffer" lucky to shoot 100, Toronto-bred Bobbett used to love golf, and in 2000 he combined his passion with his knowledge of technology to tee up a venture, called 4everSports. Founded in Cape Breton, N.S., with his two brothers-in-law, 4everSports sold a product dubbed the TeePod, a high-tech system that linked the Internet to the links. Touch-screen kiosks located next to each tee box allowed players to score their rounds and later track them online, as well as get detailed information on the hole and order food and drinks from the clubhouse. The system even used solar power and a wireless network to connect to a central server.

Today, however, 4everSports has been bankrupt for more than a year, and Bobbett hasn't picked up a putter since the day his business went under. "We were in the process of raising capital, and we weren't successful in raising enough before we ran out of money," he says. In its five fledgling years, the company burned through $3.2 million that it had raised through the personal investment of its principals, their friends and family, and grants from two regional government funding agencies. "There are a fair number of people who at the end of the day lost money in this, myself and partners included," says Bobbett. "But that was a risk we all took when we went into it."

Business, like golf, can humble the best of us. And as entrepreneurial tech stories go, 4everSports is not unique. Inventing a new product and turning it into a thriving concern is as tough as qualifying to play on the PGA tour. But Bobbett still holds out hope that even if his golf game is beyond saving, his company can be revived. But how can he turn this failed venture into a success?

Bobbett's assessment of what went wrong has little to do with technology. In fact, the TeePod system continues to operate at the Lingan Golf & Country Club in Sydney, N.S., the

© LINDA NOLAN / ALAMY. USED WITH PERMISSION.

semi-public course where it was first prototyped, in 2001. "A lot of our members use it all the time. It's like a running leaderboard throughout the day," says Lingan's head pro, Chris Bunting. "We have probably 700 members, and I would think at least half of them use it on a regular basis, for sure."

But just like in golf, even the most advanced equipment won't get you very far without the right strategy. 4everSports' real problem? It couldn't find the right revenue model to work in the hyper-competitive golf industry. Initially, Bobbett's plan was to cover the cost of installing the TeePod System, and the course would charge golfers an extra $2 a round to pay 4everSports. The golf club would benefit from new sales opportunities (the screens could display local ads), a fresh way to attract more tournaments with the system's scoring tabulation features, and it could drive increased food and beverage sales.

But Bobbett found the industry too price sensitive for the surcharge. "The courses are always cutting their prices in an effort to get people to play," he says. "That's their idea of marketing: a fire sale on tee times." Golf courses viewed $2 per round as a cost they would have to absorb. At an average of 30,000 rounds per year, it added up to an additional $60,000 annually—and for an unproven concept at that. "We had a technology that worked," says Bobbett, "but a revenue model that didn't."

Source: Andrew Wahl, *Canadian Business,* September 10, 2006, pp. 73–74. Used with permission.

business's sales are for cash. Revenues are determined at the time a sale is made. Cash receipts, on the other hand, are not recorded until the money actually flows into the business. This may not be for a month or two in the case of sales made on credit, which would be reflected in your *accounts receivable.* Similarly expenses are incurred when materials, labour, and other items are purchased and used, but payments for these items may not be made until sometime later when the cheques are actually issued. These deferred payments would be reflected in your *accounts payable*.

In addition, your net cash flow will typically be different from your net profit. Net cash flow is the difference between your cash inflows and cash outflows. Net profit is the difference between your expected sales revenue and expenses. One reason for this difference is the uneven timing of cash receipts and disbursements mentioned above. Another is that some items on the income statement, such as depreciation are non-cash expenses. They represent a charge against the business's income for the use of fixed assets owned by the firm but do not involve a direct outlay of cash.

Cash flow from operating activities can be determined from the following formula:

(+) Cash received from customers
(+) Any other operating cash receipts
    (=) Total Cash Receipts from Operations (A)
(−) Cash paid to suppliers
(−) Cash paid to employees
(−) Interest paid
(−) Taxes paid
(−) Other cash payments for expenses
    (=) Total Cash Payments from Operations (B)
    Total Net Cash Provided by Operations = (A) − (B)

Cash Flow from Investment Activities

Cash flow from investment activities includes changes to your expected cash position owing to the purchase or sale of any assets owned by the business. This might include land and buildings, vehicles, equipment, securities, or anything else the business may have sold or acquired that resulted in the receipt or outlay of cash.

Cash flow from investment activities can be determined from the following formula:

(+) Cash proceeds from the sale of assets
(−) Cash disbursements for the purchase of property or equipment
    (=) Total Net Cash Provided by Investment

Cash Flow from Financing Activities

Financing activities on a cash flow statement reflect cash received from borrowing money, issuing stock, or other cash contributions to the business, as well as any payments made on loans, dividends paid to shareholders, or other similar payments.

Cash flow from financing activities can be determined from the following formula:

(+) Cash received from bank and other loans
(+) Proceeds from issuing stock
(+) Capital contributions by owners
    (=) Total Cash Received from Financing (A)
(−) Repayment of principal on loans
(−) Dividends paid to shareholders
(−) Cash withdrawals by owners
(−) Other funds removed from the business
    (=) Total Cash Payments for Financing (B)
    Total Net Cash Provided by Financing (A) − (B)

ENTREPRENEURS IN ACTION

CHAMBAR RESTAURANT

Nico and Karri Schuermans spent four frenzied months getting ready to open their restaurant in downtown Vancouver. By the time they threw open their doors in late 2004, they were flat broke. "We had $11 left in the bank a month into operating," says Karri, part of the husband-and-wife team behind Chambar. It's a modern twist on classic Belgian cuisine that has quickly grown into one of Vancouver's most talked-about hot spots. The mix of high-end elegance and mid-range prices proved popular enough to turn a profit in just five months.

But things weren't always so rosy for Chambar. Karri says she and Nico estimated they'd need $400,000 to get the doors open. They developed a detailed business plan that laid out how much money they'd need to get started, how much they'd need to actually run the place, and how much cash to keep in reserve. But they weren't prepared for a few nasty snags. For one thing, two of their investors pulled out: One bailed during construction, taking $200,000 out of the project and halting work for two weeks; the other reneged on $100,000 of a $150,000 pledge two weeks before opening. The couple managed to come up with another $200,000, though they opened $100,000 short of their plan. They paid for kitchen equipment with cash flow, in instalments.

Costs ran over, too, because the couple decided to rent a heritage building, which meant construction regulations were more stringent. They couldn't touch the exterior of the building, for example, so they had to cut a 1.2-metre hole through three floors to accommodate some of their kitchen equipment. Although they did a lot of the work themselves—Karri's dad handled the carpentry—the couple still had to hire pros for a few jobs, like refinishing the floors.

Nico, who had previously worked in two Belgian restaurants—each with three Michelin stars—would have been happy cooking for an intimate crowd of 30 to 40 people, but Karri wouldn't agree to the venture unless they could make money. Eventually they settled on 120 seats.

One month in, construction and equipment costs had hit $500,000. They realized they needed "more flatware, more cutlery, more everything," Karri says. Rather than buy used refrigerators and other equipment, the couple opted to go new, adding 20 percent to their budget. "We decided it was better that way," she says. "We couldn't risk having food go off."

But Karri's business background paid off (she spent nine years as a marketing director in various industries). She and Nico signed a 10-year lease, with a right of first refusal for another five, thereby keeping the rental costs on their 2,800 square feet well below the recommended 11 percent of total costs. Thanks to word of mouth and a warm reception from locals, the restaurant did as much business in six months as they'd expected to do in a year.

Maintaining that goodwill requires spending money. Restaurant food costs are generally about 30 percent of the menu price, but costs at Chambar run about 4 percent higher because the duo place an emphasis on fresh ingredients—they use only seasonal vegetables and fish, and seafood from a sustainable harvesting program in Vancouver. While food costs of 34 percent are the average for some of their menu, staples like lamb and other dishes make little or no money. The $15 foie gras, for example, is on the menu not because it's profitable but because it attracts affluent customers who have a taste for the delicacy.

Based on her experience at Chambar, Karri recommends any prospective restaurant owner bank at least six months' worth of cash flow before opening their doors. "You have to leave some breathing room," she says. "The stress can be unbelievable." And one more thing: "Don't sign a lease or start construction until you have the money in the bank." (www.chambar.com)

Source: Omar el Akkad, *The Globe and Mail, Report on Small Business,* June 20, 2006. Used with permission.

DEVELOPING YOUR STATEMENT OF CASH FLOWS

Estimate Your Revenues

In most small businesses, not all sales are for cash. It is normal practice to accept credit cards or to extend terms to many customers. As a result, the revenue from a sale may not be realized until 30 days, 60 days, or even longer after the actual sale is made. In developing your cash flow forecast, you must take into account such factors as:

- Your ratio of cash to credit card or credit sales
- Your normal terms of trade for credit customers
- The paying habits of your customers
- Proceeds from the sale of any auxiliary items or other assets of the business

Sales should be entered on the cash flow forecast only when the money has actually been received in payment.

Determine Your Expenditures

To estimate your cash outflow, you must consider:

- How promptly you will be required to pay for your material and supplies. It is not uncommon that a new business will have to pay for its inventory and supplies up front on a cash on delivery (COD) basis until it establishes a reputation for meeting its financial commitments. Then it may be able to obtain more favourable credit terms from its trade suppliers. These terms of trade should be reflected in the cash flow forecast. For example, if you have to pay your suppliers' invoices right away, the cash payouts would be reflected in the cash flow forecast during the same month in which the purchases were made. However, if you have to pay your suppliers' invoices within 30 days, the cash payouts for July's purchases will not be shown until August. In some cases, even longer-term trade credit can be negotiated, and then cash outlays may not be shown for two or even three months after the purchase has been received and invoiced.
- How you will pay your employees' wages and salaries (weekly, biweekly, or monthly).
- When you must pay your rent, utility bills, and other expenses. For example, your rent, telephone, utilities, and other occupancy costs are normally paid every month. Other expenses like insurance and licence fees may be estimated as monthly expenses but not treated that way for cash flow purposes. Your insurance annual premium of $5,000 may have to be paid in five instalments: $1,000 in each of January, March, May, July, and September. That is how it must be entered on the cash flow worksheet. Your maintenance expenses may have to be paid as they are incurred and would be reflected as part of your estimated expenses for that month. Other expenses, such as licence fees and club memberships, might be in the form of an annual fee paid in a particular month of each year and would be shown when the actual expenditure is expected to be made.
- The interest and principal payments that you must make each month on any outstanding loans.
- Your plans for increasing your inventory requirements or acquiring additional assets.

Reconciling Your Cash Revenues and Cash Expenditures

To illustrate, let us continue to consider the situation of Tough Guys Sporting Goods. Tough Guys plans to open its doors at the beginning of the new year. Its owner wants to develop a monthly cash flow forecast for the expected first year of operation of the business and has made the following forecasts (Figure 4.4):

- Total sales for the year are projected to be $833,333, with a strong seasonal pattern peaking in June and July.
- Of the store's monthly sales, 60 percent are cash sales, and 40 percent are credit card sales, for which the cash is received in the following month.

FIGURE 4.4 PRO FORMA CASH FLOW FORECAST FOR TOUGH GUYS SPORTING GOODS

12-MONTH CASH FLOW PROJECTIONS

Minimum Cash Balance Required = $5,000

	January	February	March	April	May	June	July	August	September	October	November	December	Year 1 TOTAL
Cash Flow From Operations (during month)													
1. Cash Sales	17,136	25,412	33,385	43,350	48,333	55,808	62,285	55,309	43,350	39,364	36,375	43,350	503,459
2. Payments for Credit Sales	0	16,942	22,257	28,900	32,222	37,205	41,523	36,873	28,900	26,243	24,250	28,900	324,215
3. Investment Income	0	0	0	0	0	0	0	0	0	0	0	0	0
4. Other Cash Income	0	0	0	0	0	0	0	0	0	0	0	0	0
A. TOTAL CASH FLOW ON HAND	$17,136	$42,354	$55,641	$72,251	$80,555	$93,013	$103,809	$92,182	$72,251	$65,607	$60,624	$72,251	$830,469
Less: Expenses Paid (during month)													
5. Inventory or New Material	−31,461	−39,427	−47,838	−54,146	−61,611	−62,767	−53,305	−44,053	−40,268	−41,319	−38,165	−21,571	−535,929
6. Owner's Salary	−3,325	−3,325	−3,325	−3,325	−3,325	−3,325	−3,325	−3,325	−3,325	−3,325	−3,325	−3,325	−39,900
7. Employee's Wages and Salaries	−5,146	−7,198	−9,405	−11,411	−12,916	−14,697	−14,973	−12,716	−10,509	−9,606	−9,857	−6,546	−85,079
8. Supplies and Postage	−750	−1,049	−1,370	−1,663	−1,882	−2,141	−2,181	−1,853	−1,531	−1,400	−1,436	−954	−18,209
9. Advertising and Promotion	−68	−95	−125	−151	−171	−195	−198	−168	−139	−127	−131	−87	−1,655
10. Delivery Expense	0	0	0	0	0	0	0	0	0	0	0	0	0
11. Travel	−3,000	−700	−700	−700	−700	−700	−700	−700	−700	−700	−700	−700	−10,700
12. Legal and Accounting Fees	0	0	0	0	0	0	0	0	0	0	0	0	−5,000
13. Vehicle Expense	0	−1,500	0	0	−1,000	0	−1,300	0	−300	0	−900	0	−5,000
14. Maintenance Expense	−3,200	−3,200	−3,200	−3,200	−3,200	−3,200	−3,200	−3,200	−3,200	−3,200	−3,200	−3,200	−38,400
15. Rent	−580	−580	−580	−580	−580	−580	−580	−580	−580	−580	−580	−580	−6,960
16. Utilities	−100	−100	−100	−100	−100	−100	−100	−100	−100	−100	−100	−100	−1,200
17. Telephone	0	0	0	0	0	0	0	0	0	0	0	0	0
18. Taxes and Licences	0	−240	−372	−500	−560	−648	−656	−520	−356	−304	−292	−304	−4,752
19. Interest Payments	−1,000	0	−1,000	0	−1,000	0	−1,000	0	−1,000	0	0	0	−5,000
20. Insurance	0	0	0	0	0	0	0	0	0	0	0	0	0
21. Other Cash Expenses	−1,874	−2,622	−3,426	−4,156	−4,705	−5,353	−5,454	−4,632	−3,828	−3,499	−3,590	−2,384	−45,522
B. TOTAL EXPENDITURES	($50,504)	($60,000)	($71,440)	($79,932)	($91,749)	($93,706)	($86,972)	($71,846)	($85,835)	($64,159)	($62,275)	($39,751)	−($838,206)
Capital													
Purchase of Fixed Assets	0	0	0	0	0	0	0	0	0	0	0	0	0
Sale of Fixed Assets	0	0	0	0	0	0	0	0	0	0	0	0	0
C. CHANGE IN CASH FROM PURCHASE OR SALE OF ASSESTS	$0	$0	$0	$0	$0	$0	$0	$0	$0	$0	$0	$0	0
Financing													
Payment of Principal of Loan	0	0	0	0	0	0	−17,000	−20,500	−6,500	−1,500	0	−31,200	−76,700
Inflow of Cash from Bank Loan	30,000	16,500	16,000	7,500	11,000	1,000	0	0	0	0	1,500	0	83,500
Issuance of Equity Positions	0	0	0	0	0	0	0	0	0	0	0	0	0
Repurchase of Outstanding Equity	0	0	0	0	0	0	0	0	0	0	0	0	0
D. CHANGE IN CASH FROM FINANCING	$30,000	$16,500	$16,000	$7,500	$11,000	$1,000	($17,000)	($20,500)	($6,500)	($1,500)	($1,500)	($31,200)	$6,800
E. INCREASE (DECREASE) IN CASH	($3,368)	($1,181)	$201	($182)	($194)	$306	($163)	($164)	($84)	($52)	($151)	$1,300	−($3,732)
F. CASH AT BEGINNING OF PERIOD	$10,000	$6,632	$5,450	$5,652	$5,470	$5,276	$5,582	$5,419	$5,255	$5,171	$5,119	$4,968	$10,000
G. CASH AT END OF PERIOD	$6,632	$5,450	$5,652	$5,470	$5,276	$5,582	$5,419	$5,255	$5,171	$5,119	$4,968	$6,268	$6,268
MEET MINIMUM CASH BALANCE	ACCEPTABLE	ACCEPTABLE	ACCEPTABLE	ACCEPTABLE	ACCEPTABLE	ACCEPTABLE	ACCEPTABLE	ACCEPTABLE	ACCEPTABLE	ACCEPTABLE	FINANCE	ACCEPTABLE	ACCEPTABLE

- Inventory is purchased one month in advance of when it is likely to be sold. It is paid for in the month it is sold. Purchases equal 65 percent of projected sales for the next month.

- Cash expenses have been estimated for such items as the owner's salary and employees' wages and salaries, advertising and promotion expenses, delivery expense, rent, utilities, taxes and licences, insurance, and other expenses.

- The store's beginning cash balance is $10,000, and $5,000 is the minimum cash balance that should be available at the beginning of every month.

- The store has negotiated a line of credit with the bank at an annual interest rate of 10 percent, but the interest due has to be paid monthly. This line of credit can be drawn on to ensure the business has its $5,000 minimum cash balance available each month up to a limit of $80,000 and will be paid down as surplus cash becomes available.

At the end of each month it shows the cash balance that is available to be carried over to the next month's operations. To this it adds the total of the next month's cash receipts and subtracts the total of the next month's cash expenditures to determine the adjusted balance to be carried forward to the following month. In summary form, this relationship can be demonstrated by the following formula:

**Forecasted Cash Flow in Month (x) = Cash Balance Carried Over from Month (x − 1)
+ Expected Cash Inflow in Month (x) − Estimated Cash Expenditures in Month (x)**

As you can see, cumulative cash surpluses or shortfalls are clearly evident well in advance of their actual occurrence. Knowing this information in advance can assist you in scheduling your initial capital expenditures, monitoring your accounts receivable, and avoiding temporary cash shortages and can enable you to plan your short-term cash requirements well in advance. Tough Guys, for example, does not achieve a positive cash flow until July. The business will be forced to draw on its line of credit in January, February, March, April, May, and June to make certain it will have the necessary minimum cash balance available to continue to run the business. Preparing a pro forma cash flow forecast enabled Bill to anticipate these needs and avoid the possibility of any nasty surprises.

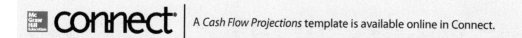

A *Cash Flow Projections* template is available online in Connect.

PRO FORMA BALANCE SHEET

One more financial statement should also be developed—*a pro forma balance sheet*. A balance sheet provides a snapshot of your business's health at a point in time. It tells you the value of your business at any point by forecasting what your business will own (*assets*) and what it will owe to other people, companies, and financial institutions (*liabilities*) to determine its *equity or net worth*. The basic formula of the balance sheet is:

Assets = Liabilities + Net Worth

The first section of the balance sheet deals with assets. *Current assets* would include an estimate of your expected average accounts receivable, startup inventory requirements, available cash, and similar items. *Fixed assets* are typically such items as buildings, furniture, fixtures, machinery and equipment, automobiles, and other capital items that you will need to operate your business. Except for land, fixed assets typically are used up over a period of years and therefore must be gradually *depreciated* in value.

The second part of a balance sheet lists liabilities. *Current liabilities* are debts you expect to incur that will fall due in less than 12 months. These usually include bills from your suppliers for the supplies and raw materials you will need for your initial inventory, short-term loans from banks and other financial institutions, any portion of your long-term debt that must be repaid during your initial year of operation, and so on. *Long-term liabilities* include any outstanding mortgages on land and buildings, notes on machinery and equipment, personal loans that you, your partners, and other stockholders may have made to the business, and any other outstanding loans of a long-term nature.

Net worth represents the value of your investment and equity in the business. Net worth can be composed of the total capital invested in the business by you and any other inside or outside investors plus any profits that have been generated by the business that have been retained within the company rather than being paid out in dividends or other means or minus any losses that may have accumulated in the business.

A typical pro forma balance sheet is illustrated in Figure 4.5.

A *Balance Sheet* template is available online in Connect.

How to Analyze Your Pro Forma Statements

Once you have created a pro forma income statement, cash flow statement, and balance sheet for your business, there are some easy calculations you can perform that will give you a better understanding of your company. You can calculate a number of *financial ratios* that can help you manage your business and make knowledgeable decisions related to some key questions, such as:

- Does the business have the capacity to meet its short-term financial obligations?
- Is the business producing adequate operating profits based on the level of assets it employs?
- Are the owners receiving an acceptable return on their investment?

A ratio shows the relationship between two numbers. It describes the relative size of the two numbers as they relate to one another and so eliminates the problem of trying to compare things on different scales.

Financial ratios can be used to compare the financial performance of two businesses of different size or to compare the performance of a company with others in the same business or the industry average (industry ratios). This application will be discussed in Stage Ten relative to analyzing the financial position of a business you might be looking to buy. Financial ratios can also be used to compare your business's performance from one time period with another, and that is the application we will look at here.

Financial ratios can be categorized into three common groups to analyze different aspects of your business:

1. **Liquidity ratios** help you understand your business's ability to meet its short-term obligations and continue to maintain its normal operations. The more liquid assets you have, the better it would be for you because they can be readily converted into cash.

2. **Profitability ratios** tell you how well you measure up in creating financial value in your business. The money you have invested in the venture could just as easily have been invested in other things, such as real estate, bonds, and other securities, so you need to know whether your business can generate the kind of returns that justify the risks involved.

3. **Leverage ratios** measure the level of debt the business has and its ability to pay back this debt over a long period of time.

Examples of some of the more commonly used ratios of each type are illustrated in the Other Considerations box on the page 125.

FIGURE 4.5 SAMPLE PRO FORMA BALANCE SHEET

TOUGH GUYS SPORTING GOODS BALANCE SHEET
End of Year 1

ASSETS

Current Assets:

1. Cash		6,300
2. Accounts Receivable		28,900
3. Inventory		231,000
4. Other Current Assets		30,500

A. TOTAL CURRENT ASSETS — **$296,700**

Fixed Assets:

5. Land and Buildings	0	
Less: Depreciation	0	0
6. Furniture and Fixtures	46,000	
Less: Depreciation	2,300	43,700
7. Equipment	0	
Less: Depreciation	0	0
8. Trucks and Automobiles	0	
Less: Depreciation	0	0
9. Other Fixed Assets	34,000	
Less: Depreciation	3,000	31,000

B. TOTAL FIXED ASSETS — **$74,700**

C. TOTAL ASSETS (C = A + B) — **$371,400**

LIABILITIES

Current Liabilities (due within 12 months):

10. Accounts Payable		150,000
11. Bank Loans/Other Loans		30,000
12. Taxes Owed		0

D. TOTAL CURRENT LIABILITIES — **$180,000**

Long-Term Liabilities:

13. Notes Payable (due after one year)	140,000	
14. Other Long-Term Liabilities	35,400	

E. TOTAL LONG-TERM LIABILITIES — **$175,400**

F. TOTAL LIABILITIES (F = D + E) — **$355,400**

Net Worth (Capital):

15. Share Capital:		
Common Shares		1,000
Preferred Shares		0
16. Retained Earnings		15,000

G. TOTAL NET WORTH (G = C − F) — **$ 16,000**

H. TOTAL LIABILITIES AND NET WORTH (H = F + G) — **$371,400**

Numbers may not match exactly due to rounding.

OTHER CONSIDERATIONS

EXAMPLES OF KEY FINANCIAL RATIOS

LIQUIDITY RATIOS

1. Current Ratio = Current Assets/Current Liabilities
2. Quick Ratio = (Current Assets − Inventories)/Current Liabilities

PROFITABILITY RATIOS

1. Gross Margin Ratio = Gross Profit Margin/Net Sales
2. Net Profit Ratio = Net Profit before Taxes/Net Sales
3. Return on Assets = Net Profit before Taxes/Total Assets
4. Return on Owner Investment = Net Profit before Taxes/Net Worth

LEVERAGE RATIOS

1. Times Interest Earned Ratio = Net Income before Interest and Taxes/Interest Expense
2. Debt-to-Equity Ratio = Long-Term Liabilities/Net Worth

DETERMINE YOUR BREAK-EVEN POINT

As your preliminary financial forecasts begin to clarify the size of the potential opportunity you are investigating, there is one other key question to explore: What sales volume will be required for your business to break even? This *break-even* point indicates the level of operation of the business at which your total costs equal your total revenue. The break-even point is important because it indicates when your business begins to make a profit. If your sales level is less than the break-even point, your business will suffer a loss.

The break-even point is affected by several factors, including your fixed and variable costs and your selling price. *Fixed costs or expenses* are those that remain constant regardless of your level of sales or production. *Variable costs* vary directly with the amount of business you do. For example, your rent is a fixed cost because it remains the same regardless of your level of sales. Your cost of goods sold, however, is variable because the amount you spend is directly related to how much you sell. Fixed costs typically include insurance, licences and permits, property taxes, rent, and similar expenses. Variable costs include supplies, salaries and wages, raw material, utilities, and delivery expenses. Variable costs are usually determined on the basis of per-unit or per-dollar sales.

The break-even point can be determined algebraically. The basic formula is:

$$\text{Break-Even Point (Units)} = \frac{\text{Total Fixed Costs}}{\text{Contribution Margin per Unit}}$$

where:

Contribution Margin per Unit = Selling Price per Unit − Variable Cost per Unit

and the *contribution margin* ratio can be determined by:

Contribution Margin Ratio = Contribution Margin per Unit Divided by the Selling Price per Unit

Algebraically, that relationship can be expressed as:

$$\text{Contribution Margin Ratio} = \frac{1 - \text{Average Variable Cost per Unit}}{\text{Selling Price per Unit}}$$

Understanding this relationship enables us to also calculate the break-even point in dollars. The basic formula for this determination is:

$$\text{Break-Even Point (Dollars)} = \frac{\text{Total Fixed Costs}}{1 - \dfrac{\text{Average Variable Cost}}{\text{Selling Price per Unit}}}$$

$$= \frac{\text{Total Fixed Costs}}{\text{Contribution Margin per Unit}}$$

Or if we are looking at the global situation for a business:

$$\text{Break-Even Point (Units)} = \frac{\text{Total Fixed Costs}}{1 - \dfrac{\text{Total Variable Cost}}{\text{Total Net Sales}}}$$

The following example may help illustrate the break-even concept. Suppose that the financial statements for Gino's Pizzeria, a pizza delivery outlet, indicate that the business's fixed costs every month for rent, utilities, interest expense, insurance, and similar items are roughly $3,600 per month. In addition, Gino has determined that his variable costs for making a typical large pizza are as follows:

Dough	$1.40
Tomato sauce	0.35
Cheese	0.75
Toppings	0.75
Delivery box	0.25
Delivery cost	0.50
Total Cost	$4.00

Rather than take a regular salary, Gino has decided to take any net income the business might generate as his income. In addition, Gino's sells a typical large pizza for $10.

From this information, you can see that after the $4 in variable costs have been covered, each pizza sold can contribute $6 toward covering the fixed costs of Gino's business. This is called his *contribution margin*. His contribution margin per unit can then be expressed as follows:

$$\begin{aligned}
\text{Contribution Margin per Unit} &= \text{Selling Price} - \text{Total Variable Cost} \\
&= \$10 - \$4 \\
&= \$6 \text{ per pizza}
\end{aligned}$$

But how many pizzas will Gino have to sell every month to break even? This can be determined as follows:

$$\frac{\text{Total Fixed Costs}}{\text{Contribution Margin per Unit}} = \text{Break-Even Volume (Units)}$$

Or, in this case:

$$\frac{\$3,600}{\$6} = 600 \text{ pizzas per month}$$

Therefore, Gino must sell a minimum of 600 pizzas every month or roughly 20 pizzas a day to cover his fixed costs of doing business. Even at that level of operation, he does not earn any income for himself. It is only after his sales exceed this level that the business starts to generate sufficient revenue to provide him with some compensation for his time and effort and give him a return on the money he has invested in the business. For example, if Gino should sell 800 pizzas one month, that would generate an income of $1,200 for him as a return on his time and money. On the other hand, if he sells only 500 pizzas, his business would incur a loss of $600.

To determine the volume of sales that Gino will have to achieve each month to reach his break-even point, we can use the formula:

$$\frac{\text{Total Fixed Costs}}{\text{Contribution Margin Ratio}} = \text{Break-Even Point (Dollars)}$$

Or, in this case:

$$\frac{\$3,600}{0.6} = \$6,000 \text{ in sales per month}$$

Therefore, Gino must sell a minimum of 600 pizzas or generate at least $6,000 in sales every month to cover his fixed costs of doing business.

As part of this exercise, Gino might ask himself, "What would happen if I raised my price to $11 for a large pizza? How would that affect my break-even point?"

Re-doing the calculation shows the following:
His Contribution Margin per pizza has now increased by $1 as follows:

$$\text{Contribution Margin per unit} = \text{Selling Price} - \text{Total Variable Cost}$$
$$= \$11 - \$4$$
$$= \$7 \text{ per pizza}$$

$$\text{Or a new break-even of } \frac{\$3,600}{\$7} = 514 \text{ pizzas}$$

So Gino would only have to sell slightly more than 500 pizzas a month if his customers would be prepared to pay an extra dollar each. That is an assessment he would have to make based on his knowledge of his customers, the competition, and his general understanding of local market conditions.

Similarly Gino might wonder if he should consider relocating to a new facility that has become available across the street. It has more parking for pick-up orders and higher traffic flows than where he is now but would increase his rent by $500/month. A similar assessment indicates that would raise his Total Fixed Costs to $4,100, assuming everything else stays the same, and would raise his break-even point as follows:

$$\text{Break-Even Point} = \frac{\text{Total Fixed Costs}}{\text{Contribution Margin per Unit}}$$

$$= \frac{\$4,100}{\$6} = 683 \text{ pizzas}$$

Or almost 15 percent more pizzas need to be sold per month than he needs to sell at his present location.

Based on his experience, Gino can now judge whether those options are changes he ought to seriously consider. Going through this type of evaluation can help him assess the implications of a range of different strategic options on the overall financial performance of his business.

Relating this notion to Tough Guys Sporting Goods store, we can also determine the volume of sales Bill would require to break even. If we assume all the operating expenses indicated in Figure 4.4 are fixed at least in the short term, including such items as salaries and wages, as well as advertising and promotion expenditures, the financial statement can be summarized as follows:

Projected sales $833,333
Projected fixed expenses $275,966
Projected variable expenses $544,166
(basically the cost of goods sold)

$$\text{Total sales needed to break even} = \text{Fixed Expenses} \div \frac{1 - \text{Variable Expenses}}{\text{Sales}}$$

$$= \$275,966 \div \frac{1 - \$544,166}{\$833,333}$$

$$= \$275,966 \div (1 - 0.652)$$

$$= \$275,966 \div 0.348$$

$$\mathbf{= \$793,000}$$

Therefore the store needs to sell at least $793,000 worth of merchandise in its first year to break even based on our estimate of its projected fixed costs and its average gross margin percentage and other variable costs. This concept is illustrated graphically in Figure 4.6.

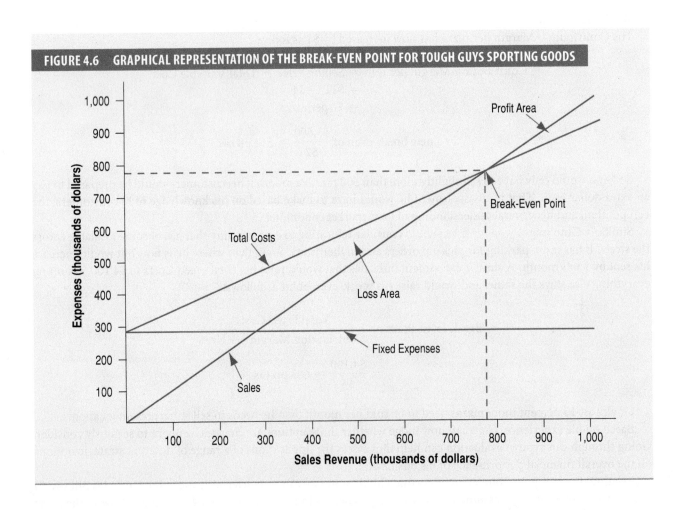

FIGURE 4.6   GRAPHICAL REPRESENTATION OF THE BREAK-EVEN POINT FOR TOUGH GUYS SPORTING GOODS

The value of break-even analysis is that it can be used to determine whether some planned course of action—for example, starting a new business, opening a new store, or adding a new item to your product line—has a chance of being profitable. Once you have estimated the break-even point for the action, you are in a better position to assess whether such a sales volume can be achieved and how long it will take to reach it.

It is essential that you determine the break-even level of operation for your business before you proceed very far with its implementation. Bankers and other financial people will expect to see this information as part of the financial documentation for your venture. In addition, if it appears that the break-even volume is not achievable, the business idea is probably destined to fail and should be abandoned before any money is invested.

COMPLETING A COMPREHENSIVE FEASIBILITY STUDY   LO2

A detailed framework template that you can use to conduct a comprehensive feasibility assessment of your own new venture idea is available online in Connect. Much of the information you have compiled in completing the worksheets in Stage four can be incorporated into the template.

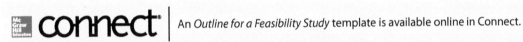

connect | An *Outline for a Feasibility Study* template is available online in Connect.

F Y I

For further information on preparing pro forma financial statements to evaluate the financial feasibility of your new venture idea, you might check out some of the following websites:

CCH Business Owner's Toolkit—Managing Your Business Finances An outline of the basic concepts of financial management as they apply to small business owners. Includes such topics as basic bookkeeping, credit management, managing your cash flow, and the evaluation of larger investments in facilities and capital equipment. (www.toolkit.com)

Business Development Bank of Canada (BDC) Ratio Calculators A ratio calculator that will compute the result of some of the most commonly used ratios for financial analysis. Brief explanations are provided. (http://www.bdc.ca)

Planning Guides: Manage Your Business and Watch It Grow. (Regions Financial Corp.) A comprehensive series of planning guides, including Creating a Profit and Loss Statement, Managing Your Cash Flow, and Preparing a Balance Sheet, which provide step-by-step instructions for the situations you may face when growing your business. (www.regions.com)

Industry Canada's SME Benchmarking Tool It offers industry-specific income statement and balance sheet data for small- and medium-sized businesses. SME Benchmarking Tool allows you to:

- Estimate the operating costs for your new business
- View financial performance averages in your industry
- Enter your own financial data to see how your business measures up to comparably sized firms

(www.ic.gc.ca)

LO1 **A cost and profitability assessment takes into account:**

- the financial components of your business, which may include, labour, materials, rent and machinery

- the collection of potential sales and cost information, which puts you in a better position to know whether you should proceed with your business and if you are in a position to look for financing

LO2 **A feasibility study includes:**

- templates you have completed

- additional information that you have provided in this stage

- the information on whether your business venture is viable or not.

For more information on the resources available from McGraw-Hill Ryerson, go to www.mcgrawhill.ca/he/solutions.

BUSINESS PLANS

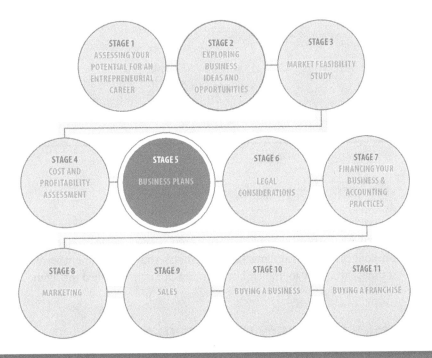

| STAGE 1 ASSESSING YOUR POTENTIAL FOR AN ENTREPRENEURIAL CAREER | STAGE 2 EXPLORING BUSINESS IDEAS AND OPPORTUNITIES | STAGE 3 MARKET FEASIBILITY STUDY |

| STAGE 4 COST AND PROFITABILITY ASSESSMENT | STAGE 5 BUSINESS PLANS | STAGE 6 LEGAL CONSIDERATIONS | STAGE 7 FINANCING YOUR BUSINESS & ACCOUNTING PRACTICES |

| STAGE 8 MARKETING | STAGE 9 SALES | STAGE 10 BUYING A BUSINESS | STAGE 11 BUYING A FRANCHISE |

LEARNING OBJECTIVES

By the end of this stage, you should be able to:

LO1 Summarize what a business plan is.

LO2 Explain the importance of a business plan in your business.

LO3 Identify what should be included in a business plan.

DOWNTOWN KIDS ACADEMY

Source: Toronto Business Development Centre (http://www.tbdc.com/stories.php). Used with permission from DownTown Kids Academy.

Research conducted by Libby Lund-Pedersen identified a viable opportunity for a daycare centre in the rapidly growing neighbourhood of King West Village. Although the potential market was confirmed, there were still many unanswered questions, and Lund-Pedersen found herself at Toronto Business Development Centre (TBDC).

TBDC helped Lund-Pedersen develop a comprehensive business plan through intensive entrepreneurial training and business adviser support. "The plan made it real," says Lund-Pedersen, adding that the business plan reinforced her commitment to the idea and proved to her that it was possible to launch the business. Another important benefit she recalls is the entrepreneurial atmosphere fostered and shared by all who are associated with TBDC.

Recognized by the National Post as one of "T.O.'s best daycares," Downtown Kids Academy expanded to almost 4,000 square feet with the addition of infant care facilities by the end of 2008 and grew from seven to nine full-time employees. Lund-Pedersen and business partner Tracy Lund-Pedersen have positioned Downtown Kids Academy for continued growth into the future.

Source: Toronto Business Development Centre (www.tbdc.com/stories.php). Used with permission from Downtown Kids Academy.

PREPARING YOUR BUSINESS PLAN   LO1

The next stage in building your dream for a new venture of your own is developing your business plan. A business plan is a written document that describes all aspects of your business venture—your basic product or service, your prospective customers, the competition, your production and marketing methods, your management team, how the business will be financed, and all the other things necessary to implement your idea. It might be called the "game plan" of your business.

BUSINESS PLANNING —THE "BIG PICTURE"

WHY CONSIDER THE "BIG PICTURE"?

When you start your business you will find that there are many things that happen that you did not expect or did not work out the way you expected. Do not worry. Your experience in this regard will not be unique. This happens to almost everyone. What is important is for you to be prepared for this to happen and be ready to make adjustments. In making these changes, it is important that you do not lose sight of what it is that you are really trying to do. This means that you need to keep in mind the "big picture," which is brought together in the business planning process.

THE STEPS IN THE BUSINESS PLANNING PROCESS

The business planning process focuses on the future. It enables you to relate what you wish to achieve to what your business concept or idea can deliver. It entails working your way through each of the following steps in a logical and sequential way. Figure 5.1 outlines the Steps in the Business Plan Process.

FIGURE 5.1   THE STEPS OF THE BUSINESS PLAN PROCESS

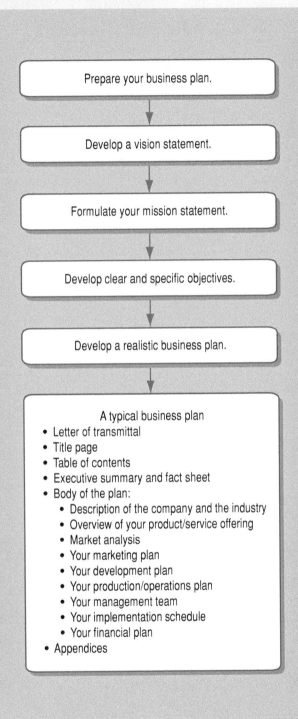

Prepare your business plan.

Develop a vision statement.

Formulate your mission statement.

Develop clear and specific objectives.

Develop a realistic business plan.

A typical business plan
- Letter of transmittal
- Title page
- Table of contents
- Executive summary and fact sheet
- Body of the plan:
  - Description of the company and the industry
  - Overview of your product/service offering
  - Market analysis
  - Your marketing plan
  - Your development plan
  - Your production/operations plan
  - Your management team
  - Your implementation schedule
  - Your financial plan
- Appendices

1. Develop a Vision Statement

A *vision statement* focuses on the "what" of your business and should describe your idealized perception of what your business will look like under perfect conditions, if all your goals and objectives have been met. It lays out the "super goal" that you would like your business to achieve. The key components of your *vision statement* will be:

- Name of your planned business venture
- Product/service offering you plan to provide
- Target market(s) you intend to serve

Your *vision statement* should be short (a sentence or two). It should also be easy to understand and easy to remember. For example, a typical *vision statement* for a new sporting goods retailer might be:

The Hockey House plans to provide a wide range of hockey-related products and services to casual skaters, minor league hockey players, community clubs and organizations, and competitive hockey teams and players.

2. Formulate a Mission Statement

A *mission statement* focuses on the "how" of your business. It defines the purpose of your venture, outlines the reason for the existence of your business, and provides some understanding of how your business will be operated. It is, in fact, the "super strategy" of your business. The key components of your *mission statement* will describe:

- What your business will do
- Its market focus, niche, or particular image
- Your planned location and the geographic market served
- How you plan to grow the business
- Your sustainable uniqueness, or what will distinguish your business from others and will continue to do so on a long-term basis

Your mission statement should be a series of short phrases that addresses each of these elements. For example, a mission statement for The Hockey House might state:

The Hockey House will provide a broad range of skates, sticks, pads, sweaters, and other related hockey equipment and services intended to meet the requirements of ice and in-line hockey players at all levels of ability, from beginners to semi-professionals and professionals. It will also sell related supplies and equipment, such as goal nets and timers, with a view to being the one-stop shop for hockey in Manitoba and northwestern Ontario. It will sell to individuals, teams, and community clubs through a retail outlet located adjacent to a major hockey complex in Winnipeg and through a website but will also produce a four-colour catalogue and call personally on groups in communities outside the city. Our principal competitive edge will be the breadth of selection we can offer and the quality of service we plan to provide.

3. Define the Fundamental Values By Which You Will Run Your Business

Many arguments, particularly in family businesses or partnerships, occur because the members do not share common values, even when they often assume that they do. For a new business to have a good chance of succeeding, all principals should agree on a basic set of values by which they will operate. The process of discussing and trying to achieve agreement on these values is likely to identify points of difference that should be addressed before the business is started. This process can be conducted in two steps. The first step requires you and any other principals associated with the business to define their own personal values. The second step consolidates the common values by which the business will be operated.

An example of a statement of business values might look like the following:

In conducting our business, we will implement our vision by conducting our affairs so that our actions provide evidence of the high value we place on:

Integrity, by dealing honestly with our customers, employees, suppliers, and the community

Responsibility, by taking into account the environment in which we do business, community views, and the common good

Profitability, by being conscious that an appropriate level of profit is necessary to sustain the business and allow our values to continue to be observed

Value, by providing quality products that are recognized as delivering value for money

Employees, by providing quality, equitable opportunities for development in a healthy workplace, with appropriate rewards

4. Set Clear and Specific Objectives

Setting objectives for your business provides you with metrics with which to measure your ability to achieve your vision. Objectives define measurable targets whose achievement can also contribute directly to the successful accomplishment of the mission of your business. Unlike "goals," which provide a broad direction for your business, "objectives" provide you with the means to measure directly the performance of your business.

Business objectives usually relate to such issues as:

- Return on investment the business should achieve
- Desired level of market position or market share
- Projected stages of technological development
- Specific levels of financial performance

To be effective an objective should:

- Refer to a specific outcome, not an activity
- Be measurable
- Be realistic and achievable based on the actual capabilities of the business
- Contain a specific time deadline

For example, a reasonable set of objectives for The Hockey House might be:

1. *To generate $xxxx in sales by the end of year one*
2. *To achieve $yyy in after-tax profits in year one*
3. *To increase inventory turnover from x times to y times during year one*

 | A framework that will enable you to develop the "big picture" for your business is available online in Connect.

5. Make It Happen! Develop a Realistic Business Plan

A business plan is an essential tool for any business. It is used to organize your thinking and development activities in advance of launching a business and to gauge your success in meeting goals as your enterprise evolves.

There is no single way to write a business plan. Its length and detail will depend on the type of business and the expectations of stakeholders, such as investors or financial institutions. Good business plans, whatever their length and level of detail, need to be clear, focused, realistic, and complete. Is your business concept easy to understand? Are your goals specific and focused on a limited number of achievable targets? Are your budget and development timeline realistic? Does your plan cover all essential considerations?

It is useful to think of a business plan as a *process* rather than a document. As circumstances change, your plan needs to adapt. Far too many business plans are introduced with pride and good intentions only to be forgotten in the hustle and bustle of running a business. But, without the guidance of a living business plan, how will you know where you stand—and where you are headed?

Preparing a business plan takes a lot of time, research, self-discipline, and commitment to complete properly; it is not a lot of fun and can be very daunting. However, regardless of whether you intend to start a small, part-time business in the basement of your home or launch a sophisticated, high-growth venture, you still need a business plan.

It is always suggested that you get help with your business plan from someone that has "been there, done that." This could be one of your volunteer business advisers or a professional who specializes in preparing business plans.

Your business plan is the culmination of all your self-evaluation, ideas, research, analysis, assessment, round-table discussions, bull sessions, schemes, and daydreams. It lays out the details so that everyone can see precisely where you are now, where you are going, and how you plan to get there. It presents everything about you and what you intend to do—your goals and objectives, opportunities and threats facing you, your business strengths and weaknesses, and so on. It is a comprehensive but concise disclosure of all aspects of your business venture.

How you define your business plan, however, affects your approach to writing it. If you view it as a very complex and boring task, your plan will come across that way to any reader. As a result, many business plans are dry, rambling, and highly technical because the entrepreneurs behind them see them largely as some sort of formal academic exercise.

Your business plan should be viewed as a selling document, not unlike a piece of sales literature you would distribute about your company. Except that with your business plan, rather than just promoting a particular product or service, you are selling the whole company as a package. If you are really excited about your company and the idea on which it is based, it should come through in your business plan. Your plan should convey to readers the excitement and promise that you feel about your venture.

WHY DEVELOP A BUSINESS PLAN? LO2

Your business plan can accomplish many things for you and your proposed venture. These can largely be categorized into two basic areas:

1. **For the internal evaluation of your business,** both as a checklist to see that you have covered all the important bases and as a timetable for accomplishing your stated objectives
2. **For external use** in attracting resources and obtaining support for your venture

From an internal perspective, developing a plan forces you to seriously consider the important elements of your venture and the steps you feel are necessary to get it off the ground. Your plan can be used to inform employees about the goals and direction of your business. It lets everyone know how they fit into the organization and what you expect of them. Your plan can also help you develop as a manager. It requires you to deal with problems relating to competitive conditions, promotional opportunities, and other situations that your business will encounter.

Externally, your business plan can serve as an effective sales document and is considered by many experts to be the heart of the capital-raising process. Any knowledgeable banker or prospective investor will expect you to be professional in your approach, fully prepared, and armed with a thoroughly researched, well-written business plan when seeking their support. Very little money has been raised for business ideas scribbled on the back of envelopes or on restaurant placemats, despite considerable folklore to the contrary.

Hans Downer became ActivDox's (see the Entrepreneurs in Action box) new president and CEO after founder and CEO David Thomson passed away suddenly. Hans found out quickly that the company was in dire need of funding and there was no solid business plan in place.

In the course of attracting external support for your venture, a number of people may have occasion to read your plan. These include bankers, suppliers, prospective customers, and potential investors. Each of them will be viewing your business from a slightly different perspective. Bankers, for example, are primarily interested in the business's fixed assets and other available collateral. They want to know if you can pay back their loan at prevailing interest rates. Venture capitalists and other private investors, on the other hand, are more interested in their expected return on investment. They tend to like innovative products and services in growth industries that promise significant returns. These differing viewpoints should be taken into account in developing your plan.

ENTREPRENEURS IN ACTION

PLANNING FOR THE WORST

When ActivDox founder and CEO David Thomson passed away suddenly last August following a heart attack, the board of the Ottawa-based document management startup scrambled to fill the void.

"There was no succession planning at all," said Hans Downer, who became the company's new president and CEO in September.

Through connections with various directors on the firm's board, Mr. Downer found out about the company and its need for someone to take the wheel. Because of his acquaintances, he gained the board's approval and jumped into his new role as head of a company that he only recently learned existed.

Beginning on September 11, Mr. Downer said there was enough money in the bank to satisfy payroll until the end of that month. His first order of business was to find funding.

"I had to do an investor presentation at the end of September. I had started (at the company) two weeks earlier," he said. "At that point, I kind of knew where the bathroom was and that was about it. It was pretty awkward."

Despite that, Mr. Downer managed to secure angel financing from the Oakville, Ontario–based Angel One Investor Network, as well as funds from Ottawa's Capital Angel Network, raising a total of $515,000 since October. That adds to the company's previous angel funding of $625,000 raised by Mr. Thomson and the $1 million in funding from the Federal Economic Development Agency for Southern Ontario— financing that was conditional on ActivDox obtaining $2 million from other sources. Mr. Downer said he expects to raise the remaining funds by the end of March. But funding wasn't the only challenge the new president and CEO faced.

"You've got a brilliant founder and some of the stuff is written down, and some of the stuff is in his head," he

MARK HOLLERON / OTTAWA BUSINESS JOURNAL

said. "Putting all the pieces back together was extremely difficult."

The startup is also in the process of changing its name to SavvyDox to avoid conflict with a company called ActiveDocs that's headquartered in New Zealand.

Yet the company is still on the path to success, with its developers—all seasoned professionals who came from Adobe Systems Inc.—working through Mr. Thomson's death to come up with a prototype.

"The demo just blew the socks off everybody," Mr. Downer said. It also landed the company two pilot projects that will begin this month: one with IT company CGI Group for a large-scale enterprise resource planning implementation in Ventura County, California; one to assist U.S.-based construction company Burns & McDonnell with the implementation of an oil pipeline in Alberta.

These 45-day projects will prepare ActivDox to launch its product in April or May, Mr. Downer said.

Source: Courtney Symons, *Ottawa Business Journal*, February 7, 2013 (www.obj.ca/Technology/2013-02-07/article-3170135/Planning-for-the-worst/1).

HOW LONG SHOULD YOUR BUSINESS PLAN BE?

Page count is not a good way to measure length of a business plan according to Tim Berry, founder of Palo Alto Business Plans.[1] You should measure a plan by readability and summarization. A good business plan should give the reader a general idea of its main contents after only skimming and browsing the main points in 15 minutes. The main points should show up in a business plan as quickly as they do in a business presentation.

When doing your plan, do not discount the importance of graphs, including infographics. The less someone has to read, the better, so if you can replace written words by using a graph, then do it.

You can ask 10 different people what they expect a business plan to be, and you will get 10 different answers. Tim Berry has sold millions of copies of his business plan software and his book, *The Plan-As-You-Go Business Plan*. He says to keep the business plan small, expect it to change, review and revise it often, and use it to steer and manage your business.

OTHER CONSIDERATIONS

10 REASONS WHY YOU SHOULD WRITE A BUSINESS PLAN

Small Business Trends asked members of the Young Entrepreneur Council (YEC): "What is a good reason to write a business plan even if you're not going for a bank loan or venture capital?"

1. **Clarity** "Writing a business plan or putting together an investor deck allows you to think more clearly about what you're doing and where you are going."

2. **Gain a Deep Understanding of Your Market** "Although it took several weeks and I've barely looked at it since, I credit my business plan for helping me understand a brand-new industry in an extremely deep way before actually entering it, and for forcing me to deeply examine how we would fit into the market."

3. **Organization** "The biggest reason to write out a business plan regardless of any financing option concerns is that it can help you stay organized and remain on track."

4. **Practice Makes Perfect** "It's great to write one simply to throw it away. The mental gymnastics are great. The plan is basically worthless the moment you're finished—but it will force you to think about things you might not have otherwise."

5. **Confirm the Math** "A lot of ideas sound great on paper and even in discussions. However, simple math can make or break an idea."

6. **Iron Out Possible Kinks** "Writing a business plan allows you to really think things through. Your plan should question the validity of your ideas, the product/service target markets, and so on."

7. **Foster Alignment** "Writing a business plan is an ideal way to make sure that everyone on your founding team is aligned with the current and future plans for the business."

8. **Hold Yourself Accountable** "A business plan is a great tool that allows founders to articulate their vision and future plans for their company."

9. **Know Your Message** "Business planning is incredibly helpful for describing what you do, understanding who your competitors are, and crafting a realistic three to five year plan."

10. **Establish Benchmarks** "Business plans are a valuable, iterative, document that can serve as a successful benchmarking tool."

Source: Anita Campbell, *Small Business Trends*, January 13, 2013 (http://smallbiztrends.com/2013/01/10-reasons-write-business-plan.html).

Companies that have adapted the lean startup methodology do not always think they need a business plan, but as Tim Berry states, "Regardless of the name or label, business planning has, in fact, changed in recent years. It has become leaner and more agile." The long-winded formal business plan is obsolete.[2]

Nobody should postpone starting a business because they do not have a business plan. A business plan should not be long winded or formal, and a realistic useful business plan becomes obsolete very quickly.

The Other Considerations box gives some tips for adopting lean business planning instead of a formal business plan. The most important parts of any business plan need to include:

- An executive summary that outlines your business, who the people are, and what the business goals are

- Market opportunity and competitive advantage—is there a need and demand?

- Goals and business strategy—how are you going to achieve your goals?

- Detailed financials

If you are looking for financing, check with the financial institution or investor to see what kind of plan they are looking for. Banks like you to get right to the point; they do not want a bunch of words, they want action. Once they

OTHER CONSIDERATIONS

IN PRAISE OF THE LEAN BUSINESS PLAN

The Lean Startup . . . relies on validated learning, scientific experimentation, and iterative product releases to shorten product development cycles, measure progress, and gain valuable customer feedback. In this way, companies, especially startups, can design their products or services to meet the demands of their customer base without requiring large amounts of initial funding or expensive product launches.[3]

The sense of flexibility, rapid change and iteration in the lean startup makes perfect sense with business planning too. Both startups and business plans need to reflect the rapid change in business landscape as technology advances.

As military leader and former president Dwight Eisenhower once said: "The plan is useless. But planning is essential."

Here are some tips for adopting lean business planning (even if I call it plan-as-you go) for your business. And this is for your business, regardless of whether or not you need a plan document to take to a bank or show potential investors. This is for running your business better:

1. The first and most essential component of the plan is the review schedule. Set up a set day of the month for taking an hour or two and reviewing the plan, looking at actual results, and comparing them to the plan, and revising as necessary.

2. Always list assumptions. The best way to tell whether you need to change a plan or stick to a plan is to look at whether assumptions have changed. In today's world, the assumptions change quickly. When assumptions change, the plan has to change.

3. Keep it short, simple and just big enough. It's not a text. It's a loosely related collection of modules. Use bullets and don't sweat the style, format, or editing. It can live on your computer in different files for different components.

4. Spreadsheets are great for financial projections, bullet points for strategy and focus, and lists for tasks and responsibilities and metrics and milestones.

5. Keep it focused on its business purpose. For most of us, it's about managing better, as in breaking long-term goals into meaningful steps and defining metrics and tracking results. In some special cases, it's for communicating with outsiders. If it's not a document for bankers or investors, don't waste time making it pretty. Don't waste time writing out what everybody in the company already knows.

6. Always include milestones. Those are specific lists of what is supposed to happen and when, how much it costs or brings in, and who is responsible for it.

7. Always include basic numbers. Cash flow is the life-blood of the business and you can't afford not to plan and manage for cash. In practice, it takes projected sales, costs, expenses, assets, liabilities, and capital to predict cash.

And that's what you can call a lean business plan. Don't ever expect to finish it, because when the plan's finished, your business is finished. And don't expect it to be right, because management isn't about guessing right, but rather knowing how and in what direction you guessed wrong and how to correct.

Source: Adapted from "In Praise of the Lean Business Plan," Tim Berry, Guest Blogger, SBA.gov, November 30, 2012. With permission. (www.sba.gov). Search for In Praise of the Lean Business Plan.

have made it past the executive summary, they will skip to the financials. They are looking for projected sales for a minimum of two years. The first year needs to be broken down monthly, with the second indicating annual projections. Banks also want you to lay out your contingency plan in the event your original idea does not work.

Bankers are experienced in most industries and know what the reasonable ask should be. Assumptions and projects need to be laid out in detail. For example, if you are opening a restaurant the bank will want to know your projected revenues and expenses for breakfast, lunch, and dinner with further breakdown of food and alcohol.

However, many people and financial institutions still use a page count as measurement for business plans, which are outlined in the following sections.

ENTREPRENEURS IN ACTION

CHANGING BUSINESS PLANS SAVE TORONTO'S WHATIMWEAR.IN

Monica Mei, the 30-year-old founder of Toronto-based software startup WhatImWear.in, was facing a potentially ruinous problem. She had begun promoting her company long before her product—a smartphone application that lets users to share photos of what they are wearing—was ready for the masses. When the app was finally finished, in fall 2011, companies with similar products had already caught wind of its features and had adapted accordingly. WhatImWear.in's niche at the intersection of social media and fashion, invitingly empty in 2010, was suddenly crowded with well-capitalized competition. Mei, meanwhile, found herself short on funding. "We just (didn't') have the luxury to sustain ourselves," she said.

Mei could have chosen to persevere in the hopes that users would suddenly flock to her product or that investors would inexplicably shower the company with money. Or she could have conceded defeat.

She picked a third option—changing her entire way of doing business. Lots of startups deal with similar situations. Any business plan, no matter how carefully crafted, is at best a working document. This means change—at a new company, anyway—is a virtual certainty. It is figuring out how to manage the process that can make things a little hairy.

"One of the great lies of entrepreneurship is persistence," said Dr. Steven Gedeon, professor of entrepreneurship at Ryerson University's Ted Rogers School of Management. "You have to be persistent to be successful. But you also have to be able to quit early and move on."

Gedeon says budding entrepreneurs must listen to their customers. It is tough to be like Apple, confidently making sure-fire products that consumers do not even know they want.

"Let's not forget Steve Jobs got kicked out of his company, and his next business was a failure," said Gedeon.

In Mei's case, customers were satisfied with other, more established products. So she decided to radically change course. She and her five employees have worked since January 2013

USED WITH PERMISSION OF WHATIMWEAR.IN.

to relaunch WhatImWear.in as a subscription-based tool for the underserved business market (they are keeping its functionality confidential to avoid the problems that plagued their first product).

The original app was free and meant to attract users with its functionality. Mei wanted to leverage that base to roll out a revenue plan over time. That model was also scrapped, and Mei thinks the new direction will bring in money from day one, because this time around, the service will not be free.

WhatImWear.in did not pivot because its product did not catch on, nor because it was targeting the wrong group. It just took too long to produce the software product and had told too many people too early. It was a communication problem between the technical and marketing teams at WhatImWear.in.

Source: Adapted from Star Business Club, Steve Kuperman, July 17, 2012 (www.starbusinessclub.ca/people/articles-people/changing-business-plans-save-torontos-whatimwear-in-spenz/#sthash.mwxdZGxJ.dpuf).

The Summary Business Plan

Summary business plans commonly run about 10 pages. Summary business plans have become increasingly popular and accepted for use by early-stage businesses in applying for a bank loan. A summary plan is a more "to the point" plan. This plan can be used for all types of business. Many tech startups think they need something different, but that is not the case, according to Doug Somers,[4] who reviews business plans on a regular basis. A summary business plan may also be enough to whet the appetite of friends, relatives, and other private investors who might subsequently request a copy of the full plan if they are sufficiently interested.

TIPS FOR DEVELOPING YOUR BUSINESS PLAN

Here are some pointers to consider in developing your business plan:

- **Business planning involves a great deal of work** Be prepared to spend weeks—or months—completing your plan.
- **Work on sections at a time** While this undertaking may appear overwhelming at first, do not get discouraged. Break the project down into manageable chunks, and work on each chunk separately.
- **Be brief but complete** Although you may have volumes of important material, aim for a plan that is brief and succinct but includes everything important to the business.
- **Focus on your intended reader** Use your plan to organize your efforts around your objectives to ensure you have all the bases covered.
- **Use lay person's terms** Avoid highly technical descriptions of your products, processes, and operations.
- **A business plan is a "living" document** Update it as your knowledge grows and whenever your plans become more concrete.
- **Be realistic** Base your projections on the results gathered from your analysis. Be honest about both positive and negative findings.
- **Discuss your firm's business risks** Your credibility can be seriously undermined if existing risks and problems are discovered by readers.
- **Do not make vague or unsubstantiated statements** Back up your statements with background data and market information.

Source: Adapted from *Entrepreneurial Edge*, Edward Lowe Foundation, "How to Develop and Use a Business Plan" (http://edwardlowe.org/erc/?ercID=7704), accessed March 7, 2013.

The Full Business Plan

A full business plan tends to slide or evolve into an operations plan that states for the next 12 months what the objectives are, who is doing what by when, how much is getting invested where, and how and when funds will be raised. Often a budget is included. The full business plan is frequently used for board approval but never used to manage the company.

The Operational Business Plan

The operational business plan will usually exceed 40 pages in length but is used only infrequently, such as when a business is planning to grow very rapidly and must try to anticipate a wide variety of issues. Or it might be part of an annual process in which it is necessary to get into great detail about distribution, production, advertising, and other areas where it is essential for everyone involved with the organization to understand clearly everything that is going on. Traditional business plans that grow to this length should be avoided as they reflect a lack of discipline and focus. But nothing says the plan has to be long. Doug Somers has seen operational plans that are more bare bones about objectives, responsibilities, and annual goals and become living documents used by management in day-to-day operations.

WHO SHOULD WRITE YOUR BUSINESS PLAN?

You should write your business plan. If someone else develops the business plan for you, it becomes his or her plan, not yours. In the case of a management team, each individual should contribute his or her part to the overall project.

Do not, under any circumstances, hire someone else to write the plan for you. This does not mean that you should not get help from others in compiling information; obtaining licences, permits, patents, and other legal considerations; or preparing your pro forma financial statements—only that the final plan should be written by you and your team.

The people who may be assessing your plan want to know that you see the big picture as it relates to your business and understand all the functional requirements of your company, not that you can hire a good consultant. It is very difficult to defend someone else's work. If you put your business plan together yourself, you have a better understanding and feel for the business. Your business plan should be a personal expression written in your own unique style, although, of course, it should look professional and businesslike.

HOW LONG DOES IT TAKE?

Putting together a business plan does not happen overnight. A plan for a relatively simple, straightforward business might be completed within a few weeks, while a plan for a complex, high growth new venture could take several months.

WHAT SHOULD YOUR PLAN CONTAIN? LO3

Your business plan is the nuts and bolts of your proposed business venture put down on paper. You will have to decide exactly what information to include, how your plan can be best organized for maximum effectiveness, and what information should be given particular emphasis. All plans, however, require a formal, structured presentation so that they are easy to read and follow and tend to avoid confusion. A number of forms and sample outlines for a business plan are available, but virtually all suggest that business plans contain the following components: (1) letter of transmittal, (2) title page, (3) table of contents, (4) executive summary and fact sheet, (5) body, and (6) appendices. The contents of a typical business plan are outlined in Figure 5.2. You can use this framework as a guideline to assist you in the development of the plan for your business.

1. LETTER OF TRANSMITTAL

The letter of transmittal officially introduces your business plan to the reader. It explains your reason for writing the plan, gives the title of the plan or the name of your business, and outlines the major features of your plan that may be of interest.

2. TITLE PAGE

The title page, or cover page, of your plan provides identifying information about you and your proposed business. It should include the name, address, and telephone number of the business as well as similar information about you. The date the plan was finalized or submitted to the recipient should also be included on the title page.

3. TABLE OF CONTENTS

The table of contents is a list of the major headings and subheadings contained in your plan. It provides readers with a quick overview of the contents of your plan and allows them to quickly access the particular sections that may be of primary interest to them.

4. EXECUTIVE SUMMARY

The executive summary is the most important part of your business plan. It must capture the attention of the reader, stimulate interest, and get the reader to keep on reading the rest of your plan. In two or three pages or less, the summary should concisely explain your business's current status; describe its products or services and their benefits to

FIGURE 5.2   A TYPICAL BUSINESS PLAN

Business Plan Contents

1. Letter of Transmittal
- Introduce your business plan to the reader.
- Outline the major features that may be of interest.

2. Title Page
- Provide identifying information about you and your proposed business: Name, address, and contact numbers for the business as well as key company contacts.

3. Table of Contents
- List the major headings and subheadings contained in your plan.

4. Executive Summary and Fact Sheet
- Include a 1–2 page summary of the most important points in your plan.
- The most important part of your business plan.
- Your Fact Sheet summarizes the basic information that relates to the venture.

5. Body of the Plan

Company and the Industry
- Provide the history and current situation of your company.
- List the goals and objectives for the business.
- Describe the principal characteristics and trends in the industry.

Product/Service Offering
- Give a detailed description of your product or service.
- Outline the stage of development and proprietary position.

Market Analysis
- Describe the profile of your principal target customers.
- Indicate current market size, trends, and seasonal patterns.
- Assess the nature of your competition.
- Estimate your expected sales and market share.

Your Marketing Plan
- Detail the marketing strategy you plan to use.
- Describe your marketing plan with respect to your sales strategy, advertising and promotion plans, pricing policy, and channels of distribution.

Your Development Plan
- Outline the development status of your product and what is still required to get it to a market-ready state.
- Are there regulatory, testing, or other requirements that still have to be met?

(continued)

FIGURE 5.2   A TYPICAL BUSINESS PLAN *(CONTINUED)*

Your Production/Operations Plan

- Outline the operating side of your business.
- Describe your location, kind of facilities, space requirements, capital equipment needs, and labour requirements.

Your Management Team

- Identify your key management people, their responsibilities, and their qualifications.
- Indicate the principal shareholders of the business, your principal advisors, and the members of your board of directors.

Your Implementation Schedule

- Present an overall schedule indicating what needs to be done to launch your business and the timing required to bring it about.
- Discuss the major problems and risks that you will have to deal with.

Your Financial Plan

- Indicate the type and amount of financing you are looking for and how the funds will be used.
- Outline your proposed terms of investment, the potential return to the investor, and what benefit is being provided.
- Provide an overview of the current financial structure of your business.
- Prepare realistic financial projections that reflect the effect of the financing, including:
  - Cash flow forecasts
  - Pro forma profit and loss statements
  - Pro forma balance sheet
  - Break-even analysis

6. Appendices

- Supporting material for your plan, including:
  - Detailed résumés of the management team
  - Product literature and photographs
  - Names of possible customers and suppliers
  - Consulting reports and market surveys
  - Copies of legal documents
  - Publicity material
  - Letters of reference

your customers; provide an overview of your venture's objectives, market prospects, and financial forecasts; and, if you are using the plan to raise external financing, indicate the amount of financing needed, how the money is to be used, and the benefits to the prospective lender or investor. The summary has to make the reader comfortable that the entrepreneur knows what he or she is doing. If you achieve this, then the reader may very well jump right to the financials. Impress the reader by ensuring your summary is concise and to the point. Do not add fluff to it.

People want to know that you know what you are doing, that you have thought through the viability of the business model and have considered the realistic steps to reach your goals, including have the right people on board. If you have reputable advisers, you should list their names to show the financiers that you have the means to make up for the lack of experience that you and your team may have.

The executive summary should give the essence of your plan and highlight its really significant points. In many instances, the summary will either sell the reader on continuing to read the rest of the document or convince him or her to forget the whole thing; the game may be won or lost on the basis of the executive summary.

The executive summary summarizes the basic information that relates to your venture and should be as short as possible—a one-pager is best, but it can go up to four pages and should include:

1. Company name
2. Company address, telephone/fax numbers, email address
3. Type of business and industry
4. Form of business organization (proprietorship, partnership, or corporation)
5. Principal product or service line
6. Registered patents or trademarks
7. Number and name of founders/partners/shareholders
8. Length of time in business
9. Current and/or projected market share
10. Funds invested in the business to date and their source
11. Additional financing required
12. Proposed terms and payback period
13. Total value or net worth of the business
14. Name of business advisers (legal counsel, accountant, others)

In some cases, businesses include some of the above information in a fact sheet, which is placed after the executive summary. If you decide to include a fact sheet, remember to include the most important points in the executive summary.

5. BODY OF THE PLAN

The body of your business plan is, by far, the longest component because it presents the detailed story of your business proposition. It should be broken down into major divisions with headings, and each major division divided into sections with subheadings. It is probably better to have too many, rather than not enough, headings and subheadings.

What follows is a typical overview of the kind of material that should be included in the body of your plan.

Your Company and the Industry

Describe the startup and background of your business, and provide the reader with some context within which to fit all the information you will be providing later in your plan.

Familiarize the reader with your company; the industry within which you will be competing, your understanding of it, and where it is headed; and what opportunities you see for your business.

Your Company

BACKGROUND Give the date your business was started, its present form of organization, its location, and pertinent historical information on the firm. Name the founders and other key people, how your key products or services were chosen and developed, and what success the business has achieved to date.

CURRENT SITUATION Discuss such issues as how you have identified your market opportunity, assessed the competition, and developed some unique factor or distinctive competence that will make your business stand out from the rest.

FUTURE PLANS Discuss your goals and ambitions for the business and your strategy for achieving them.

The Industry

PRINCIPAL CHARACTERISTICS Describe the current status and prospects for the industry in which your business will operate. How big is the industry? What are its total sales in dollars? In units? What are typical industry standards, gross margins, seasonal patterns, and similar factors?

MAJOR PARTICIPANTS Identify the major industry participants and describe their role, market share, and other performance measures. What are their principal strengths and weaknesses, and how do you think you will be able to successfully compete in this situation?

INDUSTRY TRENDS Discuss how you feel the industry will evolve in the future. Is it growing or stable? What do you feel industry sales will be five and ten years from now? What general trends are evident, and how is the industry likely to be affected by economic, social, technological, environmental, and regulatory trends?

Your Product/Service Offering

DESCRIPTION Describe in detail the product or service you plan to sell, explaining any unique characteristics or particular advantages. How will features of your product or service give you some advantage over competitors?

Indicate the stage of development your product is at and whether prototypes, working models, or finished production units are available. Include photographs, if possible.

PROPRIETARY POSITION Describe any patents or trademarks you may hold or have applied for, or any licensing agreements or other legal contracts that may provide some protection for your product or service. Are there any regulatory or government-approved standards or requirements your product must meet? How and when do you plan to obtain this certification?

POTENTIAL Outline your market opportunity as you see it and explain how you plan to take advantage of it. What are the key success factors in this business and how do you plan to exploit them to your advantage?

Most entrepreneurs do not have marketing experience and do not understand that a solid marketing strategy is essential to the success of a business. Others know but do not know where to start. It is important because if no one knows about you, how will they find you?

Market Analysis

This section of your plan should convince the reader that you thoroughly understand the market for your product or service and that you can deal with the competition and achieve sufficient sales to develop a viable and growing business. You should describe the total market and how you feel it can be broken down into segments. You can then indicate the segment or niche you plan to concentrate on and what share of this business you will be able to obtain.

Your analysis of the market may be based on:

1. Market studies available from private research firms and government departments and agencies
2. Statistics Canada or U.S. Census Bureau data
3. Information from trade associations and trade publications
4. Surveys or informal discussions with dealers, distributors, sales representatives, customers, or competitors

This is often one of the most difficult parts of the business plan to prepare, but it is also one of the most important. Almost all other sections of your business plan depend on the sales estimates developed from your market analysis. The outline provided in Stage Three can help you in this process.

TARGET MARKET AND CUSTOMERS Identify who constitute your primary target markets—individual consumers, companies, healthcare or educational institutions, government departments, or other groups.

Examine beforehand if these target markets can be segmented or broken down into relatively homogeneous groups having common, identifiable characteristics, such as geographic location, age, size, type of industry, or some other factor. Present these facts in the most logical or appropriate format.

Describe the profile of your principal target customers. Who and where are they? What are the principal bases for their purchase decisions? What are their major applications for your product? What principal benefit will they obtain from using your product rather than one of your competitors'?

Identify, if possible, some major buyers who may be prepared to make purchase commitments. If possible, get a purchase order.

MARKET SIZE AND TRENDS Estimate the size of the current total market for your product or service in both units and dollars. How are sales distributed among the various segments you identified? Are there any strong weekly, monthly, or seasonal patterns? Ensure you include the answers to these questions.

Describe how the market size for each of these segments has changed over the past three to four years in units and dollars. Outline how it is expected to change over the next three to four years.

Include the major factors that have affected past market growth (e.g., socioeconomic trends, industry trends, regulatory changes, government policy, population shifts). What is likely to happen in these areas in the future?

COMPETITION Identify each of your principal competitors. Make a realistic assessment of each of these firms and its product or service offering. Compare these competing products or services on the basis of price, quality, performance, service support, warranties, and other important features.

Present your evaluation of the market share of each segment by each competitor, its relative profitability, and its sales, marketing, distribution, and production capabilities. How do you see these factors changing in the future?

ESTIMATED SALES AND MARKET SHARE Estimate the share of each segment of the market and the sales in units and dollars that you feel you will acquire for each of the next three to five years. This should be developed by month for the next year and annually for each year thereafter. This information can be presented best in tabular form. Indicate on what assumptions you have based these projections.

F Y I   BUSINESS PLAN OUTLINES AND TEMPLATES

Here are some examples of websites that have detailed instructions, outlines, or templates for developing a comprehensive business plan.

Business Development Bank of Canada BDC Business plan templates let you prepare a professional business plan—a necessity when seeking financing for your project. (www.bdc.ca)

Canadian Bank Association The Small Business section within The Canadian Bankers Association website provides the information that small business owners need to start and run their own business, including things to consider when operating a small business, how to write a business plan, and the different financing options available to you. (www.cba.ca)

Canada Business Network The section under Business Planning gives you access to business plan templates and sample business plans. (www.canadabusiness.ca)

LivePlan LivePlan makes it easy for you to create a professional business plan. The site contains a collection of free sample business plans. (www.liveplan.com)

Community Business Development Corporations Online business plan is a web-based application allowing new and aspiring entrepreneurs the ability to prepare a three-year business plan online. (www.cbdc.ca)

Canadian Youth Business Foundation (CYBF) The CYBF Interactive Business Planner is a tool designed to guide both new and experienced entrepreneurs through the process of writing a comprehensive business plan. (www.cybf.ca)

BizPlanIt's Virtual Business Plan This unique and free online resource mirrors the major sections of a business plan and enables you to learn the fundamentals of writing a business plan. (www.bizplanit.com)

Your Marketing Plan

Your marketing plan outlines how your sales projections will be achieved. It details the marketing strategy you plan to use to establish your product or service in the marketplace and obtain a profitable share of the overall market. Your marketing plan should describe *what* is to be done, *when* it is to be done, *how* it is to be done, and *who* will do it insofar as your sales strategy, advertising and promotion plans, pricing policy, and channels of distribution are concerned.

PRICING Summarize the general financial characteristics of your business and the industry at large. What will be typical gross and net margins for each of the products or services you plan to sell? How do these compare with those of other firms in the industry? Provide a detailed breakdown of your estimated fixed, variable, and semivariable costs for each of your various products or services.

Discuss the price you plan to charge for your product. How does it compare with your major competitors' prices? Is your gross margin sufficient to cover your transportation costs, selling costs, advertising and promotion costs, rent, depreciation, and similar expenses—and still provide some margin of profit?

Detail the markups your product will provide to the various members of your channel of distribution. How do these compare with those they receive on comparable products? Does your markup provide them with sufficient incentive to handle your product?

Indicate your normal terms of sale. Do these conform to industry norms? Do you plan to offer cash, quantity, or other discounts?

Indicate how long it will take you to break even, basing your opinion on your anticipated cost structure and planned price.

SALES AND DISTRIBUTION Indicate the methods you will use to sell and distribute your product or service. Do you plan to use your own salaried or commissioned salespeople, rely on manufacturers' agents or other wholesalers and distributors, or utilize a more non traditional means of distributing your product, such as export trading companies, direct-mail selling, mail-order houses, party plan selling, or other means of selling directly to the final consumer?

If you plan to use your own salesforce, describe how large it will be and how it will be structured. Indicate how salespeople will be distributed, whom they will call on, how many calls you estimate it will take to get an order, the size of a typical order, how much you estimate a typical salesperson will sell each year, how he or she will be paid, how much he or she is likely to make in a year, and how this compares with the average for the industry.

If you plan to use distributors or wholesalers, indicate how they have been or will be selected; who they are, if possible; what areas or territory they will cover; how they will be compensated; credit and collection policies, and any special policies, such as exclusive rights, discounts, and cooperative advertising programs.

Indicate any plans for export sales or international marketing arrangements.

ADVERTISING AND PROMOTION Describe the program you plan to use to make consumers aware of your product or service. What consumers are you trying to reach? Do you plan to use the services of an advertising agency? What media do you plan to use—radio, television, newspapers, magazines, billboards, direct mail, coupons, brochures, trade shows? How much do you plan to spend on each medium? When? Which specific vehicles?

Outline any plans to obtain free publicity for your product or company.

SERVICE AND WARRANTY PROGRAM Indicate your service arrangements, warranty terms, and method of handling service problems. Describe how you will handle customer complaints and other problems. Will service be handled by the company, dealers and distributors, or independent service centres? How do these arrangements compare with those of your competitors?

Your Development Plan

If your product or service involves some further technical development, the planned extent of this work should be discussed in your business plan. Prospective investors, bankers, and others will want to know the nature and extent of any additional development required, how much it will cost, and how long it will take before your business has a finished, marketable product.

DEVELOPMENT STATUS Describe the current status of your product, and outline what still remains to be done to make it marketable. Do you presently have only a concept, detailed drawings, a laboratory prototype, a production prototype, or a finished product? Is further engineering work required? Has the necessary tooling to produce the product been adequately developed? Are the services of an industrial designer or other specialist required to refine the product into marketable form?

COSTS Indicate how much money has been spent on product development to date and where it has been spent. Present a development budget indicating the additional funds required, how they will be spent, and the timing involved in completing the project.

PROPRIETARY ISSUES Indicate any patents or trademarks that you own or have or for which you plan to apply. Are there any regulatory requirements to produce or market the product? Has the product undergone standardized testing through the Underwriters' Laboratory, the Canadian Standards Association, or some other agency? If not, what are your plans? Have you tested the product at all in the marketplace? What was the result?

Your Production/Operations Plan

Your production/operations plan outlines the operating side of your business. It should describe your plant location, the kind of facilities needed, space requirements, capital equipment needed, and your labour requirements.

If your plan is for a manufacturing business, you should also discuss such areas as your purchasing policy, quality control program, inventory control system, and production cost breakdown and whether you plan to manufacture all subcomponents of the product yourself or have some of them produced for you by someone else.

LOCATION Describe the planned location of your business, and discuss any advantages or disadvantages of this location in terms of the cost and availability of labour; proximity to customers; access to transportation, energy supplies, or other natural resources; and zoning and other legal requirements.

Discuss the characteristics of your location in relation to market size, traffic flows, local and regional growth rates, income levels, and similar market-related factors.

FACILITIES AND EQUIPMENT Describe the property and facilities currently used or that will be required to operate your business. This should include factory and office space, selling space, storage space, property size and location, and so on. Will these facilities be leased or purchased? What are the cost and timing of their acquisition?

Detail the machinery and equipment that is required for your manufacturing process. Is this highly specialized or general-purpose equipment? Is it leased or purchased? New or used? What is the cost? What will it cost for equipment set up and facility layout? What is its expected life? Will it have any residual or scrap value?

If possible, provide a drawing of the physical layout of the plant and other facilities.

MANUFACTURING PLANS AND COSTS Develop a manufacturing cost outline that shows standard production costs at various levels of operation. Break down total costs into raw material, component parts, labour, and overhead. Indicate your raw material, work-in-process, and finished goods inventory requirements at various sales levels. How will seasonal variations in demand be handled?

Indicate your key suppliers or subcontractors for various raw materials and components. What are the lead times for these materials? Are back-up suppliers or other alternatives available?

Outline the quality control procedures you will use to minimize service problems. Do you need any other production control measures?

On the basis of this configuration of facilities and equipment, indicate your production capacity. Where can this be expanded? Do you have any plans to modify existing plant space? What is the timing and cost?

LABOUR Describe the number of employees you have or need and their qualifications. Will they be full-time or part-time employees? Have you developed a job description for each position? What in-house training will be required? How much will each employee be paid? What kinds of pension plan, health insurance plan, profit-sharing plan, and other fringe benefits will be required? Have you registered with the necessary government departments?

Indicate whether your employees will be unionized or not. If employees will be members of a union, describe the principal terms of their contract and when it expires.

ENVIRONMENTAL AND OTHER ISSUES Indicate any approvals that it may be necessary for you to obtain in relation to zoning requirements, permits, licences, health and safety requirements, environmental approvals, and so on. Are there any laws or regulatory requirements unique to your business? Are there any other legal or contractual matters that should be considered?

Your Management Team

Your management team and your directors are the key to success. You should identify who your key people are; their qualifications; what they are being paid; who has overall authority; who is responsible for the various functional areas of the business, such as sales, marketing, production, research and development, and financial management; and so forth.

In most small businesses, there are no more than two or three really key players—including yourself. Concentrate on these individuals, indicating their education, qualifications, and past business achievements. Indicate how they will contribute to the success of the present venture. Do not hire friends, relatives, or other people for key positions if they do not have the proper qualifications.

Many external investors are more concerned about the management of the business than the business itself. They invest in the people rather than in the project. They will conduct a thorough and exhaustive investigation of each of your key players to determine whether they are the kind of people in whom they wish to invest. This portion of your plan should instill confidence in the management of your business in the mind of the reader.

DESCRIPTION OF MANAGEMENT TEAM Outline the exact duties and responsibilities of each key member of your management team. Prepare a brief résumé of each individual indicating education, professional qualifications, employment experience, and other personal achievements. (You will include a complete, more detailed résumé for each of these individuals in an appendix to your plan.)

DIRECTORS Indicate the size and composition of your board of directors. Identify any individuals you are planning to invite to sit on your board. Include a brief statement about each member's background, indicating what he or she will bring to the company.

MANAGEMENT AND DIRECTORS' COMPENSATION List the names of all members of your management team and board of directors and the compensation they will receive in fees or salary. Initially, at least, you and your management team should be prepared to accept modest salaries, perhaps well below what you received in your previous job, if you hope to attract external investors to your business.

SHAREHOLDERS Indicate the name of each of the individual shareholders (or partners) in your business, the number of shares each owns, the percentage of ownership, and the price paid.

Describe any investors in your business other than your management team and members of your board. How many shares do they have? When were these shares acquired? What price did the investors pay?

Summarize any incentive stock options or bonus plans that you have in effect or plan to institute. Also, indicate any employment contracts or agreements you may have made with members of your management team.

What do you like about being an Entrepreneur?

Being an entrepreneur is tough, stressful, and tiring. It's often like running a double marathon and then, at the finish line, being giving a stick by your team mate and told to run a sprint! Many times I feel like the weight of the world is on my shoulders. Yet, even after feeling drained of energy, beaten up, and sometimes extremely discouraged, one idea, one thought, one crazy challenge is enough to spark another whirlwind of excitement, passion, and drive, and there I go again, back at the forefront, trying to prove the impossible, to make a difference in the world.

Chris Arsenault
entrepreneur and
founder of iNovia Capital
www.inoviacapital.com

PROFESSIONAL ADVISERS Indicate the name and complete address of each of your professional advisers, for example, your lawyer, accountant, banker, insurance broker, and management or technical consultants. Disclose any fees or retainers that may have been paid to any of these people.

Implementation Schedule and Risks Associated with the Venture

It is necessary to present an overall schedule indicating the interrelationship among the various events necessary to launch your business and the timing required to bring it about. A well-prepared schedule demonstrates to external investors that you have given proper thought to where you are going and have the ability to plan ahead. This schedule can be a very effective sales tool.

Your plan should also discuss the major problems and risks you feel you will have to deal with in developing your business.

MILESTONES Summarize the significant goals that you and your business have already reached and still hope to accomplish in the future. What still needs to be done for the business to succeed? Who is going to do these things? When will they be completed?

SCHEDULE Develop a schedule of significant events and their priority for completion. What kind of strategic planning has been done to see that things occur as necessary? Have you developed a fallback or contingency position in case things do not come off as you have planned?

RISKS AND ASSUMPTIONS You might start by summarizing the major problems you have already had to deal with and how they were resolved. Were any particularly innovative or creative approaches used in addressing these issues?

Identify the risks your business may be faced with in the future. What are you attempting to do to avoid these? How will you deal with them if they arise? How can their impact on your business be minimized?

Summarize the downside risk. What would happen in the "worst case" scenario? What, if anything, could be salvaged from the business for your investors? Have you developed any contingency plans in case any of these risks should occur?

Your Financial Plan

Your financial plan is essential to enable a prospective investor or banker to evaluate the investment opportunity you are presenting. The plan should illustrate the current financial status of your business and represent your best estimate of its future operations. The results presented should be both realistic and attainable.

Your financial plan should also describe the type of financing you are seeking, the amount of money you are looking for, how you plan to use these funds in the business, the terms of repayment and desired interest rate, or the dividends, voting rights, and redemption considerations related to the offering of any common or preferred stock.

FUNDING REQUESTED Indicate the amount and type (debt or equity) of funding you are looking for. For what do you intend to use the money? How will it be applied in your business—to acquire property, fixtures, equipment, or inventory or to provide working capital?

Give an overview of the current financial structure of your business. Indicate the level of investment already made in the business and where the funds came from. What effect will the additional capital have on your business in terms of ownership structure, future growth, and profitability?

Outline your proposed terms of investment. What is the payback period and potential return on investment for the lender or investor? What collateral, tax benefit, or other security is being offered?

CURRENT FINANCIAL STATEMENTS If your venture is already in operation, you should provide copies of financial statements (profit and loss statement and a balance sheet) for the current year and the previous two years.

FINANCIAL PROJECTIONS In developing your financial plan, a number of basic projections must be prepared. These should be based on realistic expectations and reflect the effect of the proposed financing. The projections should be developed on a monthly basis for the first year of operation and on a quarterly or annual basis for another two to four years. These projections should include the following statements:

1. **Profit and loss forecasts** These pro forma income statements indicate your profit expectations for the next few years of operation of your business. They should be based on realistic estimates of sales and operating costs and represent your best estimate of actual operating results.

2. **Pro forma balance sheet** Your pro forma balance sheet indicates the assets you feel will be required to support your projected level of operations and how you plan to finance these assets.

3. **Projected cash flow statements** Your cash flow forecasts are probably your most important statements because they indicate the amount and timing of your expected cash inflows and outflows. Typically, the operating profits during the start up of a new venture are not sufficient to finance the business's operating needs. This often means that the inflow of cash will not meet your business's cash requirements, at least on a short-term basis. These conditions must be anticipated so that you can predict cash needs and avoid insolvency.

4. **Break-even analysis** A break-even analysis indicates the level of sales and production you will require to cover all your fixed and variable costs. It is useful for you and prospective lenders and investors to know what your break-even point is and how easy or difficult it will likely be to attain it.

An example of each of these statements and a discussion on how to determine the break-even point for your venture is presented in Stage Four of this book.

6. APPENDICES

The appendices are intended to explain, support, and supplement the material in the body of your business plan. In most cases, this material is attached to the back of your plan. Examples of the kind of material that might be included in an appendix are:

1. Product specifications and photographs
2. Detailed résumés of the management team
3. Lists of prospective customers
4. Names of possible suppliers
5. Job descriptions for the management team
6. Consulting reports and market surveys
7. Copies of legal documents, such as leases, franchise and licensing agreements, contracts, licences, patent or trademark registrations, and articles of incorporation
8. Letters of reference
9. Relevant magazine, trade journal, and newspaper articles

OTHER CONSIDERATIONS

THE SEVEN DEADLY SINS OF BUSINESS PLANS

Less than five minutes. That's the amount of time your plan has in the hands of many potential investors before they decide to turn "thumbs up" or "thumbs down" on it. In other words, they evaluate a document that may have taken you weeks or even months to prepare in just a few moments. For this reason, it is absolutely imperative that you avoid errors that will doom your plan to the rejection pile no matter how good other sections of it may be. We term these blunders the "Seven Deadly Sins of Business Plans," and here they are for you to recognize—and avoid:

Sin #1: The plan is poorly prepared and has an unprofessional look (e.g., no cover page, a cover page without contact information, glaring typos). This carelessness triggers the following investor reaction: "I'm dealing with a group of amateurs."

Sin #2: The plan is far too slick (e.g., it is bound like a book, is printed on shiny paper, and uses flashy graphics). This leads investors to think: "What are they trying to hide behind all the glitter?"

Sin #3: The executive summary is too long and rambling—it doesn't get right to the point. This failure to be concise leads investors to think: "If they can't describe their own idea and company succinctly, I don't want to waste my time—and certainly not my money—on them."

Sin #4: It's not clear where the product is in terms of development—does it exist or not? Can it be readily manufactured? If investors have to ask these questions, they may conclude: "I can't tell whether this is real or just another pipedream; I'll pass on this one."

Sin #5: No clear answer is provided to the question: "Why would anyone ever want to buy one?" Many entrepreneurs seem to assume that their new product or service is so wonderful that it will virtually sell itself. This kind of blind faith on the part of entrepreneurs leads investors to think: "How naive can you get? Even a machine that grew hair on the heads of bald men would need a marketing plan. These are truly amateurs."

Sin #6: It gives no clear statement of the qualifications of the management team: This oversight leads investors to conclude: "They probably have no relevant experience—and may not even know what relevant experience would be!"

Sin #7: Financial projections are largely an exercise in wishful thinking: This over-optimism leads potential investors to conclude: "They have no idea about what it is like to run a company, or (even worse) they think I am incredibly naive or stupid. Pass!"

The moral is clear: Keep a sharp lookout for these deadly errors, because if you commit even one, your chance of obtaining financial support and other forms of help from sophisticated investors will fade quickly.

Source: Robert A. Baron and Scott A. Shane, *Entrepreneurship: A Process Perspective*, 2nd edition (Thomson South-Western 2008), p. 220.

CONCLUSION

It is important that your plan make a good first impression. It should demonstrate that you have invested a significant amount of thinking and work on your venture. You should ensure your material is presented to prospective investors, lenders, and others in an attractive, readable, and understandable fashion.

The length of your business plan should not exceed 40 double-spaced, typed pages, not including appendices. Each section should be broken down into appropriate and clearly identifiable headings and subheadings. Make sure your plan contains no errors in spelling, punctuation, or grammar.

Once you have completed your business plan from one of the templates you have chosen that works best for your business model, click on the link below.

 | Use a checklist to assess your finished plan for completeness, clarity, and persuasiveness online in Connect.

Prepare a number of copies of your plan, and number each one individually. Make sure each copy is appropriately bound with a good-quality cover on which the name of your business has been printed or embossed.

BUSINESS PLANS

Business plans are available online in Connect.

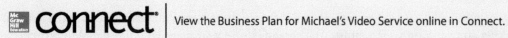 View the business plan for Third Degree ID online in Connect.

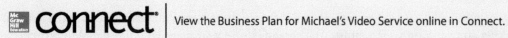 View the Business Plan for Michael's Video Service online in Connect.

LO1 **A business plan is a written document that:**

- describes all aspects of your business
- includes your product or service, your prospective customers, your competition, production and marketing methods, your management team, financing, and implementation of your business

LO2 **A business plan is important in your business because it:**

- outlines what you are planning and how you are going to get there
- acts as a guide and reference for operating your business
- can be used to potentially secure financing and attract investors
- can be referred to on a regular basis to ensure you are on track with your goals or to make adjustments due to possible changes to the market or industry

LO3 **A typical business plan includes:**

- an executive summary and fact sheet
- background information on your company
- product/service offering
- market analysis and your competition
- a marketing plan
- a development plan
- a production/operations plan
- information about the management team
- an implementation schedule
- a financial plan
- appendices for additional material not included in the body of the plan. These will include resumés of your management team, potential customers, letters of references, market surveys, to name a few.

For more information on the resources available from McGraw-Hill Ryerson, go to www.mcgrawhill.ca/he/solutions.

STAGE 6

LEGAL CONSIDERATIONS

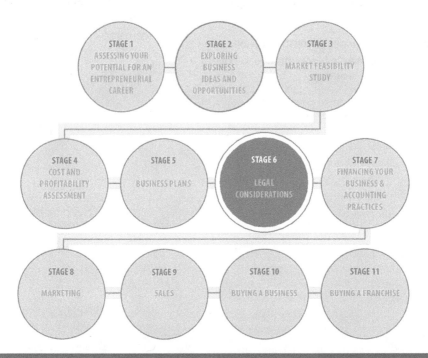

STAGE 1
ASSESSING YOUR POTENTIAL FOR AN ENTREPRENEURIAL CAREER

STAGE 2
EXPLORING BUSINESS IDEAS AND OPPORTUNITIES

STAGE 3
MARKET FEASIBILITY STUDY

STAGE 4
COST AND PROFITABILITY ASSESSMENT

STAGE 5
BUSINESS PLANS

STAGE 6
LEGAL CONSIDERATIONS

STAGE 7
FINANCING YOUR BUSINESS & ACCOUNTING PRACTICES

STAGE 8
MARKETING

STAGE 9
SALES

STAGE 10
BUYING A BUSINESS

STAGE 11
BUYING A FRANCHISE

LEARNING OBJECTIVES

By the end of this stage, you should be able to:

LO1 Describe the different business structures for starting your business.

LO2 Choose a name for your business.

LO3 Identify the business licenses you may need when starting your business.

LO4 Explain the importance of having mentors, a board of directors, or an advisory board.

LO5 Protect your intellectual property.

365 PRODUCTIONS
A GOOD PARTNER

Used with permission of 365productions.com.

The journey to success looked like smooth sailing for Ben Patience and Christopher Moreno in the first few years after they founded their event planning and production business in Vancouver.

The pair started 365 Productions in 2006 with an investment of just $5,000 each and quickly established a market among major clients for producing high-profile shows, exhibitions, and other events. However, they soon navigated toward hidden shoals that threatened to sink the young company. Ben Patience and Christopher Moreno admit that inexperience and rapid growth led to a blurring of responsibilities and increasing tension between the partners.

"We were learning as we were going along and trying to do everything," Patience says. "But eventually we found ourselves stepping on each other's toes." By the summer of 2010, there was a risk the business could spin out of control.

The partners were increasingly wasting time and energy on disagreements over daily operations. They feared "something big was going to fall off the assembly line" and realized swift action was necessary to save the company.

When Patience and Moreno joined forces after working as freelancers in Vancouver's event production industry, they founded their partnership on complementary skill sets. Those skills allow 365 Productions to bill itself as "a unique blend of creative vision and military precision." Patience is a former British military engineer, while Moreno's background is in the studio recording business.

The arrangement worked well in the early years. But as the number of employees increased, cracks began to appear. The partners faced what Moreno calls "the Mommy-said/Daddy-said syndrome" with employees. Workers used an unclear division of responsibilities between the partners to play one boss off against the other.

"If you haven't defined whose role it is to say yes or no in a particular area, it's very easy to send conflicting messages to staff," Moreno says. "It was a big challenge to keep employees on the same path and maintain standards."

At the same time, the complexity of the business was growing, and mistakes were beginning to crop up. For example, the partners were too busy to invoice clients promptly or keep a proper eye on money flowing to suppliers.

"Mistakes didn't matter so much when we were a small operation and there was not so much to lose," says Moreno. "But it's different when the jobs of 30 to 40 people with families are at stake."

"It came to a head one day when we realized we had to re-evaluate our roles and have faith in the other to do their own job and make the right decisions."

"I've dealt with a lot of clients, contracts, financial accounting and tax law, so my skill set is really from the corporate side," Moreno says. "Ben is the guy on the ground delivering the event with a technical perfection I've never had.

"Our differences have become a friendly joke. He actually shows up at my house at Christmas and makes fun of the way I've put up the lights on the tree." To ensure the partnership stays on track, they schedule regular meetings where they go over developments and track progress on the strategic plan.

With a recent expansion into Australia and further operations planned for the U.K., the company has far exceeded its profit targets and anticipates sales this year of $3.2 million with eight full-time and 30 part-time employees.

In reflecting on the partnership, Patience makes the common comparison to a marriage. "There'll be good times and bad times," he says. "But if you pick the right person at the beginning, you'll be able to work through them all."

Source: Adapted from Business Development Bank of Canada (BDC), Profit$, Fall 2012 article (www.bdc.ca) by Richard Andrews: Patience and Moreno turned to BDC Consulting Manager Christopher Lythgo to help reshape their partnership as part of a larger strategic planning process. The pair not only clarified their relationship but looked at every aspect of their operations—from employees, to sales and marketing, to technology and equipment needs.

ORGANIZING YOUR BUSINESS

One of the key issues you must resolve when starting your new venture is the legal form of organization the business should adopt (Figure 6.1). Making that decision means you should consider such factors as:

1. The complexity and expense associated with organizing and operating your business in one way or another

2. The extent of your personal liability

3. Your need to obtain startup capital and operating funds from other sources

FIGURE 6.1 ORGANIZE YOUR BUSINESS

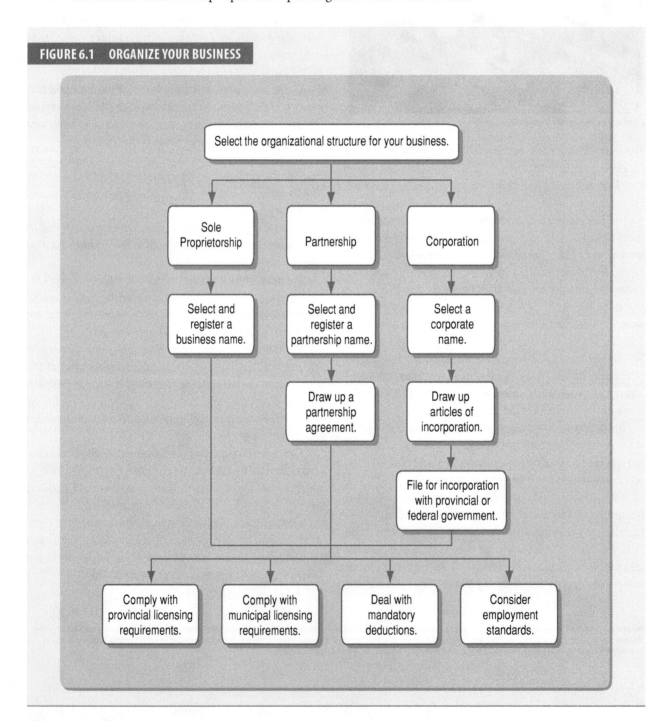

4. The extent to which you want ownership, control, and management of your business to be shared with others (if at all)

5. The distribution of your business's profits and losses

6. The extent of government regulation you are willing to accept

7. Tax considerations and implications

8. The need to involve other principals in your venture

The most prevalent forms your business might take are:

- An individual or sole proprietorship
- A partnership (general partnership or limited partnership)
- A corporation

INDIVIDUAL OR SOLE PROPRIETORSHIP

The *individual* or *sole proprietorship* is the oldest and simplest form of business organization. As owner or proprietor, you have complete control over the conduct and management of your business. You alone are accountable for all business activities and their consequences. You control the business's profits and are liable for its debts. You and the business are one and the same. The sole proprietorship is the most common form of organization for small businesses, particularly in the early stages of their development.

ADVANTAGES OF SOLE PROPRIETORSHIP

- **Simple and inexpensive to start** A sole proprietorship is simple and inexpensive both to create and dissolve. It can be brought into existence with a minimum of legal formalities and terminated just as readily. Startup costs are minimal—usually they are confined to registering your business name with the appropriate authorities and obtaining the necessary licences.

- **Individual control over operations** As a sole proprietor, you own 100 percent of your business. You are literally your own boss. If the business is not successful, you are free to dissolve it. And if the business does well, you can have a strong sense of accomplishment.

- **All profits to the owner** If the business is successful, you will reap the benefits of your efforts. No one will share in the profits of the business. You work for yourself and determine your own destiny.

- **Tax simplicity** As a sole proprietor, you declare your business on your personal tax return rather than having to file a separate form. If part of your home or your car is used for business purposes, you may be able to write some of these expenses off against the business income. In addition, if your business should incur a loss during its early stages, that loss is deductible from any other income you may have as well.

DISADVANTAGES OF SOLE PROPRIETORSHIP

- **Unlimited liability** Since the business and the proprietor are not recognized as being separate by law, you can be held personally liable for all the debts of your business. That means you may have to satisfy business debts with personal assets, such as your house and car, if the business is unable to meet its obligations. You may be able to protect some personal assets by putting them in your spouse's name before starting your venture, but there is no real guarantee against domestic breakdown.

- **Higher tax rate** Any profits generated by a sole proprietorship are taxed at your higher personal tax rate, rather than at the more favourable small-business tax rate.

EVERYTHING I WISH I KNEW RUNNING A SOLE PROPRIETORSHIP BUSINESS

2013 marks the beginning of a new fiscal year for many businesses so I thought I would share a few things I have picked up over the past few years. I've run my Web consulting business as a proprietorship the past three years and have picked up quite a few nuggets of useful information along the way. These things seem simple and almost laughable now, but as a greenhorn I wish I had known these before I started.

These tips are best if you are thinking about running a sole proprietorship (a business that is owned and run by a single person) in Canada but are helpful for others outside of the country.

HIRE A GOOD ACCOUNTANT

I'm putting this one first because it's by far the most important thing you should do when starting a business. My first year I paid someone $50 to do my taxes and I really got what I paid for. I had my taxes reassessed three times and had to pay the government more each time. The second year around I paid around $700 for the fantastic services of Waterford Tax & Advisory who did an amazing job straightening everything out and giving me some fantastic advice that saved me tons in the long run. A good accountant will always be around to answer questions and give you advice. You can't afford to use a cheap accountant, trust me.

DITCH EXCEL, USE FRESHBOOKS

This is a no-brainer for taking care of estimates, expenses, and invoicing clients. At $33 a month, this is one of the more expensive services I subscribe to, but it is worth every penny. At the end of the year I'm able to export a few reports and send them off to my accountant—no dealing with spreadsheets. My clients love Freshbooks too—I often get compliments on both how easy it is to manage invoices and how professional my invoices look like.

UNDERSTAND TAXES—PERSONAL AND HST

Starting a business, you are probably coming from a job where all your taxes are taken care of and, at the end of the year, you get a nice little return from the government. Not so when you are on your own, take the time to educate yourself on what sort of taxes you need to pay in your area.

Personal Income Taxes Running a sole proprietorship in Canada means you get taxed at the same rates as everyone else who isn't self-employed. There are both provincial and federal tax rates that vary depending on how much income you bring in. You can run your numbers for both at the CRA website.

HST I run my business in Ontario, and I need to charge all my clients who live in Ontario 13% HST—your province or state will have something similar setup. If you are making more than

$30,000 a year you will need to register for an HST number and start collecting.

So, the biggest lesson learned here is *you need to pay a ton of taxes.* As soon as you get a cheque, you should cut out anywhere from *35–50 percent* (13% HST, 22–37% income tax)—depending on how high your taxable income is—and place it in another account to pay the tax man at the end of the year.

KEEP EVERY RECEIPT AND EXPENSE EVERYTHING

The best thing you can do to reduce how hard you get hit by taxes is to expense every single dollar you pay to run your business. Again, this may seem like easy stuff to some, but it's worth noting how this stuff works.

You only get taxed on *net income,* not gross income. So, if you get paid $1,000 for a project, but spent $200 on hosting for it, you will only be taxed on $800.

So, think of every little thing you use to run your business. Buying a new laptop, conference tickets plus flights, printer ink, online subscriptions, software licenses… It all adds up quickly and can really help you reduce your taxable income.

As a business, you also don't have to pay HST. So any receipt you have that includes 13% HST, you will get that back from the government when you pay your taxes.

MAX OUT YOUR RRSP

This is a good tip for anyone around tax time. Up until the end of February, you can contribute to the previous year's RRSP. Anything you contribute to your RRSP is not taxed, so you can treat it as a huge expense. The amount you can contribute depends on your previous year's income, but it could be as much as around $20,000. In Canada, this money is meant to only be taken out at retirement, but there is a special clause that lets you cash it out, without penalty, when you buy your first house.

HEALTH INSURANCE IS CHEAP

My wife recently quit her job to work independently beside me. While we are super happy with that decision, we lost the perk of health benefits. In Canada residents are covered for the big stuff like surgeries and doctors' appointments, but not things like medicine, dental work and eyeglasses. Insurance plans are surprisingly affordable, starting at $60 for basic coverage. Kait and I went for pretty good dental, eye, and prescription coverage and it was around $160/month.

One other thing, we shopped around on the Net for insurance and we didn't find any good rates, only after getting in touch with a broker did we find out its much cheaper to have a human do it for you.

INCORPORATE TO SAVE $$

Coming full circle to having a good acceptance, mine suggested that once you start earning decent income or are working in an arrangement like Kait and I are, it would make sense to ditch the sole proprietorship and incorporate as a business. It's more expensive to incorporate a business ($500 vs. $60) and it's more work to get up and running, but it's well worth the tax savings in the long run.

Source: Wes Bos Blog, posted January 1, 2013 (www.wesbos.com).

- **More difficult to obtain equity financing** Unlimited liability obviously limits the capital base of the business unless substantial security is available. It is not uncommon for sole proprietors to obtain the bulk of their initial funding by "maxing out" personal credit cards or by pledging their homes, cottages, or other personal assets as collateral for a loan.

- **Limited resources and opportunity** A sole proprietorship usually holds limited opportunity and incentive for employees, as it is not a form of ownership conducive to growth. One person can only do so much and may not have all the skills and knowledge necessary to run all phases of the business. Employees may have to be hired to perform these tasks. The life of the business in a proprietorship is limited to the life of the proprietor. If you should die, become ill, or encounter serious personal problems, your business is immediately affected, and unless other provisions are made, your business will die with you. This could lead to a forced sale of the business's assets by your beneficiaries, perhaps at a substantial loss.

PARTNERSHIP

A *partnership* is an association of two or more individuals carrying on a business for profit. The *principals* (partners) should jointly prepare a written partnership agreement outlining the following issues in terms that are clearly understood and mutually acceptable to all of them:

1. The rights and responsibilities of each partner
2. The amount and nature of the partners' respective capital contributions to the business
3. The division of the business' profits and losses
4. The management responsibilities of each partner involved in the operation of the business
5. Provision for termination, retirement, disability, or death of a partner
6. Means for dissolving or liquidating the partnership

Some of the potential problems that can occur in a partnership are illustrated in the case of Debie Rothenberger. She and a long-time friend launched their picture framing business in 2003. Three years later, the partner wanted to leave the business, but the pair could not agree on a fair price for the partner's interest. The partners ended up in a very acrimonious dispute and had to divide up the business and its assets. Rothenberger had to start over again with a new business name, phone number, and so on, and the two old

TIPS FOR A SUCCESSFUL PARTNERSHIP

Choose Your Partner Carefully Identify your strongest capabilities, and consider a partner who complements them. Make sure you share the same business goals, work ethic, and values.

Get it in Writing Before entering a partnership, structure it legally with an agreement drafted by an experienced lawyer. Detail everything from ownership, roles, and responsibilities and how profits should be shared to how the partnership could be terminated. Outline how much money each partner will invest in the company.

Define Roles Establish clear responsibilities and expectations for each partner. Decide who does what work and how much of it.

Communicate, Communicate, Communicate Talk, meet, and email regularly and openly to avoid mistakes and misunderstandings.

Remain Flexible Just like personal relationships, business partnerships can change over time, and the original arrangements may no longer suit the operations of the company as it develops. Be prepared to adapt.

Some other things to include are:

- What happens if the business later requires additional working capital and only one of the partners has more money to invest? Does he or she lend some money to the other partner, and if so, on what terms?
- What kind of business will be carried on and what happens if one of the partners later wants to diversify into other areas? There should be a clause stipulating that all of the partners must agree to it before such a move can be made.
- What happens if one of the partners becomes permanently disabled and no longer able to perform his or her regular duties? And how will you define the term "permanently disabled" as it relates to your business?
- What happens if one of the partners dies or wants to leave the business? And what formula do you use to determine a fair value for his or her share of the company if the remaining partner wants to buy that share and continue operating the business?
- If one partner does buy out the other, should the payment be in one lump sum, or can it be made in installments?
- What happens if one partner becomes bankrupt or is caught stealing from the company? Does the other partner have the right to buy out that partner's share of the company, and at a discounted price? If so, at how much of a discount?

Source: Adapted from BDC, Profit$, Fall 2012, Murray McNeill, *Winnipeg Free Press*, September 2, 2006.

friends wound up no longer speaking to one another. In hindsight, it is clear that one major issue in the partners' attempt to deal with this situation was that they had no mechanism in place to resolve serious disagreements between them. Such a process or agreement would have made things much easier on everyone concerned and enabled them to resolve their differences without jeopardizing the entire business and their friendship.

GENERAL PARTNERSHIP

A *general partnership* is similar to a sole proprietorship except that responsibility for the business rests with two or more people, the partners. In a general partnership, all the partners are liable for the obligations of the partnership and share in both profits and losses according to the terms of their partnership agreement.

Advantages of a General Partnership

- **Pooling of financial resources and talents** The partnership is useful for bringing together two or more people who can combine their skills, abilities, and resources effectively. Management of the business is shared among the principals.

- **Simplicity and ease of organization** A partnership, like a sole proprietorship, is easy and inexpensive to establish and is subject to a minimum amount of regulation.

RULES OF ENGAGEMENT

METALCRAFT MARINE—THE SALE OF PATROL BOATS PROMPTED A HIGH-SPEED ALLIANCE

Selling naval patrol boats, fire boats, and police boats for MetalCraft Marine Inc. has led Bob Clark around the world and into many memorable situations. But his fondest memory is sharing his cramped office on the Kingston, Ontario, waterfront last year with U.S. Navy Combat Craft Crewman (SWCC) Master Chief Kelly Webb, a Special Warfare veteran and 30-year "boat guy." Over late-night pizza and beer, Clark, representing the 100-employee MetalCraft, worked with Webb, a project manager representing Brunswick, the world's largest boat-builder, to fine-tune the design for an ultra-fast patrol boat the two firms would sell together.

One Saturday night, near the end of the process, Clark and Webb could not quite agree on the width of the side deck. So, they built a life-sized mock-up out of empty beer cases. "We had to go out and buy a few more cases," Clark jokes. Last spring, the Brunswick/MetalCraft team scored a $10-million contract from the U.S. Coast Guard for 10 long-range patrol boats—and possibly 20 more. Clark has done a lot of deals, but he still gushes about the long nights redesigning patrol boats with Webb: "As a Canadian, you don't have access to that kind of person very often."

That is just one of the benefits of alliances. For entrepreneurs who feel like lowly muggles at the Hogwarts Yule Ball when they are chasing big contracts, partnerships and strategic alliances represent leverage, contacts, and credibility. Got a surefire idea for a new product, but no one to execute it? Are your margins so slim you cannot give your great product the marketing push it needs? By teaming up with a company with market knowledge and existing sales platforms, you can save hefty upfront investment while sharing in a bigger upside.

But there is nothing magical about alliances. You have to work hard to find compatible partners, then work harder to define how the alliance will work. Consultants Jonathan Hughes and Jeff Weiss of Boston-based Vantage Partners estimate that

© JIM KIDD/ALAMY

60 percent to 70 percent of alliances fail. As they wrote in a 2007 *Harvard Business Review* article, "Because alliances involve interdependence between companies that may be competitors and may also have vastly different operating styles and cultures, they demand more care and handling than other business arrangements."

Clark has lots of advice on handling bigger partners. For 25 years, MetalCraft has been a small fish in a big ocean, building one-off aluminum patrol boats, fire boats, and police boats for the U.S. Navy, U.S. cities, and government customers from Nigeria to the Middle East. Brunswick, maker of the near-legendary Boston Whaler, also serves this market, but with fibreglass boats. While these boats are easier to mass produce, they do not have the same toughness, speed, or bulletproof capability as aluminum craft. So, when Brunswick went looking to expand its share of the patrol boat market, its commercial and government unit teamed up with MetalCraft to create a new line of 11-metre patrol boats. The deal gives Brunswick access to new markets while enabling MetalCraft to leverage Brunswick's worldwide sales force. (To dodge the "Buy American" sentiment, MetalCraft will build its joint-venture boats just across the St. Lawrence River at a new facility in Cape Vincent, NY.)

Source: Adapted from *Profitguide*, Rick Spence, October 29, 2010 (www.profitguide.com/opportunity/rules-of-engagement-42334).

- **Increased ability to obtain capital** The combined financial resources of all the partners can be used to raise additional capital for the business. Income from the partnership is taxed as part of the personal income of each of the partners.

- **Potential for growth** A partnership has a higher potential for growth than a proprietorship, since a valuable employee may be offered a partnership to dissuade him or her from leaving the firm. Growth, however, is still quite restricted compared with that possible with a limited company.

OTHER CONSIDERATIONS

CONTENTS OF A TYPICAL PARTNERSHIP AGREEMENT

1. Names of the partners
2. Name of the business
3. Term of the partnership agreement
4. Extent of each of the partners' interest in the partnership and the capital each has contributed to the partnership
5. The financial records and banking arrangements of the partnership
6. A description of the capital accounts and salary and draw arrangements of each of the partners
7. An outline of each partner's responsibilities for the management of the business and what each can or cannot do without the approval of other partners
8. Partners' responsibilities to work within the business and their ability to assign their interest in the business to others
9. Procedures for the termination or dissolution of the partnership
10. Procedures for the resolution of any disputes among the partners
11. Insurance coverage to be carried by the partnership
12. Any process for amending the agreement

Disadvantages of a General Partnership

- **Unlimited liability** Partners are personally liable for all the debts and obligations of their business and for any negligence on the part of any of them occurring in the conduct of the business. This is similar to the situation with a sole proprietorship except that the partners are liable both as a group and individually—not only for their own actions (severally) but also for the actions of all others in the partnership (jointly).

- **Divided authority** There is less control for an individual entrepreneur in a partnership with divided authority. There may be possible conflicts among partners that can be difficult to resolve and could affect the conduct of the business.

LIMITED PARTNERSHIP

In a *limited partnership*, the partners' share in the liability of the business *is limited to the extent of their contribution to the capital of the business*. In such a partnership, however, there must also be one or more general partners, that is, partners with *unlimited liability*.

The limited partners may not participate in the day-to-day management of the business of the partnership, or they risk losing their limited-liability status. Also, a limited partner is entitled to interest on his or her capital and some agreed-on share of the profits. Limited partners have one major power—the ability to remove the general partner(s).

Advantages of a Limited Partnership

- **Limited liability** If properly established and registered, the liability of the limited partners is restricted to the extent of their investment. Thus, you may find it easier to recruit investors.

Disadvantages of a Limited Partnership

- **Centralized management** In a limited partnership only a small subgroup of the owners—the general partners—have decision-making authority and can participate in the management of the business.

- **Difficulty in changing ownership** It is generally difficult to change ownership in a partnership, since the partnership must be dissolved and reconstituted every time a partner dies or wants to retire. So it is important that the procedure for dealing with this issue be laid out in a partnership agreement.

LIMITED LIABILITY PARTNERSHIP

A limited liability partnership (LLP) is typically only available to groups of professionals, such as lawyers, accountants, and doctors, to enable them to limit the liability between partners. These agreements are governed by provincial legislation, so the regulations vary from province to province. In Ontario, for example, only lawyers and some designated accountants may form an LLP.

CORPORATION

The *corporation* is the most formal of the various forms of business organization. A firm that is *incorporated* is a separate legal entity from its owners—that is, legally, it is regarded as a "person" with a separate, continuous life. As a legal person, a corporation has rights and duties of its own: It can own property and other assets; it can sue or be sued; and it files its own tax return. Ownership of a corporation is recognized through the purchase of *shares*, or *stock*, which can be held by as few as one or as many as thousands of *shareholders*.

Often sole proprietors move to incorporation when they have a significant amount of contracts and business activities.

As in the case of a partnership, it is a good idea for the shareholders of a corporation to have a shareholders' agreement to protect their interests in case of friction or other conflicts that might arise among the principals. This agreement should be developed prior to the incorporation of the business and should deal with many of the same issues typically included in a partnership agreement (see the Other Considerations box).

A business need not be large to be incorporated. A sole proprietorship regularly earning in excess of $40,000 to $50,000 of taxable income annually probably should be incorporated.

Legislative changes in Ontario, Alberta, British Columbia, and other provinces now permit many groups of regulated professionals to enjoy the benefits of incorporation. These groups include lawyers, doctors, chartered accountants, dental hygienists, engineers, and management consultants. These professionals can now incorporate their practices in professional corporations.

Not-for-profit organizations may also incorporate as *corporations without share capital*. The organization does not necessarily have to be a charity. It may be an industry association, a social organization, or other non-profit entity. The difference is that there are no "owners" and it does not pay dividends. Any "profits" are retained by the corporation and used to support the purposes of the organization. Doing so enables them to operate under some kind of formal structure. Incorporation may enable them to apply for financial support from government, foundations and other organizations, make them eligible for charitable status, enable them to hold title to property and land, and limit the personal liability of their members.

Occasionally you may see references to other corporate forms, such as S Corporations or a Limited Liability Company (LLC). These are U.S. corporate structures and not applicable to Canadian registered companies, and the terms cannot be used in this country.

ADVANTAGES OF A CORPORATION

- **Limited liability** The owner or shareholder of a corporation is liable only for the amount he or she paid or owes for the shares except where statutory provisions may create personal liability for the directors or officers of the company for outstanding wages, taxes, or similar obligations. In case of bankruptcy, creditors cannot sue shareholders for outstanding debts of the business.

- **Continuity of the business even if the owner dies** Since it is an entity under the law, a corporation is not affected by the death or withdrawal of any shareholder. The shares of its stock can be sold or transferred to other individuals without difficulty. This ease of transfer allows for perpetual succession of the corporation, which is not the case with a sole proprietorship or partnership.

- **Easier to raise capital** Incorporation makes it easier to raise capital, which is done by selling stock. In addition, corporations with some history and a track record can negotiate more effectively with outside sources of financing than either a proprietorship or a partnership can.

CONTENTS OF A TYPICAL SHAREHOLDER AGREEMENT

1. The structure of the company and how equity is divided among shareholders
2. Parties to the agreement
3. Officers and directors of the company and their responsibilities
4. Right of first refusal and pre-emptive rights to acquire new shares or those of another shareholder
5. Buy-out provisions for voluntary or involuntary withdrawal of shareholders
6. Option to purchase on death or disability of a shareholder
7. Restrictions on the transfer of shares
8. Any management contracts or key person agreements
9. Any ongoing shareholder financial obligations
10. Provisions for termination of the agreement
11. A mechanism for ongoing valuation of the business and the shares

A shareholder agreement template is available on the MaRS Discovery District website (www.marsdd.com/articles/shareholders-agreement-sample-template/).

- **Employee benefits** A corporation has a better opportunity to provide benefits to employees and stockholders in a variety of ways, such as salaries, dividends, and profit-sharing plans.
- **Tax advantages** Being an independent entity in the eyes of the law, a corporation receives different tax treatment from that for either a proprietorship or a partnership and is taxed separately on its business profits. This may provide some opportunity for tax deferral, income splitting, or the reduction of actual tax costs through the deductibility of certain personal fringe benefits.

DISADVANTAGES OF A CORPORATION

- **Cost** Corporations are more expensive to start and operate. Initially, incorporation can cost in excess of $1,000 in legal and regulatory fees. In addition, a lawyer may charge upward of $300 per year to maintain the registered office and keep the *corporate book*, that is, the record of annual meetings, directors' meetings, and so on.
- **Legal formalities** A corporation is subject to more numerous and complex regulatory requirements than a proprietorship or partnership. Corporations must typically file annual reports, hold annual meetings, and file federal and provincial tax returns. This can be expensive and time consuming for a small business person and may require the ongoing services of an accountant and a lawyer.
- **Inability to flow losses through** It is not uncommon for a new business to incur substantial startup costs and operating losses during its first few years. These losses are "locked in"—a corporation must accumulate them for its own use in future years and cannot use them to offset income a shareholder may have from other sources. If your business never becomes very profitable, it is conceivable that its losses could never be used to reduce your tax liability.

    This is in contrast to a proprietorship or partnership, in which early losses would "flow through" to the owners of the business to be deducted on their personal income tax returns in the year the losses were incurred. Therefore, it may be more beneficial financially not to incorporate, so you can offset other income for tax purposes. This can improve your overall cash flow when your business is just getting started and cash flow is most critical. You can always decide to incorporate later without any tax consequences.

- **Guarantee** Lenders often require a personal guarantee. This largely negates the advantage of limited liability.

No matter what form of organization you decide to establish, things do not always work out as originally planned. Wovenfare International, for example, was set up as a corporation but had many of the elements of a partnership. Jodi Maxwell and Michelle Shaw Williams teamed up with Cecilia de la Rocha and Justine Brown to create an online meal planning service for families too busy to plan diverse and nutritious meals on their own. Together they fine-tuned the concept of selling customized meal plans to subscribers and set about developing their website and building their database of recipes on which to base the meal plans targeted toward a January 2007 launch date.

After working for six months and overcoming numerous issues, Wovenfare was launched on time, but then the women had to turn their attention to actually running the business. Some envisioned the company as a part-time business that could fit around their family schedules. Others were already engaged full time. Running the day-to-day affairs of the company was not nearly as exciting as the pre-launch activities, and no one had ever really decided who would do what once the company was operational. They all thought they should be the boss. In July, the partnership dissolved, as Brown and de la Rocha bought out the two original founders in a relatively amicable parting of ways.

CO-OPERATIVES

As the public demand for financial security, fair wages, employment opportunity, sustainability, fairer trade, local/organic products, and bottom-up structuring has grown, a well-established (though previously under-the-radar) business model has gained prominence on a global scale. Co-operative enterprises have been flourishing since their inception in Rochdale, England, in 1884; however, the model has become increasingly notable with the U.N.' s choice to name 2012 the "International Year of Co-operatives." No business model has ever before been awarded such an honour, which has led some to dub *co-operatives* the "best-kept secret in business."

In Canada alone, there are 9,000 co-operatives, with more than $370 billion in assets, employing over 150,000 people and providing services to over 18 million members!

Just like all businesses, co-operatives exist to benefit their owners. However, co-operative enterprises have a distinct structure, different from other forms of business. First and foremost, co-ops are democratic enterprises that are owned and controlled by their members. The democratic structure of a co-op is maintained by a one-member/one-vote system. This means that every member, regardless of financial investment, has an equal say in the direction of the business. The membership can consist of customers, employees, producers, or any combination of the above.

A co-op's primary purpose is to meet the needs of its member-owners, unlike most other businesses that exist solely to maximize profit. Co-ops can be formed as profit or non-profit organizations and may have branches and subsidiaries. No matter what its size or scope, each co-operative is independent, and there is no one "corporate office" for the entire movement.

The co-operative enterprise model can be applied to any kind of business or need. Co-ops are often initiated by a group of people who share a common need (e.g., a local grocery store), want to capitalize on a new market opportunity (e.g., the provision of renewable energy), lack the capital or specific skill set to go into business independently (in the case of worker co-operatives), or provide a niche product or service (e.g., housing or funeral services). By pooling their resources and working together, the members can satisfy that need or seize that opportunity, a feat they may not have been able to accomplish individually.

In more than 25 Ontario communities, credit unions (financial co-operatives) are the sole providers of banking services to clients after major banks close their doors to them.

A co-operative's startup capital usually comes from the sale of member shares in the co-op. Startup enterprises must have a minimum of five members to incorporate as a co-operative, but there is no maximum: Mountain Equipment Co-op has over 3.3 million members. After payment of fair return on capital, surplus (i.e., profit) is generally distributed in proportion to the business that members transact with the co-op in the form of *patronage* dividends or as lower prices or more favourable interest rates. Patronage return is different from profits earned on invested capital, since it is based on how much the member uses the co-operative's service, instead of the number of shares the member holds in the co-operative. Shares in co-operatives do not significantly appreciate or depreciate in value. Co-op shares generally are not considered investment vehicles as they must be sold back to the co-operative upon termination of membership and are not freely traded on stock exchanges.

Perhaps what is most interesting about co-operatives (and most appealing to entrepreneurs) is the sustainability and diversity of the model. Co-operatives around the globe are united by a set of seven core principles—making it the only business model that operates based on a common code. Principle number seven—"autonomy and independence"—for example, means that co-ops are focused on their membership and that their mission and vision guide the types of partnerships or relationships entered into by the co-operative. Other principles include concern for community, education, training, and information. By law, these seven principles must be followed by all co-operatives, effectively enshrining the concept of the triple bottom line (people, planet, profit) into the co-ops' mandates. Compare this with the values and focus of other types of business that may shift with ownership, a marketing campaign, or the drive for profits.

The strong bond between co-ops most certainly plays a role in their impressive sustainability. Three recent Canadian studies determined the survival rate of a co-operative enterprise to be more than twice that of other business corporations after 10 years (44.3 percent to 19.5 percent).

Some well- known Canadian co-operative enterprises include Mountain Equipment Co-operative, Desjardins, Vancity Credit Union, Agropur, The Co-operators Insurance, United Farmers of Alberta, Federated Co-operatives, and Gay Lea Foods. Some of the brand names you may recognize include Northumberland milk, Organic Meadow dairy, Scotsburn butter, Camino chocolate bars, Blue Diamond almonds, Ocean Spray, Sunkist, Bee Maid honey, and Citadelle maple syrup.

Another attractive feature of the co-op model is its *flexibility*. Unbeknown to many, co-operatives in one or more of the four categories (consumer, producer, worker, and multi-stakeholder), exist in almost every sector of the economy. The largest sectors include financial services (credit unions, caisses populaires, insurance, and mutual funds corporations), housing, daycare, healthcare, agriculture and food supply, retail, transportation, communication, renewable energy, community and social services, tourism, recreation, art, culture, and even funeral services.

ADVANTAGES OF A CO-OPERATIVE

- Money and jobs stay in the local economy.
- Form of control is democratic—one member, one vote regardless of investment.
- There is limited liability.
- Earnings surplus, after meeting the needs of the co-op, is distributed to the members according to their use of the services of the co-op, and/or given back through reduced prices or fees.
- Survival rate over 10 years is more than double other forms of business.

DISADVANTAGES OF A CO-OPERATIVE

- Democratic process may increase decision-making times and add complexity to record keeping.
- Ability to raise capital is generally limited to the membership.
- Startup requires five or more members (three or more for worker co-ops).
- Co-op consultants and developers are not as readily available as for other forms of business enterprise.

GETTING INTO BUSINESS

REGISTRATION AND INCORPORATION—MAKING IT LEGAL

For a sole proprietorship, no formal, legal *registration* is required as long as the business is operated just under your own name. However, if a specific business name, such as "Regal Dry Cleaners" or "Excel Construction," is used or if more than one owner is implied by the use of "and Associates" or "and Sons" in conjunction with your name, your business must be logged with the Registrar of Companies or the Corporations Branch of the province in which the business is located. Registration is a relatively simple and inexpensive process that you can probably take care of yourself. Partnerships must be registered in a similar fashion.

Incorporation is a more complex and can be considerably more expensive process that usually requires the services of a lawyer. If your business activities will initially be confined to a single province, you need incorporate only as a provincial company. Should your business plans include expansion to other provinces; however, you will be required to register in each province in which you wish to do business as an extra-provincial company, or register as a federally incorporated company. See Figure 6.2.

FIGURE 6.2   SAMPLE OF FEDERAL ARTICLES OF INCORPORATION

Industry Canada   Industrie Canada

Canada Business   Loi canadienne sur les
Corporations Act (CBCA)   sociétés par actions (LCSA)

Form 1

FORM 1	FORMULAIRE 1
ARTICLES OF INCORPORATION	STATUTS CONSTITUTIFS
(SECTION 6)	(ARTICLE 6)

1 -- Name of the Corporation

Dénomination sociale de la société

2 -- The province or territory in Canada where the registered office is situated (do not indicate the full address)

La province ou le territoire au Canada où est situé le siège social (n'indiquez pas l'adresse complète)

3 -- The classes and any maximum number of shares that the corporation is authorized to issue

Catégories et tout nombre maximal d'actions que la société est autorisée à émettre

4 -- Restrictions, if any, on share transfers

Restrictions sur le transfert des actions, s'il y a lieu

5 -- Minimum and maximum number of directors (for a fixed number of directors, please indicate the same number in both boxes)

Minimum: [   ]   Maximum: [   ]

Nombre minimal et maximal d'administrateurs (pour un nombre fixe, veuillez indiquer le même nombre dans les deux cases)

Minimal : [   ]   Maximal : [   ]

6 -- Restrictions, if any, on the business the corporation may carry on

Limites imposées à l'activité commerciale de la société, s'il y a lieu

7 -- Other provisions, if any

Autres dispositions, s'il y a lieu

8-- **Incorporator's Declaration:** I hereby certify that I am authorized to sign and submit this form.

Déclaration des fondateurs : J'atteste que je suis autorisé à signer et à soumettre le présent formulaire.

Print Name(s) - Nom(s) en lettres moulées	Signature

Note:
Misrepresentation constitutes an offence and, on summary conviction, a person is liable to a fine not exceeding $5,000 or to imprisonment for a term not exceeding six months or both (subsection 250(1) of the CBCA).

Nota :
Faire une fausse déclaration constitue une infraction et son auteur, sur déclaration de culpabilité par procédure sommaire, est passible d'une amende maximale de 5 000 $ ou d'un emprisonnement maximal de six mois, ou de ces deux peines (paragraphe 250(1) de la LCSA).

IC 3419 (2008/08), Page 1

Canada

Source: Industry Canada, Canada Business Corporations Act (CBCA), IC 3419 (2008.08), Page 1 (www.ic.gc.ca), accessed March 17, 2013.

INC. OR LTD.: WHICH SOUNDS BETTER?

For his first two years in business as a corporate responsibility consultant, Paul Klein was content to operate as a sole proprietorship.

Then, in his third year, he picked up business from larger clients, his revenues surged by 250 per cent—and Mr. Klein was left wondering why no one had ever advised him to incorporate.

"I suddenly owed a huge amount of tax, and it was all at the personal tax rate, rather than the corporate tax rate, which is much lower," recalls the founder of Toronto-based Impakt Corp. "If I had incorporated, I would have saved $40,000."

Mr. Klein says that, as a one-person operation, he had never thought about which business ownership structure might be the most appropriate for him.

That's not uncommon. In her experience, fewer than half of entrepreneurs who are starting out do, says Dorothy Brophy, senior legal counsel with Toronto-based Brophy Professional Corp., which provides legal advice to expanding businesses.

Yet choosing the right structure can have serious consequences for their business, she says.

"Most entrepreneurs are very creative and they get right in there and pursue a dream, and they do it without thinking about a structure," Ms. Brophy says. "It doesn't stop them from carrying on business, but it could have important tax and liability implications."

There are three common forms of business ownership in Canada—a sole proprietorship, which is owned by one person; a partnership, which is owned by two or more people; and a corporation, which can be owned by any number of people.

The main difference is whether the business or the business owner bears personal responsibility for the firm's taxes, business decisions, and possible lawsuits.

Sole proprietors or partners are considered to be part of their business, and are personally liable for everything the business does. Entrepreneurs who incorporate their business are treated as a separate entity and are protected from personal liability.

That means incorporating can be an especially important move for firms working in a high-risk area, Ms. Brophy says.

"If I'm importing something from China and there's a possibility it could be contaminated by lead, I would want to incorporate," she says.

"It's also important once they start making concrete decisions such as signing leases and hiring people," she adds, because the owner avoids personal responsibility in the case of a default.

The decision to switch from a sole proprietorship or partnership to a corporation often also depends on revenues and tax considerations.

PHOTO COURTESY OF PAUL KLEIN

Sole proprietors or partners pay the higher personal income tax rate, but can also gain a tax advantage by writing off losses against personal income.

Mitchell Stein, an expert on corporate governance and organization at the Richard Ivey School of Business at the University of Western Ontario in London, says that, for that reason, new business owners, especially those who need to have a second income, may prefer to set up as a sole proprietorship or partnership.

But owners should consider incorporating and taking advantage of lower tax rates once revenues start to exceed their annual living expenses, he says.

A corporate structure can also qualify businesses for small business and employment grants, suggest greater legitimacy, and help to attract certain clients, Ms. Brophy says.

Many large companies work only with corporations, which have access to omissions and general liability insurance that partnerships and sole proprietorships cannot get, Mr. Klein notes.

Since getting hit with his giant tax bill, Mr. Klein has incorporated his consultancy, moved from his basement to a downtown Toronto office, and hired four employees.

Aside from the tax advantages he now enjoys, he says setting up as a corporation has been great for business.

"I think companies are more rigorous than ever before about selecting clients, and I think they may feel a greater sense of confidence in a corporation," he says. "They know that they're working with someone legitimate who isn't working out of the basement and may or may not deliver."

Source: Anita Elash, special to the *Globe and Mail*, June 6, 2011, updated August 24, 2012 (www.theglobeandmail.com/report-on-business/small-business/sb-money/business-funding/inc-or-ltd-which-sounds-better/article4258956/).

Companies can be classified as either private or public. *Public companies,* such as Alcan and Great-West Life, trade their shares on one of the country's public stock exchanges. They typically employ professional managers, external directors, and a number of shareholders who are the owners of the business.

Private companies, on the other hand, tend to have only one shareholder or, at most, a small number of shareholders. There is some restriction on the transfer of their shares in their *articles of incorporation*, and their shares cannot be offered for sale to the public. A private corporation is sometimes called an *incorporated partnership* because it usually consists of one, two, or three people who are personal friends, business associates, or family members, each of whom may play two or three roles, serving, for example, as an officer, director, and a shareholder of the company all at the same time.

PairoWoodies Publishing is a good example of an incorporated partnership. Ian Scott first met Wendy Woudstra through the Internet. He was an experienced entrepreneur who knew something about marketing but had almost no computer skills, while she had a technical background and experience at building websites. Both work in the business and have quite different roles and responsibilities but have had to learn to be flexible and willing to cover for each other when required. Oh, and how did they happen to acquire the unusual name? It turns out that Ian and Wendy both had the same nickname when they were kids—Woody. Ian came up with the name when they were discussing possible business names. While at first they were hesitant to use the name, it has paid off for them. No one ever forgets it.

If you choose to incorporate, a private corporation is probably the type you will establish. However, as most business owners become overwhelmed and nervous about incorporating, it is suggested you work with a lawyer. They will simplify the process for you. They will explain in detail what is best for your company, with regard to shares, shareholders, and partnership agreements. Depending on which firm you choose, they may very well walk you through the process by providing you with the templates and help you do the initial steps yourself, which will save you money. Many legal firms are looking for long-term relationships with new businesses and are willing to help out. Build a relationship with your lawyers—they will, in turn, have a vested interest in you and your business. And always remember, you cannot be good at everything, so let the experts do it for you. With starting a business, you have enough on your plate that you can and should do on your own.

CHOOSING A NAME LO2

Like people, all businesses must have a name. The simplest procedure is to name the business after yourself—Harry Brown's Printing, for example. In most provinces, this type of name does not require formal registration for a sole proprietorship, but it does have disadvantages. For example, you might have people phoning you at home at all hours if you and your business's name are the same. In addition, your personal reputation may be tarnished if you experience some financial problems and are forced into receivership or bankruptcy. And if you ever sell your business, your name would go with it, and the new owner's actions could reflect negatively on your reputation.

For businesses to be registered or incorporated, the most important consideration in selecting a name is that it be acceptable to the Registrar of Companies in your province. All provinces require that a search be conducted of proposed names. Any name that is similar to a name already registered will be rejected to avoid public confusion. It is not uncommon to have to submit several names before one is finally approved. To avoid this problem, some individuals use a series of numbers rather than letters for the name of their corporation. On acceptance, the name is typically reserved for your exclusive use for 90 day so that you can proceed with your registration or the filing of your articles of incorporation.

The best approach is usually to choose a distinctive name for the firm that *accurately describes* the type of business you plan to carry on. That is, a name like "Speedy Courier Service" or "Super-Clean Automobile Washing" is probably much better than one like "Universal Enterprises" or "General Distributing." A good way to check out names is to search online or local business directories and get some idea of the range of names currently in use in your business area and perhaps some inspiration for a brilliant new possibility.

ENTREPRENEURS IN ACTION

THE NAME GAME

When it came to the decision of determining a name for my maternity boutique that sold high-end organic clothing and accessories for the urban mother-to-be, I hashed out a series of common names that came to mind: The Organic Bump, Whole Wheat Bun-in-the-Oven, Babes in Momland, The Urban Organic Mama, Phat Mat. . . you name it, I wrote it down.

I wondered how I could combine my specialty niche market with more creativity and meaning to make it distinctive. Then one day, I thought of my own mother and my first experience of motherhood. The name Nima'ma came to me as though it had been there all along. The words "ni mama" were taken from my own mother's Woodland Cree dialect that simply meant "My Mother." It referenced the pivotal experience of becoming a mother and the reverence to our Mother Earth and all things organic.

It was beautiful. It was unique. It was mine! And with the approval of close friends and family, I moved the apostrophe, added an incorporated legal element to it, and voila! Ni'Mama Maternity Inc. was born.

However, if I had taken the time to research more about the universal meaning of this word, I would have found out that it is a derogatory Chinese slang phrase meaning "Your mama!" Thankfully, many of my Chinese customers jokingly mentioned it to me with a smile in my store.

So while playing The Name Game, consider the impact it will have on your audience's perception.

The Right Name Can:

- Describe what your business does
- Project the image you want your target market to understand and relate to

PRESSUREUA/DREAMSTIME.COM

- Connect with your customers thus developing a brand that they will recognize and trust

The Wrong Name Can:

- Mislead or confuse your customers
- Drive away potential business
- Offend your customers (please refrain from using obscene or vulgar terms)

If I had called my maternity retail store TEENA, customers would have thought Teena what? Who's Teena? Who cares! So do consider selecting a name that will help people understand what your company sells.

Once you have played all angles of The Name Game, by questioning, detailing, and describing your business elements, then the business playing field awaits. Go forth and prosper!

Source: Adapted from Small Business BC, Teena Legris, April 13, 2012 (www.smallbusinessbc.ca/post/name-game).

Names that are likely to be rejected and should be avoided are those that:

1. Imply any connection with or approval of the Royal Family, such as names that include the word "Imperial" or "Royal"
2. Imply approval or sponsorship of the business by some unit of government, such as names containing "Parliamentary," "Premier's," or "Legislative"
3. Might be interpreted as obscene or not really descriptive of the nature of the firm's business
4. Are similar to or contractions of the names of companies already in business, even though they may be in a different field, such as "IBM Tailors" or "Chrysler Electronics"

The firm's name can become one of your most valuable assets if your business is successful, as has happened in the case of such companies as McDonald's and Holiday Inn. Do not go for the first name that comes to mind, and make sure that you are able to register a domain with the same name. Too often, companies do not think this through before

DO'S AND DON'TS OF NAMING YOUR BUSINESS

Coming up with a great name for your business should never be taken lightly. You want something that grabs people's attention, is easy to remember, has long-lasting appeal, and reinforces your burgeoning brand. This is trickier even than it sounds. What's more, when you're trying to think of a name, you're just starting out and have plenty on your plate already. But think through this decision carefully. You want to get it right the first time. It can be confusing to customers and colleagues if you attempt a name change down the road.

DO: MAKE IT CATCHY

Obviously, you'll want a brand name that people will recognize in the crowd. Remember, the shorter the better. Anything more than a few syllables will usually be difficult to remember. Gimmicks like alliterations or rhymes can be helpful as long as they appropriately express the idea you're trying to convey. The name should both look good on paper and sound good to the ear.

DON'T: GET TOO CREATIVE OR DESCRIPTIVE

Creativity and imagination are fantastic and essential for any entrepreneur. But don't go over board when naming your business. Feel free to make up words (Google or Yelp anyone?) but consider the auditory implications if you're trying to burst on the scene with a made-up phrase or word. Both Google and Yelp are simple, aesthetic, and auditory pleasing words that can also act as verbs. Something like FizzleMondo might just be confusing. Additionally, don't try and stuff a description of your service or product into your business name, unless you can do so tersely and without sacrificing other considerations.

DO: CONSIDER A TRADEMARK

If your business is successful and begins to grow, you'll probably want to trademark the name. Do your research beforehand or you risk discovering that your name has already been trademarked.

DON'T: FALL VICTIM TO TEXT MESSAGE SYNDROME

A lot of businesses do this successfully, so take this with a grain of salt. But if you use alternative spellings in your name, or insert punctuation marks or numbers to try to add a bit of flair, you run the risk of not being remembered. The last thing you want is for a potential customer to try to look for your business based on the name they've heard, and then give up when they can't figure out how to spell it.

DO: TEST THE WATERS

Utilize everyone at your disposal to gather opinions on your business name. Friends, colleagues, family members, even existing customers, can all contribute to a great name. You want something that resonates with a large number of people. Additionally, do some testing with Google Adwords to see if there are other businesses with names that are too similar. Finally, make sure your business name does not mean something offensive in a foreign language. This happens more than you may think.

DON'T: RESIST CHANGE IF IT'S NECESSARY

It's a tough decision to have to change your business name, but if things simply aren't working, you may have no choice. If you realize early on that your name is not accurate or doesn't reflect the concepts and ideals you're trying to convey, go for the change. It's better to change early than try to grow your business with a name that's not working.

Source: Adam Toren, blogtrepreneur.com, January 14, 2013 (www.blogtrepreneur.com/2013/01/14/dos-and-donts-of-naming-your-business/).

registering the name they have chosen. Search the Internet for names that you are thinking of. You can also go to Whois.com to find out if the name you want has been taken. It will also give you extensions for that name that may not already have been taken, for example, .net, .org, or .ca. Take your time and think it over very carefully before deciding on a name. The repercussions down the road can be costly.

You may require both municipal and provincial licences to operate your business. Your need for the former depends on the location and nature of your business; requirements for the latter depend solely on the nature of your business.

Municipal

Not all types of businesses require a municipal licence. Every municipality regulates businesses established within its boundaries and sets its own licensing requirements and fees. In Winnipeg, for example, 114 types of businesses and occupations require a licence. In general, these are amusement operations or ones that may affect public health and safety. The licensing fees can be as high as several thousand dollars, but in most cases, the fees are quite nominal—a few dollars.

In addition, all businesses—whether or not they require a licence—must conform to local zoning regulations and bylaw requirements. In fact, zoning approval is usually a prerequisite to licence approval. Companies operating in their own facilities in most cities must also pay a business tax, assessed as a percentage of the rental value of their business facilities.

Provincial

Various provincial authorities also require a licence or permit. In Ontario, for example, all establishments providing accommodation to the public, such as hotels, motels, lodges, tourist resorts, and campgrounds, must be licensed by the province. Businesses planning to serve liquor, operate long-haul cartage and transport operations, process food products, produce optical lenses, or manufacture upholstered furniture or stuffed toys may also require licensing. You should check with the local authorities to determine the types of licences and permits your business might require or consult with BizPal (www.bizpal.ca), an online project of Industry Canada and some of the provinces to simplify the business permit and licensing process for entrepreneurs and others.

Land Use and Zoning

You should check with the local municipal authorities to ensure that your business conforms to zoning and building regulations.

MANDATORY DEDUCTIONS AND TAXES

If your business has a payroll, you will be required to make regular deductions from employees' paycheques for income tax, Employment Insurance (EI), and the Canada Pension Plan (CPP). These deductions must be remitted to the Canada Revenue Agency every month.

In addition, you may also be required to pay an assessment to your provincial Workers' Compensation Board. The size of your payment will be based on the nature of your business and its risk classification, as well as the estimated size of your annual payroll. These funds are used to meet medical, salary, and rehabilitation costs of any of your employees who may be injured on the job.

Depending on the size of your venture, you may also be responsible for remitting taxes of various kinds to either the provincial or the federal government. All provinces, except Alberta, apply a retail sales tax to almost all products and services sold to the ultimate consumer. Exceptions in some provinces include food, books, children's clothing, and medicine. The size and the application of these taxes vary from province to province, but if your business sells to final consumers, you must obtain a permit and are responsible for collecting this tax and remitting it to the government on a regular basis.

Federal taxes largely fall into the categories of the Goods and Services Tax (GST) and income tax. A number of provinces have integrated their provincial sales tax with the federal government's GST to create a Harmonized Sales Tax (HST). The GST/HST is levied on virtually all products and services sold in Canada. There are some minor exceptions for certain types of products. If your taxable revenues do not exceed $30,000, you do not have to register for the GST or HST, but you can still choose to register voluntarily, even if your revenues are below this level. You should check and see whether these taxes apply in your business. If so, you will be required to obtain a Business

Number (BN) and remit any taxes collected on a regular basis. GST/HST is covered in more detail in Stage Seven, Financing.

How income tax is collected depends on the form of organization of your business. Sole proprietorships and partnerships file income tax returns as individuals, and the same regulations apply. Federal and provincial taxes are paid together, and only one personal income tax form is required annually for both, although payments may have to be remitted quarterly on the basis of your estimated annual earnings.

A corporation is treated as a separate entity for income tax purposes and taxed individually. The rules, tax rates, and regulations that apply to corporations are very complex and quite different from those that apply to individuals. You should obtain professional advice or contact the local tax authorities to determine your obligations under the Income Tax Act and to keep the amount of tax you have to pay to a minimum.

EMPLOYMENT STANDARDS

Not sure you are being treated fairly at work? Federal and provincial employment standards cover minimum wage, working hours, vacations, termination and complaints, as well as other working conditions. These requirements deal with such matters as:

1. Hours of work
2. Minimum wages
3. Statutory holidays
4. Overtime pay
5. Equal pay for equal work
6. Termination of employment
7. Severance pay
8. Working conditions
9. Health and safety concerns

You should contact the office of your provincial Ministry of Labour or its equivalent and request a copy of the *Employment Standards Act* in effect in your province as well as a copy of the *Guide to the Act*. This will provide you with specific information on all of these topics, or you can use the services of an accountant or lawyer. The Government of Canada has established minimum standards for employment and the Federal Labour Standards apply if you are a federally regulated employer (the standards are available on their website at www.labour.gc.ca).

RISK MANAGEMENT

Starting a new business involves taking risks. The time and money you spend getting your new venture off the ground could prove to be a wise investment if the business is successful and makes a lot of money, or it could be an expensive flop. Every decision you make along the way carries a risk, and only time will tell whether you made the correct choice or not.

It is not helpful to spend all your time worrying about problems—worrying does not help, and sometimes a quick decision now can be better than a good decision later. But at the same time, you cannot afford to be too bullish—ignoring risks completely is very dangerous.

Instead, you need to take a balanced approach between these two extremes. You need to think carefully about every potential problem your business might face and determine whether you can take any action to mitigate it. This calm appraisal and considered assessment is known as *risk management.*

Some common threats to new firms include:

- The entry of new unexpected competition

- Increased cost of labour, supplies, or raw materials

- Changes to the economic landscape, such as a recession, increased interest rates, higher taxes, currency fluctuations, and inflation

- Catastrophic events or so-called acts of God, such as fire, flood, and similar events, or the sudden death of a partner

- Criminal acts, such as shoplifting, burglary, or embezzlement by employees

In addition to these things, you probably have some unique and more specific threats that you can identify in relation to your particular business. You need to look systematically at all these possible risks and prioritize them. Identify those that would be most damaging to your business if they occurred and those with the highest probability of occurring.

Once you have identified a problem, there are three broad approaches you can take to managing it:

- You can *reduce* it by taking some defensive action and possibly reducing its impact. This could include deciding to avoid taking an action entirely that you have determined to be too risky.

- You can *transfer* it or shift the risk to another party, for example, by outsourcing the work or by obtaining insurance

- You can *retain* it, accepting it as a possible cost of doing business and budgeting for it accordingly

Of course, each of these categories encompasses a range of techniques. The specific action you need to take will depend on the risk you are dealing with, but a useful first step is to decide whether you intend to reduce, transfer, or retain it.

One of the most common means of shifting at least some of the risk associated with the occurrence of a major catastrophe is through insurance. With insurance, you pay a relatively small amount in premium rather than run the risk of not protecting yourself against the possibility of a much larger financial loss.

Your business may include a number of valuable assets, such as computers, product inventory, machinery and equipment, vehicles, documents, and even yourself, among other things. Therefore, unexpected events, such as fire, flood, or the death of your partner, are some of the hazards against which you have to protect yourself. For example, you need to ask yourself:

- What would happen if the contents of my business premises were destroyed by fire?

- What if there was a break-in and my equipment was stolen?

- What if an employee or a client was badly hurt on my premises?

- What if I or my partner passed away unexpectedly?

Would your business be able to absorb the costs associated with these events and still be able to continue? After weighing the risks against the costs, you may decide that you need some protection if your business is likely to survive. This can be done through the use of insurance.

There are a number of different types of insurance you should consider obtaining for your business. You should discuss your situation with your insurance agent to arrange an appropriate program.

1. **General liability insurance** covers your liability to customers injured on your premises or injured off your premises by a product you have sold to them.

2. **Business premises insurance** will protect your business premises and equipment from loss due to fire, theft, and other perils.

3. **Business-use vehicle insurance** must be obtained for cars and other vehicles used in the conduct of your business.

4. **Business interruption or loss-of-income insurance** will enable you to continue to pay the bills if your business should be closed down by damage due to fire, flood, or other catastrophe.

5. **Disability or accident and sickness insurance** can continue to provide you with a source of income if you should become seriously sick or disabled and unable to continue to run your business for a period of time.

6. **Key-person insurance** can protect your business against the death of its key personnel. It is life insurance purchased by the business with the business being the sole beneficiary.

7. **Credit insurance** protects you from extraordinary bad debt losses due to a customer going out of business.

8. **Surety and fidelity bonds** protect you from the failure of another firm or individual to fulfill its contractual obligations.

9. **Partnership insurance** can protect you against suits arising from the actions of other partners in your business.

10. **Workers' compensation** provides compensation for your employees in case of illness or injuries related to their employment.

Even with insurance, things can be tough. Jay Jennings opened his new trendy clothing store for 20-something snowboarders, and six weeks later, a fire destroyed all his clothing stock, causing him to miss the key Christmas selling season. Over the summer, local road construction made it very difficult for customers to find and access his store, and a leaky roof damaged some of his inventory and store fixtures. Just as he was gearing up for the next Christmas, thieves broke into his store and stole some of his inventory and computer equipment. And then, just as he was getting things up and running again, a second break-in occurred, causing $100,000 in damage to his merchandise and equipment. Despite having insurance for most of these disasters and submitting three claims to his insurance companies, Jay admitted he was at the end of his rope and running out of money. Jay preserved and has expanded his business over the years.

An insurance program will not protect you from *all* the risks associated with running your business, but it will provide you with some financial protection against unpredictable occurrences in several areas that could threaten the survival of your venture.

Your lease may or may not contain a penalty clause limiting your exposure should you breach the lease. A penalty of three months' rent is common in many situations, although the landlord will want you or the directors of an incorporated business to sign personal guarantees for the amount of the penalty.

MENTORS   LO4

Everyone needs help when starting a business in one way or another. When you are small and starting out, it is always good to have a mentor who can walk you through the challenges and decisions that you have to make. A mentor will not tell you what to do but will help you work through the process of making the decision that is right for you.

Mentors are normally business owners with whom you have formed a relationship over time and respect them for what they offer to small business. Most incubator centres have Entrepreneurs in Residence, who will act as a mentor to small business. However, it is important for you to be confident that an assigned mentor is the right fit

OTHER CONSIDERATIONS

STARTING A NEW BUSINESS

1. **Plan for success** A business plan will help you think through a number of important aspects of your new business.

2. **Select the form of business** that is right for you.

3. **Register your business** The process and requirements vary from province to province.

4. **Do you need a business licence?** Check with your municipality and/or BizPal.ca to find out.

5. **Do you meet zoning and local bylaw requirements?** You will need to check your local bylaws to find out.

6. **Register for provincial taxes and local permits, if they apply.** Depending on the type of business you are in, you may need to collect provincial sales tax and apply for a vendor licence or other permits.

7. **GST, PST, HST basics** The two main taxes that businesses collect are the Goods and Services Tax (GST) and retail or provincial sales tax (PST). Several provinces combine the two taxes into a single tax known as the harmonized sales tax (HST). Check out Stage Seven, Financing, for more information on this related to your province or territory.

8. **Research and purchase business insurance** Running a business carries some risks. There are many types of insurance that offer protection.

9. **Understand HR issues and responsibilities** If you will be hiring staff, you will need to understand your obligations in three principal areas:
   - Payroll obligations regarding the remission of taxes
   - Local labour laws
   - Workers' Compensation Board (WCB) requirements

10. **Keep necessary records** When you run a business, you are required to keep permanent books and records for a specified period of time.

Source: CanadaOne (www.canadaone.com/ezine/oct03/checklist.html), accessed March 14, 2013.

for you and your business. You do not want someone to be a bully and tell you what to do, but you want and need someone that you trust and has a vested interest in you and your company.

BOARD OF DIRECTORS

A *board of directors* is a body of elected or appointed members who jointly oversee the activities of a company or organization. Other names include *board of governors, board of managers, board of regents, board of trustees,* and *board of visitors.* It is often simply referred to as "the board." Typical duties of boards of directors include:

- Governing the organization by establishing broad policies and objectives
- Selecting, appointing, supporting, and reviewing the performance of the chief executive
- Ensuring the availability of adequate financial resources
- Approving annual budgets
- Accounting to the stakeholders for the organization's performance
- Setting the salaries and compensation of company management

The legal responsibilities of boards and board members vary with the nature of the organization and with the jurisdiction within which it operates. For companies with publicly trading stock, these responsibilities are typically much more rigorous and complex than for those of other types.

Typically, the board chooses one of its members to be the *chairman*, who holds whatever title is specified in the bylaws.[1]

ADVISORY BOARDS

An advisory board is a group set up to meet regularly to review business plans and new projects and also to give feedback, as needed, whenever special questions arise. No business is too small to benefit from having an advisory board and an advisory board is such a powerful management tool that no small business should be without one.

An advisory board is composed of people with a genuine interest in your business and a desire to see it do well. Advisory board members will serve as a sounding board and as a source of ideas and expertise—and they will give you honest advice.

SUMMARY

There is no pat answer to the question of the legal form of organization you should adopt. A lot will depend on such issues as the expected size and growth rate of your new venture, your desire to limit your personal liability, whether you plan to start the business on a part-time or a full-time basis, whether you expect to lose or make money from a tax point of view during your first one or two years of operation, your need for other skills or additional capital, and so forth. Take a look at Table 6.1, which summarizes many of the important differences between the various forms of organization available to you and may help you make your decision.

One word of caution: If you are considering any type of *partnership* arrangement, be extremely careful. In hard reality, partners should fulfill at least one of two major needs for you: They should provide either needed *money* or needed *skills*. If you allow any other factors to overshadow these two essential criteria, you may be taking an unnecessary risk.

F Y I

RESOURCES

Federal Incorporation The Corporations Canada website provides information and instructions on incorporating your business. A sample federal incorporation form that can be completed online is available on this website. (www.ic.gc.ca)

Provincial Incorporation The Corporations Canada website provides a list of provincial registrars for incorporating your business within a province. (www.ic.gc.ca)

Shareholder Agreements Template MaRS has created a sample template of a shareholders' agreement to help streamline business for investors, founders, and their respective legal advisers. (www.marsdd.com)

Organizing Your Business—Shareholder Agreement The website provides a checklist to use when creating a shareholder agreement. (www.ic.gc.ca)

The International Co-operative Alliance (ICA) This is an independent, non governmental organization established in 1895 to unite, represent, and serve co-operatives worldwide. (www.ica.coop)

The Canadian Co-operative Association It provides leadership to promote, develop, and unite co-operatives and credit unions for the benefit of people in Canada. (www.coopscanada.coop)

The Ontario Co-operative Association It helps with Ontario co-operatives but provides a comprehensive list of co-operative resources and links around the world. (www.ontario.coop)

BizPal This is a website where Canadian provinces, territories, and hundreds of municipalities have collaborated to provide permits and licences that may be required to start and grow your business. (www.bizpal.ca)

Portail Québec This website provides access to permits and licensing information for doing business in Quebec. (www2.gouv.qc.ca)

TABLE 6.1   WHICH FORM OF BUSINESS ORGANIZATION IS BEST FOR YOU?

This table summarizes many of the important differences between the various forms of business available to you. Review each of the alternatives on the dimensions indicated and select which one best fits with your particular circumstances. This may vary from characteristic to characteristic, since there are pros and cons of each form. Once you have reviewed all dimensions, you should be able to select the organizational form that appears to be the best overall for your particular situation.

Form of Organization	(a) Initial Requirements and Costs	(b) Liability of Owners	(c) Control	(d) Taxes	(e) Transfer of Ownership	(f) Continuity	(g) Ability to Raise Money
(1) Sole Proprietorship	Minimum requirements; perhaps only registration of your business name	Unlimited liability	Absolute control over operations	Income from business taxed as personal income	May transfer ownership of assets	Business ceases to exist when owner quits or dies	Limited to what the owner can personally secure
(2) General Partnership	Easy and inexpensive to establish	Each partner is personally liable for all debts of the partnership	Requires majority vote of all general partners	Income from business is taxed as personal income of the partners	Requires agreement of all partners	Dissolved on withdrawal or death of partner unless specified in partnership agreement	Combined resources of all the partners can be used to raise capital
(3) Limited Partnership	Moderate requirements; should be registered provincially	Liability limited to the extent of their individual investment	May not participate in the day-to-day management of the business	Same as for general partners	May sell interest in the company	Same as general partnership	Limited liability may make it easier to raise capital but can be complicated
(4) Corporation	Most expensive; usually requires a lawyer to file Articles of Incorporation	Liability limited to investment in company	Control rests with shareholders	Corporation taxed on its income and shareholders taxed on dividends received	Easily transferred by selling shares of stock	Not affected by the death or withdrawal of any shareholder	The most attractive form for raising capital

Which form best meets your needs on each dimension (select one)?

(a) _____ (b) _____ (c) _____ (d) _____ (e) _____ (f) _____ (g) _____

Which form of organization do you feel best meets your overall needs? _____

One of the primary reasons new venture teams often fail is ill-advised partnerships. Partnerships entered into principally for reasons of friendship, shared ideas, or similar factors can create considerable stress for both the partnership and the individuals involved. It has often been said that a business partner should be chosen with as much care as you would choose a spouse. However, in contemporary society, perhaps even greater care should be exercised, since a partnership may be even more difficult to dissolve than a marriage. An unhappy partnership can dissolve your business much faster than you can dissolve the partnership.

INTELLECTUAL PROPERTY

Many entrepreneurs are also inventors. One of the primary problems faced by these inventor/entrepreneurs is how to protect the idea, invention, concept, system, design, name, or symbol that they feel may be the key to their business success. These ideas, inventions, and so on are commonly referred to as "intellectual property." Legislators have long recognized that society should provide some protection for the creators of this "intellectual property." The laws they have developed provide a form of limited monopoly to the creators of intellectual property in return for their disclosure of the details of the property to the public (Figure 6.3). You may not realize it, but your business may be creating valuable intellectual property assets that should be protected.

Intellectual property is broken down into five components under the law:

1. **Patents** are rights, granted by government, to exclude others from making, using, or selling your invention in Canada.
2. **Trademarks** are words, symbols, or designs, or a combination of these, used to distinguish a product or service.
3. **Copyrights** mean the right to copy. In general, only the copyright owner, often the creator of the work, is allowed to produce or reproduce the work or to permit anyone else to do so.
4. **Industrial designs** are the visual features, such as shape, configuration, and pattern, applied to a finished article.
5. **Integrated circuit topographies** are the three-dimensional electronic circuit designs used in technology.

Protection of your intellectual property can be expensive. While government costs may range from only a small fee for registration of a copyright to several hundred dollars for registration of a patent, many of the procedures can be quite complex and require you to obtain the services of a registered patent agent. This can increase the total cost of obtaining a patent by several thousand dollars, depending on the complexity of the application. Therefore, it is important that you understand the advantages and disadvantages provided by this protection, and its likely impact on the success and financial viability of your business.

APPLYING FOR A PATENT

A *patent* is a government grant that gives you the right to take legal action, if necessary, against other individuals who without your consent make, use, or sell the invention covered by your patent during the time the patent is in force. Patents are granted for 20 years from the date on which the application was first filed and are not renewable.

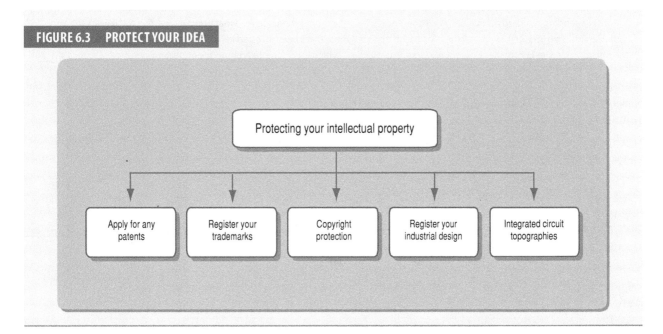

FIGURE 6.3   PROTECT YOUR IDEA

Protecting your intellectual property

| Apply for any patents | Register your trademarks | Copyright protection | Register your industrial design | Integrated circuit topographies |

OTHER CONSIDERATIONS

GENERIC VERSUS BRAND-NAME DRUG WAR HEATS UP

PHARMACIES TO SUFFER AS VICTORIA CUTS GENERIC DRUG PRICES

Any savings that might accrue at the provincial level from lower generic drug costs could be wiped out if Ottawa concludes an agreement with the European Union that would harmonize branded drug patent laws, warns Pharmasave's outgoing CEO.

The Comprehensive Economic Trade Agreement with the EU covers intellectual property rights. It includes a proposal that would extend by about two years the exclusivity period Canadian-branded drug makers now enjoy. Generic drug makers would have to wait a couple of years longer before they could start knocking off cheaper no-name variations of the drug.

"If you extend those patents, you have effectively wiped out all of the savings that you've garnered through the very aggressive pricing strategies that some provinces have deployed on generic pricing," said Pharmasave CEO Sue Paish.

She referred to the moves by B.C., Ontario, and Quebec to rewrite agreements with generic drug makers to reduce drug costs, which, according to one estimate, account for between 8 percent and 10 percent of the total healthcare budget in most jurisdictions.

Paish warns that both policies—extending drug patents and capping generic drug prices—are fraught with problems.

She points to Ontario, where generic drug pricing policies have already resulted in some drug makers simply withdrawing their products from the Ontario market. Canada represents only 3 percent of the global drug market, Paish said, so generic drug makers can always find buyers elsewhere.

"We could find ourselves in a situation where we've got a great drug price and no drugs, because the suppliers will sell somewhere else," Paish said.

Generic drug makers can produce pharmaceuticals at much lower costs than branded drug makers because they make products that another company invested hundreds of millions in dollars researching and developing, once the patents on those products expire.

"They copy what's been done by others," said Simon Pimstone, CEO Xenon Pharmaceuticals. "They don't actually invest in R&D in Canada, whereas the branded companies last year invested almost $1.5 billion in Canada."

It can cost tens of millions in clinical studies just to conclude that a new drug is ineffective.

"For a company to get a drug just into the clinic, it probably takes $20 million," Pimstone said. "Once it's in the clinic, you have still a 90 percent chance of failure. That's the odds in biotech. Of every 100 drugs that get in the clinic, 90 are going to fail."

Patents for branded drugs have 20-year terms. But it takes eight to 10 years—and up to $1 billion—to move most new drugs through three phases of clinical trials and another 12 to 18 months to get regulatory approval. During that time, the drug generates no revenue.

Only three out of every 10 drugs that make it to market will generate revenue that equals or exceeds R&D costs, according to a recent Canadian Chamber of Commerce report on intellectual property rights in Canada's pharmaceutical sector.

"After spending hundreds of millions, we'll only end up having patent protection for, what's on average, five to 10 years," Pimstone said. "Generic drug [makers] can use all the information that's out there that's been invested in by others, at hundreds of millions of dollars."

Jurisdictions like Europe have patent restoration provisions, which credit the dead time spent getting regulatory approval. This can extend the exclusivity of a branded drug by up to five years. Canada has no patent-restoration policies.

B.C.'s biotech and pharmaceutical companies warn they need the same kind of patent protection enjoyed in other jurisdictions, like the EU, if Canada wants its biotech sector to remain innovative.

There are about 130 companies or organizations in B.C. involved in biotechnology. Roughly 11,000 people are employed in the health-related life sciences sector, which has a GDP of about $1 billion, said Don Enns, president of LifeSciences BC.

"If we want to look at improving innovation, which should improve productivity within Canada, IP is one of those pillars we have to address," Enns said.

Because consumers only see the huge price differential between branded and generic drugs—and not the hundreds of millions spent getting the drug approved—Pimstone said his industry faces monumental public relations problem when arguing for stronger patent protection.

But he and others in the industry warn that, without stronger intellectual property rights, B.C.'s biotechs will be less inclined to do the original research needed to come up with new cures for diseases.

And ultimately, those discoveries may eventually reduce healthcare costs, said Gordon McCauley, CEO of Allon Therapeutics.

"If you have a drug that prevents a patient from being hospitalized, that's a dramatic saving to the healthcare system," he said. "If you want to talk about the costs, you also have to talk about the savings."

Source: Nelson Bennett, *Business In Vancouver*, June 5, 2012 (www.biv.com).

WHAT CAN YOU PATENT?

Yes	No
• New kind of door lock	• $E = MC^2$
• Apparatus for building door locks	• *Romeo and Juliet*
• Process for lubricating door locks	
• Method of making door locks	
• Improvements on any of these	

Source: Canadian Intellectual Property Office (www.cipo.ic.gc.ca), accessed March 19, 2013.

On expiration of its patent, a patented device falls into the *public domain*—anyone may make, use, or sell the invention.

To be patentable, your device must meet three basic criteria:

1. Have "absolute novelty." The invention must be new (first in the world).

2. Be useful. A patent cannot be obtained for something that does not work or has no useful function.

3. It must show inventive ingenuity and not be obvious to someone skilled in that area.

The invention can be a product (e.g., a door lock), a composition (e.g., a chemical composition used in lubricants for door locks), an apparatus (e.g., a machine for making door locks), a process (e.g., a method for making door locks), or an improvement on any of these.

You *cannot* patent a scientific principle, an abstract theorem, an idea, a method of doing business, a computer program, or a medical treatment.

A patent may be applied for only by the legal owner(s) of an invention. You cannot apply for a patent for an invention you may have seen in another country, even though that invention may never have been patented, described, or offered for sale in Canada.

Patents are now awarded to the *first inventor to file an application* with the Patent Office of the Canadian Intellectual Property Office (CIPO). This means you should file as soon as possible after completing your invention (though not prematurely if certain key elements or features of your idea would be missing from your application). It is also important that you not advertise or display or publish information on your invention too soon, as this may jeopardize your ability to obtain a valid patent later on. There is a one-year grace period for disclosure by an applicant, but it is suggested that the following rule of thumb be adopted: *Your application for a patent should be filed before your product is offered for public sale, shown at a trade show, or otherwise made public.*

How to Apply

If your idea is patentable and you wish to obtain patent protection, you should take the following steps:

1. **File online** You can go the Canadian Intellectual Property Office website (www.cipo.ic.gc), where you will find the information and forms that you need to complete. Once completed you can file online. A word of caution: Do not register just to save money. You might misunderstand or miss something completely that may be very costly down the road.

2. **Find a patent agent** The preparation and prosecution (assessment) of patent applications is quite complex. You should consult a patent agent trained in this specialized practice and registered to represent inventors before the Patent Office of the CIPO. Though hiring such an agent is not mandatory, it is highly recommended. The Patent Office provides a list of registered agents (www.ic.gc.ca) but will not recommend any particular one to you. The list of agents is available at the CIPO website (www.cipo.ic.gc).

3. **Conduct a preliminary search** The first step your agent will recommend is a preliminary search of existing patents to see if anything similar to your idea has already been patented, in which case you may conclude the process immediately. This can save you a lot of time and money that might otherwise be spent pursuing a futile application. The database search can be conducted in person by visiting the CIPO Patent Office or on the CIPO website. The online database has descriptions and drawings of patents issued in Canada since 1920.

4. **Prepare a patent application** A patent application consists of an abstract, a specification, and drawings. See Figures 6.4 and 6.5.

    An *abstract* is a brief summary of the material in the specification. The *specification* is a document that contains (1) a complete description of the invention and its purpose and (2) *claims*, which are an explicit statement of what your invention is and the boundaries of the patent protection you are seeking. *Drawings* must be included whenever the invention can be described pictorially. Typically, all inventions except chemical compositions and some processes can be described by means of drawings.

5. **File your application** Filing your application means submitting it along with a petition asking the Commissioner of Patents to grant you a patent. In Canada, filing must be done within one year of any use or public disclosure of the invention.

    If your application is accepted, you will be required to pay an annual maintenance fee to keep it in effect for the 20-year period. Independent inventors and small businesses whose gross annual revenues are less than $2 million pay lower maintenance fees than businesses classified as "other than small." Fees range from $0 in the first year to $225 in 15 to 19 years of the patent's life for these small entities.

6. **Request examination** Your application will not automatically be examined simply because you have filed it. You must formally request examination and submit the appropriate fee. This request can be made any time within five years of your filing date.

    Filing an application and not requesting examination can be a cheap and effective way of obtaining some protection for your invention without necessarily incurring all the costs of obtaining a patent. For example, let us assume you want to protect your idea but do not wish to spend all the money required to obtain a patent until you have assessed the financial feasibility of your invention. Filing an application establishes your rights to the invention, and publication of the application by the Patent Office informs other people of your claim to the product or process. If someone infringes on your invention after your application is published, you have five years to decide whether to pursue the grant of a patent and seek retroactive compensation.

    Requesting an examination, however, is no guarantee that a patent will be granted. And if it is not, you will have no grounds to claim damages for infringement on your idea.

    The CIPO Patent Office receives over 35,000 applications a year, mostly from U.S. inventors and companies. As a result, the examination process can be very slow, commonly taking two to three years to complete.

7. **If necessary, file amendment letters** When you request an examination, the patent examiner will assess your claims and either approve or reject your application. If your application is rejected, you can respond by filing an *amendment letter* with the Commissioner of Patents. The letter will be studied by the examiner. If the patent is not then granted, there may be a request for further amendments. This process will continue until the patent is granted, your application is withdrawn, or your application is rejected.

Protection Provided by Your Patent

As you can see, the patenting process is complex, costly, and time consuming. If you have a patent application in process and are concerned that someone else may attempt to patent your invention, you may use the label "Patent Pending" or "Patent Applied For" to inform the public that your application for a patent has been filed. This, however, has no legal significance and does not mean that a patent will necessarily be granted. Of course, it is illegal to use this term if, in fact, no application is on file.

If your patent application is granted, the onus will be entirely on you to protect your rights under the patent because the Patent Office has no authority to prosecute for patent infringement. If infringement occurs, you may (1) bring legal

FIGURE 6.4   PATENT APPLICATION FORM

FORM 3—PETITION FOR GRANT OF A PATENT

(Subsection 27[2] of the *Patent Act)*

1. The applicant, _____, whose complete address is _____, requests the grant of a patent for an invention, entitled _____, which is described and claimed in the accompanying specification.

2. This application is a division of application number _____, filed in Canada on _____.

3. (1) The applicant is the sole inventor.

3. (2) The inventor is _____, whose complete address is _____ and the applicant is the legal representative of the inventor.

4. The applicant requests priority in respect of the application on the basis of the following previously regularly filed application:

Country of Filing	Application Number	Filing Date
_____	_____	_____

5. The applicant appoints _____, whose complete address in Canada is _____, as the applicant's representative in Canada, pursuant to section 29 of the *Patent Act.*

6. The applicant appoints _____, whose complete address is _____, as the applicant's patent agent.

7. The applicant believes that in accordance with the *Patent Rules* they are entitled to pay fees at the small entity level in respect of this application and in respect of any patent issued on the basis of this application.

8. The applicant requests that Figure No. _____ of the drawings accompany the abstract when it is open to public inspection under section 10 of the *Patent Act* or published.

_____
signature

Instructions

In section 1, subsection 3(2) and sections 5 and 6, names and addresses must be presented in the following order with a clearly visible separation between the various elements: family name (in capital letters), given name(s), initials, or firm name, street name and number, city, province or state, postal code, telephone number, fax number and country.

Sections 2 and 8 should be deleted if they do not apply.

The contents of sections 3 to 7 may be included in the petition or submitted in a separate document.

In section 3, in accordance with section 37 of the *Patent Rules,* only subsection 3(1) or subsection 3(2) should be included.

In general, the inclusion of a signature in the petition is optional. However, in accordance with paragraph 3.01(1)(e) of the *Patent Rules,* a signature is required if a small entity declaration is included in the petition.

FIGURE 6.5 PATENT ABSTRACT

CA 02602012 2007-09-18

(12) INTERNATIONAL APPLICATION PUBLISHED UNDER THE PATENT COOPERATION TREATY (PCT)

(19) World Intellectual Property Organization
International Bureau

(43) International Publication Date
28 September 2006 (28.09.2006)

PCT

(10) International Publication Number
WO 2006/100436 A1

(51) International Patent Classification:
F03B 13/18 (2006.01)

(21) International Application Number:
PCT/GB2006/000906

(22) International Filing Date: 15 March 2006 (15.03.2006)

(25) Filing Language: English

(26) Publication Language: English

(30) Priority Data:
0505906.8   23 March 2005 (23.03.2005)   GB

(71) Applicant *(for all designated States except US)*: **AQUA-MARINE POWER LIMITED** [GB/GB]; Barony House, Stoneyfield Business Park, Inverness IV2 7PA (GB).

(72) Inventors; and
(75) Inventors/Applicants *(for US only)*: **THOMSON, Allan, Robert** [GB/GB]; Wester Aultlugie, Daviot Muir, Inverness IV1 2ER (GB). **WHITTAKER, Trevor, John** [GB/GB]; 8 Cuttles Ridge, Comber, Northern Ireland BT23 5YT (GB). **CROWLEY, Michael, David** [GB/GB]; 11 Glebe Close, Frampton on Severn, Gloucestershire GL2 7E2 (GB).

(74) **Agents: NAISMITH, Robert, Stewart** et al.; Marks & Clerk, 19 Royal Exchange Square, Glasgow G1 3AE (GB).

(81) **Designated States** *(unless otherwise indicated, for every kind of national protection available)*: AE, AG, AL, AM, AT, AU, AZ, BA, BB, BG, BR, BW, BY, BZ, CA, CH, CN, CO, CR, CU, CZ, DE, DK, DM, DZ, EC, EE, EG, ES, FI, GB, GD, GE, GH, GM, HR, HU, ID, IL, IN, IS, JP, KE, KG, KM, KN, KP, KR, KZ, LC, LK, LR, LS, LT, LU, LV, LY, MA, MD, MG, MK, MN, MW, MX, MZ, NA, NG, NI, NO, NZ, OM, PG, PH, PL, PT, RO, RU, SC, SD, SE, SG, SK, SL, SM, SY, TJ, TM, TN, TR, TT, TZ, UA, UG, US, UZ, VC, VN, YU, ZA, ZM, ZW.

(84) **Designated States** *(unless otherwise indicated, for every kind of regional protection available)*: ARIPO (BW, GH, GM, KE, LS, MW, MZ, NA, SD, SL, SZ, TZ, UG, ZM, ZW), Eurasian (AM, AZ, BY, KG, KZ, MD, RU, TJ, TM), European (AT, BE, BG, CH, CY, CZ, DE, DK, EE, ES, FI, FR, GB, GR, HU, IE, IS, IT, LT, LU, LV, MC, NL, PL, PT, RO, SE, SI, SK, TR), OAPI (BF, BJ, CF, CG, CI, CM, GA, GN, GQ, GW, ML, MR, NE, SN, TD, TG).

Published:
— *with international search report*

For two-letter codes and other abbreviations, refer to the "Guidance Notes on Codes and Abbreviations" appearing at the beginning of each regular issue of the PCT Gazette.

(54) Title: APPARATUS AND CONTROL SYSTEM FOR GENERATING POWER FROM WAVE ENERGY

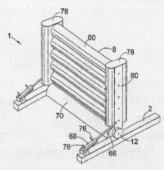

(57) **Abstract:** The present invention relates to a wave energy conversion device (1) , for use in relatively shallow water, which has a base portion (2) for anchoring to the bed of a body of water (6) and an upstanding flap portion (8) pivotally connected (12) to the base portion. The flap portion is biased to the vertical and oscillates, backwards and forwards about the vertical in response to wave motion acting on its faces. Power extraction means extract energy from the movement of the flap portion. When the base portion (2) is anchored to the bed of a body of water (6) with the flap portion (8) facing the wave motion, the base portion (2) and the flap portion (8) extend vertically through at least the entire depth of the water, to present a substantially continuous surface to the wave motion throughout the full depth of water from the wave crest to the sea bed. A plurality of devices can be interconnected to form one system. The distance between the plurality of flaps is dependent on the wavelenght.

WO 2006/100436 A1

OTHER CONSIDERATIONS

BENEFITS OF A PATENT SEARCH

If you are a small business person, a patent search can help you:

- Identify trends and developments in a particular field of technology
- Discover new products that you may be able to license from the patentee or use without needing a licence
- Find information that keeps you from duplicating the research
- Identify unproductive areas of inquiry by reading about the current state of the art
- Keep track of the work of a particular individual or company by seeing what patents they have been granted
- Find a solution to a technical problem you may have
- Gain new ideas for further research in a particular field

Source: "Summary of benefits of a patent search"—adapted and reproduced as "Other considerations: Benefits of a Patent Search." Reproduced with the permission of the Minister of Public Works and Government Services Canada, 2002. Accessed March 19, 2013.

action to compel the offender to account for any profits made, (2) seek an injunction to prevent further use of your patent, or (3) obtain a court order for the destruction of any materials produced that infringe on your rights. This, however, can be a very expensive and time-consuming process, which may prohibit a small business from enforcing its rights.

A patent granted in Canada or the United States provides you with no protection outside the country in which it was originally granted. To obtain protection in other countries, you must register your patent in each country within the time limit permitted by law (typically one year from your initial application). You can apply for a foreign patent either from within Canada via the Canadian Patent Office or directly through the patent office of the country or countries concerned. Under the terms of the Patent Cooperation Treaty, it is possible to file for a patent in as many as 43 countries, including the United States, Japan, and most of Europe, by completing a single, standardized application that can be filed in Canada. Ask your patent agent about these procedures before you decide to file in another country.

You should realize that holding a patent on a worthy idea does not necessarily mean commercial success.

An invention succeeds by acceptance in the marketplace. Your patent may be perfectly valid and properly related to your invention but commercially worthless. Thousands of patents are issued each year that fall into this category. A patent does not necessarily contribute to the economic success of an invention. In some high-technology fields, for example, innovations can become obsolete long before a patent is issued, effectively making the patent worthless.

Holding a patent may improve your profitability by keeping similar products off the market, giving you an edge. But there is no guarantee you will be able to prevent all competition. In fact, disclosing your idea in a patent might open the way for a competitor to steal your concept and introduce an imitation or "knock-off" of your product. Litigation, if it becomes necessary, can require considerable financial resources, and the outcome is by no means assured. A high percentage of patent infringements challenged in court result in decisions unfavourable to the patent holder.

However, there are many instances where patenting a product concept or idea has led to commercial success. An example is Ron Foxcroft's pea-less whistle, the Fox 40. Foxcroft developed the whistle after his regular whistle failed to blow while he was refereeing a key basketball game during a pre-Olympic tournament in Brazil. To date, his company has sold almost 100 million whistles in 126 countries around the world. However, it has also spent $750,000 registering dozens of patents and trademarks in an effort to protect Foxcroft's invention, and in 2001 was involved in 11 infringement cases against other firms that are making a cheaper version of the Fox 40, selling an identical product under another name, or just passing a cheaper imitation off as a genuine Fox 40 whistle.

Applying for a patent for a tangible product is easier to understand. But, when it comes to technology, it is a different ball game. In the Entrepreneurs in Action box, Alexander Fernandes, CEO of successful surveillance technology company Avigilon, shares how to take a technology innovation to market.

ENTREPRENEURS IN ACTION

HOW TO TAKE A TECHNOLOGY INNOVATION TO MARKET

ALEXANDER FERNANDES, CEO OF THE HIGHLY SUCCESSFUL VANCOUVER SURVEILLANCE TECHNOLOGY COMPANY AVIGILON, SHARES HIS SECRETS

Nine years ago, I saw an opportunity. At a time when technology was accelerating at a robust pace, the surveillance industry stayed stagnant. Back then, so many industries where safety and security are a top priority were relying on outdated, grainy, analogue video surveillance systems.

As a former user of video surveillance in business myself, I had always found the blurry footage provided little, if any, value. I knew that plenty of companies and organizations could benefit from a high-definition surveillance system. This was the spark that inspired who Avigilon is today. But the road to such successful position is fraught with challenges and lessons, some of which I'd like to share with other technology entrepreneurs.

So once you have identified an unmet need in the market, the question becomes: How do you take it there?

Taking an innovation to market can be an intimidating process. You have to thoroughly understand the competitive landscape and assess where your product fits into the equation. Where is your differentiation and competitive advantage going to lie? Where and how are you going to sell your product? Who are you going to sell to? If you can't sell your product for a good profit, reassess your plan.

Once you conduct your market and industry research, and validate that there is a need for your technology, the next step is the proof of concept stage. This is the time when you put together and test a design to see if your product has legs. One of the most common mistakes technology entrepreneurs make is they build their product on current technology. If possible, build your product on future technology. That way by the time you get to market you're bringing something cutting edge to the market rather than something stale.

You also want to develop a strategy to protect your intellectual property such as copyright, inventions, trade secrets, and patentable inventions. However, financing your intellectual property and building a prototype does not come cheap. With getting significant loans becoming more challenging in tough economic times, securing seed funding is absolutely crucial at

USED WITH THE PERMISSION OF AVIGILON.

this stage. One of the big advantages young companies have operating their businesses out of Vancouver is that the area is conducive for developing technology. Ideally, you will be fortunate enough to have some startup capital at your disposal. But for new tech companies that need assistance, there are many alternate resources available, at a price.

After your business model is established and your seed capital is in place, the product development stage is the period to rigorously assess your innovation—whether that is software or hardware. It's the time you take your customer feedback and industry requirements and take your best shot at creating a unique product or service that ideally meets the unmet needs of a large and growing market. You should also be growing your team beyond engineers and researchers. There should be employees that focus on marketing your product as well people to assist with customer support, production, and the supply chain. They will be the ones who will get your product from an idea to revenue.

Part of the great challenge in bringing innovative products and solutions to market is the fact that things seldom go exactly as planned. Be ready to deal with unforeseen expenses, changes in the market, or delays in development or production. Make sure to hire great minds that are adaptable as well as disciplined in managing your capital.

One of the keys to your longevity will lie in your ability to stay ahead of your competition. Because it's not about just taking your product to market, it's about staying there and dominating it.

Source: BIV is published by BIV Media Limited Partnership. Alexander Fernandes, March 5, 2013, BusinessVancouver (www.biv.com).

Having a patent does not keep counterfeiters away either. Canada Goose founded in a small warehouse in Toronto, Canada, over 50 years ago, has grown to be recognized internationally as one of the world's leading manufacturers of extreme weather outerwear. But, like many world-leading brands, their success has led to their products being copied by counterfeiters. Canada Goose took action and, as you will read in the Entrepreneurs in Action box, they won their case.

ENTREPRENEURS IN ACTION

CANADA GOOSE WINS LANDMARK COUNTERFEIT AND TRADEMARK INFRINGEMENT CASE IN SWEDEN

DISTRICT COURT OF STOCKHOLM, SWEDEN, AWARDS DAMAGES AND SENTENCES DEFENDANTS TO SERVE TIME IN PRISON

Canada Goose, one of the world's leading manufacturers of extreme weather outerwear, today welcomed a recent decision from the District Court of Stockholm in one of the most significant counterfeit cases in Sweden, which found five individuals jointly and severally guilty of felony fraud, trademark infringement, and customs offences. The Court sentenced two of the defendants to serve time in prison and also awarded Canada Goose damages for a total judgment of 701, 000 SEK (approximately $105,000 Canadian)

The defendants—five Swedish nationals—who used a number of aliases and false Swedish business name, operated the business from Thailand and sold thousands of counterfeit Canada Goose jackets alongside other luxury goods, between 2009 and 2012 in Sweden. Purchased in Thailand and repackaged in Sweden, the fake goods were found to be of poor quality in fabric and detailing, and used raccoon dog fur instead of coyote around the jacket hoods. Despite a blatant disregard for the law and confidence that he would not be caught, the main culprit was arrested in Bangkok in May 2012 and extradited to Sweden to be tried.

In its judgment, the District Court of Stockholm indicated that counterfeiting is a significant problem—estimating that 10 percent of all goods in the European Union are counterfeit—and that the practice has a harmful impact on the economy, including causing unemployment.

"This is a clear victory in protecting intellectual property and consumers, and it sends a strong message that counterfeiters will

not be tolerated," said Kevin Spreekmeester, VP Global Marketing, Canada Goose Inc., and co-chair of the Canadian Intellectual Property Council (CIPC). "Not only do these fake products impact our business and our brand reputation, but more importantly, they put consumers at risk for potential health issues."

GETSTOCK/ RICK MADONIK

Previous analysis of imitation Canada Goose jackets have shown that they include feather mulch and other fillers which are often coated in bacteria, fungus, mildew, and even feces. As well, because the jackets don't use real down or fur, which provide the necessary warmth and protection from the elements in extreme cold climates, the threat of frostbite or freezing to death becomes a reality. To educate and protect consumers, Canada Goose has made significant investments in the fight against counterfeit goods:

- Every Canada Goose jacket and accessory includes a hologram in its seam as proof of authenticity.
- On the Canada Goose website, consumers can enter the URL of any website they believe may be selling counterfeit merchandise, to verify whether or not it is an authorized retailer.
- Canada Goose continuously works with law enforcement agencies, border protection services, and financial institutions and has hired third-party online brand protection agencies to stop the sales of counterfeit products.

Source: Posted by Canada Goose Press Release, Toronto and Stockholm, October 23, 2012, accessed March 20, 2013.

You have to watch for more than counterfeiters; you have to watch for infringements. In 1993, Michel Vulpe founded a company called Infrastructures for Information, Inc. (see the Entrepreneurs in Action box), known as i4i, the Toronto company specialized in the delivery of XML-based document processing solutions. In 1994, Vulpe and his business partner, Stephen Owens, filed to patent an invention that made it possible to use consumer word-processing software, such as Microsoft Word, to edit XML and SGML. In patent language, the innovation was a "system and method for the separate manipulation of the architecture and content of a document, particularly for data representation and transformations." Essentially, Vulpe and Owens' invention gave regular computer users the ability to create documents with XML functionality, enabling sharing, searching, and updating within and between companies, and over the Internet. With his patent application making its way through the U.S. Patent and Trademark Office (USPTO), Vulpe began to seek out likely investors to help grow his company. Thanks to an accidental meeting with investment manager Neil Nisker, Vulpe raised some seed money and won an introduction to Loudon Owen, managing director of venture capital firm McLean Watson.

HOW i4i TOOK ON MICROSOFT AND WON

Almost immediately after the patent was granted, the USPTO itself became one of i4i's clients. The software helped the government agency implement a new electronic workflow for filing patents by designing a system to guide lawyers and patent agents through the process of creating XML-based patent applications in Microsoft Word.

i4i's products have been used in the intelligence and defence industries, in aircraft and vehicle maintenance and manufacturing, and in database software for galleries, museums, and libraries. Pharmaceutical companies make up one of i4i's largest client groups. They use i4i's technology to create product labels, keep track of side effects, drug interactions, dosages, and so on. NASA, the FDA, Bayer, Novartis, Baxter, Boeing, the US Social Security Administration, and the U.S. Marine Corps are all customers of i4i.

Between 2000 and 2002, Microsoft was in talks with i4i about joining forces to pitch their combined services to certain clients. Chief among these clients were intelligence officials in Washington who needed to sort through enormous quantities of data related to 9/11. i4i had the tools to distill essential patterns from the data, while Microsoft did not. In the end, Microsoft elected to pursue the project on its own, but provided no clear explanation for the change of heart. At the time, and later via an email exchange, Microsoft representatives acknowledged the value of i4i's patented technology.

In 2003, Microsoft introduced a version of Word with XML-editing capability. i4i's share of the market dropped off sharply and the word on the street was that Microsoft was offering the same customizable XML capability as i4i.

Although Vulpe and Owen suspected that Microsoft was infringing on their patent, they had no way of knowing for sure. They couldn't simply look at Microsoft's source code because it was proprietary. They painstakingly documented i4i's interactions with Microsoft, as well as their patent application process and approached a leading patent litigation management firm for help in making their case. Ownership of the patent was transferred to a new entity, i4i LP, and an exclusive licence was issued to i4i, Inc. to allow for the company's ongoing operations. The suit that i4i eventually brought against Microsoft was financed by Northwater Patent Fund, in exchange for an equity stake in the new company. As a partner, Northwater brought important expertise in patent litigation. The case was first filed in May 2007 in the eastern district of Texas. This area of Texas is known for its speedy "rocket docket" treatment of patent infringement cases, and also for its plaintiff-friendly record of case decisions.

A seven-day jury trial began in May 2009 and concluded with the ruling that i4i's patent was valid and had been knowingly and willfully infringed by Microsoft. The district court awarded i4i US$290 million in damages and Microsoft was issued an injunction against the continued sale of i4i's patented technology in its products.

Source: MaRS Discovery District (www.marsdd.com/articles/case-study-how-i4i-took-on-microsoft-and-won/), accessed March 18, 2013

Microsoft appealed the decision to the U.S. Court of Appeals for the Federal Circuit. Dell and HP filed *amicus curiae* briefs alongside Microsoft's appeal asking the court to overturn the injunction. In December 2009, the appeals court issued a ruling upholding the decision of the district court with one exception; the appeals court extended the grace period within which Microsoft would be forced to comply with the injunction. Microsoft filed a petition with the U.S. Court of Appeals for the Federal Circuit for a rehearing of the case. In June 2011, the U.S. Supreme Court ruled to uphold the verdict against Microsoft for infringing i4i's patent.

The following key points emerge from i4i's story:

- **Document your intellectual property (IP) meticulously and clearly** Had Owen and Vulpe not kept thorough records of their IP filings as well as their dealings with Microsoft, they may not have had sufficient evidence to support their case.
- **IP-related lawsuits are time-consuming and expensive** Vulpe estimates that the Microsoft case has cost his company at least $10 million over the years. In addition, a case of this magnitude can demotivate and otherwise damage a company's regular operations. As it was, Vulpe and Owen had the managerial resources to continue to support operations at i4i during the case. This helped to discredit Microsoft's claims that i4i was a "patent troll" hoping to strike it rich on a lawsuit.
- **Get help** Vulpe and Owen recognized that to confront an organization the size of Microsoft, they needed a partner with experience in IP litigation. With a creative contingency-plus-equity compensation agreement, a relatively small company was able to leverage a powerful and experienced ally in their suit against Microsoft.
- **Know the system** While the IP litigation community may know that software IP cases are best fought in east Texas, and the reasons why, the average technology entrepreneur may not. Thus it's important to consult a lawyer experienced in IP litigation as early as possible in the run-up to a potential lawsuit. IP litigation lawyers differ from lawyers that help companies apply for patents, so be wise to the difference, and choose well.

- **Consider alternatives** While Microsoft (apparently) elected to use i4i's patented technology without permission, one alternative might have been to negotiate a cross-licensing agreement. If both parties had technology that would add commercial value to the other's offering, a royalty-free cross-licensing agreement would have given both companies access to proprietary technology without patent infringement. Microsoft already has such agreements in place with Novell, Autodesk, SAP, HP, and others.

- **Some companies choose free** While i4i's document architecture/XML patent was at the core of their commercial offering, many companies opt to allow unlimited, royalty-free licence access to patented software technology that is peripheral to their business. Companies that have made use of this "open source" model of technology licensing include Novell, Red Hat, Sun Microsystems, and Microsoft.

Source: MaRS Discovery District (www.marsdd.com), articles/case-study-how-i4i-took-on-microsoft-and-won/), accessed March 18, 2013.

Vulpe and Owen hit it off and, in 1996, sealed a deal for a $2-million venture capital investment over a coffee-shop handshake. By 1998, the USPTO had issued patent #5,787,449, recognizing i4i's innovation as novel, useful, and non-obvious (the three pillars of patent eligibility), and granted i4i the exclusive right to capitalize on its innovation in the marketplace.

Bob Dickie of Spark Innovations Inc. has built his whole business around patentable products. He holds 80 patents for his inventions and thinks patent protection is crucial to business success these days. Dickie's first product was the FlatPlug, billed as the first innovation in electrical plug design in 75 years. The FlatPlug lies flat against the wall, unlike a conventional electrical plug that sticks out perpendicular to the wall. As a result, it does not waste space behind furniture and is more difficult for children to pry out. Dickie got the idea when he saw his daughter reach through her crib bars for a conventional plug. FlatPlug is protected by eight U.S. and worldwide patents. Even the package—a cardboard sleeve that keeps the extension cord and the plug in place—is patented.

Dickie has a number of strict criteria that he feels a product idea should meet to have commercial potential:

- **It must be 10 times better** Rather than evolutionary improvements in product design, Dickie looks for concepts with enough of a "story" to make distribution channels take serious notice.
- **It must be patentable** "If we can't get a patent, the business is absolutely dead," says Dickie.
- **It must be a mass-production item** High-volume products have a higher turnover, reducing much of the risk of holding inventory.
- **It should be smaller than a bread box** Small items are easier to make and less costly to design, package, and transport.
- **It must lend itself to distribution through existing channels** Going through established market lines speeds the acceptance of a new product.
- **It should have no government involvement** Spark Innovations stays away from products that are motivated by or are dependent on government support at any level.
- **It must be useful** Dickie works only with products that have long-term, practical usefulness. No novelties, fads, or games.[2]

Commercializing Your Patent

Once you have taken steps to protect your idea, you will have to give some thought to the best way to market it and hopefully turn a profit. There are a number of possible options.

- Setting up your own business, like the individuals profiled in the Entrepreneurs in Action boxes, is the option that usually comes to mind. It allows you to retain full control of your idea but also means you assume all the risk.

- Another possibility is to license the invention. With a licence you grant one or more individuals the right to manufacture and sell your innovation in exchange for royalties. The licence can apply generally or only to a specific market or geographic region, as long as you have obtained patent protection for that area.

- A third option is to sell your patent. By selling your patent, you give up all rights to the idea in return for a lump sum of money. However, then you do not have to worry about whether the product becomes a commercial success.

Watch Out for Invention Scams

Many people with a new idea immediately start looking for a company that they think will buy or license their idea. Any number of companies advertise on radio, TV, or in magazines, offering to help you patent your idea and market it for you. They offer their assistance as a "one-stop" do-it-all-for-you ticket to success for your great new idea. Most of these offers are outright scams. These firms generally follow a three-step process:

1. They send you a free kit with a pre signed *confidentiality* or *non disclosure* agreement and some general information about the services they provide.

2. Next, they offer to do a marketing evaluation of the potential for your idea. This may cost several hundred dollars.

3. They then present a package offering to patent your invention and promote your idea by submitting it to manufacturers, potential licensees, and industry in general. This time the fee can be anywhere from $3,000 to $10,000 or higher.

Only after a year or two of unfulfilled promises and zero activity do you begin to realize that you might have been scammed, but by then it is too late. It is best to avoid these kinds of operators in the first place. The truth is that commercializing a new idea is a long, complex process that takes time, energy, knowledge, and persistence. No one can guarantee you success.

REGISTERING YOUR TRADEMARK

A *trademark* is a word, symbol, picture, design, or combination of these that distinguishes your goods and services from those of others in the marketplace. A trademark might also be thought of as a "brand name" or "identifier" that can be used to distinguish the products of your firm. For example, both the name "McDonald's" and the symbol of the golden arches are (among others) registered trademarks of the McDonald's Corporation.

To *register* a trademark means to file it with a government agency for the purpose of securing the following rights and benefits:

1. Exclusive permission to use the brand name or identifier in Canada

2. The right to sue anyone you suspect of infringing on your trademark to recover lost profits on sales made under your trade name, and for other damages and costs

3. The basis for filing an application in another country should you wish to export your product

To be registerable, a trademark must be distinctive and not so similar in appearance, sound, or concept to a trademark already registered, or pending registration, as to be confused with it. For example, the following trademarks would not be registerable: "Cleanly Canadian" for a soft drink (too close to Clearly Canadian, a fruit-flavoured mineral water); "Extendo" for a utility knife (too close to Exacto).

The value of a trademark lies in the goodwill the market attaches to it and the fact that consumers will ask for your brand with the expectation of receiving the same quality product or service as previously. Therefore, unlike a patent, a trademark should be registered only if you have some long-term plans for it that will result in an accumulation of goodwill.

It is possible for you to use a trademark without registering it. Registration is not mandatory, and unregistered marks have legal status. But registration is advised for most commonly used identifiers, since it does establish immediate, obvious proof of ownership, particularly if the business is looking to expand geographically.

Failing to properly register your trademarks can sometimes lead to future problems. Robert Arthurs of the True North Clothing Company learned this lesson the hard way. Despite consulting with a lawyer and a government agency, his company's failure to do appropriate due diligence and search out previous registrations of the "True North" trade name ended up costing it a lot of money in legal and other fees. In the end, the company had to buy the rights to use the name from the registered owner despite assurances that the term was part of the "public domain" and available for use by anyone.

How to Register Your Trademark

In Canada, it is possible for you to register your trademark before you actually use it, but the mark will not be validated until it is actually put into service. Registration of a trademark involves the following steps:

1. **A search of previous and pending registrations** As with a patent, a search should be conducted to determine that your trademark does not conflict with others already in use. The search can be conducted at the CIPO Trade-marks Branch in Gatineau, Quebec, where a public inventory of all registered trademarks and pending applications is maintained. You can also conduct a search electronically at the CIPO website.

2. **An application to register your trademark** This involves filing an application for registration of your trademark.

Once your application is received, it is published in the *Trade-marks Journal* to see if anyone opposes your registration.

Even though registering a trademark is relatively simple compared with applying for a patent, it is recommended that you consult a trademark agent who is registered with the CIPO Trade-marks Branch.

One of the most vexing issues facing new companies or product developers is to protect their brands with trademark registration. Simon Pennel of St. Moritz Watch Corp. (see the Entrepreneurs in Action box) learned about the quirks of intellectual property when it encountered trademark opposition from the town of St. Mortiz, Switzerland.

Maintaining and Policing Your Trademark

It normally takes about a year from the date of application for a trademark to be registered. Registration is effective for 15 years and may be renewed for a series of 15-year terms as long as the mark is still in use.

As with a patent, it is up to the owner of the trademark to police its use, since the government provides no assistance in the enforcement of trademark rights. Some firms have gone to considerable lengths in an effort to enforce what they feel are their legal rights. For example, The Brick Warehouse, an Edmonton-based national chain of furniture stores, sued Fred and Cynthia Brick of the family-owned Brick's Fine Furniture in Winnipeg to get them to stop using the name "Brick" for their store. This was despite the fact that the Brick family began operating their provincially registered

EARLY TRADEMARK INITIATIVES CAN TRUMP BRAND TROUBLE LATER

Money is always in short supply; will a trademark really matter at the early stages?

Vancouver-based St. Moritz Watch Corp. learned about the quirks of intellectual property when it encountered trademark opposition from the town of St. Moritz, Switzerland.

St. Moritz founder and president Simon Pennell relates a very modern story.

The 31-year-old Vancouver company earns millions annually by selling Momentum® brand watches in North America, Europe, and Asia at hundreds of locations, via distributors and, increasingly, online.

"Money was tight when I started the business," Pennell said. "Registering trademarks was very expensive then, so I registered in Canada, the U.S.A. and Japan, where we had a big customer."

Though Pennell considered European protection, it then meant country-by-country registration, which, at $5,000 per country, would have been prohibitively expensive.

The town of St. Moritz, Switzerland, later registered trademarks for virtually every product category, everything from luggage and jewellery to cigars.

About 15 years ago, when Pennell's company started selling to a large European customer, the "St. Moritz" watch brand came to St. Moritz town's attention, which sought to block the watch trade.

Despite approaching the town, Pennell couldn't acquire rights for his watches, so he embarked on a dual-brand strategy intended to avoid trademark infringement in Europe while retaining brand value built under "St. Moritz" elsewhere.

About six years ago, this strategy fully migrated to branding watches solely under the "Momentum" label.

Other factors supporting the brand shift included availability of the "Momentum" brand in all relevant geographies, and the "action" appeal of Momentum to the critical, younger demographic.

It wasn't cheap to shift brand. Directly related legal costs for all countries totalled nearly $100,000. Fifteen years later, it's still costing the company to change market awareness.

"To this day, we have customers who are surprised that Momentum and St. Moritz are the same company," said Pennell.

If he were starting his company today, what would Pennell do?

"If you can register your trademark in key markets worldwide, do it. If we could have secured EU registration back then, we would have done it—no question."

"With the importance of online sales, a powerful URL that links to your brand is almost more important than a trademark

SOURCE: JUDY BISHOP, BUSINESS IN VANCOUVER, SEPTEMBER 27, 2011 (WWW.BIV.COM).

registration." Happily, today's landscape is different, according to Roger Kuypers, intellectual property lawyer at Fasken Martineau.

For companies considering Europe, there's a pan-European trademark registration that covers all 27 European Union states—a market of more than 400 million people. It takes less than a year and costs between $3,000 and $5,000 per mark. (It's worth noting that although there is an EU trademark, national registries trump the more global EU protection.)

North American trademark registration takes between a year and 18 months. The cost of registration is about $5,000 for the U.S.A. and about $2,000 for Canada.

But what's a new company to do?

At minimum, Kuypers suggests doing free online trademark database searches to see if anyone has registered the mark for similar wares. Still, phonetics or slight variations matter, and online searches would mostly miss these.

Full availability search through a lawyer would cover identical hits, marks that are similar, and "common law" searches. These are especially relevant to Canada, U.S.A. and England, where rights are conferred based on history of trademark use, not simple registration.

"If someone has used a mark for 20 years, but never registered it, you could still be liable for trademark infringement if the original user launched an action," Kuypers said.

Winnipeg outlet in 1969, while The Brick began operating under that name in Edmonton only in 1977 and was incorporated federally in 1987. After four years of legal battles and hundreds of thousands of dollars in legal fees, the sides finally agreed to an out-of-court settlement. Part of the agreement is that both stores will display a sign at their entrances stating that there is no association between The Brick or The Brick Warehouse and Brick's Fine Furniture.[3]

More recently, in another David-versus-Goliath situation, Starbucks Corp., the Seattle-based multinational coffee retailer, threatened legal action for trademark infringement against a small cafe/restaurant called HaidaBucks Cafe in Masset on the Queen Charlotte Islands, off the coast of British Columbia. Starbucks demanded that the owners of the small local cafe change its name and logo because these were creating confusion in the marketplace by being too similar to their own, even though there are no Starbucks coffee shops in Masset. The owners refused to comply, and the assistance of a high-powered Victoria law firm, the exchange of correspondence, and a considerable outpouring of public support appear to have won the battle. HaidaBucks eventually received a letter from Starbucks that concluded, "Starbucks considers this matter closed."[4]

Similarly, lululemon athletica, a Vancouver-based clothing chain, accused Madmax Worldwide Sourcing Inc. of selling a copycat version of its popular line of "yoga-inspired" clothing in Vancouver-area Costco stores and at a number of smaller retailers. Chip Wilson, the founder of lululemon, said he is not "hung up" on the trademark infringement but is acting only because his lawyer said that failing to protect the trademark could mean losing his rights.[5]

Interestingly, in late 2009, lululemon[6] itself was accused of engaging in "ambush marketing" and questionable practices. They released a line of clothing named the "Cool Sporting Event That Takes Place in British Columbia Between 2009 & 2011 Edition," an apparent reference to the 2010 Winter Olympics. The name does not infringe Canada's Olympic and Paralympic Marks Act in that it does not use the terms "Olympic(s)," "Vancouver," "2010," or any other term protected under that law, but the clothing is in the national colours of Canada, the United States, and Germany. Representatives from the Vancouver Olympic Organizing Committee, while acknowledging that no explicit infringement had taken place, nevertheless expressed disappointment at lululemon's tactics.

Registration of a trademark in Canada provides no protection of your trademark in other countries (Figure 6.6). If you are involved in or contemplating exporting to any other country, you should consider registering your trademark in that country as well.

Marking Requirements

The *Trade-marks Act* does not contain any marking requirements. However, trademark owners can indicate their registration through the use of certain symbols, namely ®(registered), ™(trademark), SM (service mark), MD (marque déposée), or MC (marque de commerce). Although the act does not require the use of these symbols, it is advisable to use them.

OBTAINING COPYRIGHT

A *copyright* gives you the right to preclude others from reproducing or copying your original published work. Materials protected by copyright include books, leaflets, periodicals and contributions to periodicals, lectures, sermons, musical or dramatic compositions, maps, works of art, photographs, drawings of a scientific or technical nature, motion pictures, sound recordings, databases, and computer programs. A copyright exists for the duration of your life plus 50 years following your death.

FIGURE 6.6   APPLICATION FOR A TRADEMARK IN CANADA

FORMAT 1

Application for Registration of a Trade-Mark in Use in Canada

To: The Registrar of Trade-marks, Gatineau, Canada.

The applicant _____ whose full post office address of its principal office or place of

business is _____

_____

applies for the registration, in accordance with the provisions of the *Trade-marks Act*, of the trade-mark identified below.

The trade-mark is the word(s) (or is shown in the attached drawing)

_____.

The trade-mark has been used by the applicant in association with all the specific wares listed hereafter, and the applicant

requests registration in respect of such wares. The trade-mark has been so used in Canada in association with the general

class of wares comprising the following specific wares _____

_____ since _____

and in association with the general class of wares comprising the following specific wares _____

_____ since _____.

The trade-mark has been used in Canada by the applicant in association with all the specific services listed hereafter, and

the applicant requests registration in respect of such services. The trade-mark has been so used in Canada in association

with the general class of services comprising the following specific services _____

_____ since _____

 and in association with the general class of services comprising the following specific services _____

_____ since _____.

The applicant is satisfied that he or she is entitled to use the trade-mark in Canada in association with the

_____ described above.

Source: Canadian Intellectual Property Office (www.cipo.ic.gc.ca), accessed March 19, 2013. Reproduced with the permission of the Minister of Public Works and Government Services, 2013.

How to Obtain a Copyright

In Canada, there is no legal requirement that your work be registered in order to obtain copyright; it is automatically acquired on creation of an original work. Nevertheless, you may wish to apply for voluntary registration. When your work has been registered, a certificate is issued that can, if necessary, be used in court to establish your ownership of the work.

You can register a copyright by completing the required application form and sending it to CIPO's Copyright Office along with the appropriate fee. You do not need to send a copy of your work with the application, but you may need to send copies to the National Library of Canada. The registration process typically takes around four weeks but may be longer if amendments are required. See Figure 6.7.

FIGURE 6.7   APPLICATION FOR REGISTRATION OF A COPYRIGHT IN A WORK

**Canadian
Intellectual Property
Office**

An Agency of
Industry Canada

**Office de la propriété
intellectuelle
du Canada**

Un organisme
d'Industrie Canada

APPLICATION FOR REGISTRATION OF A COPYRIGHT IN A WORK

Please print. For assistance in completing the form, please refer to the "Assistance" page.

**NOTICE: INFORMATION ENTERED IN THIS APPLICATION WILL BE PUBLISHED ON THE COPYRIGHT ONLINE
DATABASE THAT IS AVAILABLE FOR PUBLIC INSPECTION ON CIPO'S WEBSITE.**

<u>Note</u>: It is the applicant's responsibility to ensure the accuracy of the included information.

1. **Title of the work:**
   Enter the title of a single work. Descriptive matter that does not form part of the title should not be included.

2. **Category of the work:**
   Select the category that best describes the work.

   ☐ Literary (works consisting of text, i.e. books, pamphlets, computer programs, etc.);

   ☐ Musical (musical compositions, with or without words);

   ☐ Artistic (paintings, drawings, maps, sculptures, plans, photographs, etc.);

   ☐ Dramatic (screenplays, scripts, plays, films, etc.).

3. **Publication:**
   *Select whether the work is published or unpublished. If the work is published, enter the full date (year, month
   and day) and the place of first publication.*

   ☐ The work is unpublished

   OR

   ☐ The work is published

   Date of first publication (yyyy/mm/dd):

   Place of publication:

   City/Town   Province/State

   Country

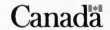

Source: Canadian Intellectual Property Office (www.cipo.ic.gc.ca), accessed March 19, 2013. Reproduced with the permission of the Minister of Public Works and
Government Services, 2013.

Indicating Copyright

There is no requirement to mark your work under the *Copyright Act*. However, you may choose to mark it with the symbol ©, your name and the year of first publication of the work, for example, © John Doe, 2008. You may use this mark even if you have not formally registered your work with the Copyright Office.

Protection Provided by Copyright

Your copyright enables you to control the copying and dissemination of your own works. This includes publishing, producing, reproducing, and performing your material. As with patents and trademarks, the responsibility for policing your copyright rests with you.

It is important to understand some of the limitations of copyright protection as well. For example, for purposes of copyright protection, the term "computer program" refers to "a set of instructions or statements, expressed, fixed, embodied or stored in any manner, which is to be used directly or indirectly in a computer in order to bring about a specific result." This means that a specific computer program, such as Microsoft Excel, can be protected as a literary work but not the idea of spreadsheet programs in general. In addition, any accompanying documentation for a program, such as a user's guide, is considered a separate work and must be registered separately.

Unlike patents and trademarks, a copyright in Canada provides simultaneous protection in most other countries of the world.

REGISTERING YOUR INDUSTRIAL DESIGN

An industrial design comprises the features of shape, configuration, pattern, or ornament applied to a finished article made by hand, tool, or machine. This may be, for example, the shape of a table or chair or the shape of the ornamentation of a knife or a spoon. The design must have features that appeal to the eye and be substantially original. Registering your design gives you exclusive rights to the design and enables you to prevent others from making, importing, renting, or selling any article on which the design has been registered and to which the design or a design not substantially different has been applied. However, no prior disclosure of the design is allowed, including publication in a college or university thesis. Unlike trademark and copyright protection, you can make no legal claim of ownership and have *no legal protection against imitation unless your design has been registered*.

How to Register Your Industrial Design

You can file your own application for industrial design registration; however, it is generally recommended that you hire a patent agent to prepare and follow through on your application. An application for an industrial design must contain:

- A completed application form
- At least one photograph or drawing of the design

Your application will be examined to ensure that it is original and registerable. It cannot be the same or similar to a design already applied to a similar article of manufacture. Following this assessment, the examiner will either approve the application or issue a report indicating what further information or amendments may be required. You have four months to reply to the report. This process can take up to a year, but once registered, designs are valid for 10 years from that date. See Figure 6.8.

Marking Your Product

You do not have to mark your design to indicate that it has been registered but marking does give you some extra protection. The proper mark is a capital "D" inside a circle along with your name or an abbreviation of it on the article itself, its label, or its packaging. If your product is marked in this way, a court may award a remedy of some kind, such as financial compensation, if someone is found to be infringing on or violating your design. Otherwise, the court can merely issue an injunction to forbid the other party from using your design.

FIGURE 6.8   INDUSTRIAL DESIGN APPLICATION TEMPLATE

Office de la propriété intellectuelle du Canada

Canadian Intellectual Property Office

Un organisme d'Industrie Canada

An Agency of Industry Canada

Direction du droit d'auteur
et des dessins industriels
Place du Portage I
50, rue Victoria
Gatineau (Québec) K1A 0C9
Téléphone : 1-866-997-1936
Télécopieur : (819) 953-6977
Internet : www.opic.gc.ca

Copyright and Industrial
Design Branch
Place du Portage I
50 Victoria Street
Gatineau QC K1A 0C9
Telephone: 1-866-997-1936
Facsimile: (819) 953-6977
Internet: www.cipo.gc.ca

DEMANDE D'ENREGISTREMENT D'UN DESSIN INDUSTRIEL

APPLICATION FOR REGISTRATION OF AN INDUSTRIAL DESIGN

Le demandeur,
The applicant, _____ ,

(nom du demandeur / name of applicant)

dont l'adresse complète est
whose complete address is _____

_____ ,

demande l'enregistrement d'un dessin pour un(e)
hereby requests registration of a design for a(n) _____

(désignation de l'objet / title identifying article)

dont il est le propriétaire.
of which the applicant is the proprietor.

À la connaissance du propriétaire, personne d'autre que le premier propriétaire du dessin n'en faisait usage lorsque celui-ci en a fait le choix.

The design was not, to the proprietor's knowledge, in use by any person other than the first proprietor at the time the design was adopted by the first proprietor.

Description du dessin :
Description of the design:

Canadă

OPIC - CIPO 45 (02-2006)

COMPANY COLLECTS DATA ON MILLIONS OF ILLEGAL DOWNLOADERS IN FIRST STEP TO CRACK DOWN ON PIRACY IN CANADA

Case Marks Beginning of Crackdown on Internet Piracy in Canada

If you're watching an illegally downloaded movie, someone could be watching you.

A forensic software company has collected files on a million Canadians who it says have downloaded pirated content.

And the company, which works for the motion picture and recording industries, says a recent court decision forcing Internet providers to release subscriber names and details is only the first step in a bid to crack down on illegal downloads.

"The door is closing. People should think twice about downloading content they know isn't proper," said Barry Logan, managing director of Canipre, the Montreal-based forensic software company.

Logan said while last week's court case involved only 50 IP addresses, his company is involved in another case that will see thousands of Canadians targeted in a sweep aimed at deterring Internet users from illegally downloading movies and other digital content.

Logan said his company has files on one million Canadians who are involved in peer-to-peer file sharing and have downloaded movies from BitTorrent sites, identifying them through Internet Protocol addresses collected over the past five months.

Logan said the court decision means Canadians must realize they could be held liable for illegal downloading and statutory damages of up to $5,000.

He said many people ignore the warnings from their ISPs that they are engaged in illegal downloading. Now, he said, they may receive litigation letters about possible court action.

Last week's court decision involved a Burnaby movie production company that went to court to force Internet service providers to provide names and addresses of subscribers who had illegally downloaded one of its movies.

The Federal Court, sitting in Montreal, ordered several Internet providers to disclose to the Burnaby company the names and addresses of their subscribers whose IP addresses were linked to illegal downloads.

The court case dealt with 50 IP addresses (unique identifiers assigned to computers and other devices on a network) who allegedly illegally downloaded NGN Prima Production's movie *Recoil*.

"Canada is a very significant country in terms of peer-to-peer file sharing and illegal downloading of copyright works," Logan said. "We have quite a significant evidence collection program that has been in place in Canada for a number of months, it doesn't discriminate between ISPs."

If ISPs hand over the subscriber data sought through court action, Logan said the copyright holders can seek statutory damages that are capped at $5,000 for non-commercial infringement.

Mira Sundara Rajan, formerly the Canada Research chair in intellectual property law at the University of B.C., said the movie industry in Canada appears to be following the lead of the United States. There, the recording and motion picture lobby was instrumental in the recent creation of a "Six Strikes" initiative, targeting Internet users who download pirated content. The graduated system starts with a notice phase and can lead to repeated offenders being blocked from certain sites. In addition to the six strike initiative, offenders can still be sued by rights holders.

"I think the end game actually is to try and make a dent in the downloading activity," said Sundara Rajan. "What we are doing is following in the footsteps of an American approach here which has been to try to target individual users and set them as examples of what can go wrong if your illegal downloading activity is discovered."

"I think that it is much more than an issue of trying to get fines in place. I think it is a question of creating an idea of deterrence in the mind of the public."

Logan said his company is looking for repeat or habitual illegal downloaders. He said they will only be identified by Internet Protocol addresses initially but if a legal action is launched, names will be released in statements of claim.

"I don't think we have to limit this to just teenagers downloading Justin Bieber's last record," he said. "We represent a lot of mature titles that would be of interest to the 30/40/50 crowd."

Logan said his clients in the industry are turning to the courts for rulings on the implementation of Bill C-11, the *Copyright Modernization Act*, which was passed in June, and took effect earlier this month. Under the act, rights holders can send copyright infringement notices to Internet providers who in turn notify subscribers who are linked to the IP address.

Source: Gillian Shaw, *Vancouver Sun*, November 27, 2012 (www.vancouversun.com/digitalife).

BODUM FIGHTS FOR INDUSTRIAL DESIGN THROUGH A GLASS, DOUBLED

Bodum Sues Canada's Trudeau Corp.

Imitation may be the sincerest form of flattery. Try it in the kitchenware business, though, and you might get a high-carbon steak knife between the eyes. The ability to defend a distinctive teapot or corkscrew is crucial for such companies. "They sell features that are pleasing to the eye," says Chris Hunter, a partner and patent agent at law firm Norton Rose. "And if they can't sell that, they don't have a product."

That helps explain Bodum's beef with Montreal-based competitor Trudeau Corp. In 2003, Bodum unveiled a double-wall glass intended to insulate hot and cold beverages, inspired by a Japanese sake bowl once seen by company owner Jørgen Bodum, son of Bodum's founder. It protected itself by registering industrial designs in Canada. In 2006, Trudeau began selling its own double-walled glasses. Bodum sued in Federal Court, claiming infringement.

This was no lark. Bodum has sued hundreds of competitors worldwide; last year it had at least 20 actions outstanding. "It has cost us a lot of money, but we have won 99 percent of the court cases," Jørgen Bodum claimed several years ago. Bodum's sparse website even features a section heralding legal triumphs. Jørgen Bodum was examined for this lawsuit, and Thomas Perez (president of its U.S. division) testified at trial—as did Robert Trudeau, the opponent's chairman.

Industrial designs aren't patents. "A design protects esthetic, visual features," explains Hunter's colleague, patent agent André Thériault. "It can be the shape of a drinking bottle or a pattern on wallpaper or carpet. A patent is more for protecting useful features and inventive concepts." Dwelling on this distinction, the court peered hard into the glasses. Its September decision noted differences in the interior curves and proportions. Ignoring the air space (which it deemed purely functional) the court found Trudeau's glasses "have almost none of the features" of Bodum's. It also accepted evidence that double-wall vessels existed as early as the late 1700s—thus invalidating Bodum's designs.

The decision is the first industrial design ruling in a generation, and Hunter and Thériault find its implications troubling. "I actually bought the Bodum glasses," Hunter says. "When you put espresso in them, the liquid inside seems to float. This decision pretty much ignores the features that made me pay $16 a glass."

Fighting perceived imitators also preoccupies Trudeau, whose 10-employee design team produces about 100 new products annually. The company resolves most disputes out of court, but still litigates occasionally, and has never lost a case. Bodum predicts that will change upon resolution of its recently filed appeal.

Source: *Canadian Business Magazine*, December 14, 2012, Matthew McClearn (www.canadianbusiness.com/companies-and-industries/bodum-glass-design-case-sparks-a-patent-war/). Used with permission.

Protection Provided by Industrial Design Registration

As with other forms of intellectual property, you may take legal action against anyone who infringes on your design in Canada. As the proprietor of the registered design, however, you have exclusive right to use it and may sell all or some of these rights to other people or authorize them to use the design, subject to certain conditions. These rights, however, relate only to Canada. To obtain similar rights in other countries you must apply for them in each country separately.

PROTECTING INTEGRATED CIRCUIT TOPOGRAPHIES

The circuits incorporated into an integrated circuit (IC) are embodied in a three-dimensional hill-and-valley configuration called a *topography*. These designs are protected by the *Integrated Circuit Topography Act*. IC products, commonly called "microchips" or "semiconductor chips" are incorporated into a variety of consumer and industrial products. The protection associated with the design of a topography is entirely distinct from that of any computer program embodied in the chip. Computer programs are subject to protection under the *Copyright Act*.

What Protection Does the Act provide?

The legislation provides exclusive rights in regard to:

- Reproduction of a protected topography or any substantial part of it
- Manufacture of an IC product incorporating the topography or any substantial part of it

- Importation or commercial exploitation of a topography, or of an IC product that embodies a protected topography or any substantial part of it
- Importation or commercial exploitation of an industrial article that incorporates an IC product that embodies a protected topography

The Act provides for a full range of civil remedies, including injunctions and exemplary damages. Protection for registered integrated circuit topographies is provided for approximately 10 years.

How to Protect an IC Topography

To protect an IC topography, you must apply to CIPO's Registrar of Topographies. Applications for "commercially exploited" topographies must be filed within two years of the date of first commercial exploitation anywhere. The application may be rejected if the topography was first exploited outside Canada. Owners must be Canadian or nationals of countries having reciprocal protection agreements with Canada. See Figure 6.9.

USE OF A NON DISCLOSURE AGREEMENT (NDA)

A *non disclosure agreement* (NDA) allows you to share details of your intellectual property with other people whose input you may be seeking without jeopardizing the information. For example, if you have a new product idea or software program in development, but need to consult an adviser for advice on how to proceed, an appropriate NDA can ensure that the adviser doesn't share the details of your new idea with anyone else.

The NDA is a legal contract between you and the other party. You agree to disclose certain information to them for a specific purpose. They agree to not disclose that information to anyone else.

There are five important elements in a typical nondisclosure agreement:

- A definition of the "confidential information"
- Material excluded from confidential information
- The obligations of the receiving party
- The time period for which the NDA is in effect
- Any miscellaneous provisions

Excluded material usually covers any information created or discovered by the receiving party prior to (or independent of) any involvement with the other party. The receiving party typically has no obligation to protect this excluded information.

You should be aware, however, that some parties routinely refuse to sign non disclosure agreements. Many venture capital companies, some R&D companies, some manufacturers and many government departments/agencies usually refuse to sign such documents. One reason is that all government employees sign a statement pledging to treat information related to their work as confidential, so they see the NDA as redundant.

TRADE SECRETS

A *trade secret* is difficult to define but may consist of a formula for a chemical compound, a process of manufacturing, a means of treating or preserving materials, a pattern for a machine or other device, a list of customers, or any other secrets that are used in a business and may give it an advantage over competitors who do not know the trade secret. The most well-known trade secrets are probably the formula for Coca Cola or how Cadbury's Chocolates gets the caramel into the Caramilk bar.

There are no government forms to file with trade secrets. You have to keep the information a secret and take reasonable measures to do so if you want trade secret protection. Trade secrets are often protected by means of an NDA. Anybody to whom a trade secret has been revealed should be asked to sign a non disclosure agreement. This could include employees, suppliers, manufacturers, sub contractors, and component manufacturers.

OPIC
Office de la propriété
intellectuelle du Canada

CIPO
Canadian Intellectual
Property Office

APPLICATION FOR REGISTRATION OF
AN INTEGRATED CIRCUIT TOPOGRAPHY

APPLICANT- Name and address

Client Number
(If already assigned by ICT)

Postal code

TITLE(S)

DESCRIPTION OF THE NATURE OR FUNCTION OF TOPOGRAPHY

INTEREST

☐ Creator of topography   OR   ☐ Successor in title

CONDITIONS OF REGISTRATION

Registrability in Canada is dependent upon the following conditions:

The creator of the topography is, at the time of its creation or on the filing date of the application:
i) a national of Canada;
ii) a national of a country recognized by Canada by convention or treaty that affords protection for topographies;
iii) a national of a country that the Minister has certified by notice published in the *Canada Gazette*; OR

The creator of the topography has, at the time of its creation or on the filing, a real and effective establishment for the creation of topographies or the manufacture of integrated circuit products in Canada or a country that is a member of the World Trade Organization (WTO) or has a reciprocal agreement with Canada; OR

The topography is first commercially exploited in Canada and the application is filed within two years thereafter.

COMMERCIAL EXPLOITATION

☐ The topography has not been commercially exploited
OR
☐ The topography was first commercially exploited in _____ on _____.
                                    (place/country)   (day/month/year)

MATERIAL FILED AND OTHER INFORMATION

AGENT - Name and address

Client Number
(If already assigned by ICT)

Postal code

REPRESENTATIVE FOR SERVICE - Name and address in Canada

Client Number
(If already assigned by ICT)

Postal code

SIGNATURE(S)

_____
Contact person (please print or type)

_____
Signature(s)

(*check appropriate box*) ☐ applicant   ☐ agent

Telephone no. (   )

Industry Canada Industrie Canada

(Français au verso)
OPIC-CIPO 148 (12-97)

Canada

Source: Canadian Intellectual Property Office (www.cipo.ic.gc.ca), accessed March 19, 2013. Reproduced with the permission of the Minister of Public Works and Government Services, 2013.

FOR MORE INFORMATION ON INTELLECTUAL PROPERTY

Further information on the protection of intellectual property can be obtained from:

Canadian Intellectual Property Office
Industry Canada
50 Victoria St., Room C-229 (in person) or Room C-114 (mail or courier)
Place du Portage, Phase 1
Gatineau, Quebec K1A 0C9
(www.cipo.ic.gc.ca)
Tel: (866) 997-1936

or contact your local Canada Business Service Centre.

The deadlines for filing, the length of time for which protection is provided, and the current registration fees for several types of intellectual property are summarized in Table 6.2.

CONCLUSION

As we have discussed, in addition to various *tangible* assets, such as land, buildings, and equipment, your business may also own certain *intangible* assets, such as patents, trademarks, and copyrights. These can be just as important as, or even more important than, your tangible assets. And like tangible assets, with the permission of their owners, they can be bought, sold, licensed, or used by someone else.

Ideas that are not patentable and are not otherwise protected may be protected by contract law either by means of a written *non disclosure* agreement or by treating them as *trade secrets*. This can be done by taking every

TABLE 6.2	INFORMATION ABOUT PROTECTION OF INTELLECTUAL PROPERTY IN CANADA			
Type	Application Deadline	Period of Coverage	Government Fees for Small Entities	
Patents	File within one year of publication (file before publication for most other countries)	20 years from filing of application	Filing fee	$200
			Examination fee	$400
			Allowance fee (Grant)	$150
			Maintenance fee:	
			Years 2, 3, & 4	$ 50
			Years 5 to 9	$100
			Years 10 to 14	$125
			Years 15 to 19	$225
Trademarks	(None)	15 years; renewable indefinitely	Filing fee	$250– $300
			Registration fee	$200
Copyright	(None)	50 years plus life of author	Registration fee	$50– $65
Industrial Designs	File within 12 months of publication	10 years from date of registration	Examination fee	$400 plus $10 for each page over 10 pages
			Maintenance of registration fee	$350

precaution to keep valuable knowledge a secret and/or by placing specific provisions in any agreement you may have with your employees that they will neither disclose to anyone else nor use for their own purposes any trade secrets they may acquire while in your employ. The advantages of this type of protection may be even greater than those of patent protection. The success of this approach depends on your ability to control the access of outsiders to the information, as there are no *legal rights* in a trade secret. Typically, once confidential information has been publicly disclosed, it becomes very difficult to enforce any rights to it.

LO1 **The different types of business structures are:**

- **sole proprietorship**—the simplest form of business ownership, particular in the early stages of starting up. As the owner you have complete control of the business and are accountable for all its activities and consequences. Your business income and expenses are filed on your personal tax return.

- **partnership**—two or more individuals carrying on a business for profit. The partners should prepare a written partnership agreement outlining issues that are clearly understood and acceptable to all partners. The agreement should include:
  - the rights and responsibilities of each partner
  - the amount and nature of the partners' respective capital contribution to the business
  - division of profit and losses
  - management responsibilities of each partner
  - provision for termination, retirement, disability, or death of one of the partners
  - means of dissolving or liquidating the partnership

- **corporation**—the most formal business organization. An incorporated business is a separate legal entity from its owners. The corporation has rights and duties of its own. It can own property and assets, it can sue and be sued, and it files its own tax return. A corporation that has more than one owner should include a partnership agreement. You do not have to be large to incorporate your business. Sole proprietors usually move to incorporation when they make in excess of $40,000 to $50,000 of taxable income in a given year.

- **co-operative**—startup capital usually comes from the sale of members share in the co-op. A minimum of five members is needed to incorporate as a co-operative, and there is no maximum number. Every member has an equal say in the direction of the business, regardless of their financial investment. A co-operative enterprise is initiated by a group of people who share a common need, want to capitalize on a new market opportunity, lack the capital or specific skill set to go into business independently.

LO2 **It is important to take time to choose the name of your business. It should:**

- be meaningful to what your business does

- should be catchy but not silly
- stay with you for the duration of your business.

Changing the name may cause confusion with your clients and the marketing efforts that you have put in place. Your name is part of your business brand.

LO3 **The types of business licences that you may need when starting a business are:**

- municipal and provincial licences to operate your business
- required licences for your province
- local zoning regulations and bylaw requirements.

Contact local municipal offices to find out what is required.

LO4 **Everyone needs help from mentors, board of directors, or an advisory board when they are starting out:**

- mentors help you out from time to time and advise you on possible solutions
- board of directors are elected or appointed members who jointly oversee the activities of a company
- advisory board acts much the same way as a mentor but are usually a group of business owners who help with large projects and give feedback

LO5 **Intellectual property is the legal rights that result from intellectual activity in the industrial, scientific, literary, and artistic fields. As an inventor or developer you must protect yourself from someone else infringing on your intellectual property (the idea or invention). Intellectual property is broken into five components under the law:**

- patents
- trademarks
- copyrights
- industrial designs
- integrated circuit topographies

The invention can be a product, a composition, an apparatus, a process, or an improvement to any of these. You cannot protect a scientific principle, an abstract theorem, an idea or a method of doing business, a computer program or a medical treatment.

The Canadian Intellectual Property Office (CIPO) looks after the application process when applying for patents, trademarks, industrial designs, and ntegrated circuit topographies. The CIPO website also lists a number of legal firms that can help you with your application.

For more information on the resources available from McGraw-Hill Ryerson, go to www.mcgrawhill.ca/he/solutions.

FINANCING YOUR BUSINESS AND ACCOUNTING PRACTICES

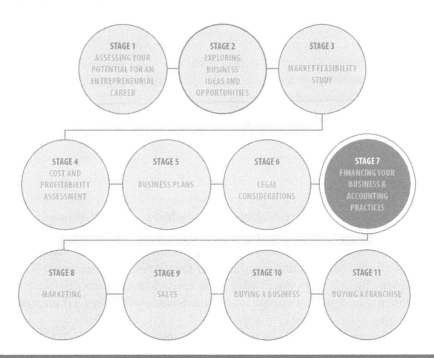

STAGE 1
ASSESSING YOUR POTENTIAL FOR AN ENTREPRENEURIAL CAREER

STAGE 2
EXPLORING BUSINESS IDEAS AND OPPORTUNITIES

STAGE 3
MARKET FEASIBILITY STUDY

STAGE 4
COST AND PROFITABILITY ASSESSMENT

STAGE 5
BUSINESS PLANS

STAGE 6
LEGAL CONSIDERATIONS

STAGE 7
FINANCING YOUR BUSINESS & ACCOUNTING PRACTICES

STAGE 8
MARKETING

STAGE 9
SALES

STAGE 10
BUYING A BUSINESS

STAGE 11
BUYING A FRANCHISE

LEARNING OBJECTIVES

By the end of this stage, you should be able to:

LO1 Identify the differences between debt and equity financing.

LO2 Summarize the major sources of funding for startups.

LO3 Evaluate your ability to secure financing.

LO4 Describe some important accounting practices.

Used with the permission of pplconnect.

Imagine the flexibility of your mobile content and functionality anywhere. The pplconnect* Virtual Smartphone* lets you access and use your real-time mobile content from any web-enabled device. Log-in to your personal pplconnect account and gain access to your mobile from a computer, laptop, tablet, and more. Driven by the desire to bring positive change, pplconnect was born from the bold idea to transform the mobile industry by handing users the power over their mobile content.

The idea behind pplconnect came from uncovering a market need. Jenviev Azzolin and her business partner Denzil D'Sa observed that more and more people, including themselves, were growing increasingly dependent on their smartphones. Often people experience separation anxiety when their mobile battery dies; when they forget their phone at home; while travelling abroad; or when switching mobile devices. After some digging, came the discovery that this phenomenon affects people on an international scale. This, combined with the desire to build a company that would have a positive impact on people worldwide (by building a customer-driven solution), led to the launch of pplconnect.

Both partners left their secure jobs at Bombardier to create pplconnect—starting from zero and building the business from the ground up by working day and night. A business plan was built and quickly submitted to the Quebec Angel Investor Challenge. Although pplconnect seemed too "early-stage" for this kind of competition, they decided to take the risk and apply anyway. This risk paid off when pplconnect won the competition! Shortly thereafter, pplconnect was selected by the Department of Foreign Affairs and International Trade Canada in collaboration with the Mobile Experience and Innovation Center to attend the India Telecom Show, as a member of the Canadian delegation (of which they were the only startup). Momentum continued to grow from there as people started gravitating towards the idea and getting on-board with the vision.

"I love what I do and feel very fortunate to be building this business, especially because I believe that we are making a difference," says Jenviev. There is no such thing as an average day for the pplconnect team. Every day they build something new and see it come to life while inspiring people to join their mission.

Source: Entrepeer Success Story, CYBF, February 11, 2013 (www.cybf.ca/entrepeer/success-stories).

ARRANGING FINANCING

Quite a number of sources of financing are available to established businesses. However, there are relatively few sources of *seed capital* for ventures that are just getting off the ground and have no track record. Obtaining such capital can require persistence and determination. Usually you must submit a formal proposal to a prospective source of funding in which you outline your needs, plans for the money, the investors' expected return, and a loan repayment schedule. Many financing proposals have to be revised several times before receiving a positive response. In addition, you may have to be prepared to combine financing from several sources to raise all the funds you require. See Figure 7.1.

Two kinds of funds are potentially available to you: *debt* and *equity*.

DEBT FINANCING   LO1

Debt financing is borrowing money that must be repaid in full, usually in periodic payments with interest. Three important parameters associated with debt financing are:

1. Amount of principal to be borrowed
2. Interest rate on the loan
3. Maturity date of the loan

FIGURE 7.1   FINANCING

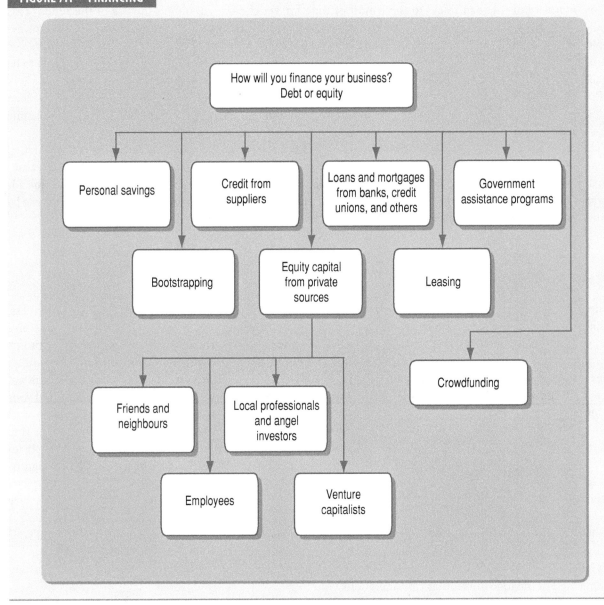

Together these three factors determine the extent of your obligation to the creditor. Until the debt has been repaid, the provider of the loan has a legal claim against the assets and cash flows of your business. In many cases, the creditor can demand payment at any time and possibly force your business into bankruptcy because of overdue payments.

The *principal* of the loan is the total amount of money you hope to borrow. This could be the difference between the amount shown on your estimate of your required startup funding and the sum you are personally able to provide to get your business started.

The *interest rate* is the "price" you will have to pay for the borrowed funds. In most cases, it will be tied to the current *prime rate*. This is generally considered to be the rate of interest that banks charge their best customers—those with the lowest risk. For example, a bank might be prepared to offer loans to a small business for prime plus some fixed percentage, perhaps 3 or 4 percent. The prime rate may fluctuate somewhat due to periodic decisions by the Bank of Canada, so the effective interest rate on your loan may also vary somewhat.

The *maturity* of the loan refers to the length of time for which you will obtain the use of the funds. This should coincide with your intended use of the money. Short-term needs require short-term financing. For example, you might use a short-term loan to purchase inventory that you intend to sell within a month or two or to finance some outstanding accounts receivables. A short-term loan, such as a *line of credit,* typically has to be repaid within a year.

Purchasing a building or a major piece of equipment may require a long-term loan or a *term* loan. This is a loan that will be repaid over an extended period of time, typically several years. The purpose of the loan will determine the maturity period.

The primary sources of debt financing are shareholder loans provided by the owners of the business and operating loans and term loans provided by banks and other financial institutions, such as trust companies, Alberta Treasury Branches, and credit unions. Providing some funds as a loan rather than as an equity investment can have some advantages for you as the owner of a small business. The interest payments made to you are income tax deductible by the business, and it may be easier to withdraw the money when necessary than if it was tied up in equity.

EQUITY FINANCING

Equity funding is money supplied by yourself or investors in exchange for an ownership position in your business. Unlike debt, equity funding does not need to be repaid. Providers of equity capital forego the opportunity to receive interest and periodic repayment of the funds they have extended to your business; rather, they share in the profits their investment is expected to generate. Other than making your own personal investment, it is not easy to attract other investors to a new business. No matter how sure you are that your business will be successful, others will not necessarily share your confidence and will need to be persuaded to invest in your idea by your enthusiasm and your business plan.

In addition to providing the funds, equity investors will usually demand a voice in how your business is run. This can substantially reduce your ability to run your business as you would like. They expect to receive their return from any dividends that may be paid out periodically from the net profits of the business or, more significantly, from the increased value of the business as it grows and prospers. They expect to be able to sell all or part of their investment for a considerable profit, although the shares of a small private company may have a very limited market.

The most common sources of equity financing for startup businesses are your own personal savings and your family and friends.

The advantages of debt versus external equity financing from your perspective as owner of the business are summarized in the following Other Considerations box.[1]

MAJOR SOURCES OF FUNDS   LO2

The major sources of funds for small business startups are personal funds, commercial loans and lines of credit, the use of personal credit cards for business purposes, personal loans provided to the business by the owner, and trade credit provided to the business by its suppliers. As you can see in Figure 7.2, these are the principal sources of financing for entrepreneurs of all ages. Most entrepreneurs are inclined to finance their businesses through their own personal funds, as well as via other informal methods, such as their personal credit and loans from relatives and friends, commonly known as "bootstrapping." It used to be that younger people had a difficult time accessing these formal sources of funding, but from this data it is not the case any longer. You may be able to "piece together" the combination of debt and equity funding that you require from a combination of these sources as well.

FIGURE 7.2 SOURCES OF FINANCING USED DURING STARTUP

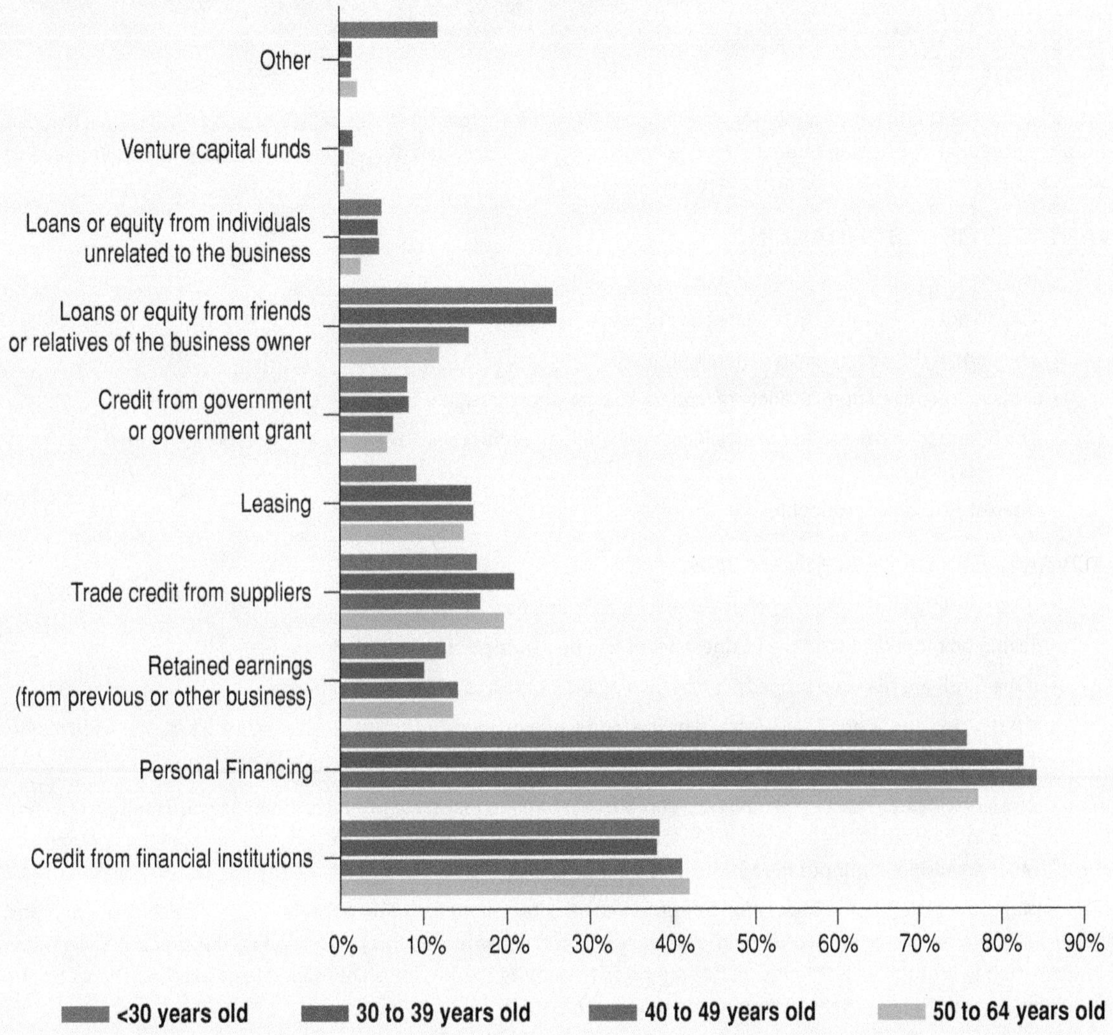
Other
Venture capital funds
Loans or equity from individuals unrelated to the business
Loans or equity from friends or relatives of the business owner
Credit from government or government grant
Leasing
Trade credit from suppliers
Retained earnings (from previous or other business)
Personal Financing
Credit from financial institutions
0%
10%
20%
30%
40%
50%
60%
70%
80%
90%
<30 years old
30 to 39 years old
40 to 49 years old
50 to 64 years old

Source: Statistics Canada, Survey on Financing of Small and Medium Enterprises, 2011.

PERSONAL FUNDS

The first place to look for money to start your business is your own pocket. This may mean cleaning out your savings account and other investments, selling your second car, postponing your holiday for this year, cashing in your RRSPs, mortgaging the cottage, or any other means you may have of raising cash.

BOOTSTRAPPING

One concept actively promoted for many new entrepreneurs is the concept of *bootstrap financing* or *bootstrapping*. Bootstrapping is essentially looking for highly creative ways of acquiring the resources you need to get your business off the ground without "kick starting" the business with external capital by borrowing money or raising equity from traditional financing sources. It means being as frugal as possible so that your business can get going

OTHER CONSIDERATIONS

DEBT VERSUS EQUITY

Debt financing is when a firm raises money for working capital or capital expenditures by selling bonds, bills, or notes to individual and/or institutional investors. In return for lending the money, the individuals or institutions become creditors and receive a promise that the principal and interest on the debt will be repaid.

ADVANTAGES OF DEBT FINANCING

- It is useful for meeting a short-term deficit in cash flow.
- You do not have to give up or share control of your business.
- The term of the debt (loan) is generally limited.
- It may be acquired from a variety of lenders. You can shop around.
- The information needed to obtain a loan is generally straightforward and normally incorporated into a business plan.
- Interest paid is tax deductible.

DISADVANTAGES OF DEBT FINANCING

- It can be difficult to obtain when the project is risky and its success uncertain.
- Taking on more debt than the business needs can be a burden on your cash flows.
- If the funds are not used properly, it may be difficult for the business to repay the loan.
- If it is a "demand" loan, it can be called by the lender at any time.
- The lender may require you to provide a personal guarantee for the loan.
- Lenders will often insist on certain restrictions being put into place. For instance, there may be a limit on how much you can draw out of the business in the form of a salary or dividends or the amount you can spend on equipment or other acquisitions without their approval.

Equity financing is the act of raising money for company activities by selling common or preferred stock to individual or institutional investors. In return for the money paid, shareholders receive ownership interests in the corporation.[2] If a company raises public money through an IPO (initial public offering), the equity shareholders are then able to sell their shares on the open market. This is one way of getting their return on investment (ROI).

ADVANTAGES OF EQUITY FINANCING

- An appropriate investor can contribute expertise, contacts, and new business, as well as money.
- Equity may be the only way to fund high-risk ventures, where the cost of debt could be prohibitive.
- It can be used to fund larger projects with longer time frames.

DISADVANTAGES OF EQUITY FINANCING

- The owner has to give up some ownership and control of the business.
- There is always the danger of incompatibility and disagreement among the investors.
- It is much more difficult to terminate the relationship if disagreements occur.

on as little cash as possible. It is estimated that between 75 and 85 percent of new startups use some form of bootstrapping to help finance themselves.[3] In some cases, it may be the only way they can get the money they need to keep their new business going until the cash generated from earnings is sufficient to fund the ongoing growth of the business.

There are a number of advantages to bootstrapping. Down the road, your business may be worth more because you have not had to raise money selling off equity positions along the way. In addition, you may be able to reduce the high interest costs on borrowed money from conventional sources. You could also find yourself in a stronger position later on to raise funds from external lenders and investors, since your business will not be saddled with a lot of debt.

Bootstrapping can take a wide variety of forms, although most of the typical techniques can be classified into specific categories, such as:

- Minimizing Your Investment
- Owner Financing
- Minimizing Accounts Receivable
- Delaying Payments
- Sharing Resources with Others

Some of the more common bootstrapping techniques are discussed below.

Personal Credit Cards

The credit limit extended by financial institutions on personal credit cards can provide you with ready access to a short-term loan, but usually at interest rates that are considerably higher than more conventional financing (upward of 18 to 22 percent or more). There may be occasions, however, where other sources of working capital are not available, and drawing on the personal line of credit associated with your cards may be the only source of funds available to sustain your business. This can be risky, since you are personally liable for the expenditures on the card, even though they may have been made for business purposes; however, it may be useful if you are expecting a major payment or other injection of cash into the business within a few days.

Suppliers' Inventory Buying Plans

In some industries, one way of obtaining working capital may be through supplier financing. Suppliers may be prepared to extend payment terms to 60, 90, or even 120 days for some customers. Other suppliers may offer floor plan financing or factoring options to help their dealers finance inventory purchases, usually in advance of the peak selling season. In addition, many suppliers offer discounts off the face value of their invoice (typically 2 percent for payment within 10 days) or penalize slow-paying customers with interest charges (often 1.5 percent a month). These programs can impact your financing requirements.

Leasing versus Buying

In competitive equipment markets, specialized leasing and finance companies will arrange for the lease of such items as expensive pieces of equipment, vehicles, copiers, and computers. Leasing, often with an option to buy rather than purchasing, can free up your scarce capital for investment in other areas of your business. While the interest rates charged on the lease contract may be somewhat higher than you might pay through the bank, the lease expenses are usually fully deductible from your taxable income. A lease contract will fix your cost of having the equipment for a specific term and may provide the flexibility to purchase the equipment at a later date at a predetermined price.

Leasehold Improvements

When locating your business in rented premises, it is usually necessary to undertake a number of leasehold improvements to make the premises appropriate for your needs. Installing new electrical outlets, adding additional partitions and walls, laying carpet, painting, installing fixtures, and similar modifications can add considerably to the cost of launching your business. Sometimes it may be possible to get the landlord of your location to assist in making these improvements, particularly if there is a lot of other space available to rent. The landlord or property manager may agree to provide a portion (an allowance of a dollar amount per square foot of space) or cover all of your leasehold improvements in return for a longer-term lease (typically three to five years). Reducing your initial expenditures in this way can reduce the startup cash and equity you require to launch your business, even though you will be paying for these improvements in your monthly rent over the course of the lease.

Advance Payment from Customers

It may be possible to negotiate a full or partial payment from some customers in advance to help finance the costs of taking on their business. In some industries, construction for example, it is customary to receive a partial payment at certain defined stages during the course of the project rather than waiting until completion. These payments can reduce the cash needs of running your business. Any work that involves special orders or custom designs for products specifically tailored to the requirements of one customer should require a significant deposit or full payment in advance.

Jen Kluger and Suzie Orol (see the Entrepreneurs in Action box) are excellent examples of young entrepreneurs who have been able to bootstrap their business successfully. They started their handmade jewellery business with very little cash and used what they had to pay for display booths at local outdoor festivals. They decided not to incur the overhead of opening their own retail store but to rely on online sales and a commission salesforce to distribute their jewellery through third-party retailers. They maintain a lean operation overall with relatively few employees, do very little advertising, rely largely on public relations to make people aware of their products, keep a minimum amount of inventory, and try to turn it over as quickly as possible. To date, the young women have never borrowed any money for their business and are well on their way to building an international company.

Examples of other ways to bootstrap are outlined in the next Other Considerations box. Bootstrapping is not without risk, however. Many of these techniques commonly associated with bootstrapping are not recommended for everyone. Try to avoid such methods as using your personal credit cards, selling your insurance policy, cashing in your RRSP, or taking out a second mortgage on your home. We often hear stories of individuals who have successfully launched their company using such methods, but we seldom hear about those who did not make it and the repercussions of facing a poor credit rating, personal bankruptcy, or other personal or family problems as a result of not being able to pay off the debt.

In general, however, there are a number of "rules of thumb" that can serve as a guide to effective bootstrapping.

1. Service businesses are easier to bootstrap than manufacturing businesses, since they do not require extensive machinery and equipment.

2. Keep your overhead low by working out of your home for as long as possible.

3. Run your business part time at the beginning, if you can. At least you may be able to do some consulting or other related work on the side to help generate some badly needed revenue.

4. Negotiate time rather than price. Try to get extensions for the payment of bills to 45, 60, or even 90 days, while also providing incentives for your customers to pay their bills as rapidly as possible.

5. Minimize your need for resources. Only lease or buy the machinery and equipment that is absolutely necessary, and try to find used rather than new equipment, if at all possible.

Once you have scraped together everything you can from your own resources and personal savings, the next step is to talk to other people. Additional funds may come from your friends, family, and close personal relations.

Recent estimates indicate that bootstrapping money, in fact, makes up more than 90 percent of the external new business startup capital in Canada. Bootstrapping may be necessary as banks and other conventional sources usually will not lend money without extensive security. Because of this, many entrepreneurs decide to do it on their own. Mike McDerment, CEO of FreshBooks, took the frugal approach by launching with no external capital and almost no internal funds. Five years later, the firm has 93 employees and more than 1.6 million users worldwide.

NO MONEY DOWN

Jen Kluger, 27, and her business partner, Suzie Orol, also 27, decided not to open a store, opting to sell their handmade jewellery online and through third-party retailers. To service the dozens of American stores that carry Foxy Originals, they employ eight U.S.-based sales reps, who are paid a 15 percent commission. "Our business model today is very similar to the one we had eight years ago," Kluger says. "We keep a nimble staff. We have minimal inventory, and we turn it around quickly."

Kluger and Orol met when they were business students at the University of Western Ontario. They discovered that they shared an interest in jewellery. Kluger had been selling her pieces to boutiques around Toronto; Orol's family worked in metal-casting, and she had drawn on this trade to design a jewellery line for teenagers. They began making necklaces and selling them on campus. Within a month, they were retailing them at local boutiques. "The idea was to make something that offered an affordable price point but was high quality," Kluger recalls.

The two women went on the road the following summer, using $900 in startup capital to book outdoor booths at local festivals. As their customer base grew, they kept overheads low by hiring interns from Ryerson University's fashion program. After one shipment of beads failed to arrive on time, Foxy Originals switched to the decorated cast-metal pieces that are now their trademark.

There's no doubt the brand is strong. "We constantly work on PR," says Kluger, pointing to the media coverage they've scored in *CosmoGIRL!, Us Weekly*, and many other publications. "It's one thing to have a good product, but it's another thing to have your market know about it." Besides firing off regular press releases, Kluger and Orol have raised their profile stateside by visiting the editors of major U.S. fashion magazines.

The most visible result of their hard work: Young celebrities like Paris Hilton, Sienna Miller and Tori Spelling have been photographed wearing their jewellery. Kluger and Orol delivered free samples to Hilton when she was in Toronto shooting *House of Wax*, and they met Spelling at the airport. "We always have jewellery on us," Kluger says with a laugh. "You never know who you're going to run into."

Kluger and Orol have never borrowed money for their business. Even more remarkable: All of their jewellery is made in Canada, at a workshop owned by Orol's parents. Although Kluger says she's happy to support the economy, there are also sound business reasons to manufacture locally. Besides ensuring quality control, it means fast turnaround for a bewildering number of product lines. "The accessories industry moves

COURTESY OF JEN KLUGER

quickly, and when you're relying on overseas imports, you can run into major trouble," Kluger warns.

Its abundance of colourful bling notwithstanding, Foxy Originals is a lean operation. Head office has just seven staff, including Kluger and Orol, who still do all the jewellery design themselves. But the duo has big plans: They've secured U.K. and Australian distributors, and expect to roll out private-label collaborations with several well-known brands sometime this year.

Foxy Originals continues to grow their business. They are now in Shopper's Drug Mart stores that have a Beauty Boutique and recently struck a deal with Target Canada to sell Foxy Originals in the 110 retail stores slated to open across Canada. Jen wouldn't disclose their sales but did say that they sold 50,000 units in 2012. Not bad for a company who, still to this day, hasn't borrowed any money and continues to manufacture their jewellery in Canada.

They continue to run a lean business with only three full-time employees. This may get harder to manage now they both have newborns, but other than that, not much has changed since 1998 when they first opened their doors.

(www.foxyoriginals.com)

Source: Nick Rockel, *The Globe and Mail Report on Small Business*, January 30, 2007. Updated, April 3, 2013, by Wendy Mayhew.

BOOTSTRAP FINANCING TECHNIQUES

Bootstrap Category	Bootstrap Financing Technique
Minimizing Your Investment	• Buy used machinery and equipment • Offer customer discount for cash payment • Hire temporary rather than permanent help • Negotiate favourable terms with suppliers • Apply for grants and subsidies
Owner Financing	• Run business out of your home • Employ relatives/friends at less than market salaries • Use income from other or part-time employment • Use personal credit cards for business • Withhold owner's salary if cash is tight • Have a working spouse • Sell other products/services
Minimizing Accounts Receivable	• Choose customers who pay quickly • Stop doing business with slow payers • Try to obtain advance customer payments • Charge interest on overdue accounts • Offer discount for early payment • Speed up invoicing
Delaying Payments	• Delay payments to suppliers • Delay tax payments • Lease equipment • Buy on consignment from suppliers
Sharing Resources with Others	• Share employees/equipment with other businesses • Share space with other businesses • Borrow equipment • Barter instead of buying/selling goods or services • Coordinate purchases with other businesses

Source: Adapted from J. Winborg and H. Lanstrom, "Financial Bootstrapping in Small Business: Examining Small Business Resource Acquisition Behaviour," *Journal of Business Venturing 16* (2000), pp. 235–254, accessed April 3, 2013.

There are also more opportunities to start a business on a shoestring, thanks to the availability of inexpensive or free online business tools and price cuts by suppliers facing fierce competition and sluggish demand.

Still, bootstrapping is not easy. Launching a business with hardly any money requires becoming a hard-core cheapskate. The following Other Considerations Box shows seven effective ways to bootstrap your startup.

THE NO-MONEY STARTUP MIRACLE

Launching a business with very little capital is an increasingly popular option. Here's how successful bootstrappers never spend a dollar unnecessarily.

1. **CULTIVATE ALLIES WHO'LL TAKE A CHANCE ON YOU** David Simpson, who lectures on entrepreneurial finance at the Richard Ivey School of Business in London, Ontario, advises finding suppliers and retailers willing to extend credit. This will minimize your costs until you land some sales.

   "If they extend you supply credit, in exchange, you can sign a contract to make them your exclusive supplier," says Simpson. And with a retailer, "If you can get them to place a pre-order based on your prototype, you can give them an exclusive for six months. Get them onside early."

   A supplier or retailer with a solid base of creditworthy clients can afford to take the risk that you'll stiff them—knowing that if you succeed, you'll generate a soaring volume of business. And other service providers, such as accountants, lawyers and Web designers, also might be open to the same deal, says Simpson: "That allows you to save thousands and thousands of dollars."

2. **UNDERSTAFF AND OUTSOURCE TO THE MAX** Never hire an employee until you have to. And use stock options to induce the few you *do* need to accept punishing workloads during the start up phase.

   But these few can't do it all. You also should take advantage of the wealth of outsourcing options. Assigning tasks such as PR to outside professionals lets you tap into skills that you lack in-house and to pay for only what you need.

3. **DECLARE WAR ON OVERHEAD** "Why do you need an office?" asks McDerment. "You don't, unless you have clients showing up. We knew we needed phone lines and servers, so we didn't skimp on those. But everything else didn't really matter." For many startups, cafes or co-workspaces are viable alternatives to conventional offices.

   Once you start asking what overhead is really necessary, you'll find plenty of other cost-cutting opportunities. Adam Epstein, founder of Huddlers, a social network for intramural sports teams, initially offered its service through a website. "We had 1,000 users," he says. "Some were active and some weren't. But it was costing us $200 per month to keep it going."

   Epstein realized even this modest outlay was an unnecessary expense for his Toronto-based startup. So, Huddlers shut down its site and is now spending what Epstein calls a "negligible" amount to develop a mobile app version of its service.

4. **DO DIRT-CHEAP MARKETING** From social media to YouTube, this is a golden age for DIY marketing. But other startups also have realized this, so you'll need a fresh angle to ensure that your marketing stands out while still costing peanuts.

   Vincent Cheung—CEO of Shape Collage, a developer of software for creating photo collages—came up with such an angle to boost his Toronto-based startup's profile. He knew that although tech bloggers are key influencers in his sector, it's tough to get coverage from the most read blogs because they're bombarded with PR pitches. So, using Technorati's search-engine ranking of the top 100 tech blogs, Cheung targeted ones at the lower end of the list, then worked his way up.

   This yielded so many posts by second-tier blogs that the top-tier ones took notice. When Lifehacker—a popular blog with "tips and downloads for getting things done"— wrote about Shape Collage, 20,000 people downloaded its software in a single day.

5. **DON'T TRY TO BE ALL THINGS TO ALL CLIENTS** It's tough to say no to a prospect, but to keep costs down; you need to resist the temptation to offer a full product range.

   Toronto-based 4ormat, which develops templates for creative-portfolio websites, has built a client base spanning more than 90 countries since its 2010 start. And that's despite narrowing its potential market by refusing to develop templates compatible with Internet Explorer (IE), the most widely used web browser.

   Lukas Dryja, 4ormat's CEO, says his company opted to avoid the development costs of making its portfolio-building interface compatible with IE, which 4ormat considers outdated technology. "Nothing upends developer velocity like spending days in a virtual machine painfully debugging an issue with Internet Explorer's woeful dev tools," says Dryja.

(continued)

Rather than craft a version of 4ormat's template that gets along with IE, the firm has targeted users of the two other leading browsers, Chrome and Firefox. And many IE users have become clients after all, heeding the suggestion on 4ormat's website that they download Chrome or Firefox so they can use 4ormat's interface.

6. **LIVE ON THE CHEAP IN A HATCHERY** Almost every big city boasts at least one startup incubator, such as Vancouver's GrowLab and Ottawa's Exploriem Entrepreneur Network, to help entrepreneurs turn promising ideas into real businesses. Although these hatcheries are best known for offering budding businesses mentoring and connections, they also can save you a ton of money. For instance, many offer free or low-cost space and shared reception services, meeting space and office equipment, as well as advice from other entrepreneurs on how to run ultra-lean.

7. **PAY YOUR LAWYER AS LITTLE AS YOU SAFELY CAN** How can you get the legal help you'll need without blowing all the money you've saved elsewhere? Start by using downloadable templates for legal documents, such as founders' agreements and intellectual property assignment agreements. Because there are major differences between the Canadian and U.S. legal systems, be sure to use templates that are valid for your location. Toronto's MaRS incubator, for instance, has developed templates for Ontario-based firms, available at ipoint.to/udqwkk.

But, cautions McDerment, you'll still need to pay a lawyer. Use the templates to create draft documents, and then have a lawyer spend a few hours reviewing these for errors and ensuring the wording would hold up in court.

Source: Lyndsie Bourgon, "The No-Money Startup Miracle," January 03, 2013, *Profit Guide,* (www.profitguide.com/startup/best-practices/the-no-money-startup-miracle-45604).

The biggest risk with this source of capital is that if your new business fails and the investors lose money, it can create considerable hard feelings among family and friends. This possibility can be reduced if you lay out all the terms and conditions of the investment in advance, just as you would for any other investors. You should explain the nature of your business, your detailed implementation plans, the risks associated with the venture, and other relevant factors. In fact, it is best if you give both yourself and your investors some measure of comfort by translating your understanding into a formal, legal shareholders' agreement. If the money is provided to you as a loan, another important reason for putting it into writing is that if, for some reason, you are unable to repay the money and your investor must write it off, the amount of a properly documented loan becomes a capital loss for income tax purposes and can be offset against any capital gains, thereby providing the investor with the potential for some tax relief from the loss.

This most basic kind of financing is often not enough to get the business started, but it is important for external funding sources to see that you and your family are prepared to invest most of your personal resources in the venture. Without a strong indication of this type of individual commitment, it will be extremely difficult to raise any other money. Why should someone not directly involved in the business risk money in your business if you are not prepared to put your own assets on the line?

BANKS, TRUST COMPANIES, CREDIT UNIONS, AND SIMILAR INSTITUTIONS

Banks and similar institutions are the most popular and widely used external source of funds for new businesses. A visit to the local banker becomes almost a mandatory part of any new venture startup situation. Banks historically have provided debt financing in the form of self-liquidating, short-term loans to cover small businesses' peak working capital requirements, usually in the form of an *operating loan* or *line of credit.*

An operating loan extends credit to you up to a prearranged limit *on an ongoing basis*, to cover your day-to-day expenses, such as accounts receivable, payroll, inventory carrying costs, office supplies, and utility bills. If you happen to be in a highly seasonal or cyclical business, for example, such a line of credit can be used to purchase additional inventory in anticipation of your peak selling period. An operating loan is intended to *supplement your basic working capital.* An operating loan can also be used to bridge unexpected cash flow interruptions and/or shortfalls. It may also give you the ability to take advantage of supplier discounts for prompt payment.

Operating loans, however, can have some restrictions. For example, your bank may prohibit you from taking retained earnings out of your company during the early stages of your business. In addition, the bank may even veto the purchase of machinery, equipment, and other fixed assets above a certain amount. These operating loans are subject to annual review and renewal by mutual agreement but can often be terminated by the lender at its option unless specific conditions have been incorporated into the loan agreement. Interest on operating loans is usually *tied to the prime rate.* That means the interest rate can change either up or down as the prime rate changes. This can be an advantage when interest rates are declining but a major issue if rates are increasing rapidly.

Banks also provide *term loans* to small businesses—loans for the purchase of an existing business or to acquire fixed assets, such as machinery, vehicles, and commercial buildings, which typically must be repaid in three to 10 years. The term of the loan is usually linked to the expected lifespan of the asset. Three to four years is common for a truck or leased office equipment, while the term of a loan to acquire a building could be considerably longer. Term loans typically have a fixed interest rate for the full term. Therefore your interest cost is predetermined in advance and your budgeting process is simplified. However, the loan amount tends to be limited to a percentage of the value of the asset being financed. In addition, term loans often command a one-time processing fee of half a percent of the value of the loan.

You should realize that business bank loans, both operating and term loans, are *demand* loans so that regardless of the term, the bank can and will demand they be paid back if it feels the company is getting into trouble. While this usually occurs only when the business has real problems, there is the potential for difficulties; what the banker may perceive as a serious situation may be perceived as only a temporary difficulty by the owner of the business.

The bank may ask for your personal guarantee of business loans as well as a pledge of collateral security for the full value of the loan or more. This means that even though your business might be incorporated, your personal liability is not necessarily limited to your investment in the business; you could lose your house, car, cottage, and other personal assets if the business fails and you are unable to repay your loans to the bank.

To qualify for a loan you must have sufficient equity in your business and a strong personal credit rating. Banks do not take large risks. Their principal considerations in assessing a loan application are the safety of their depositors' money and the return they will earn on the loan. It is critical that you take these factors into account in preparing your loan proposal and try to look at your situation from the banker's point of view.

WORKING CAPITAL

Working capital is the backbone of any business, so learning how to maintain or generate more cash in your company is vital to success. Working capital is the cash you need to operate, or your current assets minus your current liabilities. Without enough working capital, you could lose your flexibility and credibility with financial institutions, suppliers, and customers. Working capital financing is usually available for the development and or launching of new products, adding e-commerce to your business, or making changes to your marketing and promotion strategy. Working capital allows you to have a steady cash flow to keep your business running while these initiatives are being developed.

FEDERAL GOVERNMENT FINANCIAL ASSISTANCE PROGRAMS

Governments at all levels in Canada have developed a proliferation of financial assistance programs for small business. It is estimated that more than 600 programs are available from both the federal and provincial governments to help people begin a business or assist those that have already started. Many of these programs are aimed at companies that are in more advanced stages of their development and are looking to grow and expand, but quite a number can be utilized by firms in the startup stage. Many of these programs offer financial assistance in the form of low-interest loans, loan guarantees, interest-free loans, or even forgivable (non-repayable) loans. Others offer incentives, such as wage subsidies, whereby the government will pay an employee's wage for a certain period of time. These programs are too numerous to describe in any detail, but let us briefly look at several of the more important ones.

Canada Small Business Financing Program (CSBFP)

New and existing businesses with gross revenues of less than $5 million may be eligible to obtain term loans from chartered banks, caisses populaires, credit unions, or other lenders and have the loan partially guaranteed by the federal government under the *Canada Small Business Financing Act* (CSBFA). These loans are provided at a reasonable rate of interest (prime plus no more than 3 percent for floating rate loans, or the lender's residential mortgage rate plus 3 percent for a fixed-rate loan). In addition, lenders are required to pay a one-time loan registration fee to the government equal to 2 percent of the amount loaned. This fee is recoverable from the borrower. These loans may be used for any number of purposes, such as the purchase or renovation of machinery and equipment and the purchase and improvement of land and buildings for business purposes. Loan proceeds may be used to finance up to 90 percent of the cost of the asset, while the maximum value of loans a borrower may have outstanding under the CSBFA cannot exceed $500,000. For more information, contact any private sector lender or the CSBFP website (www.ic.gc.ca).

Industrial Research Assistance Program (IRAP)

The National Research Council of Canada Industrial Research Assistance Program (www.nrc-cnrc.gc.ca) provides financial support to qualified small- and medium-sized enterprises in Canada to help them develop technologies for competitive advantage. There are two program elements:

1. Financial support may be provided to small- and medium-sized enterprises in Canada that have 500 or less full-time equivalent employees for an eligible research and development project, supporting up to 100 percent of salary costs associated with the project or up to 75 percent of contractor fees.

2. The *Youth Employment Strategy* provides small- and medium-sized enterprises with financial assistance to hire highly skilled postsecondary graduates. Firms can receive a financial contribution geared toward supporting a portion of the salary costs of the postsecondary graduate up to a maximum of $30,000.

Community Futures and Community Business Development Corporations

Industry Canada's Community Futures Development Corporations (CFDCs) and Community Business Development Corporations (CBDCs) (www.communityfuturescanada.ca) are a network of 269 offices across Canada that provide their communities with a variety of business development services, including, but not limited to, the following:

Business Development Loans

- CFDCs/CBDCs each offer specific loan programs that target their community's needs, assisting entrepreneurs who may have had trouble accessing capital from traditional lenders. In some cases, these include special loans to youth entrepreneurs and entrepreneurs with disabilities.
- Normally, they can lend a maximum of $150,000 to new or existing businesses.
- Loans are fully repayable and are negotiated at competitive interest rates.

Contact your nearest CFDC/CBDC for further information on the entire cross-Canada network (www.communityfuturescanada.ca).

Technical Support

CFDCs/CBDCs provide services that include:

- Business advice, counselling, information, and referrals
- Help with business plans
- Advice on export readiness and supplier development

Training

Training may be available in, among other areas:

- Self-employment skills
- Business management training
- Marketing
- Bookkeeping
- Financing
- Computer literacy

Information

CFDCs/CBDCs can provide information on relevant federal and provincial programs and services, as well as access to business libraries and business databases (www.communityfuturescanada.ca).

Women's Enterprise Initiative Loan Program

Western Economic Diversification, through the local Women's Enterprise Initiative in each western province, provides access to a loan fund for women entrepreneurs seeking financing for startup or expansion of a business. To qualify, the business must have a fully completed business plan and be 50 percent owned or controlled by a woman or women. Loans up to $150,000 are available.

For more information, contact the Women's Enterprise Initiative in your province (www.wd.gc.ca).

Aboriginal Business Canada

Canadian status and non-status Indians, Inuit, and Métis individuals over the age of 18 are eligible for support with the preparation of business plans, marketing, and financing the startup, expansion, modernization, or acquisition of a commercially viable business under Industry Canada's Aboriginal Business Canada program. The business opportunity can be in any sector. The minimum cash equity required by the applicant is equivalent to 10 percent of eligible project costs and the contribution level can range from 30 to 75 percent, depending on the nature of the project. These contributions are non-repayable.

For more information, contact one of the Aboriginal Business Canada offices located in each of the provinces and territories, the program's head office in Ottawa, or their website (www.ainc-inac.gc.ca).

The Self-Employment Program

The Self-Employment Benefit Program is an initiative of Human Resources and Skill Development Canada but designed and delivered by each province separately. It is intended to provide financial assistance to eligible individuals to help them create jobs for themselves by starting a business. Not everyone is eligible for the program. While the requirements may vary somewhat from province to province, in order to qualify, individuals need to:

- Be currently receiving Employment Insurance (EI); or
- Have received EI benefits within the past three years.

Other conditions may have to be met as well depending on the province.

The program will provide regular EI benefits throughout the individual's benefit period or financial assistance for living expenses and other necessary expenses instead, and, like the other regular benefits, the assistance does not have to be paid back. In addition, the program typically provides entrepreneurial training and advice, one-on-one mentoring, and assistance with developing a business plan. If accepted into the program you have to commit to working full time on starting a business of your own for close to a year. If you qualify, it can be a great opportunity to get the money to support yourself while working on starting your own business.

To locate a program in your area, search the Internet by using the keywords "self-employment benefit program." Include your province and city within the search (e.g., self-employment benefit program Calgary Alberta).

Business Development Bank of Canada

The Business Development Bank of Canada (BDC) is a federal Crown corporation that provides a wide range of financial, management counselling, and information services to small business through its broad network of over 100 branches across the country. Its financial services complement those of the private sector by providing funds for business projects, when funds are not available from the commercial banks and other sources on reasonable terms. The BDC will provide term loans for the acquisition of fixed assets, working capital or operating loans, venture loans, and venture capital. Its primary focus is on small- and medium-sized businesses operating in knowledge-based, growth-oriented industries and export markets.

Brian Titus was able to obtain a BDC loan to help launch his successful micro brewery in Halifax. To do so, he had to prepare a comprehensive business plan and overcome some other obstacles, but his determination and perseverance paid off as he was able to attract the capital necessary to get the business off the ground.

For further information, contact one of the BDC offices located in each of the provinces and territories or the BDC head office in Montreal, or visit their website (www.bdc.ca).

PROVINCIAL GOVERNMENT FINANCIAL ASSISTANCE PROGRAMS

Most of the provincial governments provide a range of grants, loans, and other forms of assistance to small business. For example, Manitoba offers the Business Start Program that provides a loan guarantee for loans up to $30,000 along with an educational component to assist new entrepreneurs in launching their business. Loan proceeds can provide funds for business registration or incorporation costs, equipment and inventory purchases, promotional costs, and working capital needs. Similarly, Ontario has the Summer Company program, which provides business coaching and mentoring and awards of up to $3,000 to full-time students between the ages of 15 and 29 who want to start and run their own summer businesses. Applicants must submit a comprehensive business plan, as well as other information, and if approved, they receive some business training, regular meetings with a local business mentoring group in their community, an award of up to $1,500 to help with their business startup costs, and an additional award of $1,500 at the end of the summer upon proof of returning to school.

The list of other programs is much too extensive to provide here, but you can obtain specific information on the programs offered in your province by contacting the appropriate government department, or you can contact your local Canada Business Service Centre (www.canadabusiness.ca).

VENTURE CAPITAL

Venture capital involves equity participation in a startup or growing business situation. Conventional venture capital companies, however, really do not offer much opportunity for firms still in the concept or idea stage. These investors are generally looking for investment situations in proven firms requiring in excess of $1 million and on which they can earn a 40 to 50 percent annual return. While these companies will often accept high-risk situations, most new venture startups do not meet their primary investment criteria.

There are some exceptions to this general rule, however. During the dot-com frenzy of the late 1990s and early 2000s, the business press was full of stories of young Canadian entrepreneurs barely out of school who had received millions of dollars in venture capital financing to launch their latest Internet idea. This situation has cooled considerably. Corporate funds, pension funds, private independent venture funds, and labour-sponsored venture capital funds still have billions of dollars looking for investment opportunities, principally in the high-technology sector, but investors are being much more careful in determining where the money goes.

Christopher Frey, Kisha Ferguson, and Matt Robinson are among the lucky few who have been successful in raising a significant amount of money for a somewhat more traditional business situation. They were looking for a $300,000 equity infusion to help develop their adventure travel magazine, *Outpost*. Sometimes, however, the price can be too high. The initial offer they received to provide the funds demanded a majority stake in the business in return. Though they desperately needed the money to grow their business, they still had sufficient funds to limp along while searching out other options, so they turned the offer down. In the end, they connected with a Toronto venture capitalist, who provided them with some bridge financing and told them how to beef up their business to make it more attractive to other investors. After 18 months, they finally hooked up with another firm in the communications business, which provided them with the money they needed to solidify their operations, and they learned a number of valuable lessons along the way.

There are a number of venture capital firms that may be prepared to consider smaller investments. However, keep in mind that of 100 proposals considered by a typical venture capital firm, only four or five are selected for investment purposes. Therefore, the probability of receiving any financial assistance from this source is very slim. For more information, however, check out the Canadian Venture Capital Association's website (www.cvca.ca).

ANGEL INVESTORS

A new business startup probably has a better chance of obtaining equity capital from small, private venture capitalists—often called "angels"—or provincially supported venture capital programs. There may be doctors, dentists, lawyers, accountants, and other individuals in your community who could be approached for investment funds. Many of these people may be looking for situations where they can invest small sums (less than $50,000) with the possibility of earning a larger return than that offered by more conventional investments, and they are often prepared to invest in startup situations.

These investors often get personally involved with the businesses they invest in and tend to focus less on technology-oriented opportunities than most venture capitalists do. They typically invest in companies that have already largely burned through the owners' own money and what they can raise from families and friends but before they are big enough to be of any interest to a venture capitalist. The angel investor's plan is to be part of the business for three to five years and then cash in when the business is sold to an outside firm or their interest is bought out by the company itself.

Typical angel investors in Canada are:

- Self-made, high-income, middle-aged, well-educated people, who have substantial business experience as the owner or manager of a company. They do not tend to be wealthy professionals, such as doctors and dentists.
- Usually those who are more in favour of investing within their own locality, close to home.
- Experienced investors who do their own due diligence and are confident in their own ability to appraise investment opportunities.
- Usually those who are opportunistic, rather than scientifically seeking out potential investment situations.

OTHER CONSIDERATIONS

ANGEL INVESTORS: THE DEFINITION

Angel investors are individuals who invest in businesses looking for a higher return than they would see from more traditional investments. Many are successful entrepreneurs who want to help other entrepreneurs get their business off the ground. Usually they are the bridge from the self-funded stage of the business to the point that the business needs the level of funding that a venture capitalist would offer. Funding estimates vary, but usually range from $150,000 to $1.5 million.

The term "angel" comes from the practice in the early 1900s of wealthy businessmen investing in Broadway productions. Today "angels" typically offer expertise, experience, and contacts in addition to money. Less is known about angel investing than venture capital because of the individuality and privacy of the investments.

The typical profile of angel investors:

- The "average" private investor is between 40 and 60 years old with an annual income of $100,000, a net worth of $1 million, has previous successful entrepreneurial experience, and invests up to $150,000 per venture.

- Most angels invest close to home and enjoy advising the entrepreneur and like to be involved with the company.

For the business seeking funding, the right angel investor can be the perfect first step in formal funding. It usually takes less time to meet with an angel and to receive funds, due diligence is less involved, and angels usually expect a lower rate of return than a venture capitalist does. The downside is finding the right balance of expert help without the angel totally taking charge of the business. Structuring the relationship carefully is an important step in the process.

F Y I DIFFERENCES BETWEEN ANGEL INVESTORS AND VENTURE CAPITALISTS

	Angel Investor	Venture Capitalist (VC)
Average minimum investment	• $50,000– $100,000	• $250,000
Why investor invests	• Likes the entrepreneur • Believes in the product • Has a relationship with the entrepreneur	• Likes the entrepreneur • The entrepreneur has shown the product is good • Knows what the market is and how large it is • Knows how to reach the potential market
Involvement of investor	• Advisory role	• On board of directors
Where does the money come from?	• From an individual	• VCs use other people's money
Pitching to an investor	• Slide deck • Business plan*	• Slide deck • Business plan*
Time it takes to receive funding	• Usually quicker, as the cheque is smaller • Angel investors take more risks than VCs do	• Minimum of nine months • A relationship needs to be formed with a VC • Due diligence takes time
Return on investment	• When the company is profitable, it may buy back the shares of the investor • The company is acquired	• When the company is acquired • If the company becomes public, then the investor may sell the shares

Source: Wendy Mayhew, used with permission.
* Both angel investors and venture capitalists are moving to slide presentations. However, some are still looking at business plans.

It can be difficult for a small business to find an angel investor. Most prefer to remain anonymous for fear of being overwhelmed with requests for investments. They typically operate through informal networks of friends and business associates, with few clearly defined channels to bring angels and entrepreneurs together. Some of these

ENTREPRENEURS IN ACTION

ANGELS STEP INTO VENTURE CAPITAL VOID

Canada's venture capital industry is far from healthy, particularly if you're a startup looking for investment to turn an idea or a prototype into a product and a business.

For entrepreneurs, there is reason for optimism as angel investors are slowly starting to emerge as an alternative source of financing. While far from abundant or easy to find, angel investors are stepping into the fray. Many of these angels are successful entrepreneurs who appreciate and understand the challenges facing new business owners looking for growth capital.

One of the more active angels these days is Jordan Banks, who spent years as general manager of eBay Canada before moving to JumpTV. After leaving JumpTV, Mr. Banks took some time off and, in the process, discovered his interest and passion for helping startups as an adviser and angel investor.

He says many of his investment opportunities have come through personal connections. Of the 10 companies in his portfolio, he says nine are operated by people he already knew, or people who were well known by close friends and business colleagues.

"At the end of the day, early stage investing is almost all about the people at the company and their character, integrity and work ethic," he says. "If you get that right, good things will happen. One of the ways to get it right is to have lots of points of reference on the people you are investing in through friends or colleagues."

In evaluating investment opportunities, Mr. Banks says he tries to keep the process as simple as possible by using a three-criteria process:

- He has to believe and have great confidence in the founder of the business and a proven history of showing a bias for action.
- The company needs a simple business model that he can easily understand and explain.
- The business can't require more than one more subsequent round of financing. Mr. Banks says one of the biggest perils of angel investing is getting materially diluted by institutional money in future rounds. By reducing the requirement of future rounds, he says it reduces dilution and increases the return upon exit.

Since angel investing is often a personal and financial exercise, Mr. Banks says the most important consideration between an investor and a founder is making sure both sides have the same expectations from the beginning. "In my experience, the most

successful companies who have secured angel funding have mapped out the skill sets they'd ideally like or need from an investor group and then mapped the angel investors to those skills," he says.

"Getting money is the easy part; getting money that can be leveraged many times over after the initial cheque has been cut is the hard part. By setting expectations from the beginning about level of expected involvement and skill sets required, the chances for a future positive outcome are dramatically increased. Unfortunately, the flip side is also true."

Other than money, Mr. Banks says angels can also provide value to investments by attracting quality investors to the board, providing advice about structure, process and strategic priorities, making introductions, and helping attract excellent talent.

As for the things that angel investors should avoid, Mr. Banks says he stays away from getting involved simply because other "smart" investors have committed to investing. He also avoids companies that are in a rush to raise money because competitors have done so at high valuations. Finally, he places no value in financial projections that extend for more than 12 months.

Mr. Banks says he's excited about the growing number of angels getting involved, particularly because the community is evolving from simply writing cheques to playing an active role in helping accelerate a company's growth.

"Having said that, our terrific budding entrepreneurs in Canada certainly need more help and support at an early stage," he says. "We need more financial incentives for talented and experienced business people to become angels. We can't lose sight of how risky angel investing is and we need more programs in place to help offset that risk."

Source: Mark Evans, *The Globe and Mail, Report on Business,* published on Wednesday, March 17, 2010 8:50AM EDT. Last updated on Thursday, September 6, 2012 4:06 PM EDT. © Copyright 2010 CTVglobemedia Publishing Inc. All Rights Reserved.

issues are gradually being overcome, however, as a number of communities and organizations have established programs to bring entrepreneurs and private investors together.

In 1996, the federal government started the Canadian Community Investment Plan (CCIP) as a means to improving access to risk capital for small- and medium-sized firms located in smaller communities across the country. One of the more successful of these demonstration projects is Capital Connexion (www.capital-connexion.com) located in Quebec. It is a continuously updated database of proposals from entrepreneurs looking for financing, along with a list of angel investors searching for business projects in which to invest. Registration of both investors and entrepreneurs on the database is free, but they must be validated by a local economic development organization.

In addition, more and more private investors are getting together to form "angel networks" to work together in vetting potential deals, doing the necessary due diligence, and sharing the risk with other small investors. The National Angel Capital Organization (NACO) has become the voice of angel investors in Canada, and many of the angel groups across the country are listed on their website (www.nacocanada.com). Many of these groups meet regularly to view investment pitches from a number of early-stage companies seeking equity investment.

Canada's chartered banks are often criticized for not providing this kind of risk capital to small businesses. Banks, however, are principally low-risk lenders of their depositor's money and traditionally provide debt financing. Venture capitalists and other private investors provide financing in exchange for shares or other interest in the company. Banks have neither the mandate nor the expertise to participate in this specialized market.

Jordan Banks, profiled in the Entrepreneurs in Action box, is a typical "angel." He had a very successful career in a couple of entrepreneurial companies, such as eBay and Jump TV, and after leaving those firms, he decided to help others, as an adviser and angel investor, get started in their own business. Many of his investments have been made in firms where he knew the principals very well or they were operated by friends or contacts of people he knew very well. The character and integrity of the individuals behind the businesses are very important to him in making a decision to invest. These investments give him a way to keep involved and participate in the growth and development of the business as well as provide an opportunity to make a good financial return on his investments.

WHAT'S ON THE TABLE?

Negotiations with private venture capital sources can be lengthy and complex. It is important to keep in mind the main issues that may be under discussion in the process. These will likely include:

- **Price** What are the business and the opportunity worth? How much will the investor pay in exchange for a position in your business? You have to have a realistic idea of the range of values you might be prepared to accept and the values an investor might be prepared to consider.

- **Control** How much of your business will the investor get for his or her investment, and how much control will the investor be able to exercise over its affairs? Most private investors are not trying to gain control of your business, but they are looking to manage their risk by putting some controls in place to protect their investment. These may include:
  - Requiring prior consultation or imposing some restrictions on your ability to make financial decisions.
  - Requiring representation on your board of directors.
  - Determining the amount of equity you may have to give up based on pre-determined performance-based targets.
  - Requiring a provision giving the investors the first opportunity to participate in the future sale of equity in the business or asking for a ban on the sale of future shares without investor agreement.

- **Establishment of performance expectations** The investment may be laid out in stages and tied to specific achievement milestones and objectives. You and the investor need to agree on the performance measures that will be used to determine if the business is succeeding as expected to trigger these additional contributions or somehow change the terms of the initial deal.

- **Exit strategy** Some of the available options by which investors might cash in their investment in your business include:

  - **Acquisition by a third party** This is an outright sale of the company, in which the investor's shares would be sold as part of the sale of the company to a third-party acquirer.

  - **Sale of the investor's interest to a third-party investor** This can be an option, but minority interests in private companies can be very difficult to sell due to the lack of control and liquidity. Significant costs can be associated with finding new investors, and the process can consume a great deal of time and effort.

  - **Buyback agreement** The investor's shares may be repurchased by the company. This could be in the form of a put option or a retraction clause in which the investor maintains the legal right to force you to repurchase his or her shares at an agreed and pre-specified price at particular points in time.[4]

  - **Management or employee buyout** The founders and early investors can often realize a gain from the business by selling it to other partners or some of the key managers in the business in a management buyout or to a number of the employees through an employee stock ownership plan (ESOP).

  - **Debt repayment** The financing structure used could include some form of subordinated debt with specific repayment terms on exit. The debt agreement may carry conversion privileges that allow the investor to convert the debt into common shares under certain circumstances.

  - **An initial public offering (IPO)** The investor's shares could be sold when the business decides to raise additional capital through the sale of shares to the public. This exit mechanism is commonly viewed as the "holy grail" for both the company and the investor and can be the most satisfying and financially rewarding. However, very few private firms ever actually achieve this level of success, and it does come with a number of potentially negative considerations. For example, going public can mean the loss of a significant portion of your ownership and can leave you in a minority position. In addition, a portion of your and the investors' shares may be held in escrow, possibly for years, forcing you to remain invested in the business. It also means that by becoming "public," a lot of previously private and sensitive information must now be shared with the public.

As you can see, obtaining money from private venture capital sources might pose a number of interesting problems for you. You will probably have to give up at least partial ownership and control of your business. In addition, angel investors usually have limited resources, so additional funds may not be available if required later. Finally, as amateur investors, these people may not have the patience to wait out the situation if things do not work out as quickly as you originally planned.

The decisions you make regarding any of these issues are very important, extremely complex, and often critical to the success of your prospective deal. You should consult with a professional financial adviser before preparing any proposal for presentation in a search for private capital.

ADDITIONAL SOURCES OF FINANCING

Canadian Youth Business Foundation

The Canadian Youth Business Foundation (CYBF) (www.cybf.ca) is a national not-for-profit organization that enables young entrepreneurs (18 to 39 years old) to pursue their aspirations of building a successful business by providing them with several forms of business support and assistance. These include:

- A loan program that will provide up to $15,000 amortized over three to five years to cover the startup costs of a business

HOW COUPLE'S PERFECT PITCH YIELDED FOUR OFFERS ON *DRAGONS' DEN*

Before he and his wife, Tonia Jahshan, stepped in front of the cameras to make a pitch for investor money on CBC's *Dragons' Den*, Hatem Jahshan thought of a comeback in case Kevin O'Leary—notorious for being the mean Dragon—called him a cockroach.

"I was going to say something like, 'Well, you may think I'm a cockroach, but I'm a cockroach that grows quickly,'" says Mr. Jahshan, who is chief executive officer of Steeped Tea, an Ancaster, Ontario company that sells loose-leaf teas at tea parties hosted by independent consultants.

Mr. Jahshan didn't need his cockroach rebuttal. Five minutes into their pitch, the couple had offers from four of the five Dragons—including Mr. O'Leary, who was willing to shell out $300,000 for a 30-percent stake in Steeped Tea.

The Jahshans decided to go with Jim Treliving and David Chilton, who each offered $125,000 for 10-percent ownership in the business. Mr. Treliving had great connections in the United States, where the Jahshans wanted to establish a presence, and Mr. Chilton showed a solid understanding of Steeped Tea's business model.

Steeped Tea's successful bid for Dragon financing stands as an example of what can happen when entrepreneurs hit all the right notes in a venture capital pitch—on or off camera. Whether they are pitching to celebrity millionaires under the glare of studio lights or to family and friends for a bit of love money, business owners need to present a compelling case.

That's easier said than done, say business and venture capital experts.

"Tragically I've seen my share of poorly executed, unsuccessful pitches," says Peter Bailey, a former venture capitalist who is general manager of Flow Ventures Inc., an early-stage business consulting firm with offices in Toronto and Montreal. "Some people come in thinking they've got a great idea, why wouldn't you want to invest in it? But it's not that simple."

It's not that complicated, either. A good pitch, Mr. Bailey says, starts with clear answers to a few basic questions: What are you selling, what problem are you solving with your product or service, and what makes you the best team to solve this problem?

"And you've got to make your story clear very quickly," he says. "In the first 20 seconds, your audience needs to understand what you're selling and why."

John Vyge, a business-plan coach in Reston, Virginia, and author of *The Dragons' Den Guide to Assessing Your Business Concept* and *The Dragons' Den Guide to Investor-Ready Business Plans*, says many entrepreneurs tend to focus on their business plans when pitching for money. They should, instead, do what Ms. Jahshan did: focus on "proof of concept."

ADRIANO VALENTINI FOR THE GLOBE AND MAIL. USED WITH PERMISSION.

"She talked about how she was hosting 15 tea parties a month before she developed her direct sales model, which showed that she proved her business concept on a small scale first," Mr. Vyge says.

At the time of the pitch, Steeped Tea had 500 consultants ringing in $500 a tea party—more proof that the Jahshans' business concept and model were working, Mr. Vyge says.

The Jahshans also showed that they knew their business and market inside and out; they were quick to answer questions about the company's revenue and profit margins and the competition. "Being prepared and knowing your numbers is important," Mr. Vyge adds.

It's important to ask for a "reasonable" level of funding—that is, just enough capital to get past the next growth stage, says Sean Wise, assistant professor of entrepreneurship and strategy at Ryerson University in Toronto and author of *Hot or Not: How to Know if Your Business Idea Will Fly or Fail*.

Prof. Wise, who used to provide behind-the-scenes coaching for *Dragons' Den* contestants, says entrepreneurs should also be able to explain exactly how they will use the money and set metrics that will show what value was generated for the business and its investors.

"Example: We are startup XYZ, and we are looking to raise $100,000, which will be used to attract 25,000 new users—we already have 10,000—through a six-month campaign using Google Adwords and Facebook ads."

Giving investors a good idea of what the business is worth is critical in a venture capital pitch, says Rabinder Kooner, a business adviser with Small Business BC, a Vancouver-based non-profit resource centre. Yet this is where many entrepreneurs fail, he notes.

"A lot of people I've come across have an overly inflated idea of what their business is worth," he says. "As a result, they lose credibility with investors because it looks like they're just picking figures from nowhere and they can come across as arrogant and greedy."

Mr. Kooner's advice: Seek help from a business valuation expert. It costs money, but it will help entrepreneurs and their prospective investors get a true picture of the business.

So many things can happen after an investor puts an offer on the table, Mr. Bailey says. That's why business owners need to be ready for the due diligence that follows the handshake offer.

"First and foremost, make sure your financial house is in order," he says. "Have your books all ready and organized, and everything outlined on paper."

With its new business partners—and their money—on board, Steeped Tea is on track to enter the U.S. market by March 2013. The company did $1.3 million in sales last year. But since their pitch on *Dragons' Den* was aired, sales have "gone right through the roof," Mr. Jahshan says. Steeped Tea's consultant network has also grown dramatically, to more than 1,300 today from about 500 last year.

"At some point in the process, bringing in investors felt like we were selling our soul," Mr. Jahshan says. "But we really wanted to enter the U.S. and we knew that to do that, we needed partners who knew that market and had the right connections. We have absolutely no regrets."

Source: Marjo Johne, "It Starts with One," *Special to The Globe and Mail*, Thursday, December 6, 2012, updated Friday, December 7, 2012. Used with permission.

- The possibility of a loan of twice the amount of the loan provided by the CYBF from the Business Development Bank of Canada (BDC)
- A mandatory mentoring orientation and mentoring program for all CYBF funded entrepreneurs
- Expansion financing of up to $30,000 through a partnership with the BDC
- Access to a wide range of business resources to help young people through the startup stage

Photo courtesy of
Dan Martell

What do you like about being an Entrepreneur?

I love the fact that every day I make the world a better place for everybody.

Dan Martell,
Founder, Clarity.fm
www.clarity.fm

Dragons' Den

The popular CBC show, *Dragons' Den* (www.cbc/dragonsden.com), has made a considerable difference to many entrepreneurs who have had the nerve to face the Dragons, both good and bad. An example is Eric Dormer, president of EventDawn, an online event planning platform. Eric had been marketing his company to some well-known hotels that hosted events on a regular basis. One was ready to sign a contract until Eric pitched to the Dragons. The Dragons did not see a value in his venture and indicated that no one would ever use it. When Eric called about the contract the day after the episode was aired, he was told there was not going to be a contract. His contact had watched Eric's pitch to the Dragons, and since they thought it was not a good idea, he did not either. As any typical entrepreneur, Eric did not give up and has recently launched a newer version of his app that is currently being evaluated by event planners, and he hopes this will lead to sales in the very near future.

Then there is Ooka Island Inc., which gathered recently at its Charlottetown office to watch the educational software company's pitch on *Dragon's Den*. One staff member's smartphone was logged on to the company's e-commerce site, which pings every time Ooka Island gets a new client.

As the pitch was broadcast, the phone began to ping continuously until it sounded like a drum roll. That started a pretty steady stream of sales for the next two weeks. Joell MacPhee, one of the company's co-founders and director of reading partnerships, did not leave *Dragons' Den* with the $1.5 million she was seeking. But, the post-*Dragons' Den* online traffic rose about 900 percent from a year earlier and sales about 500 percent without spending a nickel on marketing.[5]

Producing vegan, organic breakfast cereals sounds like a nice little business. That is what Corrin Mullins figured. When the CEO of HapiFoods Group Inc. wrote the business plan for her Sechelt, B.C.–based firm, she aimed to sell 1,000 bags of Holy Crap cereal a month. But when Mullins and her husband Brian appeared on *Dragons' Den*, sales went nuts: 10,000 online orders flooded in the week after the show aired. Although Jim Treveling was to finance the business the deal did not materialize. The company lined up bridge financing so that HapiFoods, which *Dragons' Den* later named the most successful business in the program's history, could fill the orders. And Mullins, seeing such huge demand, scaled up operations radically. More than 1,800 stores now carry HapiFoods cereals, and sales top 4,000 bags a day.[6]

The producers of *Dragons' Den* are always looking for entrepreneurs to pitch to the Dragons on the show and travel across Canada once a year where they do auditions. If you are up to facing the Dragons, it might be a way of getting the financing you are looking for. Even if you do not win over the Dragons, it is a huge marketing opportunity. The *Dragons' Den* tour schedule is available at www.cbc/dragonsden.com.

CROWDFUNDING

"Crowdfunding" is the raising of funds through the collection of small contributions from the general public (known as the "crowd") using the Internet and social media. Crowdfunding has its origins in the concept of "crowdsourcing," which is the broader concept of an individual reaching a goal by receiving and leveraging small contributions from many parties.

The key to crowdfunding in the present context is its inextricable link to online social networking and its ability to harness the power of online communities to extend a project's promotion and financing opportunities. The non profit sector was the first to successfully employ crowdfunding in its present online form.

Crowdfunding is becoming an increasingly common form of raising funds in the technology and media industries, including music, film, and video games. Traditionally, crowdfunding is used to raise money to fund the development of a well-defined, singular project. The new form of crowdsourced private financing has lowered the barriers to entry not only for financing projects but also for the average citizen to play the role of investor. Crowdfunding also has a unique dual function of providing both private financing and generating publicity and attention for a project.

Kickstarter is one of several crowdfunding sites (www.kickstarter.com), with others popping up regularly. Canada now has a site (www.kickstarter.com/canada) for anyone looking for crowdfunding dollars in Canada. This did not keep University of Waterloo graduate Eric Migicovsky from launching a campaign for a project that has become the most successful crowdfunding project on Kickstarter to date.

The product, Pebble, is the first watch built for the twenty-first century. It is infinitely customizable, with beautiful downloadable watchfaces and useful Internet-connected apps. Pebble connects to iPhone and Android smartphones through Bluetooth, alerting you with a silent vibration to incoming calls, emails, and messages. While designing Pebble, the company strove to create a minimalist yet fashionable product that seamlessly blends into everyday life.

Eric Migicovsky launched the fundraising drive on April 11, 2012, for his Pebble watch, with a goal of raising US$100,000. He gave the date of May 18 to raise the required funds. Within two days, the watch had raised more than US$1.8 million. By the May 18 deadline, he had raised more than $10 million. To see the campaign results, go to the Kickstarter website (www.kickstarter.com), and search for Pebble Campaign.

By turning to the crowd, entrepreneurs are finding a low-risk way to test the market for their products and fund production without having to take on debt or source venture capital. But, there is no guarantee that your campaign will be successful, and it does take time to prepare your campaign.

What Are the Dangers of Crowdfunding?

Critics say there are several dangers associated with crowdfunding, both for the project owner and the public.

Ideas that are set out on Indiegogo, for example, are not protected in any way, and their exposure may inspire someone else to run with the concept. (Experts recommend early patent filing and use of copyright protection to head off these concerns.)

Rose Levy says that her company is not responsible for any money contributed to Indiegogo once the donor requirements have been met. In other words, once a cause has reached its specific cash target and had its month of fundraising expire, the money becomes entirely the property of the project lead, and donors having second thoughts are out of luck.

Also, while donating to charitable causes can bring instant gratification, it is different when the money is being invested in the more multi-year requirements of new business ventures.

In addition, crowds can often over-invest in a newly popular industry, some caution, leading to bubbles that pop once the true revenue power of an industry is revealed

What Are the Current Models of Crowdfunding in Canada?

Currently, there are two broad forms of crowdfunding in Canada.

The first is the straightforward Indiegogo model of a hands-off, donation-based system where project owners directly receive money from willing donors, based on the sales pitch. Some, such as Indiegogo, offer a broad range of genres to suit almost every taste, while others, such as Kickstarter, have gatekeeper filters in place to keep out certain types of projects.

Another type of platform is SoKap, which has the unique feature of also incorporating revenue distribution into the model. According to David Geertz, its founder, SoKap "is the first crowdfunding platform that allows people to fund a project and make a financial return without the sale of a security."

"We're not selling equities; we're actually selling micro licences or small promotional opportunities," says Geertz. The SoKap model allows a person to buy the rights to small geographic areas and realize small revenue when a creative product is purchased in that area.

Money raised from these rights sales goes toward supporting the particular project. Project owners also see revenues from digital sales on SoKap's website.

What Lies Ahead for Global Crowdfunding?

The U.S. recently legalized the concept of equity-based crowdfunding in its so-called *JOBS Act;* JOBS stands for "jumpstart our business startups."

Although trades will not be permitted until 2013, equity crowdfunding allows members of the public to invest directly in a company's stock without having to go through or have the protections of a stock exchange.

Funding Brokers

Agents and brokers are available to help you find financing and facilitate the deal for a fee. The fee is usually a percentage of the amount raised. Before approaching an agent or broker find out what their fees are and if they will guarantee you the financing you are looking for. Some will want money up front without any promise or commitment. Before working with an agent or broker, find out as much as you can about the person. Ask for references. Remember you are looking for financing, not an additional cost.

With a little research, networking, and advice from your advisers, you will more than likely find financing on your own. A good rule of thumb before meeting with anyone is to ask about any fees that you may have to incur.

Canadian Community Loan Funds

Canadian Community Loan Funds are non profit organizations that help people who cannot get a loan from a conventional lending institution, such as a bank or credit union, because they do not have the credit history or the collateral required by the traditional institution to backstop the loan. There are a number of these institutions across the country.

They are independent organizations, so each fund has its own lending parameters. Almost all provide loans, loan guarantees, or investments to start up or expand micro-businesses, small businesses, co-ops, and social enterprises that support their local community, as well as for other purposes. Almost all require any funding request to be backed by a solid business plan.

SCAM ARTIST FACES SOCIAL MEDIA BACKLASH

Those who use the Internet to scam people can be brought down by the Web as well.

Alleged scam artist Alanna Steinberg prefers the term "self-employed financial broker" and she claims to link angel investors to delinquent debtors seeking off-the-grid business loans. In reality, it appears she has connected loan seekers with misfortune.

A wide network of alleged victims across North America walked into her trap, baited with assurances of unsecured loans, credit cards with high limits, improved credit scores, and a suite of financial solutions on Internet sites such as Craigslist and Kijiji.

All for an advance fee that ranges from $2,000 to $10,000. And just to make it more believable, she also negotiated a back-end fee, sometimes up to 20 percent of the eventual loan.

Of course, as many victims discovered, the money never arrived. When they challenged her in small claims courts, most were awarded the amount they were owed and other costs, but few were able to collect.

That's when social media vigilantes saddled up. Google her name and you are as likely to find spoof profiles, as invitations to use her services. When cornered by a camera-toting Toronto journalist, the social media-savvy Steinberg was less than smooth-talking, dropping several F-bombs.

A report in the *Toronto Star* noted: "you will also get a number of postings by alleged victims warning potential clients to give the 'Toronto Scammer' a wide pass. One calls her 'a true wolf in sheep's clothing.'"

To read the *Toronto Star* article go to www.thestar.com and search Alanna Steinberg.

Source: "Scam Artist Face Social Media Backlash," Vikram Barhat. Advisor.ca, February 15, 2012, accessed March 29, 2013.

EVALUATING YOUR ABILITY TO SECURE FINANCING   LO3

With this extensive number of alternatives available to you as potential sources of financing, it may be useful for you to give some thought to the range of possibilities you might tap into in putting together the startup requirements for your new venture. Figure 7.3 provides a framework for you to identify how much money you think you will need to launch your business and where you think that financing might possibly come from: your personal resources; friends, relations, and other personal contacts; lending agencies; grant programs; and other sources that may be available to you.

Financing is not a business's right. All lenders are in business to make (not lose) money. Consequently when a bank lends money, it wants to ensure that it will get paid back. Johanne Dion, the CEO of Trans-HERB Inc. and one of Canada's top women entrepreneurs, says, "Banks are not there to lend you dollars. They're there to make a profit. If you don't have a good plan, if you don't do your (financial) statements every year, they'll say 'Sorry we need our money.'"[7]

When seeking a loan, it is wise to shop around for the best available terms. This includes comparing obvious features of the loan, such as the interest rate, but also evaluating:

- Size of transaction fees
- Prepayment policies
- Flexibility of payment terms
- Fixed or floating interest rate
- Security and personal guarantees required
- Quality of overall service provided by the institution
- Expected processing time

An important aspect of your financial condition is your ability to obtain financing. In assessing your capacity, any lender will consider the five "C's" of credit in deciding whether or not to extend you a loan.

FIGURE 7.3   WHERE WILL YOU GET THE MONEY?

Starting a business usually requires some money. As we have pointed out in this stage, there are any number of sources from which this financing can be obtained. You may need to give some thought to approximately how much money you think you will need to launch your business and just where you feel you will be able to obtain it. Completing a form, such as the one below, will give you a good estimate of roughly what your startup financial requirements are likely to be.

How much money do you think you will need to launch your business? $ _____

Where can you get the funds?

SOURCE	POSSIBLE AMOUNT
Personal Sources	
Cash	$ _____
Stocks/Bonds	_____
Mutual Funds	_____
Term Certificates	_____
RRSPs	_____
Cash Value of Life Insurance	_____
Other Investments _____	_____
Real Estate	_____
Vehicles	_____
Other Assets _____	_____
Credit Card Limits	_____
Other Personal Sources	_____
Total Available from Personal Sources	$ _____
Personal Contacts	
Family Members	$ _____
Friends	_____
Colleagues and Acquaintances	_____
Partners	_____
Other Private Investors _____	_____
Total Available from Personal Contacts	$ _____
Lending Agencies	
Chartered Banks	$ _____
Business Development Bank	_____
Caisse Populaires and Credit Unions	_____
Finance Companies	_____
Government Agencies	_____
Other Lending Agencies _____	_____
Total Available from Lending Agencies	$ _____
Grant Programs	
Federal Government Programs	$ _____
Provincial Government Programs	_____
Municipal Programs	_____
Other _____	_____
Total Available from Grants	$ _____

(continued)

FIGURE 7.3   WHERE WILL YOU GET THE MONEY? (*CONTINUED*)

Other Sources

Supplier Credit $ _____

Customers   _____

Others _____   _____

    Total Available from Other Sources $ _____

    TOTAL AVAILABLE FROM ALL SOURCES $ _____

Character is the general impression you make on the potential lender. The lender will form a subjective opinion as to whether or not you are of sufficiently good character to be given a loan. You must be known as a morally responsible person.

Collateral is the security you can provide the lender as a pledge for fulfillment of the obligation. It is a secondary source for repayment of the loan if your cash flow from the business in insufficient to fulfill the obligation. In real estate transactions, this generally means the property, or it may mean a pledge of other personal assets to assure the lender it will get its money back.

Capital is the cash and other liquid assets you personally have or are prepared to invest in the business. The more of your own money you have invested, the more likely that you will do all you can to maintain your payment obligations for any loan. In addition, the higher your net worth, the more you have as a cushion for repayment of the loan in case the business runs into financial difficulty.

Credit is the assessment of your previous performance in meeting your credit obligations. The information about your credit history is stored at the "credit bureau" and indicates how well you have paid your bills in the past. All major credit cards, auto loans, leases, and so on are reported to the credit bureau. A lender will evaluate your past history and your ability to maintain your obligations and try and determine how well you live within your means.

Capacity to repay the loan is probably the most critical of the five factors. The lender will want to know exactly how you intend to repay the loan. They will consider the current or expected level of income from the business and your income that may come from any other sources.

In preparing to approach a banker regarding a loan, the following are several suggestions you should keep in mind to increase your probability of getting the funds:

- Do not just drop in on your bank manager; make an appointment.

- Start your presentation by briefly describing your business and the exact reason you require a loan.

- Be prepared to answer any questions your banker may have. He or she wants to determine how well you really understand your business. If you cannot answer certain questions, explain why, and say when you will be able to provide the information.

- Be prepared to discuss collateral and other security you may be required to provide.

- If your business is currently operating, invite the banker to stop by to see it firsthand.

- Ask when you can expect a reply to your request. If there is a delay, inquire whether there is additional information you need to provide.

PROFIT magazine asked entrepreneurs, bankers, and financial consultants their most successful time-tested secrets for getting the best from bankers. Here are their suggestions:

- **Know what your banker is looking for** Before you set foot inside a bank, you should understand the ground rules of credit. Banks are not in the business of financing risk. Before signing on the dotted line, the banker needs evidence that you have a comprehensive plan and the management skills to successfully implement it.

Ask yourself the question, "If I were a banker, would I lend money to me?" The bank needs to be reassured that you can repay your loan. The bank will also look for an existing strong base of equity investment in the company. Do not expect the bank to invest in something you would not invest in. To reduce its risk the bank will want some form of collateral security. In many cases, the bank will require collateral worth two or three times the amount of the loan.

- **Do not "tell" but "show" your banker** Do not just tell your banker about the great new product you have devised. Bring it or a prototype of it along, and demonstrate what makes it so great. Bring in a sample of whatever it is you plan to sell, and let your banker see it, taste it, or try it firsthand.

- **Interview your banker** There are no good banks, only good bankers. Be prepared to shop around. Make certain you are dealing with the right person and the right branch for you. Visit at least three different banks before making a decision. Ask your accountant, lawyer, customers, or suppliers for a referral.

- **Passion makes perfect** The most persuasive thing entrepreneurs can do when negotiating a loan is to show how much passion they have for what they are doing. You should try to project the attitude that you are prepared to do everything possible to make the business succeed.

- **Ask for more money than you need** One of the worst mistakes you can make is to not consider your future requirements when calculating the size of the loan or the line of credit you think you will need. If you have to go back to the bank in five or six months to ask for an increase, the bank is going to be very concerned. It reflects badly on your ability to plan, and you are also making extra work for the bank that could be reflected in extra charges for your loan.

- **Get your banker involved in your business** Invite your banker over, at least every six months, even if it is just for coffee. Make time to get to know your banker, to get him or her involved, and ask for advice. Take advantage of opportunities to network with bankers and their colleagues. If the bank holds a reception, or open house, make an effort to attend.

- **Increase your credit when you do not need it** Many entrepreneurs begin looking for outside financing only when their own resources are tapped out. You should start to begin sourcing funds at least a year before you need it. Advanced planning will give you time to adequately explore all your options, meet with several banks, and ultimately work out the best deal for your business.

- **Make professional introductions** Introduce your lawyer and your accountant to your banker. Make sure your accountant reviews the bank's proposal outlining the terms and conditions of your loan or line of credit.

- **If all else fails, keep looking** Finding the money to start or expand a business is hard work. Most entrepreneurs have been turned down many times for financing. The key is continuing to pursue every available means of securing the capital you need.[8]

A financial institution may turn down your loan application for any of a number of reasons, and it is important that you ask what they are. This knowledge may help you in future attempts to secure funding. Some of the most frequent reasons why a loan application can be rejected are as follows:

1. The business idea might be considered ill advised or just too risky.
2. You may not have offered sufficient collateral. Lenders want some assurance that they will be able to recover most or all of their money should you default on the payments.
3. The lender may feel there is insufficient financial commitment on your part.
4. You have not prepared a comprehensive and detailed business plan.
5. Your reason for requesting the loan is unclear or not acceptable to the lender. It is important that you specify the intended application of the requested funds and that this application be outlined in detail. This outline should also show your planned schedule for the repayment of the loan.
6. You do not appear confident, enthusiastic, well-informed, or realistic enough in your objectives. The lender's assessment of your character, personality, and stability are important considerations in his or her evaluation of your loan application.

OTHER CONSIDERATIONS

THE FOUNDER PROJECT

The Founder Project is an organization run almost entirely by students whose purpose is to get students to build startups.

With 286,000 postsecondary students (the highest student per capita ratio in North America), Montreal is a hotbed for new and innovative ideas. However, students struggle to obtain the necessary capital to take their businesses to the next level. The Founder Project bridges this gap by investing in student tech startups and by generating excitement for startups at the student level.

The team consists of highly motivated students from all universities in Montreal (McGill, Concordia, UQAM, Poly, ETS, HEC, and Sherbrooke), many of whom have interned at Microsoft and Google or have founded startups in the past. They have a three-phase approach that is being implemented in Montreal and are laying the groundwork to do the same in other Canadian cities.

- The Founder Project is organizing a university-wide challenge to generate excitement for startups at the universities.

- The Founder Project is raising a fund so they can begin making small investments ($10,000–$20,000) into student startups at all Montreal universities (see roughdraft.vc and dormroomfund.com for inspiration). The ultimate goal is to raise funds so that they can invest nation-wide in startups at all universities in Canada.

- The Founder Project will implement build-a-company for credit programs/courses at the universities, and potentially a startup curriculum of sorts at the universities in Montreal (and ultimately in other cities as well).

For more information on The Founder Project, to see what types of companies are being funded, and for a list of universities that are participating, visit www.TheFounder Project.com.

The worksheet shown in Figure 7.4 will allow you to assess some of the critical factors that may affect your ability to secure external funding. It will also give you some indication of what aspects of your personal character, development of your business plan, or quality of the basic idea underlying your new venture could be improved. On the worksheet, indicate your assessment of your personal situation for each of the indicated factors as honestly as you can. How do you rate? Could some factors be improved upon? What can you do to strengthen these areas, or how might you overcome these negative factors?

One question you should consider is "How much can I possibly lose on my venture should it fail?" The losses in some types of businesses can wipe out virtually all of the funds you have invested or personally guaranteed. This tends to be true in such situations as a financial planning and counselling business, travel agency, or hair salon, in which very little property or equipment is owned by the business. In other situations, such as manufacturing, construction, or real estate, there is usually an opportunity to sell the assets solely or partially owned by the business to recover at least part of your initial investment.

The way to explore this question is to consider alternative scenarios for different ways the business might fail and to estimate the liquidation value of any residual assets. To the extent that this value falls short of the initial cost of those assets less any outstanding claims, you could lose that amount of money plus the opportunity cost of the time and effort you spent in trying to develop the business.

For more information on obtaining financing for your new business, you could consult the following websites:

Canada Business

1. This site provides information on private sector associations whose members provide debt and equity financing to businesses. (www.canadabusiness.ca)
2. This is another Canada Business site that directs you to government loans, grants, and other financing programs specifically tailored to your financial needs, provincial or territorial location, demographic group and the industrial classification within which your business falls. (www.canadabusiness.ca)

Canadian Youth Business Foundation This organization is a non profit, private-sector initiative designed to provide mentoring, business support, and loans to young Canadian entrepreneurs who are starting new businesses. (www.cybf.ca)

Canadian Bankers Association, Small Business Financing This site provides information on sources and types of small business financing. It also provides a list of charters banks in Canada. (www.cbc.ca)

Business Development Bank of Canada This site provides an overview of Business Development Bank financial products aimed at small business in general. (www.bdc.ca)

Atlantic Canada Opportunity Agency (ACOA) Programs This site provides an overview of a number of programs provided by ACOA to help Atlantic Canada entrepreneurs start new businesses or upgrade existing ones. (www.acoa.ca)

Community Futures and Community Business Development Corporations CFDCs and CBDCs provide their communities with a variety of services, including business development loans, technical support, training, and information. (www.communityfuturescanada.ca)

Western Economic Diversification Canada, Funding for Business This provides a link to information about financing programs available through WD and such organizations as Community Futures, the Women Enterprise Initiative and their Growth Capital Loan program. (www.wd.gc.ca)

Fundica.com Fundica catalogues all available grants, tax credits, loans, and equity funding offered by the federal, provincial, and municipal governments, as well as private sector funders. (www.fundica.com)

Canadian Venture Capital Association (CVCA) CVCA represents the majority of private equity companies in Canada. (www.cvca.ca)

National Angel Capital Organization The National Angel Capital Organization (NACO) is Canada's industry association representing angel capital in Canada. The site provides a list of angel investors that are members of the organization. (www.nacocanada.com)

C100 The C100 is a non profit, member-driven organization that supports Canadian technology entrepreneurship through mentorship, partnership, and investment. (www.thec100.org/)

TheFounderProject TheFounderProject bridges the gap between students and investors by investing in student startups. (www.thefounderproject.com)

Kickstarter Kickstarter is a crowdfunding site, where you can put together a project and look for funding. If the project succeeds in reaching its funding goal, all backers' credit cards are charged. If the project falls short, no one is charged. (www.kickstarter.com)

Indiegogo Indiegogo is another popular crowdfunding website. This is different from Kickstarter in that you have two options for funding. You can have either a fixed or a flexible project. As with Kickstarter, if you do not reach your goal with a fixed amount, then you do not receive any funding. If you use the flexible model, you will receive the funds, even if you have not reached the full amount of funding you are looking for. (www.Indiegogo.com)

Idea Cafe, Financing Your Biz This is a U.S. site but has a lot of interesting information. (www.businessownersideacafe.com)

America's Business Funding Directory This provides a guide to over 4,000 business loan and venture capital sources of funding (principally in the U.S.). (www.businessfinance.com)

FIGURE 7.4   LOAN APPLICATION ASSESSMENT WORKSHEET

Assessment Factor	Poor 1	2	Good 3	Excellent 4	5
Personal credit rating	___	___	___	___	___
Capacity to pay back loan from personal assets if business fails	___	___	___	___	___
Collateral to pay back loan from personal assets if business fails	___	___	___	___	___
Character (as perceived in the community)	___	___	___	___	___
Commitment (your personal investment of time, energy, and money)	___	___	___	___	___
Clarity and completeness of your business plan	___	___	___	___	___
Viability of business concept (e.g., moderate risk)	___	___	___	___	___
Personal experience in the proposed business	___	___	___	___	___
Successful experience in your own business	___	___	___	___	___
Balanced management team available	___	___	___	___	___
Suitability of your personality to the pressures and responsibilities of the business	___	___	___	___	___

What can you do to improve the weak areas (where you have rated yourself 1 or 2)?

_____

_____

_____

_____

_____

Source: Adapted from D. A. Gray, *The Entrepreneur's Complete Self-Assessment Guide* (Vancouver: International Self-Counsel Press Ltd., 1986), p. 123.

ACCOUNTING PRACTICES   LO4

THE CANADIAN TAX SYSTEM

The GST is a tax that applies on most supplies of goods and services made in Canada. The GST also applies to supplies of real property (e.g., land, buildings, and interests in such property) and intangible property, such as trademarks, rights to use a patent, and digitized products downloaded from the Internet and paid for individually.

The participating provinces (New Brunswick, Newfoundland and Labrador, Nova Scotia, Prince Edward Island, and Ontario) harmonized their provincial sales tax with the GST to implement the HST. Generally, the HST applies to the same base of goods and services as the GST.

It is important to register for an HST or GST account when you open your business. It is not mandatory to open an account until you have had an income of $30,000. However, by registering early, you are able to claim for the

THE GST/HST RATES ARE AS FOLLOWS:

Province	On or after April 1, 2013	On or after July 1, 2010, and before April 1, 2013	On or after January 1, 2008, and before July 1, 2010	Before January 1, 2008, and after June 30, 2006	On or after April 1, 1997, and before July 1, 2006	Before April 1, 1997
Alberta	5%	5%	5%	6%	7%	7%
British Columbia	5%	12%	5%	6%	7%	7%
Manitoba	5%	5%	5%	6%	7%	7%
New Brunswick	13%	13%	13%	14%	15%	7%
Newfoundland and Labrador	13%	13%	13%	14%	15%	7%
Northwest Territories	5%	5%	5%	6%	7%	7%
Nova Scotia	15%	15%	13%	14%	15%	7%
Nunavut	5%	5%	5%	6%	7%	7%
Ontario	13%	13%	5%	6%	7%	7%
Prince Edward Island	14%	5%	5%	6%	7%	7%
Saskatchewan	5%	5%	5%	6%	7%	7%
Yukon	5%	5%	5%	6%	7%	7%

It is the responsibility of the business owner to keep track of any tax changes that may be implemented to ensure the correct amount of tax is being collected.

Source: Canada Revenue Agency (www.cra-arc.gc.ca/tx/bsnss/tpcs/gst-tps/rts-eng.html), accessed April 1, 2013.

HST/GST refund that you have paid on your purchases. Once you register your business, you will be given a business number and will have to complete a HST/GST report, usually quarterly. To register, go to the Canada Revenue Agency website (www.cra-arc.gc.ca).

In Quebec, Revenu Québec administers the GST/HST. If your business is located in Quebec, visit the Revenu Québec website (www.revenuquebec.ca).

RECORDKEEPING

Keeping records may not be top of mind to entrepreneurs but it is necessary for businesses to keep track of their income and expenses. Many business owners keep receipts and throw them in a box or bag until the end of the year and then take them to an accountant to sort out. Once you receive the bill from the accountant, more than likely, you will be shocked at how much it costs.

Recordkeeping does not have to be expensive at year-end if you keep records during the year. When starting out, you do not need a sophisticated accounting package; a spreadsheet will work just fine. Most business owners are familiar with how spreadsheets work, with Excel being the most commonly used spreadsheet software.

There are several software accounting packages available for small business, with the most popular being Sage Accounting and Quick Books. Relatively new is cloud accounting. There are currently two Canadian companies that offer accounting software online, FreshBooks and Wave.

Cloud computing offers you the convenience of using the software regardless of where you are without having to have your own computer with you. The other advantage is that your account is backed up regularly and will always be there; no more worrying about computer issues or loss of your own computer. Some accountants have not

FIVE TIPS FOR SMALL BUISNESS BOOKKEEPING

1. **Plan for Major Expenses**

   Be honest about the expenses that could be coming up in the next one to five years. Is it likely that you will need to upgrade your facilities? Is your office equipment on its last legs?

   It is important to acknowledge the seasonal ups and downs of your business, and how they will affect your ability to spend during those times.

   By making sure that you have forecasted for major upgrades, or peaks in staffing costs, you will avoid taking money out of the company in good months and finding yourself short in slow months.

2. **Track Your Expenses**

   Expenses can be hard to track, which means that you may be missing tax write-offs that you could have benefited from. Business credit cards can be handy tools to make sure all expenses are kept together and tracked. As long as you keep up to date with your payments that is. Most providers have now adopted the service of categorizing your bill into types of expenses, meaning one less task for you to do.

   To help prepare for audits, it is also useful for you to make notes in your calendar of the clients that you are meeting for each of those coffee dates, lunches, and events. This will help substantiate your expenses for your tax records, should you be audited.

   That goes for car mileage too. When driving long distances to meetings, make sure you either keep track of your mileage or do a calculation with Google Maps to log how far you travelled and the associated costs.

3. **Record Deposits Correctly**

   Whether it's a pocket notebook and pencil, an Excel spreadsheet, or financial software, make sure you keep track of what is being deposited into your business bank account.

   You are likely to make a variety of deposits in your account throughout the year—from loans, to sales revenue, to cash infusions from your personal savings. If you cannot account for where each of the deposits have come from you're leaving yourself open to paying taxes on money that isn't income.

4. **Set Aside Money for Taxes**

   You know that you're going to have to pay taxes and you know when. So systematically put money aside for it. Unpaid taxes can incur penalties and interest from the Canada Revenue Agency, so make sure the money is there when you need it.

   By putting money aside each month, or each time a contract is paid, it will come as less of a sting when they are due.

5. **Keep an Eye on Your Invoices**

   Late and unpaid bills can hurt your cash flow. Assign someone to track your billing. Then put a process in place for if a bill goes unpaid. That can be issuing a second invoice, making a phone call, and even levying penalties such as extra fees at certain deadlines

   Make a plan for if clients are 30, 60, and 90 days late. Remember, every late payment is an interest-free loan that hurts your cash flow.

Source: Small Business BC, Five Bookkeeping Tips for Small Business (www.smallbusinessbc.ca).

gotten into the cloud yet and still prefer to use a software program that they are familiar with. But as the future of the cloud unfolds, accountants are going to have to get on board with this new way of recordkeeping.

Regardless of whether you use a spreadsheet, a software accounting package, or the cloud, it is important to understand that you need to keep track of income and expenses. Make a list of the various expenses you have, such as office equipment, phone, advertising, salaries, and rent. Some packages already have categories set up for you to use, and if they do, make sure you are able to add more yourself, if necessary. You will also need to find out how the software handles GST/HST. Always remember to ask for a receipt for anything to do with your business. If you do not have a receipt, then you will not be able to benefit from any tax write-offs.

Most purchases can be made by using a credit card, which can make it easier to keep track of your expenses. However, you still have to have the receipts to go with the credit card statement.

You should also keep a calendar of meetings and events to do with your business: who you met and the date you met with them. Keep any receipts from any expenses you may have incurred, such as coffee or lunch. You may be able to expense a percentage of the amount. Keep a travel log of your mileage, whether you are going to the bank, picking up office supplies, or attending a meeting with your accountant or client. Mark down your mileage when you leave and again when you return. If you forget to keep track, then use Google Maps to log the distance.

If accounting seems overwhelming to you or you do not have the time to do it on your own, you will need to hire a bookkeeper. A bookkeeper will work with you and provide all the reports and files necessary at the end of the year for you to forward to your accountant.

LO1 There are differences between debt and equity financing:

- debt financing is borrowing money that must be repaid in full. Banks are an example of debt financing. Until the debt has been repaid, the provider of the loan has a legal claim against the assets and cash flows of your business.

- equity funding is money supplied by yourself or investors in exchange for an ownership position in your business. Equity funding does not need to be repaid. Providers of equity share the profits their investment is expected to generate.

LO2 The major sources of funding for startups are:

- personal funds. Invest in yourself by using your own personal funds.

- bootstrapping. Borrowing money to get started by borrowing from family and friends.

- personal credit cards or line of credit. This is easy access to a short-term loan; however, the cost of borrowing is quite high.

- supplier financing. Some suppliers may extend payment terms. This will give you time to generate sales before paying the supplier.

- leasing versus buying. Although you will have to make monthly payments for something that is leased, you do not have to have the full purchase cost in a lump sum.

- advance payment from customers. There is nothing wrong with asking for partial or full payment when a customer places an order. Online orders need to be paid in full when the order is placed.

- crowdfunding. Crowdfunding is a relatively new concept for raising money. It is both debt and equity free. When putting your project together you need to come up with something to give to the investors to entice them to give money for your project. Pebble, for example, gave each investor one of their watches.

LO3 Not everything is in your control when looking to secure financing. Being prepared with what you can control is essential. Be ready:

- to offer sufficient collateral. Lenders want assurance they are going to be repaid.

- to be clear on what you are requesting and why you are requesting it.

- with a comprehensive business plan.

- to appear confident, enthusiastic, and well informed about your product.

You also need to be prepared in the event you are turned down; however, always ask why and what you could do better to improve your chances of getting funded down the road.

LO4 There are important accounting practices to keep in mind, such as:

- you do not need to register for a GST/HST number until you have sales of $30,000. However, you should register for a number before you reach that threshold, as it enables you to claim for taxes paid on any purchases you make.

- it is important to keep track of your income and expenses. There are several options available to you, such as using a spreadsheet, off-the-shelf software, or online accounting software.

- you should speak to an accountant prior to setting up your recordkeeping to see how he or she would like you keep records. This will potentially save you money at year-end.

For more information on the resources available from McGraw-Hill Ryerson, go to www.mcgrawhill.ca/he/solutions.

STAGE
8

MARKETING

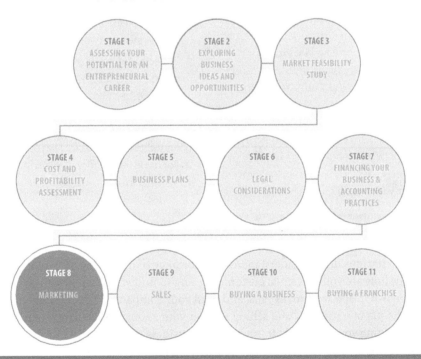

STAGE 1
ASSESSING YOUR POTENTIAL FOR AN ENTREPRENEURIAL CAREER

STAGE 2
EXPLORING BUSINESS IDEAS AND OPPORTUNITIES

STAGE 3
MARKET FEASIBILITY STUDY

STAGE 4
COST AND PROFITABILITY ASSESSMENT

STAGE 5
BUSINESS PLANS

STAGE 6
LEGAL CONSIDERATIONS

STAGE 7
FINANCING YOUR BUSINESS & ACCOUNTING PRACTICES

STAGE 8
MARKETING

STAGE 9
SALES

STAGE 10
BUYING A BUSINESS

STAGE 11
BUYING A FRANCHISE

LEARNING OBJECTIVES

By the end of this stage, you should be able to:

LO1 Explain why marketing is important to your business and the two different ways of marketing.

LO2 Evaluate the different marketing tools associated with content marketing.

LO3 Identify what is involved with traditional marketing and learn to use it to your advantage.

DAN MARTELL WANTS TO IMPACT A BILLION PEOPLE WITHIN 10 YEARS!

Dan Martell is one of the most well known and respected entrepreneurs there is in Canada. He is a master marketer and loves to help entrepreneurs with their businesses.

Dan started his first business at the age of 18 when his father asked him to build a website so that he could rent out his summer cottage. As there were close to 200 other summer properties for rent, Dan decided to build a site for everyone in the area. MaritimeVacation.ca was born. However, Dan learned very quickly that having a dot-ca website limits you to a specific location and did not draw the market they had hoped. He also realized that the business was not a problem that he wanted to solve and was not passionate about it because it was not his problem. However, Maritime Vacation gave him experience.

Since his first business, he has started several more, with two of them being sold along the way. Dan is now financially sound, and at the age 26 started investing in small businesses. In 2012 alone, he invested in six businesses.

Dan's latest venture is Clarity.fm. He wanted to build a business that would impact a billion people within 10 years. Dan started Clarity because people kept looking for advice from him. It started simple enough, with people contacting him and him returning their call. As more and more people started taking notice of what was going on through social media, Dan had to re-write the code—Dan is known for his marketing ability, but he also writes code—and people started using the website. The next thing he knew he had a thousand people using it to engage with their audience on email and social media.

In December 2012, Dan posted the following:

"Almost a year ago I asked for a favour—a birthday wish—that everyone entrepreneur I know donate one hour of their time giving advice to another entrepreneur over the phone. That was the seed that has now grown into Clarity.

Since then we've:

- Retooled the product and launched publicly in May
- Completed over 12,000 calls
- Connected entrepreneurs from across 47 countries
- Signed up over 7500+ experts and advisers

Today I'm super excited to announce that Clarity has raised $1.6 million in a round of funding from some of the best investors from Silicon Valley and across Canada."

With over 14,000 experts and new customers signing up every day for advice from the Clarity experts, it is hard to think that it will take 10 years for Dan to impact 10 billion people.

For more information on Dan Martell and Clarity.fm, go to www.clarity.fm.

Source: Interview by Wendy Mayhew. Used with permission courtesy of Dan Martell. July 2013.

Unfortunately, most startups do not understand the importance of marketing. If you do not market your product or service properly, how are your potential customers going to find you? You have to go after their business.

As a small business owner, you wear many hats, and until your company is large enough to employ both marketing and sales teams, the job of marketing and selling falls on your shoulders. To some, marketing and sales is very daunting, but it is something you have to do to succeed as a business owner.

Mark Evans, startup marketing expert, wrote a recent blog post entitled "Are Marketing and Sales the Same Thing for Startups?" In the post, he says, "It used to be that marketing and sales were two separate creatures. In one corner, marketing focused on building brand awareness among target audiences and in the other corner sales was about driving leads and deals.[1] The two worlds rarely converged."

Mark goes on to say that for startups, this model does not work when you are operating with limited or modest resources. You need to mesh sales and marketing together—marketers need to be salespeople, and salespeople have to be marketers.

MARKETING

LO1

As a small business owner, you will be juggling many jobs at the same time. Unless you have a team to work with you, you best get used to being very busy. The first order of business is to work toward your first customer, which is done through marketing.

What most entrepreneurs do not understand is that they market themselves every day. When you did your survey in Stage Three, you were marketing. When you meet someone at an event and tell them what you do, you are marketing.

As with almost everything, the Internet has changed the way marketing is done. It allows you to reach a vast audience much more easily and quickly than the traditional way of marketing your business. A healthy marketing mix includes both traditional and content marketing.

Content Marketing

Content marketing, also known as *inbound marketing*, is a marketing technique of creating and distributing relevant and valuable content to attract, acquire, and engage a clearly defined and understood target audience—with the objective of driving profitable customer action.

In a nutshell, content marketing is the art of communicating with your customers and prospects without selling. It is non-interruption marketing. Instead of pitching your products or services, you are delivering information that makes your buyer more informed. The essence of this content strategy is the belief that if we, as businesses, deliver consistent, ongoing valuable information to buyers, they ultimately reward us with their business and loyalty.[2]

Blogging, podcasts, webinars, videos, downloadable ebooks or white papers, email blasts, and infographics are all part of the mix of content marketing.

Traditional Marketing

Traditional marketing revolves around the five P's of marketing—Person, Place, Product, Pricing, and Promotion—which you learned about in Stage Three. Traditional marketing is often over shadowed by content marketing. However, it should to be part of your overall marketing mix. Face-to-face meetings with potential customers give you the advantage of demonstrating and allowing customers to see, touch, and learn about your product. They will feel the energy and passion that you have. A face-to-face meeting is also the basis of building a relationship with your customer.

Other traditional marketing channels include print advertisements, tradeshows, and direct mailings. With face-to-face meetings you can get a reaction from the customer, whereas with print and direct mailings, it is left up to the will of the recipient to reach out to you. Designing and printing can also be costly. Tradeshows on the other hand can be great exposure for your business. Attending tradeshows is a close second to a face-to-face meeting. People can see and touch your product, and you are able to capture their contact information either electronically or by asking for a business card. It is also an opportunity to ask the potential customer for a follow-up meeting or call.

It is important for you to have a good mix of both content marketing and traditional marketing as part of your marketing strategy. It is extremely important to be prepared before jumping into marketing your business. The first thing you need to do is create an elevator pitch.

Develop Your Elevator Pitch

The idea of an "elevator pitch" is that you are alone with a prospective customer or investor for the length of a typical elevator ride, say, 30 to 60 seconds, and wish to communicate the key aspects of your business concept to that person during that time. The idea is to stimulate sufficient interest on the part of the listener within that brief period of time to open the door to a more in-depth dialogue or a "tell me more" kind of conversation. Your pitch should be carefully prepared and written out. You want to practise it until you have mastered the material and can deliver it in a comfortable, conversational style. It should not appear memorized. You want to sell your prospective customer/investor on your idea and generate some enthusiasm to know more about it.

Your pitch should contain the following elements:

- Start with a "hook," something about your concept or idea that people will remember and that will stick with them.

- Focus on the market, and describe what your product or service actually does for the customer.

- Explain how your firm is different from other firms that are in the same or similar business and why you have some sort of competitive advantage.

- Outline the current situation of your business. If it is a startup, state clearly what you are looking for—financing, distributors, partners. If you are already in business, say where people can buy your product or service, and in a few sentences say how you dominate your market. There is always someone better than you, so you need to get people to pay attention to you and be able to explain what makes you better than your competition.

The more comfortable you are with your business, the easier the delivery of your pitch will be. Keep refining and practising. At this point, you are still in the process of starting your business, so you have time to perfect it. Ensure that you have perfected your pitch before delivering it to potential investors or clients. It can make or break the deal.

CONTENT MARKETING LO2
DEVELOP YOUR WEBSITE

According to a recent RBC small business survey, only 46 percent of Canadian small businesses have a dedicated website, and less than half of those businesses say they sell their products and services through their websites.[3]

The report goes on to say that with the majority of consumers choosing to research and shop for products and services online, businesses without a Web presence are missing a significant opportunity.

If you are serious about building your business to be successful, then you need to have a website.

Register a Domain Name

If you decide you want to do business online, the first thing you will need is a *domain name*. A domain name gives your website an Internet address. It consists of three components—a server prefix (www), a domain name (blueskycorp), and a domain extension (dot-com or dot-ca). Your domain name should be something that not only identifies your business but is easy to remember. The name of your business is probably the best choice for you if it has not already been taken.

In most cases, you will probably want to register both the generic top-level domain extension (dot-com) as well as the country code domain extension (dot-ca) if only to prevent someone else from registering that domain. You may choose to use either one, depending on whether you wish your business to have a distinctively Canadian identity for some reason or if you hope to be able to do business in other countries as well. You could choose to register other similar variations of your preferred domain name and make certain that no one else is able to register them.

Once you have decided on the domain name you might like, it needs to be registered with an accredited registrar. If you are going to register for a dot-ca extension, then you need to log onto the website of the Canadian Internet Registration Authority (CIRA). They maintain an extensive list of Accredited Registrars, and you must use one of them to register a dot-ca domain name. You can register generic domain names, such as dot-com or dot-org, there as well. The CIRA's website and the registrar's websites (www.cira.ca) also have a link where you can search the availability of the domain name(s) you have selected. Once you have found a domain name that is available, it is just a matter of following the directions on the website to register the name. If you serve the U.S. (or other countries) or have a customer base split between Canada and other countries, then you should use dot-com as your main website. A dot-com extension reaches a wider audience and most people are less likely to click on a site with a different country extension.

Domain names can typically be registered for one year or for up to five years. Registrars set their own fee schedules but averages between $5 and $15 per name per year. Many registrars will host the website you set up for your domain name for a fee as well.

Choose an Online Business Model

If you intend to set up an Internet-based business, the next step is to figure out how you are going to make any money. Numerous websites generate a lot of traffic but never make any money because they do not have a well-developed business model, such as the following:

1. **E-commerce site** The classic, conventional site is designed to make money online by selling products. Today most bricks-and-mortar retailers also have an e-commerce site, although more and more we are seeing businesses that only sell over the Internet. You can set up your own online store from scratch or choose one of the many complete "business in a box" solutions, such as Shopify, eBay Stores, or Amazon Webstore.

2. **Sales letter e-commerce website** These websites are like infomercials on TV and make a pitch focusing on educating potential customers on the merits or benefits of the products or services being promoted and sold. These websites tend to be long on copy and short on pictures and are generally based on some theme, such as losing weight, getting into better shape, curing some medical problem (e.g., arthritis or migraine), increasing sales in your business, and so on. Special "buy-now" offers are common to encourage customers to act right away.

3. **The eBay auction model** The eBay auction model can be especially attractive to people just starting an on-line business. It is a cheap and easy way to get started and test the demand for the products you want to sell. Then, if things go well, you can move on to your own online store in conjunction with eBay or on your own. All you have to do is register with eBay or eBay Canada, sign up for Paypal if you wish, and fill out a "Sell Your Item" form.

4. **Blog** Blogs are popping up all over the Net, in many cases just to get someone's thoughts and ideas "out there," but anyone can self-publish their work online very easily or find other ways to make money from their blogs. The standard business model to make money is to run ads on the blog, but there are also other methods, for example, joining affiliate programs such as Amazon and others: getting yourself hired or sponsored by a company; creating a blog to advertise a specific product or service; or selling your own intellectual property, such as books, educational courses, or consulting services over the Net.

5. **Service business website** A service business website is typically designed to sell the services and skills of the individual or the group of individuals behind the site. These are difficult to show online, so the sites focus on biographies of the people and testimonials from previous users of their service. Such sites are usually supported by some sort of free service, such as a newsletter, to which viewers can subscribe or tips that may be helpful to people who are interested in the service area. These sites can also be used for selling books and/or CDs and tapes prepared by the owner of the site.

6. **Info-site** An info-site is a website that focuses on presenting information usually on a specific topic, such as small business, gardening, video gaming, or similar areas of interest to many people. They are developed on the theory that enough people will be interested in the information to seek it out, visit the site, and support it by clicking on or buying something. Notable.ca, developed by Julian Brass, is a social networking and info-site letting young professionals know what is happening around town in Toronto, Montreal, and Vancouver that may be of interest to them. Info-sites can make money by selling their content through subscription or syndication or through advertising and affiliate programs. Some may sell products directly related to the information they provide as well.

7. **Brochure site** A brochure site is really an adjunct to a business that already has a strong offline presence. It is essentially an online business card presenting the name of the business, some information about the products and services the business provides, and information on how to contact the business for further information. A brochure site is not likely to make money online in and of itself. It is essentially an Internet billboard providing people with a way to quickly obtain basic information about the business, such as phone numbers and directions to the offline location. As a business model, it can be useful for such purposes as a registration site for conferences, conventions, and special events.[4]

Any of these business models have the potential to be successful. They are presented as being distinct situations, but that does not have to be the case. You might decide to combine more than one of these models into a single site. Add a blog to your conventional e-commerce business site, or have more than one site, each based on a different model, to reach different markets or to drive more business to your primary site.

Andrew Youderian, founder of e-commerce Fuel.com (www.ecommercefuel.com), started his first e-commerce business in 2008 and became very successful. Andrew now has a team running several e-commerce sites and helps others through his blog, where he shares insights and lessons learned from running his own business with individuals and small teams hoping to start, grow, and operate their own online stores. The Other Considerations box features one of Andrew's posts, "5 Reasons e-Commerce Makes a Great First Business."

Whatever business model you decide on, you need to carefully plan out all aspects of your website, including your brand and content. Websites have evolved over the years from being static sites where general information on your business is given to Content Management Systems (CMS), where you are able to make changes yourself to the information instead of paying someone else to make them for you. Although there are many companies offering their own CMS software, usually for a monthly or yearly fee for the use of it, most websites are now developed using open source software, such as WordPress (www.wordpress.org), Joomla (www.joomla.org), and Drupal (www.drupal.org). Reach out to friends and associates who have a website, and discuss with them which CMS they like and who they can recommend as a web developer to help you put your website together, if you are not tech savvy enough to do it yourself. Unfortunately, not everyone is as knowledgeable as they say they are, so always ask for references as well as their rates. Chances are if you go with someone very cheap, you will have problems and end up spending more in the long run. Be very careful.

Now that you have chosen the software platform, you need to start planning your website. Start with the design of your site. It should be professionally designed, look good, and be engaging for anyone that lands on your site. You also need to ensure that it is easy for visitors to find the information they are looking for.

The content on your website needs to be relevant and interesting to anyone visiting your site. What are you selling, and is it something that the visitor wants or needs? You want to turn visitors into customers, so content must be fresh and up-to-date. Once you have customers, ask them for testimonials, and use them on your website. As well, include case studies from satisfied customers. Putting a case study together may sound daunting and very old school, but it is an effective marketing tool for start ups. Mark Evans recently wrote a blog on case studies and why they are no-brainers for start ups (available in the Other Considerations box).

As well as relevant content on your website, you need to be mobile ready as well. Just about everywhere you look, you are seeing people glued to their smartphones or tablets. As Internet providers and device manufacturers continue to improve the browsing experience, it is becoming more and important for businesses to have a website that is mobile friendly. Everyone wants to find everything they are looking for very quickly, and once there they only want a couple of links to get the information they are looking for. Mobile users want to see large buttons and text that is easy to read, as well as contact information. You have a very short period of time to grab their attention and keep them on your site. Having a mobile-friendly website is not just shrinking your text to fit a mobile browser. You will need to either make changes yourself or have a web developer make your website mobile friendly. Make sure you test your mobile-friendly website on different phones, tablets and platforms to make sure it gives viewers the experience they are looking for.

SEARCH ENGINE OPTIMIZATION

Search Engine Optimization (SEO) is the process of making it easy for search engines, such as Google, Bing, Yahoo!, and MSN engines, as well as anyone searching for products or services that you may offer to find your website. When someone searches for information they type a word or phrase in the search box—these are called *keywords*.

When you use keywords in your titles, those keywords show up in your URL, which makes it easy to see what that specific article is all about. The search engines see the word "earrings," and they index that article on the same page as all the other articles on jewellery.

OTHER CONSIDERATIONS

6 REASONS E-COMMERCE MAKES A GREAT FIRST BUSINESS

EASILY IDENTIFIABLE DEMAND

We've all heard stories of founders who spend years building a product only to find that no one wants it. In business, determining that a viable demand exists for your service or product BEFORE investing the time to create it will significantly increase your likelihood of success. It's possible to do this in all industries, but for physical products, it's incredibly simple.

Want to gauge the potential demand for inkjet printers? Head on over to the Google Keyword Tool and BAM! You immediately know that approximately 22,000 people are searching for the phrase "inkjet printers" on Google each month. Now, I'm not advising that selling inkjet printers would be a good idea. In fact, I can't think of many WORSE things to sell online. But the ability to easily determine relative demand for an existing physical product is a great advantage over "hoping" someone is going to want a new product you create.

SCALABLE

If your "business" involves trading your time for a paycheque, it's not a business—IT'S A JOB! Our ultimate goal when starting a business is to create something that can function without our constant involvement. I want to put in a lot of time and energy upfront, and then enjoy a steady income stream without the demand for continual attention and maintenance. This doesn't mean you get to abandon your business—upkeep and re-investment are crucial—but we DO want something that can go for long stretches of time without needing to be micromanaged.

E-commerce fits the bill perfectly. Assuming you invest the time to create the proper site, systems, and team, a drop-shipping website can process 100 daily orders almost as easily as it can process 10. There will be a few operational and customer service costs that increase, but they will rise significantly slower than your increases in revenue and profitability. Again, this assumes you set things up properly.

Compare this with a freelance or consulting model, where you're simply trading hours for dollars. It's a great model for those with marketable skills looking for some extra income, and it can provide a lot of flexibility. But at root, it's a job—and one that you ultimately can't scale.

LEVERAGE OTHER PEOPLE'S CAPITAL

"But I don't have $20,000 to go out and buy inventory to stock a warehouse!" It's a predicament often shared by budding entrepreneurs. This is why the drop-shipping e-commerce model is so wonderful.

Instead of buying, stocking, and shipping your own products, you partner with a wholesale warehouse. They stock the entire inventory and pay for it upfront. When you receive a new order you need to fill, you simply forward it to the drop-ship wholesaler. They charge you only for the product you need to fulfill the order, and they ship it directly to the customer. No massive up-front inventory costs. No having to stock, store, or ship the product. It's like having your own warehouse and inventory without actually having to pay for it upfront.

There are a few trade-offs, of course. The margins will be a bit smaller than if you purchased in bulk from the manufacturer. And because there's a third party between you and your customer, there are a few more logistical issues to work out. But overall, it's an amazing way to start a business, especially in the early stages when you're trying to prove market viability. Remember, you always have the option of purchasing and stocking your own product once you grow.

YOU DON'T NEED CRAZY PROGRAMMING SKILLS

Have a great idea for a new web app or piece of software? Great! Either learn to program or pony up the cash to PAY a developer to create it. Your chances of convincing a programmer to create it based on your "great idea" are almost non-existent. Ideas are a dime a dozen. Execution and the ability to actually CREATE something yourself comprise about 90 percent of business success.

You don't have to be a programming genius to build a successful e-commerce business. With companies like Shopify, which make it incredibly easy to get an e-commerce store off the ground, just about anyone can get a shop live.

Most successful online entrepreneurs have a working knowledge of web basics like HTML and CSS, and I think there's a lot of value in spending time to understand how these work so you're not at the mercy of someone else for basic changes and updates.

(continued)

However, tools exist that make it possible to get started without being a programming ninja. Once you're up and running, you can then invest some time in learning about the intricacies of the Web so you better understand your business infrastructure and how to improve it.

THE BENEFITS OF THE INTERNET

An e-commerce business is an INTERNET BUSINESS, bearing all the wonderful benefits of working online.

Work from anywhere in the world. Reach a global audience. Enjoy incredibly low overhead and operational expenses. And perhaps the best benefit: tap into the incredible power of recurring free traffic using SEO (search engine optimization).

SEO is not really free. A LOT of work goes into improving your Google rankings. But I promise you that in terms of advertising ROI (return on investment, or how much value you get back from your invested time/money) there's no better method of building long-term, sustainable traffic than SEO. I receive tens of thousands of dollars of free traffic each month (compared to paying for this traffic with ads), and it's a key component to my businesses' profitability.

IT'S THE PERFECT BUSINESS MODEL!

In fact, definitely not. There are a few fairly serious disadvantages to starting an e-commerce site, which are available on the commercefuel.com blog, Four e-Commerce Pitfalls and Ways to Overcome Them.

Source: 5 Reasons e-Commerce Makes a Great First Business, April 18, 2013. Andrew Youderian, e-commerceFuel.com founder (www.commercefuel.com). Used with permission.

When identifying keywords, select words and phrases in the content of your website that someone is most likely to use when searching for your online business or website.

Each of your web pages should have keywords that include phrases found throughout the page content, title tag, headings, attributes, and link text. If you have words and phrases that occur often, rearrange the order to keep each tag unique. Using the same string of keywords on every page is not recommended, as it could interfere with your SEO.

The Google keyword tool will show you a list of similar keywords with the number of times the word or phrase is searched for over a certain amount of time. This will assist you in choosing the correct keywords for your website. However, just because you use the words does not mean success. You need to be constantly aware of the traffic to your website, and make any changes to your website to increase traffic. You will need to set up a website analytical tool, which will provide you with the information on the amount of traffic to your website. Google offers a free analytic tool that can be accessed on its website (www.googlekeywordtool.com).

Backlinks

Another way to generate more traffic is through backlinks. Backlinks are links that are directed toward your website from other websites or blogs. The number of backlinks is an indication of the popularity or importance of that website. Backlinks are important for SEO, as search engines, especially Google, give more credit to websites that have a good number of quality backlinks. These websites are considered more relevant and appear higher in results when there is a search query.

A search engine considers the contents of the sites to determine the quality of links. When inbound links to your site come from other sites and those sites have content related to your site, these inbound links are considered more relevant to your site.

Backlinks enable you to keep track of other pages on the Web that link to your posts. For example, Alice writes a blog entry that Bob finds interesting. Bob then goes to his own blog and writes his own post about it, linking back to Alice's original post. Now Alice's post will automatically show that Bob has linked to it, and it will provide a short snippet of his text and a link to his post. What it all works out to is a way of expanding the comment feature such that related discussions on other sites can be included along with the regular comments on a post.

If your website is about construction, backlinks from websites that have anything to do with construction are more relevant than backlinks that have nothing to do with construction. The more relevant the site linking back to your website, the better is the quality of the backlink. Be cautious when you are asked to backlink to sites—check them out to see if they are relevant to your business.

OTHER CONSIDERATIONS

CASE STUDIES ARE A NO-BRAINER FOR STARTUPS

Case Study: "A documented study of a specific real-life situation or imagined scenario, used as a training tool in business schools and firms."

From the outside looking in, case studies are far from glamorous or sexy. Heck, they sound downright boring. But if you dismiss case studies, you're making a mistake, particularly for startups looking to attract new users.

WHY IS THAT?

The biggest reason is case studies (aka success stories) bridge the gap between what your product does and how people actually use it. This is an important gap to close because it lets customers take three steps:

- Understand what your product does and how it works.
- See how it could benefit them.
- Buy your product.

One of the biggest challenges in making this happen (aka the sales funnel) is potential customers need to not only grasp how your product works and the benefits it delivers but they have to know how they can successfully embrace it to do their jobs better, differently, more efficiently, etc.

This is where case studies can play a critical role. By creating case studies that highlight how different people are successfully using your product, it provides potential customers with a better idea of how the product works in the wild.

In other words, case studies let you put the spotlight on how the product is being used as opposed to what it looks and feels like on paper.

HOW SHOULD YOU APPROACH CASE STUDIES?

To get going, it is important to think about case studies as stories rather than a "documented study of a specific real-life situation or imagined scenario." To get people to read a case study, it needs to be engaging, educational, or even entertaining.

Next, think about the different kinds of customers who are having success with your product. This gives you the opportunity to provide a variety of stories that could resonate with potential customers based on the idea your product meets the needs of different users in different ways.

Then, you want to interview customers to get their stories. Some of the questions include:

1. How did you learn about our product?
2. How do you use the product?
3. What are the biggest benefits? Can you provide an example of how it worked for you?
4. Have you discovered new or different users for the product, compared with original expectations?
5. Does the product deliver good value?

Another key question is how the product isn't working, or how it could be improved. It is always difficult to hear criticism but it's invaluable to hear this kind of feedback. And you would be surprised by how customers like it when you ask for their opinion because it shows you value their contributions.

Bottom line: If case studies are leveraged opportunities to tell a story about your product AND customers, they can be effective marketing and sales vehicles.

Source: Case Studies are a No-Brainer for Startups, Mark Evans Tech, March 21, 2013 (www.markevanstech.com).

Branding and Visual Identity

It is important to start building your brand immediately. A brand is not just a logo, it is you, your business, and how you are portrayed. Your brand defines your business. And your brand needs to be carried through all parts of your business.

The first step in developing your brand is to think carefully about what you want your brand to be: what product or service you want to focus on, what your competitive advantage is, and what your target market is. Once you have thought everything through and have it on paper, the next step is to find a graphic design company that will work with you to start building your brand.

Choose your design company carefully as you will be working with them over time. Everyone has a friend or family member that is, or thinks is a graphic designer and is either free or almost free. The problem with "free" is your work will get done when he or she is not working on a paid project. Most often, you end up going with the design that has been presented to you whether you like it or not, as the designer will not want to spend any further time on it. Working with family members or friends is a good way to end the relationship. You may not like their work, or they do not like that you do not like their work.

Finding a reputable firm can be as easy as asking for referrals from other businesses. If you see a logo or website that you like, reach out to that company, and ask for the name of the design firm they work with. Choose a few different design firms, and arrange a meeting with each of them. Describe what you are looking for and what your budget is. Be sure to ask for references, and contact the references before making your final decision.

Promotional Material

A business card is the first project for your design firm. You have already discussed your business model with them, so the firm has an idea of where to start. A business card is the basis for all the branding and visual identity for your company. When discussing the logo and text that you want on the business card, you also need to be thinking about a letterhead and a promotional piece that you will leave with prospective clients, a as well as the layout of your website and, in the case of a retail location, signage. Using email and pdf files for delivery of letters and invoices has cut down on the cost of having printed material. A word document will suffice nicely for your letterhead. Digital printing has made it more affordable for printing the necessary business cards and promotional material. Digital printing also allows you to have smaller print runs, which will be easier on your startup budget. Bear in mind you need to choose your printer in the same fashion as you chose your graphic designer. A design firm usually works with printers, so they could be a good starting point. A good printer will help you choose the stock that works best for your project. Again, communicate with them about your budget.

Building Your Email List

You need to make it easy for people to give you their email address. The most common and vastly used way to attract subscribers is to give something away in return for their email address. When someone visits your website or blog, you can have either a subscription form or a landing page, where they can provide you with the contact information. Once the email has been captured by an email program, the subscriber is then able to download the information you have promised or is given access to the material on your website. The form needs to appear on every page.

The information you are looking to obtain from the subscriber should not be too detailed and personal. Only ask for the information you need. As you build a relationship with the subscriber, you will be able to gather more information.

The following outlines the information you will be looking to get from the subscriber:

- First name
- Last name
- Email address
- Website address

All of the above should be mandatory information. In other words, if they do not give the information to you, then they will not have access to your "promotion." You will also need to include a note or a copy of your privacy policy that will indicate that the information they are providing is for your use only and will not be given, shared, or sold to outside parties.

Landing Pages

Landing pages are another way of building your email list. A landing page is a standalone web page, distinct from your main website and is designed to guide your visitors to one spot on your website. There are two types of landing pages: Click-Through and Lead-Generation.

Click-Through Landing Pages

The goal of a click-through landing page is to have a visitor to your website click through to another page. A click-through landing page is normally used with an e-commerce website, where a product or offer is explained in detail to encourage the visitor to purchase. The shopping cart or registration page should be on this page to make it very easy for your visitor to become a customer.

Lead-Generation Landing Pages

Lead generation landing pages are used to capture data from your visitor. Normally, you collect their name and email address, as this allows you to contact them for marketing purposes. It is common practice to give something to the visitor that entices them to give you their information. Some suggestions for giveaways are:

- Discount coupon
- Free webinar
- Contest entry
- Free trial
- Free e-book
- Free consultation

Figure 8.1 shows an example of a typical landing page.

BLOGGING

The best way to build your audience is through blogging. A blog post is content that has been written by you to share information that will inform or educate others on a particular subject that is relative to your product or service. A blog is not about selling, it is about engaging the readers and having them comment on your posts. To engage the readers, your material needs to come from you as an expert in your subject. At the end of a blog, there is always a link to your website. And when the readers get to your website, you may have a landing page where you will give something away in return for an email address.

It is never too early to start blogging, even as you are developing your other marketing material.

Danny Iny, founder of Firepole Marketing and also known as the Freddy Krueger of Blogging (see the Entrepreneurs in Action box), started guest blogging in 2010 to promote a project he was working on for a client. He also started blogging for his own business, and within six months, he had over 7,500 subscribers and now has over 20,000 subscribers to his daily email digest. Did blogging increase his revenue? Absolutely—but it did not happen overnight: it takes time to build trust before you see a return on your investment.

Before starting to blog, you should put an editorial blogging calendar in place. There are many templates that you can use, but a spreadsheet will do. An editorial blogging calendar will make it easier for you to keep on track and be accountable for your blog posts. The calendar should include:

- Date you will post the blog
- Title of the post
- Author of the post (have your employees blog as well)
- Where the blog post will be posted (your own blog, or guest blog)
- Category of the post (e.g., social media, small business)
- Tags—a short description (e.g., starting a business)
- Call to action—what you want to achieve from your blog post
- Keywords—words that will help you be found by search engines
- Comments and notes—both before and after you post the blog

Once you have your template, you need to decide how often you will blog—weekly, monthly—and if you will be the sole blogger or have employees who will blog as well. If it is a team project, then meet with the team and decide

FIGURE 8.1   EXAMPLE OF A LANDING PAGE

YOUR LOGO ⏀ HERE @ 280X55

This is your hero image, make it count.

This is your Primary Heading.

Try testing different variations to see which works best!

1 Very Important Point

This is the first and best key benefit or feature that describes the value of your product.

2 Another Key Point

This is the second best key benefit that talks about a different aspects of your product.

3 Third Important Point

This is the last key benefit or feature and it should mention another awesome thing you do.

More about this Service

Add some more descriptive content here to describe your product or service in a more detailed way. This could also be an explanation of the details of your offer if you are running a promotion

Get A Free Consultation

Enter your details below and one of our representatives will contact you.

Name*

Email*

Company

Phone

*Required Fields   **Download Now!**

We will never sell your email address to any 3rd party or send you nasty spam. Promise.

"I have been using GreatCompany for all my company needs for the last 3 years and couldn't be happier with their service and expertise. They've surpassed all of my expectations and customer service!"

Mark Wainright

Founder & CEO, AnotherGreatCompany

Copyright 2012 ThatGreatCompany

Privacy Policy   Terms & Conditions

Source: This sample lead generation landing page was provided by Unbounce—The DIY Landing Page Platform (http://why.unbounce.com/for-entrepreneurs/).

on the topics. Then start writing. Try and keep ahead of the calendar. When you have free time, write the post, and have it ready when the date arrives.

Before posting, remember to spell-check and proofread the blog. Check for grammatical errors. Include links that open in a new window—you do not want anyone leaving your page before finishing the article. If possible, include an image that relates to the post. Many icons and images are available for free or at a very low cost.

Once the blog is live, remember to promptly reply to anyone that comments on your post. Share your blog through social media networks to gain more attention.

With so much to do, it is difficult to find the time to blog. The Other Considerations box gives you 13 tips on how to find time to blog. Do not underestimate the power of blogging. It is now the most talked about marketing tool for businesses.

ENTREPRENEURS IN ACTION

HOW I BECAME THE FREDDY KRUEGER OF BLOGGING

It started innocently enough.

I was in Jon Morrow's guest blogging program, and received the latest lesson in my inbox, explaining that list posts were the easiest way to break into a big blog, because they usually performed well and were exhausting to produce.

As luck would have it, I had just developed a curriculum of business books for a client. So I emailed Jon and asked him if he thought it would be a good fit for Copyblogger. Jon said that he couldn't make any promises, but that I should send him a draft, so I worked my tail off to write a stellar post, and Copyblogger ran it.

The post performed well; 200+ comments, 900+ tweets, and tons of traffic back to Firepole Marketing. I even got an email from Guy Kawasaki (I had mentioned one of his books on the list) that eventually turned into an interview, book reviews, and Guy's excellent contribution to my book *Engagement from Scratch!*

I figured that since Copyblogger had worked so well, I'd try my hand at another guest post, and emailed Problogger to see if they wanted to publish the story of my experience.

It was a total shot in the dark, and there wasn't any kind of "in"—just a cold email through the contact form. It was a long shot, but it never hurts to try. To my great (and pleasant) surprise, they went for it. The result was my first post on Problogger. This led to more notoriety, and more traffic back to Firepole Marketing.

I realized that guest blogging was a great idea, and that I needed to do more of it. But where? And how? I felt that I'd been lucky with Copyblogger and Problogger. What now? Who would take my posts? Who would even answer my emails?

I did some research, and made a list of blogs that I wanted to guest post on. (Interesting note: even though my first guest post was on Copyblogger, I was so intimidated by their size and quality that it took another 14 guest posts before I worked up the courage to pitch them again.)

I emailed about a dozen bloggers, figuring that I would probably only hear back from a fraction of them, and most of

the responses would be rejections. At best, I was hoping to end up with one guest post, maybe two.

Oh, crap, they all said yes!

Except that it turns out that bloggers are a lot easier to reach than I thought they would be, and if you do your homework and make a solid, concise pitch, they're likely to respond in your favour. And they did—all of them.

My first thought: "Great!"

My second thought: "Oh, crap, now I have to write a dozen posts, and I have to do it all in the next week or two!"

I was under the gun. This was a great opportunity, but if I blew it, or showed them that I wasn't reliable, I probably wouldn't get another chance.

So I buckled down and wrote. And wrote. And wrote. And wrote some more.

Then the posts all started to go live. And people started to notice me—everywhere.

So much so that Eugene Farber over at Content Strategy Hub left a comment on a few of my posts, saying *"Wow, Danny, it's like you're Freddy Krueger. Wherever I turn, you're there!"*

Source: Danny Iny, Firepole Marketing (www.firepolemarketing.com).

OTHER CONSIDERATIONS

13 TIPS TO FIND TIME TO BLOG

1. **Start small** If you are just starting to blog set yourself a small target. Whether that is once a week, or once a month, it's better to start small and stay consistent than not do anything at all. As you find the time, you can post more regularly.

2. **Break blogging tasks into smaller chunks** Just as readers snack on content, find ways to divide your blogging activities into pieces that can be done in smaller time segments. Although you may not have an hour to write an entire post, you have 10 minutes while you're waiting for your child or spouse. Instead of playing a game on your smartphone, outline an article or brainstorm some potential title ideas.

3. **Collect blog post ideas** Jot ideas when you have them. Many bloggers find that they get their best ideas in the shower or just before they fall asleep. Keep a pad nearby at all times so that you can capture those fleeting ideas. Don't think that you'll remember those points in the morning but, like the rest of us, you don't.

4. **Use scheduling tools** Every major blogging platform has the functionality to schedule blog posts to be published in the future. If there are times when you are less busy earmark those times to work on your blog. Write as many as you can and then schedule them to publish whenever you can.

5. **Outline your blog article in advance** Don't show up at the blank screen! Sketch out the major points you plan to cover in an article in advance. This helps to jump start your thinking because your brain can work on the idea while you're doing other things.

6. **Use a blog post framework** Have an established structure for your blog posts. This can be helpful for creating content since it always follows the same arrangement. For example, The 12 Most blog always starts with the words, The 12 Most, and contains 12 points about a topic. Before you view this as limiting, test it out on a few posts on your blog to see how it enables you to add content to the blog a few tidbits at a time.

7. **Set a date to blog** This can be effective if you blog on a less frequent basis. Set an appointment to write. Don't just mentally set the time aside. Block off the time on your calendar so that no one can claim a right to it. To maximize effectiveness, it should be early or late in the day so that you're less likely to skip it.

8. **Develop a writing habit** Like exercise or other routines, it takes constant practice to get it to be second nature. Choose a time to sit down at your computer for at least a half hour to blog. Most writers work best either early in the morning when their head is clear or late at night. Determine what works best for you.

9. **Make it fun** Blogging might be more of a business tool for you, but that doesn't mean it can't be fun. If you are finding it a chore, think about what you can do to make it more exciting. Could you adjust the subjects that you're blogging about? When you enjoy a task it is much easier to start and finish it.

10. **Go offline** Disconnecting makes for a distraction-free hour of writing. While you are at it, turn off your phone, social networks, email box, and anything else that is going to distract you from getting your thoughts down. If you get the inspiration to Tweet, take the 140 characters and expand it into a blog post. Make these platforms work for you, not the other way around.

11. **Start writing where the energy is** Many of us were taught that we have to start writing at the beginning. How many pieces of paper did you ball up in frustration writing, "What I did for My Summer Vacation" because you mistakenly believed that you have to write from the first word to the last word in order. Set yourself free and realize there are no content order police.

12. **Accept guest posts** To keep feeding the content machine, reach out to some folks you trust for regular contributions. Adding a different perspective to your site often brings in new readers as well as encourages those you trust to help build and promote your brand when they post.

13. **Get up early or stay up late** Instead of checking your inbox or going online start writing early in the morning when ideas are fresh in your mind. If you stay up late turn everything off, relax, and write about something that happened during the day.

EMAIL MARKETING

Email marketing is the electronic delivery of information to a list of email addresses. It is also referred to as "email blasts." Email delivery is used when you have an announcement to make or perhaps a promotional offer. The primary intent of the email is to build brand awareness and to acquire or convert customers. Your emails can be very short, perhaps announcing a blog you have posted, or longer using a newsletter style. You will need to decide on the frequency of the emails and ensure you keep to the schedule.

Email marketing still strikes many as being old-fashioned. Social media and mobile marketing are getting all the attention, however, with a strong content marketing approach, email is more powerful than ever, thanks to social media. The reason for this is because it moves the conversation about your business to a more personal environment—your inbox. With an astounding 4,300 percent,[5] email practically pays for itself.

To get your emails read, you need to have a catchy subject line, compelling content, and a call to action that will keep your readers engaged. Do not be discouraged if someone unsubscribes from your email list. Some may have shown interest earlier but have now changed their mind. This could be due to several reasons. When someone unsubscribes, you need to remove their name permanently and immediately from your list.

Do not rush to put your email marketing campaign together. Doing it right the first time will help build a relationship with your potential customers. The Other Considerations box, The Seven Sins of Email Marking, outlines what you should not do. Following the list will ensure you are doing your email marketing right.

OTHER CONSIDERATIONS

SEVEN SINS OF EMAIL MARKETING

1. **Send irrelevant content** You need to use call to actions and landing pages with content offers in order to collect information about sales prospects. Based on the type of content your lead downloaded you should send additional information related to that content. Don't just send all the same generic content to everyone. That's a sure way to get a lot of unsubscribes.

2. **Ignore their preferences** If someone has signed up for a specific email list, such as a monthly newsletter, don't automatically subscribe them to all your other email lists. Email is a fairly personal thing and access to it shouldn't be abused.

3. **Don't honour unsubscribes** If you're not sure on the rules of email marketing, check out the CAN-SPAM Act. Don't wait before opting someone out of your list who asked to unsubscribe or worse, just ignore their request altogether. A low percentage of unsubscribes is normal; focus instead on those who want your content.

4. **Email people who didn't opt-in** This one goes along with #3. Don't email people who haven't chosen to receive content from you. This includes buying or renting lists so you can email people who have no idea who you are. If you have a specific person you want to connect with, try engaging with them on Twitter or in a LinkedIn group before "spamming" them with an email.

5. **Send email with broken dynamic tags** Have you ever gotten an email that looked something like this: *"Hi [%FirstName%], Does [%CompanyName%] need a more sophisticated widget?"* It's very likely you have. And you probably immediately deleted the email. Always send a test email to yourself or a colleague before sending out mass emails that use dynamic tags. This way if one of them is broken you'll know and can fix it before the mailing goes out.

6. **Send HTML version only** Some email clients and mobile phones don't support HTML emails or the recipient may prefer a plain text version. Make sure you always include a plain text version of your email just in case.

7. **Don't mobile-optimize your emails** There's only 4.6 billion devices worldwide . . . and it is anticipated that by 2014 mobile Internet usage will take over desktop Internet usage. So if you haven't made your emails mobile-friendly, get on it! The number of people who use their mobile device to access the Internet continues to skyrocket. Make sure you are reaching them with properly configured emails.

Source: Seven Sins of Email Marketing, Lydia Di Francesco, Prosar Inbound Inc. Blog, April 5, 2013 (www.prosar.com). Used with permission.

Scott Vetter of Prosar Inbound Inc. goes on to say there are many SMEs sending out emails that are destined to fail and that their email tactics seem to be void of any strategy. He believes the top three reasons for this are:[6]

1. **Insufficient budget** The focus of your campaign should be on return on investment, not spending as little as possible. A poor email campaign will not only fail to bring any financial results but can also cost you dearly in brand equity.

2. **Lack of strategy** Simply sending out an email to everyone on your list is not going to increase sales. You need to define who you want to target and what you have to offer. Then put a step-by-step process in place to woo them with a series of sequential emails that provide insight and incentive. Demonstrating value not only in your product/service but also in a relationship with your company is essential to building trust. Once you have earned trust, you will have developed a loyal client.

3. **Ignorance** If you do not have the in-house ability to develop and implement a successful online campaign, outsource the task.

SOCIAL MEDIA MARKETING

Video Marketing

YouTube announced in March 2013 that it hit one billion monthly users. YouTube is available on all devices, which means people are watching video after video, anywhere at any time. With an audience eager to watch and learn, you should not hesitate to jump onto YouTube. Sounds easy, but how are you going to compete with all the videos that are attempting to do the same thing as you are? You hear of videos going viral, with hundreds of thousands and, in some cases, millions of views within a very short period of time. This accounts for a miniscule percentage of the videos that are hosted on YouTube, so do not think you should run out and post a video without thinking it through.

You have to do more than hold the attention of the viewer—you need viewers to fall in love with what you have made so that they will want to stop what they are doing and tell their friends. Viral video is about sharing, which is different.

One Saturday morning in 2006, Stephen Voltz and Fritz Grobe dropped 500 Mentos mints into 100 bottles of Coke in front of a video camera. Their video went viral in a matter of hours, and before they knew it, David Letterman, Conan O'Brien, and NPR were calling.

Since then, more than 100 million people have watched "The Extreme Diet Coke & Mentos Experiments." Why? Because they did everything right. In their book, *The Viral Video Manifesto*, they explain how you can make a video guaranteed to pack a major punch by applying four core principles:

- Be True . . . Don't fake it. Make it real.
- Don't Waste My Time . . . Get down to business right away.
- Be Unforgettable . . . Show us something we've never seen before.
- It's All About Humanity . . . An emotional connection is the key to sharing.

The most successful viral videos follow all four of these rules, and the legions of unsuccessful viral video attempts almost always make the same kinds of mistakes.[7]

The one thing you need to remember when producing a video, regardless of whether you upload it to YouTube or one of many other video-sharing sites, you need to incorporate your branding into the video.

Social Media

The rise in the use of Facebook, Twitter, LinkedIn, and other social media networks has changed the way we interact with each other and the way we do business. Experts say if you are not actively involved in social media, you are missing business opportunities. Like blogging, social media is about content and not about promoting your business. It is about building relationships with people and experts in the same field as you. It is about carrying on conversations with other like-minded people.

The first thing you need to do is set up an account on Facebook, Twitter, and LinkedIn. Go to the help section of each site to find out how to use the site for business. Once you are familiar with the how and what of each social media site, it is time to start listening to conversations and using search tools to look for your business. People may already be talking about you and your business. It they are, jump into the conversation, and interact with them—they will want to hear from you. Also, research products that have to do with your business as well as any competitors you have.

The important thing is to get a feel for what is being said and how it is being said. Follow companies or individuals that you are interested in, and engage with them. Learn from what they are doing—the kind of content they are sharing, how often they are posting, and the strategies they are using to gain new followers.

Posting and reading messages on your Twitter timeline is easy, but not knowing the top basic terms will have you feeling lost. The Other Considerations box provides the basic terms to help you ease into Twitter smoothly.

Many social media users think that the more followers you have, the better. This is not true unless the followers are people that you want to interact with—individuals and businesses that are relevant to you and your business.

Once you are comfortable with moving around the social media sites, you need to put a social media strategy in place. Planning a strategy will keep you on track with your goals.

The Business Development Bank of Canada's *Social Media, A Guide for Entrepreneurs* (www.bdc.ca), explains how to create a social media strategy, which is outlined below.[8]

Goals   With the help of key employees, determine the main goals of your social media presence. Are they to attract more customers? Boost recognition of your brand? Improve customer service? Based on your goals, decide how you will measure your social media success (e.g., number of visits, number of followers and comments, how much your content is being shared, number of new sales leads, etc.), and set targets.

Audience   Determine your target audience and its receptivity to various social media platforms. Focus your initial social efforts on platforms your audience likely uses most, experimenting as you go.

Content strategy and key messages   Think about what kind of content will appeal to your target audience. Shoot for a balance of entertaining and educational material. Above all, avoid being overly self-promotional—a huge social media no-no. Frame your content around key messages aligned with your marketing strategy and overall business plan. "Develop a storyline for your business. What makes your company interesting?" says Michelle Blanc, an Internet marketing expert in Montreal. How do you develop your key messages? Use your market knowledge and research, organize a focus group, or seek professional advice. But do not rely only on intuition, which could be misleading.

Engagement   Your content should encourage your fans and followers to engage with your company and ultimately become or remain your customers. To do so, it should present the human side of your business and provide followers with benefits, such as information, advice, or entertainment. Periodically, you can go further and make direct calls to action—asking people to purchase a new product, take advantage of a special offer, or sign up for your newsletter.

What do you like about being an Entrepreneur?

I love that every day is filled with unique opportunities and challenges and that you are the only limit to your success.

Ryan Holmes
CEO, Hootsuite Media Inc.
www.hootsuite.com

BASIC TWITTER TERMS YOU MUST KNOW

When you've created a Twitter account, the next step is to understand the corresponding jargon that comes alongside your seamless operation of the platform. Posting and reading messages on your Twitter timeline is easy, but not knowing the top basic terms will have you feeling lost. Here are the basic terms to help you ease into the micro-blogging universe smoothly.

TWEET

The message you post and send out to your followers is called a "tweet." You can also use this word as a verb, as with "tweeting a message." Twitter has limited the length of tweets to less than 140 characters, so the best tweets are those that are concise and direct to the point. Also, tweets are on a public domain, so they are searchable.

FOLLOWER

A "follower" is a Twitter user who has subscribed to your account so he or she can see all your posts and updates on your own page. Generally, if you "follow" another user, that user follows you back. This is not symmetrical, however, as that user may also choose not to follow back. The more followers you have, the wider audience your tweets will get and the greater influence you will likely have in the micro-blogging community.

RETWEET

Also used as either a noun or a verb, a "retweet" simply is a sharing of your original post by another user in his or her own page. Some retweet manually by typing "RT @username" before adding comments to the post. The "username" is the original source of the post. A retweet is used when a user thinks that your post is interesting or entertaining enough to share with his or her own followers.

UNFOLLOW

You don't want this to happen to you on Twitter. Used as a verb, "unfollow" happens when one of your followers decides he or she doesn't want to be updated with your posts anymore and gets out of your network. Usual reasons for being unfollowed include poor Twitter Etiquette, uninteresting or crass posts, too much spamming, and basically, too much "noise."

MENTION

To communicate with another Twitter user you can either send a direct message (privately) or mention the user in your public post so others can also see. To mention, simply insert an "@" sign before the username. For example, "@CaptainCook I agree with what you're saying!" Using the mention automatically drives the tweet into the "@Mentions" section of the targets Twitter account.

DM

Short for "direct message," the DM is a tweet-like message that is sent privately and can only be seen by the sender and the receiver. You can only send a DM to somebody who is following you. The limit for DMs is still under 140 characters.

HASHTAG

A "hashtag" is a keyword or phrase that is preceded by a pound (#) sign, as with "#improvesmysmartquota" or "#BEInformed." Anybody who clicks the hashtag will be led to a page that lists all Twitter users who have applied the hashtag in their own posts

ENGAGEMENT

When you "engage" with another user, you are making conversation on Twitterverse with a string of responses and exchanges. Engagement is important to keeping Twitter followers because it shows that you are human and are capable of having meaningful online connections. Businesses often make engagement a priority in their Twitter marketing strategies to reach out to clients and their target markets.

FEED

A "feed" is a list of updates or tweets that are constantly being updated. They are usually arranged in chronological order, with the most recently updated ones at the top for easier viewing. Your home page, for instance, is a feed of tweets of accounts you follow; your own profile page presents a feed of your own tweets, while the search results on Twitter shows a feed of tweets that contain the word/s you are searching for.

URL SHORTENER

Sometimes, aside from posts, you will want to share URLs or websites to your followers. Because tweets are limited to less than 140 characters, online marketers have thought of a way to shorten URLs into clickable tags that will allow your posts to be within length restrictions, i.e., URLs that start with bit.l.y, tinyurl or ow.ly. A URL shortener creates the micro version of the address that automatically transfers anybody who clicks it to the longer address of the page you want to share.

TREND

When a hashtag is particularly popular on Twitter, it becomes a "trend" or a "trending topic." The Twitter home page presents a list of the most popular hashtags at a certain time. Your home page also shows a list of trends at the left side, although these trends are tailored according to who you are following.

Social media action plan   Now you are ready to create your action plan. Here are the important elements:

- **Who will do what?**—Tasks to assign in your company include monitoring social media traffic, creating content, and posting to your sites and other social media sites. Allocate adequate resources to employee training, and consider hiring a social media manager.

- **Communication**—Be sure to communicate your social strategy to employees, working to secure the buy-in of staff, from top managers on down.

- **Publishing schedule**—The lifeblood of social media is regular updates. Without them, you will not build the kind of engagement with your followers that you are looking for. Work out a publishing schedule specifying how often each of the platforms will be updated and by whom. There is no firm rule on the best publishing frequency. Your audience may respond differently than another company's. The ideal frequency can range from several times a day for a fast-moving site, such as Twitter, to several times a week for Facebook. Revisit your publishing schedule if you are not getting enough feedback from followers or your online community is not growing.

- **Experiment**—Experiment with the timing of your posts during the day to see when you are getting the most interaction with your followers.

- Take stock of your existing digital assets. Interesting content that readers find useful is critical in building your social media following. But you do not have to create all your content from scratch. You may have a lot in your files to get you started. Make an inventory of your existing assets, such as guides, articles, presentations, videos, and photos. Consider what you could rework for social media. Keep in mind, however, that existing content will only take you so far. Successful companies usually create fresh material geared specifically to each social media platform. For more content ideas, check with suppliers and business partners to see what they could contribute. Think about innovative ways to get your audience to contribute content.

Follow up   Monitor your efforts to ensure you are hitting your targets. Also, revisit and update your social media strategy regularly.

Social Media, A Guide for Entrepreneurs, is available for download on the BDC website (search for social media guide; www.bdc.ca).

It is hard not to want to be part of such impressive social media sites as Facebook, Pinterest, Twitter, and Instagram, and you should be (Figure 8.2). However, you need to ensure your messaging is consistent across all the different social networking sites.

The attraction to social media and social networking for many entrepreneurs is quick results, or so they think. Then again, they also think their products are the next big thing, with people waiting with bated breath for their next product launch, new service, or magic formula.

Granted, social networking sites are quick paced, full of information, and a wonderful place to stay connected. But at the end of the day, to use social networking as a marketing tool, you need to build a loyal following. Think about it as your own community within the network.

Lisa McKenzie, a business and social marketing strategist specializing in social branding and marketing to women and founder of McKenzie Moxie Media (www.LisaMcKenzie.com), offers the following tips for anyone engaging with social marketing:[9]

1. **Know your market intimately**
   - Who is your ideal client? Who are you looking to attract by using social media as a marketing tool? There are millions of consumers and businesses online, so you need to focus on those who need what you have to offer and are in a position to purchase.

2. **Find your market online**
   - When evaluating where to spend most of your marketing hours, it is important to consider where your market lives. Do they congregate on Facebook, chat on Twitter, pin on Pinterest, or network on LinkedIn? Maybe they live on all four. The more you listen and discover about your market, the better equipped you will be in knowing what they need and where to spend your time.

FIGURE 8.2   FACEBOOK'S GROWTH FROM 2012–2013

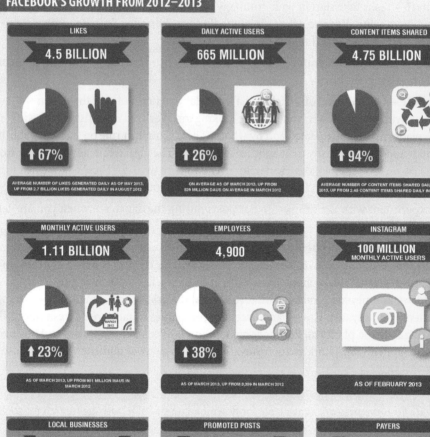

LIKES

4.5 BILLION

↑ 67%

AVERAGE NUMBER OF LIKES GENERATED DAILY AS OF MAY 2013, UP FROM 2.7 BILLION LIKES GENERATED DAILY IN AUGUST 2012

DAILY ACTIVE USERS

665 MILLION

↑ 26%

ON AVERAGE AS OF MARCH 2013, UP FROM 526 MILLION DAUS ON AVERAGE IN MARCH 2012

CONTENT ITEMS SHARED

4.75 BILLION

↑ 94%

AVERAGE NUMBER OF CONTENT ITEMS SHARED DAILY AS OF MAY 2013, UP FROM 2.45 CONTENT ITEMS SHARED DAILY IN AUGUST 2012

MONTHLY ACTIVE USERS

1.11 BILLION

↑ 23%

AS OF MARCH 2013, UP FROM 901 MILLION MAUS IN MARCH 2012

EMPLOYEES

4,900

↑ 38%

AS OF MARCH 2013, UP FROM 3,359 IN MARCH 2012

INSTAGRAM

100 MILLION
MONTHLY ACTIVE USERS

AS OF FEBRUARY 2013

LOCAL BUSINESSES

16 MILLION

↑ 100%

NUMBER OF LOCAL BUSINESS PAGES AS OF MAY 2013, UP FROM 8 MILLION IN JUNE 2012

PROMOTED POSTS

7.5 MILLION

NUMBER OF PROMOTED POSTS MADE FROM JUNE 2012 TO MAY 2013

PAYERS

24% MORE

↑

INCREASE FROM MARCH 2012 TO MARCH 2013

MOBILE MONTHLY ACTIVE USERS

751 MILLION

↑ 54%

AS OF MARCH 2013, UP FROM 488 MILLION MOBILE MAUS IN MARCH 2012

AD REVENUE

$1.25 BILLION

↑ 43%

IN THE FIRST QUARTER OF 2013, UP FROM $872 MILLION IN THE FIRST QUARTER OF 2012

REVENUE

$ 1.46 BILLION

↑ 38%

IN THE FIRST QUARTER OF 2013, UP FROM $1.06 BILLION IN THE FIRST QUARTER OF 2012

Source: Adapted from Facebook.com (www.facebook.com/facebook/photos_stream).

3. **Treat your website or blog as your HUB**
   - Facebook, Twitter, Pinterest, LinkedIn, and any other social networks you have an active profile on are marketing channels in your marketing mix.
   - To effectively get the most out of your social marketing efforts, you will want to use these channels to syndicate your communications with clear calls-to-action to drive your audience back to your website or blog.
   - Build your list by writing regular blog posts or newsletters, allow your visitors to sign up for your updates by having a sign-up box, and give them a free gift for signing up (e.g., a free report—*Top 10 ways you can save taxes this year.*)

4. **Establish a clear and congruent brand**   With all the noise on social networking sites, you must make a crisp impression to get noticed. Your brand must be clear and congruent across all platforms by keeping the same:
   - Branding
   - Logo
   - Profile picture
   - Calls-to-action

5. **Content is king—Write to establish your expertise**
   - Keywords are like social gold. Search engines love keywords that help them categorize sites and serve up the best results for searches.
   - To stay focused on attracting the right audience, you should keep a list of your brand's keywords close at hand when writing any content for your blog and social posts.
   - Once you have written a blog post, be sure to syndicate your post to all your social profiles. Repurpose and breakdown the points of your article to bite-sized headlines, and add a link to lead people back to your website to read more.

6. **Monitor your brand, reputation, industry, and keywords**
   - Make Google your best friend; there are many free tools and resources available from Google, but you will need a Gmail address to access them so sign up for one stat.
   - With your Gmail account, access Google Alerts, and set up alerts for your business name and your target market, such as "women in direct selling" and "women in multi-level marketing," as well as your keywords. You can set up daily, weekly, or up-to-the-minute alerts that will be sent directly to your inbox anytime these words appear in Google.
   - These alerts will keep you abreast of when your business name is mentioned and will keep you up-to-date with news about your market, industry, and opportunities you would not have known about otherwise.

7. **Leverage the "know, like, and trust" factor**
   - Social networks are where people congregate, connect with people they "know, like, and trust," and share aspects of their personal and professional lives.
   - People are not on Facebook and Twitter to find new products or services. They will, however, be open to watching and learning about people and companies their friends are talking about. They are also attentive to people's experiences with brands and will chime in with good or bad reports. If someone is raving about how great your company or product is, then be sure to show your appreciation. If someone is expressing a complaint, this is your opportunity to show your audience that you take your customer's feedback seriously, and do what you can to turn the communication into a positive one. Your community is watching.

8. **Build your online community**
   - In communicating about your brand online, give your audience a voice, and be the brand that cares about its customers.
   - Care enough to give your customers a voice.
   - Create an open environment for your visitors, prospects, and clients to ask questions and share ideas. Setting the stage to share your expertise and giving back to your community is smart business.
   - Host online events to grow your community.

LinkedIn

LinkedIn is very different from Facebook, Twitter, and other social media sites. LinkedIn has been designed for professionals to connect in order to do business together. At this point in time, LinkedIn boasts more than 200 million users worldwide. Of that number, approximately seven million are Canadian. Of those seven million, only a small percentage of users understand how to use the tool effectively.

Techvibes, a Canadian technology media company, asked FixedSocial, an Edmonton digital marketing consultancy group, to break down data on Canadian users to provide a comprehensive look at LinkedIn members in Canada. The infographic in Figure 8.3 shows the number of LinkedIn users in each major Canadian city and the most popular industries, among other data.

LinkedIn has many tools that allow you to quickly build a large network of business contacts to whom you can send messages and post information about your company. You can join groups relevant to your business and either join or start discussions. All of this raises your profile and establishes you as an expert in your field.

Social media are here to stay, so you need to embrace them. Social media networks are popping up on a daily basis. Some you will want to join, others you will not. Visit websites to see if any fits with your business model and your products and services, if it does not, do not worry about it. Always remember your final goal—building relationships by using content that will engage others—and show that you are an expert in your field. When done right, your efforts will profit you. It is very easy to spend hours on social media, tweeting, retweeting, uploading posts, reading posts, and making new contacts, but this should not be your only means of marketing; so ensure you keep to a schedule of being on social media networks between 30 and 45 minutes per day.

Word of Mouth

Want to generate word of mouth? Get people talking about you? One way is to help them look good. Make people feel special, or like insiders, and they will tell others—by word of mouth—about you along the way.

Chris Hadfield initially balked when his sons began preaching the merits of Twitter and Facebook. It took some time to convince him, but eventually it was decided to set up Facebook and Twitter accounts for him before he left on his five-month space mission. A few months later, he had about 1,000 followers on Twitter and about 600 Facebook friends.

During an interview prior to leaving, Chris announced that he was planning on making full use of social media during his space trip. He told the Canadian Press, "It's an amazing human adventure. ..." "The more people that can access it and look at parts of it that are interesting for them, the better."

He had increased his Twitter followers to 20,000 when he blasted off to space with Russian space colleague Roman Romanenko and NASA astronaut Tom Marshburn on December 19, 2012.

Upon his return to Earth, Hadfield had around one million Twitter followers and more than 325,000 "Likes" on Facebook. His photography and music, distributed mainly through social media, eventually earned him mainstream news coverage around the world.

During the mission, Evan Hadfield acted as a self-described "Internet janitor" for his father. The 28-year-old said recently that he read up to 13,000 online comments a day, from people writing about Chris Hadfield.

"They're all very excited. They're saying they haven't paid attention to the space industry in their entire life, but now they really want to," the younger son said during an interview in March.

Evan also played a big role in producing the now-famous "Space Oddity" video, the David Bowie cover; it was the most-watched video on Tuesday, May 14, 2013, on YouTube, with more than seven million views.

Not only did Chris Hadfield make space sexy again, his endorsement of HapiFoods (see the Entrepreneurs in Action box) has been a big win for them. Not everyone will be as lucky as HapiFoods to have such free word-of-mouth advertising from a Canadian celebrity who reached so many people around the world, but there are certainly opportunities for you to get the word out about your business.[10]

FIGURE 8.3   LINKEDIN CANADA BY THE NUMBERS

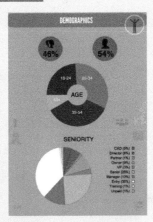

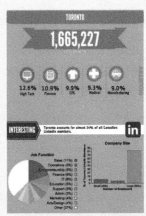

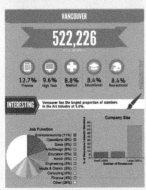

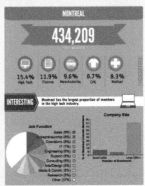

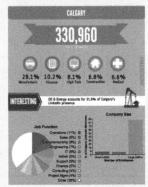

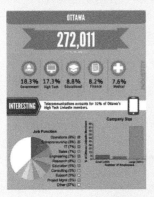

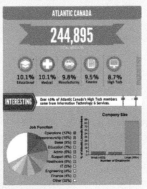

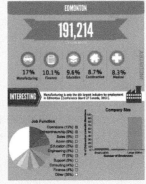

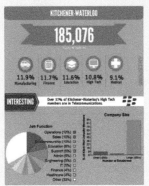

Source: Image and data courtesy of Brady Cassidy and FixedSocial, May 2013 (http://fixedsocial.com/linkedin-marketing-canada). Used with permission.

ENTREPRENEURS IN ACTION

HOW HAPIFOODS GOT ITS CEREAL ON THE INTERNATIONAL SPACE STATION

An out-of-this-world endorsement opens doors worldwide.

Like so many entrepreneurs, our niche is extremely competitive. We sell gluten-free, organic, vegan cereals. Our turf is the cereal aisle of grocery stores, hallowed retail territory dominated by major manufacturers battling it out for "stomach share." That we've managed to become the No. 1 player in Canada in our category is no small accomplishment.

In Canada, it actually hasn't been too difficult to get our Holy Crap cereal on store shelves because here, store managers listen to their customers and have major input on what products they stock. It's not like that in the U.S. Every new product must be approved by grocers' head offices and their approved distributors. It's a top-down process that can take up to a year and a half to navigate.

We've been able to cut that time down and get on the shelves of a number of key independent retailers in the U.S. And it's largely been due to an advocate located 350 km above the earth.

THE BACK STORY

In 2011, just a few months after we appeared on *Dragons' Den*, a nine-year-old fan of our cereal named Riley noticed a contest on the Canadian Space Agency's website. The contest invited Canadians to submit ideas for Commander Chris Hadfield's diet for his then-upcoming five-month mission to the International Space Station, which is scheduled to end next week.

To be eligible, the snacks had to be made in Canada, boast a long shelf life, and be easy to prepare and nutritious.

Riley, a huge space fan, nominated our Holy Crap cereal because his sister loved it. We knew it had a lot of advantages going in: it's made right here in B.C., it's space-friendly (meaning: no crumbs, no powder, no need to refrigerate) and, most importantly, it's tasty—not something astronauts in zero gravity situations are used to.

A year before launch, Cmdr. Hadfield met with CSA and NASA nutritionists to review the submissions. After measuring nutritional requirements and his personal preferences, our cereal made the cut. Holy Crap would be one of 12 Canadian foods to accompany Cmdr. Hadfield on his mission.

But the job wasn't done then. Both the CSA and NASA had to evaluate and test the product, and then package it into specialized single serving pouches that hook up to the ISS's water system. It took 14 months to get the "all-clear" from both agencies.

A BIG WIN

Getting aboard the ISS is a big win for us. Cmdr. Hadfield has become a Canadian superstar. While NASA and CSA rules prevent formal endorsements, Cmdr. Hadfield has been vocal in his appreciation for our cereal. A few weeks ago, he sent a note to his family stating that "Despite the name, [Holy Crap] is delicious."

For clients in the U.S., China, and Europe, it's proving to be a very big deal that we are on the ISS, and that a high-profile astronaut loves our product. In recent food industry trade shows in Anaheim, California, San Francisco, and Chicago, foreign buyers were lining up to talk to us about how our cereal has "the right stuff" to get on their shelves.

It's early still, but we estimate that this high-profile product placement will be worth tens of millions in export and military sales. In fact, the exposure is already helping us shorten the get-on-the-shelves process by about six months.

As soon as Cmdr. Hadfield gets back to earth safely we will all breathe a sigh of relief. Space travel is dangerous with a capital "D," and the ISS is humankind's furthest manned outpost in space. It's not for the faint of heart.

But neither is the cereal business. And getting our product on the ISS is proving to be our biggest competitive advantage ever.

Source: www.profitguide.com/industry-focus/manufacturing/want-to-land-an-out-of-this-world-endorsement-51833. Used with permission.

Mobile Marketing

With almost everyone, within every age group, from young teens to seniors, owning a mobile device of some sort, you cannot ignore the opportunity of reaching your target market through mobile marketing.

Consumers may be browsing on his or her smartphone or tablet instead of watching a TV commercial, and businesses need to view this as an opportunity to complement their marketing efforts by including their message on these devices.

OTHER CONSIDERATIONS

AVENUES FOR MOBILE MARKETING

Mobile Video, Display, or Audio Ads Mobile display ads and are an effective way to engage customers and prospects. There are a number of different formats for mobile displays ads. The Mobile Marketing Association recommends a Universal Mobile Ad Package UMAP to make it easier for marketers to create mobile ads for smartphones, feature phones, and tablets. Additionally there are rich media formats, mobile video, as well as mobile audio ads, all used to drive deeper brand engagement and revenue.

Mobile Websites This is a version of your desktop website that has been specifically designed to be compatible with mobile devices. Mobile websites deliver an engaging and streamlined mobile experience that appeals to a mobile visitor who is using their smartphone or tablet to connect with your brand.

Mobile Applications (Mobile Apps) Not to be confused with mobile websites, mobile apps are software programs that can be downloaded on a smartphone or tablet. Apps can be used by brands to educate, entertain, engage, and/or sell products to users.

Mobile Search Marketing Mobile Search, like desktop search, is a powerful way to connect consumers with your brand. It is important to note that search behaviour and motivations can differ in the mobile environment and that search results will appear differently on mobile devices versus a desktop or laptop. It is also critical to take your customers to mobile optimized pages to deliver a completely enhanced mobile experience. Lastly, consumers can amplify and share your messages more easily on mobile devices, thereby increasing the viral potential of your mobile search marketing.

Short Message Service (SMS) and Multimedia Message Service (MMS) These are systems that enable brands to send texts or rich media (graphics, video, audio) to customers.

Location-Based Marketing (LBM) There are two sub-categories of LBM, which include location-based services, such as foursquare, SCVNGR, and WHERE, as well as location-based advertising, which uses mobile display ads to geo-target prospects within a certain location.

Near Field Communications (NFC) Similar to BlueTooth, NFC uses a small chip embedded in a phone to connect wirelessly to another chip embedded in a kiosk, point-of-purchase poster, debit card terminal, or turnstile.

Source: Adapted from Mobile Marketing Roadmap, Mobile Marketing Association (www.mmaglobal.com).

It is important to understand the multitude of options available with mobile marketing. Unlike other media that are predominantly focused on a single marketing objective, mobile marketing has solutions and vehicles that drive against any and all marketing objectives. Once marketers have a good understanding of the available tools, the next step is to understand how they intersect with each other and the other media channels.

The Other Considerations box outlines some of the various ways that you can use mobile marketing to target your audience.

An effective and integrated mobile marketing strategy uses a combination of some or all of these tools to engage with consumers. Marketers should be prepared to meet consumers where they are, study their usage patterns, and, ultimately, understand what makes them go from search to purchase. For more information on mobile marketing, visit the Mobile Marketing Association website (www.mmaglobal.com).

TRADITIONAL MARKETING   LO3

NETWORKING

All cities have networking events around almost every type of business model. Events are usually held monthly and almost any day of the week. Ask other business owners that are in the same field as you what events they attend and join in. You can also set up an account on Eventbrite (www.eventbrite.ca) and explore events in your area. Most events are free. Paid events usually are put on by such organizations as your local Chamber of Commerce and will include a meal and speaker. There is always time put aside before the event starts for networking.

For some business owners, it is difficult to walk into a room where you do not know anyone and start talking to someone. But remember, everyone was in the same position as you at one time or another. If you notice someone standing alone, approach that person and introduce yourself, and ask what he or she does—make the conversation about him or her, not you. You can also approach a group that is already talking. Do not interrupt, but just listen to start with, and if you have something to add to the conversation, by all means do so. You will be given the opportunity to introduce yourself at some point during the conversation. Some organizations have ambassadors that make you feel welcome and will do introductions for you.

TRADESHOWS

Planning is important if you are going to exhibit at a tradeshow. Organizers want to fill booths and, in most cases, will tell you that the show is the right fit for you, whether it is or not. Before deciding on participating in the show, go to the website of the organization that is holding the show, and look for past exhibitors. Contact a few of them to find out what they thought of the show and if they are exhibiting again.

Ensure you ask the organizer what is included in the cost for the exhibit space. In most cases, electricity and Internet connections are additional costs. Normally, a table and tablecloth are included.

Once you have decided to exhibit at the show, you need to put your focus on how you are going to drive traffic into your booth. Some type of signage that explains what you do will need to be designed and printed. There are many different types of display units available. Seek out a company that sells exhibit booths to see the vast array available. It will also be able to design the banner for you. However, it is best to get the design firm you work with, as it already knows your business and what you are trying to portray.

As well as having your product available for demonstration, you will also need some type of promotional material that you can give to booth visitors. Most exhibitors also give some type of "trinket" with the company name on it as a way to be remembered. Most trinkets end up in the garbage unless the item is very creative and useful. Decide if you really want to give something away.

When exhibiting at a tradeshow always remember the following:

- Do not sit down while you are exhibiting.
- Always be aware of the traffic going by your booth.
- Do not ignore traffic by talking to your colleagues or other exhibitors.
- You will get tire kickers in your booth, and you will have to learn to deal with them and not let them take you away from talking to interested parties.

Stand at the front of your booth, and engage people who are walking the show floor by starting a conversation with them while drawing them into your booth for a demo or further information. If you are not comfortable speaking to potential customers, then do not be the front person. Perhaps you are the developer of the product and are better at demonstrating the product.

You do not want visitors to walk away from your booth without getting their contact information, and hopefully they want either a follow-up call or a meeting. You should have a place for visitors to drop their cards into. All visitors attending the show will have been given a badge by the organizer, which includes their name and what company they are from. It is now common practice for these badges to have a bar code that gives further information, such as email address and telephone number. However, to have access to this information, you will need a scanning device provided by the organizer for a cost. The scanning device allows you to scan the visitor badge and receive the information electronically after the show closes.

The show may be over, but your work is just beginning. You have spent a considerable amount of time, energy, and money on the show and have leads that you need to follow-up within a very short period of time. To start with, you should send a personal email or card thanking the visitors for attending the show and for their interest in your business. The next thing to do is follow-up by phone to discuss further and arrange a meeting. You may find that although they were very interested when they talked to you at the show, their enthusiasm has now cooled. It could be that they are overwhelmed by all the information they received at the show or hesitant to tell you that they are not interested. Do not be discouraged by this turn of events. It is part of being in business.

ENTREPRENEURS IN ACTION

HOW TO RUN A TRADE SHOW BOOTH

"We definitely made the most of it. It went surprisingly well," she said. "Although it's a little daunting to exhibit as a startup, knowing there are all these larger organizations there with lots of cash to spend and extravagant booths."

In fact, humbling as it might seem, prioritizing efforts and investments was one of the first and important lessons the startup learned, even prior to the show. It originally had extravagant booth plans itself, with interactive elements to draw crowds, but ultimately recognized that a small company like TitanFile can better focus its efforts on a well-placed, basic booth with the right staff and the right collateral and materials.

For TitanFile that staff was a tripartite representation from sales, marketing, and technology, including CTO Tony Abou-Assaleh. "Focus on having a good team at your booth. It was very beneficial to have myself, a sales guy and to have the CTO."

One of the biggest lessons, which the team at TitanFile hopes to factor into future shows, is a maxim in real estate whether it's a city neighbourhood or show floor: "Location is everything." "It's tiring walking around a trade show, especially one such as LegalTech with three floors at the New York Hilton. More than once I heard people mention that they only stumbled across the second floor by accident—unfortunately for us, we were on the second floor."

It's an error they plan to rectify. "In future, we make our way down to the first floor. It comes at extra expense, but I think it's well worth it."

PCRUCIATTI / DREAMSTIME.COM / GETSTOCK.COM

Finally, Barnes said not to ignore the opportunities that exist outside the show floor. Exhibitors, startup or otherwise, need to be aggressive and TitanFile found opportunities to share its vision everywhere, from the fetching of the morning's coffee to attending an evening party held by larger exhibitors. That "aggressiveness" and the company's vision for collaboration and secure file sharing served the company well.

Barnes said although it was "quite a dip in the pocket," TitanFile will definitely be attending LegalTech New York in 2014. But they'll have a chance to put in action the lesson learned much sooner: the startup will be attending the American Bar Association's Annual Spring Conference in Chicago from April 3 to 6.

Source: Lawrence Cummer, *Backbone Magazine*, March 5, 2013 (www.backbonemag.com).

To support its goal of expanding into the U.S. legal market, innovation contest runner-up TitanFile targetted top industry trade shows in 2013. The first of these—LegalTech New York 2013—provided the startup with "extraordinary" success and also a number of lessons, according to Emily Barnes, community manager at TitanFile (see the Entrepreneurs in Action box).

PUBLIC RELATIONS AND MESSAGING

Everyone dreams of being featured as a TV news story, in a major newspaper or an online newsmaker, such as Fast Company or Mashable, and everyone thinks that their story is newsworthy. Although you may think this, the media may not. You have to convince the media that you are newsworthy, and that means writing a great press release.

A news release at one time was only intended for journalists, but the Web allows a release to reach different audiences, such as investors, competitors, suppliers, consumers, and bloggers. Because of this, there is pressure for you to write a an excellent news release to get noticed. The basic rules for communicating your information are as follows:

- Get the facts right.
- Know your audience.
- Build strong relationships.

Canada Newswire's *How to Craft a Great News Release*[11] (http://info.newswire.ca) provides all the information you need to write a press release.

Headline

- Be sure to include a brief, compelling headline that conveys what your release is about. This is your opportunity to get an influencer's attentions. Use subheads to expand on headlines when communicating a complex idea.
- Write a concise headline that highlights the newsworthiness of the topic. Focusing on the relevance of your news for the media or for consumers (not just the fact you have launched a new product, but the benefits of the product) is likely to generate more interest. The reader wants to know why they should care.

Dateline

- State the date and origin city of the release. It lets the writers know where and when the information originated.

The Lead

- Your lead needs to quickly convey the news and compel a writer to pen a piece. Do not include fancy words and background details. Explain what is new. Answer some or all of the 5 W's: who, what, where, when, and why.

Body

- The body should include context and possibly background information, statistics, study results, and quotes. Answer the question: Who cares? Always keep in mind that journalists, bloggers, and editors are usually short on time and may not read the release word-for-word. Important information should be upfront and easy to find.

Quotes

- Quotes from company executives or subject-matter experts add credibility and may alert a writer to a potential interview subject. Do not include clichés or interviews of anyone from the company.

Boilerplate

- Boilerplate statements provide a quick snapshot of your organization: the products and services it offers, its location, how long it has been in operation, ownership structure and its status in the marketplace. Keep it short and sweet.

Contact Information

- Include the names, phone numbers, and email addresses for at least one contact, who that can be contacted immediately for interview requests for additional information. Include links to your website and online media room.
- Make sure the contacts are available for a potential interview when the release goes live.

VIDEO MARKETING

Video is dominating the Internet and cannot be overlooked. A video showcasing your product or service is a great way to help your customers feel more comfortable when deciding to purchase. It also gives you credibility as being an authority on your product or services.

You have a very short period of time to engage visitors when they land on your website. They expect to find information they are looking for at their fingertips, and videos can deliver what they are looking for in a quick and concise way.

Lisa Larter, owner and founder of the Lisa Larter Group (www.videocreationformula.com), published an online resource guide on Video Creation Formula. The guide gives information on the equipment and software Lisa uses to film her videos. Below are some tips from the guide on what else is important to know before producing your video:

1. Great lighting makes a difference, so pick a spot where natural light is abundant.
2. Sound is important; people will stop watching your video immediately if the audio is poor.
3. Ladies, wear a bit of extra make-up, nothing shiny or sparkly. Guys, powder is your friend; get some.

4. Look through the camera lens, and see the background where you are shooting. Is the camera straight? Make sure you do not have a plant or picture on the wall growing out of your head!

5. Make a list of words to help you stay on track, *but,* do not over script your video. Speak from your heart.

6. Do your video from start to finish, pretending that editing is *NOT* an option. You can do this. Remember, practice makes perfect.

7. Get a friend to help you shoot the video, and make sure it is someone you are comfortable with and trust. It is easier when you have help.

8. Relax and have fun with it. Be yourself and let your personality shine through!

COLD CALLING

Picking up the phone and calling someone to talk about your business seems foreign to most startups, yet it is an effective way of doing business. Talking about your business allows the prospective clients to hear the passion in your voice about your product. If they are interested in a product such as yours, they will embrace this passion and, in most cases, will want to hear and see more. This is the perfect opportunity for you to get in front of the person to give a live demonstration and let him or her touch and feel the product. It also is the beginning of building a relationship with the person.

If the thought of cold calling makes your stomach drop to your toes, the tips in the Other Considerations box, even if they will not eliminate your fears, will help you make cold calling a more successful experience.

ADVERTISING

Print Advertising

Print advertising is on the downturn. If you subscribe to newspapers, magazines, or any other print publication, you will no doubt notice how thin they are getting. That is because fewer people are advertising. But is that such a bad thing for you as an advertiser? Not necessarily—if there are fewer businesses advertising, then it may just be beneficial for you to advertise. But before making any drastic decisions, find out if your competition is placing ads in the same publication.

Some questions you need to ask yourself before taking the plunge into print advertising are:

- How many subscribers does the publication have?
- Are the subscribers relevant to your business?
- Cost versus potential return on investment (ROI)—will it be worth it? You have to take into account that you are going to have to run a series of ads—consistency is important to draw attention to your product or service.
- Most publications will design the ad for you but if you, have to design it yourself, then you have an added expense.

Online Advertising

Online advertising is advertising that is done over the Internet. With more and more users connected to the Internet through tablets, mobile, and video on-demand services, online advertising has become the way to get the word out about your business. You can advertise on Twitter, Facebook, and YouTube. Costs vary per network, but all these media are worth checking out.

One of the most popular ways to advertise on the Internet is by using Google Adwords, also known as *pay-per-click advertising*. In other words, you only pay when someone clicks through to your website from your ad. If your Adwords campaign is set up and managed properly, it will be one of the best sources for attracting new business. According to Phil Frost, co-founder of Main Street ROI, you need to start with a checklist—it is like baking a cake. You need all the key ingredients, and you never take shortcuts if you want it to turn out the way you are expecting it to. The Other Considerations box has a condensed version of Phil's blog post on "How to Create a Profitable Google AdWords Campaign (from Scratch)," which appeared on the Kissmetrics blog. The full post is available on the Kissmetric website (www.kissmetrics.com).

COLD CALLING

1. **Focus on the goal** Beginners tend to think that cold calling is about making the sale. It's not. It's about getting the chance to make the sale. Specifically, the purpose of a cold call is to set an appointment to make the pitch.

2. **Research your markets and prospects** You need to target your cold calling to the right audience. Use market research to focus on your target market. Then find out as much as you possibly can about the company or individual you're going to call in advance. This gives you the huge advantage of being able to talk about their business and their needs when you call them.

3. **Prepare an opening statement for your call** This lets you organize your thoughts before calling, and helps you avoid common mistakes in the opening that would give the person you're calling the chance to terminate the conversation. For instance, you should never ask, "Is this a good time to talk?" or "How are you today?" Don't read your opening statement into the phone, but use it as a framework to get the cold calling conversation off to a good start.

4. **What should be in the opening statement?** Include a greeting and an introduction, a reference point (something about the prospect), the benefits of your product or service, and a transition to a question or dialogue. For example, "Good afternoon, Ms. Marshall. This is Ken Brown with Green Works. I read in the local paper that you recently broke ground for a new office complex. We specialize in commercial landscape services that allow you to reduce in-house maintenance costs and comply with the city's new environmental regulations. I'd like to ask a few questions to determine whether one of our programs might meet your needs."

5. **Prepare a script for the rest of your call** Lay out the benefits of your product or service and the reasons your prospect should buy. Write out possible objections and your answer to them. Without a cold calling script, it's too easy to leave something out or meander. Once again, it's not that you'll be reading your script word for word when you call, but that you've prepared the framework of the cold call in advance.

6. **Ask for an appointment at a specific time** Say, "Would Wednesday at 11 a.m. be a good time to meet?" instead of saying, "Can I meet with you to discuss this next week?"

7. **Remember that gatekeepers are your allies not your foes** Be pleasant to whoever picks up the phone or is guarding the inner sanctum when cold calling. Develop strategies to get the gatekeeper on your side. Sometimes asking, "I wonder if you could help me?" will help you get the information you need, such as the name of the right person to talk to or when the best time to contact the prospect is. Learning the names of gatekeepers and being friendly when cold calling helps, too.

8. **Smooth the way for your call by sending prospects a small, unique promotional item** This helps break the ice and makes your business stand out from the crowd. Pat Cavanaugh (sales guru of Inc.com), says, "It's amazing. A $2.15 crazy little item we've sent out has helped us get Fortune 500 accounts. When we call, they say, 'Oh yeah. . . . you were the one that sent me that . . .'"

9. **Do your cold calling early in the morning, if possible** That's the best time to reach the decision maker directly, and for most people, the time that they're most energized.

10. **Be persistent** "Eighty percent of new sales are made after the fifth contact, yet the majority of salespeople give up after the second call."[12]

And above all, practise, practise, practise. While cold calling may never be much fun for you, you can get better at it, and the more you practise, the more effective a sales tactic it will be. So get your script and your call list together and reach for the phone. The people who want to do business with you are out there—but you have to let them know about you first.

HOW TO CREATE A PROFITABLE GOOGLE ADWORDS CAMPAIGN (FROM SCRATCH)

Ingredient #1: *Customer Demand* If your customers are not searching for your product or service in Google, then obviously, AdWords search advertising is not going to work for you. Before creating your first campaign, you need to verify there is in fact search volume for what you're going to offer.

The tool to use is the Google AdWords Keyword Suggestion Tool (https://adwords.google.com/select/KeywordToolExternal). The tool acts much like a thesaurus. You enter in phrases you think your prospects are searching, and Google tells you other similar, relevant phrases. Google also will tell you how often people search these phrases, how competitive the keywords are in AdWords, and how much it'll cost to advertise on each keyword. This information will help you determine which keywords you want to use in your first campaign. You should also use the keyword match type setting called Phrase. This gives you an accurate sense of how many relevant phrases there are per month. Type the phrases you think your ideal clients are searching for and click the search button.

When the Keyword Tool refreshes, you'll see a list of keyword ideas that are based on the phrases you typed into the search box. Plus, you'll see the AdWords Competition, the Local Monthly Searches, and approximate CPC for each keyword—how much it will cost each time someone clicks on your ad.

There are three questions you should ask to determine whether or not to advertise on a particular keyword:

1. **Is the keyword searched in Google**? If there is no search volume, then that tells you no one is typing that phrase into Google. There is no point in advertising on keywords no one is searching for.

2. **Is the person searching this keyword likely to buy my product or service**? When starting out, you'll want to advertise on what is called "buying intent" keywords where the person is clearly looking to buy.

3. **Can I afford to advertise on the keyword**? This question is important, but it requires a bit of math to calculate.

Ingredient #2: *Fourth Grade Math* Before you can finalize your keyword list, you must first make sure some basic "fourth grade math" makes sense. This will prevent you from going after keywords where there's no chance of being profitable. It's better to run these numbers now before you've sunk time and money into a campaign destined to fail.

To answer the question "Can I afford to advertise on this keyword?" you need to calculate your maximum cost per click (Max CPC). You'll compare your business's Max CPC to the estimated keyword CPC in the Keyword Tool to see if you can afford to advertise.

Your Max CPC is determined by your website conversion rate, your profit per customer, and your target advertising profit margin. If you don't know these numbers, then you'll need to guesstimate, or set up tracking to more accurately calculate them.

Use the formula below to calculate your Max CPC and then compare to the estimated CPC you found above:

$$\text{Max CPC} = (\text{profit per customer}) \times (1 - \text{profit margin}) \times (\text{website conversion rate})$$

For example, let's say your average profit per customer is $500, and out of 1,000 website visitors you convert 10 into customers. That means you have a 1 percent website conversion rate. If you are comfortable with a 30 percent profit margin, then here's how you would calculate your Max CPC:

$$\text{Max CPC} = \$500 \times (1 - 0.30) \times 1\% = \$3.50$$

Again, your Max CPC must be in the neighborhood of the estimated CPC in Google's Keyword Tool. If your Max CPC is $3.50 and the estimated CPC for a keyword is $10, then you'll need to first increase either your profit per customer or your conversion rate before you can profitably advertise on that particular keyword.

Ingredient #3: *Competitor Intelligence* At this point, you now have a list of "buying intent" keywords that you're confident you can afford. The next step is to reduce your risk by leveraging competitor intelligence. In most industries, you'll find competitors who already have tested and optimized their AdWords campaigns. That means they have figured out which keywords, ads, and landing pages work and do not work in your market. You can do this as well through KeywordSpy.

KeywordSpy (www.keywordspy.com) collects, organizes, and provides easy access to all of your competitors' historical advertising information.

Ingredient #4: *Powerful USP* Your USP, or unique selling proposition, is what differentiates your business from your competitors and gives your prospects a compelling reason to choose you. Your USP answers the question *"Why should I, your prospect, choose to do business with you, versus any and every other option, including doing nothing?"*

(continued)

When it comes to AdWords, there are three important reasons to create a powerful USP:

1. A strong USP will generate more traffic from qualified prospects (encourage clicks on your ads) and repel unwanted leads (prevent clicks on your ads).

2. A strong USP will skyrocket your sales conversion rates and convert more of your traffic into paying customers.

3. A strong USP can eliminate price comparison shopping. This can be a game changer for your business because you're no longer seen as a commodity. If you give your prospects a compelling reason to do business with you versus your competition, then price becomes a secondary issue, and you'll be able to demand higher prices than your competition without hurting your sales.

Ingredient #5: *Irresistible Offer* What can you offer in your AdWords campaign that is so compelling your prospect would be a fool to not take action? And how can you stand out from all the other ads your prospect is going to see in the search results? The answer is your irresistible offer, which consists of the following four components:

A. Valuable Your product or service must be more valuable than the price. This doesn't mean your offer has to be cheap. You just need to clearly define all of the value your product or service provides to your customer and make sure it outweighs your price tag.

B. Believable When you make an offer that appears to be too good to be true, then your prospect may be a little skeptical. So you must provide a believable reason for your offer.

C. Reduce or reverse risk Everyone is scared of getting ripped off online. One of the best tactics to minimize the risk to your customer is with a money back guarantee. A money back guarantee puts all the risk on your business to deliver excellent service, or else you'll have to give all the money back to the customer.

D. Call to action Use the KISS method… Keep it simple, stupid. If you want your prospect to pick up the phone and call you, then make it crystal clear and simple to call you. Don't expect your prospect to connect the dots or search around your website to figure out the next step. Use a strong call to action and keep it simple.

Ingredient #6: *Compelling Ads* With AdWords search advertising, you pay only when people click on your ads. Therefore, your ads have two very important jobs:

1. Attract qualified prospects so they click on your ad instead of competitors' ads.

2. Repel unqualified prospects so they do not click and waste your ad budget.

That means more traffic, more sales, and less wasted money on unqualified traffic, which all leads to higher profits for you. Compelling ads with a high click-through rate (CTR) will boost your AdWords Quality Score, which in turn will lower the cost per click of your keywords. So your ads will directly affect how much you pay per click for each of your keywords. Great ads will lower your costs while lousy ads will raise your costs.

There are four key components to your AdWords text ads:

Headline The headline is the most important component as it's the first thing your prospect will read. Try to include your key-word in the headline of your ads because Google will boldface the text, which makes it stand out from other ads. This also is the easiest way to ensure your ad is 100 percent relevant for the prospect searching.

A strategy is to ask a question in the headline. For example, if the keyword is "new york city dentist" then a compelling headline is "Need a New York Dentist?" Not only is part of the keyword in the headline, but the question will get the prospect nodding her head yes. As all great salespeople know, just one yes is sometimes all it takes to start a chain reaction leading to the sale.

Description Line 1 and 2 In your two description lines, reiterate the benefits of your service, state your USP, provide social proof, and/or describe your offer. And, of course, include your call to action.

Display URL The display URL is an easily overlooked area of your ads. Don't just copy and paste your domain name. Instead use your Display URL to include your offer, your call to action, your USP, or anything else that will make your ads stand out.

Examples for a display URL are:

- www.domain.com/Whiter_Smile
- www.domain.com/NYC_Dentist
- www.domain.com/Free_Whitening

Ingredient #7: *Congruent Landing Pages* At this point, your prospect has searched for your product or service. She found your ad to be compelling versus all of the other options. She clicked to learn more and landed on your website.

Now what? Well, if you're like a lot of first-time advertisers, then your prospect is now on your home page scratching her head trying to figure out what just happened. The ad made a promise the home page couldn't keep.

That's because your home page is not an advertising landing page! Home pages explain everything your business does, all of your products and services, and all of the different customers you serve. In other words, your home page could never, ever, be 100 percent relevant to the keyword searched and the ad clicked. Do not make this mistake.

Instead, create a dedicated landing page that matches the keyword and the ad. The goal is to make the entire sales process *congruent* so your prospect is continually reassured she's going down the right path.

The most important component on your landing page is your headline, which is the first thing your prospect will read. Your headline must grab attention, reiterate the offer made in the ad, and compel your prospect to keep reading the rest of the page.

The copy of your landing page should again be relevant to the keyword searched and the ad clicked on. Include your USP, benefits of your product or service, details about your irresistible offer, social proof, credibility that you're a legitimate business, and a strong call to action.

Ingredient #8: *Conversion Tracking* If you skip this step, then you'll never know which keywords and ads are generating sales and which are just losing money. In other words, you will not be able to optimize your campaign once it's up and running.

Conversion tracking is simply the method of measuring sales generated by your AdWords campaign. More specifically, you want to know which keywords and which ads are generating sales.

If some or all of your sales occur online with an e-commerce shopping cart, then conversion tracking is pretty straightforward. Just use the built-in Google AdWords conversion tracking.

But what if you have an "offline" sales process? What if you generate leads online, but you ultimately close the sale "offline"—over the phone or in person—rather than online? Clearly, you can't add conversion code to your cash register, so what can you do?

The three tactics recommended for tracking offline sales are:

1. Create a conversion page in your sales process. For example, send all of your customers to a special page to get their receipt, create an account online, or download an important document. Think of some way to get your customers to go to a web page and add the AdWords code to that page. Now you can track the sales.

2. Use unique coupon codes in your ads and landing pages. If you use unique coupon codes in your ads and landing pages, then you can match the codes back to the ad and keyword that generated the sale.

3. Use tracking phone numbers in your ads and landing pages. Again, if you use unique tracking phone numbers, then you can match the calls and subsequent sales to the ads and keywords that generated the sale.

Ingredient #9: *AdWords Settings for Success* AdWords does a great job of making it fairly easy to set up your campaign. The process is pretty simple; however, a lot of the default settings are not in your best interest. The most important settings to watch out for are:

Search vs. display Select Search Network Only for your campaign type so you're targeting only the Google Search Network and not the Display Network.

Device bids According to a recent study by Constant Contact, only 34 percent of small businesses have a mobile optimized website. If you're among the 66 percent who do not have a mobile-friendly website, then it should be obvious you don't want to spend money advertising to mobile devices.

Keyword match types There are three main keyword match types:

- Broad
- Phrase
- Exact

Broad match is the default match type. If you leave your keywords as Broad match, then Google will show your ads to any search phrase Google thinks is relevant to your keyword. This means your ads will get more impressions, but you'll likely show ads to irrelevant search phrases that will just waste your budget. So I do not recommend Broad match.

Phrase match keywords will trigger ads when the exact phrase is part of the keyword typed into Google. For example, if your Phrase match keyword is "office space," then your ad will display for "New York office space" and "office space in New York." However, your ad would not display for "office in space" because the phrase "office space" is broken up by the word "in."

Exact match simply tells Google to display your ad only when the exact keyword is typed into Google. You'll get the most control with Exact match, but you'll limit your exposure.

(continued)

I recommend starting with Phrase match because you'll get the best of both worlds with regard to targeting and reach. However, when you use Phrase match, you need to make sure you include negative keywords.

Negative keywords Negative keywords give you the ability to block phrases from triggering your ads. For example, if you're an office space rental company advertising on the Phrase match keyword, "office space," then you will want to block the keyword "movie." That way your ads for an office space rental will not be displayed for folks searching for the *Office Space* movie.

To add negative keywords, go to the Keywords tab in your account.

Ingredient #10: *Optimization* Most campaigns are not profitable from the start and they always require continual optimization to stay profitable. There are three main areas to improve your AdWords campaign performance:

1. **Your keyword bids.** Once you start to generate clicks and sales, you need to adjust your bids accordingly. If your keywords are generating sales profitably and you're not ranked #1, then continue to raise your bids. If your keywords are not generating sales profitably, then obviously, you'll need to lower your bids or pause the keyword entirely.

2. **Your ad click-through rate (CTR).** Your ad CTR directly affects your quality score, which in turn determines how much you pay per click. To optimize your CTR, test different ads to see which version gets the most clicks.

3. **Your landing page conversion rate.** The final area to optimize is your landing page. There are many tools to help you test different landing page versions, but if you're just starting out, I recommend you use Google Analytics Experiments (formerly known as Google's Website Optimizer). It's easy and free to get started. Go to http://analytics.google.com to set up your free account. Then create an experiment to test two different versions of your landing page and measure to see which one generates the most conversions.

Source: This article was written by Phil Frost, who is co-founder of Main Street ROI, an online marketing, training, and coaching company based in New York City. To learn more, go to www.mainstreetroi.com.

PIVOTING

Pivoting is changing the direction of where you are taking your business. When you first start your business, you have a vision of where you want to go and how you are going to get there. You have researched your target market and know what it wants and needs. Although you think you have it all figured out, your sales numbers may tell you something very different.

Companies such as YouTube and PayPal are much different today from when they launched their business. For example, YouTube, founded in 2005, began as a video dating site called Tune In Hook Up. When the site failed to gain traction, the founders scrapped the idea and instead focused on simply sharing videos online. They were acquired by Google for $1.65 billion in stock. Statistics show that:

- More than one billion unique users visit YouTube each month.
- Over four billion hours of video are watched each month on YouTube.
- About 72 hours of video are uploaded to YouTube every minute.

PayPal started as a way to exchange money via Palm Pilots. After securing a relationship with eBay, PayPal was acquired by eBay in 2002 for $1.5 billion.

Canadian co-authors Alistair Croll and Benjamin Yoskovitz published a book titled *Lean Analytics—Use Data to Build a Better Startup Faster.* The book gives examples of companies that successfully pivoted, which are highlighted in the Other Considerations box.

Pivoting does not mean you have failed—it is merely taking a new direction than what you originally planned. There are very few companies that have never pivoted from their original business model.

OTHER CONSIDERATIONS

CONCLUSION

There are many ways of marketing your product or service, but the most important thing to understand is that you have to market your product or service to be successful. If you are not comfortable doing it, then you will have to hire someone to do it for you. If you do not market, you will not survive in business for very long.

Always remember:

1. Pick the target market segment and know your customer profile in that segment intimately.

2. Ensure that your offering is unique and that your point of differentiation is desirable and wanted by your target segment.

3. Your brand is not your logo or visual look. Your brand is your promise of value to your market and how you live and deliver it. Your brand is how you behave, the quality of your business, your differentiation, your price, your customer service, your market messages.

4. Service companies must live by the law of inseparability. The service cannot be separated from the person providing it. Use it to your advantage, and work on your personal brand. Customer service is key. And in a service-based business, it is the only thing that matters, since how you behave is the brand.

5. Service companies must also live by the law of intangibility. A service cannot be tried before it is purchased. Therefore, service companies must work on building credibility. Use testimonials to counteract perceptions of risk, showcase the experience of your staff, be approachable, but do not look like you are an amateur.

6. Know your competitors inside and out.

7. Word-of-mouth is the most powerful form of promotion for strapped startups, so encourage it through delighted customers, social media, and referral programs.

8. The difference between successful companies and unsuccessful companies is most often a function of promotion. The person who promotes best wins. Do not choose promotion as the place to economize. If people do not know about you, they cannot buy from you. Brands get built through awareness.

9. Protect your differentiation. Service is tied to the person, which can be a key point of defendable differentiation. When it comes to a product realize how easily it can be copied by another firm, and build on your experience and expertise to help make it more difficult to steal.

Although you may be successful in getting the media to take notice of you, it can be very short lived. You need to continuously work on your marketing through blogging, engaging, and interacting with social media, as well as through traditional marketing.

F Y I

MARKETING RESOURCES

The following list of books, blogs, and guides will provide you with more information on marketing.

BOOKS

How to Work a Room: A Guide to Successfully Managing the Mingling by Susan RoAne.

Content Rules: How to Create Killer Blogs, Podcasts, Videos, Ebooks, Webinars and More that Engage Customers and Ignite Your Business by Ann Handley and C.C. Chapman.

Power Friending: Demystifying Social Media to Grow Your Business by Amber Mac.

UnMarketing: Stop Marketing. Start Engaging by Scott Stratten.

BLOGS

Mark Evans Tech Mark blogs about marketing for startups. He also has a weekly newsletter about Canadian startups. (www.markevanstech.com)

RocketScope A marketing blog for helping startups market their business. (www.rocketscope.com)

Clarity Blog Clarity thinks that sometimes entrepreneurs lose sight of how important they are. The blog is to remind them they are important. (http://blog.clarity.fm)

Unbounce Unbounce empowers marketers to act-independently from technical teams, improving their efficiency and their ability to generate sales. (http://unbounce.com)

Prosar Inbound Marketing The inbound marketing blog that covers insights, opinions, guidance, and random thoughts regarding online and strategic marketing. (www.prosar.com/inbound_marketing_blog/)

Kissmetrics A blog about analytics, marketing, and testing. (blog.kissmetrics.com)

Chris Brogan A blog about marketing and sales. (www.chrisbrogan.com)

Content Marketing Institute The website is full of practical, how-to guidance, insights, and advice from experts, and an active community for discussing the latest news, information, and advances that are moving the industry forward. (www.contentmarketinginstitute.com)

GUIDES

Profit Magazine—Special Report Low Cost Marketing, Spend Less Money, Get More Results. (www.profitguide.com). Search for Low Cost Marketing Guide.

LO1 Marketing involves reaching out to prospective clients to let them know who you are, what you do, and why they should buy from you. Marketing is essential to the success and growth of your business, and if you do not know how to market, you have two options: either learning how you can do it yourself or hiring someone to do it for you.

Marketing is broken down into two categories: content marketing and traditional marketing. It is important to incorporate both into your marketing:

- content marketing is creating and distributing relevant and valuable content to attract, acquire, and engage your target audience and drive them to purchase from you

- traditional marketing revolves around the 5 P's of marketing: person, place, product, pricing, and promotion

LO2 Content marketing starts with your elevator pitch and moves through your website and social media platforms. It is extremely important to have compelling content that people will want to listen to, read, and engage with you. Distribution of your content can be:

- through blog posts, either your own or as a guest blogger
- email campaigns
- testimonials and success stories from satisfied customers
- promotional material
- videos
- Twitter, Facebook, and LinkedIn

LO3 Traditional marketing is not dead and should not be overlooked. As with content marketing, there are many ways of getting the word out about your business. Some of these include:

- networking at events
- exhibiting at tradeshows
- face-to-face meetings
- cold calling
- press releases
- advertising, both online and offline

For more information on the resources available from McGraw-Hill Ryerson, go to www.mcgrawhill.ca/he/solutions.

SALES

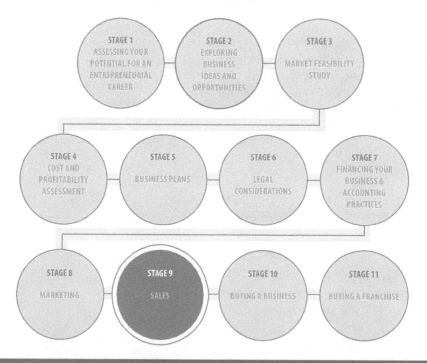

RETHINKING THE SALES PROCESS

COLLEEN FRANCIS, PRESIDENT AND FOUNDER, ENGAGE SELLING.
Courtesy of Collen Francis

The Right Teacher

When I formally began my sales career, I was really, really lucky. I was given a great teacher, named Fred Carr. He didn't just help light a fire under my career—he also was instrumental in helping me dig myself out of a rather deep financial hole I had created for myself.

I was six months into my sales career selling life insurance, and I was failing miserably. The company had provided me with all kinds of sales techniques—including many that had been given cute names, like the Puppy Dog Close or the Hot Potato or Good Cop–Bad Cop. Because I was new and eager, I followed those selling instructions diligently. And after having invested half a year of my life memorizing the techniques, as well as learning my product and following my leads, I hadn't sold a thing. Nothing. My sales performance chart was a big empty graph with a zero in the corner.

Since I was paid a draw against commission, I also was $12,000 in debt to that employer. They had been paying me $2,000 a month whether I sold anything or not—the plan being that I would pay them back when I enjoyed some good months of sales. But six months had passed and those good months—even just one—remained out of my reach.

And what's even worse, I discovered that when you're financially strapped you develop into an emotional wreck, and an unhappy person. Relationships are squandered as you blame others for your failure. I know because I did just that. I blamed everyone else, for my failure, including my (now ex) husband. Truth be told, failing at sales also caused the failure of my first marriage.

Despite this dismal situation, my sales manager refused to give up on me. Granted, he was in a tight spot because he knew that if he fired me, he'd be on the hook for that sizeable draw I had been pulling for so many fruitless months. Thank god, he also saw some potential in me.

That's when Fred entered the picture. When my sales manager partnered me with Fred, I learned quickly that he was the top performer in the office. That $12,000 debt I had accumulated over six months? Fred was earning that . . . in a week. And I learned something even more important from him. He taught me how he had become so successful in his work.

Rethinking Sales

Fred and I talked a lot about the approaches I was using to sell life insurance. I explained how I had been following all the sales techniques the company had taught me to use. And I also offered my own—and now obvious—opinion: "Fred, I have to admit that I really don't think these techniques work." He agreed.

Fred taught me to rethink my sales approach—to trust my instincts and to be wary of sales techniques (especially the ones with the cute names). The trouble with most of the techniques that are out there is that they belong to someone else—there's no room for your personal stamp (although I've often wondered if there really is somebody out there who has been wildly successful for all these years, thanks to all these techniques they've authored).

Techniques also tend to impose a tightly systematized way of doing things—telling you what to say and when to say it, sometimes in such excruciating detail you'd swear that the author was programming a robot rather than teaching a human being how to sell to others. There's a real danger in sticking to that approach. If you devote all your energies to following one of these techniques, you can become more preoccupied with adhering to its processes and its steps than with listening to the needs of your prospects and clients. That's what happened to me when I was striking out month after month before Fred put me on the right track.

Fred's lesson to me, and it's one I've never forgotten, is that all these old-school sales techniques are a nuisance that keep you from your real job as a sales professional—to build great relationships with prospects and turn them into repeat customers.

Once I started looking at sales in this new light, I was able to rethink what I was doing right and what I was doing wrong. What was missing from my approach were the very things that had the potential of turning me into a great salesperson—being a good listener, being a problem solver, being sincerely interested in others. Let me be clear. Those aren't just qualities that I alone possess—we all have these traits. Rethinking the sales process is all about finding a commonsense approach, building on those strengths, so you can work with, listen to, and tend to the needs of your customers.

Whether it's adapting your approach to suit a buyer's behaviour, working to build reciprocal relationships with prospects and clients, or changing the way you tackle cold calling so that it becomes the start of a conversation that you want to initiate—there's a lot you can do to develop a winning sales approach that is custom fitted to your needs and your sales targets.

I was lucky to have Fred as a teacher (and to have had a boss whose faith in me was unwavering). I learned a lot (and probably just in the nick of time, too). That's why I'm always pleased to share these personal experiences with you. Being successful in sales doesn't hinge on following a process or a technique. It's all about having the right mindset and persevering.

Success leaves clues. That's a favourite saying of mine. I was dumb enough to make a lot of mistakes that hurt me and others and at the same time was at least smart enough to recognize that if Fred could do it I could do it too. Always be on the lookout for smart successful people to learn from in your life. They are the best teachers of your own success.

Source: Rethinking the Sales Process. Author: Colleen Francis, president and founder, Engage Selling (www.engageselling.com). Used with permission.

As mentioned in Chapter 8, Marketing, as a small business owner, it is difficult to separate sales and marketing unless you have a large staff or are outsourcing your marketing and sales efforts. Marketing is the beginning of making a sale but now you need to close the sale. This sales chapter will walk you through the steps and help you face the challenges that you may experience when trying to make the sale.

THE SALES PROCESS   LO1

What exactly is meant by the sales process? The sales process is what you do to close the sale and get a signed contract for work to be performed and payment issued for the completed work.

By now you know what your target market is. But do you know who the decision maker is and how to contact them to make an appointment? There are many ways to find your contacts, but once you do, you need to know what to do and what not to do. Not knowing what to do can very quickly keep you from getting the appointment with the person you want to meet.

BEING PREPARED

It goes without saying that you need to be prepared for making the sale. You need to know your product inside and out and know how to present it to prospective clients, but there are other things that you need to do to make sure you are making a great first impression. You need to stand out from the rest. You can easily do this by:

- Ensuring your branding and visual identity are professional looking.
- Having an updated website that contains everything that you want your customers to know about.
- Dressing professionally—no jeans or shirts hanging out; stay away from low-cut tops or short skirts. Stand out from the rest by wearing a suit to your meeting.
- Leaving a copy of your brochure or documentation of some sort that outlines what you have discussed at the meeting.
- Sending a personal thank-you note—not an email, but a handwritten note thanking the prospect for their time and interest in your product or service.

GENERATING LEADS

Although you are attending events, joining organizations, and blogging, it is not enough. You need to be constantly looking for leads to increase your sales. Figure 9.1 presents an infographic from Clarity.fm, which shows the most common challenges entrepreneurs face today, with slow or lost sales being the greatest struggles for entrepreneurs.

FIGURE 9.1   STARTUP STRUGGLES

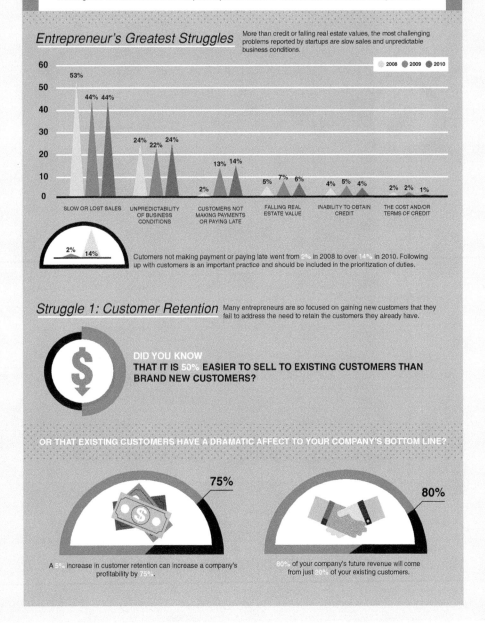

STARTUP STRUGGLES

THE MOST COMMON CHALLENGES ENTREPRENEURS FACE TODAY

Every entrepreneur encounters challenges while trying to get their business off the ground. Though it may seem over-whelming, with trusted advice and focused passion you can overcome these obstacles and build a lasting business.

Entrepreneur's Greatest Struggles

More than credit or falling real estate values, the most challenging problems reported by startups are slow sales and unpredictable business conditions.

● 2008 ● 2009 ● 2010

Cutomers not making payment or paying late went from 2% in 2008 to over 14% in 2010. Following up with customers is an important practice and should be included in the prioritization of duties.

Struggle 1: Customer Retention

Many entrepreneurs are so focused on gaining new customers that they fail to address the need to retain the customers they already have.

DID YOU KNOW
THAT IT IS 50% EASIER TO SELL TO EXISTING CUSTOMERS THAN BRAND NEW CUSTOMERS?

OR THAT EXISTING CUSTOMERS HAVE A DRAMATIC AFFECT TO YOUR COMPANY'S BOTTOM LINE?

75%

A 5% increase in customer retention can increase a company's profitability by 75%.

80%

80% of your company's future revenue will come from just 20% of your existing customers.

Source: Startup Struggles, Clarify.fm (http://blog.clarity.fm/startup-struggles-common-problems-startups-face/). Used with permission.

(continued)

FIGURE 9.1 *(CONTINUED)*

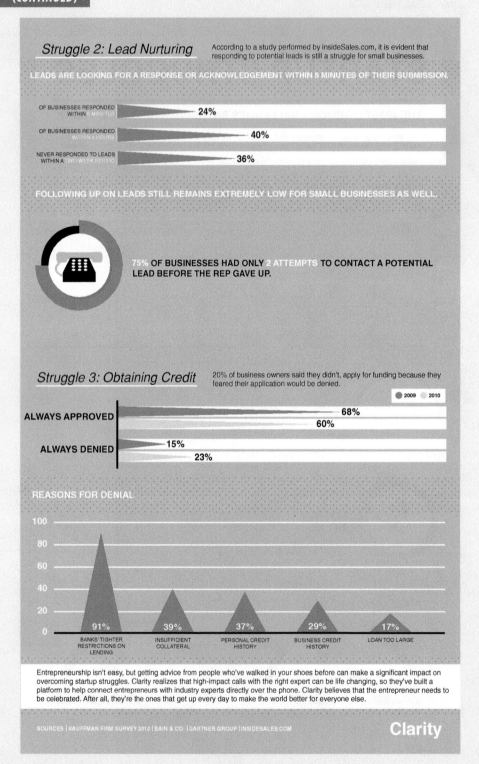

Struggle 2: Lead Nurturing

According to a study performed by insideSales.com, it is evident that responding to potential leads is still a struggle for small businesses.

LEADS ARE LOOKING FOR A RESPONSE OR ACKNOWLEDGEMENT WITHIN 5 MINUTES OF THEIR SUBMISSION.

OF BUSINESSES RESPONDED WITHIN 5 MINUTES — **24%**

OF BUSINESSES RESPONDED WITHIN 4 HOURS — **40%**

NEVER RESPONDED TO LEADS WITHIN A TWO WEEK PERIOD — **36%**

FOLLOWING UP ON LEADS STILL REMAINS EXTREMELY LOW FOR SMALL BUSINESSES AS WELL.

75% OF BUSINESSES HAD ONLY 2 ATTEMPTS TO CONTACT A POTENTIAL LEAD BEFORE THE REP GAVE UP.

Struggle 3: Obtaining Credit

20% of business owners said they didn't apply for funding because they feared their application would be denied.

● 2009 ○ 2010

ALWAYS APPROVED — **68%** / **60%**

ALWAYS DENIED — **15%** / **23%**

REASONS FOR DENIAL

BANKS' TIGHTER RESTRICTIONS ON LENDING	91%
INSUFFICIENT COLLATERAL	39%
PERSONAL CREDIT HISTORY	37%
BUSINESS CREDIT HISTORY	29%
LOAN TOO LARGE	17%

Entrepreneurship isn't easy, but getting advice from people who've walked in your shoes before can make a significant impact on overcoming startup struggles. Clarity realizes that high-impact calls with the right expert can be life changing, so they've built a platform to help connect entrepreneurs with industry experts directly over the phone. Clarity believes that the entrepreneur needs to be celebrated. After all, they're the ones that get up every day to make the world better for everyone else.

SOURCES | KAUFFMAN FIRM SURVEY 2012 | BAIN & CO. | GARTNER GROUP | INSIDESALES.COM

Clarity

Source: Startup Struggles, Clarify.fm (http://blog.clarity.fm/startup-struggles-common-problems-startups-face/). Used with permission.

In earlier chapters, finding leads through networking events and friends was discussed. But there are other ways of generating leads as well, such as:

- Working with other consultants who offer services that complement your business.

- Offering referral rewards to current customers by giving them something in return such as a gift certificate to a nice restaurant or something that they will remember you by. Make the gift worthwhile for your customers to want to help you.

- Writing for an established publication. Publishers are always looking for interesting articles that offer advice and assistance that will help others.

- Participating in user forums. The number of forums available is staggering. Start listening, and add your comments to these forums. It will give you credibility and be the start of building relationships with prospective clients.

- Cold calling. Gain confidence in making cold calls and setting up meetings. It is the beginning of a relationship when you meet and talk to potential customers.

Many sales reps and managers complain that they cannot create a consistent flow of revenues or commissions month after month. Instead of a nice, straight line increasing consistently over time, like an upward-pointing arrow, they find themselves staring repeatedly at sales results that look more like a hockey stick: nothing for two months, a sharp increase for a month or two, and then back down again to nothing a month later.

So, what can you do to keep your sales funnel full of leads and to ensure a consistent, reliable flow of revenues all year round?

Ninety-nine times out of a hundred, lack of consistent revenues—the "hockey stick syndrome"—is caused by lack of consistent prospecting. A failure to prospect on a regular basis will inevitably result in irregular revenues, and inconsistent commissions. It is that simple.

Successful new business development requires careful planning and organization. A tried and proven method of organizing this process is called the *prospecting funnel* (Figure 9.2). The prospecting funnel is a four-stage process, starting from the broad global marketplace and narrowing down through four steps to a new customer.

The first stage entails selecting from the global marketplace a *target market* or list of possible customers, called *suspects* or *suspect accounts*. To determine suspects, we must define and employ various qualifying criteria, such as size, credit worthiness, sales potential, location, and more, depending on the business you are in.

Stage two involves verifying the customer's need or interest in your product/service, thus converting some of these *suspects* into genuine *prospects*.

Stage three requires using various consultative selling techniques, skills, and tools to convert the *prospect accounts* into *hot ones* that are ready to start doing business with you and your organization.

The fourth and final stage involves moving the *hot ones* through further selling efforts toward making a favourable buying decision so that they become *new customers*.

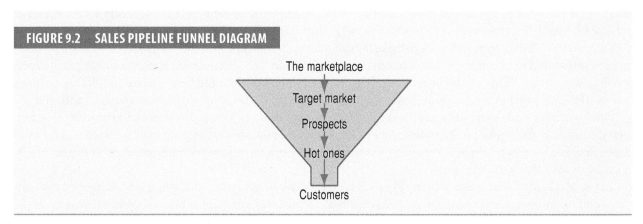

FIGURE 9.2   SALES PIPELINE FUNNEL DIAGRAM

The marketplace

Target market

Prospects

Hot ones

Customers

Source: The Canadian Professional Sales Association (CPSA) is committed to helping sales professionals improve their effectiveness, efficiencies, and professionalism through sales resources, professional sales training and development, as well as membership savings programs. (www.cpsa.com).

The prospecting funnel achieves three important objectives:

- It organizes all the prospecting activities.
- It causes the salesperson to focus efforts on maintaining a constant flow of new business.
- It provides an objective way of distributing time as well as a means of avoiding the fear of rejection and resultant procrastination.

Marketplace

This refers to the global marketplace as a whole—all countries, all industries, all organizations—and is located above the funnel. In most cases, of course, this marketplace is too broad a starting point for your business-creation efforts. Therefore, the task is to identify *suspects*.

Suspects

Suspects are those accounts that *may* have a need or interest in your product or service. They are at the top level of the funnel. Suspects *may* become new customers and are also described as *leads*. Their viability as customers is unconfirmed, however, and the job is to find out which ones qualify as worthwhile *prospects*. Suspects comprise what is commonly known as the *target market* and are defined based on specific qualifying criteria that you and your organization define.

Prospects

Prospect accounts are those suspects that have a *verified* need or interest in your products and/or services. Prospects are found at the middle level of the funnel and can only be converted through a conversation with the customer.

Hot Ones

Through effective consultative selling, prospect accounts will become *hot one*s. Hot ones are those accounts that are *ready and likely* to do business with you—and where an initial order is *probable*. All buying influences (people who make or influence the buying decision) have been contacted and support your proposition. The next step is clear and should result in the hot one committing to start doing business—that is, becoming a *new customer*.[1]

THE COLD CALL
PREPARING BEFORE MAKING THE CALL

The thought of picking up the phone to make a call to talk about your business is a harrowing experience to some but something that, at some point in your business, will have to be done. To prepare yourself for the call, write down what you want to say, and practise it over and over again before making the call. Role play with a friend or relative who will offer constructive criticism about what they think could be done to improve the call.

Once you feel comfortable and ready to make the call, start with someone that you have met at a networking event or been introduced to by someone. It is easier to start a conversation with someone you already know. As well, a great opening statement is "That so-and-so referred me to you and thought you would be interested in what my business has to offer." More often than not, such persons will give you the opportunity to talk to them and meet with you.

Once you have made some "soft calls," you will be able to start making "cold calls" without too much of an effort. Being passionate about your product/service goes a long way. The passion is felt by potential customer, and they will more than likely want to arrange a meeting—how could they not want to work with someone that is so totally engaged in what they are offering?

Art Sobczak, president of Business By Phone Inc., specializes in authoring, designing, and delivering content-rich training programs and resources that help business-to-business salespeople begin showing results from the very next time they get on the phone. He works with sales reps helping them get more business by phone. Art has seen and heard it all and shares his insights in the Other Considerations box.

OTHER CONSIDERATIONS

A MISTAKE-FILLED CALL

I answered the phone. The salesperson immediately jumped in:

Caller: *"Hi, I'm Carl Kelly with Web Marketing and Design. Boy, you are sure a hard guy to reach."*

Art: "OK."

Caller: *"We're a web design and search engine marketing company. As you know, more and more companies are making the Internet a major part of their marketing programs. We can help you get a web presence and more business from the Internet. Have you ever considered using the Internet to market your business?"*

Art: "Let me get this right. You are an Internet marketing business, right?"

Caller: *"Yeah."*

Art: "And you're asking me if I now use the Internet."

Caller: *"Well, yeah."*

Art: "Do you even know what we do here?"

Caller: *"Let's see, ummm, Business By Phone. Something to do with selling phones I'd assume. That or a telemarketing company."*

Art: "Wrong on both accounts. Am I crazy to assume that maybe you would have checked our website first, to find out what we do, and to see how we market online?"

Caller: *"Hey, I have to make a lot of calls here. I don't have time for that. What I do know is that we can help you increase your business online."*

I pretty much ended the call at that point. This guy did not have a clue.

Mistake 1: *"Boy, you are sure a hard guy to reach."* This adds nothing to the call, and, worse, immediately gets the listener thinking, "Alright, bad salesperson on the line here. How can I get rid of him?"

Mistake 1a: Since he said I was hard to reach, he must have reached my voice mail numerous times. On the voice mail I give an option to get our website address. Which, of course, he did not take the time to visit. Too busy, I guess.

Mistake 2: *"As you know, more and more companies ..."* As you should know, you should never use, *"As you know..."* at the beginning of a call, or anywhere for that matter. First, maybe they don't know, or agree. It could make them defensive. Plus it sounds cheesy.

Mistake 3: No pre-call planning. This is so obvious, it's laughable. I was actually looking around my office to be sure I wasn't on Candid Camera. An Internet marketing company and he didn't even check out my website first?

Mistake 4: Bad opening. Which was a result of no planning. Worse, he made the definitive statement, *"We **can** help you get a web presence and more business from the Internet."* Even when you do know, from a position of intelligence, that you can help someone, it's still not a good idea to state it definitively. If they don't know you, it can raise the question in their mind, "Well, who are **they** to make that statement? He doesn't know me."

Mistake 5: Lame, argumentative excuse:*"Hey, I have to make a lot of calls here. I don't have time for that."* He could have just said, "You are not important enough to me to take the time to find out anything about you."

Source: A Mistake-Filled Call, Art Sobczak, Business By Phone Inc. (www. smartcallingonline.com). Used with permission.

Art goes on to say that a skilled caller would have avoided most of these mistakes by simply doing the research, and using that in an interest-creating opening, which then would have easily moved to the questions. An example that would have gotten the attention of Art would sound something like this:

"Hi Art, I'm Carl Kelly with Web Marketing and Design. We specialize in working with web marketers, including training firms that sell lots of electronic online products like you do, improve their search engine rankings, traffic, and overall sales. We do this through some unique methods, and I'd like to ask a few questions about your strategy and plans to see if I could provide you with more information."

Always do your research and planning before you think of making a call. Once you have your research and planning in place, then use it to create interest in the opening statement.

THE GATE KEEPER

It can be difficult, and sometimes frustrating, trying to reach the person you want to meet with or even trying to find the name of the person you need to speak to. Although it is less common for businesses to have a receptionist or administrative assistants answering the phone, there are some executives/decision makers who still do have someone to assist them in keeping up with their day-to-day routine. These people are also known as "Gate Keepers." As well as assisting their employers administratively, they have been taught to protect them and screen their calls to keep them from being inundated by the many requests for their time.

Approaching the Gate Keeper positively and outlining the benefits of your business to their business may very well open the door to the decision maker. Start by introducing yourself, and explain why you are calling and what the benefit of your product or service is to the company; say that you would like to arrange an appointment to discuss the benefits in more detail with her employer. If you do not know the decision maker's name, then ask the Gate Keeper if they could help you by giving you the information. Most people like to help others, and this will give them a sense of importance. Always get the name of the Gate Keeper, and use it—everyone likes to hear their name. This makes the conversation personal. Once you have the information you are looking for, ask for the telephone number (for future reference), and then ask if they would mind transferring your call.

Receptionists and administrators do not always get the recognition they deserve. Send a thank-you note to them for helping you get to the decision maker. This will go a long way for you and your business.

OVERCOMING SALES OBJECTIONS LO2
TYPES OF SALES OBJECTIONS

It would be nice if you walk into a meeting and give your sales presentation and the client looks at you and says, "I want this. When can I have it?" Unfortunately, that rarely happens.

In this very competitive world, you have to stand out from your competitors. Chances are the company you are trying to present to or are presenting to has already been approached by other companies and will have many questions for you on why they should choose you over your competitor. Being prepared for any objections will turn something negative into a positive and help you get the sale.

Some objections you may run into are:

- I'm too busy to meet with you
- The timing isn't right
- Pricing
- What makes you different from your competitor?
- We don't know who you are
- Already working with a supplier and don't want to make a change
- Have to get approval or discuss with others
- We don't need it

How do you overcome these objections? You do not want to just say, "Thank you for your time,"—not at least until you have provided good reasons why they should buy from you. The Other Considerations box offers some tips on how to handle sales objections. Remember, although you may handle the objections well, it still does not mean you will get the sale. You have to realize at some point that you have to move on.

I'm Too Busy to Meet With You

You need to get the attention of the person you are contacting. First and foremost, know something about your customer and their business, and then promise them something. An example might be that your product will increase productivity and save them time and money.

The Timing Isn't Right

It is tough to get an appointment if your contact is busy. If they are in the middle of something that needs to be done, then ask them when you might meet with them. If your product or service will help them with their time, then give them the benefits of why they should meet with you now and not wait.

Pricing

If pricing is an issue, then you need to overcome this objection immediately. Show prospects the value and benefits of what you are selling, how it will benefit them by saving them time and money by being productive, or how it will make their job much easier.

You may also be told that they have already been given a cheaper price from a competitor. Deal with this by asking the client if the offering was identical to yours, and offer to go over their proposal with them to ensure they are comparing apples to apples.

What Makes You Different from Your Competitor?

Since you should know everything there is to know about your competitors, this should be a no-brainer. Explain the differences, and why you are better suited to the company. Do not ever put down your competition—only explain the benefits of purchasing from you.

We Don't Know Who You Are

It can be difficult as your client does not know who you are and you have yet to build a relationship with them. Share testimonials, case studies, and references from other clients. Be honest with them, and start building the relationship by staying in touch and meeting for a coffee to get to know each other away from the office.

Already Working with a Supplier and Don't Want To Make a Change

This can be a difficult one to overcome, but do explain that you understand their point of view. Offer a free trial for them to evaluate your product. Stay in touch while the free trial is in place to see if they are using the product, what they like and dislike and make changes, if necessary. This will help you close the sale at the end of the trial.

Have to Get Approval or Discuss with Others

Not everyone makes a decision on the spot, although we would like them to. Accept their response, but stay in touch periodically. Do not be pushy, but if you see something that may be of interest to them send it along. This keeps you in their minds. Every so often make a call to see if they have made a decision yet, and ask if there is anything you can do to help with the decision.

We Don't Need It

There is a saying—"You don't know what you don't know." Since you have done your homework on the business and genuinely believe that there is a fit for your product within the organization, you need to explain the value and benefits to them. If they see that it will benefit them, it will make it much easier to overcome the objection.

When overcoming objections, always remember to be polite and understanding—they may not be ready to purchase now, but they may well remember you in the future as someone they will want to work with.

THE SALES PRESENTATION

LO3

Once your cold calls have paid off and you have an appointment scheduled to meet with your prospective client, you need to be prepared with the sales presentation. Being prepared is critical to your success in getting the sale.

Start outlining your presentation by:

- Writing down your objectives.
- Knowing who the decision maker is. Find out as much information as you can about the decision maker—know their needs, objectives, and interests.
- Developing a schedule for completion of your presentation.

Although the above points are the basis of your presentation, every presentation needs to be tailored and relevant to the client you are meeting with. Having some insight about your client beforehand will go a long way when doing your presentation.

Keep these points close as you write out your presentation. Points that need to be covered in your presentation are:

- **Build rapport with your customer.** Put yourself in the same position as your prospect.
- **Demonstrate your product/service to the client**. Give a sample of your product to the client. Let them see, touch, and feel it.
- **Ask questions**. Poise your questions in a way that the customer will have to respond with other than a yes-or-no answer. There is nothing worse than trying to pull information from someone. Use the five W's; who, what, why, when and where.
- **Answer their questions.** Be prepared by knowing your product/service inside and out. If, for some reason, you do not know the answer, tell them and promise to get back to them with the information. Make sure you respond to them—another way to connect with them.
- **Ask for the business**. Do not ever leave a meeting without asking when they will be making their decision will be made and what can you do to help them with it, and arranging a follow-up meeting.

Once you have your presentation together, rehearse it until you feel comfortable. However, make sure you do not sound like you are rehearsing in front of the client. Be natural, professional, and passionate.

When entering the meeting, introduce yourself, and if possible, sit across the table from the decision maker. Never sit beside them, if you can help it. When doing a demonstration, it is best to stand, especially if there is more than one person in the meeting, and position yourself where everyone can view the demonstration easily.

Do not do all the talking—listen to your customer. If they have questions, answer them before continuing on with the meeting. There is nothing worse than a salesperson rambling on and not paying attention to the customer.

Once the meeting is finished write a personal thank-you note to the decision maker, thanking them for their time and how you look forward to working with him or her in the near future.

Stay in touch. It may take several weeks, months, or even longer for a decision to be made. Stay in touch with the prospect, and do not give up until they tell you they are not interested. If they are not interested, find out why so that you can learn from them how you can make your product/service better.

Gayle Hinkley (see the Entrepreneurs in Action box), winner of the $10,000 Visa Elevator Pitch, was prepared when she made her sales pitch to the judges. Not only had she rehearsed, but she also had a tent card created in the shape of a uniform to show the judges what type of kiosk she also would use the money for. Gayle knew her customers and what they wanted but did not have the funding to go ahead with her project.

ENTREPRENEURS IN ACTION

AND THE WINNER IS . . . MEET GAYLE HINKLEY, OUR 2012 VISA $10,000 ELEVATOR PITCH WINNER

She researched. She brainstormed with people. She wrote out her script, again and again, and practised for hours—and it was over in 60 seconds.

But it was one minute that made all the difference.

For a decade Hinkley has been selling uniforms primarily to people in the medical field (though she sells a huge range of uniforms for anyone from vets to waitresses to costume designers for movies). The idea she pitched to our judges? It was brilliantly simple: Bring the product to the people rather than wait for them to come to the shop. She proposed creating a kiosk right in the hospital itself so that buying a new uniform or a more comfortable pair of shoes is as easy as getting a coffee.

"I kept hearing from my customers that they hardly ever get downtown, and I know how busy they are," she says.

The idea had been germinating for a while. At the request of a hospital in Victoria she did a three-day sale and the results were positive. Not only did her selection sell well, the staff was impressed with the quality and the style of the uniforms she carries. "I was sitting in this nearly empty hospital cafeteria with my husband and we looked around at all the empty space and he said, 'You know, you should have a kiosk right here.' And that was it. It was a great idea and I thought it would really work."

She put together a business proposal and submitted it to the hospital administration. However, the actual startup money she'd need to build the space would have been a stretch for her.

"That's when I saw the advertisement for the Elevator Pitch contest and I thought well, I wonder if I have a chance to win the prize."

Visa was already a trusted ally in her business. "I use my Visa Business card with rewards for all my products and inventory, and that means I build up enough reward points that I can book flights to go to the uniform trade shows—I haven't missed a conference in all the years I've been in business. I can manage my cash flow without tying up thousands of dollars in travel expenses."

So, she decided to give the Visa contest a try. That's when her preparation started.

"I sat in my office with a pen and paper and plotted out exactly how my business would work and worked on bringing that down to just 60 seconds, focusing on what I thought would be most important," she says. She called on the services of her son to be her cameraman and practised for a few hours. She put on one of her most stylish uniforms, filmed her pitch, submitted it, and waited.

GAYLE HINKLEY
Source: Used with permission of Gayle Hinckly

Then she got word she was selected as a finalist.

"I was so nervous, I thought oh no I can't really do this," says Hinkley. But instead of giving in to the impulse of "no I can't," her entrepreneurial "yes I can" spirit came out and she got down to work, again honing her pitch and her presentation. She had her idea for a kiosk drawn out on a tent card created in the shape of a uniform, and had her goods and services listed on the other side. She was armed and ready for the judges.

In the end what does she think wooed them to her idea? "I think it was a few things. I think it helped that I was wearing a uniform that looked as good as street clothes, and I had a prop so they could visualize the idea. I had my numbers down, in terms of the size of the opportunity. I think the need for my kiosk is obvious and easy to understand."

Hinkley says other marks in her favour were likely that she has a business track record already, knows her market and the prize could make a huge difference in terms of achieving a business goal of creating her first kiosk, which she hopes will be just a pilot and something she can roll out to other hospitals.

And what might have been that added extra? "They could tell I'm really passionate. I've been in this business a long time and I still get excited about helping people look professional."

Source: And the Winner is . . . Meet Gayle Hinkley, Our 2012 Visa $10,000 Elevator Pitch Winner, Tracy Nesdoly, July 2012 (www.visa.ca). Used with permission of Gayle Hinkley.

Whether you are a business owner or part of a sales team for a medium- or large-sized company, your performance as a salesperson is determined by how often you successfully close sales—sealing the deal that translates goods or services into revenue. To close more business effectively, you must be the one who is controlling and directing the customer through each step of a sales process. Do not expect the customer to know what to do next. Most people are commitment-phobic. They are not going to make a decision until they are presented with options.

Stay in control of your sales process by adopting a strategy that gets your customers to commit to a series of steps—and to stick to it. Colleen Francis advises that you need to be following up with each of your customers at *a minimum of every 30 days* in some way. It does not necessarily have to be by phone, but you need to be doing something to stay in that top-of-mind position.

Colleen's article in the Other Considerations box outlines what you need to do close the sale.

OTHER CONSIDERATIONS

ONE STEP AHEAD: TAKING CONTROL OF EVERY SALES RELATIONSHIP SO YOU ARE CLOSING ON EVERY CONVERSATION!

PLAN AND BACKUP

Before you engage any customer in a conversation, you need to have a plan on how you're going to close more business with that person. You also need to have a backup plan. For example, if you can't meet your primary objective—to get a commitment to meet with a decision maker in your client's firm, for instance—your backup can be to get the name and contact information of that decision maker.

KNOW WHAT'S NEXT

If your best efforts don't result in closing a deal with a customer, you need to decide what is going to happen next. It's not enough to simply agree to talk again later. When will you talk again? Be specific. Your goal needs to include setting a date, and a well-defined set of next steps.

Those who have attended one of our Engage Sales Mastery Workshops have seen me map out a series of possible next steps in great detail. In this article, however, let me give you a glimpse of what we cover. When attempting to close a sale, your customer can choose to say "Yes," "No" or "Maybe." If they say "No," find out why. It is because there are no projects going on? Is it because they have chosen another supplier? It is simply the wrong time for a new project? The answers you receive to those questions will give you something to build on for your follow-up strategy.

Apply the same approach when the answer is "Maybe." If, for example, a customer says: "We are not doing anything until the end of the fourth quarter of this year, call me back in December," you would respond by asking some probing questions. "I'd be happy to call you in December...is that when you expect to have your project ready to go, or will that just be when you're ready to start investigating a possible start to the project?" Similarly, if the customer says: "What you're proposing sounds like a great idea, but we really just don't have the budget yet," you can respond by asking: "When is your budgeting process starting?" The answers you obtain give you added insight on formulating your next steps with each customer.

USE THE RIGHT TOOLS TO HELP KEEP YOU ON TRACK

Keeping track of every conversation and every commitment you make to pursue next steps in sales...these are not the kinds of things you can simply commit to memory. This is why a customer relationship management database (or CRM) is absolutely vital. It could be as simple as a PC-based ACT! database, as intuitive as Daylite for Mac, or as substantial as a Salesforce.com account. No matter which one best suits your needs, a CRM is a wise investment. It's far from being an administrative nuisance. Think of it as an extension of your brain. It remembers all the commitments you make and the people you talk to, and it doesn't get sidetracked the way all of us do in our day-to-day lives. Deals get lost too easily by simply forgetting to make a note to follow-up with a prospect. Don't take that risk! Rely on your CRM instead.

ACCOUNT MANAGEMENT

Managing customer accounts with artful care, attention, and skill ripens the opportunity to close a deal. You need to nurture relationships and manage accounts as you work toward closing the sale. But you cannot overdo it. You do not want to scare the customer away.

In the Other Considerations box, the Canadian Professional Sales Association provides an article on nine mistakes to avoid for superior account management performance. By following these steps, you will get that much closer to having your customer become a client.

These account management mistakes cost sales professionals dearly, but they can easily be avoided by developing standardized ways for paying attention to all aspects of a sales account.

OTHER CONSIDERATIONS

ARE YOU MAKING THESE 9 ACCOUNT MANAGEMENT MISTAKES?

1. **Too much follow-up** There is a delicate balance between giving the customer the amount of attention they want, and smothering them with too much. Don't be afraid to ask your client what is comfortable for them. Be sure to let them know when you'll follow-up with them and gauge their response. Be sure that each time you do follow-up with them, you make it count and provide value.

2. **The buyer feels sold** Nobody likes to feel sold. It puts unneeded pressure on a relationship if a person is not ready to buy. The salesperson who pushes too hard, too early creates tension, and this can result in an unresponsive prospect or a reluctant buyer. A better approach is to position yourself as a friendly adviser. As much as we all claim that we "focus on relationship-building and client needs" do we really?

3. **The customer does not feel understood** Even if you may have seen the same problem multiple times, the customer wants to know that you care about and understand their specific situation. Using a cookbook approach or a broad stroke brush to describe their problems shows a lack of empathy. Speak in the first person to show the prospect that you can identify with them. For example, "I can understand what you are dealing with..." and "If it were me, I would be looking at this situation differently..."

   Ask questions about the obstacle and how it affects the client's business. Do not just pretend to understand the situation; make sure that you gather adequate information that allows you to actually grasp their concerns.

4. **Too much dead air** Relationships are delicate and require attention, but with the many accounts that you have to manage, you may let a bit too much time pass without a follow-up. A long span without communications can make any follow-up difficult. The perception could be that you are looking for something selfishly rather than coming with

(continued)

better intentions to help. Keep in mind, too, that all the hard work you put into an initial call or presentation could all be undone simply because the prospect doesn't recall what you spoke about the last time, or worse yet, doesn't recall you at all.

Be sure to use your CRM or calendar to schedule an appropriate follow-up within a reasonable time for all your accounts. Expedite the delivery of follow-up materials such as information packages, quotes, proposals, etc. by templating or standardizing the process in advance and tweaking as needed for individual clients. Also, as mentioned before, let the client know when they can expect a follow-up; setting an expectation with your client will keep you accountable, ensuring that you deliver on your follow-ups on time every time.

5. **Letting competitors outdo you** Customers that need answers/solutions to problems immediately could easily look elsewhere. Delayed or unresponsive behaviour due to neglect or being disorganized can leave the door open for competition to better serve your customers. Always assess the urgency of your prospects' requests, and make yourself available via multiple communication channels such as email, phone, cellphone, Twitter, live chat, etc. Remember, the easier you make it for a customer to contact you, the more likely they will choose you to help them resolve their needs.

6. **Majoring on the minors** It is easy to get caught up in a transaction and forget the relationship. If a customer relationship will mean continued business for months or years, then haggling over money, features, or minutiae that can cause resentment is not worth it in the long run. Have a clear picture of the lifetime value of a customer and make long-term decisions on how you will handle any negotiations to build goodwill over time.

7. **Placing their own interests above those of the customer** Selling is based on trust and the sales representative that violates trust, loses sales. If a customer senses that you have guided them to product or service for your benefit more than for theirs, this can compromise your relationship. Avoid this, by always being transparent and ensuring that the customer feels that you are acting in their best interest. Help them with the best deals and go the extra mile in proving you care about their needs.

8. **Irrelevant marketing overload** The advent of automated workflows and marketing messages means more leads in your pipeline. However, if current leads are being bombarded with irrelevant messaging, it may sour their experience.

Customers that are subscribed to unrelated product or brand messages from your company can get confused about the salesperson's positioning. The marketing messages the customer receives should be selective and relevant to the conversations they have had with their account manager. Systems that ensure that the communication tracks match their interest need to be tightly controlled by the salesperson.

9. **Lack of expertise** The customer is engaging a sales representative because that person is familiar with the industry, challenges, and their own offerings. It is critical to continually stay aware of all the current industry issues and share what is happening with customers. With the ease of access to information online, the experienced salesperson will expect that the customer will come prepared with tons of information. The salesperson needs to help the customer sift through this information and direct them to appropriate statistics, facts, and answers that are relevant to their situation. Pertinent information should be packaged and proactively provided to customers.

Source: The Canadian Professional Sales Association (CPSA) is committed to helping sales professionals improve their effectiveness, efficiencies, and professionalism through sales resources, professional sales training and development, as well as membership savings programs (www.cpsa.com). Used with permission.

Growing relationships over time and building trust with accounts make a skilled sales professional indispensable to both their company and their respective customers. It is a daily choice of paying attention to details, being organized, and being eager to help the customer.

Small businesses have many ups, downs, and considerable challenges as they launch, manage, and grow their business. The one thing that every small business owner needs to ask themselves, even before starting the business, is: Who is going to be responsible for generating sales? Are you, as the business owner, a salesperson? With all the responsibilities that go with being an owner, do you even have the time to be a salesperson? Perhaps you are best suited to be the spokesperson for the company and pass any leads to a salesperson. If you are not a salesperson then you need to hire someone that will do the sales for the company.

As you move toward hiring a salesperson, it is important that candidates understand that you are in the early stages of your business, but even more importantly, you need to make it very clear what they are expected to bring to your business. Mark Evans, owner of Mark Evans Tech, outlines the five must-haves for startup salespeople.

OTHER CONSIDERATIONS

FIVE MUST-HAVES FOR START-UP SALESPEOPLE.

1. **The willingness to work for a small, non-established company** It sounds straightforward but salespeople like selling, but working for a startup can mean trying to push a small rock up a big hill—without the compensation and perks. A salesperson needs to be excited about a startup's ability to resonate with customers who may have not known the product exists.

2. **The ability to multi-task** In a startup, salespeople need to do a lot more than just sell. They have to do business development, marketing, customer service, and administrative duties. In a sense, all of the above involves selling but in a different and indirect way. While salespeople like to be out there selling, working for a startup has to be a lot more.

3. **Good listening skills** The products sold by startups are created to solve a problem but it doesn't mean customers know they need or want them. It means salespeople have to listen as much as they speak, which can be a challenge. It means taking a soft-sell approach in which a salesperson learns what a customer needs rather than what a salesperson wants to sell them.

4. **Embrace the idea of being product developers** The one thing salespeople do is talk with potential and existing customers on a regular basis. As a result, they can get a good understanding of the problems or needs faced by potential customers, the products or features they would like to see, their budgets, and the competition.

5. **Be team players rather than lone wolves** While salespeople need to be out talking to potential customers, they also have to understand the different parts of the company, and be willing to get involved in other parts of the business. They need to have a willingness to accept recommendations and ideas from other people and, at the same time, be willing to bring their ideas and feedback to the table.

Source: Five must-Haves for Startup Salespeople, Mark Evans Tech, April 16, 2013 (www.markevanstech.com). Used with permission.

What do you like about being an Entrepreneur?

There are many things I love about being an entrepreneur but flexibility and freedom probably top the list. I started the business with three other moms after my eldest child was diagnosed with autism and striking a work/life balance became essential. Now a mom of six young children, I split my time 50/50 between my home and office, though as company spokesperson, I travel quite a lot too, sometimes with a kid or three. Of course, the well-known adage that 'with freedom comes responsibility,' is true and I enjoy giving back by sharing knowledge and expertise as much as possible. I love connecting with other entrepreneurs through my blogs and social media (Twitter@juliecole), and mentoring those starting out. Freedom by no means equals less work, just a different kind, and I love it!

Julie Cole
Co-Founder & VP of Public
Relations & Customer Service
Mabel's Labels
www.mabelslabels.com

Customers are the backbone of your business, and without them your business probably will not survive. Customer service can be the difference between you and your competitor. You have to stand out from the rest when you are making the sale and continue to do so after the sale. Keeping a customer happy will potentially lead to future sales.

When someone is pleased with the service they receive, they will tell someone else about it but probably not as much as if they receive poor customer service. Customers want to feel important and they actually mean something to your business.

Take for example, a restaurant. You and your spouse are planning a nice dinner at a restaurant that you have heard and read good reviews about. You have made reservations and arrive on time only to be kept waiting and completely ignored. You are finally seated and given menus. Your server is polite and takes your order. Your drinks arrive, but it takes forever to get your food. You ask your server when the food will be coming. She says she does not know and that the kitchen has been slammed with orders. It is a busy night. She goes and checks and comes back saying it will be out shortly. Time goes by, and you are still waiting.

Finally, your food arrives without any apology. You mention that you are not pleased that it took so long. The server says she could not do anything about it. You eat your food and leave angry and frustrated and, of course, will never return again and probably will tell everyone how bad the service was. The Internet has made it so easy to spread the word through social media sites and, in this case, the many restaurant review sites. This can be devastating to a business.

What could have been done to prevent this?

Upon arrival, the guests should have been approached and explained that their table was not quite ready and the restaurant was busier than they thought they were going to be. The staff should have apologized for the inconvenience and asked if the guests would prefer to wait in the lounge until their table was ready. They should never have been ignored.

Management should have stepped in and apologized, perhaps provided another beverage on the house while the guests were waiting, or offered a discount on the bill, which would have indicated that the restaurant at least cared enough about its guests to try and make them happy.

Restaurants, for the most part, do not train their staff in customer service, and they do not look at the repeat customers and how word-of-mouth advertising can either help or hinder business.

Victoria Sopik, CEO of Kids & Company (see the Entrepreneurs in Action box), one of *Profit Magazine's* Fastest-Growing Companies, says that in other child-care centres, parents are happy enough with the care their children receive but not with the customer service. To differentiate themselves from the others, they offer a very high level of customer service. With 50 child-care centres across Canada and revenue of more than $50 million, they must be doing something right.

Victoria understands what customer service is all about, but unfortunately not every business does. Why is that? Cellphone companies are notorious for their poor customer service. With the ever-increasing demand for cellphones you have to wonder how long they will be able to continue this way, especially with the possibility of U.S. carriers moving into the Canadian market.

Implementing a customer service plan in your organization should be done immediately. If you are wondering how to do this, it is quite simple. Ask yourself how you like to be treated by someone you have bought something from and go from there.

For the most part, technical people should not be part of support unless they are skilled at solving problems at a level that customers can understand. This is not only frustrating for the customer but can end in the customer taking their business away from the company.

LITTLE THINGS COUNT IN CUSTOMER SERVICE

Help Your Customers Make a Decision

People generally like to be helped. They may not be sure exactly what they are looking for, but they like to be offered assistance. Ask them questions, and help them make the decision that is best suited to their needs. Do not oversell or be pushy. Give them options, if possible, but let them make the final decision.

SURPRISE 'EM WITH GREAT CUSTOMER SERVICE

In many other child-care centres, parents are happy enough with the care their children are getting, but not with the customer service. So we've differentiated ourselves by offering a very high level of customer service.

We hear from families that they phone other centres and they don't hear back or they're put on a long waiting list. Our centres serve our corporate clients' employees, and parents can log on to register their child and get an immediate response and a guaranteed space. In the old model, there's often an attitude of "You're lucky to have a spot in our centre." But our message is "We're grateful that you've chosen to send your child to us."

We now have hundreds of corporate clients, and this year we'll reach 50 child-care centres across Canada and revenue of more than $50 million. One of the biggest challenges we've faced getting to this point is ensuring our people have a customer service mindset. We do all kinds of things to incentivize that. For instance, we give our centre directors a bonus for every child who is registered on our directory, and we reward employees who go above and beyond. If a parent says a child has lost a mitten and the teacher searches everywhere and finds it, we'll give the teacher a Tim Hortons' gift card.

We have a far more rigorous entry process than most centres do. We'll ask in interviews, "What would you say to a parent who told you they'll be 10 minutes late picking up their child?" At some centres, they'd say, "It's $1 a minute, so make sure you show up with $10." But we'd say, "Don't worry, we'll stay open for as long as you need us to." The interviewee may not know that that's our policy. But we're looking for someone who thinks about how they can help the parent instead of telling them they'll be fined for being late.

ANTIL / DREAMSTIME.COM

Source: Surprise 'em with Great Customer Service, Jim McElgunn, Profitguide, March 18, 2013 (www.profitguide.com). Used with permission.

Greet Your Customers By Name

People like to feel that they mean something to you and your business. They like to be recognized. How many times have you talked about a business that calls you by name when they speak to you? This makes you feel special and important.

Listen to Your Customers

If a customer calls or emails, be courteous, and respond to their questions professionally. Listen to them—only ask questions when you need to. Let them do the talking. Do not send a customer who has contacted you to the FAQ or video section of your website. Listen to their questions, and respond accordingly. If you do not have the answer, promise to get back to them with the answer. Make a point of responding as soon as you can. If there is a delay, reach out to the customer, and let them know you are still working on it. Customers like to be treated with respect and know that you care.

Be Transparent and Take Responsibility

The worst thing you can do is not admit that a mistake has been made. You need to admit and apologize when something has gone wrong. And then fix the problem as soon as you can. Once the problem has been fixed, stay in touch with your customer to make sure they are satisfied. Send them a note or gift card when the problem has been resolved.

Always remember that word of mouth goes both ways—it can help or hinder any business. Ensure your customer service stories will help you. Social media are a driving force for bad customer service reviews. The Other Considerations box explains the importance of resolving customer issues quickly and responsively.

OTHER CONSIDERATIONS

SELL. SLEEP. #FAIL

At first, it seems like no big deal. A customer tweets one morning about a problem she's having with a firm's product. But then, some of her Twitter followers repost her tweet to their followers, who do the same. By the end of the day, thousands of people have seen the complaint.

What they *haven't* seen is a response from the company. Even though there's an easy fix for this customer's problem, this firm hasn't told her about it; in fact, the company hasn't even noticed her tweet. That's because it isn't systematically monitoring and responding to social media posts about its business that raise customer service issues. As a result, the firm's reputation has taken a hit—and it doesn't even know it.

The company is far from alone in this. A survey of U.S. Twitter users by market research firm Maritz Research found that only 29 percent of businesses respond to complaints tweeted about them. You'd never see companies ignore most complaints coming in by phone or email, so why do they blow it when it comes to social media?

Probably, they simply haven't realized that many consumers prefer raising issues via social media because it's so easy. "Before, if you had a complaint, you had to find a phone number, pick up the phone, sit on hold, go through a call tree and speak with someone who might or might not be helpful," says Ryan Holmes, CEO at Vancouver-based HootSuite Media Inc., creator of a popular social media dashboard. "Social media has flipped that on its head."

It's only natural for social media users to post about your business using those channels. But few companies are set up to respond to these posts, says Sajan Choksi, CEO of Innovative Vision Marketing Inc., a Toronto-based call-centre operator: "The same thing happened when email came along and companies initially didn't understand how to use email for business."

It's time to figure it out for social media. "The old axiom was that one unhappy customer will tell 10 people; but, with social media, they'll tell thousands," says Holmes. "The stakes are much higher."

But the rewards are bigger if you get on top of this issue while rival firms haven't even realized it is an issue. If you respond quickly to customer service concerns, you can nip unfounded criticism of your company in the bud before it spreads widely. What's more, you can convert disgruntled clients into fans. The Maritz study showed that when a company responds to a tweeted complaint, 83 percent of consumers said they liked or loved the firm for doing so—regardless of the outcome of the complaint.

There's another upside: you can boost your sales by replying speedily to people who are thinking about buying from you but first need some questions answered. Maggie Fox, CEO of Social Media Group, a Toronto-based social media marketing agency, says many posts are of this sort. "You need a process to ensure that you send this post to the right person in your company," she says. "Otherwise, you'll miss out on that sale."

A growing number of firms are experimenting with how best to adapt to this new era. Choksi says a significant number of his clients, including SMEs, have outsourced management of customer contacts via social media to his firm this year. But things are still at the trial stage.

The first step in developing a response system is to settle on criteria for determining whether to respond to a given post. Not all social media messages that refer to a company or product are tied to a customer service issue.

Choksi's firm uses software tools such as the response-management systems Tracx and Convers IQ to aggregate feeds from Twitter, Facebook, LinkedIn, blogs, and other sources, then does keyword searches to spot posts that need replies. Next, a customer service agent drafts a response and sends it to a designated person at the client, who approves or rewords the response, then posts it. Innovative Vision and its clients agree on canned responses to recurring issues—say, advising a customer: "Here's a URL for our FAQ page, on which point 4 answers your question."

There's an art to identifying the best search terms to use along with your brand and product names—and misspellings of these. Fox says you can spot complaints by trying terms such as "broken," "sucks," "unhappy"—or the harshest hashtag in the Twitterverse: #fail.

But searches are imperfect. "Computers understand only content, not context," says Choksi. "The best method is to have a human read the posts at high speed to identify which ones you should respond to."

Social media users expect a quick response. Fox recommends posting a reply within 12 hours—24 at most. And that includes weekends, she says: "If someone posts a complaint on Facebook on a Friday evening, it will fester all weekend."

Choksi suggests a far more demanding standard: reply within five minutes. "If you don't respond to a negative post for even four hours," he says, "it can go viral."

You'll have to judge which standard makes sense for your firm. Whatever your choice, be sure to avoid a common blunder. "Companies often don't respond because they don't have the answer yet," says Fox. "Big mistake. To consumers, it's perfectly acceptable to say, 'I'm looking into your problem. Let's take it offline to resolve.'"

Consumers who read a posted complaint look for whether the business has responded and promised to address the concern, but generally not at what happened after that. So, be sure to reply in public and invite the customer to continue the discussion through her medium of choice, such as phone, email, or private chat. Holmes says most people realize that "it's difficult to resolve a customer service issue in a 140-character snippet on Twitter." Besides, the customer probably doesn't want personal details posted publicly as you work with her to resolve her concern.

Fine, you may be thinking, but what's this going to cost? As with most things, that depends. "If you get more than 100 posts a day, it may make sense to outsource this so someone at your company doesn't have to stare at a screen all day," says Choksi. He says that his company can provide 24/7 coverage for an all-in cost of $10 per hour—totalling about $87,000 per year. If you opt instead for 9-to-5 coverage, the cost would be about $21,000. But if you get no more than a few dozen posts per day, says Choksi, you'd probably decide to handle them in-house.

If you do, you could use the free version of HootSuite to notify a designated employee on his mobile any time someone posts about a customer service issue. Or you could set up the software for the employee to check posts once a day—which, if there aren't many, might take half an hour. This employee could use the software's assignment tool to forward the post to the right colleague, such as someone who handles billing issues.

However you manage your responses to social media posts, says Fox, you must make it crystal clear whose responsibility this is: "Does marketing own this issue? Customer care? If it belongs to everyone, it belongs to no one."

Above all, companies should ensure that when someone posts a customer service issue about their business, they don't default to the worst possible response option: total silence.

Source: Sell. Sleep. #Fail, Jim McElgunn, Profit Guide (www.profitguide.com). Used with permission.

The bottom line in customer service is to keep your customer happy and coming back to you for future purchases. You also have to understand that you cannot please everyone. However, you must address this with the customer—never be rude. Try to solve their problem; if you cannot, apologize, and offer them either a discount or a refund. You do not want customers who are not satisfied. They will be very verbal about your poor customer service.

Research has shown that it costs as much as 15 times more to find a new customer than it does to keep an existing one. What's more, an increase of just 5 percent in your customer retention rate—that is just 5 percent more of your customers who come back to buy again and again—can increase your profits by as much as 75 percent.

So, why do most businesses focus much of their time and effort on tracking down new business, when the most profitable customers are the ones you already have?

In the Other Considerations box, sales expert Colleen Francis gives nine tips for the best ways to consistently and reliably exceed customers' expectations and build greater loyalty and higher profits—for life.

LOVE THE ONE YOU'RE WITH: 9 TIPS FOR BUILDING LOYALTY—AND COMMISSIONS!

1. **Be nice and say thank you!** You'll be surprised how much this matters—and how dramatic the results can be!

   For new customers, always say "thank you" within days (or if it's online, within hours) of receiving your first order. After that, if it doesn't make sense to offer thanks for every order, make sure you do it at least once a year.

   I encourage you to use handwritten thank you notes—preferably ones that aren't branded with your logo to look like an advertisement. Depending on the size of the order, you might also encourage your managers or executives to thank the customer as well.

   In addition, many of our clients have gone one step further and developed a special "welcome kit" for new clients, complete with a thank you note, a small but meaningful present, and useful information or perks for doing business with them. For instance, my karate school includes a 20 percent discount coupon for Dairy Queen in their welcome package, as a reward for having a good workout!

2. **Make it easy to be a customer** Find ways to remove the voice mail maze, long login forms, and other barriers you set up for prospects (or "suspects"). For example, get a dedicated phone line for repeat customers, or even have a separate customer-only website that makes it easier for them to re-order.

   To make your business more customer-friendly, start by pulling in one person from each department (preferably not management) for a brainstorming session, and ask each of them what changes they would implement to make it easier to do business with your company. Prioritize the list, and then starting working on the new ideas one at a time.

   If brainstorming isn't reasonable at your office, consider hiring an outside firm to "mystery shop" your organization. Have them act as a prospect or client to see what an outsider really experiences when they deal with your company. Then take their findings, and take action to improve those things that need fixing.

3. **Reward loyalty** Most companies make the mistake of rewarding only new customers. I know that I for one always get irked when my current suppliers give a better deal to new customers who may only be with them for a single order, than they offer to me, a client who has already proven my loyalty.

   No matter how thin your profit margins, you can afford to give your best customers discounts, special services, and even the red carpet treatment. Don't think so? Just do the math. Remember that new customers cost you up to 15 times more than repeat customers, and factor that into your profit-loss equations.

   In many cases, it's not even necessary to invest in a formal "loyalty" program. Simply invite your best customers to "inner circle" events, focus groups, or exclusive training. Even if the customer has to pay for the trip, at least they'll feel appreciated, and many of them will go out of their way to attend.

4. **Make it about them** Think about how good it feels when the waiter at your favourite restaurant greets you by name, brings you your favourite aperitif, and always remembers exactly where you like to sit. You tend to return again and again, and always tip a little more than usual, right?

   Believe me, that waiter knows exactly what he or she is doing. The good news is, the same approach works just as well with even the most battle-hardened enterprise IT buyers. Give them advice, counsel, and content specific to their needs, without being asked. Make sure any emails, phone calls, and special offers are customized to them, and their needs. And remember, it's all about them—not you.

5. **Ask them what they want** Most people want their opinions heard, and love being asked for their point of view. That's why simply surveying your customers will not only gain you some valuable information and insights into their needs and preferences. It can also communicate that you care what your customers think - and what they want.

   While you don't want to conduct surveys too often, you can ask for feedback after a particular transaction, or on an anniversary date. Remember: your clients care more about their own opinions than they do about yours. If you also report the results of the survey back to them, you'll give them a double confirmation of your concern.

6. **Ask them how you can help** Be truly interested in your customers, and show them that you sincerely want to help them. After all, they can't continue to do business with you if they don't continue to have a successful business of their own!

   One client of mine doubled her referrals almost instantly just by asking, *"Now…how can I help you?"* at the end of every client meeting. By putting the needs of her customers first, she demonstrated how much she cares about them. You'll find that many of your customers are genuinely surprised by a question like this, because as often as not, no one has ever asked them that before! And that's why your follow-up question is indispensable:

"You've helped my business grow by becoming part of our family network. I would like to help your business grow, too. So let me ask you, what type of people do you want to meet to help increase your revenues?"

7. **Get "buy" with a little help from their friends** The happier your customers are, the happier they will be to refer you to their own friends, colleagues, and associates.

   A referral from a customer is the highest form of trust. Trust is built on consistent behaviour over time, starting with continuously showing your customers that you're focused on *their* needs. Once you've established that level of trust, identify "apostles" among your most loyal customers, and empower them to crusade for your product or service.

   Of course, always reward customers who send business your way. At a minimum, a handwritten thank you note will show them you appreciate the effort they made. At the maximum, a gift will help you secure that relationship— and likely lead to even more referrals in the future.

8. **Get your customers involved** Build a customer panel or advisory board, and invite your customers to join. You'll be surprised by how many will be more than happy to join—and how many of those who do join will also start to share, refer, and buy more as a result of their participation.

   As an added bonus, if you listen and act on what they have to say, you'll not only build their trust and loyalty, but you'll also make them more willing to reach out to new prospects on your behalf.

9. **Ensure everyone in your company is involved** Last, but most definitely not least, make sure everyone in your company knows how important the customer is, and develop a foolproof communications plan that puts that knowledge into practice.

   It takes years to build a great relationship, and just one big mistake to end it. The last thing you want after putting all this work into building loyalty is to have one of your representatives thanking a customer one day, and then having another treat them like an anonymous prospect the next!

   Remember: whether they're responsible for shipping products, setting up accounts, collecting payments, or running a marketing event, everyone in your company who will talk to your customers at some point is a customer service rep. So make sure they all know who your most important customers are—and how they should be treated.

   In fact, many of my clients find that putting all of their employees through basic customer service and sales training can be an exceptionally profitable investment. Every time anyone talks to a customer, they have the potential to either earn more business and loyalty, or lose it. Make sure you maximize every opportunity you have to treat your customers well, and the results will speak for themselves.

   It's easy these days to complain about needy, demanding, or high maintenance customers and clients. The only thing worse is not having needy, high maintenance, demanding—or any—customers at all!

   Get over it! Refocus your time, energy, and budget on building profitable relationships with your existing customers, and do everything you can to keep the people who keep the lights on happy.

Source: Love the One You're With: 9 Tips for Building Loyalty—and Commissions! Author: Colleen Francis, president and founder, Engage Selling (www.engageselling.com). Used with permission.

MANAGING YOUR TIME

With so much to do, it is critical for businesses to organize and manage their time to ensure they are doing everything that needs to be done when it needs to be done. As a small business owner, time is one thing that you do not have a lot of, and it is important that you know how to be more effective with it.

Plan your Day

Before you leave your office for the day, create a to-do list for the next day. Block out time for specific tasks that you need to complete. Always add some time for the unexpected items that will invariably happen during the day. Prioritize your tasks.

Start Your Day Early

Starting your day early has its advantages. The time can be used to respond to emails and make phone calls (you will be amazed at the number of people that start work early), and for the most part, you will not have any interruptions. It is much easier to work when no one else is around.

Do not Let Distractions Get in the Way

Make a point of keeping distractions at bay. Set specific times during the day to read and respond to email. Do not let unwanted phone calls get in the way. If someone is calling to catch up, tell them you are in the middle of something, and arrange a time to get together for lunch or coffee. You need to stay focused on what you want to accomplish during the time you have allotted to complete the task.

Take a Break

Always make time to take a break during the day. This will clear your mind and help you think through any challenges you might be facing. Often, walking away from something is the best way to find the answer you have been looking for.

Delegate

If you have employees then delegate some tasks to them. Give them a time to complete the task, and follow-up to ensure they are on top of it.

F Y I

Canadian Professional Sales Association The knowledge base contains articles on sales techniques. (www.cpsa.com)

Engage Selling Solutions Colleen Francis, a successful sales trainer and speaker has numerous articles on her website to do with selling. Sign up on her website to receive news articles. (www.engageselling.com)

Mark Evans Tech Mark Evans works with small business to help them with their marketing. As marketing and sales are usually intertwined when you are starting your business, you will find articles to do with sales on the website. You can also sign up for his blog. (www.markevanstech.com)

SmartCallingOnline A collection of articles on how to prospect and telesales training. (www.smartcallingonline.com)

LEARNING OBJECTIVES SUMMARY

LO1 The sales process is what a small business owner does to close the sale and get a signed contract for work to be performed and payment issued for the completed work. To close a sale, you have to start with being prepared by:

- ensuring your branding and visual identity are professional looking
- having an updated website
- dressing professionally
- leaving a copy of your brochure or documentation of some sort that outlines what you have discussed at the meeting
- sending a personal thank-you note
- generating leads by:
  - working with other consultants who offer services that complement your business
  - offering referral rewards to current customers
  - writing for an established publication
  - participating in user forums
  - cold calling

LO2 Overcoming sales objections:

- I'm too busy—know your customer and their business, and then promise them something, for example, your product will increase productivity, save them time and money
- the timing isn't right—if your product or service will help them with their time, then give them the benefits of why they should meet with you now and not wait
- pricing—show prospects the value and benefits of what you are selling, how it will benefit them by saving them time and money by being productive, or how it will make their job much easier
- what makes you different from your competitor?—explain the differences and why you are better suited to the company
- we don' know who you are—share testimonials, case studies, and references from other clients. Be honest with them and start building the relationship by staying in touch and meeting for a coffee to get to know each other away from the office

- already working with a supplier and don't want to make a change—offer a free trial for them to evaluate; stay in touch while the free trial is in place to see if they are using the product and what they like and dislike; and make changes, if necessary
- have to get approval or discuss with others—do not be pushy, but if you see something that may be of interest to them, send it along; this keeps you in their mind. Every so often make a call to see if they have made a decision yet, and ask if there is anything you can do to help with the decision
- we don't need it—explain the value and benefits to them. If they see that it will benefit them, it will make it much easier to overcome the objection

LO3 The following points should be covered in your presentation:

- how to build rapport with your customer
- demonstrate your product/service to the client
- ask questions
- answer their questions
- ask for the business

LO4 To successfully close the sale, you should:

- make sure you are talking to and working with the decision maker
- control and direct the customer through each step of the sales process
- give the customer options and help them make their decision
- ask what it will take to get their business

LO5 Without customers, you do not have sales; and if you do not have sales, then you will not be in business long. Treat your customers with kid gloves, and:

- help your customer make a decision
- greet your customer by name
- listen to your customer
- be transparent, and take responsibility

For more information on the resources available from McGraw-Hill Ryerson, go to www.mcgrawhill.ca/he/solutions.

STAGE 10

BUYING A BUSINESS

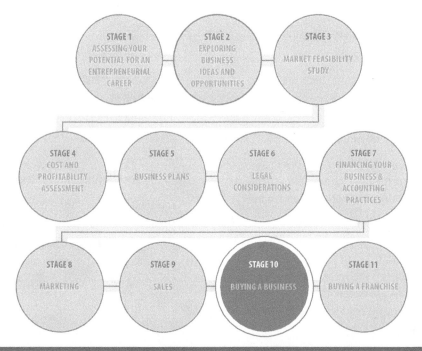

| STAGE 1 ASSESSING YOUR POTENTIAL FOR AN ENTREPRENEURIAL CAREER | STAGE 2 EXPLORING BUSINESS IDEAS AND OPPORTUNITIES | STAGE 3 MARKET FEASIBILITY STUDY |

| STAGE 4 COST AND PROFITABILITY ASSESSMENT | STAGE 5 BUSINESS PLANS | STAGE 6 LEGAL CONSIDERATIONS | STAGE 7 FINANCING YOUR BUSINESS & ACCOUNTING PRACTICES |

| STAGE 8 MARKETING | STAGE 9 SALES | STAGE 10 BUYING A BUSINESS | STAGE 11 BUYING A FRANCHISE |

LEARNING OBJECTIVES

By the end of this stage, you should be able to:

LO1 Recognize the advantages and disadvantages of buying an existing business.

LO2 Identify the factors to consider when buying a business.

LO3 Determine an appropriate price to pay for a business.

BUFFERBOX—PARCEL DELIVERY: THE WAY IT SHOULD BE

You experience this all too often—coming home to see a failed delivery notice on your door or your precious package left sitting in plain sight at your doorstep. Online shopping is supposed to be cost effective and time saving, but parcel delivery makes it anything but that.

Founded in May 2011, BufferBox, a technology startup in the eCommerce and logistics industry located in Kitchener–Waterloo, Ontario, came up with an idea that would ease the frustration of deliveries. BufferBox's technology allows online shoppers to pick up their purchases anytime, at their convenience, from automated, self-serve parcel pick-up stations.

BufferBox makes rage-inspiring missed deliveries a thing of the past. You ship your product to one of BufferBox's network of self-serve parcel pick-up stations and enter the PIN code you were emailed at the pick-up station at your convenience. A door will then magically pop open with your package.

It did not take long for the three young founders, Aditya Bali, Jay Shah, and Mike McCauley to see the results of their hard work. On November 30, 2012, BufferBox posted the following announcement on their blog:

We are excited to announce that BufferBox has been acquired by Google!

We have been able to achieve more than we could have ever imagined since we started working on our idea a couple years ago, and the team couldn't be more excited about the future. As online shopping becomes a bigger part of how you buy products, we look forward to playing a part in bringing that experience to the next level. We are happy to share that it will be business as usual for our users and we are looking forward to continuing to build out the service.

It has been an incredible journey and we'd like to thank everyone who has played such an important part in enabling us to make it this far. We couldn't be happier to be able to continue building out our vision within Google.

To learn more about BufferBox, visit their website (www. bufferbox.com).

Source: www.bufferbox.com

Google is known for purchasing companies and making many young entrepreneurs very wealthy before they hit the age of 30. In fact, some are still in university and in the early stages of building their startup and have not really given any thought to selling their businesses.

Stages One and Two of this book have provided you with a means of evaluating your personal potential for an entrepreneurial career and a procedure for generating and evaluating the basic attractiveness of an idea on which to base your own business. The obvious route to self-employment is to start a business of your own based on this idea. Another route that should be explored is that of buying an existing firm. For many people, this may even be their preferred course of action. How do you decide which route to take?

But not everyone wants to start from scratch and think buying an established business is what they would prefer to do. Stage Ten discusses the various aspects that should be evaluated in considering whether you should start a new business or buy an existing one.

ADVANTAGES AND DISADVANTAGES OF BUYING AN EXISTING BUSINESS

LO1

The case for buying an existing firm, as against setting up a new one of your own, is not clear-cut either way. Each situation must be decided on its merits. There are distinct advantages and disadvantages to each course of action. You must consider how well your personal preferences fit into each of these options. Table 10.1 gives both some of the advantages and disadvantages of buying a business.

As you can see, there are both pluses and minuses in choosing to acquire an established business. You should view this option in terms of whether it will enable you to achieve your personal objectives. How do these advantages and disadvantages compare with those of starting a new business of your own? In buying an existing business do you see a reasonable opportunity to succeed? No one else can really advise you what to do. Instead, you must "do your own thing" and match the alternatives with your abilities and interests. Refer to Figure 10.1.

HOW TO FIND THE RIGHT BUSINESS TO BUY

Just finding a business to buy is as easy as searching for listings in newspapers or online, but finding a business acquisition to match your desires and experiences is a time-consuming and difficult process. Hundreds of businesses change hands every year, so it should be possible to find one that appeals to you if you are sufficiently determined and persistent. However, rather than being sold as a result of an advertisement in some newspaper, most businesses are sold to people who had some active business relationship with the company when it became available. It is usually not sufficient for an individual determined to acquire a business to sit and wait for the right opportunity to come along. You must go looking and do so with a plan of how you are going to assess whether this is the right fit for you.

TABLE 10.1 ADVANTAGES AND DISADVANTAGES OF BUYING A BUSINESS	
ADVANTAGES OF BUYING A BUSINESS	**DISADVANTAGES OF BUYING A BUSINESS**
• Buying an existing business can reduce the risk. The existing business is already a proven entity. And it is often easier to obtain financing for an established operation than for a new one.	• The physical facilities (the building and equipment) and product line may be old and obsolete.
• Acquiring a "going concern" with a good past history increases the likelihood of a successful operation for the new owner.	• Union/management relationships may be poor.
	• Present personnel may be unproductive and have a poor track record.
• Established business has a proven location.	• The business may have a poor location.
• The established firm already has a product or service that is presently being produced, distributed, and sold.	• The inventory may contain a large amount of "dead" stock.
• The equipment needed for production is already available, and its limitations and capabilities are known in advance.	• As a buyer, you inherit any ill will that may exist toward the established firm among customers or suppliers.
• The business has an established clientele.	• A high percentage of the assets may be in poor-quality accounts receivable.
• The business has established relationships with banks, trade creditors, and other sources of financial support.	• The financial condition of the business, and its relationships with financial institutions, may be poor.
• An existing firm can often be acquired at a good price. The owner may be forced to sell the operation at a low price relative to the value of the assets in the business.	• As an entrepreneur, you have less freedom of choice in defining the nature of the business if you purchase an existing firm.

FIGURE 10.1   BUYING A BUSINESS

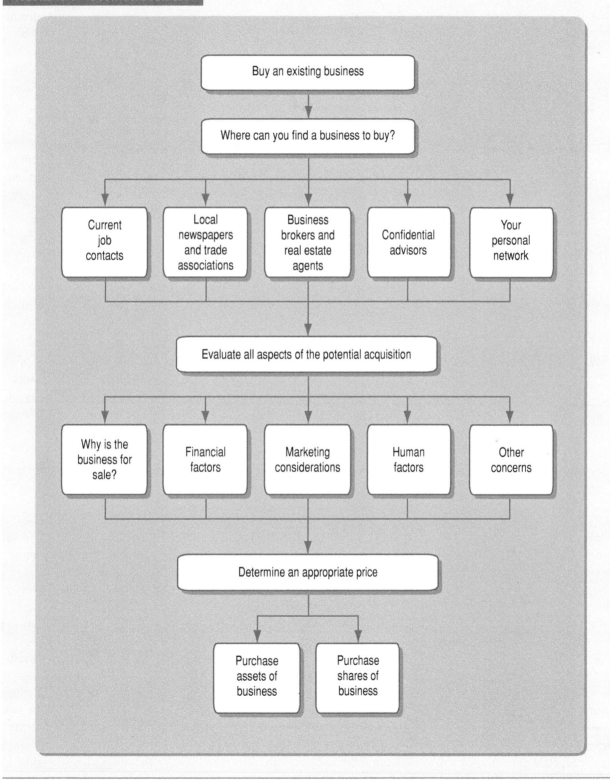

There are basically five different sources through which you may obtain information regarding attractive companies to buy:

1. **Current job contacts** Acquisition candidates may include present or potential competitors of your current employer, suppliers, customers, and perhaps even your present employer. These situations probably provide the best match between your experience and strengths and the unique requirements of the business. This was how Scott Hallam came to buy Delfino Roofing from its previous owner after having worked in the business (see the Entrepreneurs in Action box).

2. **Local newspapers and trade associations** This may involve making "cold calls" to firms that look good or that you have an interest in; such firms may be identified from Chamber of Commerce directories and trade association membership lists. Another way is to place "Acquisition Wanted" advertisements in several major newspapers. In addition, despite what has been said earlier, you may wish to follow up on some advertisements in the "Business Opportunities" section of the major financial papers. Every now and then, an advertisement that would warrant your consideration may appear in these sections.

3. **Business brokers and commercial real estate agents** These individuals are professionals who work at bringing buyers and sellers together for a commission. The commission, typically payable by the seller, varies with the size of the deal but may be as high as 10 percent of the negotiated purchase price.

4. **Confidential advisers** These include the loans officer at your bank, securities brokers, professional accountants, and lawyers. These advisers are often aware of what businesses are or may soon be available for sale. These sources may be difficult to use, however, because their information is shared mostly with other clients with whom they have developed some relationship over time. In many cases, it may be necessary for you to have gained the confidence of the source over an extended period.

5. **Your personal network** These include venture capital firms, personal friends and acquaintances, and insurance brokers and agents. Essentially, you should consider all individuals within your personal network of business contacts that may have access to information on attractive businesses for sale. This requires letting many of these people know about your search and the kind of business that you are looking for. You will need to keep reminding them about your interest so that when the information comes along, there is a good probability that it will make its way to you.

IMPORTANT FACTORS TO CONSIDER LO2

Before starting the process of evaluating a business, you should review your own personal requirements. This includes understanding your strengths and weaknesses, what you enjoy and do not enjoy, type of lifestyle you are seeking (work hours etc.), and your personal income requirements. You may find a business in an industry that you have never worked in before, but the qualities of the business may match your strengths. If your strength is operations and efficiencies, look for businesses where this is the key to the business being successful, such as manufacturing or logistics. If your sales skills are poor or you dislike sales, you may wish to avoid businesses where a strong sales team is critical to the company's success, even if it is the perfect business on paper.

An essential requirement for the successful purchase of an existing firm is to know how to assess and evaluate the operation. This is a complicated process, so you are well advised to have professionals, such as an accountant, lawyer, or business evaluator, assist you in negotiations when buying a business. As a potential buyer, you should also have a good understanding of the nature of the target business and the industry in which it competes to be able to assess its future performance, strengths, weaknesses, unexploited market opportunities, and other factors. No business is perfect, but you should ensure you have done your research and sought the appropriate guidance for you to make an informed decision. A number of basic factors must be considered in determining the value of the business to you. Some of these are more complex and involved than others, but each one must be carefully investigated and studied. Why the business is for sale is the most important of these concerns.

ENTREPRENEURS IN ACTION

FROM LABOURER TO OWNER

Scott Hallam started working for Delfino Roofing part time while he was studying business at college. He was introduced to the owner by someone in the program he was taking. The company was just starting one of its first jobs when Scott agreed to help. He put in time on weekends and whenever he didn't have class or obligations for his own online startup during the week. Scott had a brief background of flat roofing for a major company with a competitive labour force but had not yet done any shingling, so it took a little getting used to. Luckily, the work ethic that he had developed with the previous company made him stand out as a labourer and allowed him to gain experience and move up quickly. Within a few months of part-time work, Scott had the summer to roof full-time and (probably thanks to some persistence) was eventually given a position as a shingler.

At the same time Scott continued to work on his online business; however, ParkInMyDriveway reached a point where the effort to launch was much greater than its potential to be successful and profitable. He and his partner, John, never fully closed down the idea. They spent months coming up with ideas to rebrand and repackage the tools they had created to provide a valuable offering to anyone they could think of. They compiled lists of potential customers for a number of the more promising ideas and cold-called people for weeks. Scott and John even went as far as meeting with larger property and asset management firms to work with them in designing management tools to solve their issues with rental management, etc.

In the end, they took the website down but left the Facebook page and other media available to the public. In their opinion, there wasn't any point in taking those tools down; if people have a related need in the future, there would be potential to connect with them about it. The business never fully went live, no one was hurt by it, and thus it is not something either partner is ashamed of; not many people hit a home-run with their first business.

After ParkInMyDriveway ended, Scott's first priority was to get a job with a guaranteed paycheque until he could get ahead on bills again and have the freedom to be entrepreneurial. He looked around for jobs that were available to someone with his experience and education, but, as he had assumed, any business development position that provided any potential for growth within a company required a university degree or 5–10 years industry experience. He had taken a two-year program in small business and entrepreneurship, so he had not expected it to launch him into a career.

By this point, he had been working with Delfino Roofing for close to three years; part time during school, full time

DELFINO ROOFING

during summers, and for a year after college (while managing ParkInMyDriveway). He had become one of the more experienced guys on the crew and had gained a wealth of knowledge about many different roofing systems, etc. Naturally, he decided to continue with the company indefinitely until he figured out what it was he wanted to do.

Scott has a love for small business as both an entrepreneur and an employee. He stayed with Delfino after ParkInMyDriveway because they had a growing business that was able to offer opportunity and room for growth. The year before he purchased the company he was given many fortunate opportunities.

He asked for, and received, more responsibility, which led to running crews. It was not long before Scott decided to offer some free marketing help to the owner. It was a sacrifice of time and effort, but a couple of decent marketing ideas led to the owner leaving him in charge of a limited budget for marketing.

After becoming head of marketing and a foreman, Scott started realizing just how much potential the company had to grow and be successful. He was itching to get involved in a business venture somehow again and so threw caution to the wind and said that he would either have to gain some more meaningful experience in business management within the company or look for it elsewhere. To his complete disbelief, the owner quickly agreed.

They had done well with every project they took on and developed a reputation that was allowing them to expand quickly, so Scott offered to help by preparing, selling, and planning the projects that he would run in exchange for a small commission. It didn't take long for Scott to realize that he had underestimated the task and had to work with the owner to revamp his sales funnel and overall system for tracking and managing information for each estimate and/or project.

As Scott started working deeper and deeper into the company he soon discovered that the owner was growing tired of the business. Furthermore, he felt unable to make his crews run efficiently enough at a consistent and worthwhile profit margin to justify taking on the extra business that was coming his way.

It was around that time that Scott began to formulate ideas of how they could make the business more successful. When the owner approached him to say he was looking to go back to school for business, Scott was more than happy to make a deal

(continued)

to purchase the company. The owner made a gracious offer and the two began negotiating a purchase arrangement.

At this point Scott had been giving a lot of sweat equity to the company and didn't have enough money on hand to make the purchase. It was another shot in the dark, but he proposed a payment plan. Thanks to the previous owner's good nature, strong relationships with his employees, and desire to keep them employed, he agreed.

In late August of 2012, Scott purchased all of the shares of the company through an agreement which stipulated that he made payments, based on his own profits, to pay off the value of all the company assets that were handed over to him at that time. Compensation was added to the total for the brand and reputation that came with the company, but the valuation of the company was significantly low in consideration of the fact that he had helped to get it to that point. Scott did as much due diligence as he could on the company. The paperwork for the company was not maintained well and certain records were lost or omitted from everything he looked over.

He felt weary but purchased the company in a manner that would allow him to exit relatively unharmed, if he were to be blindsided with debt or other unforeseen issues. Overall, he took a calculated risk because he saw the potential of the company and believed in his plan to make it profitable.

Since purchasing the business, Scott has faced tons of challenges; enough to make him want to pull his hair out at times. But he's learned to manage the stress and enjoy the process. The biggest challenge he faced was a WSIB audit that was done before his first winter of ownership. All of the existing paperwork indicated that they were on par with safety insurance, but due to poor bookkeeping in the company's first three years, Scott ended up being faced with significant debt. He had the choice to pack it in or pay the debt but decided it was worth it to pay the debt and start growing the company.

The business had about four to five steady full-time employees when he purchased Delfino Roofing and is projecting to have 13 by the summer. Expanding a business this quickly is challenging, Scott says, but necessary in a market so dependent on price and reputation.

Although there have been many challenges Scott is dedicated and determined to make his business grow, while maintaining a solid reputation.

With Scott's two new business partners, Joshua Thornley and John Ouellette, who bring a wealth of experience to their team, Delfino Roofing and their dedicated professionals work hard to provide reliable, efficient, and customer-friendly service for their customers and hope to continue growing to better serve Ottawa and surrounding areas for years to come.

Source: Delfino Roofing. Interview by Wendy Mayhew, used with Permission. April 2013.

WHY IS THE BUSINESS FOR SALE?

You should have this question in mind at all times during the evaluation of a possible acquisition. When the owner of a business decides to dispose of it, the reason presented to the public may be somewhat different from the facts of the situation. Owners may be quite willing to express some reasons for wanting to sell their businesses. They wish to retire, or they want to move to another city, or illness is pressuring the owner to leave the business. But there are a number of others that the current owner may not be quite so likely to volunteer. For example, the owner may be experiencing family pressures or marital problems, or perhaps the owner sees a better business opportunity somewhere else. None of these reasons is cause for concern. But what if the company needs more financing than the owner can raise, or the current market for the firm's products is depressed? What if competitors are moving in with more effective products or methods, or the current plant and equipment is worn out or obsolete, and the firm is no longer able to compete successfully? And what if the firm has to contend with new government regulations that are creating some difficulties, or certain key employees are leaving the firm to set up a similar business of their own?

As you can see, there are many possible reasons why a business may be up for sale. It is important that you retain a skeptical attitude because behind each of the offered explanations may be a number of hidden ones. A skeptical attitude forces you to examine the situation from all angles and not necessarily accept at face value everything you are told. When the real reasons for selling are factors that may lead to the eventual collapse of the company, the present owner may be hard-pressed to justify your purchase of the enterprise.

This is not to say that all businesses for sale are bad opportunities. Many companies are sold for very plausible and honest reasons. However, to keep from losing your shirt as well as your savings, a detailed evaluation should be conducted to determine the true character of the business.

FINANCIAL FACTORS

An analysis of the financial statements of the firm being sold, preferably with the help of a professional accountant, can help you assess its current health. You should not fall into the trap, however, of accepting these statements as the absolute truth. Even in those situations where the statements have been audited (small businesses rarely have audited statements), many accounting techniques allow business owners to present a less than accurate picture of the financial situation of their company. One reason why seeking the advice of an accountant is so important is small business owners often have items on the financial statements that may not be required for the normal operations of the business, such as bonuses paid to the shareholders or rent that is above or below market rate because it is owned by a family member. Will you have the same rental arrangement? You need to understand the difference between the historical financial statements of the business as well as how the financials would look if you owned the business. There can be items that impact the statements in both positive and negative fashions. Adjustments such as these are made to determine Normalized Financial Statements. Preparation of these statements goes beyond the scope of this book, but you should be aware that this is normal practice and a cause for concern. Your adviser can review the types of adjustments and help you assess if there are any that could be a liability to you.

The most important financial factors are (1) the trend in profits, (2) ratio analysis, (3) the value of the business's tangible assets, (4) the value of the business's intangible assets, and (5) cash flow. Let us discuss each in turn.

The Trend in Profits

A study of the records of the business will indicate whether sales volume and profits have been increasing or decreasing. If they have been going up, it is useful to know which departments within the business, or products within the firm's product line, have accounted for this increased sales and/or profitability.

If sales and profits are declining, the question may arise as to whether this is due to a failure by the firm to keep up with the competition, to its inability to adjust to changing circumstances, or perhaps to a lack of selling effort. Some experience with this type of business situation, plus a few questions directed to appropriate sources, may elicit an explanation.

Ratio Analysis

For every size and type of business, there are certain financial ratios that have become generally accepted as reasonable for that kind of operation. Some information on these ratios is collected and published by trade organizations and associations, such as the National Retail Hardware Association or the National Association of Retail Grocers. Ratios have also been developed by various manufacturers for use by retailers that handle their product lines. Ratios for firms in a wide variety of retail, service, and manufacturing sectors are published by Dun & Bradstreet (www.dnb.com), the Risk Management Association (formerly Robert Morris Associates) (www.rmahq.org), and other companies. Industry Canada, as part of its SME Benchmarking Tool website (sme.ic.gc.ca), can provide information as well. A study of the ratios of any business offered for sale, compared with standard ratios for that industry and size of company, will quickly indicate any discrepancies. These discrepancies may be due to mismanagement, neglect, carelessness, or perhaps even the lack of appropriate financing. You should calculate the ratios for the business over a period of three to five years so that you can see trends year-over-year and compare them to the industry ratios. If you see positive or negative trends, you should gather information and ask questions to try to understand why these trends are occurring. Table 10.2 provides examples of the most frequently considered ratios, including the formula and sample calculation for each one.

All ratios are calculated from information on the firm's income statement or balance sheet. Figures 10.2 and 10.3 illustrate simplified financial statements for a hypothetical firm called the Campbell Co.

Other detailed financial and employment data on small businesses in Canada, by industry, are available from the SME Benchmarking Tool database of Industry Canada. These profiles are usually produced every two years, with 2010 being the most current available. These data can provide performance benchmarks for the financial planning of both startup and established businesses.

Keep in mind that financial ratios are open to wide interpretation and should be relied on only to get a general perspective of the relative financial health of the business, to measure the financial progress of the business from one period to another, or to flag major deviations from an industry or sector norm.

TABLE 10.2 FREQUENTLY CONSIDERED RATIOS

Formula	Description
Current Ratio $\text{Current Ratio} = \dfrac{\text{Current Assets}}{\text{Current Liabilities}}$	This is a measure of short-term solvency or whether the business has enough liquid assets to cover its short-term debts.
Quick Ratio $\text{Quick Ratio} = \dfrac{\text{Current Assets} - \text{Inventories}}{\text{Current Liabilities}}$	The quick ratio can be used to estimate the ability of a firm to pay off its short-term obligations without having to sell its inventory.
Debt to Net Worth Ratio Debt-to-Net-Worth Ratio $= \dfrac{\text{Total Outstanding Current and Long-Term Debt}}{\text{Net Worth}}$	The debt-to-net-worth ratio indicates the firm's obligations to its creditors relative to the owner's level of investment in the business. Debt includes current liabilities, long-term loans, bonds, and deferred payments; the owner's net worth includes the value of common stock, preferred stock, any capital surplus, and retained earnings. Any outstanding shareholders' loans to the business should be considered part of the owner's net worth rather than as part of the business's present debt.
Debt Service Ratio Debt-Service Coverage Ratio = Net Operating Income/Total Debt Service Net Operating Income = (Annual Net Income Before Tax + Interest Expense + Amortization & Depreciation + Other Discretionary and Non-cash Items, Such As Non-contractual Items Provided by Management) Total Debt Service = (Principal Repayment + Interest Payments + Lease Payments)	This ratio shows whether the company has enough cash to make its debt payments. Lenders will use this as one of the factors to determine whether the company can take on any further debt.
Gross Profit to Sales Ratio $\text{Gross-Profit-to-Sales Ratio} = \dfrac{\text{Gross Profit}}{\text{Net Sales}}$	This ratio is determined by dividing gross profit or gross margin by net sales. Gross profit is determined by deducting costs of goods sold from net sales. No general guidelines exist for this ratio or even among companies within an industry, as it can vary substantially.

Interpretation	Sample Calculation
A general rule of thumb is that a current ratio of 2:1 could be considered satisfactory for a typical manufacturing business. Service firms typically have a lower ratio, since they tend to have less inventory. However, as with any rule of thumb, extreme care should be exercised in evaluating this ratio. A cash-poor firm may be unable to pay its bills, even though its ratio appears to be acceptable. On the other hand, many businesses with a current ratio less than the rule of thumb are quite solvent. Too high a ratio can indicate the business is not utilizing its cash and other liquid assets very efficiently (not reinvesting in the business); too low a ratio may raise questions about the firm's ability to meet its short-term obligations. In practice, however, what is more important than the absolute level of the current ratio is how the ratio is changing over time. An improving current ratio would tend to indicate improved short-term financial solvency unless the business is building up excessive or obsolete inventories. Using both the current and quick ratio is important to identify the impact of inventories.	$\text{Current Ratio} = \dfrac{\$158,000}{\$95,000} = 1.66$
Inventories tend to lose their value faster than other assets if disposed of in a hurry. The quick ratio is probably a more valid test of the firm's ability to meet its current liabilities and pay its bills than the current ratio. Inventories can be obsolete or not saleable due to current market conditions (seasonal, recession, too much supply). If inventory cannot be converted to cash quickly, or for its fair value, inventory can give a misleading result of the short-term health of the business.	$\text{Current Ratio} = \dfrac{\$78,000}{\$95,000} = 0.82$
This ratio is commonly used by creditors to assess the risk involved in lending to the firm. For example, if the debt-to-net-worth ratio is too high, say, about 2:1 or 3:1, you may find it difficult to borrow additional funds for the business. Too low a ratio, on the other hand, may indicate the business is not being operated very efficiently and some profits are being sacrificed. Keep in mind that many smaller businesses may not operate with debt, especially if they do not require investment in equipment or other capital items.	Debt to Net Worth $= \dfrac{\$135,000}{\$50,000} = 2.70$
If the ratio equals one, then there is just enough cash to cover the annual debt payments. Below 1, there is not enough cash; and more than 1, there is cash left over; so the higher the ratio, the better. Depending on the lender, company, and industry, a lender will require this ratio to be 1.15:1.4 with the new debt in place, before considering approval of the loan.	Debt-Service Coverage Ratio $= 37/44 = .84$ Net Operating Income $= 18 + 9 = 10 = 37$ Total Debt Service $= 35 + 9 + 0 = 44$
What sales level do you need in order to cover your basic overhead? If you pick an industry with low gross profit margins, you need to understand that it takes a lot more sales to just cover basic overhead than a business with higher gross profit.	Gross Profit to Sales $= \dfrac{\$133,000}{\$425,000} = 0.31 \text{ or } 31\%$

(continued)

TABLE 10.2   FREQUENTLY CONSIDERED RATIOS (*CONTINUED*)

Formula	Description
Gross Profit to Sales Ratio (continued)	This ratio is very important because it shows how profitable the business is by providing its product or service, before overheads, such as rent, advertising, and administration.
Net Profit to Sales Ratio $$\text{Net-Profit-to-Sales Ratio} = \frac{\text{Net Profit (Before or After Taxes)}}{\text{Net Sales}}$$	This ratio is calculated by dividing net profit by net sales. You may use net profit either before or after taxes. This ratio helps assess the overhead structure of the business. For instance, if gross profit is at industry norm but net profit is below, what in the firm's overhead structure is too high? The trend of this ratio can also show cost structure increasing or decreasing.
Return on Assets $$\text{Return on Assets} = \frac{\text{Net Profit (Before or After Taxes)}}{\text{Total Assets}}$$	This ratio is determined by dividing net profit (before or after taxes) by total assets. It is an excellent indicator of whether all the firm's assets are contributing to its profits and how effectively the assets are being employed—the real test of economic success or failure.
Sales to Inventory Ratio $$\text{Sales-to-Inventory Ratio} = \frac{\text{Net Sales}}{(\text{Beginning Inventory} + \text{Ending Inventory})/2}$$	This does not indicate actual physical turnover, since inventories are usually valued at cost, while sales are based on selling prices, including markups, but this ratio does provide a reasonable yardstick for comparing stock-to-sales ratios of one business with another or with the average values for the industry.
Average Collection Period $$\text{Average Collection Period} = \frac{\text{Accounts Receivable}}{\text{Net Sales}/365}$$	To determine the average collection period for the business's outstanding accounts receivable, annual net sales are divided by 365 days to determine the business's average daily credit sales. These average daily credit sales are then divided into accounts receivable to obtain the average collection period.

Interpretation	Sample Calculation
As well, if you wish to scale the business to a much larger size, a company with low gross profits may not be that interesting to you, as the cost of acquiring new customers may not generate enough profits for it to be worthwhile. If this ratio is different from the industry norm, make sure gross profit is being calculated properly (includes all the right costs). Is there anything that can be done to improve it (such as investment in better equipment).	
As with the previous ratio, no general guidelines exist because of the variability among companies and industries. This figure can be as low as 1 percent or less for retail food stores and supermarkets and as high as 8 or 9 percent in some service sectors. Keep in mind that in small businesses, the owner's tax planning can impact these figures. Owners sometimes change their salary or bonuses every year, depending on the profitability of the business. See discussion on normalized earnings (Financial Factors).	Net Profit to Sales $$= \frac{\$13,500}{\$425,000} = 0.03 \text{ or } 3\%$$
If the firm purchases assets that do not generate operating income, such as purchasing vacant land that sits idle, it will lower this ratio. You may have initially thought that the higher asset value on the balance sheet was a positive aspect of the company. In buying the business, do you want to also buy the vacant land? Could your cash be invested with better return, such as new equipment or more labour? Or just held for future investment? Generally, the higher the ratio, the better, but it must be done in comparison with similar companies in the industry.	Return on Assets $$= \frac{\$13,500}{\$185,000} = 0.07 \text{ or } 7\%$$
This helps find out whether a firm is holding too much inventory (sales are slowing, too much investment in inventory) or not enough (missed sales opportunities, supply/buying/production problems).	Sales-to-Inventory Ratio $$= \frac{\$425,000}{\$75,000 + 80,000/2} = 5.48$$
This ratio is helpful in assessing the collectability of any outstanding receivables. It also can help understand the company's customer base or potentially the financial management or close oversight of the business. If the collection period is longer than others in the industry, are their customers having cash flow problems, or are they very large customers that pay slowly? These are important to understand the cash flow risks of the business. For most small businesses, 30–60 days is a normal range, but exceptions apply.	Average Collection Period $$= \frac{\$53,000}{\$425,000/365} = 45 \text{ days}$$

FIGURE 10.2   EXAMPLE OF SIMPLIFIED BALANCE SHEET

THE CAMPBELL CO. BALANCE SHEET
AS OF DECEMBER 31, 201Y

ASSETS (000s)

Current Assets

Cash	$ 25	
Accounts receivable	53	
Inventory	80	
Total current assets		$ 158 **(A)**

Fixed Assets

Machinery	$ 40		
Less: Accumulated depreciation	25	15	
Equipment and fixtures	30		
Less: Accumulated depreciation	18	12	
Total fixed assets			27 **(B)**
Total Assets (C = A + B)			$ 185 **(C)**

LIABILITIES AND OWNER'S EQUITY

Current Liabilities*

Accounts payable	$ 60	
Notes payable	35	
Total current liabilities		95

Long-Term Liabilities

Notes payable[†]	$ 40	
Total long-term liabilities		40
Total liabilities		$ 135 **(D)**

OWNER'S EQUITY

Capital investment	20	
Retained earnings	30	
Total owner's equity		50 **(E)**
Total Liabilities and Owner's Equity (F = D + E)		$ 185 **(F)**

*Debt is due within 12 months.

[†] Debt is due after 1 year.

Value of Tangible Assets

In assessing the balance sheet of the prospective acquisition, you must determine the actual or real value of the tangible assets. A physical count of the inventory must be taken to determine if the actual level corresponds to the level stated on the balance sheet. This inventory must also be appraised in terms of its age, quality, saleability, style, condition, balance, freshness, and so on. Most large inventories will have some obsolescence. You must determine whether the present inventory is consistent with current market conditions. Also, take care that the seller does not sell this inventory after you have checked it. Any consignment goods in inventory should be clearly identified as well. This evaluation is best performed by someone with considerable experience in the industry involved. Perhaps you can hire the services of the owner of a similar but noncompeting firm to assist you in this appraisal.

FIGURE 10.3   EXAMPLE OF SIMPLIFIED INCOME STATEMENT

THE CAMPBELL CO.
INCOME STATEMENT
FOR YEAR ENDING DECEMBER 31, 201Y

	(000s)	
Gross sales	$428	
Less: Returns	3	
Net Sales		**$ 425 (A)**
Cost of goods sold:		
Beginning inventory	$ 75	
Plus: Net purchases	297	
Cost of goods available	372	
Less: Ending inventory	80	
Cost of Goods Sold		**292 (B)**
Gross Profit (C = A − B)		**$ 133 (C)**
Selling Expenses		**$ 29 (D)**
Administrative expenses:		
Office salaries	$ 60	
Interest	9	
Depreciation	10	
Other administrative expenses	7	
Total Administrative Expenses		**86 (E)**
Profit Before Income Tax (F = C − D − E)		**$ 18 (F)**
Income Tax (G = 25% of F)		**4.5 (G)**
Net Profit (G = F − G)		**$ 13.5 (H)**

You must also check the age of any outstanding accounts receivable. Some businesses continue to carry accounts receivable on their books that should have been charged off as bad debts, resulting in an overstatement of the firm's profit and value. Generally, the older the receivables, the lower is their value. Old outstanding accounts may reveal a slack credit policy of the present owner. These old accounts will have to be discounted in determining the present value of the business.

The fixed assets of the business must also be scrutinized. You should determine if the furniture, fixtures, equipment, and building are stated at their market or depreciated value. Some questions you should ask include: How modern are these assets? Are they in operating condition? How much will it cost to keep these assets in operation? Are the assets all paid for? You must be aware of any liens or chattel mortgages that may have been placed against these assets. This pledging of assets to secure a debt is a normal business practice; however, you should know about any such mortgages. Other liabilities, such as unpaid bills, back taxes, back pay to employees, and so on, may be hidden; you must be aware of the possibility of their existence and contract with the seller that all claims not shown on the balance sheet will be assumed by him or her.

Value of Intangible Assets

In addition to the more obvious physical goods and equipment, certain intangible assets may also have a real value to a prospective purchaser. Among the most important of these are goodwill; franchise and licensing rights; and patents, trademarks, and copyrights.

You must be very realistic in determining what you can afford or are prepared to pay for goodwill. Is the public's present attitude toward the business a valuable asset that is worth money, or is it a liability? Typically, few businesses that are for sale have much goodwill value. Is any goodwill associated with the business personal to the owner or largely commercial due to the location, reputation, and other characteristics of the business? If largely personal, this goodwill may not be transferable to a new owner, so you should not pay very much for it. Many business owners, however, often have very unrealistic and inflated ideas of the goodwill associated with their business because they have built it up over the years with their own "sweat equity" and, therefore, are not very objective. So you should be careful and talk to customers, suppliers, neighbours, employees, and perhaps even competitors to determine if this level of goodwill does actually exist.

In fact, quite often, things are not always as they appear. It did not take long for Tom Kramer to get his first shock after purchasing Grant Cameron's pump distribution business. Within the first week, Kramer received a letter from a supplier who had no idea that Tom had purchased the business. Despite everybody's best efforts to create a smooth changeover, the supplier had been left out of discussions because he represented a very small percentage of revenue. The supplier cancelled his contract, but to make matters even worse, the previous owner had made a large commitment to the supplier by hiring someone for his contract (Tom had no choice but to let the employee go). See the Entrepreneurs in Action box.

If franchise, licensing, or other rights are involved in the business, you should make certain that you understand the terms and conditions associated with such rights and that these rights will be transferred to you on acquisition of the company. An effort should also be made to determine the market value of any patents, trademarks, or copyrights the company may hold and to ensure these are part of the sale—that is they do not remain with the current owner on completion of the transaction.

What do you like about being an Entrepreneur?

I love to build things and I love to see other people build things. You start with this little idea—there is something missing that has not yet been created— and you start working on it. You show it around and get other people excited. They join to help you build it. Overnight, you have turned into an entrepreneur. You're not just building it, you are also building the thing that builds it: A Company. More and more things need to be built—people, systems, processes, value systems, channels, and so on. Entrepreneurship is beautiful because it allows people who like to build things to build things. Then, overnight, it ratchets up the difficulty. Overnight there are hundreds more things that need building, then thousands. There are always infinite challenges for the builder.

Tobias Lüke
Founder & CEO
Shopify
www.shopify.com

Cash Flow

You must also observe the cash flows generated by the operation. A business can be very profitable but chronically low in cash due to overly generous credit terms, excessive inventory levels, or heavy fixed-interest payments. You must assure yourself that upon your entry into the business you will have sufficient inflows of cash to meet your cash outflow requirements. Constant cash problems can indicate that the business is possibly being run by ineffective management or that the firm's resources have generally been badly allocated. You must ask yourself if you have the know-how to overcome this misallocation of resources. If the firm's cash flow is very low and the long-term debt is quite high, the business may be eating up its capital to pay the debt or possibly defaulting on its debt. If you are to contend with such issues, you may have to increase the firm's debt or be prepared to invest more capital in the business to ease the cash flow problem.

ENTREPRENEURS IN ACTION

A NEW BUSINESS OWNER PUMPS IT UP

After all the bankers and lawyers went away, Tom Kramer sat down to take a good long look at the business he'd just bought.

He wanted to move slowly. As the former vice-president of a large organization, he'd been involved in many acquisitions. This time, he had Smith Cameron Process Solution's previous owner Grant Cameron by his side for a year, but it was also Kramer's first time as owner.

The first shock came almost immediately.

"The first week, Grant received a letter from a supplier who had no idea that we'd made the transition," Kramer said. Despite everybody's best efforts to create a smooth changeover, this supplier had been left out of earlier discussions because he represented a very small percentage of revenue.

The supplier cancelled its contract, but that wasn't the worst of it. "Grant had made a rather large commitment to this supplier by hiring a guy," Kramer said. "It became clear the only option we had was to let the guy go with the contract."

So much for moving slowly.

Kramer, 50, turned his attention to Cameron.

Kramer knew from previous experience that most sellers start with euphoria and then move on to seller's remorse. They have "those anxiety moments—feeling like they've lost all sense of direction even though they knew this was coming," Kramer said. He was fortunate. Cameron felt neither grief nor remorse after selling Smith Cameron, which distributes industrial and commercial pumps and fluid control systems.

"Tom had a fantastic owner in Grant," said business consultant Tara Landes, president of Bellrock Benchmarking Inc., whom Kramer hired to implement a thorough strategic plan. "Having been in this situation many times before, I can tell you, this guy was great. He stuck around, he did his job, he didn't try to make waves with the staff."

That's not to say it was easy.

Cameron was a day-to-day manager who ran into the middle of every fire. Kramer could drive an excavator if need be, but he lacked technical depth in his new industry.

Where Cameron was self taught, Kramer attends an annual Harvard business management program. Where Cameron had built up a business from scratch, Kramer had attained senior management posts with large organizations.

To Kramer's initial discomfort, he was forced to put a lot of trust in three key employees, and he desperately needed new business systems.

"The whole company reported to Grant," Kramer said. "It was perfectly pancake flat. The shipper/receiver reported to Grant!"

OlivierI/Dreamstime.com

Meanwhile, Cameron's 30 loyal employees "seemed to be waiting for the ice to crack beneath their feet," Kramer recalled. His quarterly "town hall" meetings were an awkward exercise in hearing his own voice.

At the same time, Kramer was quietly battling his own self doubt. "The guy's done this for 30 years, the business was built this way, maybe it only operates this way!" he told himself. "What if I make a decision in no longer doing it exactly this way? Maybe I lose all the money I just invested. I bet the farm!"

Kramer ultimately invested six figures in outside consulting that first year to engage employees and really understand the company's value proposition. One of his first big moves was exactly what Cameron had identified as a key strategy but hadn't had the energy or ability to do—expand into Alberta. Kramer bought a five-employee service company in Edmonton.

Looking back, Cameron remembers the strategic plan implementation as "a very painful" process. "My blood pressure went up quite a bit," Cameron said. "I understand why he wanted to do it and perhaps needed to do it, but it wasn't how I ran the company so it was very foreign to me."

Eight or nine months after the sale, Cameron concluded he was hindering more than helping. "I was spending a lot of time avoiding train wrecks for specific projects and Tom took me aside: 'As much as I appreciate you keeping things on the rails, I'd appreciate you letting the train wreck happen.'"

Kramer, on the other hand, knows he held back on some needed changes because it felt uncomfortable going ahead while Cameron was still around. "Some of the mistakes I made? Not listening to my gut enough," Kramer said. "My gut was telling me to do something, but my heart was telling me 'Maybe

(continued)

just delay it.' . . . So far, all of them except for one have turned out fine. We just didn't get as far as fast."

Not as fast?

Smith Cameron's revenue has grown 34 percent in 22 months. The three key employees have become part owners. Employees are no longer silent and their numbers have swollen to 43. Kramer and Cameron still talk about company issues.

SOME TIPS FROM BUSINESS CONSULTANT TARA LANDES

Buying a business is like getting married and everybody focuses only on the wedding and forgets about the marriage, Tara Landes says. Even people who know what they want to do differently forget to look at how, and that's the hard part.

- Plan an exit strategy for the old owners. Knowing their departure date is not enough. How, specifically, will you disengage them from the day to day? Confront difficult issues head on. "While you may feel uncomfortable talking about particular issues, that's not a good enough reason not to do it. It's too expensive," Landes said. "At a minimum, do some sort of cost benefit analysis and figure out how much it will cost you to delay until that owner's gone."

- Reassure staff. "One thing Tom did very well was telling everyone again and again that they were not going to be fired," Landes said. "You know you've done it enough times when the staff say to you 'OK, I get it, stop telling me that.' Until they do that, you haven't done it enough.'"

- Examine business systems, not just computer systems. What managerial reports are they using, what regular meetings do they hold and what are the agendas? Do job descriptions exist? Many buyers think they are doing this during due diligence, but don't really think it through, Landes warned. If you can't do it yourself in the first few weeks post-purchase, a consultant can do the job in about two weeks for about $5,000, she said.

- Ask for employee and client surveys pre-purchase, or conduct them yourself post-purchase. What is morale really like? What do employees see as the challenges? Bellrock discovered that Smith Cameron does a superior job of communicating with its 800 active clients, "but who knew?" Landes said. "It's not necessarily because of a systematic way Grant had of communicating. It's because he hired great people and trained them well." As the new owner, you want to know this, Landes said. "You better make sure those employees stick around."

Source: Jenny Lee, *The Vancouver Sun*, February 19, 2013 (blog: vancouversun.com/smallbusiness). © Copyright *The Vancouver Sun*.

MARKETING CONSIDERATIONS

The previous section dealt with the internal aspects of the firm's profitability; there has been no discussion of the external determinants of these conditions. But you must be concerned with analyzing markets, customers, competition, and various other aspects of the company's operating environment.

You must carefully examine the company's current market situation. Each market segment served by the firm must be analyzed and understood. Studying maps, customer lists, traffic patterns, and other factors can help you to determine the normal market size for the business. Once the market and its various segments are understood, the composition of these segments should be determined to identify the approximate number of customers in the total market. As a buyer, you should be concerned with five key areas:

1. The company's trading area
2. Population demographics
3. The trend and size of the market
4. Recent changes in the market
5. Future market patterns

All these factors help in determining whether the firm's market area is changing, if there is a declining relevant population, or if technological or other changes may be creating an obsolete operation.

This kind of information can assist you in assessing trends in the level of the business's market penetration. For example, if its market share has been increasing, perhaps you should anticipate further growth. But if the business's market penetration has been declining or static, you should be aware that something could be wrong with the operation. It may be that the business is nearing the end of its life cycle. A shrewd seller, aware that the operation is approaching a natural decline, may be bailing out.

At the same time, a business that is not presently being marketed very well may represent a significant opportunity with the right management. John and Elisa Tait bought a store, Elements of Nature, which was little more than a museum gift boutique. Sales were often as low as $50 per day. During the first five years, they turned the business around so that in-store sales grew to as much as $4,000 on some days and developed a thriving web-based business as well, attracting orders from all over the world. The business has become so successful the Taits have expanded to Calgary, where they can pursue not only new business opportunities but more personal interests and their new store, The Discovery Hut (www.discoveryhut.com), continues to be a huge success.

Competition facing the business must also be evaluated and understood. First and foremost, you should make sure that the present owner will not remain in competition with you. Very often an owner will dispose of a business only to open up a similar operation. If the business is largely based on the personality and contacts of the owner, you may be hard-pressed to maintain the necessary rapport with customers, suppliers, and financial sources. A legal agreement may help ensure that the vendor will not go on to compete with you.

Another aspect of assessing competition is to look at that presently faced by the firm. You should be aware of the business's major competitors and what trends can be foreseen in the nature of their activity. Most of this information can be obtained either from direct observation or by talking with other people in the business.

Other aspects of the environment also should not be overlooked. You must be tuned in to developments in the economy, changes in technology, government policy and regulations, and trends in society at large that can affect your business situation. Your banker or other professionals may be able to tell you what the experts are saying about such variables. Both national and regional economic factors must be studied to develop accurate projections as to the size of the market opportunity available to the business.

HUMAN FACTORS

When a business is being purchased, personnel must be considered equal in importance to financial and marketing factors because usually it is desirable to retain certain key people to provide some continuity. As a prospective buyer, you should assess the value of the company's personnel and try to become acquainted with the attitudes of the present employees. For example, will key employees continue to work for the firm under your management? If these key people are likely to leave, you must anticipate the consequences.

Both the quality and the quantity of trained personnel must be evaluated. The skill level of the employees has some bearing on the sale value of the business. Highly trained staff, for example, can increase the seller's bargaining power. On the other hand, inefficient and poorly trained staff may permit you to negotiate a lower purchase price because of the long-term expense involved in retraining or hiring additional employees.

OTHER CONCERNS

In assessing a business to buy, you will also have to take into account a number of other factors. These include various legal considerations as well as past company policies. The legal aspects of doing business are becoming increasingly more complex and the use of a lawyer is practically a fact of business life. A lawyer can help you in such areas as deciding on an appropriate form of legal organization; identifying real estate documents, such as zoning restrictions and covenants, that may put you at a disadvantage; labour laws and union regulations; complying with all licensing and permit requirements; the transferability of intangible assets, such as copyrights, patents, dealerships, and franchises; and whether buying the shares or the assets of the firm is the most advantageous way of purchasing the company.

You should also have some understanding of the historical practices of the firm relating to employees, customers, and suppliers if future policies are to enhance your opportunities for business growth. An evaluation of these practices and policies will determine if you should continue with past practices or make modifications. If you fail to make this evaluation, you may eventually find yourself in a situation where you have to continue policies that are ill-advised in the long run. For example, it may be necessary to tighten credit policies or make a change in labour practices, even though this may cause a short-term loss of customers or employees.

OTHER CONSIDERATIONS

KEY POINTS TO CONSIDER IN BUYING A BUSINESS

- Take your time and verify the information you are given before you commit yourself.
- Don't fall in love with the business before you do your homework.
- Be careful not to pay too much for goodwill.
- Buy a business within an industry you know well, with a product or service you are comfortable selling.
- Buy based on the return on investment not the price.
- Don't use all your cash for the purchase and then run into cash flow problems.
- Investigate before you buy.

Source: "Buying a Business," Canada Business Network (www.canadabusiness.ca), accessed May 21, 2013.

HOW TO DETERMINE AN APPROPRIATE PRICE TO PAY FOR A BUSINESS

LO3

Buying a business is a serious matter involving a substantial financial and personal investment. A business bought at the wrong price, or at the wrong time, can cost you and your family much more than just the dollars you have invested and lost. After you have thoroughly investigated a business opportunity according to the factors in the previous section, weighed the wealth of information you have gathered, and decided that your expectations have been suitably fulfilled, a price must be agreed upon with the seller.

Valuing a business is a very complex procedure, so it is impossible to do it justice to this topic here. Any explanation short of an entire book is probably insufficient. The process takes into account many variables and requires that you make a number of assumptions. Determining an appropriate price to pay for a business is a very technical process, and understanding what methods are applicable to the unique situation requires an in-depth understanding of business valuation. If you are trying to make this determination on your own, you should either have a sound knowledge of general accounting principles or use the services of a professional accountant or business valuation expert who has taken formal training and is accredited by the Canadian Association of Business Valuators. This section is to provide you with an overview of the various types of valuation methods.

Setting the purchase price for a going-concern typically involves two separate kinds of evaluations:

1. **Balance sheet methods**—evaluation of the firm's tangible net assets
2. **Earnings-based methods**—evaluation of the firm's expected future earnings

Balance sheet methods are generally less reliant on estimates and forecasts than earnings-based methods; however, it should be remembered that balance sheet methods totally ignore the future earnings capability of the business.

BALANCE SHEET METHODS

This approach calls for making some evaluation of the assets of the business. It is used most often when the business being valued generates its earnings primarily from its assets, as with retail stores and manufacturing companies.

There are a number of balance sheet methods of evaluation, including *book value, modified or adjusted book value*, and *liquidation value*. Each has its proper application, but the most useful is the adjusted book value method.

Modified Book Value

If the company has a balance sheet, the quickest means of determining a valuation figure is to look at its net worth as indicated there. You simply take the total assets as shown in the financial statement and subtract total liabilities to get the *net book value*. The advantage of this method is that for most firms the numbers are readily available.

Its drawbacks, however, are numerous. The company's accounting practices will have a big impact on its book value. Similarly, book value does not necessarily reflect the fair market value of the assets or the liabilities. For example, buildings and equipment shown on the balance sheet may be depreciated below their actual market value, or land may have appreciated above its original cost. These differences will not be reflected on the company's balance sheet. Despite these drawbacks, however, net book value may be useful in establishing a reference point when considering the asset valuation of a business. This approach is illustrated in section I of Figure 10.4 on the basis of the balance sheet for The Campbell Company presented in Figure 10.2, and shows a value of $50,000.

Adjusted Book Value

The adjusted book value method is the most useful balance sheet method. It is simply the book value adjusted for differences between the stated book value and the fair market value of the business's fixed assets

---

FIGURE 10.4   APPLICATION OF BALANCE SHEET METHODS

BUSINESS VALUATION—THE CAMPBELL CO.
BALANCE SHEET METHODS

		(000s)
I.	**NET BOOK VALUE**	
	Total stockholders' equity*	$ 50
	Net Book Value	**$ 50**
II.	**MODIFIED BOOK VALUE**	
	Net book value	$ 50
	Plus:	
	Excess of appraised market value of building and equipment over book value	25
	Value of patent not on books	10
	Modified Book Value	**$ 85**
III.	**LIQUIDATION VALUE**	
	Net book value	$ 50
	Plus:	
	Excess of appraised liquidation value of fixed assets over book value	9
	Less:	
	Deficit of appraised liquidation value of inventory over book value	(5)
	Deficit due to liquidation of accounts receivable	(3)
	Costs of liquidation and taxes due upon liquidation	(8)
	Liquidation Value	**$ 43**

*Item E from Figure 10.2.

and liabilities. Adjustments are most frequently made to the book values of the following items on the balance sheet:

- Accounts receivable—often adjusted downward to reflect the fact that some receivables may be uncollectable.
- Inventory—usually adjusted downward, since some of it may be dated or stale and difficult to sell off at prices sufficient to cover its cost.
- Real estate—often adjusted upward, since it has commonly appreciated in value after being acquired by the business.
- Furniture, fixtures, and equipment—adjusted upward if they are relatively new and have been depreciated below their market value or adjusted downward if they are older and worn out or technologically obsolete.

This refinement of the plain book value approach still has a number of drawbacks, but it does give a more accurate representation of the value of the company's assets at current market value than book value does. The application of this method is illustrated in section II of Figure 10.4 and shows a value of $85,000.

Liquidation Value

A third approach is to go beyond the books of the company to get a more detailed evaluation of specific assets. Generally, this involves determining the *liquidation value* of the assets or how much the seller could get for the business or any part of it if it were suddenly thrown onto the market. This approach is ordinarily a highly conservative evaluation and, as such, is frequently useful in determining the lowest valuation in a range of values to be considered. The liquidation value approach is presented in section III of Figure 10.4, and shows a value of $43,000. Note that the liquidation value of the firm's fixed assets may be considerably less than their appraised market value, largely due to the distressed nature of their disposition.

RULE-OF-THUMB APPROACHES

In some situations, especially the purchase of small businesses or businesses with low capital assets, such as service businesses, certain rules of thumb have been developed to serve as useful guides for the valuation of a business. They typically rely on the idea of a "price multiplier."

In companies where there are relatively few tangible assets, another rule of thumb is to calculate the selling price as a percentage of the net or gross annual receipts of the business. This method is illustrated in Table 10.3 for various types of businesses.

One word of advice, however. Many valuation professionals discourage the use of such rule-of-thumb formulas. They contend that the formulas do not address many of the factors that impact a business's actual value and rely on a "one size fits all" approach when no two businesses are ever actually alike. These rule-of-thumb formulas do, however, give you an easy way to at least get a ballpark figure on what a business might be worth. But keep in mind that using one of these rules of thumb does not mean that the balance sheet and the income statement for the business can be ignored. These rules are merely a starting point for business valuation and must be reviewed in the context of the other business factors discussed earlier in this section.

WHAT TO BUY—ASSETS OR SHARES?

The acquisition of a business may be structured under one of two basic formats:

1. You can purchase the seller's stock or shares in the business.
2. You can purchase part or all of the business's assets.

Although these alternatives are treated somewhat the same for financial reporting purposes, the tax consequences can differ significantly. A major consideration in the purchase or sale of a business may be the effect on the tax liability of both the buyer and the seller. The "best" form of a particular transaction will depend on the facts and

TABLE 10.3 RULES OF THUMB FOR VALUING A SMALL BUSINESS

CAUTION: These rule-of-thumb valuations are only appropriate for average companies in the industries below. Fast growing, unusually risky, declining, or unusually low-risk companies would not be appropriate valued using these methods.

Type of Business	"Rule-of-Thumb" Valuation
Accounting Firms	100–125% of annual revenues
Auto Dealers	2–3 years net income + tangible assets
Auto Parts	4–5 times monthly sales plus inventory
Beauty Salon	15–25% of net profit +$2,500 per station
Book Stores	15% of annual sales + inventory
Camp Grounds (with real estate)	8 times annual net profit
Coffee Shops	40–45% of annual sales + inventory
Courier Services	70% of annual sales
Day Care Centers	2–3 times annual cash flow
Dental Practices	60–70% of annual revenues
Distributors	25–50% of annual gross sales
Dry Cleaners	70–100% of annual sales
Employment & Personnel Agencies	50–100% of annual revenues
Engineering Practices	40% of annual revenues
Florists	34% of annual sales + inventory
Fast Food Restaurants	40–50% of annual gross sales
Food/Gourmet Shops	20% of annual sales + inventory
Furniture & Appliance Stores	15–25% of annual sales + inventory
Hotels	2 to 3 times annual gross sales
Gas Stations	15–25% of annual sales + equip/inventory
Gift & Card Shops	32–40% of annual sales + inventory
Grocery Stores	11–18% of annual sales + inventory
Insurance Agencies	100–125% of annual commissions
Janitorial & Landscape Contractors	40–50% of annual sales
Law Practices	40%–100% of annual fees
Liquor Stores	25% of annual sales + inventory
Manufacturing	40–50% of annual gross sales
Marinas (with real estate)	8–10 times annual net profit
Motels	$20,000 per room
Property Management Companies	50–100% of annual revenues
Pharmacies	Total daily sales times 80-120, plus inventory
Publishers (books)	2–3 times gross annual sales
Restaurants (nonfranchised)	30–45% of annual sales
Retail	25–50% of annual gross sales + inventory
Sporting Goods stores	30% of annual sales + inventory
Taverns	55% of annual sales
Travel Agencies	40–60% of annual commissions
Trucking Companies	$2,000 to $5,000 per driver
Veterinary Practices	60–125% of annual revenues

Source: "30 Second or Less Business Valuation," Business Valuation for Busy People, (www.communityfutures.com/cms/fi leadmin/fi les/cfdc/pdf/30SecValuation.pdf), accessed May 11, 2010.

circumstances of each case. Since the tax implications of acquiring or disposing of a business can be very complex and a poorly structured transaction can be disastrous for both parties, it is suggested that you seek competent tax advice from your accountant or lawyer regarding this matter. Another factor to consider in deciding whether to buy assets or shares is "contingent liabilities." If assets are acquired, in most instances, the buyer takes no responsibility for any contingencies that may arise subsequent to the sale, such as lawsuits, environmental liabilities, or tax reassessments.

In some cases, there may not be any choice. If the company is a sole proprietorship, for example, there are no shares, only assets and liabilities accumulated in the course of doing business that belong to the proprietor personally. So, when acquiring the company, you and the owner must decide which of these assets and liabilities are to be transferred and which are to stay with the present owner. You may feel that some of the assets are not really essential to carry on the business and the seller may desire to keep something—often the real estate, which you may be able to lease rather than buy from him. This may be one way of reducing the cost of the business to you. These are matters that would have to be discussed in detail between you and the prospective seller.

FINANCING THE PURCHASE

Personal Equity

Any number of sources of financing can be used to purchase a business. Because you are buying something that already exists and has a track record, you may find this financing easier to obtain than if you were starting a business from scratch. However, the place to begin is with your own personal equity. In most transactions, anywhere from 20 to 50 percent of the money needed to purchase a business comes from the buyer and his or her family and close friends. The notion of buying a business by means of a highly leveraged transaction with a minimum amount of up-front cash is not a reality for most buyers.

Seller Financing

If you do not have access to enough cash to make the purchase, you might consider asking the seller to finance part of the purchase. This is very common in the sale of many small businesses. In most small business sales, it is important to have the seller's help for a period of time after the sale to transition the business to the new owner. Seller financing is one of the best ways to ensure this support is provided, as they have a vested interest to help you be successful. The seller's willingness to participate will be influenced by his or her own requirements, such as tax considerations or cash needs. For example, the seller might carry a promissory note for part of the purchase price, or you might lease rather than buy a portion of the facilities, equipment, or other assets. Another option is that you may be able to get the seller to agree to tie repayments to the actual performance of the business after the sale. Terms offered by sellers are usually more flexible and often more favourable than those available from a third-party lender, such as a bank. In addition, there may be some real advantages to the sellers, since many of these options will provide them with a steady source of revenue instead of a lump-sum payment, so they do not immediately face a tax liability on any capital gains realized from selling the business.

Third Parties

Banks and other lending institutions may provide a loan to assist in the purchase of a business, although the rate of rejection tends to be quite high on these transactions. When a bank will consider financing an acquisition, its focus tends to be on the physical assets associated with the transaction. The bank might, for example, provide financing for up to 50 to 75 percent of the value of any real estate, 75 to 90 percent for any new equipment acquisitions, or 50 percent of any inventory. The only other assets that might be attractive are the accounts receivable, which it may finance to 50 or 60 percent as well.

With any of these financing options, buyers must be open to creative solutions. They must also be prepared to take some risks. There is no sure thing, even though the business may appear to have had a long and successful operating history.

Structure of the Transaction

There are many alternatives to structuring a business sale, such as the types of financing, terms of any consulting agreements (to retain key owners or management for a period of time), leases (particularly if the seller owns the premises), payment terms, noncompetition agreements, and so on. These and other factors can impact the purchase price of the transaction. The best structure meets both the needs of the buyer and the seller.

If the company you are purchasing the business from does not own the premises, it may sublet the premises to you. If this is the case, you will need to discuss the lease with the landlord of the building and find out the terms and conditions with the existing lease or if it would be more advantageous for you to negotiate a new lease.

Earn-out

In some situations, especially where there is a high rate of growth expected, an earn-out may be included in the structure. For example, the seller had negotiated, before the sale of the business, a new contract that would double the company's sales. The contract will not be confirmed until after the sale of the business. The buyer is unlikely to pay the seller up-front for that value, in case the new order does not take place. The seller however, has created the value to the business and deserves some share. A calculation would be negotiated should certain targets be met. For instance, if the sales should double in the year after the sale, the seller would receive a percentage of the sales or profits in addition to the purchase price already paid. This type of structure is also seen in technology or high-risk industries where the sales projections are very aggressive and volatile.

A WORD OF WARNING

As you have seen, there are a lot of things you need to worry about in buying an existing business, including undisclosed debts, overstated earnings, poor employee relations, overvalued inventory, and potential lawsuits. Therefore, you should have a good accountant and a lawyer on your team for all but the simplest business acquisitions. The lawyer can either represent you in the actual negotiations or just serve as your coach and can also act as your trustee in handling the exchange of money. It is a good idea, if possible, to retain a lawyer who is very familiar with the tax aspects of business transfers, as this can often save you a lot of money. In addition, if you are buying a business for more than the value of its tangible assets, you should consider consulting with a professional business appraiser who has some experience in valuing businesses in the same industry.

STRIKING A DEAL

When the negotiations to acquire a business actually begin, you will discover that the value you may have assigned to the business during your assessment process serves as a useful benchmark to begin the negotiations, but it is not likely to be the final purchase price. At this point, a number of intangibles may enter the process, and depending on the factors that motivate each party to the deal, the final purchase price may be higher or lower than the price you calculated during the valuation process. At the end of the day, a good deal is one where both parties are satisfied with the price and other terms of the deal.

The question is: How can you negotiate this type of "win–win" scenario? Here are a few things to consider:

1. As a buyer, you must know the highest amount you are willing to pay for the business before negotiations start.

2. Avoid confrontational language that will offend the other party and shut negotiations down; stick to calm, factual reasoning and arguments as you negotiate back and forth.

3. When entering negotiations, it is important to understand that intangible assets can drive up the price of a business. Sellers typically want to allocate as much to goodwill as possible so they will be better off for tax purposes, while you may want to minimize the amount allocated to goodwill and maximize the amount allocated to tangible assets, which depreciate at a faster rate.

4. As the buyer, if you are firm on one point, such as the purchase price or the allocation of goodwill, then you should look for other areas where you can be flexible, such as vendor financing, to facilitate the closing of the deal.

5. If the deal is not working, always be willing to walk away.[1]

TAKING OVER A FAMILY BUSINESS

Another route to entrepreneurship for you may be taking over or joining a family business, perhaps a firm founded by your parents or grandparents. In fact, many family leaders actively strive to continue the family involvement in their businesses over several generations. This is a situation that has some unique opportunities and risks.

Family businesses are characterized by having two or more members of the family who may already control, are directly involved in, or own the majority of a business. It is estimated that roughly 80 percent of all businesses in North America are family businesses. What distinguishes these firms from non-family businesses is:

1. The interrelationship between family members interacting with each other and interacting with the business.

2. The complex issue of succession planning.

As illustrated in Figure 10.5, a family business can be thought of as an integrated system with three different subsystems, each with its own boundaries that separate it from the other subsystems. These three overlapping perspectives must be integrated to facilitate effective functioning of the entire system, and a change in one subsystem has ramifications for both of the other subsystems. This is further complicated by the fact that the major subsystems—family and business—are fundamentally different.

For example, if we think for a moment about the values of a typical family, they would include such things as unconditional acceptance of each member, permanent relationships, and a nurturing environment intended to foster the well-being of the entire group. This is basically an emotion-based system, as shown in Table 10.4. On the other hand, a business system tends to be goal focused and task focused and all about making money. It values such qualities as competence, productivity, and performance and tends to be task based in its orientation. So, at a very basic level, these two subsystems have widely divergent goals and values. What makes a family business so challenging is that family members have to find a way to make these two differing subsystems co-exist so that family members not only work effectively together but do so in the best interests of the business.

FIGURE 10.5　A SYSTEMS VIEW OF FAMILY BUSINESS

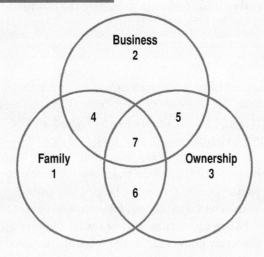

Source: M. Voeller, L. Fairburn, and W. Thompson, *Exit Right: A Guided Tour of Succession Planning for Families-In-Business Together* (Toronto: Summit Run Inc., 2000), p. 15.

This situation can become further complicated when the third subsystem—ownership—is factored into the equation. The ownership group may include both family and non-family members who may or may not also be actively involved in managing the business. In addition, these individuals can have totally different experiences and expectations of the system that need to be factored in.

Figure 10.5 also depicts the interaction of these three subsystems to create seven possible sets of circumstances in which you might find yourself in relation to a family-owned enterprise:

1. A family member who neither works in the business nor is a shareholder

2. A non-family member who works in the business but is not a shareholder

3. A non-family shareholder who does not work in the business

4. A family member who just works in the business

5. A non-family shareholder who works in the business

6. A family member who is a shareholder but does not work in the business

7. A family member who owns shares and works in the business

TABLE 10.4　MAJOR DIFFERENCES BETWEEN A BUSINESS SYSTEM AND A FAMILY SYSTEM

BUSINESS SYSTEM	FAMILY SYSTEM
Task-based system	Emotion-based system
Mission: To produce goods/services profitably	Mission: To nurture offspring into competent adults
Competency prevails	Equality rules
Acceptance is based on performance	Acceptance is unconditional
Relationships are temporary and contractual	Relationships are permanent
Power: Based on authority and influence	Power: Based on generational stage/birth order

Source: Adapted from M. Voeller, L. Fairburn, and W. Thompson, *Exit Right: A Guided Tour of Succession Planning for Families-In-Business Together* (Toronto: Summit Run Inc., 2000), p. 14.

Individuals in different circumstances will have totally different experiences and expectations for the business as a whole, yet all of them are in a position to significantly impact the ongoing success of the enterprise. These different needs and expectations need to be taken into account in managing the business.

THE QUESTION OF SUCCESSION

It is generally conceded that the most important issue facing most family businesses is the question of succession. Death or retirement of the founders or principals of all businesses is inevitable, yet most family firms lack any kind of clear succession plan. A report by the Canadian Federation of Independent Business (CFIB) indicated that four out of 10 current small- and medium-sized business owners intend to exit their businesses within five years, largely due to retirement, with that number increasing to seven out of 10 within 10 years.[2] This means there are thousands of Canadian businesses in transition, and millions of jobs are likely to be impacted. The interesting part of this report is the lack of any formal process on the part of most SME owners to provide for this transition. The CFIB survey, for example, found that only a third of these owners were currently planning for their future succession, and of those, the majority had made only informal, unwritten plans that had not even been communicated to the intended successor. There are three main reasons for this omission:

1. The owners are often too busy keeping their business alive and operating to plan for their own departure.
2. The owners do not have any confidence in the ability of their children or the relatives who might take their place to continue to run the business.
3. The owners do not see the perpetuation of their business in the family as a major concern.

This lack of a succession plan can create difficulties for a number of people, including family members, bankers, employees, managers, lawyers, spouses, and friends. Planning with foresight for succession can create a much more favourable transition than trying to implement these changes after the fact.

Planning a Successful Transition

A number of important issues must be considered in developing a successful succession plan, including the following:

1. **Understanding the context for the transition** Several key aspects that contribute to a successful succession plan include the timing, the type of business, the hopes and desires of the principal owner, and business environment considerations.

Timing

The earlier the owner starts to plan for a successor, the better the chance of getting the right person. Otherwise death, illness, or other issues can create a major problem for the business if a contingency plan is not in place.

Type of Business

Some owners may be easy to replace. With others it may be a lot more difficult. Situations that require a high level of technical expertise or where the business has been built on the principal owner's personal network of connections may make transition difficult. However, finding someone to run a business that requires minimal knowledge or experience may not be very difficult.

The Hopes and Desires of the Principal Owner

Family business succession includes the transfer of ethics, values, and traditions, as well as transfer of the actual business. A successor is typically expected to share these standards and continue adherence to them in the business.

Business Environment Considerations

The business environment usually changes over time and often an accompanying change is needed at the top to address these changing circumstances. It is critical to ensure that the successor and the environment have the "right fit" if a change in leadership is to be effective.

2. **Identifying the qualities needed in a successor** Successful successors may need to possess a number of qualities or characteristics. Some of the more common of these characteristics include:

   - Knowledge of the business or the ability to acquire that knowledge within an acceptable time frame
   - Honesty and the basic capacity to operate the business successfully
   - Good health
   - Energy and perceptiveness
   - A genuine enthusiasm for the business
   - A personality compatible with the requirements of the business
   - A high level of perseverance
   - Stability, maturity, and aggressiveness
   - Problem-solving skills and resourcefulness
   - The ability to plan and organize
   - The ability to help other people to develop
   - A general agreement with the owner's basic philosophy about the business[3]

   If it is difficult to identify an individual with all these traits, emphasis should be placed on selecting a successor with the capacity to develop most of these characteristics within a reasonable time frame.

3. **Implementing the succession plan** A number of important steps can be followed in the successful implementation of a succession plan, including the following:

Grooming an Heir

In some cases, the heir-apparent to take over the business may be obvious, or the principal owner may pick a successor and let it generally be known to be able to openly help that person to develop. In others, the owner may hesitate to actually announce a choice. While one family member may appear to have the inside track, there may be a number of other possibilities, and no one may know for sure who will get the job. Even if the successor has been chosen, it is not uncommon for the owner to have difficulty delegating the authority needed to effectively help that person develop the skills required to take over the business.

Family Acceptance of the Plan

Whatever succession plan is developed requires the general acceptance of the rest of the family. A detailed discussion with all family members about their expected duties, obligations, and responsibilities is imperative to the success of the plan. All those who will be most affected by the plan need to be included, so that hopefully the plan will gain their general acceptance and support.

A "family council" may be effective for this purpose—a formal, periodic meeting where family members share information, discuss issues, and make decisions about matters that affect them as a group. The family council should include all family members, regardless of their roles in the business, and usually also involves those who may not have a direct involvement in the business but who are nevertheless impacted by its direction and success.[4] It can be a valuable tool for enhancing family relationships and improving communication about the business.

The Use of Outside Assistance

Developing a succession plan and running a family business in general is a complex task involving complicated financial matters, buy–sell agreements and other legal issues, the resolution of conflict among family members, and a lot of other specialized tasks that are best handled by outside consultants and advisors. These may include expert consultants, such as accountants, lawyers, financial planners, industrial psychologists, and others, who have a specialized field of knowledge that can be useful for resolving a particular kind of problem.

This phase might also include "process" consultants or facilitators, who help the family members to see the entire picture and move toward their broader-based goals in a coordinated way. For example, most experts recommend using a facilitator skilled in dealing with family dynamics and conflict, in conjunction with family council meetings.

The succession plan outlined for McNally International Inc. (see the Entrepreneurs in Action box) illustrates how it can be done in such a way that the probable successors gain the necessary experience to run the business, and learn the skills to be effective leaders.

HOW CAN YOU PREPARE FOR RUNNING THE FAMILY BUSINESS?

If you are involved in a family business, you cannot start too soon to prepare yourself for your future role in that business. The five important steps in this preparation are as follows:

1. **Tell others of your interest in being involved in the family business** Do not keep your aspirations secret. Announce your goals to others, and look to them for assistance, advice, and support in helping you achieve them. It is especially important that your intentions be made clear to the principal stakeholders in the business, such as parents, siblings, and employees.

2. **Take responsibility for your personal development** This might include an informal apprenticeship in the business, perhaps starting with summer and part-time jobs. You should also consider an appropriate educational program, perhaps taking a diploma or degree in business or a related field so that you understand the general parameters of operating a company.

3. **Gain experience outside the family business** Working for another firm outside the family enterprise, even in another industry, can be an effective way of gaining valuable experience and building your credibility as a manager or the boss in your own business. It can also be a useful learning experience, as you have an opportunity to see different management styles, observe different operating techniques, and solve different problems—valuable skills that you can bring back to the family business. It is also an opportunity to obtain accountability training by holding positions that teach responsibility and provide important opportunities for decision making.

4. **Build relationships** Build contacts with individuals who are part of the family business's current network, including customers, suppliers, lawyers, bankers, and other professional advisers. These connections are often made in community-service settings and social situations, such as at sporting events, at a golf club, or in similar circumstances. You might also start building up your own network through school alumni and membership in the Chamber of Commerce, service clubs, professional associations, and other organizations.

5. **Avoid family feuds** Work *with* other members of the family, not against them. Learn to blend family traditions and values with your future business goals. This will help pave the way for a smooth transition when a clear takeover plan is in place.

THE RIGHT WAY TO SELL A FAMILY BUSINESS

Family business owners who are thinking about selling their companies and want to tilt the process to their advantage should start planning immediately.

"One reason our family business had a successful succession was because we started the process early," says Laura McNally, part of the third generation at McNally International Inc., a leading Canadian tunneling and marine contractor.

Ms. McNally says her father and uncle decided to bring in an outside adviser and embrace the creation of a family forum to plan for succession. One of the tools introduced was a "three circle" decision-making model that directed three questions: Is this a decision for the family? Is it for the shareholder? Or is it a challenge for management? Each circle involved different stakeholders, which added complexity to the process, but it worked.

Even though the third-generation family employees were not shareholders, it was decided that it would be sensible to include them in ownership transition discussions because they held important positions in the company. As Ms. McNally's father and uncle started to step back from day-to-day operations, they needed a plan to do it in an orderly way. Ms. McNally played a key role as change agent working closely with other senior managers.

Many owners underestimate the effort needed to prepare a company for ownership succession and the scrutiny of a buyer. They often think a fresh coat of paint is all it takes or that the business will sell itself. "However, this may not get you the best price or the right buyer," Ms. McNally says.

Based on first-hand experience, the McNally story shows that a team effort is required to prepare a business for sale. Here are key actions to think about:

THE CLASSIC CHESTNUT—STRATEGY

Regardless of timing, a business will be more attractive to a buyer if there is a defined strategy. Not only did McNally's senior management understand the segments of the market that were most attractive, they also developed a plan to capitalize on these opportunities, and they had a proven track record that demonstrated credibility to buyers.

FIGURE OUT WHAT DRIVES PROFITABILITY

Management realized that as the company grew it needed to focus on its systems and processes and bring them to a

Monkeybusinessimages / Dreamstime.com

higher standard. This required them to extract information from Ms. McNally's father and uncle and to institutionalize their knowledge into procedures and training that would be in place when they were ready to step away.

HIRE YOUR EXPERTS EARLY

The shareholders wanted all of their advisers—lawyers, tax planners, family succession and investment bankers—to work as a cohesive team. This required all parties to have an understanding of each other's roles and required effective communication within the team. The advisers were brought in early and they were given ample time to meet management, assess the go-forward leadership team, and become intimately familiar with the business and where it was headed so they could address the key questions that buyers would no doubt have.

"Selling a business and planning for succession is emotional," Ms. McNally says. "It creates not only work stress, but family stress as well. That's when you need to lean on your advisers."

By 2010, the family forum moved into the final stage. All the preparation by management and advisers provided the family and shareholders with the ability to set realistic expectations regarding value and business fit in the event of a sale.

Ms. McNally and her husband Colin Brown now run a consulting practice called McNally Brown Group, which specializes in preparing family businesses for a sale.

Source: Jacoline Loewen, director, Crosbie and the EMDA Canada and author of "Money Magnet: How to Attract Investors to Your Business," *The Globe and Mail*. Used with permission.

OTHER CONSIDERATIONS

THE ENDURING TRAITS OF SUCCESSFUL FAMILY FIRMS

Many people argue against family members working together in a business, yet numerous business dynasties have been created by family firms. One famous business consultant, David Bork, recommends recognizing some of the "enduring traits" that successful family firms have exhibited over the years:

1. Shared values about people, work, and money
2. Shared power by respecting one another's talents and abilities
3. Traditions that set them apart from other families
4. Willingness to learn and grow and openness to new ideas
5. Engaging together in other activities besides business to maintain relationships
6. Genuine caring for other family members
7. Mutual respect and trust for other family members
8. Assisting and supporting one another through times of grief, loss, pain, and shame
9. Respect for one another's privacy
10. Well-defined interpersonal boundaries to avoid conflict between family members

Source: S. Nelton, "Ten Keys to Success in Family Business," *Nation's Business*, April 1991, pp. 44–45.

CHECKLIST FOR A BUSINESS ACQUISITION

Should you start a new business or buy an existing one? At this point in your deliberations, this is the critical question. The material, in the Business Acquisition Questionnaire, available online with Connect, will aid you in making this choice.

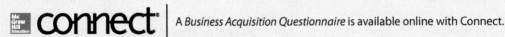

A *Business Acquisition Questionnaire* is available online with Connect.

F
Y
I

CAFÉ The Canadian Association of Family Enterprise (CAFE), is a not-for-profit national organization dedicated to promoting the well-being and understanding of families in business. There are CAFE chapters in most major business regions from British Columbia to Nova Scotia. CAFE offers an outsider's perspective and an insider's understanding of family businesses. Its objective is to educate, inform, and encourage its members in areas of unique interest to family businesses, through a program of activities that provide sources of information and professional advice. (www.cafenational.org)

LO1 The following are the advantages of buying an existing business:

- it can reduce the risk of starting a business as it is already a proven entity (it is often easier to obtain financing for an established operation)
- acquiring a "going concern" with a good past history increases the likelihood of a successful operation for the new owner
- the business has a proven location for successful operation
- the business has a product or service that is already being produced, distributed, and sold
- the business an established clientele
- financial relationships have already been established
- an existing business can often be acquired at a good price

The following are the disadvantages of buying an established business:

- the physical facilities (the building and equipment) may be out of date
- the union/management relationship may be poor
- present personnel may be unproductive
- it may be in a poor location
- inventory may contain a large amount of "dead stock"
- you may inherit ill will that may exist with customers or suppliers
- a high percentage of the assets may be in poor-quality accounts receivable
- the financial condition of the business may be poor

LO2 Why is the business for sale? It is important to do your research when looking to buy an established business to ensure you have all the facts before moving forward with the purchase. Some factors to take into consideration are as follows:

- when the owner of a business decides to dispose of it, the reason presented to the public may be somewhat different from the facts of the situation

- owners may be quite willing to express some reasons for wanting to sell their businesses, such as they wish to retire, or they want to move to another city, or illness is pressuring the owner to leave the business
- there are a number of other reasons for selling that the current owner may not be quite so likely to volunteer, such as the owner may be experiencing family pressures or marital problems, or perhaps the owner sees a better business opportunity somewhere else
- what if the company needs more financing than the owner can raise, or the current market for the firm's products is depressed?
- what if competitors are moving in with more effective products or methods, or the current plant and equipment is worn out or obsolete, and the firm is no longer able to compete successfully?
- what if the firm is having to contend with new government regulations that are creating some difficulties, or certain key employees are leaving the firm to set up a similar business of their own?
- you will need to conduct an analysis of the financial statements of the firm being sold with the help of a professional accountant that will help you assess the current health of the business—do not fall into the trap of accepting the seller's statements as the absolute truth

LO3 Determining an appropriate price to pay for a business is a very technical process, and understanding what methods are applicable to the unique situation requires an in-depth understanding of business valuation. If you are trying to make this determination on your own, you should either have a sound knowledge of general accounting principles or use the services of a professional accountant or business valuation expert who has taken formal training and is accredited by the Canadian Association of Business Valuators.

For more information on the resources available from McGraw-Hill Ryerson, go to www.mcgrawhill.ca/he/solutions.

11

BUYING A FRANCHISE

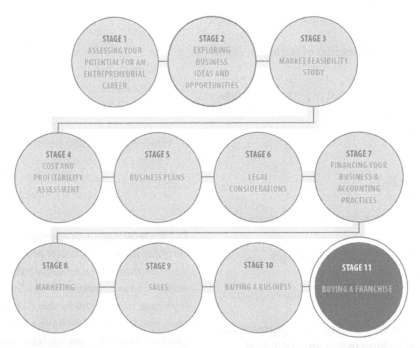

STAGE 1
ASSESSING YOUR POTENTIAL FOR AN ENTREPRENEURIAL CAREER

STAGE 2
EXPLORING BUSINESS IDEAS AND OPPORTUNITIES

STAGE 3
MARKET FEASIBILITY STUDY

STAGE 4
COST AND PROFITABILITY ASSESSMENT

STAGE 5
BUSINESS PLANS

STAGE 6
LEGAL CONSIDERATIONS

STAGE 7
FINANCING YOUR BUSINESS & ACCOUNTING PRACTICES

STAGE 8
MARKETING

STAGE 9
SALES

STAGE 10
BUYING A BUSINESS

STAGE 11
BUYING A FRANCHISE

LEARNING OBJECTIVES

By the end of this stage, you should be able to:

LO1 Explain what franchising is.

LO2 Recognize what the advantages and disadvantages of franchising are.

LO3 Describe the types of franchises available.

LO4 Explain the buying process of a franchise.

LO5 Identify the advantages of franchising your own business.

FRANTECH MEDIA

Photo courtesy of Rob Lancit, President, Frantech Media. Used with permission.

Rob Lancit got his first taste of working with folks south of the border (Canadian border, that is) while working for a Montreal-based clothing manufacturer during his college years. This coincided with his first taste of sweet success, as Rob was able to grow the business from $7 million revenue to $15 million—in just two years!

In 1995, Rob headed west and started a national video distribution company. While in Vancouver, he was head-hunted to lead the franchise division of a new technology startup. This led to his direct and active involvement with the IFA and attendance at several U.S. trade missions to Australia, New Zealand, Singapore, the United Kingdom, and Italy.

During this period, Rob worked with several top U.S. franchise systems, learning the ropes and discovering, as the only Canadian in these organizations, the pitfalls American franchise systems he invariably stumbled into while attempting to develop Canadian versions of their U.S. models.

In 2000, Rob launched the CANAM Franchise Development Group with the express intention of assisting U.S. franchisors expanding into the Canadian markets. As time went on, however, the business branched out to Canadian franchisors requiring assistance, and the company's name was changed to FranTech Media.

Then, in 2002, Rob perceived a need in the marketplace for a web portal geared toward franchising opportunities in Canada—BeTheBoss.ca was the result. Soon thereafter, he developed a franchise system with wife and partner, Elana, and became a franchisor.

Being needs focused enabled Rob to spot another opportunity back east and enter a niche market with planetefranchise.ca, a specialized web portal aimed exclusively at the Quebec market.

In 2009, he saw the launch of his latest web portal: buythatfranchise.ca. This site has rapidly become Canada's leading online directory for all franchise directory listings; it contains sophisticated "browse and match" tools that make it a market leader in the franchise industry.

CANAM has come a long way since the humble launch in 2000. It is just over a decade later, and the landscape has changed dramatically. One thing is as true today for FranTech Media as it was then: Rob Lancit remains the undisputed Canadian franchise authority!

In 2012, Rob acquired the U.K.'s top franchise portal: www.franchiseexpo.co.uk. Rob is excited to help international franchisors enter the U.K. marketplace and assist U.K. franchisors with expanding their concepts domestically.

Source: Frantech Media, Rob Lancit. Used with permission.

CONSIDERING A FRANCHISE

In addition to exploring the possibilities of starting your own business or buying an existing one, you may want to investigate the opportunities presented by *franchising*. Canada is said to be one of the franchise capitals of the world, led only by the United States. A Canadian franchise opens every two hours, 365 days a year, and represents over $100 billion, or almost 50 percent of total retail sales in Canada annually and continues to grow. There are close to 76,000 franchised outlets employing over 1.5 million people in Canada. Approximately 500 of the largest U.S. franchisors have introduced their franchise systems to Canada.[1]

Franchising allows you to go into business for yourself and at the same time be part of a larger organization. This reduces your chances of failure because of the support that the established company can provide. If this appears to be an attractive situation, then a franchise may be the answer for you. Let us look at what this means in the context of starting a business of your own.

AN INTRODUCTION TO FRANCHISING   LO1

Franchising has often been referred to as an industry or a business. However, it is neither. It can be best described as *a method of doing business*—a means of marketing a product and/or service that has been adopted and used by a wide variety of industries and businesses. See Figure 11.1.

FIGURE 11.1   INTERESTED IN A FRANCHISE?

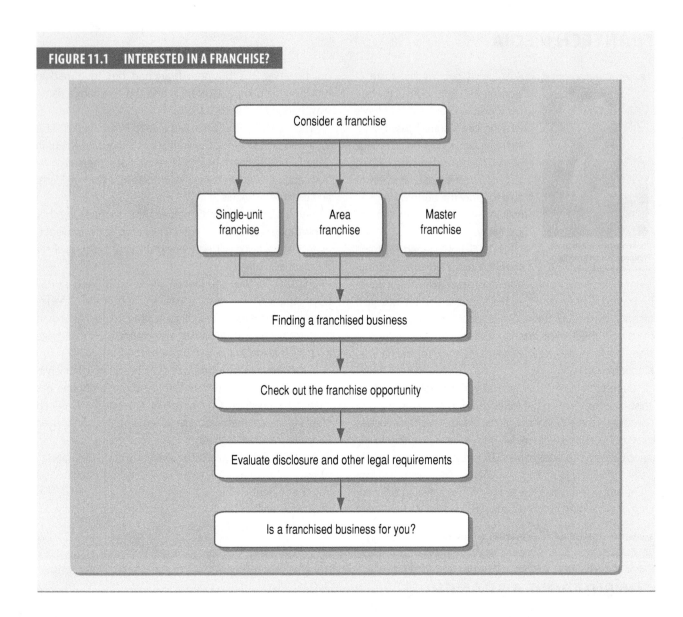

WHAT IS FRANCHISING?

There is no single, simple definition of franchising. For example, Statistics Canada defines it as a system of distribution in which one enterprise (the franchisor) grants to another (the franchisee) the right or privilege to merchandise a product or service. The International Franchise Association, the major trade association in the

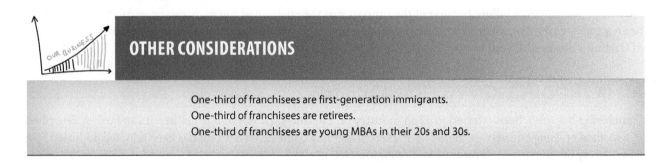

OTHER CONSIDERATIONS

One-third of franchisees are first-generation immigrants.
One-third of franchisees are retirees.
One-third of franchisees are young MBAs in their 20s and 30s.

field, defines it as a continuing relationship in which the franchisor provides a licensed privilege to do business plus assistance in organizing, training, merchandising, and management in return for consideration from the franchisee. These are just two of the many definitions that have been offered.

Regardless of the formal definition, however, it is best to think of franchising as a legal and commercial relationship between the owner of a trademark, trade name, or advertising symbol and an individual or group of people seeking the right to use that identification in a business. A franchisee generally sells goods and services supplied by the franchisor or that meet the franchisor's quality standards. Franchising is based on mutual trust and a legal relationship between the two parties. The franchisor provides business expertise, such as a proven product or service offering, an operating system, a marketing plan, site location, training, and financial controls, that otherwise would not be available to the franchisee. The franchisee brings to the franchise operation the motivation, entrepreneurial spirit, and often the money to make the franchise a success.

Virtually all franchise arrangements contain the following elements:

1. A continuing relationship between two parties
2. A legal contract that describes the responsibilities and obligations of each party
3. Tangible and intangible assets (e.g., services, trademarks, and expertise) provided by the franchisor for a fee
4. The operation of the business by the franchisee under the franchisor's trade name and managerial guidance

Franchise arrangements can be subdivided into two broad classes:

1. **Product distribution arrangements,** in which the dealer is to some degree, but not entirely, identified with the manufacturer/supplier
2. **Entire-business-format franchising,** in which there is complete identification of the dealer with the supplier

In a *product distribution arrangement*, the franchised dealer licenses its trademark and use of logo to a franchisee and typically does not provide any systems or procedures on how to run the business. This arrangement is just the ability to sell the franchises products. Examples of this type of arrangement are Coke, Pepsi, Ford, BMW, and Goodyear tires.

Entire-business-format franchising is characterized by an ongoing business relationship between franchisor and franchisee, which includes not only the product, service, and trademark but also the entire business format—a marketing strategy and plan, operating manuals and standards, quality control, and continuing two-way communications. Restaurants, personal and business services, rental services, real estate services, and many other businesses fall into this category.

Entire-business-format franchising has been primarily responsible for most of the growth of franchising since 1950. Most of our comments will relate to this form of franchising.

ADVANTAGES OF FRANCHISING LO2

As has been pointed out, franchising is one way for you (the franchisee) to go into business for yourself and yet at the same time be part of a chain, with the support of an established company (the franchisor) behind you. This can enable you to compete with other chains through the use of a well-known trademark or trade name. In addition, the franchisor may provide you with assistance in such areas as site selection, equipment purchasing, national advertising, bookkeeping, the acquisition of supplies and materials, business counselling, and employee training. See Table 11.1 for the pros and cons of owning a franchise.

As a franchisee, you will have the opportunity to buy into an established concept with reduced risk of failure. Statistics show that a typical franchisee has an 80 percent chance of success. Several factors may explain this result. First, your risk is reduced because you are supposedly buying a successful concept. This package includes proven and profitable product or service lines, professionally developed advertising, a known and generally recognized

TABLE 11.1 THE PROS AND CONS OF OWNING A FRANCHISE

The Pros	The Cons
Reduced Risk Franchising does not guarantee success, but a good franchise should help reduce the chances of failure.	**Loss of Independence** The loss of independence can be viewed negatively by some franchisees. Although most franchisees invest in a franchise because they want the guidance of the franchisor, the moment they enter the franchise system they want to make changes.

A Proven System
With a tried and tested operating system, the franchisee loses the obstacles and gains the opportunities. A franchisee should receive a completely proven system that includes initial training, opening assistance, accounting systems, established suppliers, manuals, and use of the trademarks. The all important "learning curve" helps prevent the franchisee from repeating previous mistakes and provides information on inventory levels, store design, competition, pricing structure and operational data drawn from the entire system.

Easier Access to Financing and Reduced Cash Requirements
Financial institutions prefer to lend to established franchised systems because of their higher success rate. The consumer awareness created by national or regional name recognition can reduce the costs of grand-opening promotional activity and advertising startup. As well, the purchasing power of the franchisor can reduce the franchisee's initial outlay for equipment and supplies.

Purchasing Power
Collective purchasing power on products, supplies, extended health and insurance benefits, equipment, and advertising can easily offset any ongoing royalties paid by the franchisee.

Site Selection Assistance
Franchisors can provide expert site selection assistance based on their operating experience and demographic knowledge. Landlords and developers prefer to deal with someone who has an established track record. This enables franchisees, as part of an established franchise system, to obtain locations in major malls and other developments that otherwise would not be available to them as an independent operator.

Advertising Clout
Most independent businesses cannot afford the services of advertising and promotional experts. Consequently, their advertising is often poorly conceived and inconsistent. They also cannot afford to invest in the level of advertising required to maintain a commanding presence in the marketplace. In a franchise system, the

Unless you are capable of working within a system and can accept a certain amount of regimentation, you should think long and hard before entering into a franchise relationship. One of the greatest strengths of franchising is consistency among units, and with consistency must come compliance.

Franchisor's Failure to Perform
Some franchisors do not deliver what they promise for a couple of reasons. A common reason for failure is the franchisor's shortage of available capital, which can be caused by:

- The franchisor's unrealistic franchise sales projections,
- The franchisor underestimating the expenses associated with the development of the franchise system;
- The franchisor's failure to meet franchise sales projections, or
- High franchisee attrition.

Alternatively, it could be that the franchisor is just not capable of providing the support and assistance or does not possess the ability to operate a franchise organization.

Misunderstanding the Franchise Agreement
Confusion over the interpretation of certain aspects of the franchise agreement can result in a problem with either the franchisor or the franchisee. A potential franchisee has probably never encountered a document anywhere near similar to a franchise agreement. A franchise agreement requires careful explanation and scrutiny, and failure to do so will inevitably result in a conflict that may end up in the courts.

Misrepresentation by the Franchisor
Misrepresentation by the franchisor can be intentional or unintentional. Projections of income and expense can be provided to the franchisee in good faith but may turn out to be inappropriate for the location because of the franchisor's inexperience or unfamiliarity with the area's demographics. Conversely, the figures may be total fabrications simply to get the franchisee to sign on the dotted line and hand over the initial franchise fee.

Caveat emptor (let the buyer beware), applies to franchising as it does to any consumer purchase or investment; however, consumers are often their own worst enemy, choosing to ignore cautionary advice and warning signals, and basing their investment decision on emotion without balancing it with logic.

advertising cost is spread over many units, enabling the franchisor to achieve economies of scale. This also allows the franchisee to create well-conceived promotional campaigns and place the advertising in the most effective medium.

Building Equity

Because of the national or regional name recognition, and territorial exclusivity, a franchised business should sell faster and for a higher value than an independent business. A buyer is often motivated to buy the franchised business for the same reasons as the original franchisee and may perceive a higher value associated with a recognized name and system.

Stress Reduction

The ability to operate more effectively and efficiently can relieve many pressures of business. Systems that control job scheduling, cash flow, and inventory levels allow the franchisee to run the business instead of the business running them.

Payment of Fees

The franchisee typically pays an initial fee for being granted the franchise, using the system, and receiving initial training. Typically, single-unit franchise fees are in the range of $25,000 to $35,000. The initial fee is paid only once during the term of the agreement; however, franchisors may charge a nominal renewal fee at the commencement of each new term of the agreement. The typical term for a franchise agreement is five or 10 years but may vary to coincide with the terms of a lease. Franchisors sometimes charge a site selection fee of $5,000 or more, in addition to the initial fee, which offsets their costs of site selection and lease negotiation.

In addition to the initial fee, some form of ongoing royalty is paid by the franchisee to the franchisor. In most instances, the royalty is based on a percentage of the franchisee's gross sales, which vary from 1 to 10 percent, or even higher, with a median range of 3 to 6 percent; however, units with high sales volumes often pay 1 percent or 2 percent less.

Franchisees are also required to contribute to a national or regional advertising fund, which is in addition to any requirement that the franchisee invests a minimum amount on local advertising.

Source: Advantages and Disadvantages of Buying a Franchise, BeTheBoss.ca (www.betheboss.ca). Used with permission.

brand name, the standardized design or construction of a typical outlet, and a proven and market-tested operating system. Second, you are often provided with training for your new job and continuing management support. You have the ongoing assistance of a franchisor who can afford to hire specialists in such areas as cost accounting, marketing and sales, and research and development. These are important assets usually not available to the small, independent businessperson.

As a franchisee, you may also be able to take advantage of the lower cost of large-scale, centralized buying. You may be able to purchase supplies at reduced cost, since the franchisor can purchase in bulk and pass the savings along. You may also have access to financing and credit arrangements that would not otherwise be available to an independent business. Banks and other lending institutions are usually more willing to lend money to a franchisee who has the backing of a large, successful franchisor than to a completely independent business.

For example, after receiving a layoff notice from his federal government job of 20 years, Allan McGuire purchased a Cody Party franchise (see the Entrepreneurs in Action box). The location had previously been run as a corporate store that had been in operation for two and a half years, had a profitable track record, and an established clientele. Allen found his own financing through a government guaranteed small business loan. He needed $200,000 for the purchase of the franchise as well as a line of credit and a corporate credit card. He was given the money for the franchise but not for the line of credit or the credit card. It was not until after the sale had closed that inventory was done, and Allen realized that the cost of the inventory was more than he had imagined. Also, other inventory needed to be added to make it through their Halloween busy season, which was approaching quickly. Cody stepped in to help financially. As with any new business, there are always challenges, fitting in with personnel who stayed with the franchise, jumping through hoops, the financial challenges, and having no spare money. At this time, Allen is not taking a salary, but he hopes that will change very shortly.

ENTREPRENEURS IN ACTION

LAID OFF PUBLIC SERVANTS BUILDING NEW CAREERS IN SMALL BUSINESS

Allan McGuire bought the Cody Party Kanata franchise in August after being laid off from the federal government where he worked for 20 years.

After a year of federal government layoffs that saw some 11,000 civil servants lose their jobs, many have turned to the entrepreneurial fire inside to find work in 2013.

"At the beginning of April, I received notice that my position was surplus," said Allan McGuire, who by August 2012 had bought a Cody Party supply franchise in Kanata after working for the Canadian government for the past 20 years.

"As a guy with that many years in, I thought I would be pretty safe," McGuire said, anticipating cuts to the Rural and Co-operatives Secretariat program, where he worked, to be a mere 5 to 15 percent. "When the budget dropped, my program suffered a 90 percent cut. It was drastic. 100 total employees were cut down to 12 or 15."

Rather than move to Kitchener or Toronto to find another position with the feds, McGuire said he began to look for something new. "I just didn't want to go back into an office environment. Even before I started working for the public service I had considered finding a business I could operate on my own."

Longing for financial freedom, as McGuire looked into how much it would cost, he found a promising franchise prospect and contacted Sandra Harvey of the Murphy Business & Financial Corporation, which specializes in the sale of small businesses.

"When I met with Allan, I could see he had a lot of drive and skill sets," Harvey said, noting that January is a popular month for new business starts since many people make resolutions at the end of the year. "I find that we're getting a lot of interest from the government world looking to be first-time business owners. For a lot of people franchises are a really

METRO/GRAHAM LANKTREE.

great fit because they take care of the business model, marketing, and tools."

In his work with the Rural and Co-operatives Secretariat, McGuire developed strong management and networking skills, along with a grasp of numbers since the department gives out funding, Harvey said. "He's far too young to retire, so I found something that I thought was a match for him from a risk perspective and the things he likes to do."

McGuire said he was able to get bank financing with Harvey's help, but it took roughly $300,000 and a $50,000 down payment to buy the business, get an inventory, and set to work.

"Sandra was willing to invest more time and effort into helping me make an informed decision," he said. "Am I going to become wealthy? Nah. Comfortable? That would be good. The first year is the toughest year, but I feel that I'm going to make it through OK."

Source: Graham Lanktree, Metro Ottawa, January 2, 2013 (www.metronews.ca/news/ottawa). Used with permission.

Cody's franchising model allows for franchisees to work together, selling inventory to each other and share rental inventory. Cody also has a wide range of suppliers for the franchisees to work with and purchase directly from the suppliers and, in some cases, allows the franchisee to purchase such items as fireworks and return what they do not sell. Allen says that Cody sets them apart from other franchisors by offering support and has the willingness to be open to discussions with the owners. They are willing to help if you are willing to help yourself.

When asked if he would do it again, he said, "Absolutely," even though he does not know what his long-term plans are yet. Buying an established franchise over starting a business from scratch has its advantages, especially for someone that is 50.

DISADVANTAGES OF FRANCHISING

While franchising has a considerable number of advantages, there are also several disadvantages that you should be aware of. One of the principal complaints is the degree of control that franchisors exert over their franchisees. While you will be an independent businessperson, in effect, you do not have complete autonomy and must operate within the operating system as defined by the franchisor. You are usually in a subordinate position to the franchisor and must abide by the often extremely rigid terms and conditions of the franchise agreement. All franchise contracts give the franchisor either an open right to terminate the contract or the right to terminate upon breach of the agreement. As a result, you may find yourself in a weak bargaining position.

Franchisees also have certain reporting obligations to the franchisor and may be subject to frequent inspection and constant supervision. To fit comfortably into such an arrangement, you must accept the necessity of such controls. These restrictions, however, may be unacceptable to some individuals. You must seriously assess your personal suitability for the role of a franchisee.

Another disadvantage of franchising is that the cost of the services provided to you by the franchisor is based on your total sales revenue. These costs can amount to 10 percent or more of your total revenue or an even larger share of your profits. A related complaint is that the markup franchisors may add to the products you must buy from them can increase your operating costs, particularly if equally good products could be purchased elsewhere at lower

OTHER CONSIDERATIONS

UNDERESTIMATING TIM HORTONS: DUNKIN' DONUTS $16-MILLION MISTAKE

There's a price to be paid for ignoring Tim Hortons—$16.4 million, to be exact. That's how much a Quebec Superior Court judge dinged Dunkin' Brands Canada Ltd. recently for failing to protect its brand.

The saga here stems back to 1996, when Dunkin' Donuts dominated the Quebec coffee market. The company had more than 200 stores across the province, and although headquartered in the U.S., was very much a distinctive Quebec entity. The rest of Canada had Tim's, Second Cup, and later Starbucks, but Quebec had Dunkin' Donuts. In Montreal, there was one it seemed on every major street corner.

And so it would last forever. Or at least that's what the parent company, at the time called Allied Domecq Retailing International, appeared to believe. Its franchisees, however, looked somewhat further afield and didn't like what they saw. Coffee was morphing from a morning drink into an all-consuming national obsession . . . and Tim's was fast becoming the embodiment of caffeine in this country.

According to court filings, 21 Dunkin' Donut franchisees alerted Allied Domecq in 1996 to the gathering storm that was Tim's. The chain only had 60 outlets in Quebec, but it was rapidly expanding across Canada, and had just merged with Wendy's International, enabling it to scale up even faster. Between 1991 and 1995, it doubled the number of stores, from 500 to 1,000.

Although the Dunkin' operators had enjoyed years of essentially no competition in Quebec, they knew a predator when they saw one. They filed a 50-point action plan with the parent company, signalling that immediate action was needed to safeguard the brand.

Allied responded, four years later, with a refurbishment program that promised a 15 percent sales increase for franchisees who participated. Daunted by the cost of the renovations, and declining sales, few pursued the option.

By 2008, Dunkin' Donuts presence in the province had tumbled from 210 outlets to 41. A partnership with Alimentation Couche-Tard, a major convenience store chain, was briefly tried. Throughout, sales slipped while Tim's rolled on.

Today there remain fewer than 15 Dunkin' Donuts in Quebec. Tim's, in the meantime, just opened its 500th store in the province. Surveying the rout, Quebec Justice Daniel Tingley offered a stinging assessment before awarding the $16.4-million plus costs verdict to the franchisees. "A successful brand is crucial to the maintenance of healthy franchises. However, when the brand falls out of bed, collapses, so, too, do those who rely upon it. And this is precisely what has happened in this case."

Source: Reprinted with permission from Yahoo! Inc. © 2013 Yahoo! Inc. YAHOO! and the YAHOO! logo are trademarks of Yahoo! Inc. Used with permission.

prices. While you might initially feel that your operating costs are likely to be lower as a result of the franchisor's central purchasing program, it may not become apparent until later that you are actually paying a huge markup on the material, equipment, and supplies you acquire.

Acquiring a franchise is not necessarily a licence to print money. Besides an initial franchise fee, you will probably also have to make periodic royalty payments and advertising contributions based on a percentage of your gross revenues. Even with these expenditures, you still run the risk of not achieving the expected sales, and thus the profit that the franchisor stated was possible.

It should also be remembered that the benefits available through franchising have not always materialized. Franchisors have not always supplied the services they promised or truthfully disclosed the amount of time and effort the franchisee would have to commit to the franchise. Termination policies of many franchisors have given franchisees little or no security in many cases.

TYPES OF FRANCHISES   LO3

FRANCHISE FORMATS

There are three major ways a franchise can be formatted:

1. **Single-unit franchise** This is the most popular and simplest format. In it, the franchisor grants you the right to establish and operate a business at a single location. This has been the most used means of franchise expansion and the method by which many independent entrepreneurs have become involved in franchise distribution.

2. **Area franchise** This format involves a franchisor's granting you the right to establish more than one outlet within a specified territory. This territory can be as large as an entire province or state, or even a country, or it can be as small as part of a city. To ensure that this territory is adequately serviced, the franchisor will usually require the construction and operation of a specific number of outlets within a period of time. Area franchising may be a means of achieving certain economies of scale and perhaps a lower average franchise cost. On the other hand, it requires a larger total capital outlay for plant and equipment. Area franchisees with a large number of outlets can sometimes acquire greater financial strength than their franchisors. This has happened in a number of instances in the fast-food industry.

3. **Master franchise** In this format, a franchisor grants you (the master franchisee) the right not only to operate an outlet in a specific territory but also to sell subfranchises to others within that same territory. Granting master franchises is the fastest way for a franchisor to expand, but it is also very complex and results in a division of fees and royalties between the franchisor and subfranchisor. A master franchisee may not need as much initial capital as an area franchisee, but he or she must learn not only how to open and operate a franchise business but also how to sell franchises.

RANGE OF AVAILABLE FRANCHISES

What comes to mind when you think of a business that is franchised? If you are like most people, you think of coffee shops (Tim Hortons and Starbucks) and fast-food restaurants (Subway and McDonalds), which is correct, but there are so many other franchise opportunities other than these. To give you an idea of the scope of franchising, the Franchise Canada Directory 2013 of the Canadian Franchise Association (www.cfa.ca) provides information on over 1,100 Canadian listings in 51 different product/service categories. The range of possibilities available to a prospective franchisee includes opportunities in the following areas and more:

- Accounting/tax services
- Advertising/marketing/promotional products and services
- Automotive and truck services
- Beauty/cosmetic supplies

- Business consultants/services/training
- Business—supplies/equipment and services
- Commercial—supplies/equipment and services
- Commercial/residential services
- Computer/software/Internet
- Consumer buying services
- Dry cleaning/clothing care
- Educational products and services
- Employment/personal services
- Environmental products and services
- Event planning
- Financial/cash services
- Food—baked goods/coffee/donuts
- Food—grocery/specialty shops
- Food—meal assembly
- Food—quick service restaurants
- Food—restaurants/dining rooms
- Furniture/upholstery repair
- Hair and nail salons/spas
- Health and fitness/nutrition
- Home—decorations/furnishings
- Home—improvement/renovation/restoration
- Home—inspection services
- Home—maid/cleaning services
- Home-based businesses
- Hospitality products/services
- Hotels/motels/campgrounds
- Janitorial and maid services
- Lawn and garden supplies/services
- Mobile businesses
- Pets—sales/supplies/services
- Printing/copying/shipping
- Real estate
- Retail
- Seniors/home care and services
- Sign products/services
- Sports/recreation/entertainment
- Tanning salons
- Travel
- Weight loss services/body contouring
- Wine making

The top 10 franchises for 2013, based on their 2012 performance, are shown in Table 11.2. You can see from the table that the top performing franchises are in varied industries and only include two food franchises.

CANADIAN LEGISLATION AND DISCLOSURE REQUIREMENTS

Many U.S. states have laws and regulations governing franchise companies, but the same is not true of Canada. Only Alberta, Manitoba, Ontario, Prince Edward Island, and New Brunswick have legislation specifically related to franchise disclosure, although other provinces are expected to adopt similar legislation. The legislation in all five provinces is quite similar in that it requires franchisors (with some exceptions) to provide prospective franchisees with a disclosure document containing a lot of information that otherwise would be very difficult for the prospective franchisee to obtain. This information includes:

- The business background of the directors and officers of the franchisor
- Details of any litigation against the franchisor

TABLE 11.2 TOP 10 FRANCHISES FOR 2013 BASED ON 2012 PERFORMANCE	
Franchise	**Description**
Anytime Fitness	Anytime Fitness is not only the largest but also the fastest-growing fitness franchise in the world.
Pizza Hut	Pizza Hut is expanding across Canada with single and multi-unit opportunities for delivery and take-out units.
Kumon	Kumon is the world's largest after-school math and reading enrichment program and one of the most established franchise businesses in the world.
Snap-on	With a Snap-on franchise, you'll sell the #1 branded product in the category, and you'll have a solid foundation of existing and potential customers to call on.
Liberty Tax Service	Liberty is led by IFA Entrepreneur of the year, John Hewitt. With 42 years of experience in the tax preparation business, John has led Liberty to open 3,800 offices in just 14 years.
Papa Murphy's	Papa Murphy's is the fifth-largest pizza chain in North American and the pioneer and leader of the Take 'N' Bake pizza segment.
The UPS Store	Enormous strength, limitless potential, and unparalleled brand recognition with over 5,900 locations worldwide.
Express Employment Professionals	Staffing generates $8 billion annually and employs 1.8 million Canadians. Express Employment Professionals averaged more than $3.37 million is sales per territory.
Minuteman Press	As Canada's leading printing company for more than 35 years, Minuteman Press has gained a reputation nationwide for providing fast, dependable graphics and print services to all types of businesses.
Maid Simple House Cleaning	Maid Simple House Cleaning is a flexible home-based business in the residential home cleaning franchise sector.

Source: Top Canadian Franchises for 2013. BeTheBoss.ca (www.betheboss.ca). Used with permission.

- Details of bankruptcy, insolvency, or criminal proceedings against the franchisor or its directors
- The names and addresses of existing and former franchisees
- The particulars of any advertising fund expenditures
- A set of financial statements

This information must be provided to the franchisee at least 14 days before signing any franchise agreement or paying any money to the franchisor. Otherwise the franchisee may have recourse to rescind the franchise agreement. For example, 3 for 1 Pizza and Wings (Canada) Inc. was found to be in violation of Ontario's franchise law by not providing a full package of disclosure information and ordered to repay $35,000 to a man who backed out of a deal. This was the second time the company was ordered to pay refunds after a judge concluded that the company had not provided sufficient disclosure.[2] The basic principle behind the legislation is that everyone entering into a franchise arrangement should have access to all the information necessary to make an informed decision. The presumption is that both parties "act in good faith and in accordance with reasonable commercial standards."

In all other provinces, franchisors are still under no legal obligation to provide any specific information or file any material with a government agency or department. As a prospective franchisee, you are on your own for the most part. If your potential franchisor does operate in a legislated province you should request a copy of the disclosure material they are obliged to provide to prospective franchisees in those provinces, although you may not be entitled to the same length of time for deliberation or legal recourse. If you are considering a franchise in a province that do not have legislation for franchising, you should check with your local government and province to find out what regulations, if any, they may have.

THE FRANCHISE AGREEMENT

Because two independent parties participate in a franchise relationship, the primary vehicle for obtaining central coordination and control over the efforts of both participants is a formal contract. This *franchise agreement* is the heart of the franchise relationship. It differs from the typical contract in that it contains restrictive clauses peculiar to franchising that limit your rights and powers in the conduct of the business. Franchisors argue that these controls are necessary to protect their trademark and to maintain a common identity for their outlets.

A franchise agreement should cover a variety of matters. There should be provisions that cover such subjects as:

- The full initial costs, and what they cover
- Use of the franchisor's trademarks by the franchisee
- Licensing fees
- Land purchase or lease requirements
- Building construction or renovation
- Equipment needs
- Initial training provided
- Starting inventory
- Promotional fees or allowances
- Use of operations manuals
- Royalties
- Other payments related to the franchisor
- Ongoing training
- Co-operative advertising fees
- Insurance requirements
- Interest charges on financing

- Requirements regarding purchasing supplies from the franchisor, and competitiveness of prices with those of other suppliers
- Restrictions that apply to competition with other franchisees
- Terms covering termination of the franchise, renewal rights, passing the franchise on to other family members, resale of the franchise, and similar topics

In considering any franchise proposition, you should pay a great deal of attention to the franchise contract. Since it is a key part of the relationship, it should be thoroughly understood. The rest of this section discusses the evaluation of an agreement for a single-unit franchise within a business-format franchise system. It is important to realize, however, that this is not a "typical" franchise agreement; there is really no such thing. While agreements may follow a fairly standard approach in terms of format, they do not do so in terms of content. Every agreement is specially drafted by the franchisor to reflect its particular objectives and the future of the business.

Obligations Undertaken by the Franchisor

The obligations undertaken by the franchisor may include any or all of the following:

1. To provide basic business training to you and your employees. This includes training in bookkeeping skills, staff selection, staff management, business procedures, and the systems necessary to control the operation. In addition, the franchisor may provide you with training relating to the operational aspects of the business.

2. To investigate and evaluate sites for the location of your franchise. You will be advised as to whether or not the site meets the franchisor's standards and what sort of performance might be expected at that location. In addition, you may be assisted in the design and layout of your franchise operation.

3. To provide either the equipment or the specifications for any necessary equipment and furniture you require.

4. To provide promotional and advertising material to you, and some guidance and training on marketing and promotional principles.

5. The franchisor may provide you with a statement indicating the amount of opening inventory required, and may make arrangements for you to purchase inventory either from the franchisor's own purchasing department or from particular suppliers established for this purpose.

6. The franchisor may provide you with on-site assistance for the opening of your franchise outlet. Quite often, the franchisor will provide a team of two to three people to assist you in getting the business off the ground.

7. The franchisor may also provide business operating manuals explaining the details of operating the franchise system and a bookkeeping/accounting system for you to follow. There may also be additional support through such things as business consultation, supervisory visits to your premises, and staff retraining.

Obligations Imposed on a Franchisee

Your obligations as a franchisee may require you to do any or all of the following:

1. Build your franchise outlet according to the plan or specifications provided by the franchisor.
2. Maintain construction and opening schedules established by the franchisor.
3. Abide by the lease commitments for your franchise outlet.
4. Observe certain minimum opening hours for your franchise.
5. Pay the franchise fees and other fees specified in the franchise agreement.
6. Follow the accounting system specified by the franchisor and promptly provide financial reports and payments of amounts due.
7. Participate in all regional or national co-operative advertising and use and display such point-of-sale or advertising material as the franchisor stipulates (this would include having all your advertising materials approved by the franchisor).

OTHER CONSIDERATIONS

FRANCHISE BREAK-UPS ARE HARD TO DO

Notwithstanding what franchise parties might have intended when they first got together, not every franchise relationship is destined to last. There are many reasons why franchise relationships fall apart. Some franchisees rush into buying a franchise without fully appreciating what is involved or required. Others expect a quicker or more substantial return on their investment, and still others discover they would prefer to run their own operation and make their own decisions.

Franchisees typically don't have the right to unilaterally terminate their franchise agreements. Simply walking away when they've had enough will usually constitute a default of their franchise agreement, entitling the franchisor to sue the franchisee for monies owing under the agreement. However, a disgruntled or unhappy franchisee may avoid a dispute by negotiating an exit strategy with the franchisor. It is rarely in the interest of the franchisor to maintain a relationship with a franchisee who has lost interest in being a part of the system.

Franchisors on the other hand, usually have wide latitude under a franchise agreement to terminate a franchisee. Most franchise agreements contain lengthy termination provisions all favouring franchisors. These are summarized in disclosure documents in those provinces with franchise legislation. Depending on the nature of the default, a franchisor may or may not have to give a franchisee notice of default with an opportunity to fix it. For more serious defaults such as fraud, abandonment, or bankruptcy, a franchisor may be permitted to terminate the franchise agreement without any notice.

If a franchisor gives notice of default or termination, the notice should be clearly written and refer to the relevant provision(s) of the franchise agreement. If the default is one that can be fixed, the franchisee must be advised of exactly what it needs to do and by when. As for a notice of termination, the effective termination date must be spelled out, as well as the franchisee's obligations. Most franchisees must de-identify and for a reasonable period of time not compete with the franchisor. Franchisees may also be exposed to unpaid royalties for the remainder of the franchise agreement.

To avoid being terminated, franchisees must comply with all of the terms of their franchise agreements. If franchisees anticipate they will have difficulty making royalty or other payments, they should communicate in advance with the franchisor to work out alternative arrangements. Franchisees are better off asking for support upfront than ignoring their obligations and facing termination.

Franchisors should be able to enforce terminations provided they act in accordance with the terms and conditions of the agreement. However, if they haven't exercised their termination rights fairly they may have difficulty doing so. Unlike some U.S. state laws that deal expressly with terminations, Canadian franchise statutes only require parties to franchise agreements to perform and enforce their obligations in good faith and in accordance with reasonable commercial standards. Examples of when a franchisor may be enjoined from terminating a franchise agreement on account of the duty of good faith and fair dealing are if the franchisor specifically promised the franchisee it wouldn't treat its non-payment as a default, or if, without a legitimate business reason, the franchisor sought to enforce a contractual provision it had not enforced against any other franchisee.

If at an injunction hearing, a franchisee can show that its only source of income is the franchise operation, and that it will go bankrupt unless it can continue operating the franchise pending trial, a court likely will restrain a franchisor from terminating the agreement. A franchisee will be expected to comply with the franchise agreement and depending on its payment history, a court may impose COD terms on the franchisee for the franchisor's supply of product.

The reality is that the last thing any franchisor wants is for one of its stores to go dark. To avoid terminations, franchisors should pay close attention to early warning signs of problems and address any issues both practically and on a timely basis. If the relationship can't be rectified and is headed for divorce, then given the uncertainty, cost and time associated with going to court to enforce any termination, franchisors may wish to consider alternative exit strategies like buying-out the franchisee, helping the franchisee find a third-party buyer, or putting a management arrangement in place.

Source: Jennifer Dolman, *Financial Post*, October 10, 2012 (www.financialpost.com). Used with permission.

8. Maintain your premises in clean, sanitary condition and redecorate when required to do so by the franchisor.

9. Maintain the required level of business insurance coverage.

10. Permit the franchisor's staff to enter your premises to inspect and see whether the franchisor's standards are being maintained.

11. Purchase specific goods or services from the franchisor or specified suppliers.

12. Train all staff in the franchisor's method and ensure that they are neatly and appropriately dressed.

13. Obtain the franchisor's consent before assigning the franchise contract to another party.

14. Maintain adequate levels of working capital and abide by the operations manual provided by the franchisor.

These are only examples of some of the obligations you might expect to incur. There will probably also be clauses involving bankruptcy, transfer of the business, renewal of the contract, and provisions for the payment of royalties and other financial considerations.

What do you like about being an Entrepreneur?

I have truly enjoyed mentoring people who want to become entrepreneurs and sharing my experience to inspire others to become successful.

Ronald V. Joyce
Chairman, Jetport
Investments

Photo courtesy of
Ronald V. Joyce

Franchise Fees and Royalties

In most cases, you will be required to pay an initial franchise fee on signing the franchise agreement. This fee generally pays for the right to use the franchisor's trade name, licences, and operating procedures; some initial training; and perhaps even assistance in site selection for your franchise outlet. The amount of the fee varies tremendously, according to the type of franchise business. For a large restaurant operation or hotel, for example, the fee may be as high as $50,000 or $100,000, but for a small service franchise (e.g., maid service or lawn care), it may be only $5,000 to $10,000. This fee is not all profit for the franchisor, as it must go to pay for franchisee recruitment, training, assistance with site selection, and other services normally provided to you. Some franchisors will charge a separate training fee, but this is usually established merely to recover the cost of providing the training to you and your employees.

In addition to this initial fee, ongoing fees may also be provided for in the franchise agreement. These will generally consist of royalties payable for ongoing rights and privileges granted by the franchisor. Royalties are usually calculated as a percentage of the gross sales, not profits, generated by your franchise. They may be paid weekly, monthly, or quarterly, and represent the main profit centre for most franchisors. These royalties must continue to be paid, even though the franchise may be losing money. For a fast-food franchise, typical royalties range from 3 percent to 8 percent. For some service franchises, the royalty may run from 10 to 20 percent or even higher.

While some franchisees come to resent having to continue to pay ongoing royalties to their franchisor, this payment may be preferable to the franchisor charging a higher initial fee to the franchisee. Ongoing royalty payments at least imply a continuing commitment to the success of the franchise by the franchisor, to the ultimate benefit of both parties.

As well as royalty fees, many franchise agreements require you to contribute a proportion of your business's gross revenues to a regional or national co-operative advertising fund. This contribution may be an additional 2 to 4 percent of gross sales. These payments are used to develop and distribute advertising material and to run regional and national advertising campaigns. These are typically not a source of profit for the franchisor.

The administration of these advertising funds has often been the subject of considerable concern to franchisees and one of the areas of greatest dispute between franchisors and franchisees. The advertising fund should be maintained as a separate trust account by the franchisor and not intermixed with its general operating revenues. The purpose of this fund should be specified in the franchise agreement. In addition, the agreement should also state how and by whom the fund will be administered.

In addition to requiring you to support a regional or national advertising program, a franchisor may require you to support your own local advertising. Typically, you must spend a specific amount on a periodic basis, calculated either on the basis of a percentage of gross sales or in terms of a fixed amount. Local advertising devised by you will normally require the prior approval of the franchisor.

In some cases, the franchisor also provides you with special services, such as bookkeeping, accounting, and management consulting services, which are billed on a fee-for-service basis. Before acquiring a franchise you should be sure that you understand all the fees that will be payable, including any extra fees that may not be mentioned in the franchise agreement.

Purchase of Products and Supplies

A key element in the success of many franchise organizations is the sameness of each of the franchise outlets. Therefore, franchisors will work to ensure the maintenance of a certain quality of product or service and to make sure that uniform standards are employed throughout their system. Consequently, many franchisors, in an attempt to exercise complete control over their operation, require you to purchase products and services from them or from designated sources. In some cases, the approved suppliers may include affiliates of the franchisor. You may also be able to purchase items from other sources of supply, provided the franchisor has approved each of those sources in advance.

If the franchisor exerts tight control over such supplies, you should try to ensure beforehand that supplies are going to be readily available when required, that they are sold to you at fair market value and on reasonable terms, and that you have the ability to choose alternative sources for any nonproprietary items if the franchisor or the designated supplier is unable to provide them to you when required.

Many franchisors earn a profit from providing supplies to their franchisees. Often, however, because franchisors exercise enormous buying power they can supply goods and services at prices and under terms that are better than those you could negotiate for yourself. You should shop around to compare prices for comparable merchandise. If the prices being charged by the franchisor are out of line, this added cost can dramatically affect your business's future earnings.

Volume rebates are often paid to franchisors by suppliers of particular products. Rather than pocket the money themselves or distribute it back to their franchisees, some franchisors will contribute this to the advertising fund. As a potential franchisee, you should ask how these rebates will be handled, as a considerable amount of money may be involved.

Leased Premises

Many franchise operations require the use of physical facilities, such as land and buildings. When these premises are leased rather than owned by the franchisee, there are a number of ways in which this lease arrangement can be set up:

1. The franchisor may own the land and/or buildings and lease it to you.
2. You may lease the land and/or building directly from a third party.
3. You may own the property, sell it to the franchisor, and lease it back under a sale leaseback agreement.
4. A third party may own the property and lease it to the franchisor, who then sublets it to you.

The franchise agreement should spell out who is responsible, you or the franchisor, for negotiating the lease, equipping the premises, and paying the related costs. If a lease is involved, its terms and renewal clauses should be stated and should correspond with the terms of the franchise. You must be careful not to have a 20-year lease on a building and only a five-year franchise agreement, or vice versa.

Franchisors generally want to maintain control of the franchise premises. Accordingly they will often own or lease the property on which the franchise business is located, and then sublet these premises to you. In other situations, the franchisor may assign a lease to you subject to a conditional reassignment of the lease back to the franchisor on termination of the franchise for any reason.

With respect to other leasehold improvements, you may also be required to purchase or lease from the franchisor (or from suppliers designated by the franchisor) certain fixtures, furnishings, equipment, and signs that the franchisor has approved as meeting its specifications and standards.

Territorial Protection

In many cases, the franchise agreement provision with respect to your territory and protection of that territory may be subject to considerable negotiation prior to inclusion in the agreement. You will generally want to have the franchisor agree not to operate or grant a franchise to operate another franchised outlet too close to your operation. This restriction may be confined to a designated territory or may be confined to a predetermined geographic radius from your premises.

Franchisors, on the other hand, like to see exclusive territorial protection kept to a minimum. As a result, some franchisors may restrict the protection provided to you to a grant of first refusal to acquire an additional franchise within your territory or may subject you to a performance quota in terms of a prescribed number of outlet openings to maintain exclusivity within your territory. Another approach taken by some franchisors is to limit exclusivity to a formula based on population, with the result that when the population within your territory exceeds a certain number, the franchisor may either itself operate, or grant a franchise to operate, an additional outlet in the territory.

Some questions you might like to have answered in the franchise agreement are as follows:

1. Exactly what are the geographic boundaries of your territory, and are they marked on a map as part of the contract?

2. Do you have a choice of other territories?

3. What direct competition is there in your territory, and how many more franchises does the franchisor expect to sell in that area within the next five years?

4. If the territory is an exclusive one, what are the guarantees of this exclusivity?

5. Even with these guarantees, will you be permitted to open another franchise in the same territory?

6. Can your territory be reduced at any time by the franchisor?

7. Has the franchisor prepared a market survey of your territory? (If so, ask for a copy of it, and study it.)

8. Has the specific site for the franchise within the territory been decided on? (If not, how and when will this be done?)

Training and Operating Assistance

Virtually every franchise agreement deals with the question of training the franchisee. Training programs may involve training schools, field experience, training manuals, or on-location training.

The franchise agreement should have some provision for an initial training program for you and should specify the duration and location of this training and who is responsible for your related transportation, accommodation, and living expenses. This initial training is generally provided for you and the managers of your franchise business. The franchisor will usually require you and your managers to complete the training program successfully prior to the opening of your franchise business. If for some reason you should fail to complete the training program, the franchisor often reserves the right to terminate the agreement and refund all fees, less any costs incurred.

Many franchise agreements also provide for startup advisory training at the franchise premises prior to or during the opening of the business. This typically involves a program lasting a specified number of days. The agreement should indicate who is expected to bear the cost for such startup training, including who will be responsible for the payment of travel, meals, accommodation, and other expenses of the franchisor's supervisory personnel.

10 QUESTIONS YOU NEED TO ASK YOUR FUTURE LANDLORD

1. **Who is the landlord?** Will you be dealing with a large institution, a bank or a small independent "Mom and Pop" landlord? Depending on your opposition, you will be using a different negotiating approach or strategy. For instance, large institutional landlords often handle leasing matters through a board of directors—not one individual making decisions. Therefore, there may be some delay with the managing of tenancy issues. Smaller landlords are typically more local and more accessible.

2. **How long has the landlord owned the property?** In commercial real estate, there are both new and established landlords. Established landlords can be either "holders" or "flippers." Holders will keep the property long-term and work to increase its value, while flippers will resell the building for a profit within a short time. Long-term landlords are more stable to work with and more knowledgeable about the property's history and any required maintenance issues. A newer landlord who is primarily interested in short-term ownership will know less about the property.

3. **Where is the landlord located?** A local landlord is often more accessible, thus making it easier to deal with potential problems before and after signing the lease. While franchisees can still rent from absentee or corporate landlords (or even landlords with a local address, but who are often absent), a local landlord is more likely to tend to his/her local properties first.

4. **Is the person in charge of property management local?** Ensure that the property manager is readily available to deal with any concerns you may have. A property manager may look after multiple sites, and if the sites are not all in the same town or city, the property manager may be out of town—and out of reach—when you need him or her.

5. **What is the building's history?** An older building may require significant maintenance, which tenants pay for in Common Area Maintenance (CAM) charges. The term of a new lease is typically five to 10 years. It may take another five to 10 years for your franchise to become profitable. Are you prepared to invest new money into an old building?

6. **Who is doing the property leasing?** Landlords may deal with the leasing themselves, hire in-house leasing staff, or turn the listing over to a real estate agent. Each party will have a different motivation for seeing the deal signed, plus each will be more or less knowledgeable about the property.

7. **Who were the two most recent tenants to move in and when?** You may want to approach these tenants and ask them how their lease negotiations went. To find the newest tenants, ask the listing agent; if he or she claims to have only recently acquired the listing and does not know the building's history, push for details. The agent will have access to the landlord who can provide occupancy records for previous and recent tenants.

8. **Who were the last two tenants to move out?** The agent will be able to answer this question, but you may want to ask other tenants in the building for more facts. When and why did the formers tenants move out? Were they unhappy with the building and moved elsewhere? Did they close their business? Speak to the former tenants, and ask for their reasons for leaving as well as their opinions of the landlord.

9. **Who is the property's biggest tenant (the anchor tenant)?** How secure is this anchor's tenancy? The anchor tenant(s) typically pulls the most traffic to a property, so you will want to confirm that they will be staying. The agent you are dealing with will be able to verify this for you. If certain tenants or anchors are important to you, protect yourself with a Vacancy Protection clause, inserted into the lease agreement. Should the anchor close, move, or terminate the lease, a Vacancy Protection clause gives you the right to either pay less rent or terminate your lease based on decreased traffic flow.

10. **Is the building for sale?** Due to the number of limited qualified buyers available, commercial buildings are not advertised for sale in the conventional way (with a conspicuous "For Sale" sign always posted out front). Instead, commercial properties are offered to other landlords through a commercial property website. Building owners looking to sell their building will have different motivations towards prospective tenants.

Source: Dale Willerton, BeTheBoss.ca expert (www.betheboss.ca), accessed May 16, 2013. Used with permission.

The franchise agreement may also make reference to periodic refresher training. It should specify whether attendance at such programs is optional or mandatory. If it is mandatory, you should ensure that a specified maximum number of such programs is indicated for each year of the franchise agreement. The duration and location of these programs should also be specified.

Most franchisors want tight control over the day-to-day operations of the franchise, and accordingly they provide extensive operating assistance to their franchisees. This assistance is often in the form of a copyrighted operations manual that spells out, procedure by procedure, how you are expected to run the business. The manual will include such information as the franchisor's policies and procedures; cover such details as the hours you must remain open, record-keeping methods and procedures, procedures for hiring and training employees; and in a restaurant franchise, contain such matters as recipes, portion sizes, food storage and handling procedures, and menu mix and prices. The franchise agreement may also indicate that operating assistance will be provided in relation to:

1. The selection of inventory for your franchise business
2. Inspections and evaluation of your performance
3. Periodic advice with respect to hiring personnel, implementing advertising and promotional programs, and evaluating improvements in the franchise system
4. Purchasing goods, supplies, and services
5. Bookkeeping and accounting services
6. Hiring and training of employees
7. Formulation and implementation of advertising and promotional programs
8. Financial advice and consultation
9. Such additional assistance as you may require from time to time

Contract Duration, Renewal, and Termination

The duration of your franchise agreement may be as short as one year or as long as 40 to 50 years. However, the majority of franchise contracts run from 10 to 20 years. Most agreements also contain some provision for renewal of the contract. Be sure you understand these renewal provisions and what the terms, conditions, and costs of renewal will be. Renewal provisions commonly contain requirements for the payment of additional fees and upgrading of the franchise facilities to standards required by the franchisor at that time. The cost of upgrading is usually borne by the franchisee.

You should be aware, however, that not all agreements necessarily contain provisions for their renewal at the expiration of the initial term. Some agreements merely expire at the end of this term, and the rights revert to the franchisor.

The part of the franchise agreement usually considered most offensive by many prospective franchisees are those sections relating to termination of the agreement. Franchisors typically wish to develop a detailed list of conditions in which you might be considered in default of the agreement. *Events of default* typically fall into two categories: (1) critical or material events that would allow for termination of the agreement without notice by the franchisor and (2) events about which you would first be given written notice, with an opportunity to correct the situation.

Most franchise agreements also allow the franchisor the right, on termination or expiration, to purchase from you all inventory, supplies, equipment, furnishings, leasehold improvements, and fixtures used in connection with the franchise business. The method of calculating the purchase price of such items is entirely negotiable by the parties prior to the execution of the franchise agreement. This has been another area of considerable disagreement between franchisors and franchisees.

When renewing franchise agreements, many franchisors do not require the payment of an additional fee, but they may require franchisees to pay the current, and usually higher, royalty fees and advertising contributions. These increases, of course, reduce your income. In addition, the franchisor may require you to make substantial leasehold improvements, update signage, and make other renovations to your outlet to conform to current franchise system standards. These capital expenditures can be expensive, so it should be clear from the beginning what improvements might be required on renewal.

Selling or Transferring Your Franchise

With respect to the transfer or sale of your franchise, most franchise agreements indicate that you are granted rights under the agreement based on the franchisor's investigation of your qualifications. These rights are typically considered to be personal to you as a franchisee. The contract will usually state that transfers of ownership are prohibited without the approval of the franchisor, but you should attempt to have the franchisor agree that such consent will not be unreasonably withheld.

For self-protection, you should be sure that the agreement contains provisions for the transfer of the franchise to your spouse or an adult child on your death. Also, it should be possible to transfer the franchise to a corporation that is 100 percent owned by you and has been set up solely to operate the franchise. These transfers should be possible without the payment of additional fees.

Most franchisors, however, require transfer of your franchise to an external party who meets their normal criteria of technical competence, capital, and character.

Another common provision is for the franchisor to have a *right of first refusal*—the option to purchase your franchise in the event that you receive an offer from an independent third party to acquire your rights. In such a situation, you may be required to first offer such rights back to the franchisor under the same terms and conditions offered by the independent third party. If the franchisor declines to acquire your rights within a specified period of time after receipt of your notice of such an offer, you can proceed to complete the sale or transfer to the third-party purchaser.

One problem with this right of first refusal is the response time the franchisor has to exercise this right. In some agreements, the allowable period is several months, during which the third-party buyer is left on hold. In your original agreement, you should try to negotiate for a more reasonable period of 15 to 30 days for the exercise of this right of first refusal.

By anticipating these and other problems during the initial negotiations, you may be able to avoid future difficulties and enhance the marketability of your franchise.

Some Examples

As mentioned above, the specific terms included in a franchise agreement can vary substantially from situation to situation. For example, under the terms of the Cultures Restaurants (www.cultures-restaurants.com) franchise agreement for its healthy choices and healthy living concept franchise, franchisees pay $30,000 for an initial franchise fee plus a monthly royalty of 6 percent of gross sales and 3 percent of gross sales for the corporate advertising program. The minimum total investment required to get into the business is $30,000, with a total average investment of between $100,000 around $200,000. For this fee, the franchisee receives the use of the company's trademark and trade names. The company also provides training and marketing support.

In contrast, franchisees of Quizno's Classic Subs (www.quiznos.com) can expect to make a total investment of around $250,000 to open a typical outlet. This includes the company's standard franchise fee of $25,000. In addition, franchisees will need further funds for deposits of various types and money for working capital. Royalties amount to 7 percent of gross sales paid monthly, and the advertising contribution is a further 4 percent (1 percent for national advertising and 3 percent for expenditures in the local market). Of this amount, franchisees should have at least $90,000 in unencumbered cash. The rest may be financed through one of the national banks' franchise programs with the assistance of the company. Franchisees receive four weeks of intensive initial training, assistance in site selection and lease negotiations, pre-opening and ongoing operational support, and national, local, and grand-opening store marketing programs.

The Keg Steakhouse and Bar (www.kegsteakhouse.com) bills itself as Canada's leading steakhouse. A typical new, stand-alone Keg restaurant requires an investment of over $3.5 million to build the facility and cover the necessary startup costs. This includes the franchise fee of $75,000. Franchisees also pay a royalty of 5 percent of their gross sales each month and contribute 2.5 percent to a corporate advertising fund. This enables them to use the "Keg" brand name on their restaurant and the company provides them with training and other support before they open their location, and ongoing support in accounting, marketing, menu development, personnel management, and financial planning.

TABLE 11.3 A SAMPLING OF CANADIAN FRANCHISORS

Franchisor	Number of Franchisees/ Dealers in Canada	Initial Fee	Royalty	Advertising Program	Approximate Investment Required	Website
Boston Pizza	340	$60,000	7%	2.5%	$600,000–$800,000	www.bostonpizza.com
Dollar Thrifty Rent-a-Car	66	$5,000–$50,000	8%	—	$50,000–$300,000	www.thrifty.com
Great Canadian Dollar Store	120	$19,880	4%	—	$150,000–$400,000	www.dollarstores.com
The UPS Store	360	$35,000	—	—	$145,000–$180,000	www.theupsstore.ca
Dairy Queen Canada	588	45,000	4%	5–6%	$300,000	www.dairyqueen.com
McDonald's Restaurants of Canada	1,136	$45,000	20% includes rent, services fee, and advertising		$500,000	www.mcdonalds.com
Midas Muffler Shop	162	$30,000	—	—	$350,000–$420,000	www.midas.com
Yeh! Yogourt	11	$30,000	6%	1%	$200,000–$300,000	www.yehyogourt.com/
Second Cup Coffee Co.	360	$40,000	9%	3%	$300,000–$400,000	www.secondcup.com
Tim Hortons	3,436	$50,000	4.5%	4%	$480,000–$510,000	www.timhortons.com
M&M Meat Shops	400	—	3%	2%	$200,000–$300,000	www.mmmeatshops.com
ATM Franchise	210	$25,000	$100.00	1%	$25,000–$50,000	www.acfnfranchised.com

Source: Adapted from the *Franchise Canada Directory 2013*, Canadian Franchise Association (www.cfa.ca) and BeTheBoss.ca (www.betheboss.ca).

A sampling of some other popular franchisors indicating their initial franchise or dealership fee, royalty rate, required advertising contribution, and their approximate total average investment to open a typical outlet is shown in Table 11.3.

BUYING A FRANCHISE   LO4

FINDING A FRANCHISE BUSINESS

Perhaps the most common source of preliminary information regarding available franchises is by searching online for franchise websites, such as betheboss.ca, lookforafranchise.ca, and frannet.ca, and for franchise consultants, such as Murphy Business & Financial Corporation. Another source is newspaper advertisements. Major business newspapers, such as the *National Post* and *The Globe and Mail,* all have special sections devoted to franchise advertisements. The "Business" or "Business Opportunities" section of the classified advertisements in your local newspaper can also be an important place to look for prospective franchise situations. Business journals and trade magazines may also contain

ENTREPRENEURS IN ACTION

THE MAN BEHIND TIM HORTONS

Ron Joyce is behind the success of Tim Hortons but many don't know that before becoming a partner with Tim Horton, he had a DQ franchise. He saw how happy customers were when they were given ice cream—huge smiles from both young and old. He absolutely loved that he was making someone happy.

Ron started his career as a police officer, but a chance meeting with an acquaintance who owned a Dairy Queen changed Ron's future. He left the police force and opened a DQ franchise—it was exciting to be self-employed, turned out to be profitable, and he found it much more fun serving ice cream than serving a speeding ticket.

It's a lot more rewarding seeing someone smile than frown. I've found my niche in life!

In the first eight months of operation, Ron had made three times the salary he received as a police officer. He secured financing to open a second DQ but was turned down by DQ Canada. That's when he saw an ad for a Tim Hortons franchise. The franchise was in its infancy at that time—no recipes, no training guides, nothing other than a Ouija board helping them decide what donuts would be made that night.

Ron did have concerns about the business, but he had borrowed the money to purchase the store and knew he had to make it work. He went on to buy a second store, but when asked about a third one, he was considering the decision to sell his stores—he knew that Tim's wasn't moving forward under current management and approached Tim Horton about taking over management and becoming a partner in the company. In late 1966, Ron became a full partner and began the journey of making Tim Hortons a national recognizable chain.

Initially, Tim Hortons stores were mostly available in small towns in Ontario. In 1973, it was decided to open the first out-of-province store in Moncton, New Brunswick. The coffee shop opened in June 1974—breaking all previous sales records for Tim's. It was a winning model that continued across Canada. However, as with any business, there are always growing pains and as the expansion of the company was so rapid the company struggled with being under-capitalized as they preferred to purchase the land and build their own stores rather than lease properties. It was a trying time at that stage in the development of the company; however, Mr. Joyce maintains that the efforts were well worthwhile.

After Tim Horton's death in 1974, Ron became partners with Tim Horton's wife. After a year, Ron approached Mrs. Horton with three options: she'd buy him out, he'd buy her out, or they would sell the company. She sold her shares to Ron in 1975 for $1 million.

As Ron put it, *it was now my business, and I could run like hell with it.* It gave him the freedom to do the things he couldn't do with a partner, and the company expanded quickly.

Ron had aggressive plans and always had the full support of his senior management team. In 1990, there were 500 stores, and his goal was to expand to 1,000 stores by 1995. Together, the goal was surpassed as the chain opened over 1,200 stores by the end of that year.

RON JOYCE

Ron's next ambitious goal was to open 2,000, stores by the year 2000 and this goal was also achieved; however, in 1996, Ron sold the company to Dave Thomas of the U.S.-based Wendy's franchise.

In the mid-90s, Tim Hortons' success was receiving a lot of attention from potential buyers, and Ron had met many food service industry executives interested in buying the company. The decision to sell to Wendy's was based on their success in the U.S., and it was Ron's vision to expand Tim Hortons across the United States. The success of the first Tim Hortons/Wendy's combination stores along highway 401 in Ontario proved that the partnership could be successful for both companies.

Throughout the early days in the late 1960s and during the expansion of the company across Canada, the store owners were always held in the highest regard by Ron Joyce. They were not considered franchisees to Ron. When asked what has made Tim Hortons so successful, Mr. Joyce responded by saying, "The distribution of the name in every community across Canada and strong partnerships with the store owners."

Did he ever want to give up—of course, he did. The long hours, seven days per week, travelling across the country took a toll, but he persevered with his passion for the people and the company he nurtured.

After selling Tim Hortons, Mr. Joyce built a successful private airport, Jetport, located in Mt. Hope, Ontario, and Fox Harb'r, a golf resort in his home province of Nova Scotia. He also started a charity—The Joyce Foundation—whose primary focus is to provide access to education for children and youth with significant financial need or facing other socio-economic barriers to success.

At 82, Mr. Joyce still enjoys going to work and helping others succeed as he has.

On giving advice to anyone thinking of starting a business—
Find something that you love to do and embrace it!

Source: Interview with Wendy Mayhew, Business Launch Solutions, February 2013. Used with permission, courtesy of Ron Joyce.

ads for many franchise organizations. Recommendations from friends, trade shows and seminars, and business opportunity shows often held in larger Canadian cities can also be excellent means of contacting franchisors.

Another important source of information is franchise directories, which list franchisors' names and addresses along with information on the type of franchise offered, the costs involved, and other useful information. One helpful directory is *FranchiseCanada* magazine's directory published annually by the Canadian Franchise Association (www.cfa.ca).

CHECKING OUT THE FRANCHISE OPPORTUNITY

After sifting through the various choices available, most prospective franchisees narrow their selection down to one or two possibilities. The next step is requesting a promotional kit from each of these franchisors. Normally, this kit contains basic information about the company—its philosophy, a brief history, a listing of the number of outlets, where they do business, and so on. Most kits also contain an *application form* requesting your name and address, information about your past business experience, the value of your net assets, and other data; for the process to continue with the franchisor, you must complete it in detail. The form may have any one of a number of titles:

- Confidential Information Form
- Personal History
- Confidential Application
- Franchise Application
- Pre-Interview Form
- Qualification Report
- Credit Application
- Application for Interview Form
- Request for Interview

Regardless of which of these titles is used, they are all different ways of describing the same thing and request much the same information. For example, you may be asked for:

1. Personal data, such as your name, address, telephone number, age, health and physical impairments, marital status, number of dependants, and the names of any fraternal, business, or civic organizations to which you might belong.

2. Business data, such as your present business, your position, the name and address of your employer, how long you have been involved in this business, your present annual salary, and any previous business history you may have, and the name and address of your bank.

3. Professional references from your bank manager, for example, and any other references you may care to provide.

4. Financial data, such as your average annual income for the past five years and a total declaration of your current assets and liabilities to establish your net worth.

5. Additional data that relate to your particular interest in the franchise.

The application form normally requires you to provide a deposit, typically in the range of $2,000 to $5,000. In most cases, the form will state that this deposit will be credited toward the initial franchise fee without interest or deduction if the transaction proceeds. However, you should make sure that if you are turned down, all or most of this deposit will be refunded, especially if it is a large amount of money and the franchise is new and unproven.

If your application is approved, the franchisor will interview you to determine your suitability as a franchisee. The focus of this interview will be on assessing your capability according to various objective criteria that have been established by the franchisor. Every franchisor has its own established criteria based on previous experience with various kinds of people. For example, many franchisors will not consider absentee owners and refuse to grant

OTHER CONSIDERATIONS

McDONALD'S—INCLUSION AND DIVERSITY

According to the McDonald's website, the company is moving from awareness to action. Its goal is to have people within its organization working and living to reach their full potential. It believes that leaders hold themselves accountable for learning about, valuing, and respecting individuals on both sides of the counter. Diversity and inclusion are part of its culture—from the crew room to the board room. The company is working to achieve this goal every day by creating an environment for everyone to contribute their best.

QUICK FACTS

- 70 percent of U.S. employees are women/minorities.
- Over 25 percent of women/minorities are in leadership.
- 45 percent of franchisees are women/minority[3].

Many Canadian franchisors are committed to diversity within their franchise system, but few, if any, have implemented partnerships, education, and global initiatives as McDonald's has.

In some cases, franchisees are left to their own means of creating diversity within their franchise.

franchises strictly for investment purposes. They feel that the success of their system rests on the motivation created by individually owned and managed outlets.

The personal characteristics desired by the franchisor will vary with the type of business. For example, a different level of education is necessary to operate a management consulting service than is needed to operate a carpet cleaning firm. Research on these selection criteria indicates that many franchisors tend to rank them in the following order:

1. Credit and financial standing
2. Personal ability to manage the operation
3. Previous work experience
4. Personality
5. Health
6. Educational background

While other factors may also be considered by particular franchisors, these criteria tend to dominate the selection process.

This interview is also an opportunity for you to raise questions about the franchisor's financial stability, trademark protection policy, the ongoing services provided to franchisees, information regarding any financial packages that may have been arranged with particular banks, the names and addresses of current franchisees, and any other questions that may occur to you. This is an opportunity for you and the franchisor to assess each other and see if you can work together on a long-term basis.

At this interview, the franchisor will also provide you with a copy of the franchise agreement. At this point, you must evaluate all the available information with the help of an accountant, your bank manager, and a lawyer to ensure that you feel comfortable with the franchisor and that you are happy your investment is secure. If you have any remaining questions or doubts, now is the time to resolve them. Then, if you are still not completely sure in your own mind that you wish to proceed, you should ask for a refund of your deposit.

Well-established and popular franchisors are unlikely to change their arrangements or legal documentation very much in response to a prospective franchisee's requests. They have successful systems in which many would-be franchisees would like to participate. For them, it is a seller's market.

If one of these franchisors accepts you as a franchisee, you may have to make up your mind very quickly. It is important to be decisive. If you are comfortable with the franchisor and the franchise agreement, you should be ready to sign. If not, you should ask for a refund and pursue other opportunities.

Some franchisors will expect you to sign the contract right away. Others wait until they have found a suitable location for your outlet, usually within a predetermined period of time. In some cases, it can take weeks, perhaps even months, for a suitable site to be found or a lease negotiated before you actually sign. It should also be remembered that popular franchisors often have long waiting lists of prospective franchisees, so one or more years can pass before you will be in business.

FRANCHISE FINANCING

One of the first steps in evaluating any franchise opportunity is to determine the total cost of getting into the business. This could include the initial franchise fee, equipment costs, startup inventories and expenses, and initial working capital requirements. This total commitment can be substantial. A study released by the International Franchise Association in the United States indicated the following median values for the minimum and maximum range within an industry for starting a franchised outlet by industry category. These figures are in U.S. dollars and do not include the cost of real estate.[4]

- Baked goods $210,000–$395,000
- Business services $51,000–$84,000
- Fast food $178,000–$2,900,000
- Lodging $4,109,000–$6,485,000
- Real estate $31,000–$98,000
- Restaurant $423,000–$920,000
- Service businesses $65,000–$136,000
- Sports and recreation $4,400–$340,000
- Travel $67,000–$135,000

You must also determine how much of this amount must be put up as an initial investment and what kind of terms might be arranged for handling the balance. Most franchisors expect the franchisee to put up 30 to 50 percent of the total franchise package cost as an initial investment. You must ask yourself whether you have enough unencumbered capital to cover this amount.

Financing of the remainder can sometimes be done through the franchisor, or the franchisor may have previously arranged a standardized financing package for prospective franchisees through one of the major banks or trust companies. Subway, the successful submarine sandwich franchise, offers its new franchisees financing via an in-house equipment leasing program. Compucentre also has arranged an in-house financing program for franchisees in conjunction with a couple of the major banks. These programs may be somewhat more expensive for the franchisee than arranging an independent bank loan, but they can be more convenient.

The initial investment required for a restaurant, for example, can be substantial. A typical quick service restaurant, such as Pizza Pizza, has an initial franchise fee of $30,000 and an average total investment of $300,000 to $500,000. The cost of a full-service restaurant, such as Swiss Chalet Chicken & Ribs, includes a franchise fee of $60,000 and a total investment ranging from $1.6 million to $1.8 million. In these cases, equipment and leasehold improvements tend to make up the largest component of the total cost.

In the retail sector, the size of the total investment will vary, depending on the nature and location of the outlet. For example, a furniture store, such as The Brick Warehouse, will require a franchise fee of $40,000 and an average total investment of $500,000 to $1 million, with the franchisee having to come up with $400,000 to $700,000 as his or her initial startup capital. An electronics store, such as The Source, has a franchise fee of $15,000 and a total investment ranging from $75,000 to $200,000. The Wine Kitz winemaking franchise has an initial fee of $15,000 and a total required investment of $120,000 to $150,000. Much of this investment is typically in inventory.

OTHER CONSIDERATIONS

WHAT DOES IT COST TO OPEN A FRANCHISE?

The estimated costs to open a Joey's Urban Restaurant (based on approximately 1,500 square feet, in Canadian dollars):

	Food Court	Joey's Urban
Based on approximate sq ft.	350 sq ft.	1200 sq ft.
Deposits, permits, and drawings	$9,000	$11,500
Leasehold improvements and fixtures	$110,000	$135,000
Furniture, equipment, and smallwares	$60,000	$95,000
Franchise fee	$25,000	$25,000
Opening inventory	$6,500	$8,250
Opening advertising and signage	$11,000	$13,000
Pre-opening and training	$3,500	$3,500
Total projected opening costs	**$225,000**	**$291,250**

Source: Joey's Urban (http://joeysurban.ca), accessed July 18, 2013. Used with permission.

The investment required for a service franchise is usually much lower. Many service franchises can be established for a total investment of less than $50,000. For example, Jani-King Canada, the world's largest commercial cleaning franchise, offers its franchises for a fee as low as $10,000 with a nominal additional amount of financing for equipment, supplies, and initial working capital. A residential cleaning and maid service franchise, such as Molly Maid, can be established for a franchise fee of $15,000 plus $15,000 to $25,000 in working capital. At the other extreme, opening a franchised hotel or motel may involve a total investment of several million dollars, although the initial amount of money required may be much less, since the land and buildings for the hotel or motel can often be externally financed.

OTHER CONSIDERATIONS

ADVICE WHEN CONSIDERING A FRANCHISE OPTION

- Do your own research, and take your time.
- Don't be afraid to cold-call current franchisees (especially those in other provinces), and ask them all kinds of questions.
- Try to talk to former franchisees whose business went under. The more reputable franchisors may help you with names and numbers.
- Talk to knowledgeable people in the franchising sector to get the latest word on the organization you're thinking of joining, and what it's like to work with.
- Have an experienced franchise lawyer review your contract.
- If you still want to jump into the world of franchising, assume that nothing will ever again work the way you are used to. The best you can hope for is to reduce the number of "omigawd" surprises you are going to have to face.

Source: M. Stern, "Franchise Fairy Tales," *Canadian Business*, June 23, 2003, p. 30.

If you have a successful business and are looking to expand you might consider franchising as one alternative to enable you to do so. As a growth strategy, franchising can provide you with the ability to improve your market share by increasing your number of points for distributing your product or service. You can grow and expand your business faster than through internal company growth and with minimal capital, since the initial investment for the additional business unit is provided by the franchisee.

Advantages of Franchising Your Business

Franchising can provide you with a number of other significant advantages such as:

Capital Since franchisees use their own capital you have no investment at the unit level so you can leverage off the assets of these franchisees.

Return on investment (ROI) Because you have a smaller investment in the overall business, your ROI should be significantly higher.

Speed of growth Establishing franchises can enable you to grow much faster without increasing your investment or adding more employees.

Reduced role in day-to-day operations As a franchisor you are primarily concerned with the overall operating performance of your franchisees, reducing the scope of your involvement in day-to-day management of the business.

Highly motivated management Franchisees are typically more highly motivated than hired managers, since the business is their own.

Quality control Franchisees generally keep their units in better operational condition than hired managers and, as part of the local community, are better able to promote the business locally.

Long-term management Franchisees are more unlikely to leave in the short term, so you can realize a better return from investment in long-term training and development.

Unit performance Franchised outlets typically outperform company outlets in terms of sales volume.

Lean organizational structure Through franchising, you can grow your organization without necessarily adding a lot of overhead.

Brand building Since you are able to grow your organization without adding a lot of investment and overhead, you are able to expand your market presence more rapidly and effectively than possible through internal organizational growth.

Advertising Franchisees will typically contribute to a common advertising and promotional fund that can be used to promote your brand under your direction.[5]

Is Your Business Franchisable?

However, while these advantages may appear to be very attractive it is important to recognize that all businesses may not necessarily lend them to a franchise development strategy. To franchise your business, you must have a successful business concept that can be readily replicated in other locations. An appropriate first step in the decision to franchise is an examination of the question of whether or not your business concept is actually "franchisable." Any organization seriously considering franchising should undertake this analysis before going ahead and implementing a franchise strategy. The iFranchise Group, a U.S. consulting firm that specializes in assisting firms in developing and implementing franchise programs, has identified a number of criteria that assess the readiness of a company for franchising and the likelihood that it will be successful as a franchisor. These include:

Credibility To sell franchises, a company must first be credible in the eyes of its prospective franchisees. Credibility can be reflected in a number of ways: organization size, number of units, years in operation, success of the prototype unit, publicity, consumer awareness of the brand, or strength of management.

Differentiation In addition to credibility, a franchise organization must be adequately differentiated from its competitors. This can come in the form of a differentiated product or service, a lower investment cost, a unique marketing strategy, or different target markets.

Transferability of knowledge The organization must have the ability to teach its operating system to others. To franchise, a business must generally be able to thoroughly educate a prospective franchisee in a relatively short period of time. Generally, if a business is so complex that it cannot be taught to a franchisee in three months, a company will have difficulty franchising.

Adaptability The business concept must be able to be adapted from one market to another. Some concepts do not travel well over large geographic areas because of regional variations in consumer tastes or preferences. Others are constrained by varying provincial laws or regulations. Still other concepts work only because they are in a very unique location or because of the unique abilities or talents of the individual behind the concept.

Refined and successful prototype operations A refined and successful prototype is necessary to demonstrate that the system is proven and works and is generally instrumental for the training of franchisees. The prototype also acts as a testing ground for new products, new services, marketing techniques, merchandising, and operational efficiencies.

Well-documented systems All successful businesses have systems. But to be franchisable, these systems must be documented in a manner that communicates them effectively to franchisees. Generally, a franchisor will need to document its policies, procedures, systems, forms, and business practices in a comprehensive and user-friendly operations manual.

Affordability Affordability must reflect a prospective franchisee's ability to pay for the franchise in question. For example, a franchise with a $100,000 startup cost that targets prospects with clerical experience might be affordable to any number of people, whereas a multi-million dollar hotel franchise might not.

Return on investment This is the real acid test of franchisability. A franchised business must, of course, be profitable. But more than that, a franchised business must allow enough profit after paying your royalty and other costs for the franchisees to earn an adequate return on their investment of time and money.

Market trends and conditions While not an indicator of franchisability as much as a general indicator of the success of any business, these trends are key to long-term planning. Is the market growing or consolidating? How will that affect your business in the future? What impact will the Internet have? Will the franchisee's products and services remain relevant in the years ahead? What are other franchised and non-franchised competitors doing? And how will the competitive environment affect your franchisee's likelihood of long-term success?

Capital While franchising is a low-cost means of expanding a business, it is not a "no cost" means of expansion. You will need the capital and resources necessary to implement a successful franchise program. The resources required to initially implement a franchise program will vary, depending on the scope of the program. If you are looking to sell just one or two franchised units, the necessary legal documentation may be completed at costs as low as $15,000. If, however, you are seeking more aggressive expansion, startup costs can run to $100,000 or more. And once the costs of printing, marketing, and hiring additional personnel are added to the mix, you may require a budget of $250,000 or more to reach your expansion goals.

Commitment to relationships Successful franchisors focus on building long-term relationships with their franchisees that are mutually rewarding. Unfortunately, not all franchise organizations understand the link that exists between relationships and profits. Strong franchisee relationships enable the franchisor to sell franchises more effectively, introduce needed changes into the system more easily, and motivate franchisees and their managers to provide a consistent level of products and services to their customers.

Strength of management Finally, the single most important aspect contributing to the success of any franchise program is the strength of its management. Often, new franchisors will try to take everything on themselves. In addition to absorbing several new jobs for which they have little to no time, you will need to exhibit expertise in fields in which you may have little or no experience, such as marketing, lead handling, franchise sales, advertising fund management, personnel training, and overseeing the management of several organizational units.[6]

How to Proceed

If you make the decision to franchise the next step is to outline a *business plan* detailing your expected growth and strategy for the next five years. You will probably need to raise some additional money and hire some people with new capabilities who will have to be integrated into your existing organization structure.

You will also need to develop a detailed *operations manual* for your franchisees. This manual will serve as a sales tool demonstrating to prospective franchisees that you have developed, tested, and refined your basic operating system so that it can be readily implemented in other locations and successfully transferred to other operators. This manual will serve as a sales tool, as a training guide for new franchisees, as a reference guide for current franchisees and as a quality control device for the entire chain.

You will need to develop *training programs* to induct new franchisees into your system and also familiarize the franchisee's employees and corporate employees with the system.

To be legally entitled to sell franchises in most jurisdictions now you will need a comprehensive *franchise agreement,* as described earlier in this stage, and a *franchise disclosure document* meeting the legal requirements of all the individual jurisdictions in which you plan to sell franchises.

Finally, you will need to sell franchises. This will require a specific marketing plan and related materials to get your message successfully across to targeted franchise prospects.

As you can see from the above discussion, franchising can be an excellent strategy for growing your business but is also a very specific and complicated concept with lots of issues and potential pitfalls. Therefore, it is important to have the expert support of professionals who specialize in franchising if you should decide to proceed with franchising your business. These franchise support services can include:

Franchise consultants, who can lead you through the franchise process in a step-by-step basis.

Legal counsel, who can advise you of the legal requirements as well as assist you in developing your franchise agreement and necessary disclosure documents.

Accountants, who can help you develop a financial model for your business that includes cash flow projections, your royalty structure, and so on that may be required for your disclosure documents.

Marketing consultants, who can assist in preparing your marketing plan, promotional materials, operations manual, and other documents that will be necessary for convincing potential investors they should become part of your franchise organization.

Should you decide to move in the franchise direction one final thing you need to appreciate is that your role in the business will change dramatically. You will go from being deeply involved in running the operational side of your business to being the CEO of a franchise company. This means you will have to redirect your time more to marketing activities trying to generate interest among prospective franchisees, attending public speaking events to familiarize the market with your franchise, and oversee new business owners trying to build a profitable business in various markets across the country.

FUTURE TRENDS IN FRANCHISING

A number of trends have emerged in the past few years that will positively impact franchising opportunities, and they are likely to continue. Among the most important are:

1. **Increasing emphasis on senior care** In North America, with the aging of the baby boomers, it is predicted that eldercare will replace child care as the number-one social issue. As they age, many seniors want to stay in their own homes, so any business that will provide them with companionship, extra help around the

house, or assistance in performing their daily activities, such as personal care and meal preparation, is likely to succeed.

2. **Child care and education** Increasingly, people want their children to have fun, become better educated, or get other forms of enrichment or special attention, and they are prepared to pay for it.

3. **Technical support** With the continual dependence of people and businesses on increasingly complex technology, advice is often needed on what to buy and what not to buy, how to handle repairs and upgrades, as well as solutions for various technological problems.

4. **Pet care** More and more, pets are being considered part of the family, and companies are springing up to provide a range of services, such as boarding facilities, cleaning and grooming, pet training, and feeding and general care services.

5. **Home improvements** Consumers are increasingly spending more on their dwellings, which has created an explosion of franchisors providing a broad range of services, such as general building services, kitchen remodelling, handyman services, interior decorating and painting, and electrical and plumbing services.

6. **Fitness** Fitness and obesity have received considerable coverage in the media, fuelling consumer interest in improved diet and exercise regimes. Gyms and fitness centres have been at the centre of this trend, particularly facilities that have emphasized women-only services.

7. **Restaurants** Restaurants of all types are expected to continue to be a very popular sector of franchising. Such concepts as Asian and healthy fast food, specialty ice cream, and neighbourhood coffeehouses continue to grow.

EVALUATING A FRANCHISE—A CHECKLIST

A checklist for evaluating a franchise is available online with Connect. The checklist can serve as an effective tool for you to use in evaluating a franchise opportunity. When reading through the questions, you will notice that some of them require you to do a little homework before you can reasonably respond. For example, you and/or your lawyer will have to review the franchise agreement to assess the acceptability of the various clauses and conditions. You will also have to give some thought to how much capital you personally have and where you might raise additional financing.

Some questions call for further research. Ask the franchisor for the names and addresses of a number of current franchisees. Select a sample of them and contact them to discuss their views of the franchisor and the franchise agreement. Make certain your interview takes place without the franchisor or his or her representative present. Check the length of time that the franchisee has operated in that particular location in comparison with the length of time that franchise has been in existence. If there is a difference, try to determine what happened to the earlier franchisee(s). If you have been provided with pro forma financial statements or other information by the franchisor indicating the level of sales and financial performance you might expect, ask these franchisees to confirm that these statements are reasonably close to reality. In addition, what you may feel you require in terms of training, advertising and promotion support, and ongoing operating assistance may be a function of the type of franchise you are evaluating.

Make a copy of this checklist for each franchise you intend to evaluate. By using a similar outline to assess each opportunity, it will be much easier for you to compare them.

 Find a *Checklist for Evaluating a Franchise* online with Connect.

For more information on franchising, you might check out the following sources:

Canadian Franchise Association The national voice of the franchise industry in Canada. (www.cfa.ca)

International Franchise Association A membership organization of franchisors, franchisees, and suppliers dedicated to providing members and guests with a one-stop shopping experience for franchise information. Check out their "Consumer Guide to Buying a Franchise." (www.franchise.org)

FranTech Media Inc. A resource for both franchisors and franchisees. Connects the right people with the right franchise opportunities by providing the complete franchise-specific marketing solution. BetheBoss.ca (a website owned by FranTech Media) has a full directory of franchise opportunities as well as a wealth of resources including articles on just about everything you need to know written by industry experts. (www.frantechmedia.com)

FranNet, The Franchise Connection An international consulting firm that provides education and support to individuals who are interested in exploring self-employment as a career option through franchised business ownership. (www.frannet.com)

DREAMERS Franchise Consultants Inc. A dynamic, respected global leader in international franchise development and business consulting, including candidate assistance with immigration to Canada and the U.S. (www.wowfranchises.com)

Canadian Franchise Opportunities An online directory of franchises and franchise business services. (canada.franchiseopportunities.com)

Canadian Franchising Magazine A bi-monthly digital publication bringing you all the latest news, expert advice, and franchising information from coast to coast. (www.canadianfranchisemagazine.com)

LEARNING OBJECTIVES SUMMARY

LO1 What is franchising?

- franchising is a legal and commercial relationship between the owner of a trademark, trade name, or advertising symbol and an individual or group of people seeking the right to use that identification in a business

- A franchisee generally sells goods and services supplied by the franchisor or that meet the franchisor's quality standards

- The franchisor provides business expertise, such as a proven product or service offering, an operating system, a marketing plan, site location, training, and financial controls, that otherwise would not be available to the franchisee

- The franchisee brings to the franchise operation the motivation, entrepreneurial spirit, and often the money to make the franchise a success.

LO2 The advantages of franchising are:

- reduced risk—franchising does not guarantee success, but a good franchise should help reduce the chances of failure

- a proven system—with a tried and tested operating system, the franchisee loses the obstacles and gains the opportunities. A franchisee should receive a completely proven system that includes initial training, opening assistance, accounting systems, established suppliers, manuals, and use of the trademarks. The all important "learning curve" helps prevent the franchisee from repeating previous mistakes and provides information on inventory levels, store design, competition, pricing structure, and operational data drawn from the entire system

- easier access to financing and reduced cash requirements—financial institutions prefer to lend to established franchised systems because of their higher success rate.

- purchasing power—collective purchasing power on products, supplies, extended health and insurance benefits, equipment, and advertising can easily offset any ongoing royalties paid by the franchisee

- site selection assistance—franchisors can provide expert site selection assistance based on their operating experience and demographic knowledge; enables franchisees, as part of an established franchise system, to obtain locations in major malls and other developments that otherwise would not be available to them as independent operators

- advertising clout—the advertising cost is spread over many units enabling the franchisor to achieve economies of scale; allows the franchisee to create well-conceived promotional campaigns and place the advertising in the most effective medium

- building equity—a buyer is often motivated to buy the franchised business for the same reasons as the original franchisee and may perceive a higher value associated with a recognized name and system

- stress reduction—systems that control job scheduling, cash flow, and inventory levels allow the franchisee to run the business instead of the business running them

The disadvantages of franchising are:

- loss of independence—unless you are capable of working within a system and can accept a certain amount of regimentation, you should think long and hard before entering into a franchise relationship; one of the greatest strengths of franchising is consistency among units, and with consistency must come compliance

- franchisor's failure to perform—a common reason for failure is the franchisor's shortage of available capital, caused by:
  - franchisor's unrealistic franchise sales projections
  - franchisor underestimating the expenses associated with the development of the franchise system
  - franchisor's failure to meet franchise sales projections
  - high franchisee attrition

- misunderstanding the franchise agreement—a franchise agreement requires careful explanation and scrutiny, and failure to do so will inevitably result in a conflict that may end up in the courts

- misrepresentation by the franchisor—can be intentional or unintentional; projections of income and expense can be provided to the franchisee in good faith but may turn out to be inappropriate for the location because of the franchisor's inexperience or unfamiliarity with the area's demographics

- payment of fees—in addition to the initial fee, some form of ongoing royalty is paid by the franchisee to the franchisor; franchisees are also required to contribute to a national or regional advertising fund, which is in addition to any requirement that the franchisee invests a minimum amount on local advertising

LO3 Franchise opportunities are vast and growing on an annual basis. Franchises are not just coffee shops and fast food restaurants, although they seem to be the most recognizable. Other types of available franchises at this time are:

- accounting/tax services
- advertising/marketing/promotional products and services
- automotive and truck services
- beauty/cosmetic supplies
- business consultants/services/training
- business—supplies/equipment and services
- commercial—supplies/equipment and services
- commercial/residential services
- computer/software/Internet
- consumer buying services
- dry cleaning/clothing care
- educational products and services
- employment/personal services
- environmental products and services
- event planning
- financial/cash services
- food:
  - baked goods/coffee/donuts
  - grocery/specialty shops
  - meal assembly
  - quick service restaurants
  - restaurants/dining rooms
- furniture/upholstery repair
- hair and nail salons/spas
- health and fitness/nutrition
- home:
  - decorations/furnishings
  - improvement/renovation/restoration
  - inspection services
  - maid/cleaning services
- home-based businesses
- hospitality products/services
- hotels/motels/campgrounds
- janitorial and maid services
- lawn and garden supplies/services
- mobile businesses

- pets—sales/supplies/services
- printing/copying/shipping
- real estate
- retail
- seniors/home care and services
- sign products/services
- sports/recreation/entertainment
- tanning salons
- travel
- weight loss services/body contouring
- wine making

LO4 The buying process of a franchise starts with finding a franchise to buy. Places to look for opportunities are:

- online searches
- newspapers and trade publications
- *FranchiseCanada* magazine's Directory
- Canadian Franchise Association
- pre-Interview form
- qualification report
- credit application
- application for interview form

Now that you have found a franchise(s) that you are interested in exploring, you will need to request information from the franchisor. You will be asked for personal information, including:

- confidential information form
- personal history
- confidential application
- franchise application

After you have submitted the requested information have been interviewed, and have decided to move forward, you need to determine the costs associated with getting into the business. These costs will include:

- initial franchise fee
- equipment costs
- start up inventory and expenses
- initial working capital
- how much will the initial investment be to the franchisor and what terms can be arranged for the remaining balance

In some cases, financing can be done through the franchisor. In other cases, they may have arrangements through major banks or trust companies in place.

LO5 Franchising your own business can provide you with a number of significant advantages, such as:

- capital—since franchisees use their own capital, you have no investment at the unit level, so you can leverage off the assets of these franchisees
- return on investment—because you have a smaller investment in the overall business, your ROI should be significantly higher
- speed of growth—establishing franchises can enable you to grow much faster without increasing your investment or adding more employees
- reduced role in day-to-day operations—as a franchisor, you are primarily concerned with the overall operating performance of your franchisees, reducing the scope of your involvement in day-to-day management of the business
- highly motivated management—franchisees are typically more highly motivated than hired managers, since the business is their own
- quality control—franchisees generally keep their units in better operational condition than hired managers and, as part of the local community, are better able to promote the business locally
- long-term management—franchisees are more unlikely to leave in the short term, so you can realize a better return from investment in long-term training and development
- unit performance—franchised outlets typically outperform company outlets in terms of sales volume
- lean organizational structure—through franchising, you can grow your organization without necessarily adding a lot of overhead
- brand building—since you are able to grow your organization without adding a lot of investment and overhead, you are able to expand your market presence more rapidly and effectively than possible through internal organizational growth
- advertising—franchisees will typically contribute to a common advertising and promotional fund that can be used to promote your brand under your direction

For more information on the resources available from McGraw-Hill Ryerson, go to www.mcgrawhill.ca/he/solutions.

ENDNOTES

PROLOGUE

1. Startups—Present and Future, Benjamin Tal (http://research.cibcwm.com/economic_public/download/if_2012-0925.pdf). Contact Benjamin Tal 416 956 3698 benjamin.tal@cibc.ca.
2. Ibid.
3. CIBC (http://research.cibcwm.com/economic_public/download/if_2012-0925.pdf).
4. Investopedia (investopedia.com/terms/e/entrepreneur.asp#axzz2ExMorntP), accessed December 13, 2012.
5. Investor Words (investorwords.com/e2.htm#entrepreneur), accessed December 13, 2012.
6. William D. Bygrave, "The Entrepreneurial Process" in William D. Bygrave, Ed., *The Portable MBA in Entrepreneurship*, 3rd. ed. (Hoboken, NJ: John Wiley & Sons, Inc., 2004), p. 2.
7. Inc.com (inc.com/eric-schurenberg/the-best-definition-of-entepreneurship.html). What's an Entrepreneur? The best answer ever (HBS Professor, Howard Stevenson), accessed December 13, 2012.
8. Peter Drucker, *Innovation and Entrepreneurship: Practice and Principles* (New York: Harper and Row, 1985), p. 25.
9. Adapted from Jeffrey A. Timmons, *New Venture Creation: Entrepreneurship for the 21st Century*, 4th ed. (Homewood, IL: Richard D. Irwin, 1994), p. 23.
10. Adapted from The Jobberman Blog, 3 Reasons Entrepreneurs make the Best Employees (blog.jobberman.com/jobs-in-nigeria/2012/09/3-reasons-entrepreneurs-make-the-best-employees)
11. The E-Myth Revisited, Why Most Small Businesses Don't Work and What to Do About It (www.michaelegerbercompanies.com/resources/products/the-e-myth-revisited).

STAGE ONE

1. www.nyu.edu/about/news-publications/news/2012/10/05/stern-study-reveals-those-with-perception-of-power-or-status-act-differently.html.
2. P. Robinson, D. V. Stimpson, J. C. Huefner, and H. K. Hunt, "An Attitude Approach to the Predictions of Entrepreneurship," *Entrepreneurship Theory & Practice,* Summer 1991, Vol. 15, Issue 4.
3. N. J. Lindsay, A. Jordaan, and W. A. Lindsay, "Values and Entrepreneurial Attitude as Predictors of Nascent Entrepreneur Intentions," Working Paper, Centre for the Development of Entrepreneurs, School of Management, University of South Australia, Adelaide (http://sbaer.uca.edu/research/icsb/2005/paper124.pdf).
4. K. Vesper, *New Venture Strategies,* rev. ed. (Prentice-Hall, Englewood Cliffs, NJ, 1990), pp. 3–9.
5. D. Roberts and C. Woods, "Changing the World on a Shoestring: The Concept of Social Entrepreneurship," *University of Auckland Business Review,* Autumn 2005, pp. 45–51.
6. Free the Children (www.freethechildren.com/about-us/our-story/), accessed January 10, 2013.
7. *The American Heritage Dictionary of the English Language*, 4th ed., William Morris, Ed. (Boston: Houghton Mifflin Company, 2000).
8. V. E. Henderson, "The Ethical Side of Enterprise," *Sloan Management Review,* Spring 1982, p. 38.
9. K. Blanchard and N. V. Peale, *The Power of Ethical Management* (New York: William Morrow and Co. Inc., 1988), p. 27.
10. J. M. Alford, "Finding Competitive Advantage in Managing Workplace Ethics," paper presented at the 19th National Conference of the United States Association for Small Business and Entrepreneurship (USASBE), Dallas, Texas, 2005.

11. M. Earl, "Note on Individuals, Corporations and Society," Note 9B04M072, Richard Ivey School of Business, University of Western Ontario, 2004.

STAGE TWO

1. R. P. Singh, G. E. Hills, and G. T. Lumpkin, "New Venture Ideas and Entrepreneurial Opportunities: Understanding the Process of Opportunity Recognition." Paper presented at the United States Association for Small Business and Entrepreneurship Annual Conference, 1999 (www.sbaer.uca.edu/research/usasbe/1999/43.pdf). Updated January 2013.
2. Ibid.
3. G. T. Lumpkin, G. E. Hills, and R. C. Shrader, "Opportunity Recognition," in H.P. Welsch (ed.) *Entrepreneurship: The Way Ahead* (London, Routledge, 2004), pp. 73–90.
4. J. A. Timmons, *New Venture Creation*, 4th ed. (Burr Ridge, IL: Irwin, 1994), p. 87.
5. 2012 CYBF Best Business Aware Winners (www.cybf.ca/cybf_initiatives/awards/best-business).
6. J. G. Longnecker, L. B. Donlevy, V. A. C. Calvert, C. W. Moore, J. W. Petty, and L. E. Palich, *Small Business Management*, 4th Canadian ed. (Toronto: Nelson Education, 2010), p. 30.
7. I would like to thank Vance Gough of Mount Royal College for permission to include this exercise.
8. Susan Ward, About.com Small Business: Canada (sbinfocanada.about.com/od/businessopportunities/a/The-Best-Business-Opportunities-2013.htm).
9. F. Popcorn and L. Marigold, *Clicking: 17 Trends That Drive Your Business—and Your Life* (New York: HarperBusiness, 1998).
10. Ronald A. Knowles and Cliff G. Bilyea, *Small Business: An Entrepreneur's Plan*, 3rd Canadian ed. (Toronto: Harcourt Brace & Company, 1999), p. 55.

11. Richard Buskirk, *The Entrepreneur's Handbook* (Los Angeles: Robert Brian, Inc., 1985), pp. 41–45.
12. David Rae, "How Does Opportunity Recognition Connect with Entrepreneurial Learning?" Working Paper, Centre for Entrepreneurial Management, University of Derby, U.K.

STAGE THREE

1. Fluid Surveys blog post, Get the Most Out of Your Survey, Tips for Writing Effective Questions. Rafal Deren. With Permission (www.fluidsurveys.com).
2. Analyzing Your Competition, Regions Planning Guides (www.regions.com/small_business/planning_guides.rf), accessed February 2013.
3. Adapted from J. G. Barnes, *Research for Marketing Decision Making* (Toronto: McGraw-Hill Ryerson Ltd., 1991), pp. 84–94.
4. M. Scott and R. Bruce, "Five Stages of Growth in Small Business," *Long-Range Planning*, June 1987, pp. 45–52.

STAGE FOUR

1. A. J. Szonyi and D. Steinhoff, *Small Business Management Fundamentals*, 3rd Canadian ed. (Toronto: McGraw-Hill Ryerson, 1988), pp. 58–65.
2. www.ic.gc.ca/app/sbp/prfpls/prfl/rprtStp/sv.do;jsessionid=0000Tf6S7XB-NRZfkAejTgFRBAk:1247mpv0c, accessed May 25, 2010.

STAGE FIVE

1. http://articles.bplans.com.
2. Adapted from blog post by Tim Berry, In Praise of the Lean Business Plan, published in SBA.gov. (www.sba.gov).
3. Wikipedia—definition of lean startup.
4. Doug Somers, Cassidy Bay Group (www.cassidybay.com).

STAGE SIX

1. Wikipedia, board of directors (http://en.wikipedia.org/wiki/Board_of_directors), accessed March 19, 2013.
2. Adapted from Ellen Roseman, "Spark of Genius," *The Globe and Mail*, September 26, 1994.
3. R. Pederson, "Legal Battle of the Bricks Finally Ends; Sides Agree to Coexist," *Edmonton Journal,* June 20, 1992, p. F1.
4. HaidaBucks, An Indigenous Experience, Latest News (www.lanebaldwin.com/hbc/news.htm), accessed May 28, 2010.
5. P. Brieger, "When Mediation Fails, Call Your Lawyer: Yoga Clothier Files Trademark Lawsuit," *National Post,* September 25, 2003, p. FP.01.F.
6. lululemon athletica (en.wikipedia.org/wiki/lululemon_athletica), accessed May 28, 2010.

STAGE SEVEN

1. Ibid.
2. J. C. McCune (1999), "Bootstrapping: Cutting Corners and Pinching Pennies to Finance Your Business," Bankrate.com (www.bankrate.com/brm/news/biz/Cashflow_banking/19991101.asp), accessed March 26, 2013.
3. G. H. Haines Jr., J. J. Madill, and A. L. Riding, "Financing Small Business Growth: Informal Investing in Canada," *Journal of Small Business and Entrepreneurship*, Spring 2003, pp. 13–40.
4. Adapted from Entrevestor.com (www.entrevestor.com/blog/ooka-islands-post-dragon-sales-soar), February 29, 2013.
5. Profit Guide, November 2012 (www.profitguide.com/microsite/profitw100/2012/14-HapiFoods-Group).
6. Kara Kuryllowicz, "Learning the Ropes," *PROFIT*, October 2001, p. 42.
7. Adapted from David Menzies, "Getting the Best From Your Bank," *PROFIT*, November, 1998, pp. 26–32. Reprinted with permission.

STAGE EIGHT

1. Mark Evans Blog, Are Marketing and Sales the Same thing for Startups? April 5, 2013. Adapted from with permission (www.markevanstech.com).
2. Content Marketing Institute (www.contentmarketinginstitute.com), accessed May 3, 2013. Used with permission.
3. Less than Half of Canadian Businesses Have a Dedicated Website, February 27, 2013 (www.rbc.com/newsroom/2013/0227-smallbus-tech.html), accessed May 23, 2013.
4. Susan Ward, *7 Online Business Models, Part 1: How to Make Money Online,* About.com Small Business: Canada (sbinfocanada.about.com/od/onlinebusiness/a/onlinebizmodels.htm), accessed May 2, 2013.
5. Direct Marketing Association (www.thedma.org).
6. Adapted from the blog 3 Reasons Why E-mail Campaigns Fail, Scott Vetter, Prosar Inbound Blog, April 8, 2013 (www.prosar.com). Used with permission.
7. The Viral Manifesto website (www.viralvideomanifesto.com/book), accessed May 24, 2013.
8. www.bdc.ca/EN/Documents/marketing/SMeBook_2012_EN.pdf?utm_campaign=social%20eBook%20-%20EN&utm_medium=email&utm_source=Eloqua
9. Adapted from Real World Entrepreneur Training. Used with permission from Lisa McKenzie, Red Carpet Strategies, www.lisamckenzie.com.
10. www.citynews.ca/2013/05/15/astronaut-chris-hadfields-sons-pushed-him-to-social-media-stardom/
11. Adapted from *How to Craft a Great News Release.* The full guide is available for download on the CNW website (http://info.newswire.ca/download-Howtocraftagreatnews-releaseEnglish.html).
12. From AllBusiness.com.

STAGE NINE

1. Sales Pipeline Funnel Diagram, Canadian Professional Sales Association (www.cpsa.com).

STAGE TEN

1. M. Collins and J. King, *A Comprehensive Guide to Buying a Business in Canada*, Canada One Toolkit (www.canadaone.com/tools/buy_a_biz/index.html), accessed May 21, 2013.
2. "Two Million Jobs in Play as Small Business Succession Issue Looms," News Release, Canadian Federation of Independent Business, June 13, 2005 (www.canadiandemocraticmovement.ca/2-million-jobs-in-play-as-small-business-succession-issue-looms/), accessed May 21, 2013.
3. R. M. Hodgetts and D. F. Kuratko, *Effective Small Business Management*, 6th ed., The Dryden Press Series in Entrepreneurship (Orlando, FL: Harcourt Brace College Publishers, 1997), p. 65.
4. M. Voeller, L. Fairburn, and W. Thompson, *Exit Right: A Guided Tour of Succession Planning for Families-In-Business Together* (Toronto: Summit Run Inc., 2000), p. 33.

STAGE ELEVEN

1. "The Growth of Franchising in Canada," BeTheBoss.ca (www.betheboss.ca). With permission.
2. J. Daw, "3 for 1 Pizza & Wings Ordered to Repay $35,000," *Toronto Star*, May 31, 2003, p. C3.
3. www.mcdonalds.com.
4. "The Profile of Franchising 2006: Series II—Initial Investment," International Franchise Association Educational Foundation, Inc., Washington, D.C. September 2006, (www.ifranchisegroup.com), accessed May 2013.
5. "Advantages of Franchising," The iFranchise Group Inc. (www.ifranchisegroup.com), accessed May 16, 2013.
6. The iFranchise Group Inc. (www.ifranchisegroup.com/franchise-your-business/criteria-for-franchisability), accessed May 21, 2013.

GLOSSARY OF FINANCIAL TERMS

Accounts payable Money owed by a firm to its suppliers for goods and services purchased for the operation of the business. A current liability.

Accounts receivable Money owed to a firm by its customers for goods or services they have purchased from it. A current asset.

Amortization To pay off a debt over a stated time period, setting aside fixed sums for interest and principal at regular intervals, such as a mortgage.

Angels Private individuals with capital to invest in business ventures.

Assets The resources or property rights owned by an individual or business enterprise. Tangible assets include cash, inventory, land and buildings, and intangible assets include patents and goodwill.

Bad debts Money owed to you that you no longer expect to collect.

Balance sheet An itemized statement that lists the total assets and total liabilities of a given business, to portray its net worth at a given moment in time.

Bankruptcy The financial and legal position of a person or corporation unable to pay its debts.

Bootstrap Using your own funds or funds from family and friends to finance your business.

Break-even point The level of sales in either units or dollars at which sales revenue and costs are equal so that a business is neither making nor losing money.

Capital asset A possession, such as a machine, that can be used to make money and has a reasonably long life, usually more than a year.

Capital costs The cost involved in the acquisition of capital assets. They are "capitalized," showing up on the balance sheet and depreciated (expensed) over their useful life.

Capital gain The difference between the net cost of an asset and the net sales price, if the asset is sold at a gain.

Capital loss The difference between the net cost of an asset and the net sales price, if the asset is sold at a loss.

Capital requirement The amount of money needed to establish a business.

Capital stock The money invested in a business through founders' equity and shares bought by stockholders.

Cash discount An incentive provided by vendors of merchandise and services to speed up the collection of accounts receivable.

Cash flow The movement of cash in and out of a company. Its timing is usually projected month by month to show the net cash requirement during each period.

Cash flow forecast A schedule of expected cash receipts and disbursements (payments) highlighting expected shortages and surpluses.

Collateral Assets placed by a borrower as security for a loan.

Contribution margin The difference between variable revenue and variable cost.

Conversion In the context of securities, refers to the exchange of a convertible security, such as a bond for shares in a company.

Cost of goods sold The direct costs of acquiring and/or producing an item for sale. Usually excludes any overhead or other indirect expenses.

Crowdfunding Funding a project from a large group of individuals who invest in your project. Crowdfunding is usually conducted through dedicated websites.

Current assets Cash or other items that will normally be turned into cash within one year (accounts receivable, inventory, and short-term notes) and assets that will be used up in the operation of a firm within one year.

Current liabilities Amounts owed that will ordinarily be paid by a firm within one year. Such items include accounts payable, wages payable, taxes payable, the current portion of a long-term debt and interest, and dividends payable.

Current ratio Current assets divided by current liabilities. Used as an indication of liquidity to show how easily a business can meet its current debts.

Debt Money that must be paid back to someone else, usually with interest.

Debt capital Capital invested in a company that does not belong to the company's owners. Usually consists of long-term loans and preferred shares.

Debt-to-equity ratio The ratio of long-term debt to owners' equity. Measures overall profitability.

Demand loan A loan that must be repaid in full, on demand.

Depreciation A method of writing off the costs to a firm of using a fixed asset, such as machinery, buildings, trucks, and equipment, over time.

Employee stock ownership plan (ESOP) A company contributes to a trust fund that buys stock on behalf of employees.

Equity The difference between the assets and liabilities of a company, often referred to as *net worth*.

Equity capital The capital invested in a firm by its owners. The owners of the equity capital in the firm are entitled to all the assets and income of the firm after all the claims of creditors have been paid.

Escrow Property or money held by a third party until the agreed-on obligations of a contract are met.

Factor A financial institution that buys a firm's accounts receivable and collects the accounts.

Financial statements Documents that show your financial situation.

Fiscal year An accounting cycle of 12 months that could start at any point during a calendar year.

Fixed assets Those things that a firm owns and uses in its business and that it keeps for more than one year (including machinery, land, buildings, vehicles, etc.).

Fixed costs or expenses Those costs that do not vary from one period to the next and usually are not affected by the volume of business (e.g., rent, salaries, telephone, etc.).

Floor plan financing An arrangement used to finance inventory. A finance company buys the inventory, which is then held in trust for the user.

Franchise The right to sell products or services under a corporate name or trademark, usually purchased for a fee plus a royalty on sales.

Goodwill The value of customer lists, trade reputation, and so on, which is assumed to go with a company and its name, particularly when trying to arrive at the sale price for the company. In accounting terms, it is the amount a purchaser pays over the book value.

Gross margin or gross profit margin The difference between the volume of sales your business generates and the costs you pay out for the goods that are sold.

GST/HST GST is a tax that applies to the supply of most property and services in Canada. Some provinces have harmonized the provincial sales tax with the GST. This is called HST (harmonized sales tax). A business must register for a GST/HST number when it has reached sales of $30,000. It is beneficial for business owners to register prior to meeting that threshold, as this enables them to apply for credit of the GST/HST they have paid for their business expenses.

Income statement The financial statement that looks at a business's revenue, less expenses, to determine net income for a certain period of time. Also called *profit-and-loss statement*.

Industry ratios Financial ratios established by many companies in an industry, in an attempt to establish a norm against which to measure and compare the effectiveness of a company's management.

Initial public offering (IPO) A company's first sale of stock to the public. Securities offered in an IPO are often, but not always, those of young, small companies seeking outside equity capital and a public market for their stock. Investors purchasing stock in IPOs generally must be prepared to accept considerable risks for the possibility of large gains.

Intangible assets Such assets as trade names or patent rights that are not physical objects or sums of money.

Interest A charge for the use of money supplied by a lender.

Inventory The supply of goods, whether raw materials, parts, or finished products, owned by a firm at any one time, and its total value.

Inventory turnover The number of times the value of inventory at cost divides into the cost of goods sold in a year.

Investment capital The money set aside for starting a business. Usually this would cover such costs as inventory, equipment, pre-opening expenses, and leasehold improvements.

Lease An agreement to rent for a period of time at an agreed price.

Leverage ratios Measures of the relative value of stockholders' capitalization and creditors' obligations and of the firm's ability to pay financing charges.

Liabilities All the debts of a business. Liabilities include short-term or current liabilities, such as accounts payable, income taxes due, and the amount of long-term debt that must be paid within 12 months; long-term liabilities include long-term debts and deferred income taxes. On a balance sheet, liabilities are subtracted from assets; what remains is the shareholders' equity.

Line of credit An agreement negotiated between a borrower and a lender establishing the maximum amount of money against which the borrower may draw.

Liquid assets Cash on hand and anything that can easily and quickly be turned into cash.

Liquidation value The estimated value of a business after its operations are stopped, the assets sold, and the liabilities paid off.

Liquidity A term that describes how readily a firm's assets can be converted into cash.

Liquidity ratios Ratios that measure a firm's ability to meet its short-term financial obligations on time, such as the ratio of current assets to current liabilities.

Loan guarantee The assumption of responsibility for payment of a debt or performance of some obligation if the liable party fails to perform to expectations.

Long-term liabilities Debts that will not be paid off within one year.

Management buyout (MBO) A leveraged buyout in which the acquiring group is led by the firm's management.

Markup The amount vendors add to the purchase price of a product to take into account their expenses plus profit.

Maturity For a loan, the date on which the principal is required to be repaid.

Net worth The value of a business represented by the excess of the total assets over the total amounts owing to outside creditors (total liabilities) at a given moment in time. Also referred to as *book value*.

Operating costs Expenditures arising out of current business activities; what it costs to do business—the salaries, electricity, rental, deliveries, and so on, that are involved in performing the operations of a business.

Operating loan A loan intended for short-term financing, supplying cash flow support, or covering day-to-day operating expenses.

Overhead Expenses, such as rent, heat, property tax, and so on, incurred to keep a business open.

Principal The face amount of debt; the amount borrowed or loaned.

Pro forma A projection or estimate. A pro forma financial statement is one that shows how the actual operations of the business will turn out if certain assumptions are realized.

Profit The excess of the selling price over all costs and expenses incurred in making the sale. Gross profit is the profit before corporate income taxes. Net profit is the final profit of the firm after all deductions have been made.

Profitability ratios Ratios that focus on how well a firm is performing. Profit margins measure performance in relation to sales. Rate-of-return ratios measure performance relative to some measure of size of the investment.

Profit-and-loss statement A financial statement listing revenue and expenses and showing the profit or loss for a certain period of time. Also called an *income statement*.

Profit margin The ratio of profits (generally pre-tax) to sales.

Put option The right to sell (or put) a fixed number of shares at a fixed price within a given period of time.

Quick ratio Current cash and "near" cash assets (e.g., government bonds, current receivables, but excluding inventory) compared with current liabilities (bank loans, accounts payable). The quick ratio shows how much and how quickly cash can be found if a company gets into trouble. Sometimes called the *acid test ratio*.

Retained earnings The profits that are not spent or divided among the owners but kept in the business.

Return on investment (ROI) The determination of the profit to be accrued from a capital investment.

Royalty Payment for the right to use intellectual property or natural resources.

Seed capital The first contribution by an investor toward the financing of a new business.

Stock buyback A corporation's purchase of its own outstanding stock.

Subordinated debt Debt over which other senior debt takes priority. In the event of bankruptcy, subordinated debt holders receive payment only after senior debt claims are paid in full.

Term loan A loan intended for medium-term or long-term financing to supply cash to purchase fixed assets, such as land, buildings, machinery, and equipment, or to renovate business premises.

Terms of sale The conditions concerning payment for a purchase.

Trade credit The credit terms offered by a manufacturer or supplier to other businesses.

Transactions fees Fees charged to cover the time and effort involved in arranging a loan or other financial package.

Turnover The number of times a year that a product is sold and reordered.

Variable expenses Costs of doing business that vary with the volume of business, such as manufacturing cost and delivery expenses.

Venture capital Funds that are invested in a business by a third party either as equity or some form of subordinated debt.

Venture capitalist The person who raises money from investors and invests that money into suitable investments that should result in a high rate of return, usually within 3 to 7 years.

Working capital The funds available for carrying on the day-to-day operation of a business. Working capital is the excess after deduction of the current liabilities from the current assets of a firm and indicates a company's ability to pay its short-term debts.

WEBSITES

PROLOGUE

www.startupcan.ca Startup Canada

www.ic.gc.ca Industry Canada, Small Business Statistics

www.purdys.com Purdy's Chocolatier

www.top100women.ca Canada's Most Powerful Women: Top 100 awarded by the Women's Executive Network

www.travelpod.com TravelPod

www.401bay.com 401 Bay Centre

www.cabi.ca Listing of incubators/accelerators

STAGE ONE: ASSESSING YOUR POTENTIAL FOR AN ENTREPRENEURIAL CAREER

www.babson.edu Babson University Academy of Distinguished Entrepreneurs

www.Equifax.ca Equifax Canada Inc.

www.transunion.ca TransUnion Canada

www.aimpersonnel.ca Association of Canadian Search, Employment & Staffing Services

STAGE TWO: EXPLORING BUSINESS IDEAS AND OPPORTUNITIES

www.oliberte.com Oliberté Limited

www.talentegg.ca TalentEgg

www.avenirmedical.com Avenir Medical Inc.

www.GrowingCity.ca Growing City

www.gofiddleheads.com Fiddleheads

www.suzyq.ca SuzyQ Doughnuts

www.shutoutsolutions.com Shutout Solutions

www.theglobeandmail.com *The Globe and Mail*

www.nationalpost.com *National Post*

www.wsj.com *The Wall Street Journal*

www.canadianbusiness.com *Canadian Business*

www.profitguide.com PROFIT

www.theglobeandmail.com *Globe and Mail Report on Business Magazine*

www.financialpost.com *Financial Post Magazine*

www.inc.com *INC.*

www.entrepreneur.com *Entrepreneur*

www.money.cnn.com *Fortune*

www.webwire.com WebWire

www.inventnet.com Inventor's Network

www.inventorscollege.org Inventors College

www.inventorscollege.org Great Canadian Inventions Show

biztradeshows.com Biz Trade Shows

tradeshowcalendar.globalsources.com Global Sources Trade Show Centre

www.eventseye.com EventsEye

www.allconferences.com Directory of conferences by AllConferences.com

www.biztradeshows.com List of conferences by Biz Trade Shows

www.flintbox.com Flintbox

patents1.ic.gc.ca Canadian Patents Database

notable.ca Notable.ca Lifestyle Guide

www.innovationcentre.ca Canadian Innovation Centre

www.canadabusiness.ca Canada Business Services Centres of Industry Canada

www.ic.gc.ca Industry Canada

STAGE THREE: MARKET FEASIBILITY STUDY

www.csa.ca Canadian Standards Association (CSA)

www.ul.com Underwriters Laboratory (UL)

www.innovationcentre.ca Canadian Innovation Centre

www5.statcan.gc.ca Statistics Canada, CANSIM database

www.CanadaBusiness.ca Canada Business Services for Entrepreneurs

www.google.ca Google

www.bing.com Bing

ca.yahoo.com Yahoo!

www.cybf.ca Canadian Youth Business Foundation (CYBF)

www.canadianbusiness.com Canadian Business Online

www.entrepreneurship.org Kauffman Foundation Entrepreneurship

www.proquest.com ProQuest

www.northernlight.com Northern Light

STAGE SIX: LEGAL CONSIDERATIONS

www.bizpal.ca BizPal

www.labour.gc.ca Federal Labour Standards

www.cipo.ic.gc Canadian Intellectual Property Office (CIPO)

www.ic.gc.ca List of registered agents from the Patent Office

STAGE SEVEN: FINANCING YOUR BUSINESS AND ACCOUNTING PRACTICES

www.ic.gc.ca Canada Small Business Financing program

www.nrc-cnrc.gc.ca National Research Council of Canada Industrial Research Assistance Program

www.communityfuturescanada.ca Community Futures Development Corporations/Community Business Development Corporations

www.wd.gc.ca Women's Enterprise Initiative

www.ainc-inac.gc.ca Aboriginal Business Canada

www.bdc.ca Business Development Bank of Canada

www.canadabusiness.ca Canada Business Service Centre

www.cvca.ca Canadian Venture Capital Association

www.capital-connexion.com Capital Connexion

www.nacocanada.com National Angel Capital Organization (NACO)

www.cybf.ca Canadian Youth Business Foundation (CYBF)

www.cbc *Dragons' Den* tour schedule

www.kickstarter.com Kickstarter

www.cra-arc.gc.ca Canada Revenue Agency for GST/HST

www.revenuquebec.ca Revenu Québec

STAGE EIGHT: MARKETING

www.cira.ca Canadian Internet Registration Authority (CIRA)

www.ecommercefuel.com Andrew Youderian's blog, founder of eCommerceFuel.com

www.wordpress.org WordPress

www.joomla.org Joomla

www.drupal.org Drupal

www.googlekeywordtool.com Google keyword tool

www.google.com Google free analytic tool

www.bdc.ca Social Media, A Guide for Entrepreneurs

www.LisaMcKenzie.com McKenzie Moxie Media

www.mmaglobal.com Mobile Marketing Association

www.eventbrite.ca Eventbrite

www.videocreationformula.com Video Creation Formula

www.kissmetrics.com Kissmetric

STAGE TEN: BUYING A BUSINESS

www.dnb.com Dun & Bradstreet

www.rmahq.org Risk Management Association (formerly Robert Morris Associates)

sme.ic.gc.ca Industry Canada, as part of its SME Benchmarking Tool website

www.discoveryhut.com The Discovery Hut

STAGE ELEVEN: BUYING A FRANCHISE

www.betheboss.ca BeTheBoss

www.cfa.ca Franchise Canada Directory 2013 of the Canadian Franchise Association

www.cultures-restaurants.com Cultures Restaurants

www.quiznos.com Quizno's Classic Subs

www.kegsteakhouse.com The Keg Steakhouse and Bar

www.cfa.ca *FranchiseCanada* magazines's directory, published annually by the Canadian Franchise Association

INDEX